enVisionmath 2.0

Scott Foresman • Addison Wesley

Volume 2 Topics 8-16

Authors

Randall I. Charles
Professor Emeritus
Department of Mathematics
San Jose State University
San Jose, California

Jennifer Bay-Williams
Professor of Mathematics Education
College of Education and Human Development
University of Louisville
Louisville, Kentucky

Robert Q. Berry, III
Associate Professor of Mathematics Education
Department of Curriculum, Instruction and Special Education
University of Virginia
Charlottesville, Virginia

Janet H. Caldwell
Professor of Mathematics
Rowan University
Glassboro, New Jersey

Zachary Champagne
Assistant in Research
Florida Center for Research in Science, Technology, Engineering, and Mathematics (FCR-STEM)
Jacksonville, Florida

Juanita Copley
Professor Emerita, College of Education
University of Houston
Houston, Texas

Warren Crown
Professor Emeritus of Mathematics Education
Graduate School of Education
Rutgers University
New Brunswick, New Jersey

Francis (Skip) Fennell
L. Stanley Bowlsbey Professor of Education and Graduate and Professional Studies
McDaniel College
Westminster, Maryland

Karen Karp
Professor of Mathematics Education
Department of Early Childhood and Elementary Education
University of Louisville
Louisville, Kentucky

Stuart J. Murphy
Visual Learning Specialist
Boston, Massachusetts

Jane F. Schielack
Professor of Mathematics
Associate Dean for Assessment and Pre K-12 Education,
College of Science
Texas A&M University
College Station, Texas

Jennifer M. Suh
Associate Professor for Mathematics Education
George Mason University
Fairfax, Virginia

Jonathan A. Wray
Mathematics Instructional Facilitator
Howard County Public Schools
Ellicott City, Maryland

PEARSON

Glenview, Illinois Boston, Massachusetts Chandler, Arizona Hoboken, New Jersey

Mathematicians

Roger Howe
Professor of Mathematics
Yale University
New Haven, Connecticut

Gary Lippman
Professor of Mathematics and Computer Science
California State University, East Bay
Hayward, California

ELL Consultants

Janice R. Corona
Independent Education Consultant
Dallas, Texas

Jim Cummins
Professor
The University of Toronto
Toronto, Canada

Common Core State Standards Reviewers

Debbie Crisco
Math Coach
Beebe Public Schools
Beebe, Arkansas

Kathleen A. Cuff
Teacher
Kings Park Central School District
Kings Park, New York

Erika Doyle
Math and Science Coordinator
Richland School District
Richland, Washington

Susan Jarvis
Math and Science Curriculum Coordinator
Ocean Springs Schools
Ocean Springs, Mississippi

Velvet M. Simington
K-12 Mathematics Director
Winston-Salem/Forsyth County Schools
Winston-Salem, North Carolina

ISBN-13: 978-0-328-82746-6
ISBN-10: 0-328-82746-0

PEARSON

13 18

Digital Resources

You'll be using these digital resources throughout the year!

Go to PearsonRealize.com

MP

Math Practices Animations to play anytime

Solve

Solve & Share problems plus math tools

Learn

Visual Learning Animation Plus with animation, interaction, and math tools

Glossary

Animated Glossary in English and Spanish

Practice Buddy

Online Personalized Practice for each lesson

Tools

Math Tools to help you understand

Assessment

Quick Check for each lesson

Help

Another Look Homework Video for extra help

Games

Math Games to help you learn

eText

Student Edition online

ACTIVe-book

Student Edition online for showing your work

PEARSON realize™ Everything you need for math anytime, anywhere

Hi, we're here to help you.
Let's have a great year!

KEY

Major Cluster

Supporting Cluster

Additional Cluster

The content is organized to focus on Common Core clusters.
For a list of clusters, see Volume 1 pages F13–F16.

Digital Resources at PearsonRealize.com

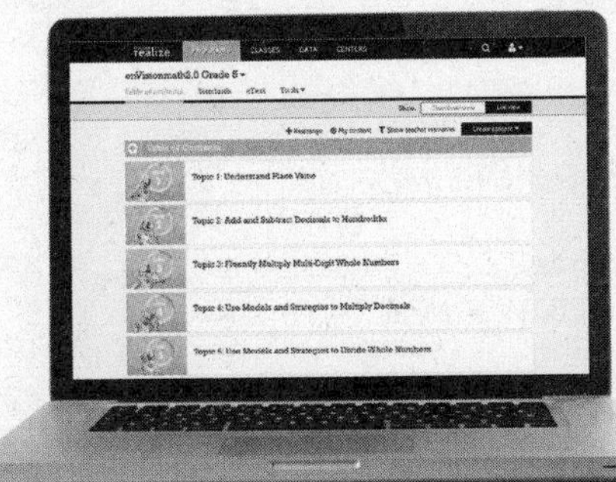

And remember your eText is available at PearsonRealize.com!

Contents

TOPICS

PearsonRealize.com

TOPIC 8 Apply Understanding of Multiplication to Multiply Fractions

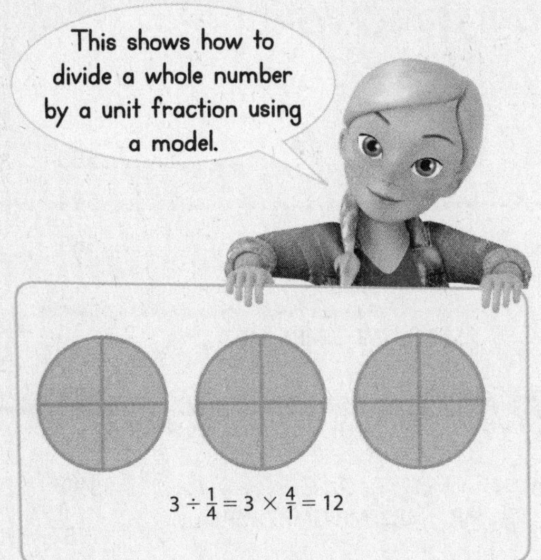
This shows how to divide a whole number by a unit fraction using a model.
$3 \div \frac{1}{4} = 3 \times \frac{4}{1} = 12$

TOPIC 9 Apply Understanding of Division to Divide Fractions

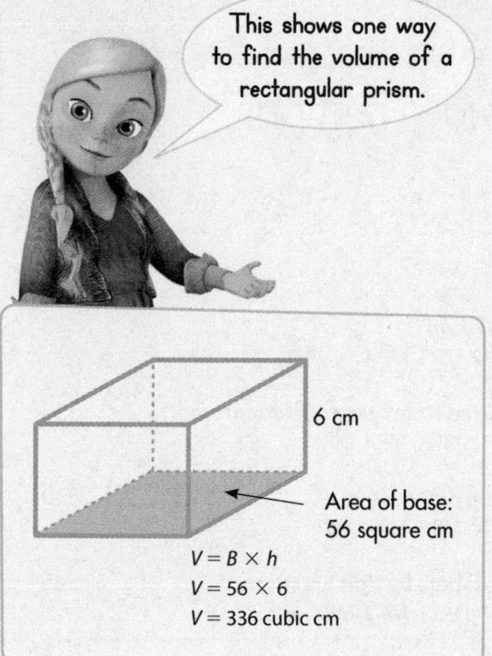
This shows one way to find the volume of a rectangular prism.
6 cm
Area of base: 56 square cm
$V = B \times h$
$V = 56 \times 6$
$V = 336$ cubic cm

TOPIC 10 Understand Volume Concepts

This shows how customary units of length are related.

1 foot (ft) = 12 inches (in.) 1 yard (yd) = 3 ft = 36 in. 1 mile (mi) = 1,760 yd = 5,280 ft

TOPIC 11 Convert Measurements

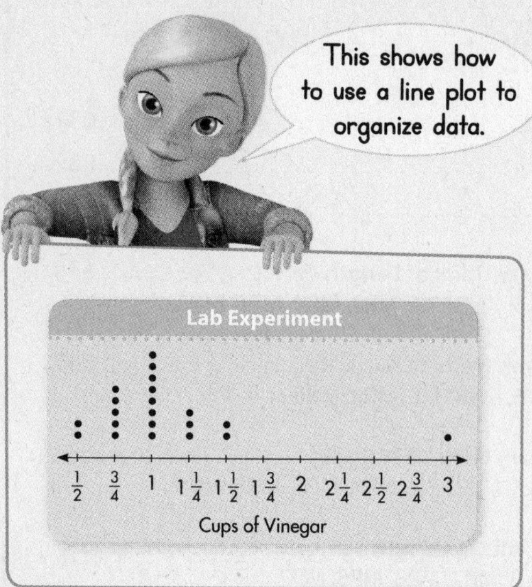

TOPIC 12 Represent and Interpret Data

This shows how to evaluate an expression using the order of operations.
12 ÷ 4 + (9 − 2) × (3 + 5)
12 ÷ 4 + 7 × 8
3 + 56
59

TOPIC 13 Algebra: Write and Interpret Numerical Expressions

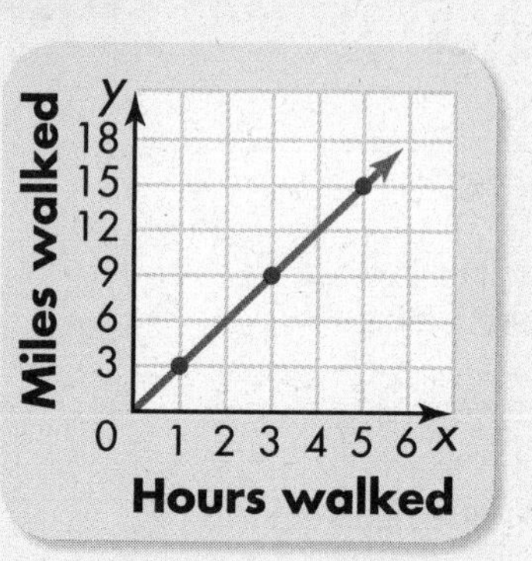

TOPIC 14 Graph Points on the Coordinate Plane

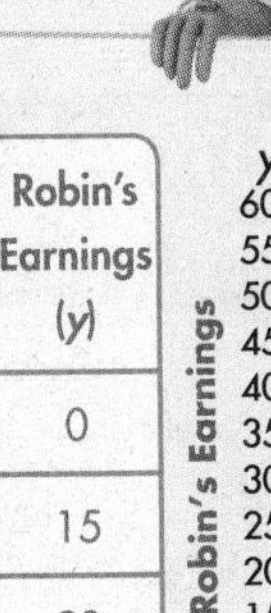

This shows how ordered pairs form a pattern on the coordinate grid.

Jill's Earnings (x)	Robin's Earnings (y)
0	0
5	15
10	30
15	45
20	60

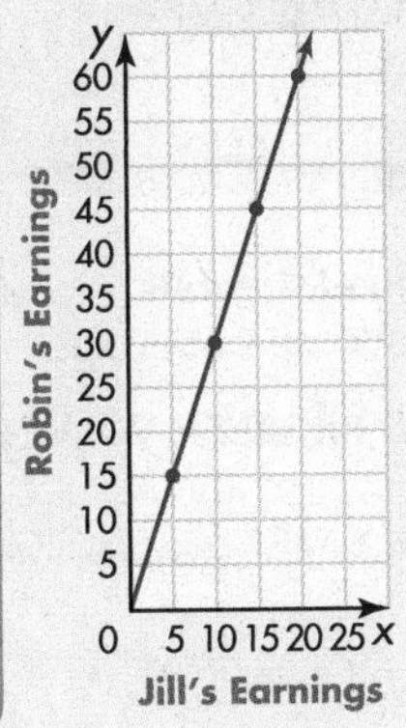

TOPIC 15 Algebra: Analyze Patterns and Relationships

These are different types of quadrilaterals.

TOPIC 16 Geometric Measurement: Classify Two-Dimensional Figures

STEP UP to Grade 6

Math Practices and Problem Solving Handbook

Math practices are ways we think about and do math.

Math practices will help you solve problems.

Math Practices

MP.1 Make sense of problems and persevere in solving them.

MP.2 Reason abstractly and quantitatively.

MP.3 Construct viable arguments and critique the reasoning of others.

MP.4 Model with mathematics.

MP.5 Use appropriate tools strategically.

MP.6 Attend to precision.

MP.7 Look for and make use of structure.

MP.8 Look for and express regularity in repeated reasoning.

There are good Thinking Habits for each of these math practices.

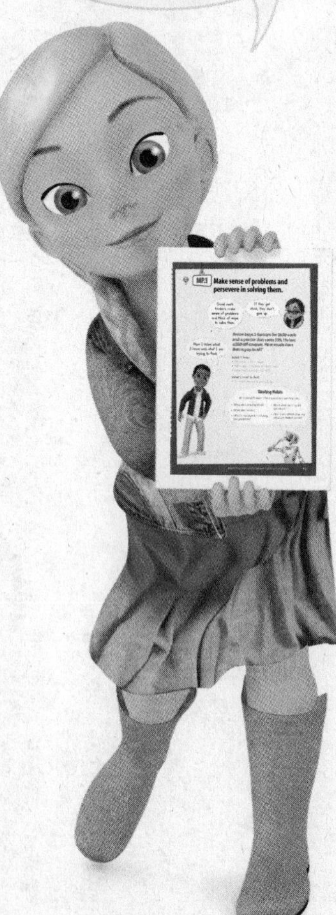

Make sense of problems and persevere in solving them.

Good math thinkers make sense of problems and think of ways to solve them.
If they get stuck, they don't give up.

Here I listed what I know and what I am trying to find.

Anton buys 2 laptops for $600 each and a printer that costs $99. He has a $50 off coupon. How much does Anton pay in all?

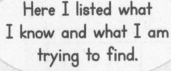

What I Know:

- Anton has a $50 coupon.
- Anton buys 2 laptops for $600 each.
- Anton buys a printer for $99.

What I need to find:

- The total amount Anton will pay.

Thinking Habits

Be a good thinker! These questions can help you.

- What do I need to find?
- What do I know?
- What's my plan for solving the problem?
- What else can I try if I get stuck?
- How can I check that my solution makes sense?

Reason abstractly and quantitatively.

Good math thinkers know how to think about words and numbers to solve problems.

I drew a bar diagram that shows how the numbers in the problem are related.

Derrick buys 6 games that cost a total of $150. How much does each game cost?

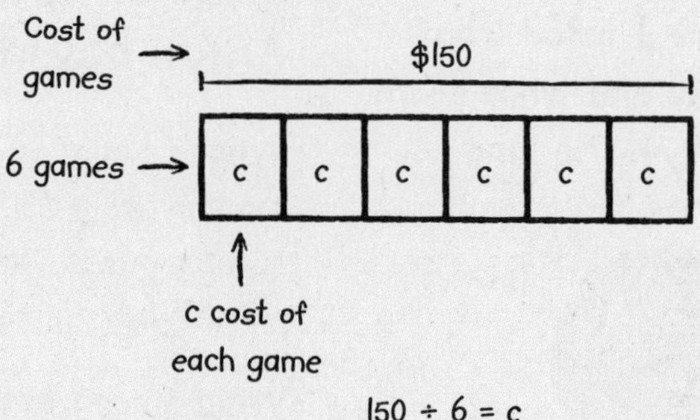

$150 \div 6 = c$

Thinking Habits

Be a good thinker! These questions can help you.

- What do the numbers and symbols in the problem mean?
- How are the numbers or quantities related?
- How can I represent a word problem using pictures, numbers, or equations?

MP.3

Construct viable arguments and critique the reasoning of others.

Good math thinkers use math to explain why they are right. They can talk about the math that others do, too.

Molly says that every fraction whose denominator is twice as great as its numerator is equivalent to $\frac{1}{2}$. Do you agree? Explain.

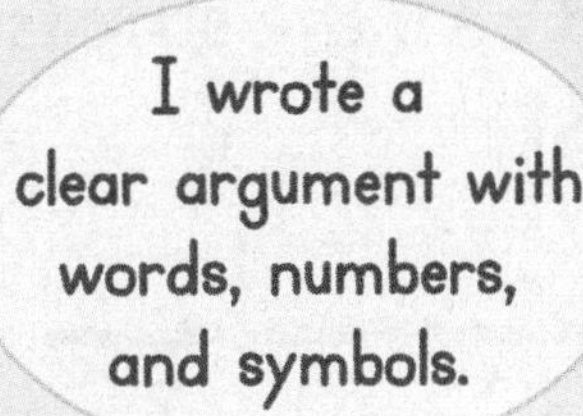
I wrote a
clear argument with
words, numbers,
and symbols.

Yes, Molly is correct. Every fraction that has a denominator that is twice as great as its numerator can be written as an equivalent fraction by dividing both the numerator and denominator by the same non-zero number.

$\frac{5}{10} = \frac{5 \div 5}{10 \div 5} = \frac{1}{2}$

Thinking Habits

Be a good thinker! These questions can help you.

- How can I use numbers, objects, drawings, or actions to justify my argument?
- Am I using numbers and symbols correctly?
- Is my explanation clear and complete?
- What questions can I ask to understand other people's thinking?
- Are there mistakes in other people's thinking?
- Can I improve other people's thinking?
- Can I use a counterexample in my argument?

Model with mathematics.

Good math thinkers choose and apply math they know to show and solve problems from everyday life.

I can use what I know about division to solve this problem. I can draw a picture to help.

Jasmine has a strip of wood that is 75 centimeters long. She is going to saw it into 5 equal pieces. How long will each piece of wood be if the strip is cut into 5 equal pieces?

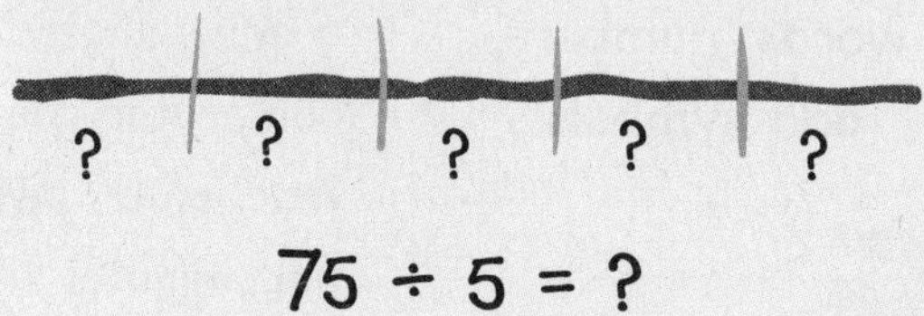

$$75 \div 5 = ?$$

Thinking Habits

Be a good thinker! These questions can help you.

- How can I use math I know to help solve this problem?
- How can I use pictures, objects, or an equation to represent the problem?
- How can I use numbers, words, and symbols to solve the problem?

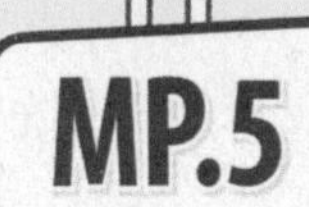

Use appropriate tools strategically.

Good math thinkers know how to choose the right tools to solve math problems.

I decided to use a protractor because I could measure the angles directly.

Harry said that the angle made at the back point of home plate is an acute angle. Is Harry correct? Justify your argument.

Harry is incorrect. The angle is a right angle because it has a measure of 90°.

Thinking Habits

Be a good thinker! These questions can help you.

- Which tools can I use?
- Why should I use this tool to help me solve the problem?
- Is there a different tool I could use?
- Am I using the tool appropriately?

Attend to precision.

Good math thinkers are careful about what they write and say, so their ideas about math are clear.

I was precise with my work and the way that I wrote my solution.

Bill has 125 oranges. He puts 6 oranges into each box. How many boxes does he need?

125 ÷ 6 = 20 R5

120 oranges will fit into 20 boxes.
So, Bill needs 21 boxes for 125 oranges.

Thinking Habits

Be a good thinker! These questions can help you.

- Am I using numbers, units, and symbols appropriately?
- Am I using the correct definitions?
- Am I calculating accurately?
- Is my answer clear?

Look for and make use of structure.

Good math thinkers look for patterns or relationships in math to help solve problems.

I broke numbers apart to multiply.

There are 5,280 feet in 1 mile. How many feet are in 3 miles?

5,280 feet = 1 mile

$$
\begin{aligned}
3 \times 5{,}280 &= 3 \times (5{,}000 + 200 + 80) \\
&= (3 \times 5{,}000) + (3 \times 200) + (3 \times 80) \\
&= 15{,}000 + 600 + 240 \\
&= 15{,}840
\end{aligned}
$$

There are 15,840 feet in 3 miles.

Thinking Habits

Be a good thinker! These questions can help you.

- What patterns can I see and describe?
- How can I use the patterns to solve the problem?
- Can I see expressions and objects in different ways?
- What equivalent expressions can I use?

Look for and express regularity in repeated reasoning.

Good math thinkers look for things that repeat, and they make generalizations.

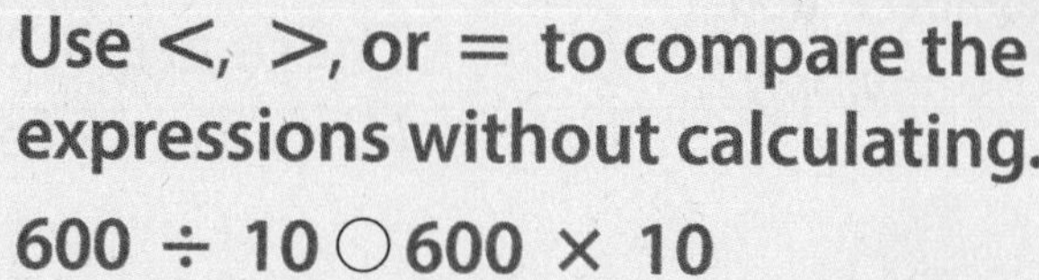

Use <, >, or = to compare the expressions without calculating.
600 ÷ 10 ○ 600 × 10

I used reasoning to generalize about calculations.

600 ÷ 10 < 600 × 10
Dividing by 10 results in a number less than multiplying by 10.

Thinking Habits

Be a good thinker! These questions can help you.

- Are any calculations repeated?
- Can I generalize from examples?
- What shortcuts do I notice?

Problem Solving Guide

Math practices can help you solve problems.

Make Sense of the Problem

Reason Abstractly and Quantitatively

- What do I need to find?
- What given information can I use?
- How are the quantities related?

Think About Similar Problems

- Have I solved problems like this before?

Persevere in Solving the Problem

Model with Math

- How can I use the math I know?
- How can I represent the problem?
- Is there a pattern or structure I can use?

Use Appropriate Tools Strategically

- What math tools could I use?
- How can I use those tools strategically?

Check the Answer

Make Sense of the Answer

- Is my answer reasonable?

Check for Precision

- Did I check my work?
- Is my answer clear?
- Did I construct a viable argument?
- Did I generalize correctly?

Some Ways to Represent Problems

- Draw a Picture
- Make a Bar Diagram
- Make a Table or Graph
- Write an Equation

Some Math Tools

- Objects
- Grid Paper
- Rulers
- Technology
- Paper and Pencil

 Math Practices and Problem Solving Handbook

Problem Solving Recording Sheet

This sheet helps you organize your work.

Name Carlos

Teaching Tool 1

Problem Solving Recording Sheet

Problem:
A store sold 20 sweatshirts. Of these, 8 were red. Twice as many were green as yellow. How many of each color sweatshirt did the store sell?

MAKE SENSE OF THE PROBLEM

Need to Find

How many sweatshirts were sold in each color?

Given

A total of 20 sweatshirts. 8 were red. Twice as many green sweatshirts as yellow.

PERSEVERE IN SOLVING THE PROBLEM

Some Ways to Represent Problems

- ☐ Draw a Picture
- ☐ Make a Bar Diagram
- ☑ Make a Table or Graph
- ☑ Write an Equation

Some Math Tools

- ☐ Objects
- ☐ Grid Paper
- ☐ Rulers
- ☐ Technology
- ☐ Paper and Pencil

Solution and Answer

20 - 8 = 12, so there are 12 green and yellow sweatshirts. If there are 2 green shirts, there will be 1 yellow shirt.

green	yellow	total
2	1	3
4	2	6
6	3	9
8	4	12

So, there are 8 green sweatshirts and 4 yellow sweatshirts.

CHECK THE ANSWER

I can add to check my work. 8 red, 8 green, and 4 yellow sweatshirts. 8 + 8 + 4 = 20. There are 20 sweatshirts in all.

Math Practices and Problem Solving Handbook

Bar Diagrams

You can draw a **bar diagram** to show how the quantities in a problem are related. Then you can write an equation to solve the problem.

Add To

Draw this **bar diagram** for situations that involve *adding* to a quantity.

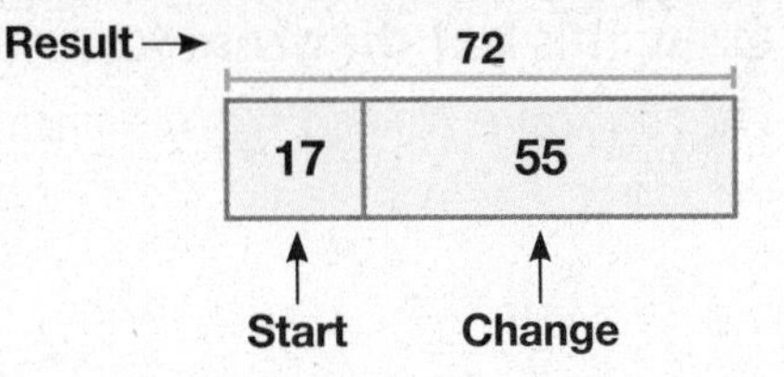

Result Unknown

Monica bought a new bicycle for $279. She also bought a used bicycle for $125. How much did she spend in all?

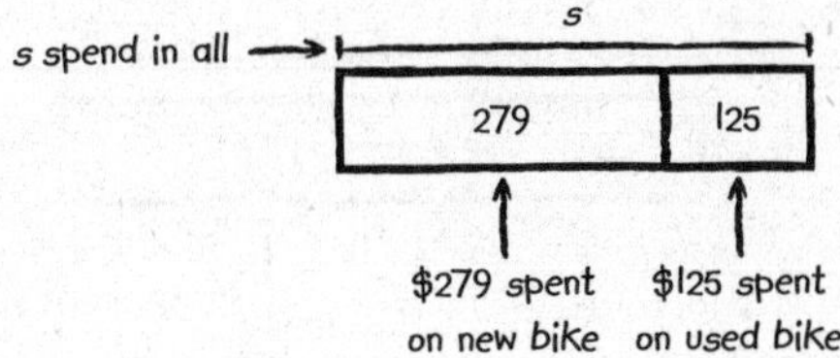

$279 + 125 = s$

Monica spent $404 on the two bikes.

Start Unknown

Vanessa deposited $750 in her bank account. After she made the deposit, she had $2,200 in her account. How much did Vanessa start with in her account?

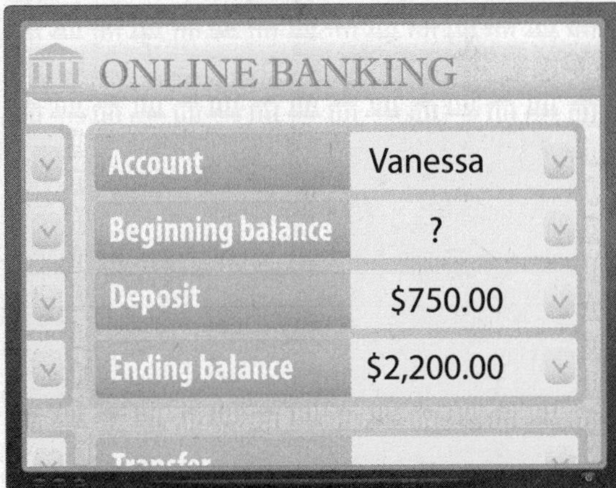

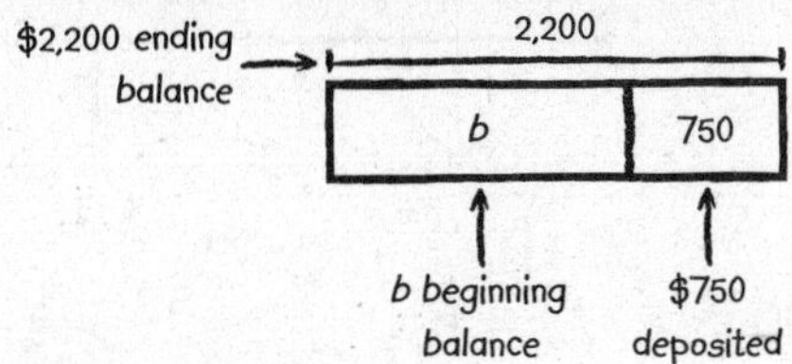

$b + 750 = 2{,}200$

Vanessa started with $1,450.

Math Practices and Problem Solving Handbook

Bar Diagrams

You can use bar diagrams to make sense of addition and subtraction problems.

Take From

Draw this **bar diagram** for situations that involve *taking* from a quantity.

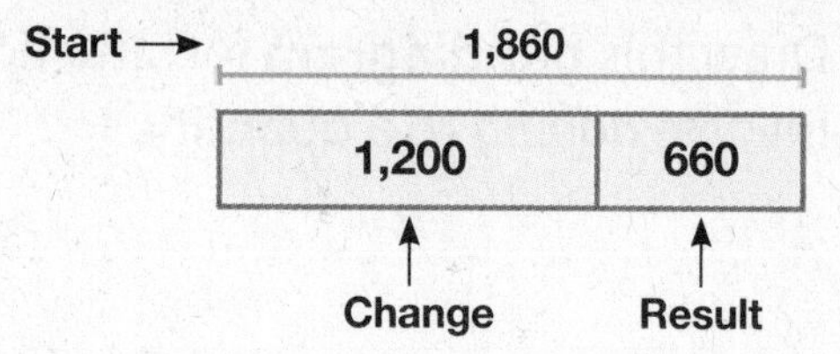

Result Unknown

Nicolas has a goal of doing 2,600 push-ups this year. He has done 1,775 push-ups so far. How many more push-ups does he need to do to reach his goal?

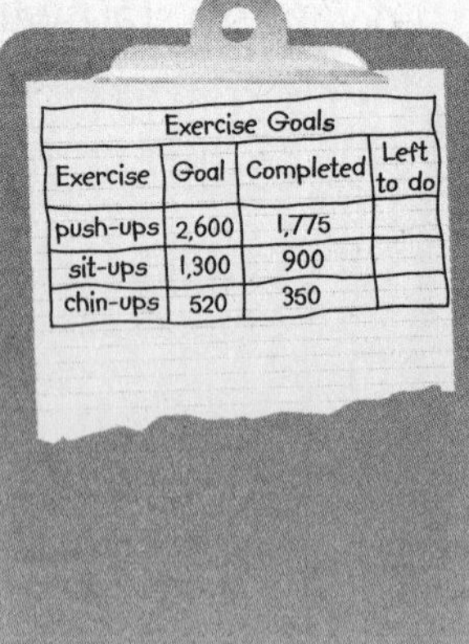

Exercise Goals

Exercise	Goal	Completed	Left to do
push-ups	2,600	1,775	
sit-ups	1,300	900	
chin-ups	520	350	

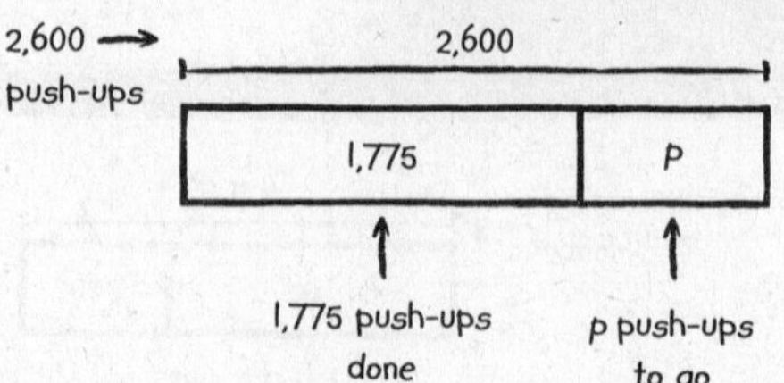

$2{,}600 - 1{,}775 = p$

Nicolas has 825 more push-ups to do to reach his goal.

Start Unknown

A store had a collection of DVDs. They sold 645 DVDs during a weekend sale. How many DVDs did the store have before the sale?

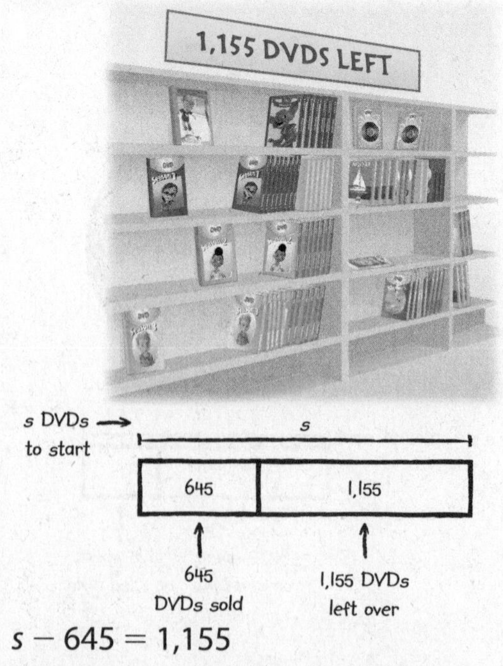

s DVDs to start →

s

645	1,155

645 DVDs sold

1,155 DVDs left over

$s - 645 = 1{,}155$

The store had 1,800 DVDs before the sale.

The **bar diagrams** on this page can help you make sense of more addition and subtraction situations.

Put Together/Take Apart

Draw this **bar diagram** for situations that involve *putting together* or *taking apart* quantities.

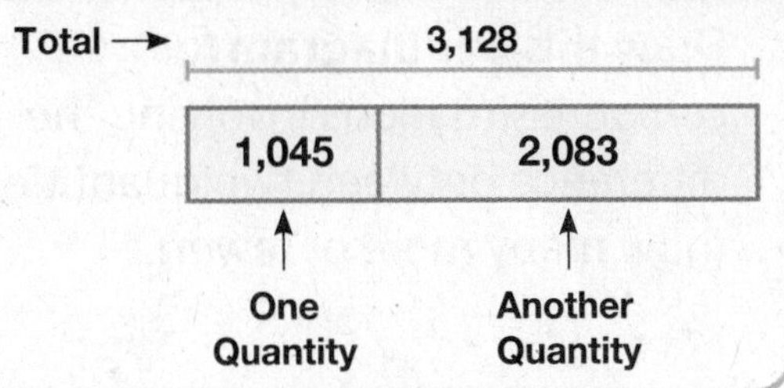

Whole Unknown

Rhode Island covers the least space of all states in the U.S. What is the total land and water area of Rhode Island?

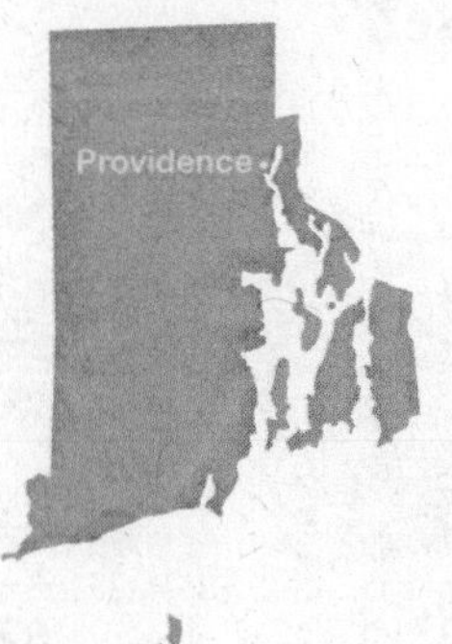

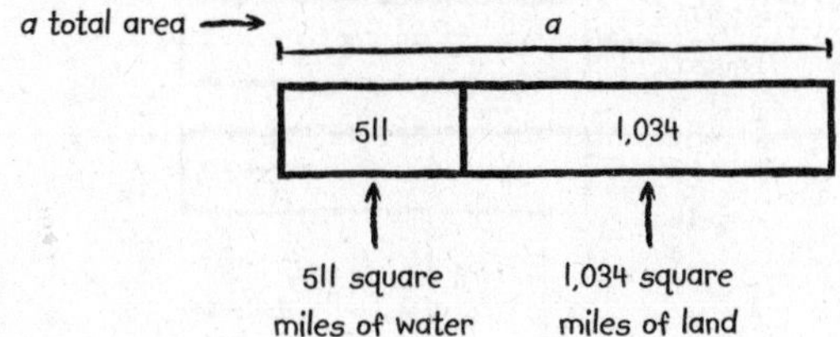

$511 + 1{,}034 = a$

The total land and water area of Rhode Island is 1,545 square miles.

Part Unknown

A farmer harvested 150 peppers on Saturday. He harvested more peppers on Sunday. He collected a total of 315 peppers over the two days. How many peppers did he harvest on Sunday?

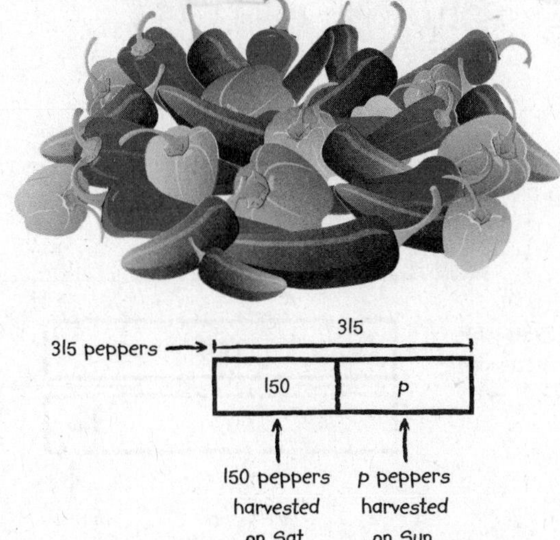

315 peppers → 315

150	p

150 peppers harvested on Sat. p peppers harvested on Sun.

$150 + p = 315$ or $315 - 150 = p$

He harvested 165 peppers on Sunday.

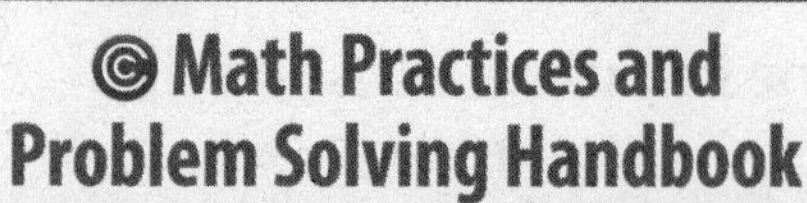

Math Practices and Problem Solving Handbook

Bar Diagrams

Pictures help you understand.

Compare: Addition and Subtraction

Draw this **bar diagram** for *compare* situations involving the difference between two quantities (how many more or fewer).

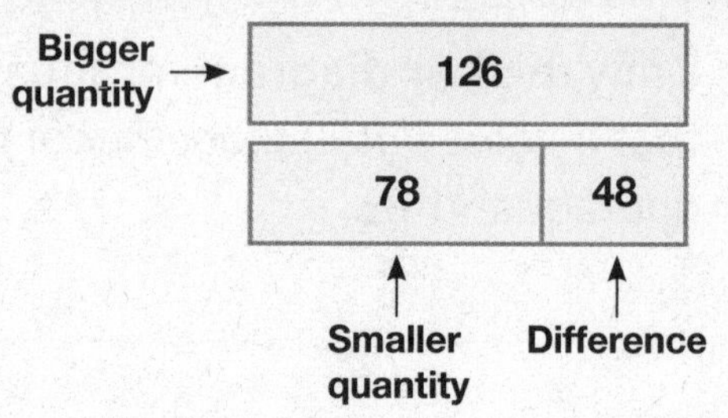

Difference Unknown

Last year, 1,796 people attended the county fair. This year 1,544 people attended. How many more people attended last year than this year?

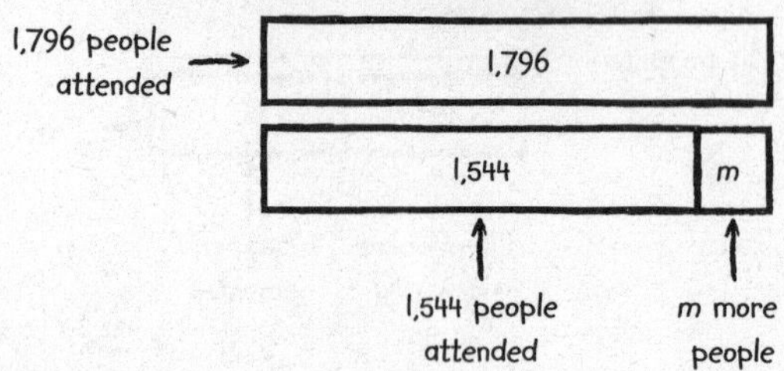

$1{,}796 - 1{,}544 = m$

Last year, 252 more people attended.

Smaller Unknown

Ann's school raised $2,375 for charity. Brian's school raised $275 less than Ann's school. How much did Brian's school raise?

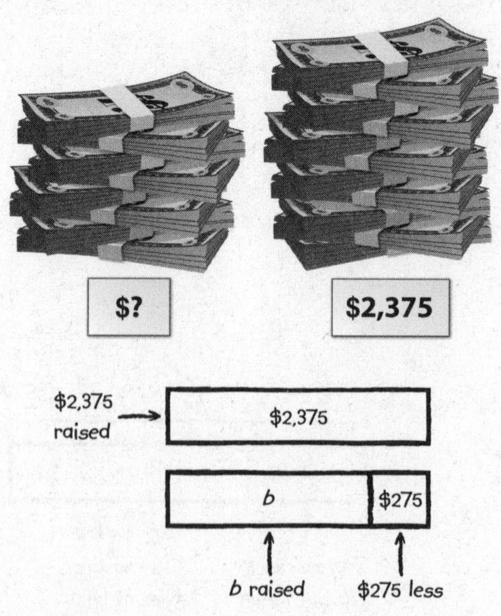

$2{,}375 - b = 275$ or $b + 275 = 2{,}375$

Brian's school raised $2,100.

The **bar diagrams** on this page can help you solve problems involving multiplication and division.

Equal Groups: Multiplication and Division

Draw this **bar diagram** for situations that involve *equal groups.*

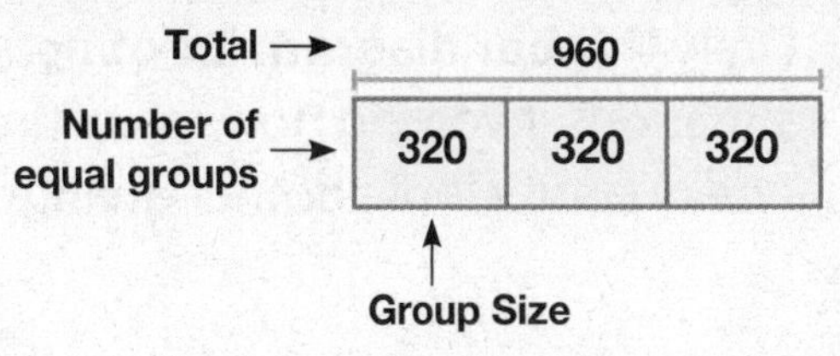

Number of Groups Unknown

Tom spent $135 on some new video games. Each game cost the same. How many video games did he buy?

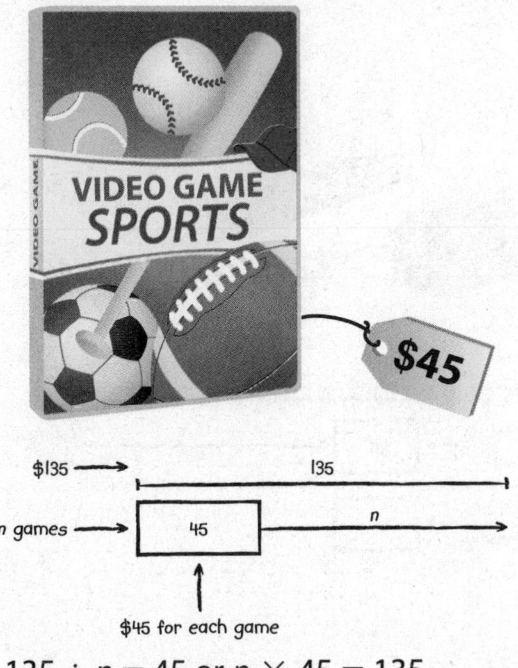

$135 \div n = 45$ or $n \times 45 = 135$

Tom bought 3 video games.

Group Size Unknown

Workers at an orchard harvested 480 apples. They separated the apples evenly into 4 bins. How many apples did they put in each bin?

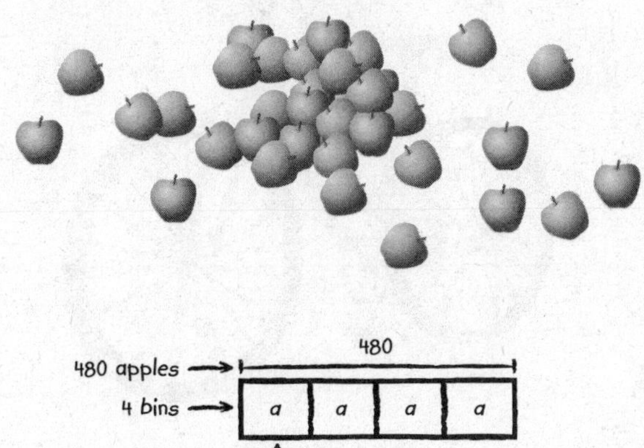

$4 \times a = 480$ or $480 \div 4 = a$

They put 120 apples in each bin.

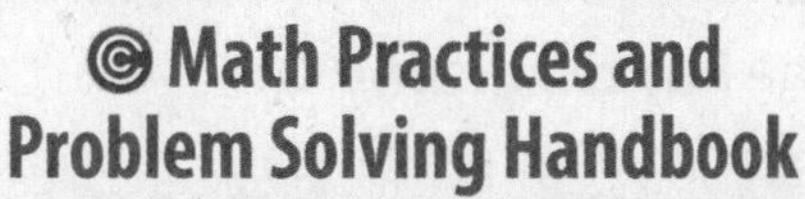

Math Practices and Problem Solving Handbook

Bar Diagrams

Bar diagrams can be used to show how quantities that are being compared are related.

Compare: Multiplication and Division

Draw this **bar diagram** for *compare* situations involving how many times one quantity is of another quantity.

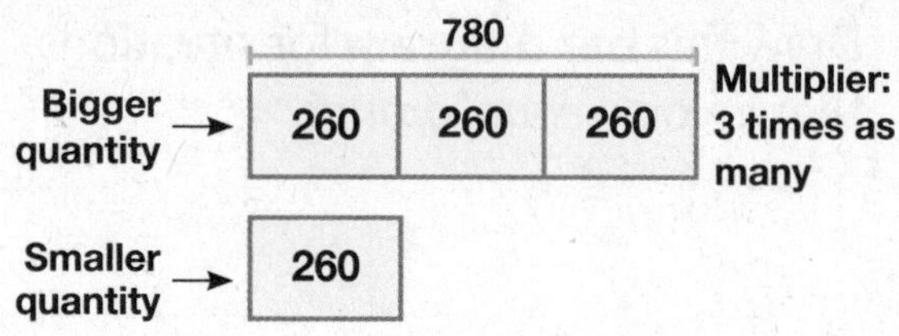

Bigger Unknown

Linda biked 175 miles last summer. Kendra biked 3 times as far as Linda. How many miles did Kendra bike?

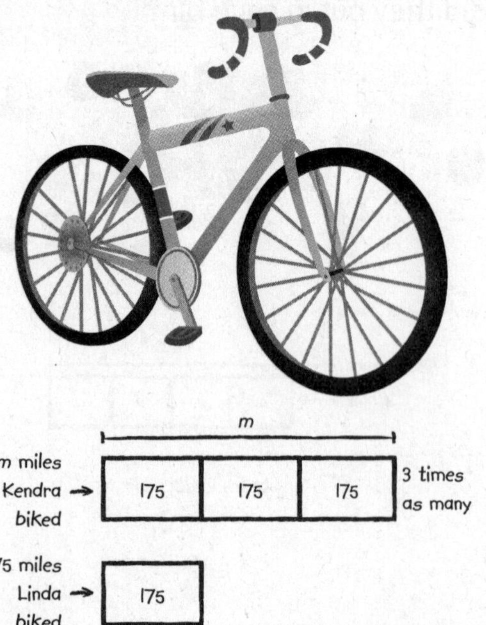

$3 \times 175 = m$

Kendra biked 525 miles.

Multiplier Unknown

Joe buys a new tent and sleeping bag. How many times as much as the sleeping bag does the tent cost?

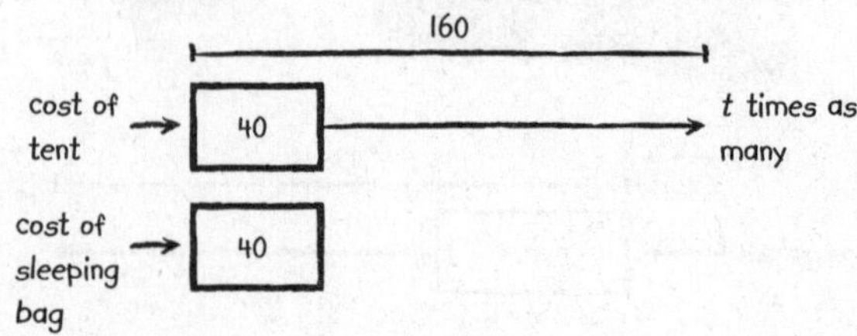

$160 \div 40 = t$ or $40 \times t = 160$

The tent costs 4 times as much as the sleeping bag.

Apply Understanding of Multiplication to Multiply Fractions

Essential Questions: What does it mean to multiply whole numbers and fractions? How can multiplication with whole numbers and fractions be shown using models and symbols?

Physical changes are reversible.

You can change a substance so that it looks and feels different, but it's still the same substance. The molecules haven't changed.

A substance can act differently because of a physical change. Here's a project about kitchen science.

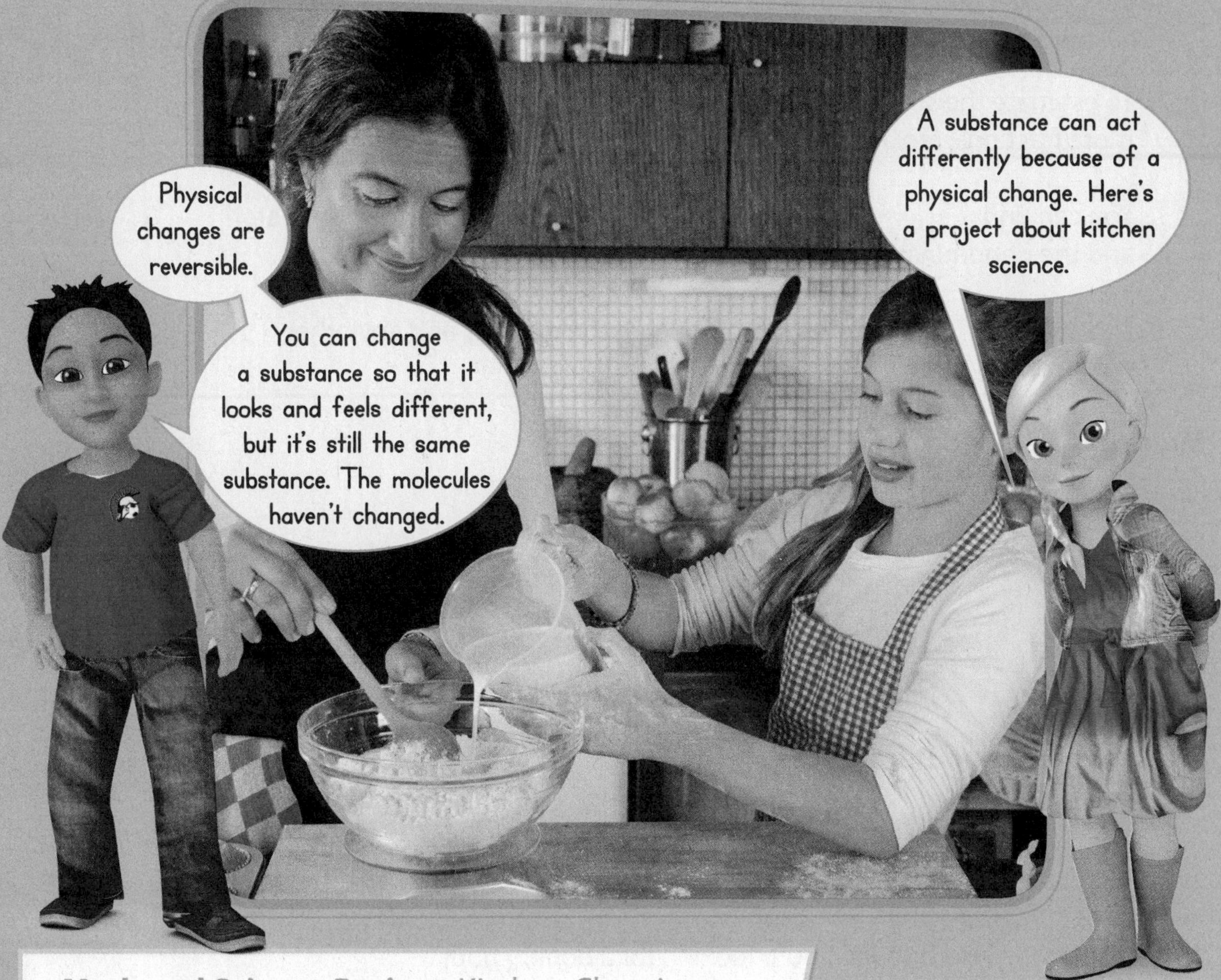

Math and Science Project: Kitchen Chemistry

Do Research Use the Internet or other sources to learn about physical changes to substances. Look for examples of physical changes that occur in the kitchen. When you condense, freeze, melt, vaporize, or whip air into a substance, you are making physical changes to that substance.

Journal: Write a Report Include what you found. Also in your report:

- Give examples of foods that are commonly condensed, frozen, melted, vaporized, or whipped.
- Write your favorite recipe that involves making physical changes to the food.
- Make up and solve multiplication problems with fractions and mixed numbers.

Name ______________________________

Review What You Know

Vocabulary

Choose the best term from the box. Write it on the blank.

- benchmark fractions
- mixed number
- equivalent fractions
- multiple
- factor

1. To estimate the sum of two or more fractions, replace the addends with ____________.

2. You can find ____________ by multiplying both the numerator and the denominator of a fraction by the same nonzero number.

3. A ____________ of a number is a product of the number and any other whole number.

Multiply and Divide

Find each product or quotient.

4. 108×2
5. $270 \div 30$
6. 243×20
7. $288 \div 24$
8. 456×11
9. $432 \div 24$

Fraction Sums and Differences

Find each answer.

10. $\frac{5}{9} + \frac{8}{9}$
11. $2\frac{2}{3} + 5\frac{1}{2}$
12. $\frac{11}{12} - \frac{2}{3}$
13. $6\frac{7}{10} - 2\frac{3}{5}$

14. At the library, Herb spent $\frac{1}{6}$ hour looking for a book, $\frac{1}{4}$ hour reading, and $\frac{1}{2}$ hour doing research on the computer. How many hours did Herb spend at the library?

Common Denominators

15. Explain how you can find a common denominator for $\frac{3}{5}$ and $\frac{5}{8}$.

Name ______________________

Solve

Lesson 8-1
Use Models to Multiply a Whole Number by a Fraction

I can ...
multiply a whole number by a fraction.

Content Standards 5.NF.B.4a, 5.NF.B.6
Mathematical Practices MP.2, MP.3, MP.4, MP.6, MP.7

Solve & Share

Sasha walked $\frac{1}{2}$ mile every day for 5 days. How far did she walk? Use the number line to help you.

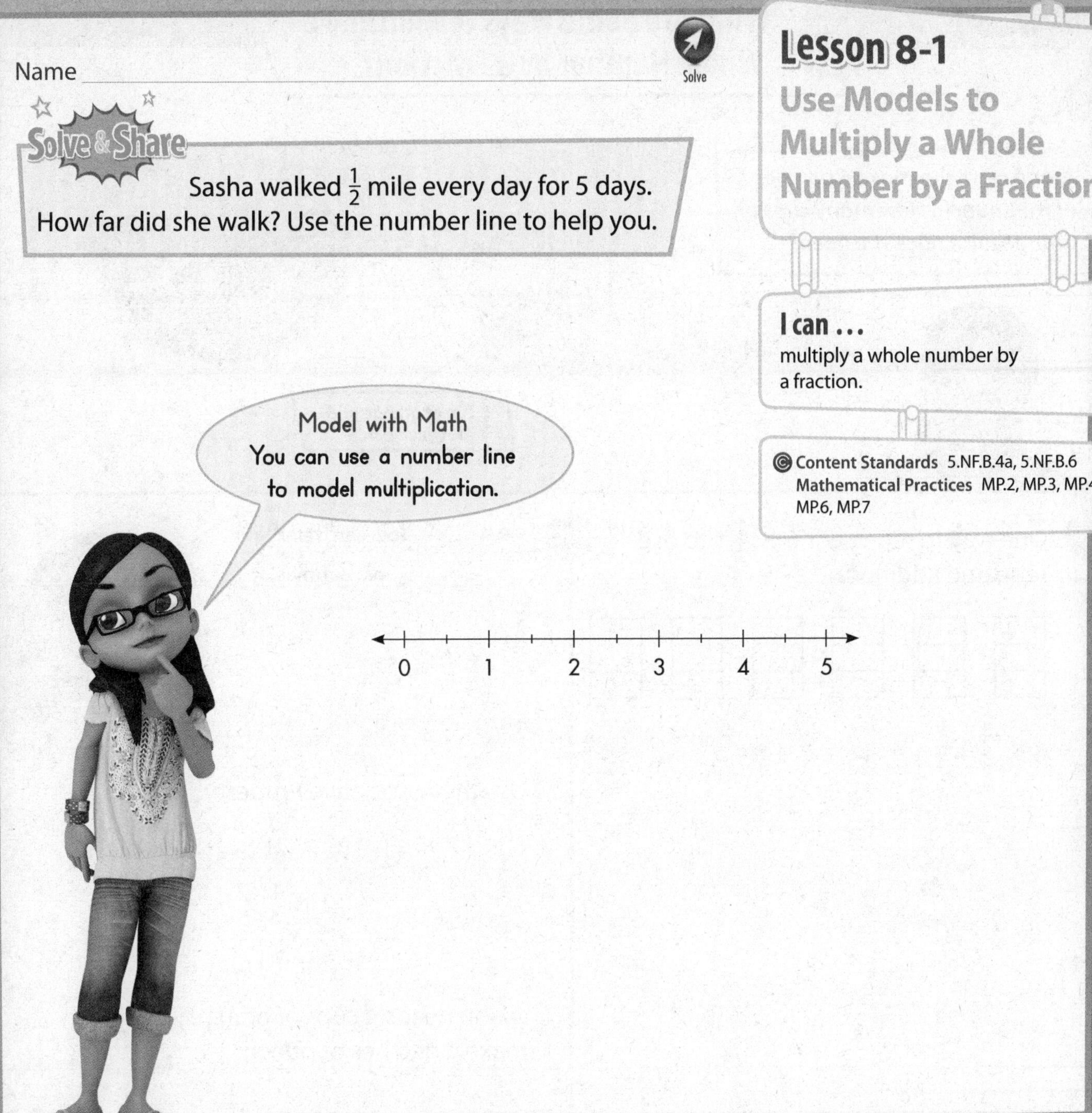

Model with Math
You can use a number line to model multiplication.
0
1
2
3
4
5

Look Back! MP.2 Reasoning How does using a model help you multiply a whole number by a fraction?

What Are Some Ways to Multiply a Whole Number by a Fraction?

A

Joann wants to make 6 batches of fruit punch. How many cups of orange juice does she need?

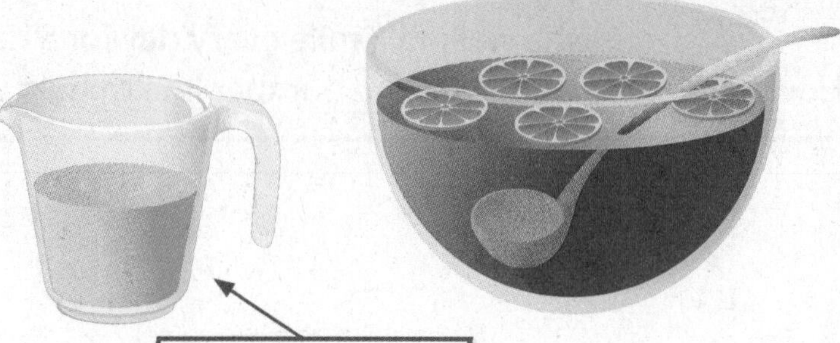

B

One way to represent $6 \times \frac{2}{3}$ is to use repeated addition.

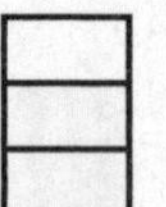 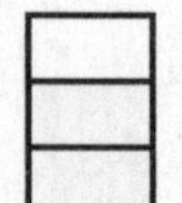 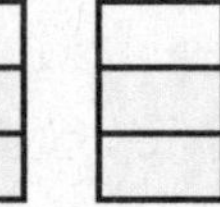 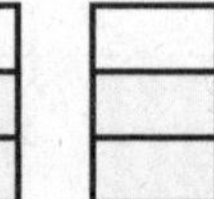 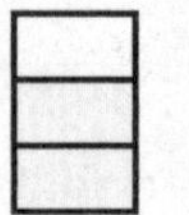 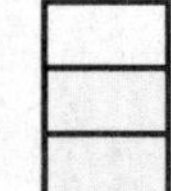

$$6 \times \frac{2}{3} = \frac{2}{3} + \frac{2}{3} + \frac{2}{3} + \frac{2}{3} + \frac{2}{3} + \frac{2}{3}$$
$$= \frac{6 \times 2}{3}$$
$$= \frac{12}{3}$$

So, $6 \times \frac{2}{3} = \frac{12}{3} = 4$.

C

You can think of $\frac{2}{3}$ as 2 times $\frac{1}{3}$.

$\frac{2}{3} = 2 \times \frac{1}{3}$

So, $6 \times \frac{2}{3} = 6 \times \left(2 \times \frac{1}{3}\right)$.

Use the Associative Property.

$$6 \times \left(2 \times \frac{1}{3}\right) = (6 \times 2) \times \frac{1}{3}$$
$$= 12 \times \frac{1}{3}$$
$$= \frac{12}{3} = 4$$

Joann needs 4 cups of orange juice to make 6 batches of punch.

Convince Me! **MP.7 Use Structure** Find $10 \times \frac{3}{5}$. Use repeated addition to check your answer. Show all of your work.

Name ______________________

Practice Buddy Tools Assessment

Guided Practice*

Do You Understand?

1. Micah wants to use Joann's recipe to make 9 batches of punch. How many cups of orange juice does he need?

2. MP.3 Construct Arguments Explain why $8 \times \frac{3}{4}$ is the same as adding $\frac{3}{4} + \frac{3}{4} + \frac{3}{4} + \frac{3}{4} + \frac{3}{4} + \frac{3}{4} + \frac{3}{4} + \frac{3}{4}$.

Do You Know How?

In **3** and **4**, find each product. Shade the model to help solve.

3. $3 \times \frac{2}{3}$

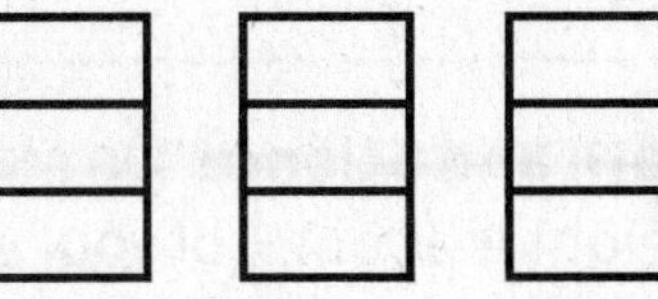

4. $2 \times \frac{3}{5}$

Independent Practice

Leveled Practice In **5–7**, complete each equation to find the product.

5. $6 \times \frac{3}{4} = \frac{\square}{\square} + \frac{\square}{\square} + \frac{\square}{\square} + \frac{\square}{\square} + \frac{\square}{\square} + \frac{\square}{\square} = \frac{\square \times \square}{\square} = \frac{18}{4} = \square$

6. $16 \times \frac{3}{8} = 16 \times \square \times \frac{1}{8} = \frac{\square \times 1}{8} = \frac{\square}{\square} = \square$

7. $500 \times \frac{2}{5} = \square \times 2 \times \frac{\square}{5} = \frac{\square \times 1}{5} = \frac{1{,}000}{\square} = \square$

In **8–15**, find each product. Use models to help.

8. $35 \times \frac{2}{5}$

9. $7 \times \frac{5}{12}$

10. $9 \times \frac{2}{3}$

11. $300 \times \frac{1}{2}$

12. $64 \times \frac{3}{8}$

13. $900 \times \frac{2}{3}$

14. $84 \times \frac{1}{4}$

15. $42 \times \frac{2}{7}$

*For another example, see Set A on page 513.

Math Practices and Problem Solving

16. **Higher Order Thinking** Explain how you would find $36 \times \frac{3}{4}$ mentally.

17. Lions spend about $\frac{5}{6}$ of their day sleeping. How many hours a day does a lion sleep? Write an equation to model your work.

18. **Math and Science** On Mars, your weight is about $\frac{1}{3}$ of your weight on Earth. If Helena weighs 96 pounds on Earth, about how many pounds would she weigh on Mars?

19. Bradley is making fruit salad. For each bowl of fruit salad, he needs $\frac{3}{4}$ cup of grapes. How many cups of grapes will he use if he makes 24 bowls of fruit salad?

20. **MP.3 Construct Arguments** Do you think the difference $1.4 - 0.95$ is less than 1 or greater than 1? Explain.

21. Write a multiplication expression that shows 10^6.

22. **MP.6 Be Precise** The table shows the number of miles each person ran this week. Who ran more miles by the end of the week? How many more?

DATA

	Monday	Wednesday	Saturday
Pat	2.75 mi	3 mi	2.5 mi
Toby	2 mi	2.25 mi	3.5 mi

Common Core Assessment

23. Choose Yes or No to tell if the fraction $\frac{3}{8}$ will make each equation true.

$96 \times \square = 36$ ○ Yes ○ No

$38 \times \square = 14$ ○ Yes ○ No

$16 \times \square = 6$ ○ Yes ○ No

$56 \times \square = 21$ ○ Yes ○ No

24. Choose Yes or No to tell if the number 56 will make each equation true.

$\square \times \frac{1}{2} = 28$ ○ Yes ○ No

$\square \times \frac{2}{7} = 16$ ○ Yes ○ No

$\square \times \frac{8}{9} = 49$ ○ Yes ○ No

$\square \times \frac{1}{4} = 14$ ○ Yes ○ No

Name ___________________________

Homework & Practice 8-1

Use Models to Multiply a Whole Number by a Fraction

Another Look!

Juan needs $\frac{3}{4}$ yard of fabric to make a pillowcase. How many yards of fabric will Juan need to sew 5 pillowcases?

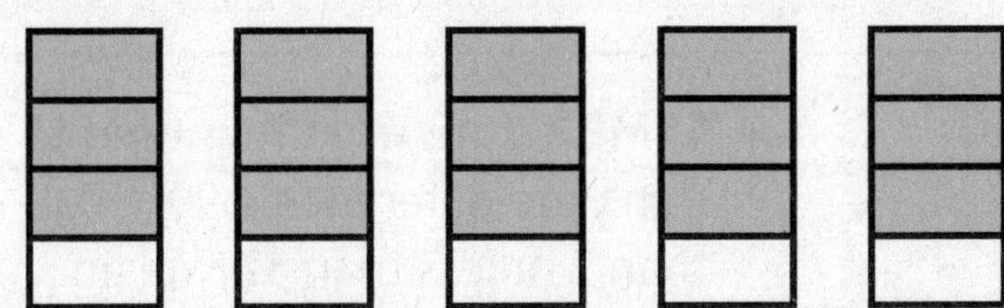

Multiply the whole number by the numerator.

$5 \times 3 = 15$

Write the product over the denominator.

$\frac{15}{4} = 3\frac{3}{4}$

Juan will need $3\frac{3}{4}$ yards of fabric.

Remember: You can check your answer using repeated addition.

Leveled Practice In **1–11**, find each product. Use models to help.

1. $72 \times \frac{5}{12} = \square \times 5 \times \frac{1}{12} = \frac{\square \times 1}{12} = \frac{360}{\square} = \square$

2. $35 \times \frac{2}{5} = \square \times 2 \times \frac{1}{\square} = \frac{\square \times 1}{5} = \frac{\square}{\square} = \square$

3. $12 \times \frac{3}{4} = \frac{\square}{\square} + \frac{\square}{\square} + \frac{\square}{\square} + \frac{\square}{\square} + \frac{\square}{\square} + \frac{\square}{\square} + \frac{\square}{\square} + \frac{\square}{\square} + \frac{\square}{\square} + \frac{\square}{\square} + \frac{\square}{\square} + \frac{\square}{\square} = \frac{\square}{4} = \square$

4. $13 \times \frac{2}{3}$

5. $70 \times \frac{9}{10}$

6. $81 \times \frac{2}{9}$

7. $57 \times \frac{2}{3}$

8. $600 \times \frac{3}{10}$

9. $16 \times \frac{3}{5}$

10. $400 \times \frac{1}{4}$

11. $48 \times \frac{5}{6}$

12. **MP.4 Model with Math** Look at the picture. Write and solve an equation to model the picture. Show your answer as a multiplication equation with $\frac{1}{2}$ as a factor.

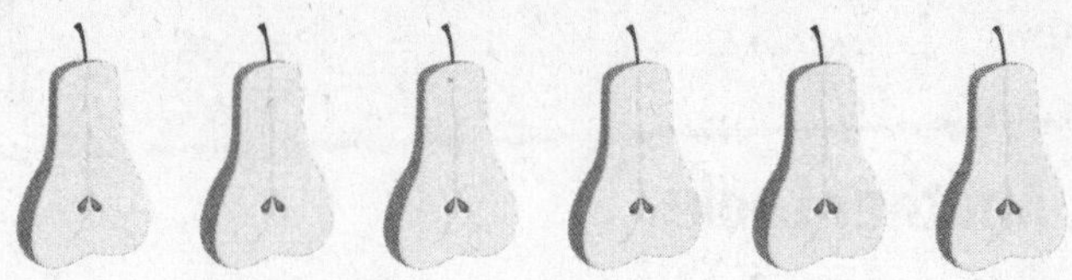

13. **Higher Order Thinking** Explain how you would find $45 \times \frac{7}{9}$ mentally.

14. **MP.3 Construct Arguments** Do you think the difference $2.99 - 0.01$ is greater than 3 or less than 3? Explain.

15. Yara saved \$440. She spent $\frac{3}{4}$ of it on a tablet. How much money did Yara spend on the tablet?

16. Write a multiplication expression that shows 10^5.

17. **Algebra** Tina had \$145. She spent \$40 on fruit at the farmer's market. Solve the equation $40 + c = 145$ to find the amount Tina has left.

\$145	
\$40	c

18. Hippos spend most of their day in water. How many hours a day does a hippo spend in water?

Hippos spend about $\frac{2}{3}$ of their day in water.

Common Core Assessment

19. Choose Yes or No to tell if the number 34 will make each equation true.

$\square \times \frac{1}{2} = 17$	○ Yes ○ No
$51 \times \frac{2}{3} = \square$	○ Yes ○ No
$\square \times \frac{3}{8} = 12$	○ Yes ○ No
$300 \times \frac{1}{9} = \square$	○ Yes ○ No

20. Choose Yes or No to tell if the fraction $\frac{2}{9}$ will make each equation true.

$81 \times \square = 18$	○ Yes ○ No
$900 \times \square = 200$	○ Yes ○ No
$72 \times \square = 16$	○ Yes ○ No
$450 \times \square = 100$	○ Yes ○ No

Name ____________________

Lesson 8-2
Use Models to Multiply a Fraction by a Whole Number

I can ...
multiply a fraction by a whole number.

Content Standards 5.NF.B.4a, 5.NF.B.6
Mathematical Practices MP.2, MP.3, MP.4

Solve & Share

Brandon has 6 eggs. He needs $\frac{2}{3}$ of the eggs to make an omelet. How many eggs does he need?

Model with Math
Would a drawing help you picture the situation?

Look Back! **MP.2 Reasoning** Should your answer be less than or greater than 6? How do you know?

How Can You Model Multiplying a Fraction by a Whole Number?

Claudia has 8 yards of fabric. She needs $\frac{3}{4}$ of the fabric to make a banner. How many yards of fabric does she need?

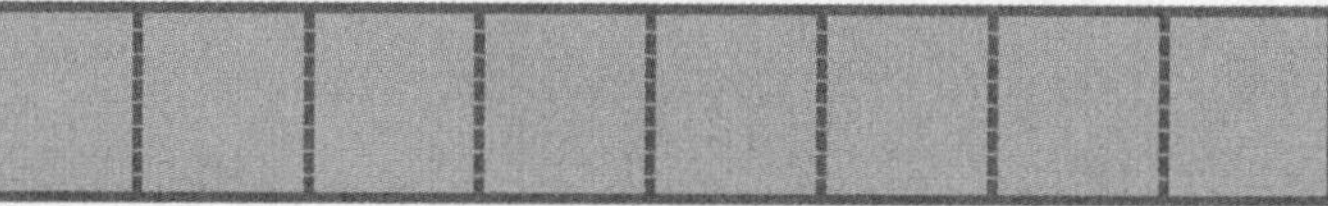

You can use models to represent the problem.
You need to find $\frac{3}{4}$ of 8.

Step 1

Since you are finding $\frac{3}{4}$ of 8, divide the model into 4 equal parts.

Step 2

Since you are finding $\frac{3}{4}$ of 8, take 3 of those parts to make 6.

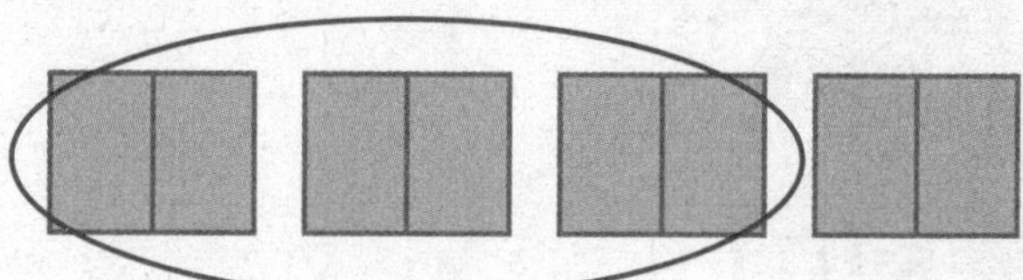

So, $\frac{3}{4} \times 8 = 6$.

Claudia needs 6 yards of fabric to make a banner.

Convince Me! MP.4 Model with Math

Here is how Lydia found the product $\frac{4}{5} \times 10$.

$$\frac{4}{5} \times 10 = 4 \times \frac{1}{5} \times 10$$
$$= 4 \times \frac{10}{5}$$
$$= 4 \times 2 = 8$$

Use the model at the right to show that Lydia's answer is correct.

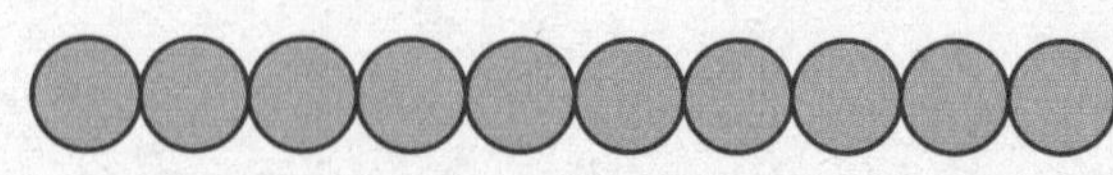

Name ______________________

Practice Buddy Tools Assessment

Another Example

Find $\frac{3}{4} \times 2$.

Divide 2 into 4 equal parts.

Circle 3 parts to get $\frac{3}{2}$.

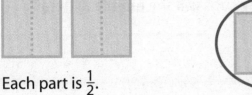

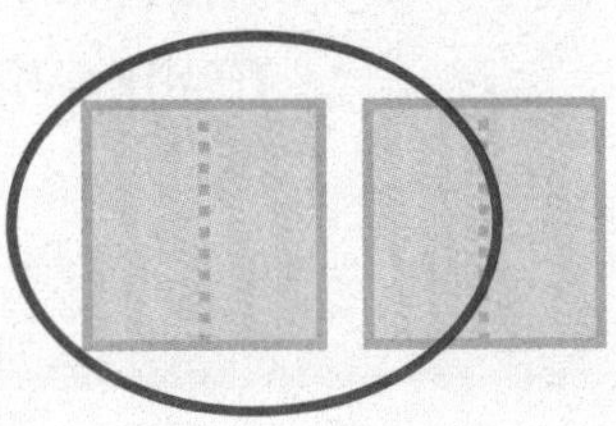

Each part is $\frac{1}{2}$.

So, $\frac{3}{4} \times 2 = \frac{3}{2}$.

Think three-fourths of 2 wholes.

Guided Practice*

Do You Understand?

1. **MP.3 Construct Arguments** Explain why the product of $4 \times \frac{2}{3}$ is the same as the product of $\frac{2}{3} \times 4$.

2. In the problem at the top of page 464, what multiplication equation could be used to find how many yards of fabric Claudia did not use?

Do You Know How?

In **3** and **4**, use the model to find each product.

3. $\frac{2}{3} \times 6$

4. $\frac{3}{8} \times 4$

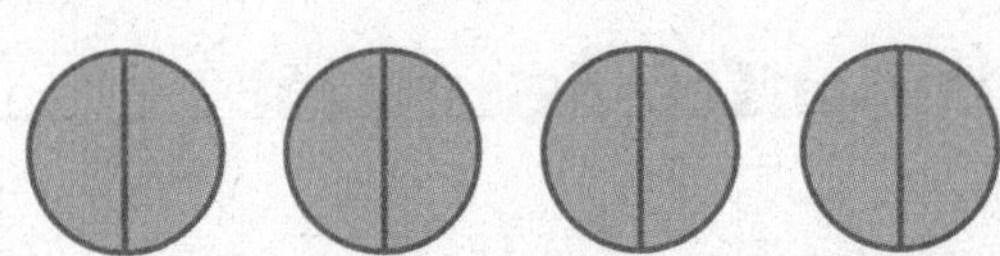

Independent Practice

In **5–7**, find each product. Draw models to help.

5. $\frac{2}{3} \times 15$

6. $\frac{11}{12} \times 6$

7. $\frac{5}{8} \times 16$

*For another example, see Set B on page 513.

Math Practices and Problem Solving

8. **MP.3 Construct Arguments** Janice said that when you multiply a fraction less than 1 by a nonzero whole number, the product is always less than the whole number. Do you agree?

9. **Math and Science** A scientist wants to find out how the properties of water change when salt is added to it. For every cup of water she has, she replaces $\frac{1}{8}$ of it with salt. If she has 24 cups of water, how many cups will she replace with salt?

10. Shanna attends school for 1 week longer than $\frac{3}{4}$ of the year. How many weeks in a year does Shanna attend school?

11. **Higher Order Thinking** Gina has 48 stickers. $\frac{3}{8}$ of the stickers have pictures of flowers. $\frac{1}{8}$ of the stickers have pictures of plants. The rest of the stickers have pictures of people. How many stickers have pictures of people? Explain how you found your answer.

12. Two paperback books cost a total of \$10. How much change will Stacy get if she buys two hardcover books and two paperback books and gives the clerk three \$20 bills?

Sale: Hardcover books, \$18.25 each

Common Core Assessment

13. Draw lines to match each expression on the left to its product on the right.

$\frac{3}{4} \times 16$	10
$\frac{5}{12} \times 12$	5
$\frac{9}{10} \times 5$	12
$\frac{2}{3} \times 15$	$4\frac{1}{2}$

14. Draw lines to match each equation on the left to the number on the right that makes the equation true.

$\frac{2}{3} \times \square = \frac{8}{3}$	4
$\frac{5}{6} \times \square = 10$	13
$\frac{1}{12} \times \square = 4$	12
$\frac{1}{2} \times \square = \frac{13}{2}$	48

Name ____________________

Help Practice Buddy Tools Games

Homework & Practice 8-2

Use Models to Multiply a Fraction by a Whole Number

Another Look!

Tyler used $\frac{2}{3}$ of a 9-yard-long piece of fabric to make a jacket. What was the length of fabric, in yards, that he used?

Remember: $\frac{2}{3}$ of 9 means $\frac{2}{3} \times 9$.

Step 1

Draw 9 circles and separate them into 3 equal groups.

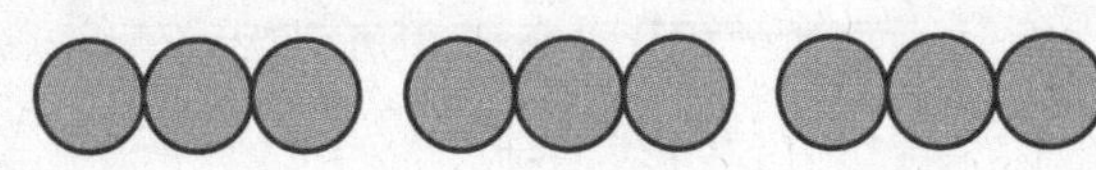

Step 2

Circle 2 of the groups.

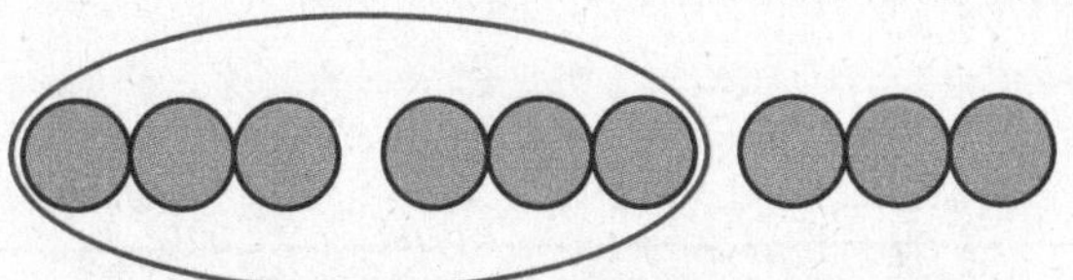

So, Tyler used 6 yards of fabric.

Leveled Practice In **1–8**, find each product. Use models to help.

1. $\frac{5}{10} \times 5$

2. $\frac{3}{5} \times 10$

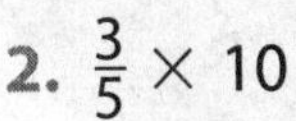

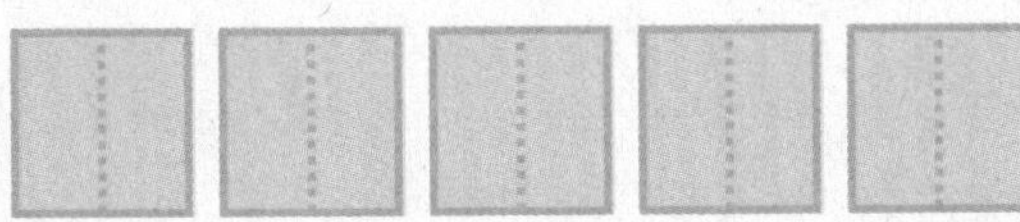

3. $\frac{5}{6} \times 3$

4. $\frac{5}{6}$ of 12

5. $\frac{3}{5}$ of 20

6. $\frac{2}{3}$ of 8

7. $\frac{2}{9} \times 3$

8. $\frac{4}{7} \times 21$

9. **MP.3 Critique Reasoning** Find the error in the work below. Then show the correct calculation.

$\frac{8}{12} \times 6 = 8 \times \frac{1}{12} \times 6 = 8 \times \frac{1}{72} = \frac{8}{72} = \frac{1}{9}$

10. A scientist measured the amount of rainfall during the afternoon. It rained 0.43 inch each hour. What was the total amount of rainfall in 3 hours?

11. **MP.2 Reasoning** A giraffe can run at a speed of 32 miles per hour. Which animal listed in the chart has a speed that is $\frac{15}{16}$ of the speed of a giraffe? Explain how you found your answer.

DATA

Animal	Speed (in miles per hour)
Cat	30
Cheetah	70
Jackal	35

12. If a frilled lizard is 90 centimeters long, how long is the tail?

The frilled lizard's tail is $\frac{2}{3}$ of its length.

13. **Higher Order Thinking** Eric has 240 coins in his collection. $\frac{11}{20}$ of the coins are pennies. $\frac{4}{20}$ of the coins are nickels. The rest of the coins are quarters. How many of the coins are quarters? Explain how you found your answer.

Common Core Assessment

14. Draw lines to match each equation on the left to the fraction on the right that makes the equation true.

$\square \times 4 = \frac{8}{3}$	$\frac{1}{2}$
$\square \times 15 = 12$	$\frac{2}{3}$
$\square \times 21 = 15$	$\frac{5}{7}$
$\frac{1}{6} \times 3 = \square$	$\frac{4}{5}$

15. Draw lines to match each expression on the left to its product on the right.

$\frac{11}{12} \times 12$	9
$\frac{7}{9} \times 18$	6
$\frac{3}{8} \times 16$	14
$\frac{3}{4} \times 12$	11

Name ______________________

Lesson 8-3
Multiply Fractions and Whole Numbers

I can ...
multiply fractions and whole numbers.

Content Standard 5.NF.B.4a
Mathematical Practices MP.2, MP.3, MP.4, MP.6

Solve & Share

Julie has 10 yards of ribbon. She divides the ribbon into 3 equal pieces and uses 2 of the pieces on gifts. How much ribbon does she use? ***Solve this problem any way you choose.***

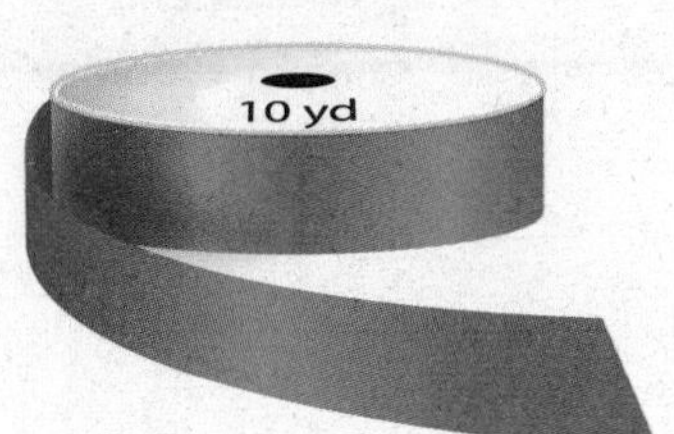

Model with Math You can use words, pictures, and equations to solve the problem. *Show your work in the space above!*

Look Back! **MP.2 Reasoning** Should the answer be less than or greater than 5? How do you know?

How Can You Multiply Fractions and Whole Numbers?

A

Hal spent $\frac{3}{4}$ hour reading each day for 7 days. How much total time did he spend reading?

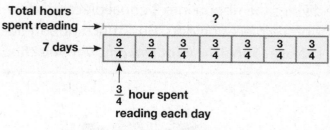

Total hours spent reading → ?

7 days → | $\frac{3}{4}$ | $\frac{3}{4}$ | $\frac{3}{4}$ | $\frac{3}{4}$ | $\frac{3}{4}$ | $\frac{3}{4}$ | $\frac{3}{4}$ |

$\frac{3}{4}$ hour spent reading each day

B One Way

Multiply to find the number of fourths.

$$7 \times \frac{3}{4} = 7 \times 3 \times \frac{1}{4}$$
$$= 21 \times \frac{1}{4}$$
$$= \frac{21}{4}$$

To rename $\frac{21}{4}$, divide the numerator by the denominator.

Rewrite as a mixed number.

$$\frac{21}{4} = 5\frac{1}{4}$$

Hal spent $5\frac{1}{4}$ hours reading.

C Another Way

Rename the whole number as a fraction. Multiply the numerators, multiply the denominators, and then write the product as a mixed number.

$$\frac{7}{1} \times \frac{3}{4} = \frac{7 \times 3}{1 \times 4} = \frac{21}{4} = 5\frac{1}{4}$$

Hal spent $5\frac{1}{4}$ hours reading.

Every whole number can be written as a fraction with a denominator of 1.

Convince Me! © **MP.6 Be Precise** Find $6 \times \frac{4}{9}$. Then use repeated addition to justify your answer.

Name ______________________________

Guided Practice*

Do You Understand?

1. MP.2 Reasoning In the example at the top of the previous page, how can finding $\frac{1}{4}$ of 7 help you find $\frac{3}{4}$ of 7?

2. If Hal spent $\frac{2}{3}$ of an hour reading each day for 7 days, how much time, in all, did he spend reading? Show how you found your answer.

Do You Know How?

In **3–5**, find each product. Write the product as a mixed number.

3. $\frac{3}{8} \times 4 = \frac{\square \times \square}{\square} = \frac{\square}{\square} = \square\frac{\square}{\square} = \square\frac{\square}{\square}$

4. $8 \times \frac{5}{6} = \frac{\square \times \square}{\square} = \frac{\square}{\square} = \square\frac{\square}{\square} = \square\frac{\square}{\square}$

5. $5 \times \frac{4}{7} = \frac{\square \times \square}{\square} = \frac{\square}{\square} = \square\frac{\square}{\square}$

Independent Practice

Leveled Practice In **6–16**, find each product. Write the product as a mixed number.

Remember: You can use division to rename a fraction as a mixed number.

6. $\frac{3}{4} \times 14 = \frac{\square \times \square}{\square} = \frac{\square}{\square} = \square\frac{\square}{\square} = \square\frac{\square}{\square}$

7. $600 \times \frac{2}{3} = \frac{\square \times \square}{\square} = \frac{\square}{\square} = \square$

8. $\frac{5}{9} \times 37 = \frac{\square \times \square}{\square} = \frac{\square}{\square} = \square\frac{\square}{\square}$

9. $\frac{4}{5} \times 500$

10. $5 \times \frac{2}{3}$

11. $17 \times \frac{6}{8}$

12. $\frac{9}{10} \times 25$

13. $\frac{7}{8} \times 320$

14. $28 \times \frac{7}{12}$

15. $\frac{2}{3} \times 1{,}287$

16. $900 \times \frac{2}{9}$

*For another example, see Set B on page 513.

Math Practices and Problem Solving

17. About 0.6 of the human body is made up of water. If a person has a mass of 75 kilograms, what is the mass of the water in this person's body?

18. **Number Sense** How can you use mental math to find $25 \times \frac{3}{10}$?

19. During a nature walk, Jill identified 20 species of animals and plants.

   a **MP.3 Construct Arguments** Jill said that $\frac{1}{3}$ of the species she identified were animals. Can this be correct? Explain.

   b If $\frac{3}{5}$ of the species Jill identified were animals, how many plants did Jill identify?

20. A rectangular painting is 2 feet long and $\frac{5}{6}$ foot wide. What is the area of the painting?

21. **Higher Order Thinking** An art teacher makes a batch of purple paint by mixing $\frac{3}{4}$ cup red paint with $\frac{3}{4}$ cup blue paint. If she mixes 13 batches, how many cups of purple paint will she have?

22. **Math and Science** A water molecule is made up of 3 atoms. One third of the atoms are oxygen and the remaining atoms are hydrogen. If there are 114 water molecules, how many hydrogen atoms are there? Show your work.

Common Core Assessment

23. Which is the product of 14 and $\frac{3}{7}$?

   Ⓐ $2\frac{3}{7}$

   Ⓑ 5

   Ⓒ 6

   Ⓓ $32\frac{2}{3}$

24. Which is the product of $\frac{11}{12}$ and 4?

   Ⓐ $1\frac{1}{4}$

   Ⓑ $3\frac{2}{3}$

   Ⓒ $4\frac{1}{3}$

   Ⓓ 33

Name ___________________________

Help | Practice Buddy | Tools | Games

Homework & Practice 8-3

Multiply Fractions and Whole Numbers

Another Look!

Lorena has a 16-inch long scarf, and $\frac{2}{3}$ of its length is red. How many inches long is the red section of the scarf?

Since you are multiplying 16 by a fraction less than 1, the answer will be less than 16.

Step 1	Step 2	Step 3
Multiply. $\frac{2}{3} \times 16 = \frac{2 \times 16}{3} = \frac{32}{3}$	Rewrite as a mixed number. $\frac{32}{3} = 10\frac{2}{3}$	Answer the question. The red section of the scarf is $10\frac{2}{3}$ inches long.

Leveled Practice In **1–16**, find each product. Write each product as a mixed number.

1. $26 \times \frac{3}{4} = \frac{\square \times \square}{\square} = \frac{\square}{\square} = \square\frac{\square}{\square}$

2. $9 \times \frac{7}{10} = \frac{\square \times \square}{\square} = \frac{\square}{\square} = \square\frac{\square}{\square}$

3. $\frac{2}{5} \times 32 = \frac{\square \times \square}{\square} = \frac{\square}{\square} = \square\frac{\square}{\square}$

4. $\frac{1}{8} \times 400 = \frac{\square \times \square}{\square} = \frac{\square}{\square} = \square$

5. $15 \times \frac{4}{5}$

6. $\frac{3}{11} \times 66$

7. $45 \times \frac{3}{8}$

8. $\frac{3}{10} \times 12$

9. $55 \times \frac{2}{5}$

10. $\frac{5}{6} \times 40$

11. $\frac{7}{9} \times 54$

12. $600 \times \frac{5}{12}$

13. $\frac{2}{3} \times 21$

14. $500 \times \frac{3}{5}$

15. $72 \times \frac{5}{8}$

16. $\frac{2}{9} \times 35$

17. **MP.4 Model with Math** Find $6 \times \frac{3}{5}$. Use the model at the right to find the product.

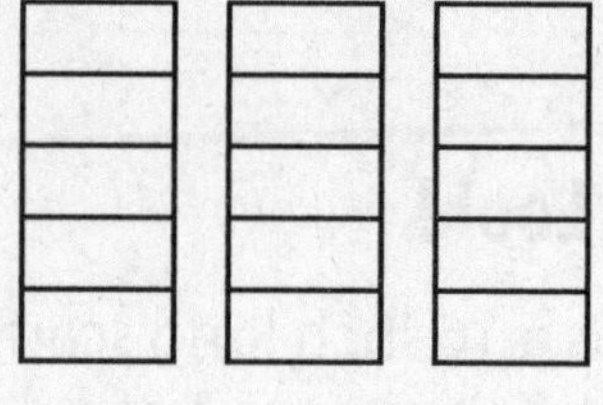

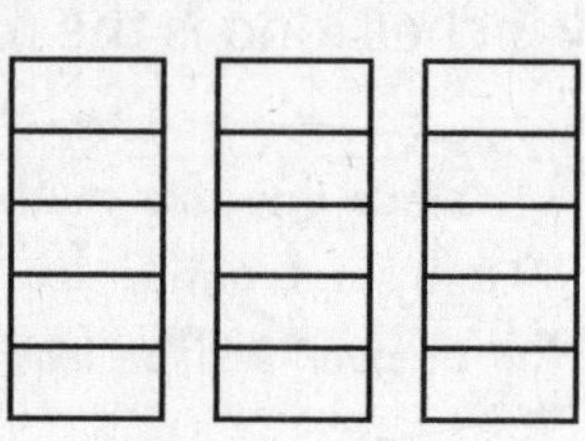

18. What mixed number represents the part of the model you did **NOT** shade for Exercise 17?

19. **MP.2 Reasoning** Without multiplying, tell which is greater: 0.75×81 or 0.9×81. Explain.

20. **MP.2 Reasoning** Without multiplying, tell which is greater: $\frac{4}{5} \times 45$ or $\frac{2}{3} \times 45$. Explain.

21. **Higher Order Thinking** The school library has 2,469 books. Two-thirds of the books are paperbacks. How many books are paperbacks?

How can you use estimation to check that your answer is reasonable?

22. The table shows the amount of apple sauce made from one apple of each size. Patrice has 17 medium apples and 23 large apples. What is the total amount of apple sauce that she can make with these apples?

DATA

Apple Size	Amount of Apple Sauce
Small	$\frac{1}{3}$ cup
Medium	$\frac{1}{2}$ cup
Large	$\frac{3}{4}$ cup

Common Core Assessment

23. Which is the product of $\frac{4}{9}$ and 72?

Ⓐ 12
Ⓑ 32
Ⓒ $32\frac{4}{9}$
Ⓓ 36

24. Which is the product of 56 and $\frac{5}{9}$?

Ⓐ $1\frac{4}{9}$
Ⓑ 30
Ⓒ 31
Ⓓ $31\frac{1}{9}$

Name ___

Lesson 8-4
Use Models to Multiply Two Fractions

I can ...
use models to multiply two fractions.

Content Standard 5.NF.B.4a
Mathematical Practices MP.2, MP.4, MP.6

Solve & Share

The art teacher gave each student half of a sheet of paper. Then she asked the students to color one fourth of their pieces of paper. What part of the original sheet did the students color? ***Solve this problem any way you choose.***

Model with Math
You can draw a picture to represent the problem.

Look Back! **MP.2 Reasoning** Should your answer be less than or greater than 1? How do you know?

How Can You Use a Model to Multiply Fractions?

A

There was $\frac{1}{4}$ of a pan of lasagna left. Tom ate $\frac{1}{3}$ of this amount. What fraction of a whole pan of lasagna did he eat?

Find $\frac{1}{3}$ of $\frac{1}{4}$ to solve the problem.

B One Way

Divide one whole into fourths.

Divide $\frac{1}{4}$ into 3 equal parts.

Divide the other $\frac{1}{4}$s into 3 equal parts.

12 parts make one whole, so one part is $\frac{1}{12}$.

$$\frac{1}{3} \times \frac{1}{4} = \frac{1}{12}$$

C Another Way

Shade 1 of the 3 rows yellow to represent $\frac{1}{3}$.

Shade 1 of the 4 columns red to represent $\frac{1}{4}$.

The orange overlap shows the product.

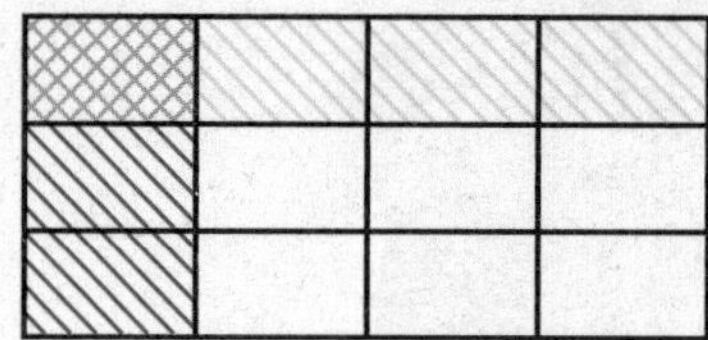

1 out of 12 parts are shaded orange.

$$\frac{1}{3} \times \frac{1}{4} = \frac{1 \times 1}{3 \times 4} = \frac{1}{12}$$

Tom ate $\frac{1}{12}$ of the pan of lasagna.

Convince Me! **MP.4 Model with Math** Find $\frac{1}{4} \times \frac{1}{5}$ using the area model. Explain your work.

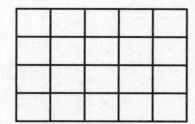

Another Example

Find $\frac{2}{3} \times \frac{3}{4}$ using a number line.

$\frac{1}{3}$ means 1 of 3 equal parts, so $\frac{1}{3}$ of $\frac{3}{4}$ is $\frac{1}{4}$.

$\frac{2}{3}$ means 2 of 3 equal parts, so $\frac{2}{3}$ of $\frac{3}{4}$ is 2 times $\frac{1}{4}$.

$\frac{2}{3} \times \frac{3}{4} = \frac{2}{4}$ or $\frac{1}{2}$

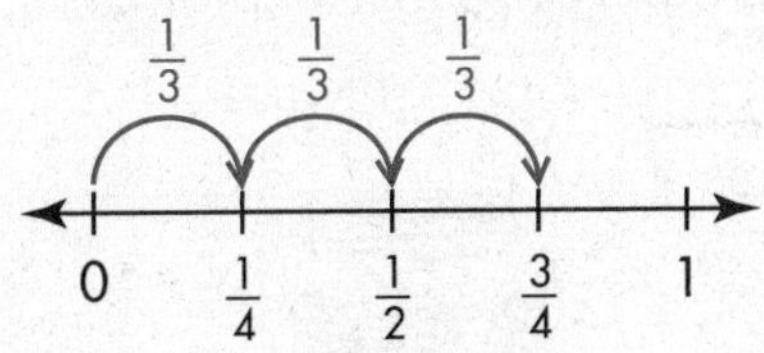

Guided Practice*

Do You Understand?

1. Tina has $\frac{1}{2}$ of a pan of cornbread leftover from a dinner party. She eats $\frac{1}{2}$ of the leftover part the next night. How much of the whole pan does she eat? Write an equation to model your work.

2. In the example on page 476, find the fraction of a whole pan of lasagna that Tom ate if he started with $\frac{7}{8}$ of a pan.

Do You Know How?

3. Find $\frac{5}{6} \times \frac{1}{2}$. Shade the model to help solve.

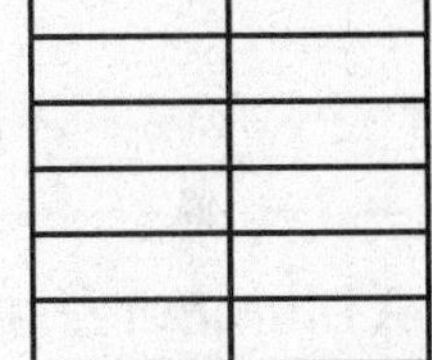

4. Find $\frac{3}{4}$ of $\frac{4}{9}$.

Independent Practice

In **5–6**, find each product. Shade the model to help solve.

5. $\frac{1}{3} \times \frac{5}{6}$

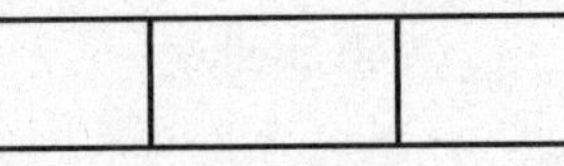

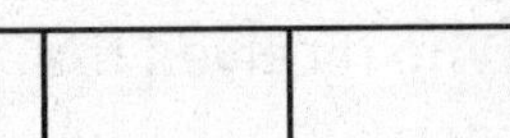

6. $\frac{2}{3} \times \frac{1}{12}$

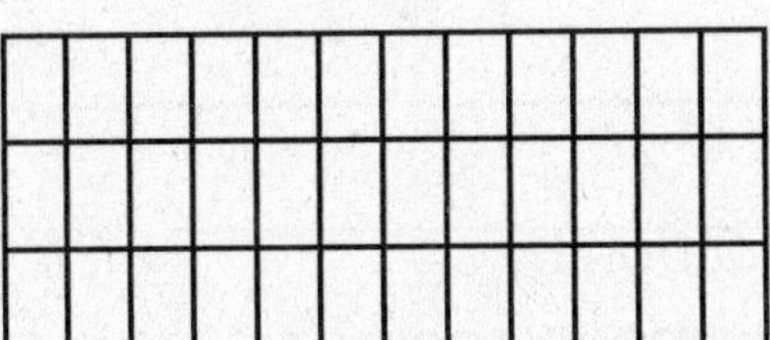

In **7–14**, find each product. Use models to help.

7. $\frac{7}{8} \times \frac{1}{2}$

8. $\frac{2}{5} \times \frac{1}{12}$

9. $\frac{5}{7}$ of $\frac{7}{9}$

10. $\frac{1}{2} \times \frac{3}{4}$

11. $\frac{1}{4} \times \frac{7}{8}$

12. $\frac{5}{6}$ of $\frac{9}{10}$

13. $\frac{1}{4} \times \frac{1}{8}$

14. $\frac{1}{3}$ of $\frac{3}{7}$

*For another example, see Set C on page 514.

Math Practices and Problem Solving

15. **MP.2 Reasoning** Will $50 be enough to buy 6 cans of paint? Explain.

16. A scientist had $\frac{3}{4}$ of a bottle of a solution. She used $\frac{1}{6}$ of the solution in an experiment. How much of the bottle did she use?

17. **Algebra** What value of n makes the equation $\frac{2}{3} \times n = \frac{4}{9}$ true?

18. Write an expression that shows 10^4.

19. A plumber charges $45 for the first hour and $30 for each additional hour. How much does he charge if it takes him 4 hours to make a repair?

20. **Higher Order Thinking** If $\frac{7}{8}$ is multiplied by $\frac{4}{5}$, will the product be greater than either of the two factors? Explain.

21. In the voting for City Council Precinct 5, only $\frac{1}{2}$ of all eligible voters cast votes. What fraction of all eligible voters voted for Shelley? Morgan? Who received the most votes?

DATA

Candidate	Fraction of Votes Received
Shelley	$\frac{3}{10}$
Morgan	$\frac{5}{8}$

Common Core Assessment

22. Majid made the model to show multiplying a fraction by a fraction. Which multiplication sentence does the model show?

Ⓐ $\frac{3}{4} \times \frac{8}{9} = \frac{2}{3}$

Ⓑ $\frac{1}{3} \times \frac{1}{8} = \frac{1}{24}$

Ⓒ $\frac{3}{4} \times \frac{3}{9} = \frac{1}{4}$

Ⓓ $\frac{3}{9} \times \frac{8}{9} = \frac{8}{27}$

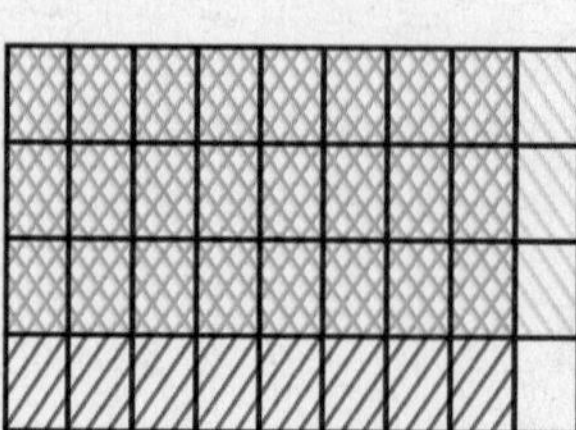

Name ______________________

Homework & Practice 8-4

Use Models to Multiply Two Fractions

Another Look!

Graeme reserved $\frac{1}{2}$ of the seats in a restaurant for a dinner party. $\frac{1}{8}$ of those seats will be needed for family and the rest for his friends. What fraction of the restaurant's seats will be used by the family?

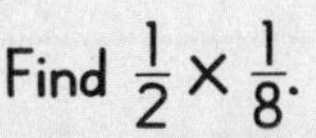

Step 1

Draw a picture to represent $\frac{1}{8}$. Draw a rectangle that has lines dividing it into 8 equal parts. Shade 1 of the 8 parts.

Step 2

Then draw a horizontal line to show $\frac{1}{2}$. Shade $\frac{1}{2}$ of the whole rectangle. The purple overlap is the answer.

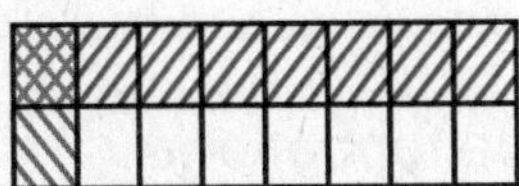

The two shadings overlap on $\frac{1}{16}$ of the whole rectangle.

$\frac{1}{16}$ of the restaurant's seats will be used by Graeme's family.

In **1–3**, find each product. Shade the model to help solve.

1. $\frac{4}{7} \times \frac{2}{3}$

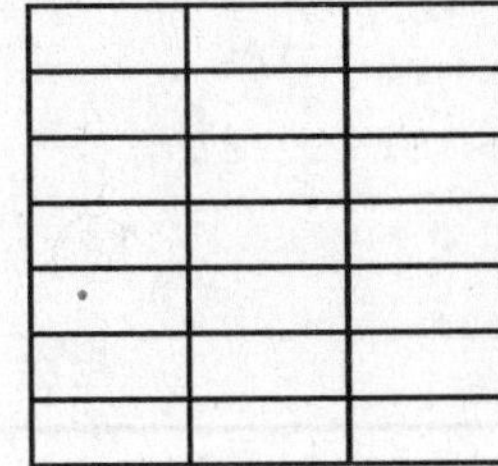

2. $\frac{1}{2} \times \frac{11}{12}$

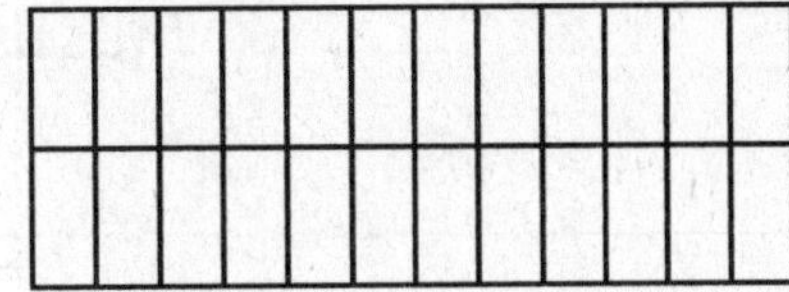

3. $\frac{2}{5}$ of $\frac{1}{4}$

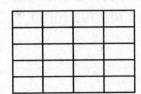

In **4–11**, find each product. Use models to help you.

4. $\frac{3}{4} \times \frac{1}{8}$

5. $\frac{8}{9}$ of $\frac{9}{10}$

6. $\frac{3}{7} \times \frac{2}{3}$

7. $\frac{1}{5} \times \frac{5}{6}$

8. $\frac{1}{6}$ of $\frac{3}{4}$

9. $\frac{7}{8} \times \frac{1}{2}$

10. $\frac{1}{12} \times \frac{3}{5}$

11. $\frac{1}{2}$ of $\frac{5}{9}$

12. **Algebra** What value of n makes the equation $n \times \frac{3}{4} = \frac{3}{16}$ true?

13. **MP.2 Reasoning** $\frac{4}{9} \times \frac{7}{8} = \frac{7}{18}$. What is $\frac{7}{8} \times \frac{4}{9}$? How do you know without multiplying?

14. **MP.6 Be Precise** The stained glass shown here is a hexagon. How can you use multiplication to find its perimeter?

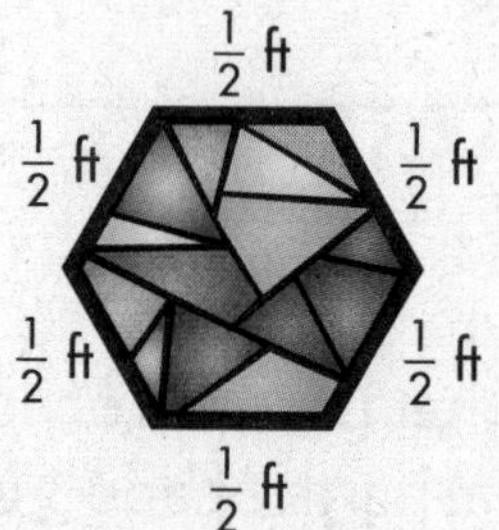

15. Vincent found a recipe for banana macadamia nut bread that uses $\frac{3}{4}$ cup of macadamia nuts. If he only wants to make half the recipe, how many cups of macadamia nuts should he use?

16. **Higher Order Thinking** If $\frac{1}{2}$ is multiplied by $\frac{1}{2}$, will the product be greater than $\frac{1}{2}$? Explain.

17. In gym class, Matthew runs $\frac{3}{4}$ mile. His gym teacher runs 3 times that distance. How far does Matthew's gym teacher run?

18. Titus had $\frac{1}{2}$ of a can of paint. He used $\frac{2}{3}$ of the paint to cover a tabletop. What fraction of a full can of paint did Titus use?

Common Core Assessment

19. Nola made the model to show multiplying a fraction by a fraction. Which multiplication sentence does the model show?

Ⓐ $\frac{1}{2} \times \frac{1}{2} = \frac{1}{4}$

Ⓑ $\frac{1}{3} \times \frac{4}{5} = \frac{4}{15}$

Ⓒ $\frac{1}{3} \times \frac{1}{5} = \frac{1}{15}$

Ⓓ $\frac{4}{9} \times \frac{4}{5} = \frac{16}{45}$

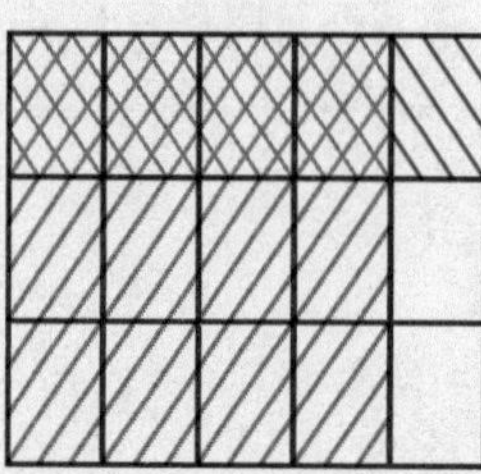

Name ____________________

Lesson 8-5
Multiply Two Fractions

I can ...
multiply two fractions.

Content Standard 5.NF.B.4a
Mathematical Practices MP.1, MP.2, MP.3, MP.4, MP.6

Solve & Share On Dan's eReader, $\frac{2}{3}$ of the books are fiction. Of the fiction books, $\frac{4}{5}$ are mysteries. What fraction of the books on Dan's eReader are mysteries? ***Solve this problem any way you choose.***

You can model with math by writing a multiplication sentence to solve the problem.

Look Back! **MP.2 Reasoning** What fraction of the books are not mysteries? Explain.

How Can You Find the Product of Two Fractions?

A

Amelia takes pictures with her smartphone. Of the pictures, $\frac{5}{6}$ are of animals. What fraction of all her pictures are of dogs?

$\frac{3}{4}$ of her animal photos are of dogs.

You need to find $\frac{3}{4}$ of $\frac{5}{6}$ to answer the question.

B

Step 1

Estimate $\frac{3}{4} \times \frac{5}{6}$.

Since both fractions are less than 1, the product will be less than 1.

C

Step 2

Multiply the numerators together. Then multiply the denominators together.

$$\frac{3}{4} \times \frac{5}{6} = \frac{3 \times 5}{4 \times 6}$$
$$= \frac{15}{24}$$

Since $\frac{15}{24} < 1$, the answer is reasonable.

So, $\frac{15}{24}$ or $\frac{5}{8}$ of all Amelia's pictures have dogs in them.

$\frac{15}{24}$ and $\frac{5}{8}$ are equivalent fractions.

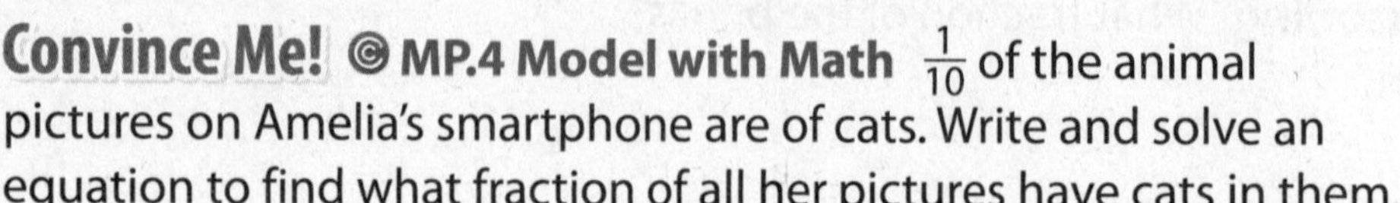

Convince Me! **MP.4 Model with Math** $\frac{1}{10}$ of the animal pictures on Amelia's smartphone are of cats. Write and solve an equation to find what fraction of all her pictures have cats in them.

Name

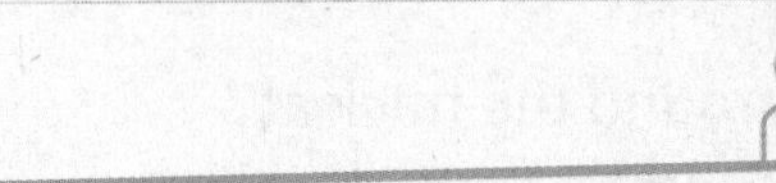

Guided Practice*

Do You Understand?

1. MP.2 Reasoning Is the product of $\frac{3}{6} \times \frac{5}{4}$ equal to the product of $\frac{3}{4} \times \frac{5}{6}$? Explain how you know.

2. MP.3 Construct Arguments Why is adding $\frac{3}{9}$ and $\frac{6}{9}$ different from multiplying the two fractions? Explain.

Do You Know How?

In **3–10**, find each product.

3. $\frac{2}{3} \times \frac{1}{2}$
4. $\frac{5}{9}$ of $\frac{1}{9}$
5. $\frac{7}{10} \times \frac{3}{4}$
6. $\frac{1}{3} \times \frac{1}{4}$
7. $\frac{5}{6}$ of $\frac{3}{7}$
8. $\frac{3}{5} \times \frac{11}{12}$
9. $\frac{4}{10} \times \frac{2}{5}$
10. $\frac{3}{4} \times \frac{2}{9}$

Independent Practice

In **11–30**, find each product.

11. $\frac{9}{10} \times \frac{1}{2}$
12. $\frac{5}{6} \times \frac{1}{3}$
13. $\frac{4}{7}$ of $\frac{7}{9}$
14. $\frac{3}{4} \times \frac{4}{5}$
15. $\frac{2}{3} \times \frac{7}{8}$
16. $\frac{5}{6}$ of $\frac{11}{12}$
17. $\frac{1}{3}$ of $\frac{3}{4}$
18. $\frac{6}{7} \times \frac{3}{8}$
19. $\frac{2}{5}$ of $\frac{5}{12}$
20. $\frac{2}{3} \times \frac{4}{5}$
21. $\frac{1}{2} \times \frac{1}{2}$
22. $\frac{1}{2}$ of $\frac{8}{9}$
23. $\left(\frac{1}{6} + \frac{1}{6}\right) \times \frac{3}{4}$
24. $\left(\frac{3}{7} + \frac{2}{7}\right) \times \frac{2}{3}$
25. $\frac{1}{2} \times \left(\frac{1}{3} + \frac{1}{3}\right)$
26. $\left(\frac{9}{10} - \frac{3}{10}\right) \times \frac{1}{4}$
27. $\frac{2}{3} \times \left(\frac{3}{5} + \frac{1}{5}\right)$
28. $\left(\frac{8}{9} - \frac{1}{3}\right) \times \frac{3}{4}$
29. $\left(\frac{5}{12} + \frac{1}{6}\right) \times \frac{5}{6}$
30. $\frac{11}{12} \times \left(\frac{3}{4} - \frac{1}{2}\right)$

*For another example, see Set D on page 514.

Math Practices and Problem Solving

31. Eduardo runs 6 laps around the track at Lincoln Park School. Then he runs $3\frac{1}{2}$ miles to get home. How far will he run in all? Show your work.

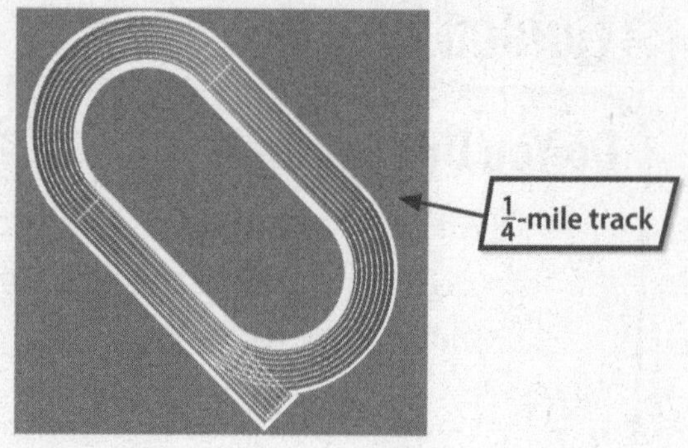

32. **MP.6 Be Precise** To amend the U.S. Constitution, $\frac{3}{4}$ of the 50 states must approve the amendment. If 35 states approve an amendment, will the Constitution be amended?

33. **Higher Order Thinking** In Ms. Barclay's classroom, $\frac{2}{5}$ of the students play chess. Of the students who play chess, $\frac{5}{6}$ also play sudoku. If there are 30 students in her class, how many play chess and sudoku?

34. One sheet of stamps is shown at the right. Emma needs to buy 50 stamps to send out invitations for her graduation party. Will 2 sheets of stamps be enough? How do you know?

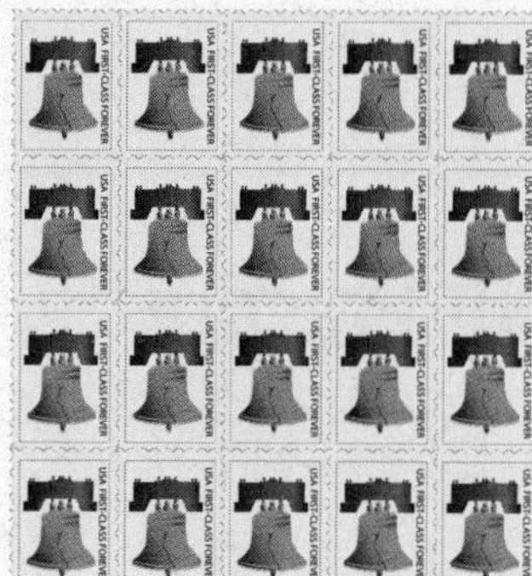

Common Core Assessment

35. Choose all the expressions that have $\frac{3}{4}$ as a product.

- ☐ $\frac{1}{2} \times \frac{1}{2}$
- ☐ $\frac{9}{10} \times \frac{5}{6}$
- ☐ $\frac{7}{8} \times \frac{6}{7}$
- ☐ $\frac{3}{4} \times \frac{3}{4}$
- ☐ $\frac{1}{4} \times \frac{1}{2}$

36. Choose all the multiplication sentences that have $\frac{1}{3}$ as the missing part.

- ☐ $\frac{4}{5} \times \frac{5}{12} = \square$
- ☐ $\frac{1}{4} \times \square = \frac{1}{6}$
- ☐ $\frac{7}{8} \times \square = \frac{7}{24}$
- ☐ $\frac{5}{6} \times \frac{2}{5} = \square$
- ☐ $\frac{1}{6} \times \frac{2}{3} = \square$

Name ______________________

Homework & Practice 8-5

Multiply Two Fractions

Another Look!

Find $\frac{3}{4} \times \frac{2}{3}$.

You can multiply the numerators and denominators to find the product.

Step 1

Multiply the numerators, and then multiply the denominators.

$\frac{3 \times 2}{4 \times 3} = \frac{6}{12} = \frac{1}{2}$

Step 2

Check that the answer is reasonable.

Since $\frac{1}{2}$ is less than 1, the answer is reasonable.

Leveled Practice In **1–24**, find each product.

1. $\frac{7}{8} \times \frac{2}{3} = \frac{\square \times 2}{8 \times \square} = \frac{\square}{24} = \frac{\square}{\square}$

2. $\frac{3}{4} \times \frac{5}{9} = \frac{\square \times 5}{4 \times \square} = \frac{15}{\square} = \frac{\square}{\square}$

3. $\frac{4}{5} \times \frac{1}{8} = \frac{\square \times 1}{5 \times \square} = \frac{\square}{\square} = \frac{\square}{\square}$

4. $\frac{4}{7} \times \frac{1}{2} = \frac{\square \times \square}{\square \times \square} = \frac{\square}{\square} = \frac{\square}{\square}$

5. $\frac{3}{5} \times \frac{3}{7} = \frac{\square \times \square}{\square \times \square} = \frac{\square}{\square}$

6. $\frac{4}{9} \times \frac{2}{3} = \frac{\square \times \square}{\square \times \square} = \frac{\square}{\square}$

7. $\frac{11}{12} \times \frac{2}{5}$

8. $\frac{2}{3} \times \frac{4}{5}$

9. $\frac{1}{6} \times \frac{2}{3}$

10. $\frac{3}{4}$ of $\frac{1}{2}$

11. $\frac{6}{7} \times \frac{1}{5}$

12. $\frac{2}{3} \times \frac{5}{9}$

13. $\frac{1}{3}$ of $\frac{3}{10}$

14. $\frac{4}{5}$ of $\frac{5}{6}$

15. $\frac{3}{7} \times \frac{2}{7}$

16. $\frac{1}{2}$ of $\frac{2}{3}$

17. $\frac{4}{5} \times \frac{2}{3}$

18. $\frac{3}{10} \times \frac{3}{10}$

19. $\left(\frac{1}{2} + \frac{1}{3}\right) \times \frac{8}{9}$

20. $\left(\frac{2}{3} - \frac{1}{6}\right) \times \frac{11}{12}$

21. $\left(\frac{3}{5} + \frac{1}{4}\right) \times \frac{2}{3}$

22. $\frac{7}{8} \times \left(\frac{1}{3} + \frac{1}{3}\right)$

23. $\left(\frac{11}{12} - \frac{5}{6}\right) \times \frac{3}{4}$

24. $\frac{1}{3} \times \left(\frac{9}{10} - \frac{3}{5}\right)$

25. **MP.1 Make Sense and Persevere** A full bottle holds $\frac{1}{4}$ gallon of juice. If $\frac{3}{5}$ of the juice has been poured out, how much juice is left in the bottle?

26. Natasha has 3 pounds of apples and $2\frac{1}{2}$ pounds of grapes. If she gives $\frac{1}{3}$ of her apples to Silvie, how many pounds of apples does she have left?

27. Keyshia is riding her bike on Bay View bike path. Keyshia's bike got a flat tire $\frac{2}{3}$ of the way down the path and she had to stop. How far did Keyshia ride?

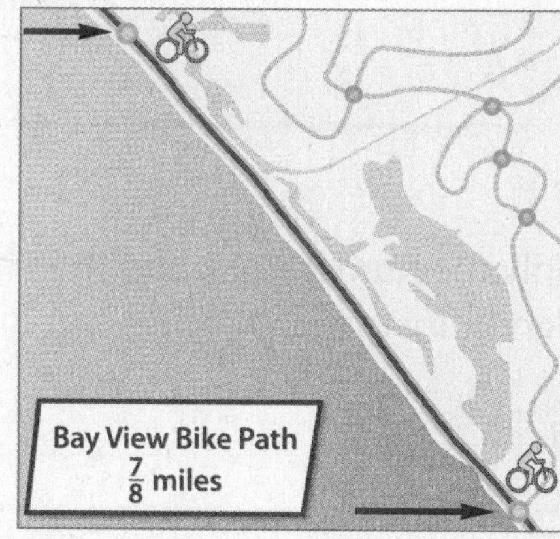

28. Of the apps on Juan's tablet, $\frac{3}{4}$ are gaming apps, and $\frac{5}{7}$ of the gaming apps are action games. What fraction of the apps on Juan's tablet are action games?

29. **Higher Order Thinking** In Mrs. Hu's classroom, $\frac{4}{5}$ of the students have a dog as a pet. Of the students who have a dog as a pet, $\frac{2}{3}$ also have a cat as a pet. If there are 45 students in her class, how many have both a dog and a cat as pets?

30. Patrick walks $\frac{9}{10}$ mile to the gym. How far has he walked when he has covered $\frac{2}{3}$ of the distance to the gym?

31. **MP.3 Construct Arguments** Which is greater, $\frac{4}{7} \times \frac{1}{4}$ or $\frac{4}{7} \times \frac{1}{6}$? Explain.

Common Core Assessment

32. Choose all the multiplication sentences that have $\frac{5}{6}$ as the missing part.

- ☐ $\square \times \frac{2}{3} = \frac{5}{9}$
- ☐ $\frac{2}{3} \times \square = \frac{7}{9}$
- ☐ $\frac{11}{12} \times \frac{10}{11} = \square$
- ☐ $\square \times \frac{1}{5} = \frac{1}{6}$
- ☐ $\frac{3}{4} \times \square = \frac{5}{8}$

33. Choose all the expressions that have $\frac{8}{15}$ as a product.

- ☐ $\frac{2}{3} \times \frac{4}{5}$
- ☐ $\frac{8}{9} \times \frac{3}{5}$
- ☐ $\frac{3}{15} \times \frac{5}{15}$
- ☐ $\frac{7}{10} \times \frac{1}{5}$
- ☐ $\frac{11}{15} \times \frac{8}{11}$

Name ______________________

Lesson 8-6
Area of a Rectangle

I can ...
find the area of a rectangle.

Content Standard 5.NF.B.4b
Mathematical Practices MP.1, MP.2, MP.3, MP.5, MP.6

Solve & Share

A rectangular poster is $\frac{1}{4}$ yard wide and $\frac{3}{4}$ yard tall. What is its area? ***Solve this problem any way you choose.***

You can use appropriate tools, like grid paper, to solve the problem.

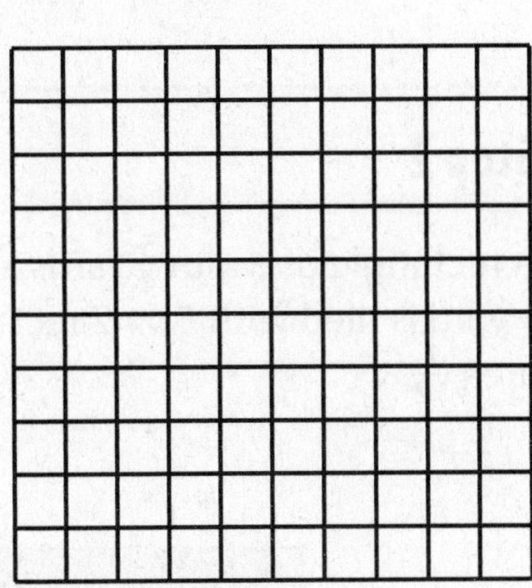

Look Back! **MP.2 Reasoning** Is the area of a poster that is $\frac{3}{4}$-yard wide and $\frac{1}{4}$-yard tall the same as the area of the poster above? Explain.

How Can You Find the Area of a Rectangle with Fractional Side Lengths?

A

Jenny has a rectangular garden. What is the area of her garden?

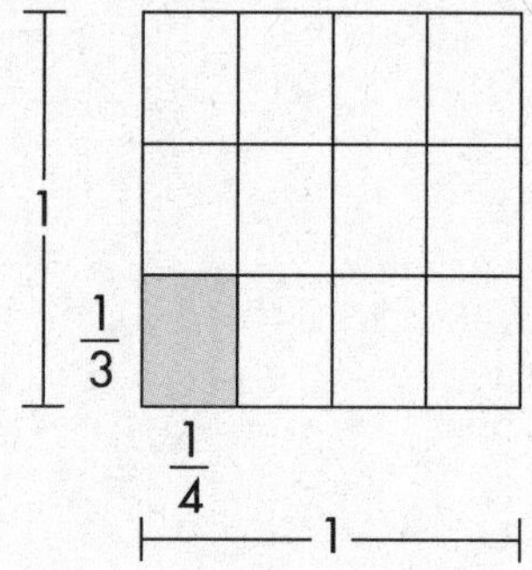

The product of two fractions can be represented by an area model.

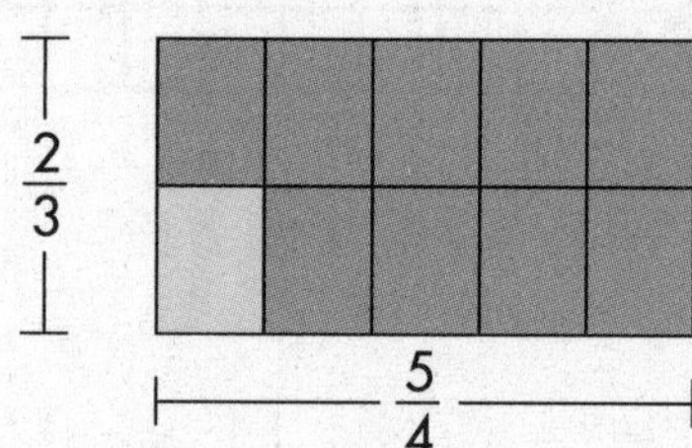

B

Step 1

$\frac{1}{4} \times \frac{1}{3} = \frac{1}{12}$ because 12 rectangles each $\frac{1}{4}$ wide and $\frac{1}{3}$ high fit in a unit square.

C

Step 2

A rectangle of width $\frac{5}{4}$ yards and height $\frac{2}{3}$ yard is tiled with 5×2 rectangles of area $\frac{1}{12}$.

So, $\frac{5}{4} \times \frac{2}{3} = \frac{5 \times 2}{4 \times 3} = \frac{10}{12}$.

The area of Jenny's garden is $\frac{10}{12}$ square yard.

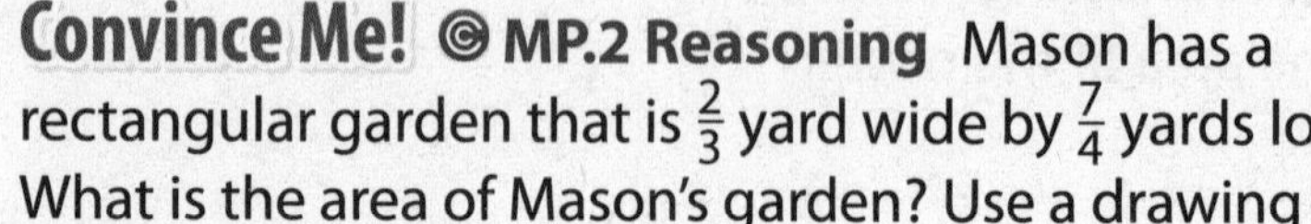

Convince Me! **MP.2 Reasoning** Mason has a rectangular garden that is $\frac{2}{3}$ yard wide by $\frac{7}{4}$ yards long. What is the area of Mason's garden? Use a drawing to show your work.

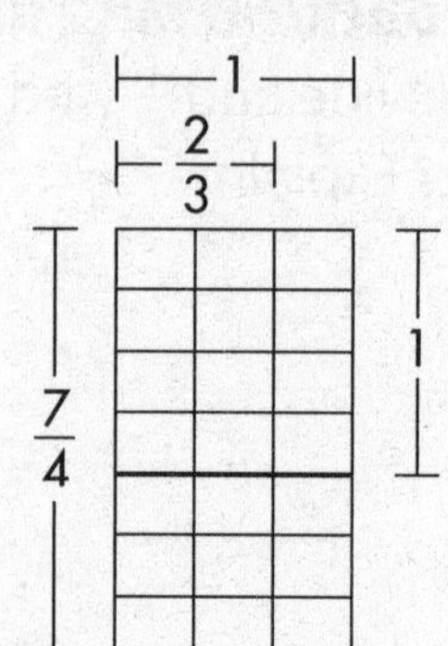

Name

Guided Practice*

Do You Understand?

1. If you do not remember the formula for finding the area of a rectangle, how can you find its area?

2. MP.6 Be Precise How could you define area?

Do You Know How?

3. Find the area of a rectangle with side lengths $\frac{2}{3}$ foot and $\frac{1}{2}$ foot.

4. Find the area of a square with side lengths of $\frac{5}{4}$ inches.

Independent Practice*

In **5–10**, find each area.

5.
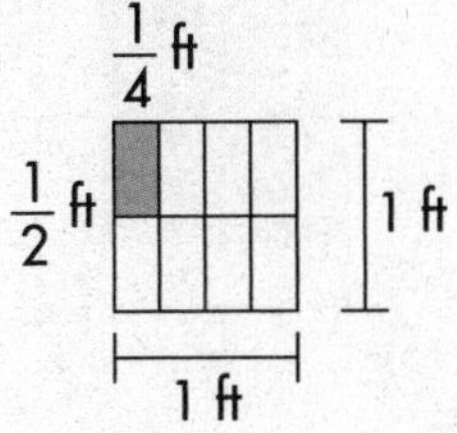

6.
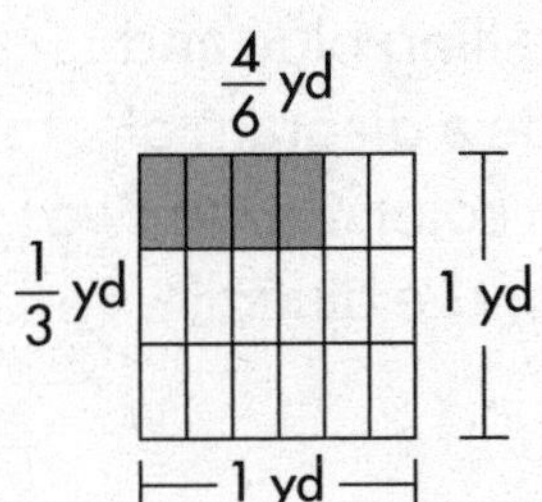

7.
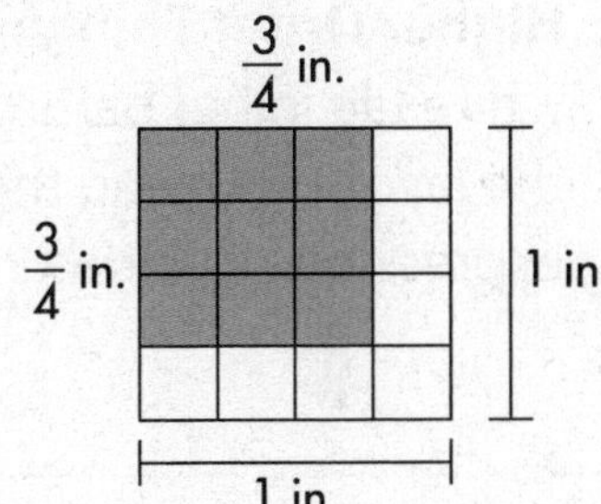

8.
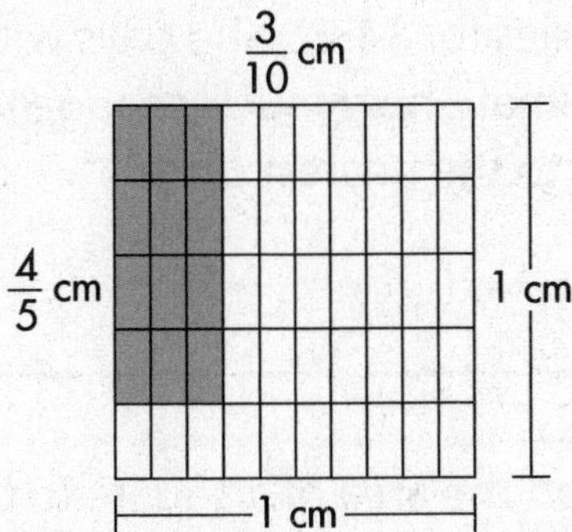

9.
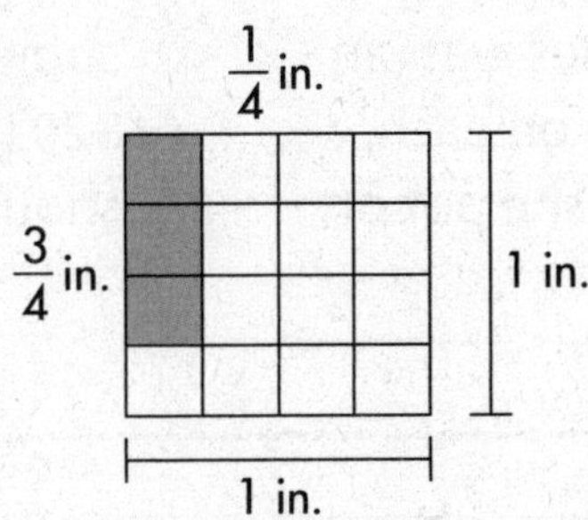

10.
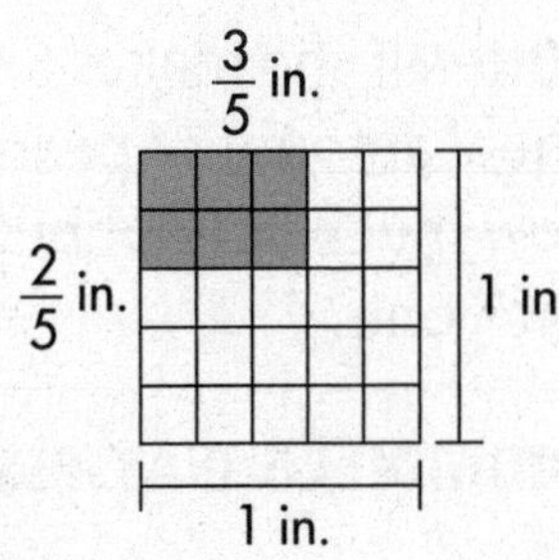

11. Find the area of a rectangle with side lengths $\frac{5}{3}$ feet and $\frac{3}{4}$ foot.

12. Find the area of a square with side lengths of $\frac{3}{8}$ inch.

13. Find the area of a rectangle with side lengths $\frac{7}{2}$ centimeters and $\frac{5}{4}$ centimeters.

*For another example, see Set E on page 514.

Math Practices and Problem Solving

14. **MP.3 Construct Arguments** Roy and Tom are working on a multiplication problem. Roy claims that $\frac{7}{4} \times \frac{3}{8} = \frac{21}{32}$. Tom claims that the correct answer is $\frac{21}{8}$. Who is correct? Explain your answer.

15. Emilio needs to know how much area to clear for his son's square sandbox. Each side of the sandbox is $\frac{3}{4}$ yard. Find the area that the sandbox will cover.

16. **MP.1 Make Sense and Persevere** Margaret purchased a doormat measuring $\frac{1}{2}$ yard by $\frac{2}{3}$ yard for her back door step. If the step is $\frac{1}{4}$ square yard, will the mat fit? Explain.

17. Each person on a Ferris wheel pays $6.50 for a ticket. There are 72 passengers. How much money is collected from all the passengers?

18. **Higher Order Thinking** Kim is installing blue and white tile in her bathroom. She made a diagram of the layout showing the area of both colors. Write two expressions that describe the area of the blue tile.

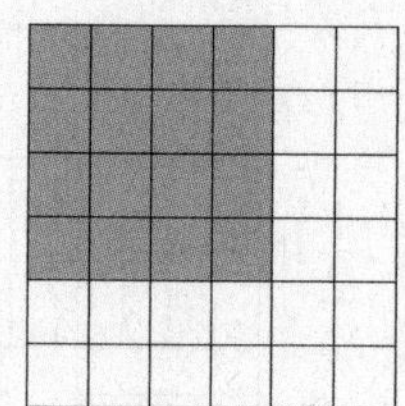

19. Wilhelmina has 8.3 ounces of peanut butter. If she makes 5 sandwiches with an equal amount of peanut butter on each, how much peanut butter does she put on each one?

20. Irene buys a talking doll for $10.66 and some batteries for $4.22. She pays with a $20 bill. Estimate how much change she should get, to the nearest dime.

Common Core Assessment

21. Juno calculated the area of a square to be $\frac{4}{9}$ square yard. Which shows the side length of the square?

Ⓐ $\frac{2}{9}$ yard
Ⓑ $\frac{4}{9}$ yard
Ⓒ $\frac{2}{3}$ yard
Ⓓ $\frac{8}{9}$ yard

22. Bo calculated the area of a square to be $\frac{25}{4}$ square inches. Which shows the side length of the square?

Ⓐ $\frac{25}{2}$ inches
Ⓑ $\frac{25}{8}$ inches
Ⓒ $\frac{5}{2}$ inches
Ⓓ $\frac{5}{4}$ inches

Name ______________________________

Help Practice Buddy Tools Games

Homework & Practice 8-6

Area of a Rectangle

Another Look!

Cole wants to cover the back of a picture frame with colorful paper. What is the area of the back of Cole's picture frame?

$\frac{1}{2}$ ft

$\frac{3}{4}$ ft

Multiply to find the area of the back of the picture frame.

$A = \frac{3}{4} \times \frac{1}{2} = \frac{3}{8}$

The area of the back of Cole's picture frame is $\frac{3}{8}$ square foot.

Multiply the length by the width to find the area of a rectangle.

In **1–5**, find each area.

1.

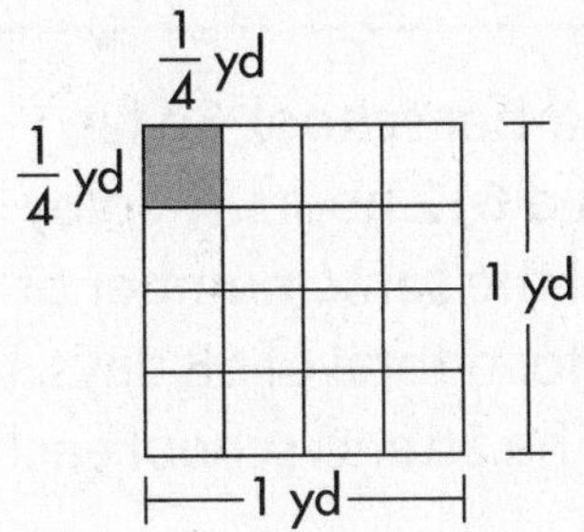

$\frac{1}{4} \times \frac{1}{4} = \frac{\square}{\square}$ sq yd.

2.

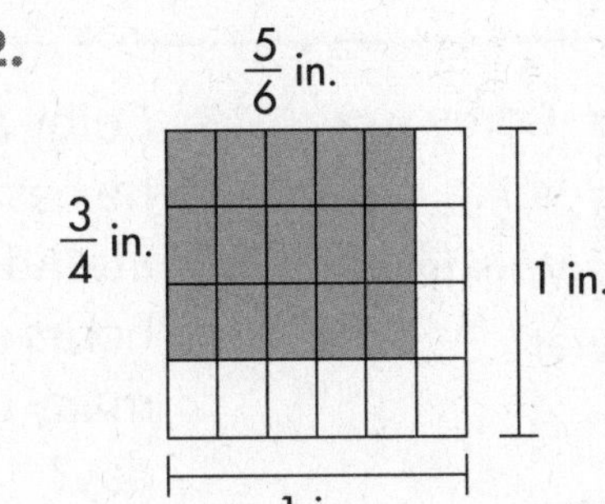

$\frac{\square}{\square} \times \frac{\square}{\square} = \frac{\square}{\square} = \frac{\square}{\square}$ sq in.

3.

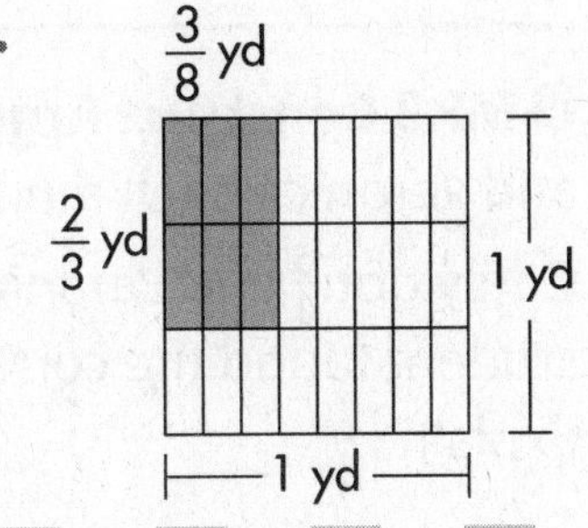

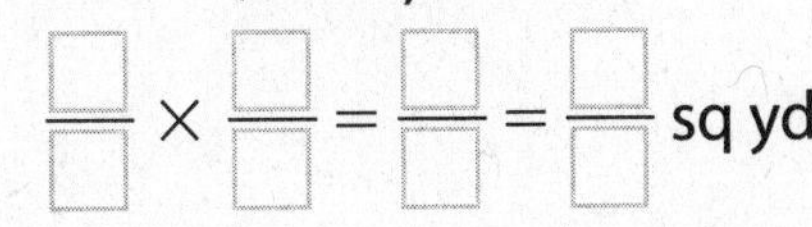

4.

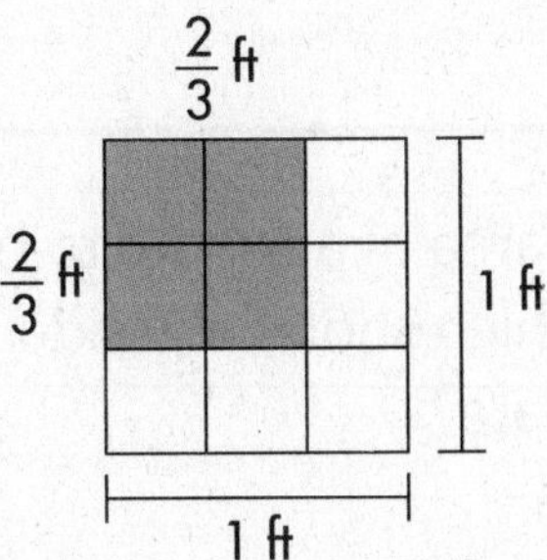

5.

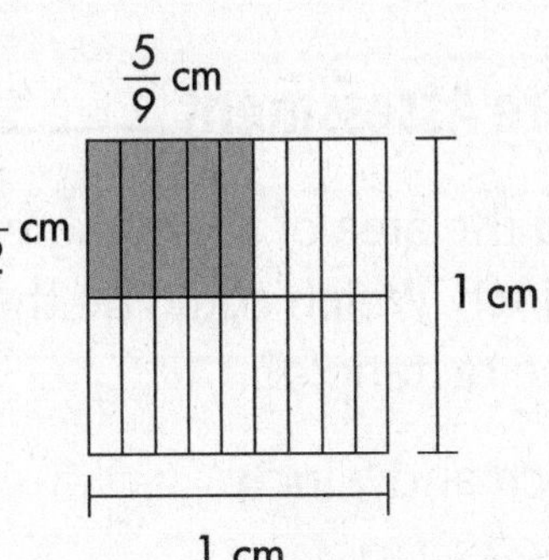

6. Find the area of a square with side length $\frac{3}{4}$ yard.

7. Find the area of a rectangle with side lengths $\frac{5}{4}$ feet and $\frac{5}{3}$ feet.

8. Find the area of a square with side length $\frac{7}{12}$ inch.

9. ◎ **MP.1 Make Sense and Persevere** A crate is $\frac{3}{4}$ yard long and $\frac{2}{3}$ yard wide. The crate is also 2 feet tall. What is the area of the top of the crate?

10. Mike is making macaroni salad. For each bowl of macaroni salad, he needs $\frac{1}{3}$ cup of macaroni. How many cups of macaroni will he use if he makes 27 bowls of macaroni salad?

11. **Higher Order Thinking** Dorothy is installing purple and white tile in her kitchen. She made a diagram of the layout showing the area of both colors. Write two expressions that describe the area of the purple tile.

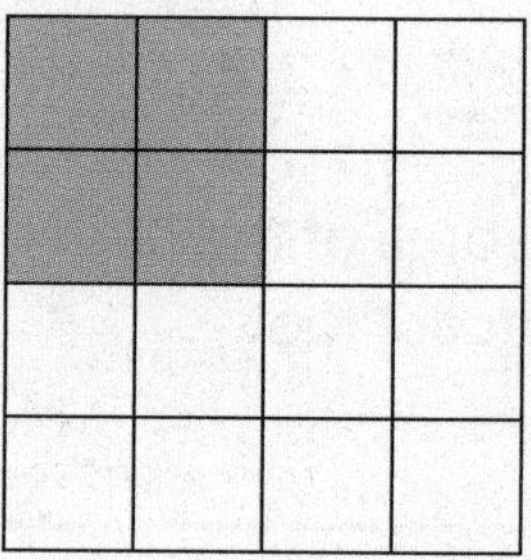

12. ◎ **MP.3 Construct Arguments** Corey and Veronica each multiplied $\frac{1}{2} \times \frac{5}{2}$. Corey got $\frac{6}{4}$ and Veronica got $\frac{5}{4}$. Which student found the correct answer? Explain.

13. Colby attends barber school. So far, he has completed 612 hours. If Colby attended school the same number of hours each day for a total of 68 days, how many hours did he attend school each day?

◎ Common Core Assessment

14. Tomás found the area of a rectangle to be $\frac{1}{6}$ square inch. Which could be the side lengths of the rectangle?

    Ⓐ $\frac{1}{4}$ inch and $\frac{2}{3}$ inch

    Ⓑ $\frac{1}{3}$ inch and $\frac{1}{3}$ inch

    Ⓒ $\frac{1}{6}$ inch and $\frac{1}{6}$ inch

    Ⓓ $\frac{1}{2}$ inch and $\frac{1}{12}$ inch

15. Jackie found the area of a square to be $\frac{25}{16}$ square feet. Which shows the side length of the square?

    Ⓐ $\frac{5}{4}$ feet

    Ⓑ $\frac{5}{8}$ foot

    Ⓒ $\frac{5}{16}$ foot

    Ⓓ $\frac{25}{4}$ feet

Name ______________________________

Lesson 8-7
Multiply Mixed Numbers

I can ...
multiply mixed numbers.

Content Standard 5.NF.B.6
Mathematical Practices MP.1, MP.2, MP.3, MP.4, MP.8

Solve & Share

Look at the ingredients needed to make Josie's special pancakes. How much pancake mix and milk will you need if you want to double the recipe? To triple the recipe? ***Solve this problem any way you choose.***

Generalize
How can you use what you know about multiplying fractions to help you multiply mixed numbers?

Josie's Pancake Recipe

$2\frac{1}{4}$ **cups pancake mix**
1 egg
$1\frac{2}{3}$ **cups milk**
$\frac{3}{4}$ **teaspoon vanilla**

Look Back! **MP.4 Model with Math** What number sentence can you write using repeated addition to show how much pancake mix is needed if the recipe is tripled?

How Can You Find the Product of Mixed Numbers?

A

A clothing factory has machines that make jackets. The machines operate for $7\frac{1}{2}$ hours each day. How many jackets can Machine A make in one day?

DATA

Jackets Per Hour	
Machine A	**Machine B**
$2\frac{3}{4}$	$3\frac{1}{3}$

$7\frac{1}{2}$ times $2\frac{3}{4}$ is about 8 times 3. So, the answer should be about 24.

B

One Way

You can use an area model to find the partial products. Then add to find the final product.

	7	$\frac{1}{2}$
2	$2 \times 7 = 14$	$2 \times \frac{1}{2} = 1$
$\frac{3}{4}$	$\frac{3}{4} \times 7 = \frac{21}{4} = 5\frac{1}{4}$	$\frac{3}{4} \times \frac{1}{2} = \frac{3}{8}$

$14 + 1 + 5\frac{1}{4} + \frac{3}{8} =$

$14 + 1 + 5\frac{2}{8} + \frac{3}{8} = 20\frac{5}{8}$

C

Another Way

You can also use an equation to find the product. Rename the mixed numbers, then multiply.

$$7\frac{1}{2} \times 2\frac{3}{4} = \frac{15}{2} \times \frac{11}{4}$$
$$= \frac{165}{8}$$
$$= 20\frac{5}{8}$$

Machine A makes 20 jackets each day.

Since 20 is close to the estimate of 24, the answer is reasonable.

Convince Me! © **MP.4 Model with Math** How many jackets can Machine B make in one day? Write an equation to model your work.

Name ______________________________

Practice Buddy Tools Assessment

Guided Practice*

Do You Understand?

1. MP.3 Construct Arguments Explain how you would multiply $5 \times 2\frac{1}{2}$.

Do You Know How?

In **2** and **3**, estimate the product. Then complete the multiplication.

2. $2\frac{3}{4} \times 8 = \frac{\square}{4} \times \frac{8}{1} = \square$

3. $4\frac{1}{2} \times 1\frac{1}{4} = \frac{\square}{2} \times \frac{\square}{4} = \square$

Independent Practice

Compare your product against your estimate to check for reasonableness.

In **4–9**, estimate the product. Then complete the multiplication.

4. $3\frac{4}{5} \times 5 = \frac{\square}{5} \times \frac{5}{1} = \square$

5. $1\frac{3}{5} \times 2\frac{1}{4} = \frac{\square}{5} \times \frac{\square}{4} = \square$

6. $1\frac{1}{2} \times 3\frac{5}{6} = \frac{\square}{2} \times \frac{\square}{6} = \square$

7. $4\frac{2}{3} \times 4 = \frac{\square}{3} \times \frac{4}{1} = \square$

8. $3\frac{1}{7} \times 1\frac{1}{4} = \frac{\square}{7} \times \frac{\square}{4} = \square$

9. $1\frac{1}{3} \times 2\frac{1}{6} = \frac{\square}{3} \times \frac{\square}{6} = \square$

In **10–20**, estimate the product. Then find each product.

10. $2\frac{1}{6} \times 4\frac{1}{2}$

11. $\frac{3}{4} \times 8\frac{1}{2}$

12. $1\frac{1}{8} \times 3\frac{1}{3}$

13. $3\frac{1}{5} \times \frac{2}{3}$

14. $3\frac{1}{4} \times 6$

15. $5\frac{1}{3} \times 3$

16. $2\frac{3}{8} \times 4$

17. $4\frac{1}{8} \times 5\frac{1}{2}$

18. $\left(\frac{1}{6} + 2\frac{2}{3}\right) \times \left(1\frac{1}{4} - \frac{1}{2}\right)$

19. $\left(2\frac{4}{9} + \frac{1}{3}\right) \times \left(1\frac{1}{4} - \frac{1}{8}\right)$

20. $\left(1\frac{7}{8} + 2\frac{1}{2}\right) \times \left(1\frac{1}{5} - \frac{1}{10}\right)$

For another example, see Set F on page 515.

Math Practices and Problem Solving

In **21–23**, use the diagram at the right.

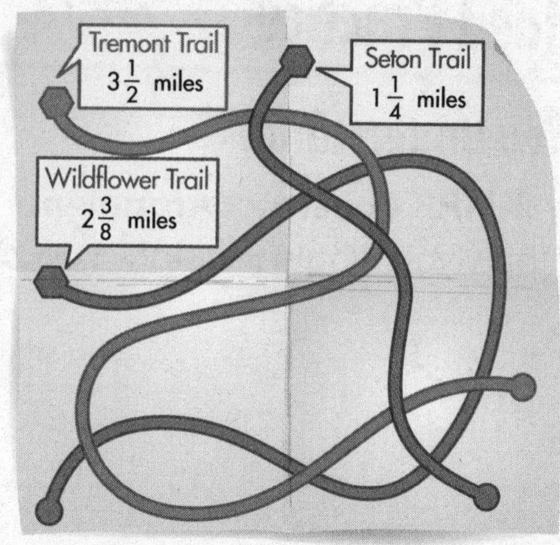

21. MP.1 Make Sense and Persevere Bernie and Chloe hiked the Tremont Trail to the end and back. Then they hiked the Wildflower Trail to the end before stopping to eat lunch. How far did they hike before they ate lunch?

22. Higher Order Thinking In one day, Ricardo hiked $2\frac{2}{3}$ times as far as Bernie and Chloe hiked before they ate lunch. How far did he hike?

23. The city plans to extend the Wildflower Trail $2\frac{1}{2}$ times its current length in the next 5 years. How long will the Wildflower Trail be at the end of 5 years?

24. MP.2 Reasoning How can you use multiplication to find $3\frac{3}{5} + 3\frac{3}{5} + 3\frac{3}{5}$?

25. The world's smallest gecko is $\frac{3}{4}$ inch long. An adult male Western Banded Gecko is $7\frac{1}{3}$ times as long. How long is a Western Banded Gecko?

26. The Akashi-Kaikyo Bridge in Japan is about $1\frac{4}{9}$ times as long as the Golden Gate Bridge in San Francisco. The Golden Gate Bridge is about 9,000 feet long. About how long is the Akashi-Kaikyo Bridge?

27. Patty spent 3.5 times as much as Sandy on their shopping trip. If Sandy spent \$20.50, how much did Patty spend?

Common Core Assessment

28. Choose all that are true.

- ☐ $4\frac{1}{12} \times 2\frac{3}{4} = 11\frac{11}{48}$
- ☐ $5\frac{1}{2} \times 5 = 25\frac{1}{2}$
- ☐ $1\frac{1}{2} \times 3\frac{1}{5} = 4\frac{1}{2}$
- ☐ $\frac{3}{4} \times 8\frac{1}{5} = 6\frac{3}{20}$
- ☐ $2\frac{1}{5} \times 6\frac{1}{4} = 13\frac{3}{4}$

29. Choose all that are true.

- ☐ $15\frac{1}{4} = 5 \times 3\frac{1}{4}$
- ☐ $4\frac{1}{3} = 4\frac{1}{3} \times 1$
- ☐ $9\frac{3}{4} = 4\frac{1}{2} \times 2\frac{1}{6}$
- ☐ $3\frac{1}{3} = 6\frac{2}{3} \times \frac{1}{2}$
- ☐ $13\frac{3}{5} = 7\frac{1}{3} \times 2\frac{2}{5}$

Name ______________________

Homework & Practice 8-7

Multiply Mixed Numbers

Another Look!

Millwood City is constructing a new highway through town. The construction crew can complete $5\frac{3}{5}$ miles of road each month. How many miles will they complete in $6\frac{1}{2}$ months?

Step 1	Step 2	Step 3	Step 4
Round the mixed numbers to whole numbers to estimate the product. $5\frac{3}{5} \times 6\frac{1}{2}$ $\downarrow \quad \downarrow$ $6 \times 7 = 42$ So, they can complete about 42 miles.	Rename the mixed numbers. $5\frac{3}{5} \times 6\frac{1}{2} = \frac{28}{5} \times \frac{13}{2}$	Multiply the numerators and the denominators. $\frac{28}{5} \times \frac{13}{2} = \frac{364}{10} = 36\frac{2}{5}$ The construction crew will complete $36\frac{2}{5}$ miles of highway in $6\frac{1}{2}$ months.	Check for reasonableness. Compare your product to your estimate. $36\frac{2}{5}$ is close to 42, so the answer is reasonable.

In **1–4**, estimate the product. Then complete the multiplication.

1. $1\frac{1}{4} \times 2\frac{1}{4} = \frac{\square}{4} \times \frac{9}{\square} = \frac{5 \times \square}{\square \times 4} = \frac{45}{\square} = \square\frac{\square}{16}$

2. $3\frac{1}{2} \times 2\frac{2}{3} = \frac{7}{\square} \times \frac{\square}{3} = \frac{\square \times 8}{2 \times \square} = \frac{\square}{6} = \square\frac{1}{\square}$

3. $5\frac{1}{3} \times 2\frac{3}{4} = \frac{\square}{3} \times \frac{11}{\square} = \square$

4. $4\frac{1}{5} \times 2\frac{1}{4} = \frac{\square}{5} \times \frac{\square}{4} = \square$

In **5–12**, estimate the product. Then find each product.

5. $4 \times 6\frac{1}{4}$

6. $3\frac{2}{3} \times 2\frac{3}{4}$

7. $\frac{7}{8} \times 4\frac{1}{6}$

8. $1\frac{1}{2} \times 2\frac{3}{4}$

9. $8\frac{1}{10} \times \frac{2}{3}$

10. $4\frac{1}{12} \times 7$

11. $3\frac{4}{5} \times 7\frac{1}{2}$

12. $6\frac{2}{3} \times 4\frac{4}{5}$

13. How can you use estimation to find $9\frac{1}{2} + 9\frac{1}{2} + 9\frac{1}{2} + 9\frac{1}{2} + 9\frac{1}{2}$?

14. A model of a house is built on a base that measures $7\frac{3}{4}$ in. wide and $9\frac{1}{5}$ in. long. What is the area of the model house's base?

15. Algebra Write a mixed number for t so that $2\frac{3}{4} \times t$ is more than $2\frac{3}{4}$.

16. A-Z **Vocabulary** Give an example of a benchmark fraction and an example of a mixed number.

17. MP.1 Make Sense and Persevere Leon and Marisol biked the Brookside Trail to the end and back. Then they biked the Forest Glen Trail to the end and back before stopping to eat. How far did they bike before they stopped to eat?

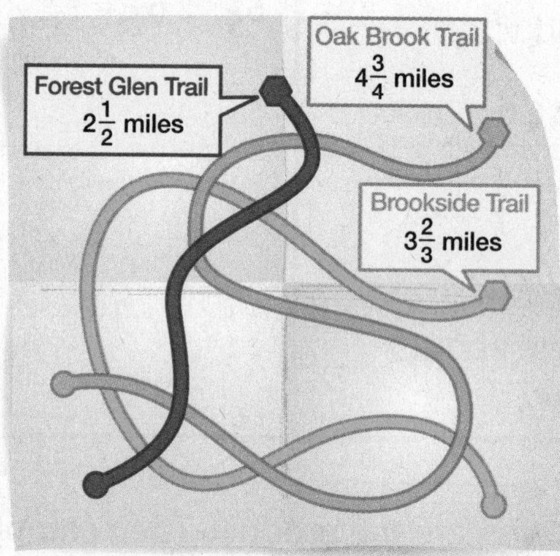

18. The One World Trade Center in New York City is about $3\frac{1}{5}$ times as tall as the Washington Monument in Washington, D.C. The Washington Monument is 555 feet tall. About how tall is the One World Trade Center?

19. Higher Order Thinking Lucie can walk about $3\frac{4}{5}$ miles each hour. About how far can she walk in 2 hours 45 minutes?

Common Core Assessment

20. Choose all that are true.

- ☐ $\frac{1}{4} \times 1\frac{7}{8} = \frac{15}{32}$
- ☐ $2\frac{1}{2} \times 2\frac{1}{2} = 5\frac{1}{2}$
- ☐ $3\frac{1}{5} \times 2\frac{1}{4} = 6\frac{2}{5}$
- ☐ $4\frac{1}{2} \times 1\frac{1}{3} = 6$
- ☐ $5\frac{1}{4} \times \frac{1}{2} = 2\frac{5}{8}$

21. Choose all that are true.

- ☐ $4\frac{1}{12} \times \frac{3}{4} = \frac{49}{16}$
- ☐ $8\frac{5}{6} \times 2 = 17\frac{2}{3}$
- ☐ $5\frac{1}{2} \times 5\frac{1}{2} = 30\frac{1}{4}$
- ☐ $9\frac{1}{5} \times \frac{3}{5} = 9\frac{4}{5}$
- ☐ $6\frac{3}{4} \times 3\frac{1}{4} = 19$

Name ______________________________

Lesson 8-8
Multiplication as Scaling

I can ...
use multiplication to scale or resize something.

Content Standards 5.NF.B.5a, 5.NF.B.5b
Mathematical Practices MP.2, MP.7

Solve & Share

Without multiplying, circle the problem in each set with the greatest product and underline the problem with the least product. ***Solve this problem any way you choose.***

Set 1

a. $\frac{1}{2} \times 2$

b. $\frac{3}{3} \times 2$

c. $\frac{4}{4} \times \frac{5}{6}$

Set 2

a. $3\frac{3}{4} \times 2\frac{1}{2}$

b. $\frac{3}{4} \times 2\frac{1}{2}$

c. $\frac{4}{4} \times 2\frac{1}{2}$

Set 3

a. $\frac{3}{4} \times \frac{6}{6}$

b. $\frac{3}{4} \times 1\frac{5}{6}$

c. $\frac{4}{4} \times \frac{5}{6}$

Reasoning
How can you use what you know about multiplying fractions to help you find the problem with the greatest product?

Look Back! **MP.2 Reasoning** How is $\frac{3}{3} \times 2$ like 1×2?

How Can You Use Number Sense to Evaluate the Size of a Product?

A

Sue knitted scarves that are 4 feet long for herself and her friends Joe and Alan. After a month, they compared the lengths of their scarves. Some scarves had stretched and some had shrunk. The results are shown in the chart. How had the lengths of Joe's and Alan's scarves changed?

DATA

Sue	4
Joe	$1\frac{1}{2} \times 4$
Alan	$\frac{3}{4} \times 4$

B

Alan's scarf

Alan's scarf shrunk.

$\frac{3}{4} \times 4 < 4$

Multiplying a number by a fraction less than 1 results in a product less than the given number.

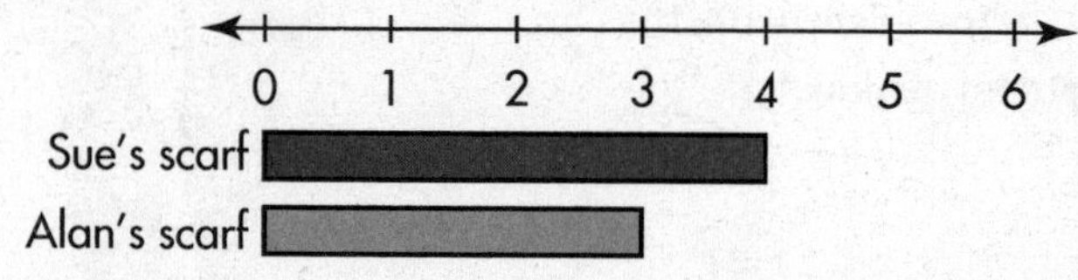

C

Joe's scarf

Joe's scarf stretched.

$1\frac{1}{2} \times 4 > 4$

Multiplying a number by a fraction greater than 1 results in a product greater than the starting number.

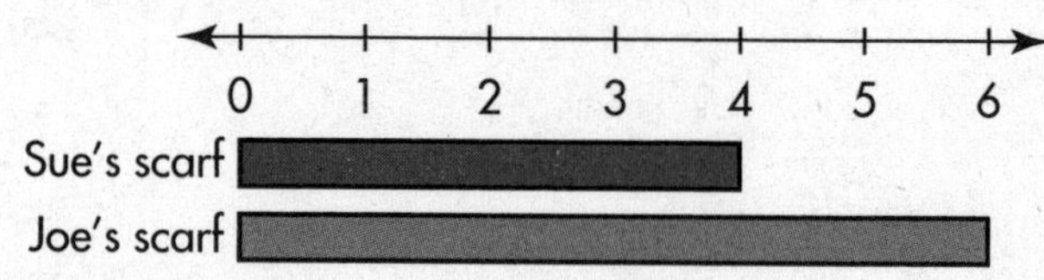

Convince Me! **MP.7 Use Structure** Sue knitted a scarf for her friend June that was also 4 feet long. After a month, the length of June's scarf could be represented by the expression $\frac{3}{3} \times 4$. How did the length of June's scarf change? Explain.

Name ____________________

Practice Buddy | Tools | Assessment

Guided Practice*

Do You Understand?

1. MP.2 Reasoning Why does multiplying a number by $3\frac{1}{2}$ increase its value?

2. Does the scaling factor always have to be the first factor in an expression?

Do You Know How?

In **3–5**, without multiplying decide which symbol belongs in the box: $<$, $>$, or $=$.

3. $3\frac{1}{2} \times 2\frac{2}{3} \square 2\frac{2}{3}$
4. $\frac{4}{5} \times 2\frac{2}{3} \square 2\frac{2}{3}$
5. $4\frac{3}{5} \times \frac{4}{4} \square 4\frac{3}{5}$

Independent Practice

In **6–17**, without multiplying, decide which symbol belongs in the box: $<$, $>$, or $=$.

6. $2\frac{1}{2} \times 1\frac{2}{3} \square 1\frac{2}{3}$
7. $\frac{3}{5} \times 4\frac{4}{5} \square 4\frac{4}{5}$
8. $1\frac{2}{7} \times \frac{5}{5} \square 1\frac{2}{7}$
9. $\frac{1}{3} \times 2\frac{2}{5} \square 2\frac{2}{5}$
10. $3\frac{3}{5} \times \frac{2}{2} \square 3\frac{3}{5}$
11. $4\frac{1}{3} \times 2\frac{2}{7} \square 2\frac{2}{7}$
12. $2\frac{1}{5} \times \frac{1}{10} \square 2\frac{1}{5}$
13. $\frac{1}{2} \times 1\frac{2}{5} \square 1\frac{2}{5}$
14. $4\frac{3}{4} \times 3\frac{1}{4} \square 4\frac{3}{4}$
15. $1\frac{1}{12} \times 1\frac{3}{4} \square 1\frac{3}{4}$
16. $5\frac{1}{3} \times \frac{5}{6} \square 5\frac{1}{3}$
17. $\frac{5}{5} \times 4\frac{2}{3} \square 4\frac{2}{3}$

In **18** and **19**, without multiplying, order the following products from least to greatest.

18. $2 \times \frac{3}{5}$ $\quad 2\frac{1}{4} \times \frac{3}{5}$ $\quad \frac{3}{4} \times \frac{3}{5}$ $\quad \frac{5}{5} \times \frac{3}{5}$

19. $\frac{1}{5} \times \frac{2}{3}$ $\quad 4\frac{1}{2} \times \frac{2}{3}$ $\quad \frac{1}{3} \times \frac{2}{3}$ $\quad 4 \times \frac{2}{3}$

In **20** and **21**, without multiplying, order the following products from greatest to least.

20. $3 \times \frac{3}{4}$ $\quad \frac{2}{3} \times \frac{3}{4}$ $\quad 1\frac{1}{4} \times \frac{3}{4}$ $\quad \frac{4}{4} \times \frac{3}{4}$

21. $\frac{3}{3} \times \frac{1}{3}$ $\quad 4 \times \frac{1}{3}$ $\quad 2\frac{2}{3} \times \frac{1}{3}$ $\quad 2\frac{1}{3} \times \frac{1}{3}$

*For another example, see Set G on page 516.

Math Practices and Problem Solving

22. Who ran farther by the end of the week? How much farther? Use the table below that shows the distances in miles.

DATA	Monday	Tuesday	Wednesday	Thursday	Friday
Holly	$1\frac{1}{2}$	$\frac{1}{2}$	$2\frac{1}{4}$	$\frac{3}{4}$	$1\frac{1}{2}$
Yu	$1\frac{3}{4}$	$1\frac{1}{2}$	$2\frac{3}{4}$	$1\frac{1}{4}$	$\frac{1}{2}$

23. **MP.2 Reasoning** Ethan took a quiz with 15 questions. If he answered $\frac{3}{5}$ of the questions correctly, how many did he get wrong?

24. At a taffy pull, George stretched the taffy to 3 feet. Jose stretched it $1\frac{1}{3}$ times as far as George. Maria stretched it $\frac{2}{3}$ as far as George. Sally stretched it $\frac{6}{6}$ as far. Who stretched it the farthest? the least?

25. **Higher Order Thinking** Without multiplying, decide which symbol belongs in the box: <, >, or =. Explain how you decided.

$4\frac{3}{4} \times 3\frac{1}{4} \; \square \; 4\frac{1}{2}$

26. Write two decimals with a product close to 6.3.

$\_\_.\_\_ \times \_\_.\_\_ \approx 6.3$

≈ is a symbol that means *is approximately equal to.*

Common Core Assessment

27. Write each expression in the correct answer space to show products less than $4\frac{1}{2}$ and those greater than $4\frac{1}{2}$.

Less than $4\frac{1}{2}$	Greater than $4\frac{1}{2}$

$4 \times 4\frac{1}{2}$ $1\frac{1}{12} \times 4\frac{1}{2}$ $4\frac{1}{2} \times \frac{3}{4}$ $\frac{4}{5} \times 4\frac{1}{2}$

28. Write each expression in the correct answer space to show products less than $1\frac{3}{4}$ and those greater than $1\frac{3}{4}$.

Less than $1\frac{3}{4}$	Greater than $1\frac{3}{4}$

$1\frac{3}{4} \times 1\frac{3}{4}$ $\frac{9}{10} \times 1\frac{3}{4}$ $1\frac{3}{4} \times \frac{1}{2}$ $5\frac{1}{6} \times 1\frac{3}{4}$

Name ____________________

Homework & Practice 8-8

Multiplication as Scaling

Another Look!

Theodore and Pam are rolling out modeling clay for an activity in art class. Theodore rolled out his clay until it was 5 inches long. Pam rolled hers $\frac{2}{3}$ times as far. Did Pam roll her clay out less than, more than, or the same as Theodore?

Step 1

Use a number line to find out how far Pam rolled out her clay. The arrows show $5 \times \frac{2}{3}$.

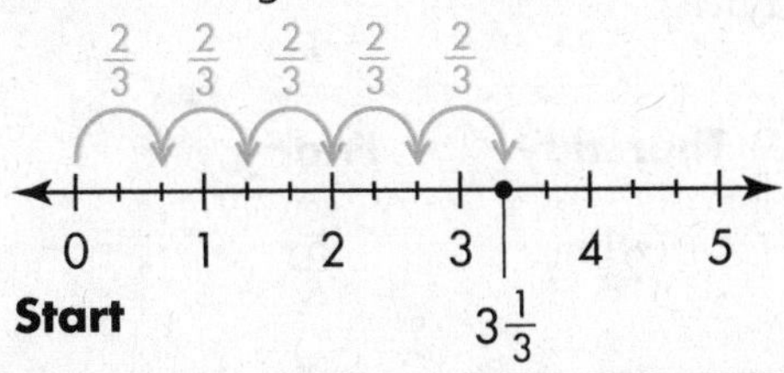

Step 2

Use a number line to compare the lengths of clay.

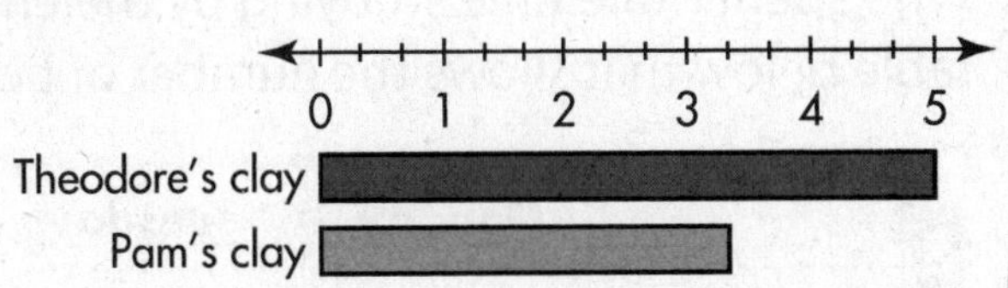

Pam rolled out less clay than Theodore.

In **1** and **2**, decide which symbol belongs in the box: <, >, or =. Use the number line to help find the answer.

1. $5 \times \frac{3}{4}$ ☐ 5

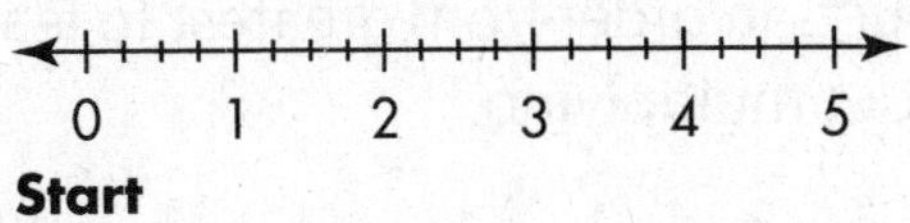

2. $1\frac{1}{2} \times 3$ ☐ 3

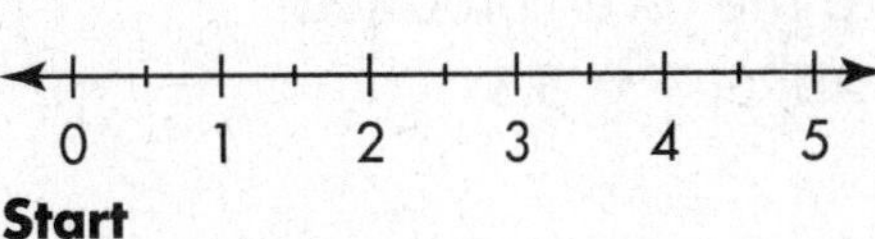

In **3–8**, without multiplying, decide which symbol belongs in the box: <, >, or =.

3. $5\frac{1}{3} \times 2\frac{3}{4}$ ☐ $5\frac{1}{3}$

4. $10\frac{3}{4} \times \frac{2}{2}$ ☐ $10\frac{3}{4}$

5. $\frac{1}{12} \times 1\frac{6}{7}$ ☐ $1\frac{6}{7}$

6. $5\frac{1}{5} \times 5\frac{1}{10}$ ☐ $5\frac{1}{10}$

7. $\frac{1}{4} \times 4\frac{1}{2}$ ☐ $4\frac{1}{2}$

8. $3\frac{9}{10} \times 1\frac{2}{3}$ ☐ $1\frac{2}{3}$

In **9** and **10**, without multiplying, order the following products from least to greatest.

9. $\frac{5}{6} \times 1\frac{8}{9}$ $\quad \frac{5}{6} \times \frac{1}{4}$ $\quad \frac{5}{6} \times 10\frac{1}{12}$ $\quad \frac{5}{6} \times \frac{6}{6}$

10. $\frac{1}{12} \times \frac{1}{4}$ $\quad 3\frac{1}{4} \times \frac{1}{4}$ $\quad 4\frac{1}{3} \times \frac{1}{4}$ $\quad \frac{1}{10} \times \frac{1}{4}$

11. **Higher Order Thinking** Without multiplying, decide which symbol belongs in the box: <, >, or =. Explain how you decided.

$2\frac{1}{3} \times \frac{1}{8} \square 2\frac{1}{2}$

12. Erin is making fruit salad. For each bowl of fruit salad, she needs $\frac{2}{3}$ cup of strawberries. How many cups of strawberries will she use if she makes 18 bowls of fruit salad?

13. Who spent more time studying by the end of the week? Use the table below that shows the number of hours spent studying.

DATA	Monday	Tuesday	Wednesday	Thursday	Friday
Mark	$2\frac{1}{6}$	$1\frac{5}{6}$	$3\frac{3}{4}$	$2\frac{1}{8}$	$\frac{5}{6}$
Diane	$2\frac{1}{2}$	$\frac{5}{6}$	$3\frac{2}{3}$	$3\frac{2}{3}$	$\frac{3}{4}$

14. Make up two decimals with an answer close to the given product.

__.__ × __.__ = 5.5

15. **MP.2 Reasoning** Put the following products in order from greatest to least, without multiplying.

$3\frac{1}{8} \times \frac{1}{8}$ $\frac{2}{3} \times 3\frac{1}{8}$ $3\frac{1}{8} \times 3\frac{1}{8}$ $3\frac{1}{8} \times \frac{4}{4}$

Common Core Assessment

16. Write each expression in the correct answer space to show products less than $\frac{2}{3}$ and those greater than $\frac{2}{3}$.

Less than $\frac{2}{3}$	Greater than $\frac{2}{3}$

$\frac{2}{3} \times 1\frac{1}{2}$ $\frac{2}{3} \times \frac{2}{3}$ $\frac{2}{3} \times \frac{1}{2}$ $2\frac{2}{3} \times \frac{2}{3}$

17. Write each expression in the correct answer space to show products less than $10\frac{1}{2}$ and those greater than $10\frac{1}{2}$.

Less than $10\frac{1}{2}$	Greater than $10\frac{1}{2}$

$1\frac{1}{12} \times 10\frac{1}{2}$ $\frac{1}{12} \times 10\frac{1}{2}$ $10\frac{1}{3} \times 10\frac{1}{2}$
$1\frac{1}{9} \times 10\frac{1}{2}$

Name ______________________

Math Practices and Problem Solving

Lesson 8-9

Make Sense and Persevere

I can ...
make sense of problems and keep working if I get stuck.

Mathematical Practices MP.1, Also MP.3, MP.4, MP.6
Content Standards 5.NF.B.6, 5.NF.B.5a, 5.NF.B.5b

Solve & Share

A rectangular dog park was built with the dimensions shown. The fencing that completely surrounds the park cost $12 a yard. Each square yard of grass sod that covers the entire park cost $8. What was the total cost for the fencing and the sod? ***Solve this problem any way you choose.***

$8\frac{1}{4}$ yd

$25\frac{1}{2}$ yd

Thinking Habits

Be a good thinker!
These questions can help you.

- What do I need to find?
- What do I know?
- What's my plan for solving the problem?
- What else can I try if I get stuck?
- How can I check that my solution makes sense?

Look Back! **MP.1 Make Sense and Persevere** Before solving the problem, how do you know that the area of the dog park must be greater than 200 square yards?

How Can You Make Sense of Problems and Persevere in Solving Them?

A

Gwen is planning to tile the entire floor of the family room and kitchen. Tile costs $12 per square foot. What is the total cost of tiling the family room and kitchen floors?

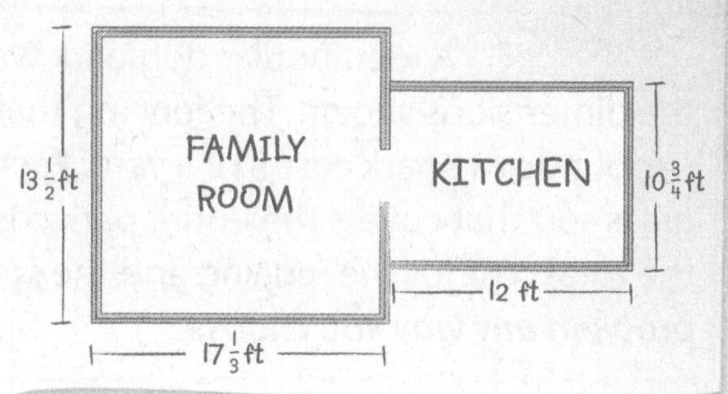

You can make sense of the problem by answering these questions. What do you know? What are you asked to find?

Here's my thinking...

B

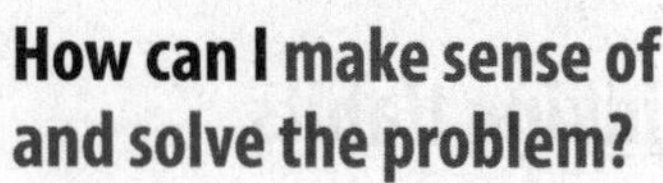

How can I make sense of and solve the problem?

I can

- identify the quantities given.
- understand how the quantities are related.
- choose and implement an appropriate strategy.
- check to be sure my work and answer make sense.

C

Find the area of the family room.

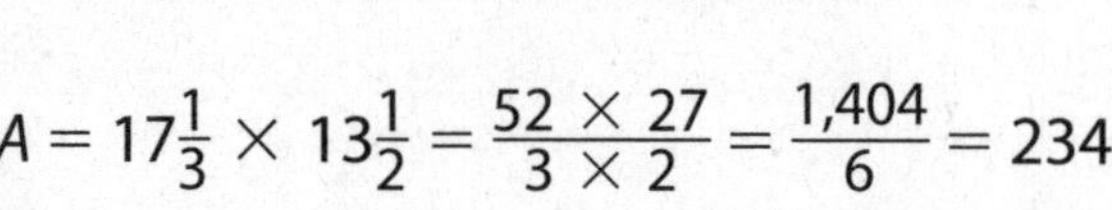

$$A = 17\frac{1}{3} \times 13\frac{1}{2} = \frac{52 \times 27}{3 \times 2} = \frac{1{,}404}{6} = 234$$

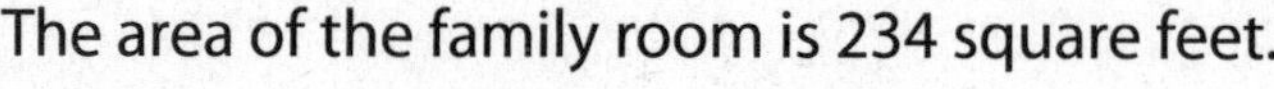

The area of the family room is 234 square feet.

Find the area of the kitchen.

$$A = 12 \times 10\frac{3}{4} = \frac{12 \times 43}{1 \times 4} = \frac{516}{4} = 129$$

The area of the kitchen is 129 square feet.

Add to find the total area. $234 + 129 = 363$

Calculate the total cost. $363 \times 12 = 4{,}356$

The total cost is $4,356.

Convince Me! **MP.1 Make Sense and Persevere** How much more does it cost to tile the family room floor than the kitchen floor? Show your work.

Name ________________________

Guided Practice*

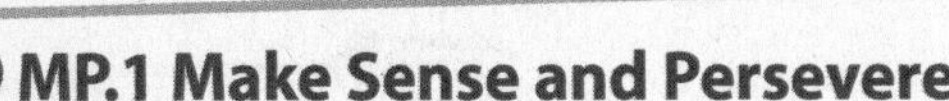

MP.1 Make Sense and Persevere

A website has a daily trivia contest. On Mondays, Wednesdays, and Fridays, you have $1\frac{1}{2}$ hours to submit an answer. On Tuesdays and Thursdays, you have $1\frac{1}{4}$ hours. On Saturdays and Sundays, you have only $\frac{3}{4}$ of an hour. How many hours each week do you have to submit an answer?

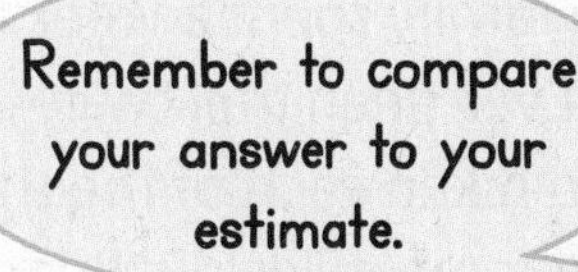

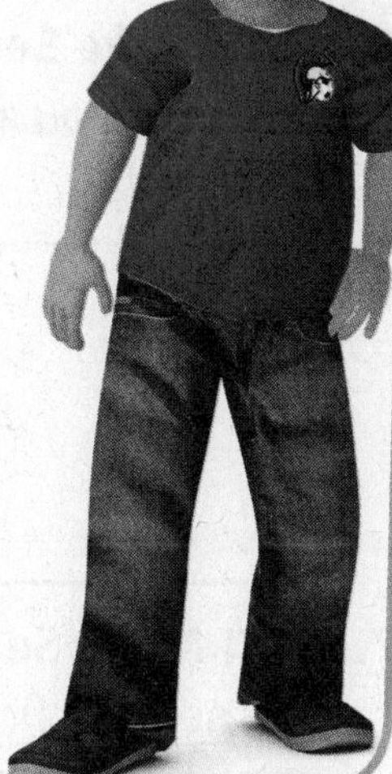

1. Estimate the total hours each week you have to submit an answer. Write an equation to show your work.

2. Write an equation using multiplication and a variable to represent the problem. Then solve the equation and answer the question.

Independent Practice

MP.1 Make Sense and Persevere

Isabel is buying framing to go around the perimeter of one of her paintings. Each inch of framing costs $0.40. What is the total cost of the framing for the painting?

3. What is the first step you need to do? What is the answer to the first step? Write an equation to show your work.

4. What is the next step to solve the problem? What is the answer to the problem? Write an equation to show your work.

5. How can you check that your answer makes sense?

*For another example, see Set H on page 516.

Math Practices and Problem Solving

Common Core Performance Assessment

Hiking Trails

The Farina family spent a week at the state park. Christine hiked the Evergreen trail twice and the Yellow River trail once. Brian hiked each of the three longest trails once. How many more miles did Brian hike than Christine?

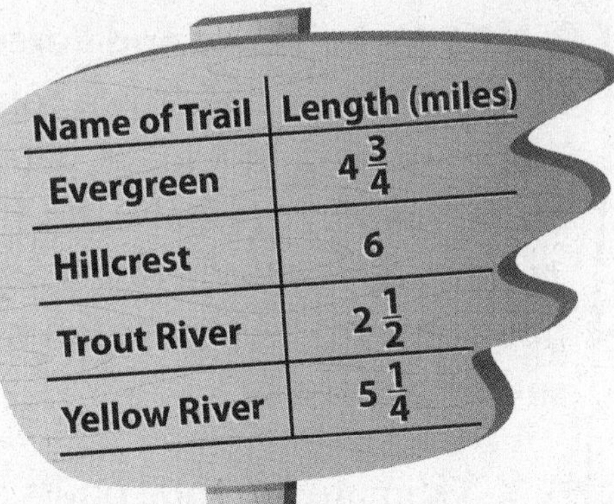

Name of Trail	Length (miles)
Evergreen	$4\frac{3}{4}$
Hillcrest	6
Trout River	$2\frac{1}{2}$
Yellow River	$5\frac{1}{4}$

6. **MP.1 Make Sense and Persevere** What do you know? What are you asked to find? What information do you not need?

7. **MP.1 Make Sense and Persevere** What information do you need to find before you can answer the final question?

Read the problem carefully so you can identify what you know and what you are asked to find.

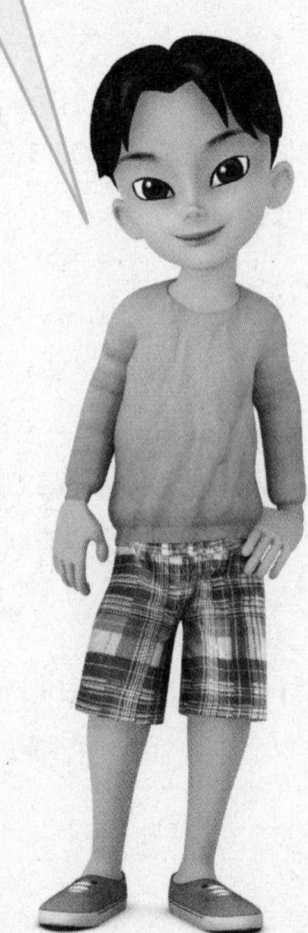

8. **MP.4 Model with Math** Write equations to represent the information in Exercise 7.

9. **MP.1 Make Sense and Persevere** Solve the problem.

10. **MP.3 Construct Arguments** Explain why your answer makes sense.

Name ______________________________

Homework & Practice 8-9
Make Sense and Persevere

Another Look!

Last weekend Troy spent $\frac{3}{4}$ hour doing math problems. He took 3 times as long to finish his science project. Then he spent $1\frac{1}{4}$ hours writing an essay. How much time did Troy spend on these assignments?

Make sense of the problem and then plan how to solve it.

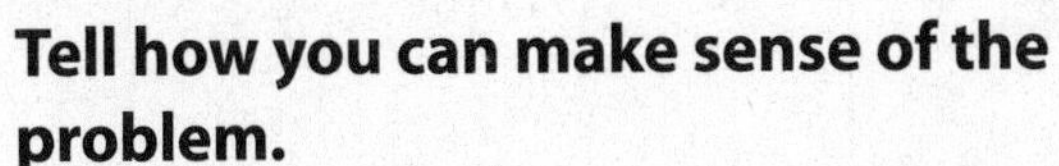

Tell how you can make sense of the problem.

I know that Troy spent $\frac{3}{4}$ hour doing math problems and 3 times as long on his science project.

He spent $1\frac{1}{4}$ hours writing an essay.

Tell how you can persevere in solving the problem.

I need to determine how much time Troy spent on the assignments.

First, you need to find the amount of time Troy spent on his science project.

$3 \times \frac{3}{4} = \frac{3}{1} \times \frac{3}{4} = \frac{9}{4} = 2\frac{1}{4}$ hours

Then add to calculate the total time.

$\frac{3}{4} + 2\frac{1}{4} + 1\frac{1}{4} = 4\frac{1}{4}$ hours

Troy spent $4\frac{1}{4}$ hours on the assignments.

MP. 1 Make Sense and Persevere

Debra's rectangular vegetable garden measures $9\frac{1}{3}$ yards by 12 yards. A bottle of garden fertilizer costs $14.79. If Debra needs to mix $\frac{1}{8}$ cup of fertilizer with water for each square yard of her garden, how many cups of fertilizer does she need?

1. How can you make sense of the problem?

Remember to check that your work makes sense.

2. Is there any information that is not needed to solve the problem?

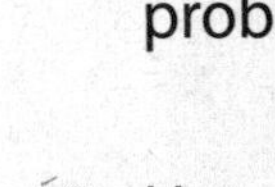

3. How can you persevere in solving this problem? What is the answer?

Common Core Performance Assessment

Children's Costumes

Mrs. Lin is sewing costumes for her grandchildren. She is making three lion costumes, one zebra costume, and two bear costumes. Fabric costs $7.49 per yard. How much fabric does Mrs. Lin need?

DATA

Children's Costumes

Costume	Fabric (yards)
Bear	$2\frac{1}{4}$
Lion	$1\frac{2}{3}$
Zebra	$2\frac{5}{8}$

4. **MP.1 Make Sense and Persevere** What do you know? What are you asked to find? Is there any information you do not need?

5. **MP.1 Make Sense and Persevere** What do you need to find before you can answer the final question?

6. **MP.4 Model with Math** Write equations to represent the information you described in Exercise 5.

7. **MP.1 Make Sense and Persevere** Solve the problem.

8. **MP.3 Construct Arguments** Explain why your answer makes sense.

Remember that good problem solvers keep asking themselves if their work makes sense.

Name ______________________________

Fluency Practice Activity

Work with a partner. Get paper and a pencil. Each partner chooses light blue or dark blue.

At the same time, Partner 1 and Partner 2 each point to one of their black numbers. Both partners find the product of the two numbers.

The partner who chose the color where the product appears gets a tally mark. Work until one partner has seven tally marks.

I can ...
multiply multi-digit whole numbers.

Content Standard 5.NBT.B.5

Partner 1
11
93
26
82
200

16,016	2,600	16,275	2,343
42,600	1,925	8,200	4,550
50,512	42,036	9,300	17,466
37,064	5,538	14,350	19,809
35,000	90,400	11,752	20,000
4,972	123,200	57,288	6,776

Partner 2
100
175
213
452
616

Tally Marks for Partner 1	Tally Marks for Partner 2

TOPIC 8

Vocabulary Review

Word List

- area model
- Associative Property of Multiplication
- benchmark fractions
- Commutative Property of Multiplication
- mixed number
- round

Understand Vocabulary

Choose the best term from the box. Write it on the blank.

1. To estimate the product of two mixed numbers, ______ each factor to the nearest whole number.

2. Using ______ can help make it easier to estimate computations.

3. The product of two fractions can be represented by a(n) ______.

4. Another way to write the fraction $\frac{19}{5}$ is as a ______, $3\frac{4}{5}$.

True or False

Estimate each product to decide if the comparison is true or false. Write T for true or F for false.

______ 5. $6\frac{3}{5} \times 5\frac{7}{8} < 42$

______ 6. $8\frac{2}{9} \times 9\frac{1}{4} > 90$

______ 7. $\frac{2}{7} \times \frac{5}{8} < 1$

______ 8. $5\frac{1}{10} \times 3 > 15$

Use Vocabulary in Writing

9. Suppose you know the answer to $\frac{4}{5} \times \left(20 \times 1\frac{7}{8}\right)$. Explain how the Commutative and Associative Properties of Multiplication can make the computation easier. Then find the answer.

Name ____________________

TOPIC 8

Reteaching

Set A pages 457–462

Find $4 \times \frac{2}{3}$ using a number line.

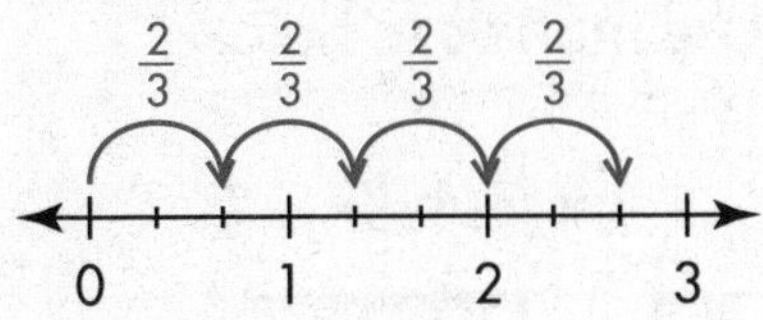

Each jump is $\frac{2}{3}$.

$1 \times \frac{2}{3} = \frac{2}{3}$

$2 \times \frac{2}{3} = \frac{4}{3} = 1\frac{1}{3}$

$3 \times \frac{2}{3} = \frac{6}{3} = 2$

$4 \times \frac{2}{3} = \frac{8}{3} = 2\frac{2}{3}$

So, $4 \times \frac{2}{3} = 2\frac{2}{3}$.

This makes sense because $\frac{2}{3}$ is less than 1, so $4 \times \frac{2}{3}$ should be less than 4.

Remember to multiply the numerator of the fraction by the whole number.

Find each product. Use number lines, fractions strips, or drawings to help you.

1. $4 \times \frac{3}{4}$

2. $7 \times \frac{1}{4}$

3. $8 \times \frac{5}{6}$

4. $10 \times \frac{1}{2}$

5. $9 \times \frac{1}{3}$

6. $9 \times \frac{2}{3}$

7. $3 \times \frac{7}{8}$

8. $7 \times \frac{3}{8}$

9. $5 \times \frac{5}{6}$

10. $12 \times \frac{2}{3}$

11. $15 \times \frac{4}{5}$

12. $2 \times \frac{9}{10}$

Set B pages 463–468, 469–474

Mary's clock uses $\frac{3}{4}$ of the batteries in the package. How many batteries does the clock need?

8 batteries in each package

Find $\frac{3}{4}$ of 8.

$\frac{1}{4}$ of 8 is 2.

$\frac{3}{4}$ is three times as much as $\frac{1}{4}$.

So, $\frac{3}{4}$ of 8 is three times as much as 2.

$\frac{3}{4}$ of 8 is 6.

Mary's clock needs 6 batteries.

Remember that the word *of* often means to multiply.

Find each product.

1. $4 \times \frac{1}{2}$

2. $\frac{3}{4}$ of 16

3. $24 \times \frac{1}{8}$

4. $\frac{4}{7}$ of 28

5. $\frac{4}{5} \times 37$

6. $\frac{7}{8} \times 219$

7. Marco weighs 80 pounds. His bones make up about $\frac{1}{5}$ of his body weight. How much do his bones weigh?

8. Monica bought 12 gallons of paint. She used $\frac{2}{3}$ of the paint to paint her house. How many gallons of paint did she use?

9. A soccer coach gives each player $\frac{1}{2}$ liter of water at halftime. If there are 11 players, how many liters does he need?

Set C pages 475–480

Find $\frac{2}{3} \times \frac{5}{6}$.

A drawing can show fraction multiplication. Start with a rectangle that has 3 rows and 6 columns. There are 18 sections in all.

For $\frac{2}{3}$, shade 2 rows.

For $\frac{5}{6}$, shade 5 columns.

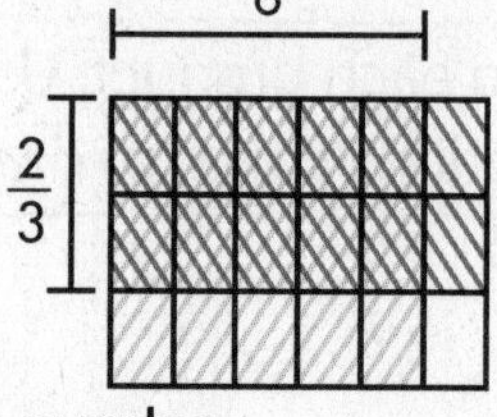

Count the sections in the overlap.

10 of the 18 squares are in the overlap area.

So, $\frac{5}{6} \times \frac{2}{3} = \frac{10}{18}$ or $\frac{5}{9}$.

Remember to use each denominator to make the grid.

Find each product. Use models to help.

1. $\frac{2}{3} \times \frac{3}{8}$

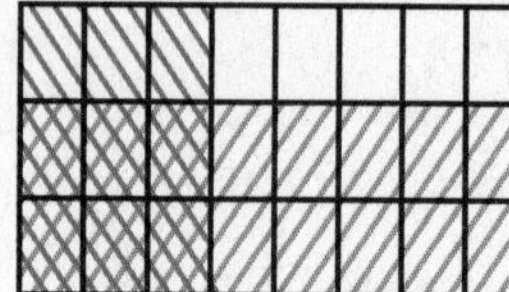

2. $\frac{1}{4} \times \frac{3}{5}$

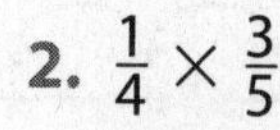

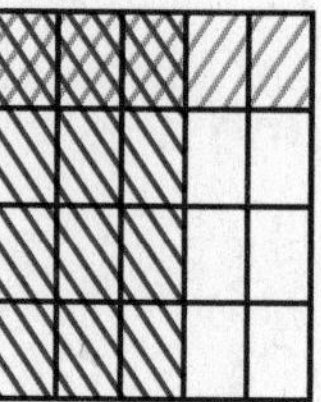

3. $\frac{1}{6} \times \frac{1}{8}$

4. $\frac{4}{7} \times \frac{4}{7}$

Set D pages 481–486

Find $\frac{4}{5} \times \frac{3}{4}$.

Multiply the numerators to find the numerator of the product. Multiply the denominators to find the denominator of the product.

$\frac{4}{5} \times \frac{3}{4} = \frac{4 \times 3}{5 \times 4} = \frac{12}{20}$ or $\frac{3}{5}$

Remember to multiply the numerators together and the denominators together.

1. $\frac{6}{7} \times \frac{1}{2}$

2. $\frac{3}{8} \times \frac{8}{3}$

3. $\frac{2}{3} \times \frac{1}{3}$

4. $\frac{7}{8} \times \frac{3}{2}$

Set E pages 487–492

Find the area of a rectangle with length $\frac{3}{2}$ and width $\frac{1}{3}$.

Because 2 × 3 rectangles $\frac{1}{2}$ long and $\frac{1}{3}$ wide fit in a unit square, $\frac{1}{2} \times \frac{1}{3} = \frac{1}{2 \times 3}$.

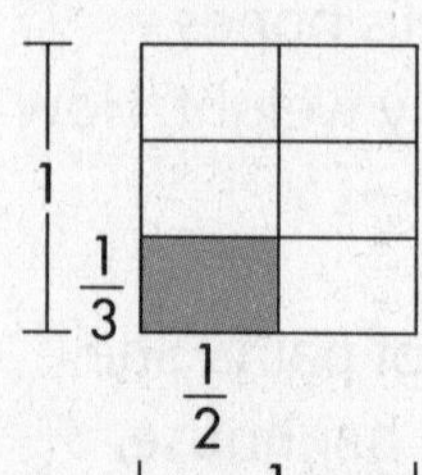

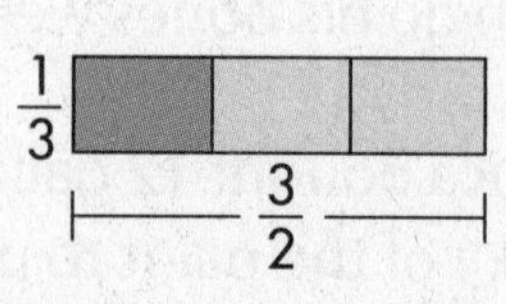

The rectangle of length $\frac{3}{2}$ and width $\frac{1}{3}$ is tiled with 3 rectangles of area $\frac{1}{2 \times 3}$.

So, the area of the rectangle is $\frac{3}{6}$ or $\frac{1}{2}$ square unit.

Remember that a unit square can be used to help find areas of rectangles.

Find the area of a rectangle with the given dimensions.

1. Length: $\frac{8}{5}$ units
   Width: $\frac{3}{4}$ unit

2. Length: $\frac{4}{3}$ units
   Width: $\frac{7}{10}$ unit

3. Gabriel has a square canvas that measures $\frac{5}{4}$ feet on each side. What is the area of Gabriel's canvas?

Name ___

Set F pages 493–498

Find $3\frac{1}{2} \times 2\frac{7}{8}$.

Estimate: $3\frac{1}{2} \times 2\frac{7}{8}$ is about $4 \times 3 = 12$.

Rename fractions, then multiply.

$\frac{7}{2} \times \frac{23}{8} = \frac{161}{16} = 10\frac{1}{16}$

The product $10\frac{1}{16}$ is close to the estimate, 12.

An area model can also represent the product of mixed numbers.

A rectangular field of crops is $4\frac{2}{3}$ miles by $2\frac{3}{4}$ miles. Calculate $4\frac{2}{3} \times 2\frac{3}{4}$ to find the area.

Estimate: $4\frac{2}{3} \times 2\frac{3}{4}$ is about $5 \times 3 = 15$.

Use an area model to find the partial products.

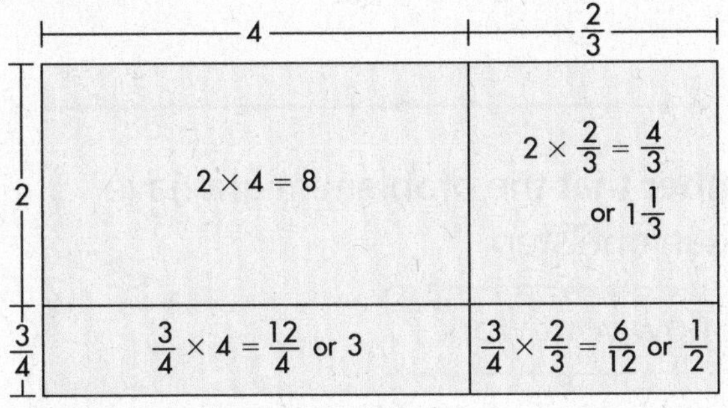

Add the partial products.

$8 + 1\frac{1}{3} + 3 + \frac{1}{2} =$

$8 + 1\frac{2}{6} + 3 + \frac{3}{6} =$

$8 + 3 + 1\frac{2}{6} + \frac{3}{6} = 12\frac{5}{6}$

So, $4\frac{2}{3} \times 2\frac{3}{4} = 12\frac{5}{6}$.

The area of the field is $12\frac{5}{6}$ square miles. The product is close to the estimate of 15, so the answer is reasonable.

Remember to compare your answer with your estimate.

TOPIC 8 | **Reteaching** Continued

Estimate. Then find each product.

1. $2\frac{1}{3} \times 4\frac{1}{5}$
2. $4\frac{1}{2} \times 6\frac{2}{3}$
3. $3\frac{3}{5} \times 2\frac{5}{7}$
4. $14\frac{2}{7} \times 4\frac{3}{10}$

Use the grid. Write the missing labels and find the product.

5. $6\frac{2}{3} \times 3\frac{3}{5}$

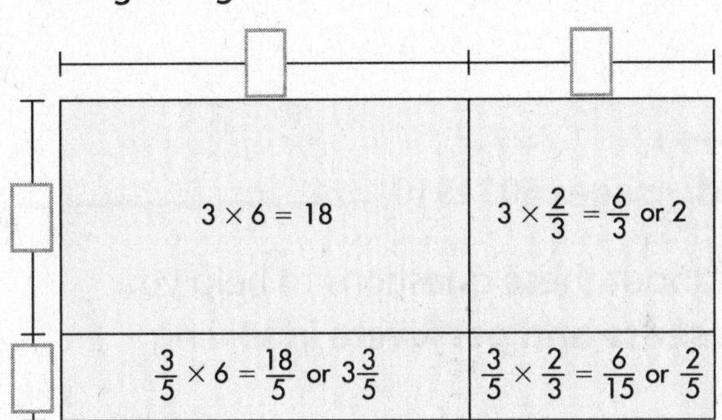

6. $2\frac{5}{12} \times 3\frac{1}{3}$

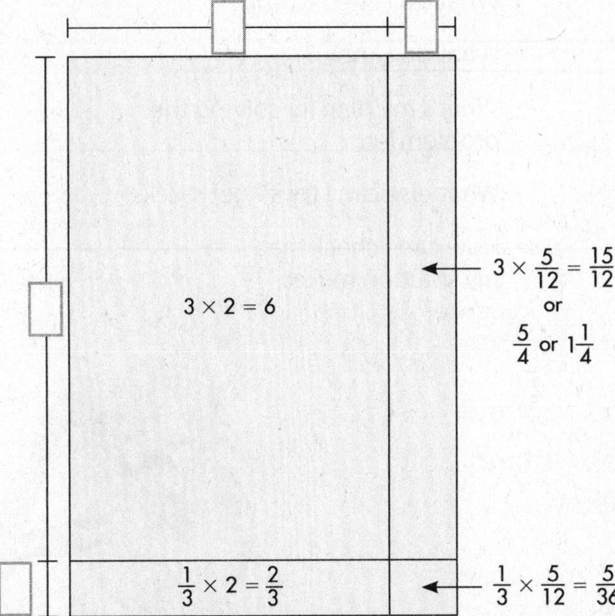

Set G pages 499–504

Multiplication can be thought of as scaling, or resizing, a fraction.

Will the product of $4\frac{1}{2} \times \frac{3}{4}$ be greater than or less than $4\frac{1}{2}$? How can you tell without multiplying?

Since $\frac{3}{4} < 1$, $4\frac{1}{2} \times \frac{3}{4} < 4\frac{1}{2} \times 1$.

So, $4\frac{1}{2} \times \frac{3}{4}$ will be less than $4\frac{1}{2}$.

Will the product of $4\frac{1}{2} \times 2\frac{1}{3}$ be greater than or less than $4\frac{1}{2}$? How can you tell without multiplying?

Since $2\frac{1}{3} > 1$, $4\frac{1}{2} \times 2\frac{1}{3} > 4\frac{1}{2} \times 1$.

So, $4\frac{1}{2} \times 2\frac{1}{3}$ will be greater than $4\frac{1}{2}$.

Remember that a fraction is equal to 1 if the numerator and denominator are the same.

Without multiplying, decide which symbol belongs in the box: <, >, or =.

1. $2\frac{1}{10} \times \frac{3}{5}$ ☐ $2\frac{1}{10}$
2. $\frac{3}{4} \times \frac{5}{5}$ ☐ $\frac{3}{4}$
3. $7\frac{1}{2} \times 1\frac{1}{6}$ ☐ $7\frac{1}{2}$
4. $\frac{8}{3} \times \frac{9}{10}$ ☐ $\frac{8}{3}$

Order each set of numbers from least to greatest.

5. $3\frac{1}{5}$, $3\frac{1}{5} \times \frac{9}{10}$, $3\frac{1}{5} \times 1\frac{1}{2}$
6. $\frac{2}{3} \times \frac{3}{4}$, $\frac{2}{3} \times \frac{5}{4}$, $\frac{2}{3}$
7. $2\frac{1}{3} \times \frac{5}{5}$, $2\frac{1}{3} \times \frac{6}{5}$, $2\frac{1}{3} \times \frac{1}{5}$

Set H pages 505–510

Think about these questions to help you **make sense and persevere** in solving them.

Thinking Habits

- What do I need to find?
- What do I know?
- What's my plan for solving the problem?
- What else can I try if I get stuck?
- How can I check that my solution makes sense?

Remember that the problem might have more than one step.

Solve. Show your work.

1. John has $1\frac{1}{2}$ hours of homework each day from Monday through Thursday and $2\frac{3}{4}$ hours over the weekend. How much homework does John have in a week?

2. Elle is buying new flooring for her kitchen and laundry room. She knows that the area of the kitchen is 132 square feet. The laundry room is $8\frac{1}{3}$ feet by $6\frac{3}{4}$ feet. What is the total area of the two rooms?

Name ____

TOPIC 8

Assessment

1. What is the area of a rectangle with length $\frac{1}{12}$ foot and width $\frac{3}{4}$ foot?

Ⓐ $\frac{1}{16}$ sq ft

Ⓑ $\frac{1}{12}$ sq ft

Ⓒ $\frac{2}{3}$ sq ft

Ⓓ $\frac{5}{6}$ sq ft

2. Alberto runs $3\frac{1}{4}$ miles each day for 7 days.

n **total miles**

$3\frac{1}{4}$	$3\frac{1}{4}$	$3\frac{1}{4}$	$3\frac{1}{4}$	$3\frac{1}{4}$	$3\frac{1}{4}$	$3\frac{1}{4}$

Part A

Write an equation using the variable *n* to model how far he runs.

Part B

How many miles in all does he run?

3. Draw lines to match each expression on the left with the correct product on the right.

$\frac{5}{8} \times \frac{7}{6}$	$\frac{48}{35}$
$\frac{5}{7} \times \frac{8}{6}$	$\frac{40}{42}$
$\frac{8}{5} \times \frac{7}{6}$	$\frac{35}{48}$
$\frac{8}{5} \times \frac{6}{7}$	$\frac{56}{30}$

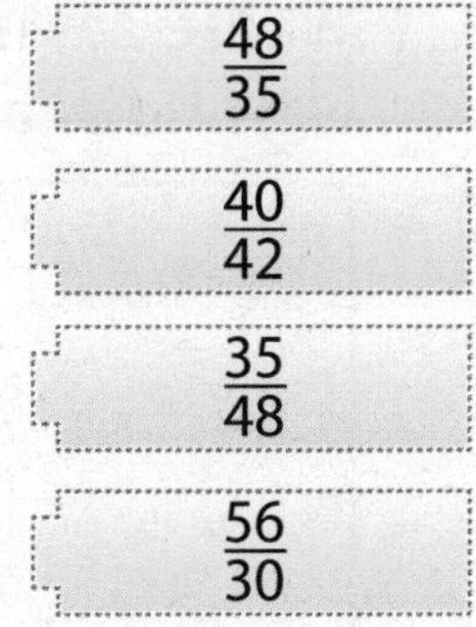

4. For questions 4a–4d, choose Yes or No to tell if the number $\frac{3}{4}$ will make each equation true.

4a. $12 \times \square = 9$ ○ Yes ○ No

4b. $18 \times \square = 12\frac{1}{2}$ ○ Yes ○ No

4c. $15 \times \square = 10\frac{1}{4}$ ○ Yes ○ No

4d. $20 \times \square = 15$ ○ Yes ○ No

5. Choose all the expressions that are equal to $\frac{4}{7} \times 6$.

☐ $4 \div 6 \times 7$

☐ $\frac{6}{7} \times 4$

☐ $6 \div 4 \times 7$

☐ $4 \times 6 \div 7$

☐ $7 \div 4 \times 6$

6. Tracy took a test that had 24 questions. She got $\frac{5}{6}$ of the questions correct. How many questions did she answer correctly? Write an equation to model your work.

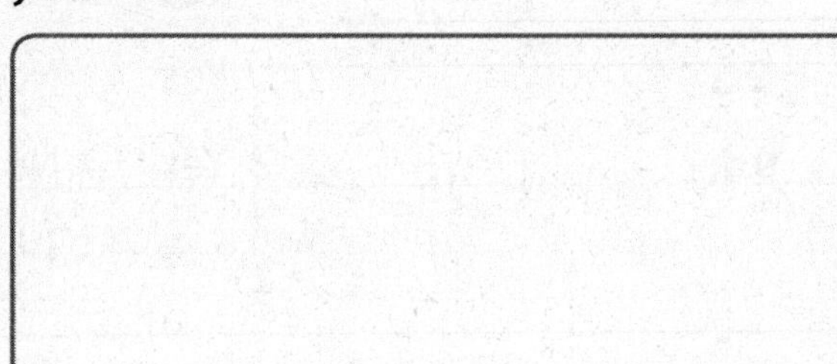

7. Mary is making a window covering that has 5 sections, each of which is $1\frac{3}{10}$ feet in width. What is the width of the entire window covering?

Ⓐ $6\frac{1}{2}$ feet

Ⓑ $5\frac{1}{2}$ feet

Ⓒ $5\frac{3}{10}$ feet

Ⓓ $3\frac{11}{13}$ feet

8. Eduardo has a recipe that uses $\frac{2}{3}$ cup of flour for each batch. If he makes 4 batches, how many cups of flour will he need? Write your answer as a mixed number. Use the number line to help.

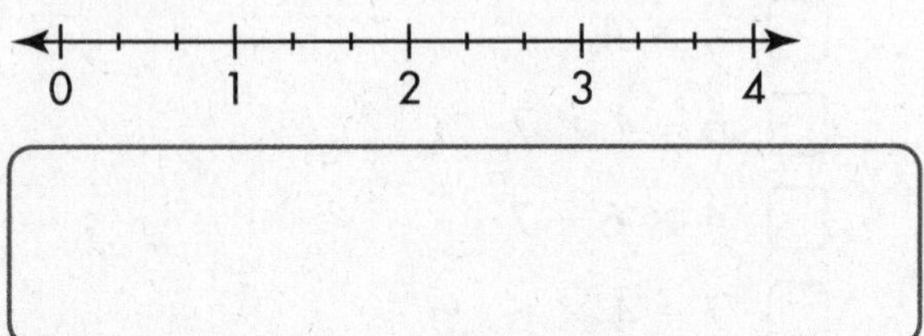

9. For questions 9a–9d, choose Yes or No to tell if the number $\frac{2}{3}$ will make each equation true.

9a. $\square \times \frac{3}{4} = \frac{1}{4}$ ○ Yes ○ No

9b. $\square \times \frac{5}{6} = \frac{10}{18}$ ○ Yes ○ No

9c. $\square \times \frac{2}{3} = \frac{4}{6}$ ○ Yes ○ No

9d. $\square \times \frac{3}{8} = \frac{1}{16}$ ○ Yes ○ No

10. Ted and his friends are rolling out clay for art class. Ted rolled out his clay until it was 2 feet long. Noah rolled out his clay $\frac{3}{5}$ as long as Ted's clay. Jeannine rolled out her clay until it was $1\frac{1}{2}$ times as long as Ted's clay. Miles rolled out his clay $\frac{5}{5}$ as long as Ted's clay.

Part A

Without completing the multiplication, whose clay is longer than Ted's clay? How can you tell?

Part B

Without completing the multiplication, whose clay is shorter than Ted's clay? How can you tell?

Part C

Whose clay is the same length as Ted's clay? How can you tell?

Name ______________________________

TOPIC 8

Assessment Continued

11. Choose all the expressions that are equal to $\frac{7}{8} \times \frac{9}{10}$.

- ☐ $\frac{7 \times 10}{8 \times 9}$
- ☐ $\frac{7 \times 9}{8 \times 10}$
- ☐ $\frac{7 \times 8}{9 \times 10}$
- ☐ $\frac{63}{80}$
- ☐ $\frac{8 \times 9}{7 \times 10}$

12. Draw lines to match each expression on the left with the correct product on the right.

$\frac{3}{8} \times 5$	$\frac{24}{5}$
$\frac{3}{5} \times 8$	$\frac{40}{3}$
$\frac{5}{3} \times 8$	$\frac{30}{8}$
$\frac{6}{8} \times 5$	$\frac{15}{8}$

13. Which of the following is equal to $\frac{4}{7} \times \frac{11}{15}$?

Ⓐ $\frac{4 \times 7}{11 \times 15}$

Ⓑ $\frac{4 \times 15}{7 \times 11}$

Ⓒ $\frac{4 \times 11}{7 \times 15}$

Ⓓ $\frac{7 \times 15}{4 \times 11}$

14. Members of a landscaping company built a retaining wall. They used brick to make the top $\frac{2}{3}$ of the wall.

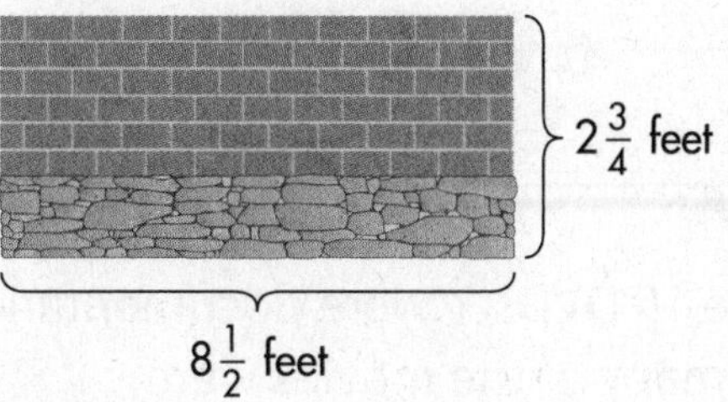

Part A

What is the height of the brick portion of the wall? Write an equation to model your work.

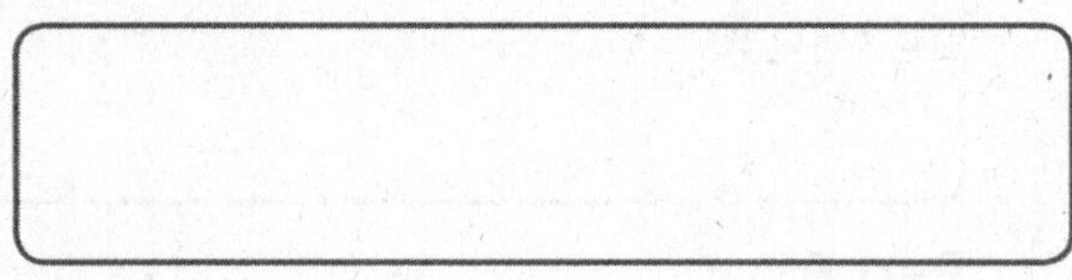

Part B

Estimate the area of the whole retaining wall.

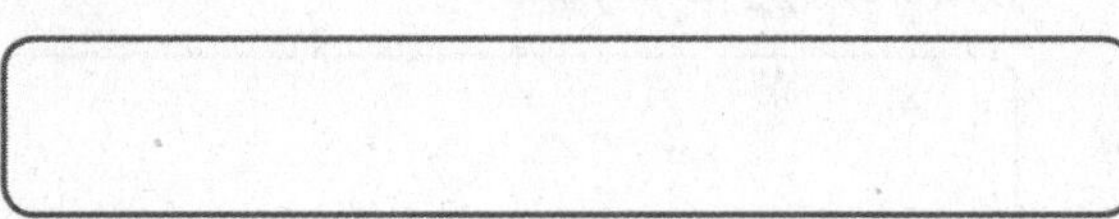

Part C

What is the area of the whole retaining wall? Write an equation to show your work. Compare your answer to your estimate to see if your answer is reasonable.

15. Tyler's family rented 15 DVDs last month.

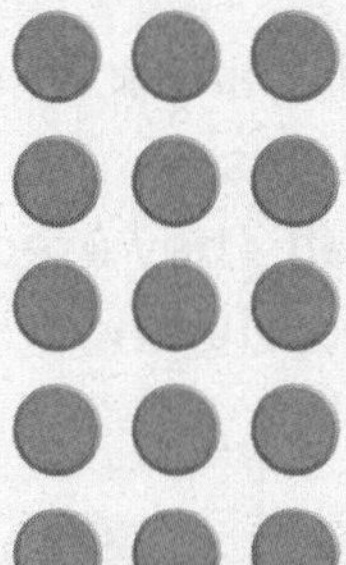

Part A

Of the 15 DVDs, $\frac{1}{5}$ were documentaries. How many of the movies were documentaries? Use the model to help you.

Part B

Of the 15 DVDs, $\frac{3}{5}$ were comedies. How many movies were comedies? Use the model to help you.

Part C

What relationship do you notice between the number of comedies and the number of documentaries?

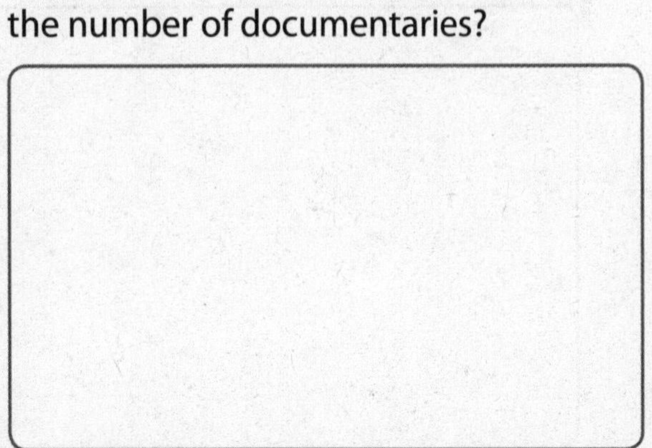

16. Kristen and Niko buy a canvas for their art studio.

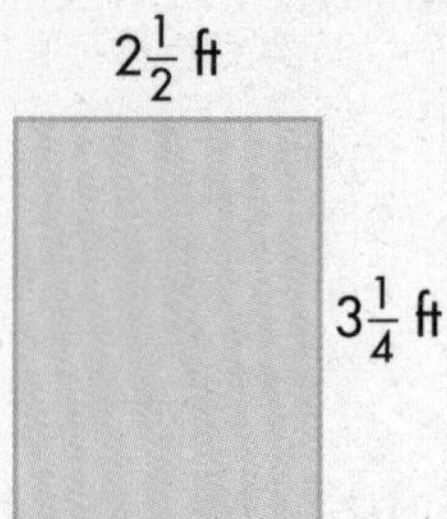

Part A

Estimate the area of their canvas. Write an equation to model your work.

Part B

Find the actual area of their canvas. Write your answer as a mixed number.

Part C

Compare your answer to your estimate to see if your answer is reasonable.

Name ____________________

What's for Dinner?

Branden and Ashley are making the casserole in the **Tuna Casserole Recipe** card.

1. Branden is trying to decide how much tuna casserole to make.

Part A

How many cups of tuna does Branden need to make 3 times the recipe? Draw a model to show how to solve.

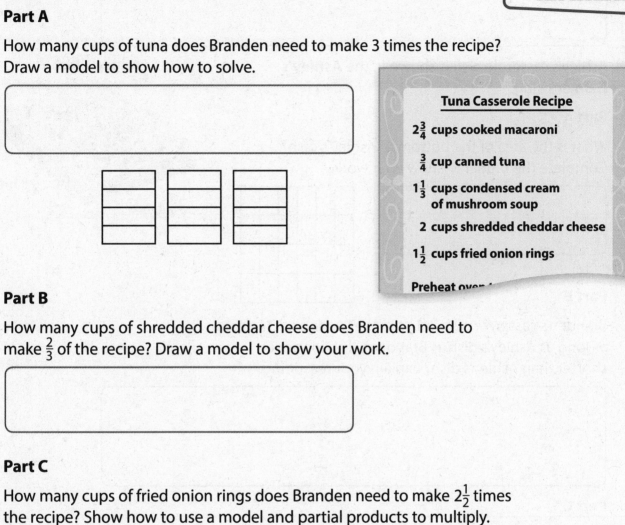

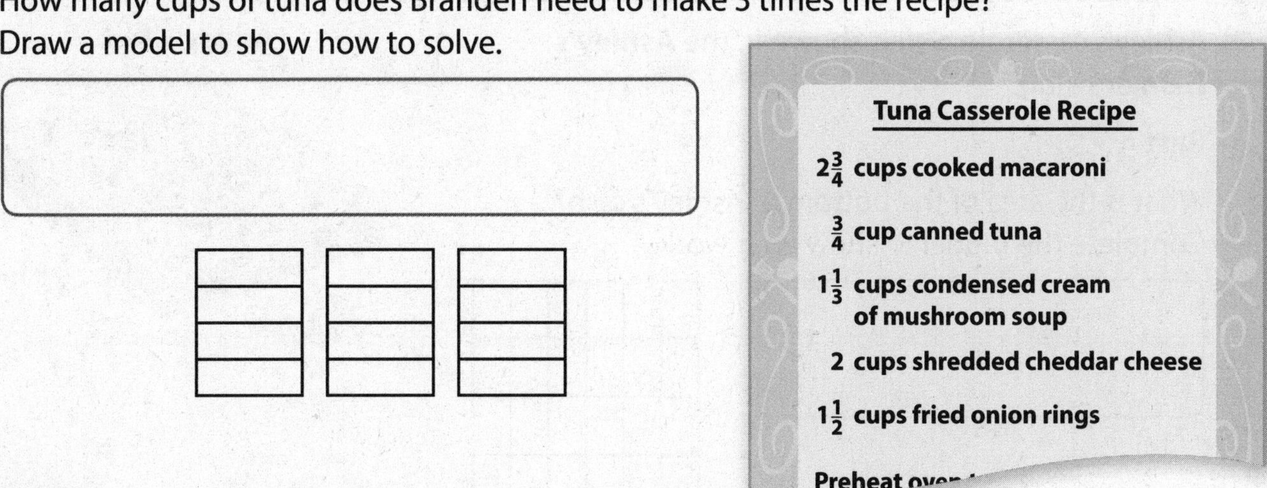

Tuna Casserole Recipe
$2\frac{3}{4}$ cups cooked macaroni
$\frac{3}{4}$ cup canned tuna
$1\frac{1}{3}$ cups condensed cream of mushroom soup
2 cups shredded cheddar cheese
$1\frac{1}{2}$ cups fried onion rings
Preheat ove

Part B

How many cups of shredded cheddar cheese does Branden need to make $\frac{2}{3}$ of the recipe? Draw a model to show your work.

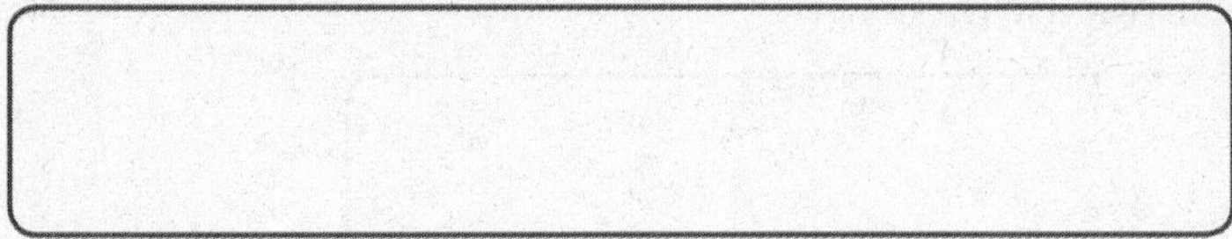

Part C

How many cups of fried onion rings does Branden need to make $2\frac{1}{2}$ times the recipe? Show how to use a model and partial products to multiply.

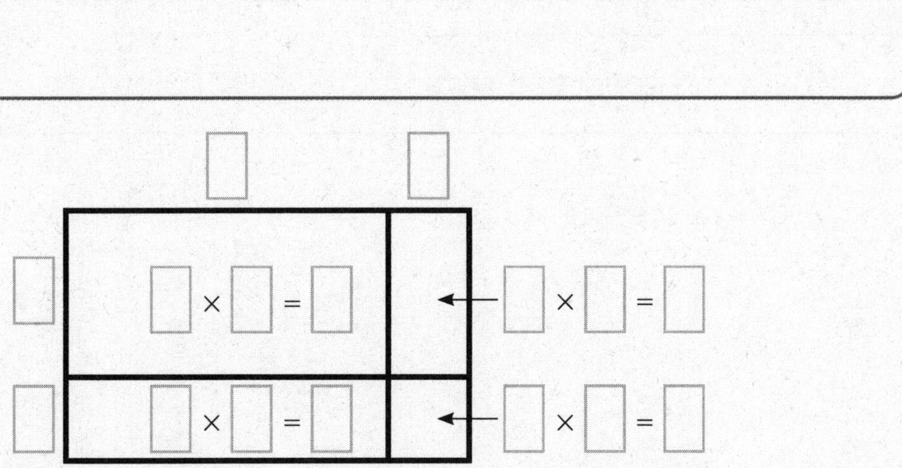

Part D

How many cups of cooked macaroni does Branden need to make $2\frac{1}{2}$ times the recipe? Show how to rename fractions, then multiply.

2. Ashley's casserole dish is shown in the **Ashley's Dish** drawing.

Ashley's Dish

$\frac{5}{6}$ ft long

$\frac{3}{4}$ ft wide

Part A

What is the area of the bottom of Ashley's dish? Complete the model to show your work.

Part B

Branden's casserole dish is $1\frac{1}{2}$ times as wide and $1\frac{4}{5}$ times as long as Ashley's dish. Is Branden's dish longer or shorter than Ashley's dish? Explain your reasoning.

Part C

What is the area of the bottom of Branden's dish? Show your work.

Apply Understanding of Division to Divide Fractions

Essential Questions: How are fractions related to division? How can you divide with whole numbers and unit fractions?

The thermal energy of an object depends on its temperature and on how many particles it contains.

A cup of hot cocoa has more thermal energy than a cup of cold milk.

I can chill with that! Five marshmallows roasting on a stick have more thermal energy than just one! Here's a project about thermal energy.

Math and Science Project: Thermal Energy

Do Research Use the Internet or other sources to learn about thermal energy. Make a list of 3 ways you use thermal energy in your home and at school. Which use is most important to you? Why?

Journal: Write a Report Include what you found. Also in your report:

- Ask each member of your household 3 ways they use thermal energy. Organize your data in a table.
- Draw conclusions from your data. How does your household use thermal energy?
- Make up and solve problems with fraction division.

Name ______________________

Review What You Know

Vocabulary

Choose the best term from the list at the right. Write it on the blank.

- common factor
- equivalent fractions
- estimate
- like denominators
- mixed number
- quotient

1. To find an approximate answer or solution is to ______________.
2. The fractions $\frac{3}{4}$ and $\frac{17}{4}$ are fractions with ______________.
3. The fractions that name the same amount are ______________.
4. The answer to a division problem is the ______________.
5. A number that has a whole-number part and a fraction part is called a ______________.

Meaning of Fractions

Each rectangle represents one whole. Write the shaded part of each rectangle as a fraction.

6. 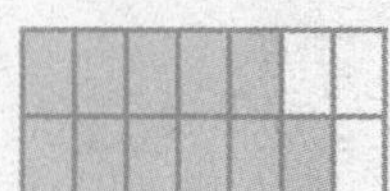

7. 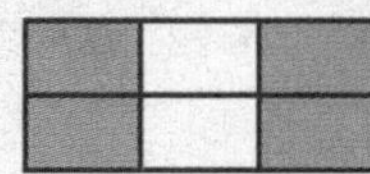

Fraction Computation

Find each sum, difference, or product.

8. $\frac{2}{5} + \frac{1}{4}$

9. $\frac{5}{6} - \frac{1}{4}$

10. $2\frac{5}{8} + 7\frac{1}{4}$

11. $14 - 3\frac{5}{8}$

12. $3\frac{2}{3} + 4\frac{1}{2}$

13. $\frac{3}{8} \times 2$

14. $\frac{1}{4} \times \frac{3}{5}$

15. $8 \times \frac{9}{10}$

16. $3\frac{1}{2} \times 2\frac{3}{5}$

A-Z Glossary

My Word Cards

Use the examples for each word on the front of the card to help complete the definitions on the back.

Examples: $\frac{1}{4}$, $\frac{1}{3}$, $\frac{1}{2}$

My Word Cards

Complete the definition. Extend learning by writing your own definitions.

A fraction with a numerator of 1 is called a ________________.

Name ____________________

Solve

Lesson 9-1

Fractions and Division

I can ...
understand how fractions are related to division.

Content Standard 5.NF.B.3
Mathematical Practices MP.1, MP.2, MP.3, MP.4

Solve & Share Four people want waffles for breakfast. There are 6 waffles left. How can 6 waffles be shared equally among 4 people? How much does each person get? Draw a picture and write a division expression to model the problem.

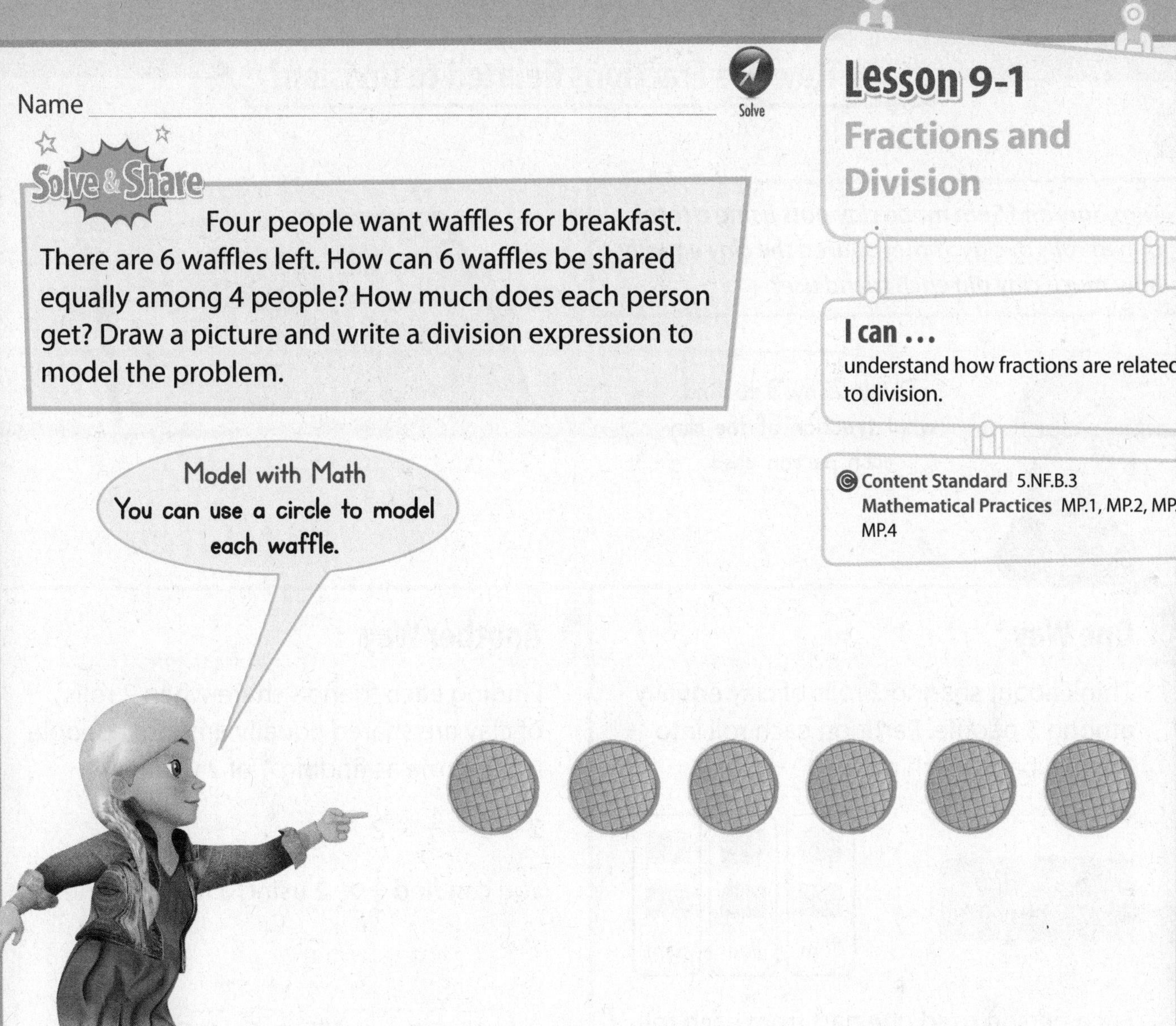

Model with Math
You can use a circle to model each waffle.

Look Back! **MP.3 Construct Arguments** One of the waffles was burnt. Explain how they can share 5 waffles equally.

How Are Fractions Related to Division?

A

Tom, Joe, and Sam made clay pots using a total of two rolls of clay. If they shared the clay equally, how much clay did each friend use?

Divide 2 by 3 to find what fraction of the clay each person used.

B One Way

Think about sharing 2 rolls of clay equally among 3 people. Partition each roll into 3 equal parts. Each part is $1 \div 3$, or $\frac{1}{3}$.

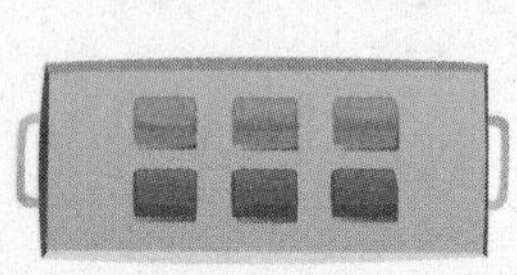

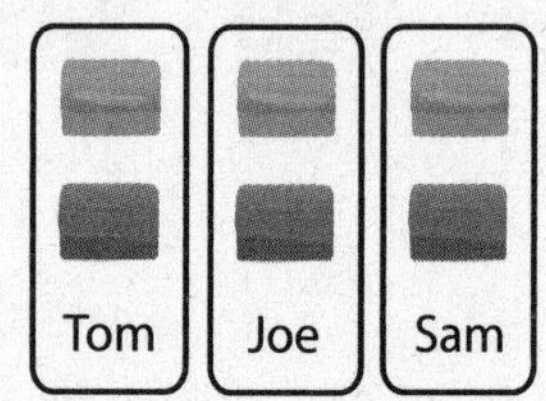

Each person used one part from each roll of clay for a total of 2 parts. This is the same as $\frac{2}{3}$ of one roll of clay.

So, $2 \div 3 = \frac{2}{3}$. Each friend used $\frac{2}{3}$ of a roll of clay.

C Another Way

Finding each friend's share when 2 rolls of clay are shared equally among 3 people is the same as finding $\frac{1}{3}$ of 2 wholes.

$2 \div 3 = \frac{1}{3} \times 2$

You can find $\frac{1}{3} \times 2$ using a number line.

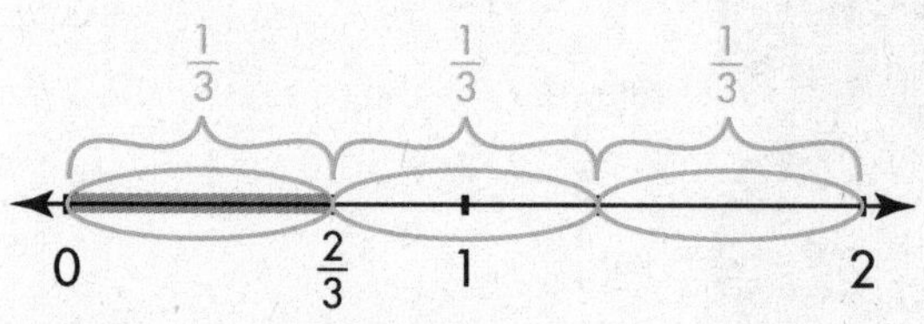

So, $2 \div 3 = \frac{2}{3}$. Each friend used $\frac{2}{3}$ of a roll of clay.

Convince Me! **MP.2 Reasoning** Amelia is sharing 4 slices of cheese with 5 friends. How much cheese will each person get? Explain how you decided.

Name

Practice Buddy Tools Assessment

Guided Practice*

Do You Understand?

1. Explain how to write $\frac{3}{10}$ as a division expression.

2. Explain how to write $2 \div 5$ as a fraction.

3. ⓒ **MP.4 Model with Math** Use the number line below to show $3 \div 4$.

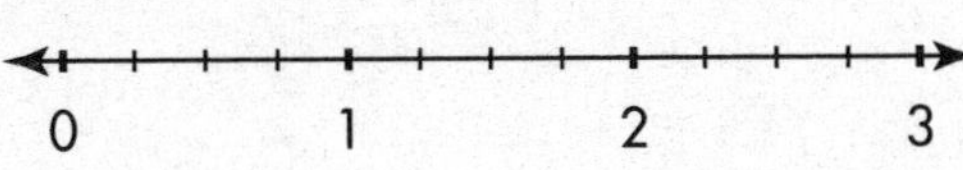

Do You Know How?

In **4** and **5**, write a division expression for each fraction.

4. $\frac{1}{9}$

5. $\frac{7}{8}$

In **6** and **7**, tell what fraction each person gets when they share equally.

6. Five friends share 8 apples.

7. Two friends share 1 bagel.

Independent Practice

In **8–12**, write a division expression for each fraction.

8. $\frac{6}{7}$

9. $\frac{1}{4}$

10. $\frac{6}{11}$

11. $\frac{4}{9}$

12. $\frac{8}{15}$

In **13–17**, write each division expression as a fraction.

13. $9 \div 11$

14. $1 \div 10$

15. $7 \div 13$

16. $11 \div 17$

17. $25 \div 75$

In **18–21**, tell what fraction each person gets when they share equally.

18. 8 students share 6 breakfast bars.

19. 6 soccer players share 5 oranges.

20. 10 friends share 7 dollars

21. 8 friends share 8 muffins

*For another example, see Set A on page 577.

Math Practices and Problem Solving

22. Four friends are baking bread. They equally share 3 sticks of butter. Write an equation to find the fraction of a stick of butter that each friend uses.

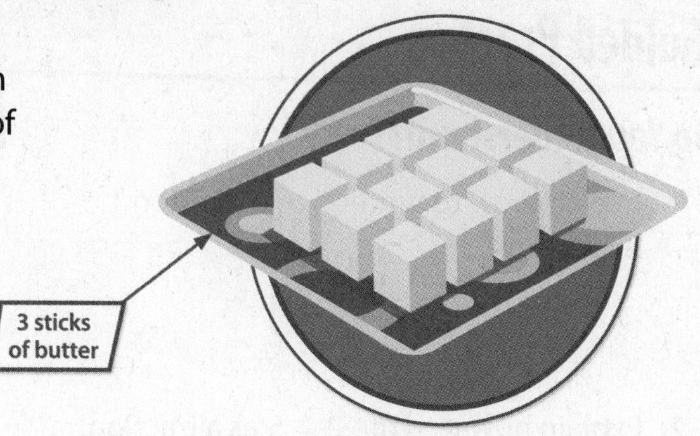

23. MP.2 **Reasoning** A group of friends went to the movies. They shared 2 bags of popcorn equally. If each person got $\frac{2}{3}$ of a bag of popcorn, how many people were in the group?

24. **Higher Order Thinking** Missy says that $\frac{5}{6}$ equals $6 \div 5$. Is she correct? Why or why not?

25. MP.1 **Make Sense and Persevere** The table shows the food and drinks Tabitha bought for herself and 4 friends for her party. How much did Tabitha spend for each person if the cost was split equally? Show your work.

DATA

Item	Number Bought	Cost Each
Sandwiches	5	\$2.89
French Fries	5	\$1.99
Pitcher of Juice	2	\$4.95

Common Core Assessment

26. Choose Yes or No to tell if the number 5 will make each equation true.

$2 \div \square = \frac{2}{5}$ ○ Yes ○ No

$4 \div 20 = \square$ ○ Yes ○ No

$\square \div 5 = \frac{3}{5}$ ○ Yes ○ No

$\square \div 6 = \frac{5}{6}$ ○ Yes ○ No

27. Choose Yes or No to tell if the number 3 will make each equation true.

$\square \div 3 = \frac{1}{3}$ ○ Yes ○ No

$2 \div \square = \frac{2}{3}$ ○ Yes ○ No

$\square \div 8 = \frac{3}{8}$ ○ Yes ○ No

$3 \div 9 = \square$ ○ Yes ○ No

Name ______________________

Help Practice Buddy Tools Games

Homework & Practice 9-1

Fractions and Division

Another Look!

If 3 pizzas are shared equally among 8 people, what fraction of a pizza will each person get?

Step 1

Partition each pizza into 8 equal pieces. Each piece is $\frac{1}{8}$ of the whole.

Since there are more people than pizzas, each person will get less than a whole pizza.

Step 2

Each person gets 1 piece of each pizza. This is the same as $\frac{3}{8}$ of one pizza.

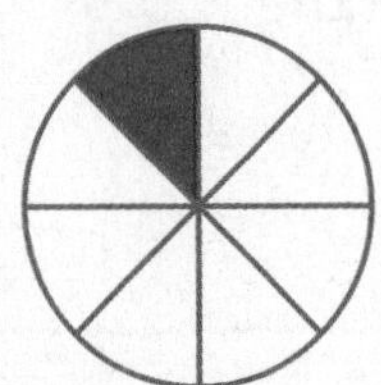
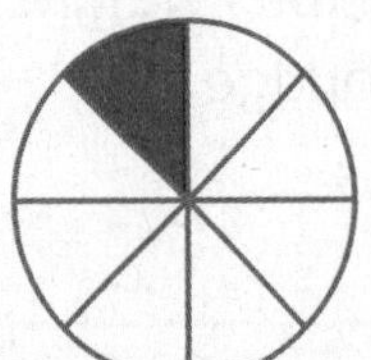
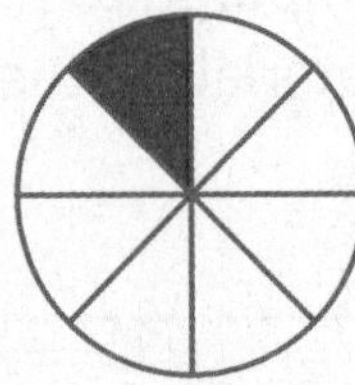

So, $3 \div 8 = \frac{3}{8}$. Each person gets $\frac{3}{8}$ of a pizza.

In **1–5**, write a division expression for each fraction.

1. $\frac{1}{2}$ **2.** $\frac{5}{6}$ **3.** $\frac{9}{15}$ **4.** $\frac{10}{25}$ **5.** $\frac{16}{31}$

In **6–10**, write each division expression as a fraction.

6. $5 \div 9$ **7.** $1 \div 12$ **8.** $4 \div 21$ **9.** $8 \div 30$ **10.** $15 \div 45$

In **11–14**, tell what fraction each person gets when they share equally.

11. 6 friends share 3 apples.

12. 8 people share 1 pizza.

13. 10 students share 1 hour to give their science reports.

14. 5 women each run an equal part of a 3-mile relay.

Use the table for **15** and **16**. The table shows the weights of different materials used to build a bridge.

15. **MP.4 Model with Math** Write a division expression that represents the weight of the steel structure divided by the total weight of the bridge's materials.

DATA

Bridge	Materials
Concrete	1,000 tons
Steel structure	400 tons
Glass and granite	200 tons

16. Write a fraction that represents the weight of glass and granite in the bridge compared to the total weight of the materials in the bridge.

17. **Higher Order Thinking** A group of students shared 3 rolls of clay equally. If each student got $\frac{1}{2}$ of a roll of clay, how many students were in the group? Explain.

18. **A-Z Vocabulary** Write a division equation. Identify the dividend, divisor, and quotient.

19. One lap around the school track is $\frac{1}{4}$ of a mile. If Patrick runs 7 laps around the track and then runs $1\frac{1}{2}$ miles to get home, how far will he run in all?

20. There were 16 teams at a gymnastics meet. Each team had 12 members. How many gymnasts participated in the meet?

Common Core Assessment

21. Choose Yes or No to tell if the number 4 will make each equation true.

$4 \div 5 = \square$ ○ Yes ○ No

$\square \div 4 = \frac{3}{4}$ ○ Yes ○ No

$1 \div \square = \frac{1}{4}$ ○ Yes ○ No

$\square \div 5 = \frac{4}{5}$ ○ Yes ○ No

22. Choose Yes or No to tell if the number 10 will make each equation true.

$\square \div 10 = \frac{1}{10}$ ○ Yes ○ No

$3 \div \square = \frac{3}{10}$ ○ Yes ○ No

$4 \div 40 = \square$ ○ Yes ○ No

$\square \div 21 = \frac{10}{21}$ ○ Yes ○ No

Name ____________________

Lesson 9-2
Fractions and Mixed Numbers as Quotients

I can . . .
show quotients as fractions and mixed numbers.

Content Standard 5.NF.B.3
Mathematical Practices MP.1, MP.2, MP.3, MP.4, MP.6

Solve & Share Jonah has an 8-pound bag of potting soil. He divides it evenly among 5 flowerpots. How much soil is in each pot? Show your answer as a fraction or mixed number. ***Solve this problem any way you choose.***

Model with Math
You can write an equation or draw a picture to help find the answer.

Look Back! **MP.6 Be Precise** Suppose one of the pots breaks, so Jonah has to divide the soil evenly among 4 pots. How much soil is in each pot then?

How Can You Show a Quotient Using a Fraction or Mixed Number?

A

Three friends are going hiking. They bought a tub of trail mix to share equally. How much will each friend get?

You can divide to share
4 pounds among 3 people:
4 ÷ 3.

Trail mix
4 pounds

B

Divide each pound into 3 equal parts. Each part is $1 \div 3$ or $\frac{1}{3}$.

Each friend gets 1 pound plus $\frac{1}{3}$ of a pound, or $1 + \frac{1}{3} = 1\frac{1}{3}$ pounds of trail mix in all.

So, $4 \div 3 = \frac{4}{3} = 1\frac{1}{3}$.

1 pound

1 pound

1 pound

1 pound

Convince Me! **MP.2 Reasoning** Kate shares a 64-ounce bottle of apple cider with 5 friends. Each person's serving will be the same number of ounces. Between what two whole number of ounces will each person's serving be? Explain using division.

Name ______________________________

Guided Practice*

Do You Understand?

1. How can you write $\frac{10}{3}$ as a division expression and as a mixed number?

2. **MP.2 Reasoning** Suppose 3 friends want to share 16 posters equally. For this situation, why does the quotient 5 R1 make more sense than the quotient $5\frac{1}{3}$?

Do You Know How?

3. Find $11 \div 10$ and $10 \div 11$. Write each quotient as a fraction or mixed number.

In **4** and **5**, tell how much each person gets when they share equally.

4. 2 friends share 3 apples.

5. 3 students share 5 breakfast bars.

Independent Practice

In **6–13**, find each quotient. Write each answer as either a fraction or mixed number.

6. $11 \div 6$
7. $1 \div 5$
8. $18 \div 4$
9. $5 \div 9$
10. $9 \div 8$
11. $23 \div 10$
12. $12 \div 17$
13. $28 \div 20$

In **14–17**, tell how much each person gets when they share equally.

14. 2 girls share 7 yards of ribbon.
15. 4 friends share 7 bagels.
16. 4 cousins share 3 pies.
17. 8 soccer players share 12 oranges.

*For another example, see Set A on page 577.

Math Practices and Problem Solving

18. Daniella made gift bows from 8 yards of ribbon. The bows are all the same size. If she made 16 bows, how much ribbon did she use for each one? Give the answer as a fraction or mixed number.

19. © **MP.6 Be Precise** Tammi has 4 pounds of gala apples and $3\frac{1}{2}$ pounds of red delicious apples. If she uses $1\frac{3}{4}$ pounds of gala apples in a recipe, how many pounds of apples does she have left?

20. Casey bought a 100-pound bag of dog food. He gave his dogs the same amount of dog food each week. The dog food lasted 8 weeks. How much dog food did Casey give his dogs each week? Give the answer as a fraction or mixed number.

21. **Higher Order Thinking** Write a word problem that can be solved by dividing 6 by 5.

22. The amount of fabric needed for an adult and a baby scarecrow costume is shown at the right. The amount of fabric for an adult scarecrow costume is how many times the amount of fabric for a baby scarecrow costume? Give the answer as a fraction or mixed number.

© Common Core Assessment

23. Which is the quotient $37 \div 6$?

Ⓐ $\frac{6}{37}$

Ⓑ $6\frac{1}{6}$

Ⓒ $6\frac{5}{6}$

Ⓓ $6\frac{1}{37}$

24. Lindsay divides 40 by 9. Between what two whole numbers is her answer?

Ⓐ 2 and 3

Ⓑ 3 and 4

Ⓒ 4 and 5

Ⓓ 5 and 6

Name ____________________

Help Practice Buddy Tools Games

Homework & Practice 9-2

Fractions and Mixed Numbers as Quotients

Another Look!

Max has 5 clementines (a type of small orange). He shares them equally with his friend Tyler. How many clementines will each friend get?

Find the quotient of $5 \div 2$ as a mixed number.

Divide each clementine into 2 equal parts. Each piece is $\frac{1}{2}$ of the whole.

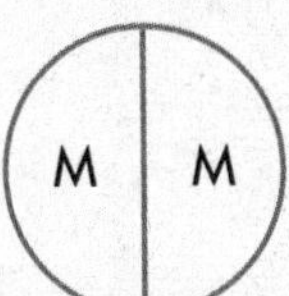

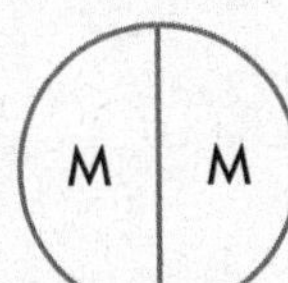

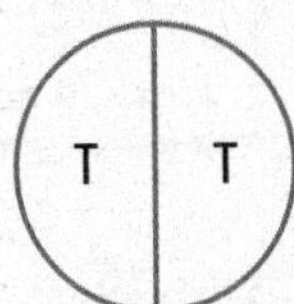

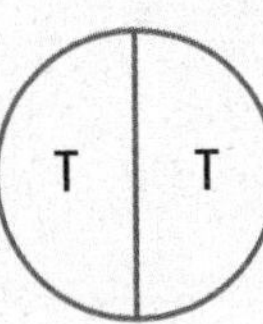

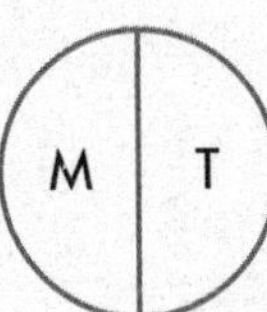

Each friend gets 2 clementines plus $\frac{1}{2}$ of a clementine or $2 + \frac{1}{2} = 2\frac{1}{2}$ clementines in all.

So, $5 \div 2 = \frac{5}{2} = 2\frac{1}{2}$.

Since there are more clementines than people, each person will get more than 1 clementine.

1. Find $5 \div 8$ and $8 \div 5$. Write each quotient as either a fraction or mixed number.

In **2–9**, find each quotient. Write each answer as either a fraction or mixed number.

2. $7 \div 5$
3. $2 \div 3$
4. $15 \div 4$
5. $51 \div 25$
6. $6 \div 11$
7. $17 \div 12$
8. $16 \div 6$
9. $92 \div 30$

In **10–13**, tell how much each person gets when they share equally.

10. 3 friends share 5 pounds of trail mix.
11. 6 people share 12 muffins.
12. 2 sisters share 3 hours of babysitting.
13. 4 students share 10 yards of fabric.

14. Carol jogged $1\frac{3}{4}$ miles on 5 days last week. She jogged $2\frac{1}{4}$ miles on 4 days this week. Was her total distance greater last week or this week? How much greater? Explain.

15. **MP.3 Construct Arguments** How can you tell before dividing that the first digit of the quotient 2,874 ÷ 3 is in the hundreds place?

16. **MP.1 Make Sense and Persevere** Which car traveled the farthest on 1 gallon of gas? Show your work.

	Distance	Gasoline
Car A	302 mi	10 gal
Car B	174 mi	5 gal
Car C	292 mi	8 gal

17. **Vocabulary** Complete the sentence using one of the terms below.

common denominator
benchmark fraction **mixed number**

A ________________ for the fractions $\frac{1}{3}$ and $\frac{1}{4}$ is 12.

18. **Math and Science** The smallest bone in the human body is the stapes bone. It is located in the ear and is about 2.8 millimeters in length. Write this number in expanded form.

19. At Dee's Pizza Kitchen, 7 pizzas were shared equally among 3 families. How much pizza did each family get? Write an equation to represent the problem.

20. **Higher Order Thinking** Everett says that $1\frac{1}{4}$ equals 4 ÷ 5. Is he correct? Explain.

Common Core Assessment

21. Which is the quotient 27 ÷ 5?

Ⓐ $\frac{5}{27}$
Ⓑ $5\frac{1}{5}$
Ⓒ $5\frac{2}{5}$
Ⓓ $5\frac{3}{5}$

22. Leonard divides 70 by 8. Between what two whole numbers is his answer?

Ⓐ 11 and 12
Ⓑ 10 and 11
Ⓒ 9 and 10
Ⓓ 8 and 9

Name ______________________

Lesson 9-3
Use Multiplication to Divide

I can ...
connect dividing by a fraction to multiplication.

Content Standards 5.NF.B.7b, 5.NF.B.7c
Mathematical Practices MP.2, MP.4, MP.7

Solve & Share

A sandwich shop prepares large wraps and cuts them into fourths. Each fourth is one serving. William buys 5 whole wraps for a party. How many servings in all does he get? ***Solve this problem any way you choose.***

Model with Math
How could fraction strips, bar diagrams, or other models help you visualize the problem?

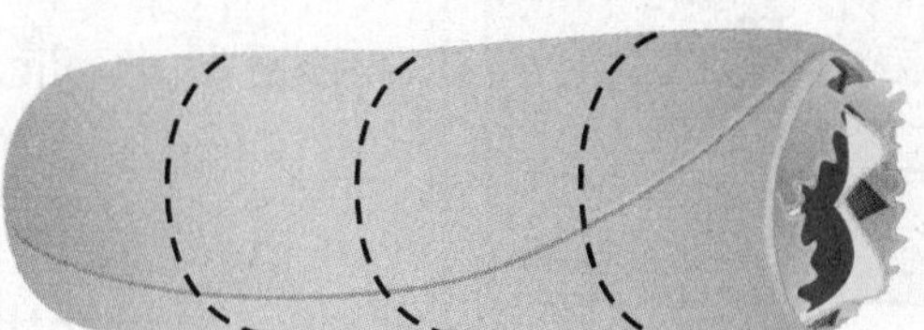

Look Back! **MP.4 Model with Math** Write an equation that represents the problem about the wraps.

How Is Dividing by a Fraction Related to Multiplication?

A

If a bottle of liquid plant food contains 3 cups, how many plants will you be able to feed? Explain why your answer makes sense.

You need to find how many eighths are in 3 cups. $3 \div \frac{1}{8} = ?$

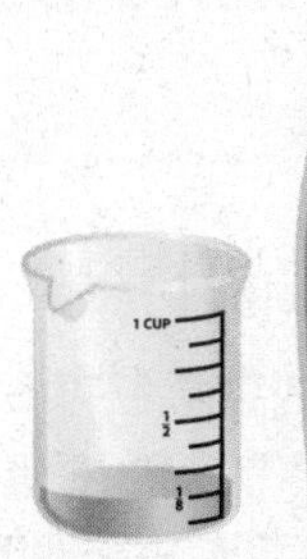

Plant Food
Use 1/8 cup per plant.

Use $\frac{1}{8}$ cup per plant.

B How many $\frac{1}{8}$s are in 3?

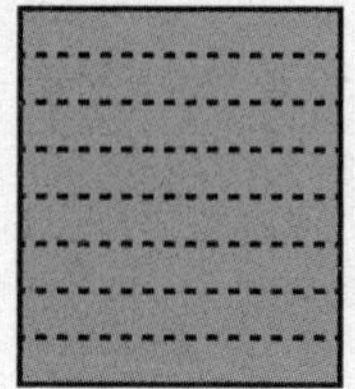
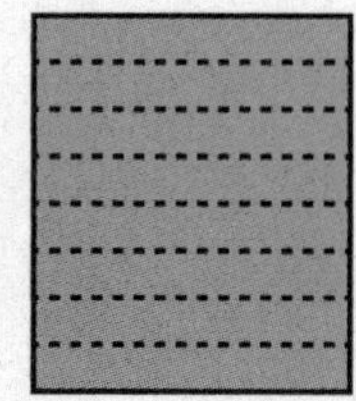
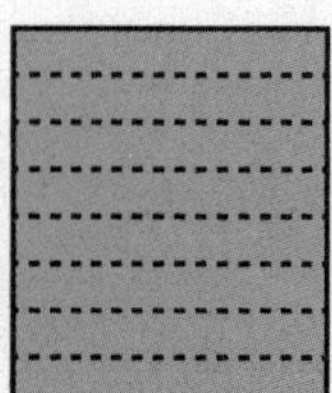

Use a model and multiplication to solve.

Since there are 8 eighths in each whole, there are $3 \times 8 = 24$ eighths in 3 wholes.

So, $3 \div \frac{1}{8} = 24$.

The plant food can feed 24 plants.

C Does the answer make sense? Do 24 eighths equal 3?

Use multiplication to check.

$24 \times \frac{1}{8} = \frac{24}{8} = 3$

Yes, 24 eighths equals 3, so the answer makes sense.

The inverse relationship between multiplication and division applies to fraction computation, too!

The division equation $3 \div \frac{1}{8} = 24$ is true because the multiplication equation $24 \times \frac{1}{8} = 3$ is true.

Convince Me! **MP.7 Use Structure** Use the same numbers in the multiplication equation $15 \times \frac{1}{3} = 5$ to write a division equation. Draw a diagram to show that your division equation makes sense.

Name ____________________

Guided Practice*

Do You Understand?

1. **MP.2 Reasoning** Explain how to use multiplication to find $4 \div \frac{1}{5}$.

2. Show how to use multiplication to check your answer to Exercise 1.

Do You Know How?

3. Find $3 \div \frac{1}{10}$.

4. Draw a model to find $2 \div \frac{1}{6}$.

5. Use a multiplication equation to check your answer to Exercise 4.

Independent Practice

In **6–9**, use the model to find each quotient. Use multiplication to check your answer.

6. $3 \div \frac{1}{4}$

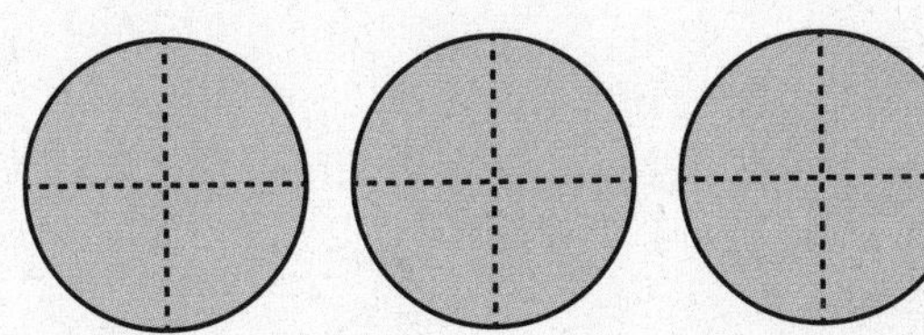

7. $2 \div \frac{1}{12}$

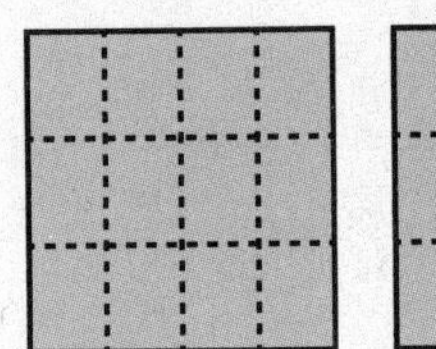

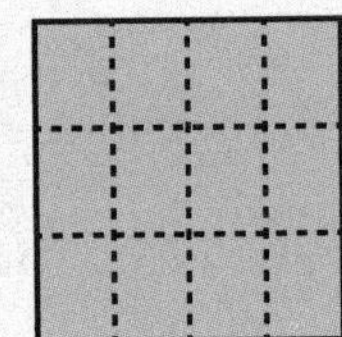

8. $4 \div \frac{1}{9}$

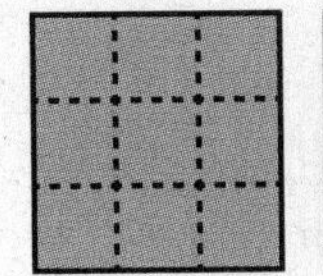

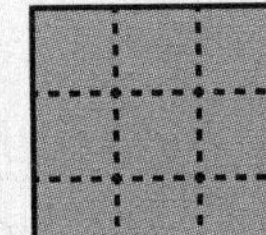

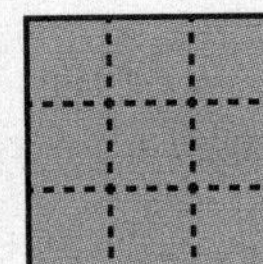

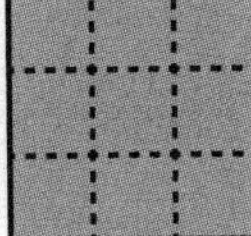

9. $3 \div \frac{1}{6}$

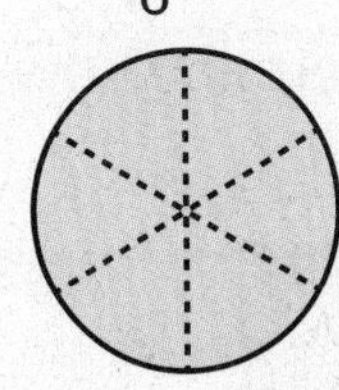

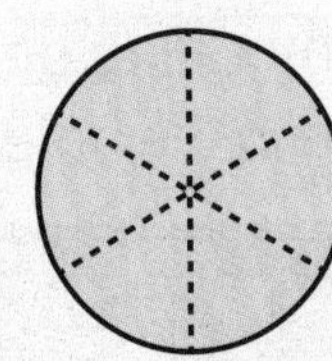

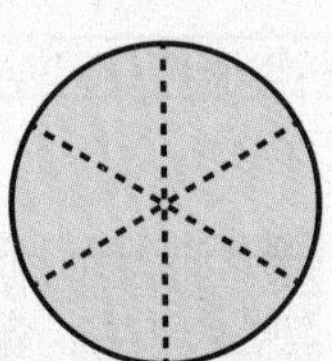

In **10–12**, draw a model to find each quotient. Use multiplication to check your answer.

10. $5 \div \frac{1}{6}$

11. $4 \div \frac{1}{8}$

12. $3 \div \frac{1}{3}$

**For another example, see Set B on page 577.*

Math Practices and Problem Solving

13. **MP.4 Model with Math** Write and solve a division equation to find the number of $\frac{1}{3}$-pound hamburger patties that can be made from 4 pounds of ground beef.

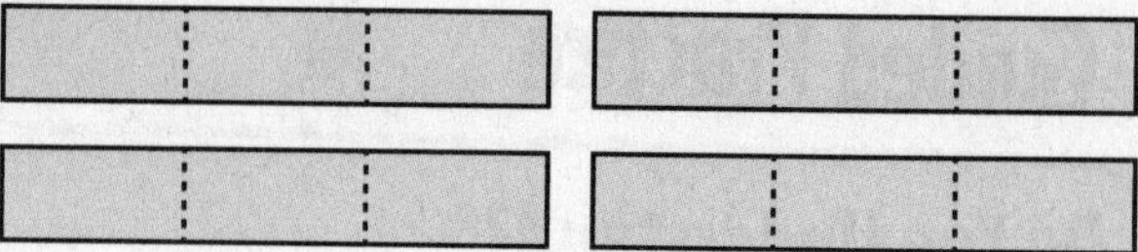

14. Write and solve a word problem for the expression $8 \div \frac{1}{2}$.

15. **MP.7 Use Structure** Use the numbers in the multiplication equation $28 \times \frac{1}{7} = 4$ to write a division equation involving division by a fraction.

16. **Number Sense** Sally and Timothy have two different answers for 1,785 ÷ 35. Without dividing, how can you tell whose answer is wrong?

Sally: 1,785 ÷ 35 = 51
Timothy: 1,785 ÷ 35 = 501

17. **Higher Order Thinking** A restaurant charges $3.50 for a slice of pie that is one sixth of a pie and $3.00 for a slice that is one eighth of a pie. One day they baked 5 pies, all the same size. If they sell all the slices, would they make more money by slicing each pie into sixths or eighths? How much more? Explain.

Common Core Assessment

18. Javier drew a model to determine how many fifths are in 6 wholes.

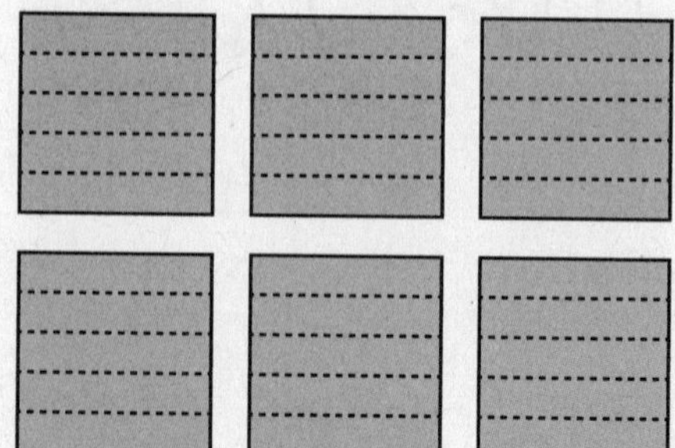

Part A

Describe Javier's work by writing a division equation that includes a fraction.

Part B

Check your answer by using the numbers in your division equation to write a multiplication equation.

Name ______________________

Help Practice Buddy Tools Games

Homework & Practice 9-3

Use Multiplication to Divide

Another Look!

How many sixths are in 4?

Find $4 \div \frac{1}{6}$. Use a model to help.

There are 6 sixths in each whole, so 4 wholes contain $4 \times 6 = 24$ sixths.

$4 \div \frac{1}{6} = 24$

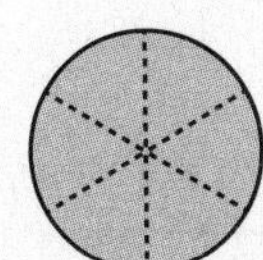 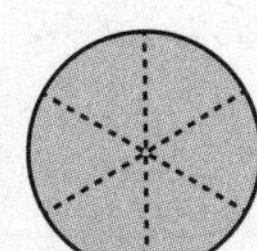 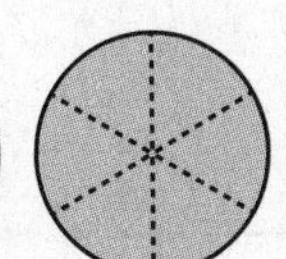 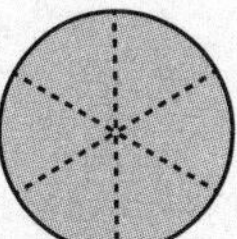

Check your answer.

$24 \times \frac{1}{6} = \frac{24}{6} = 4$

The answer checks.

You can use multiplication to check division.

In **1–4**, use the model to find each quotient. Use multiplication to check your answer.

1. $2 \div \frac{1}{9}$

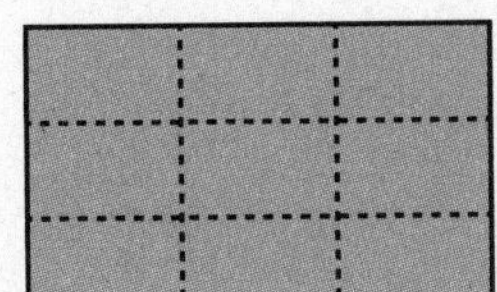 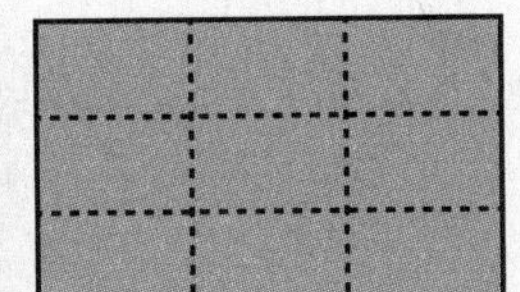

2. $4 \div \frac{1}{4}$

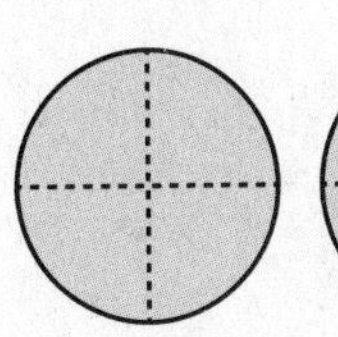 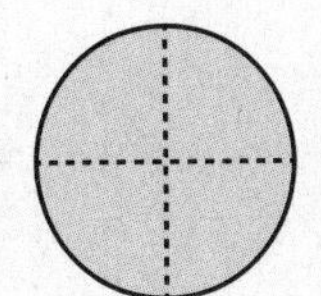 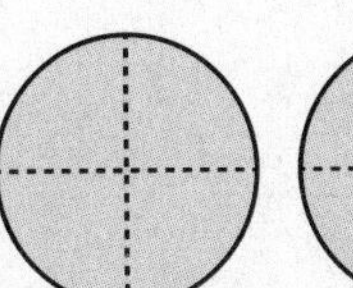 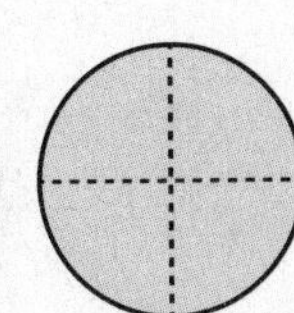

3. $7 \div \frac{1}{3}$

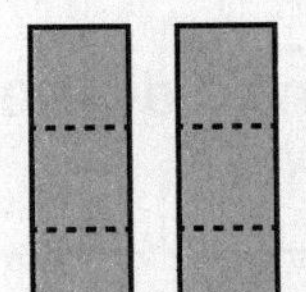 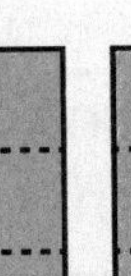  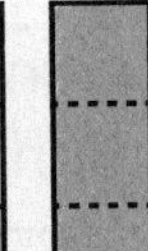  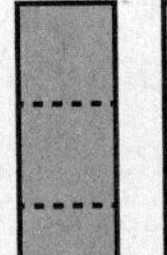 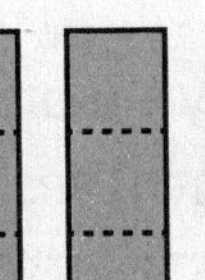 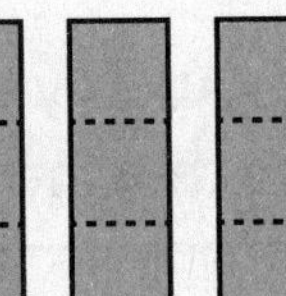 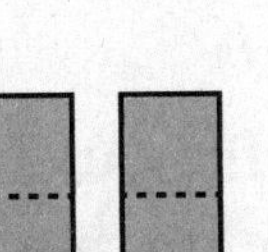

4. $3 \div \frac{1}{2}$

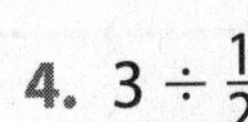 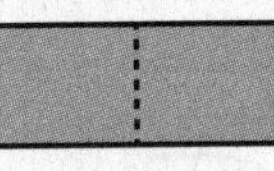 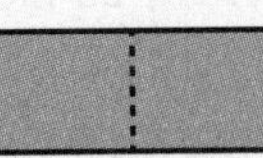 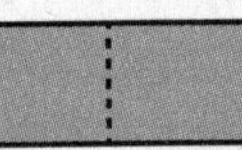

In **5–7**, draw a model to find each quotient. Use multiplication to check your answer.

5. $4 \div \frac{1}{6}$

6. $2 \div \frac{1}{8}$

7. $3 \div \frac{1}{12}$

8. **MP.7 Use Structure** Use the numbers in the multiplication equation $45 \times \frac{1}{9} = 5$ to write a division equation involving division by a fraction.

9. A square has a side length of 6.2 centimeters. What is the perimeter of the square?

10. Denise makes beaded bracelets for a craft fair. She uses $\frac{1}{4}$ yard of yarn for each bracelet. How many bracelets can she make from 10 yards of yarn?

11. Arthur paid $0.84 for 0.25 pound of potato salad. How much does one pound cost?

12. **Higher Order Thinking** A company donated 5 acres of land to the city. How many more small garden plots would fit on the land than medium garden plots? Explain.

DATA

Community Garden Plots	Size (fraction of an acre)
Small	$\frac{1}{6}$
Medium	$\frac{1}{4}$
Large	$\frac{2}{3}$

Common Core Assessment

13. Audrey drew a model to determine how many eighths are in 5.

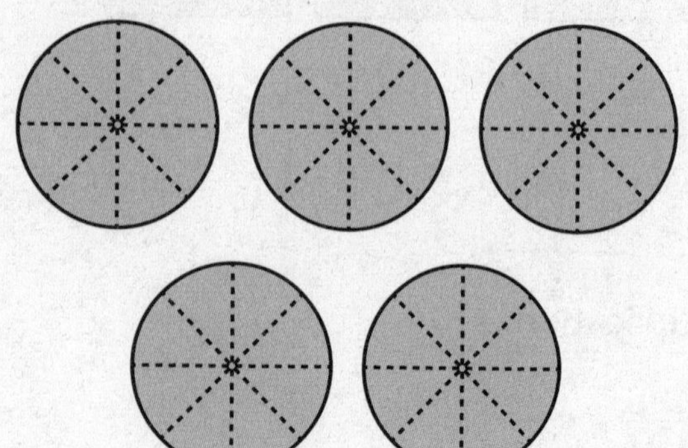

Part A

Describe Audrey's work by writing a division equation that includes a fraction.

Part B

Check your answer by using the numbers in your division equation to write a multiplication equation.

Name ______________________

Lesson 9-4
Divide Whole Numbers by Unit Fractions

I can ...
divide a whole number by a unit fraction.

Content Standards 5.NF.B.7b, 5.NF.B.7c
Mathematical Practices MP.1, MP.2, MP.4, MP.5

Solve & Share One ball of dough can be stretched into a circle to make a pizza. After the pizza is cooked, it is cut into 8 equal slices. How many slices of pizza can you make with 3 balls of dough? ***Solve this problem any way you choose.***

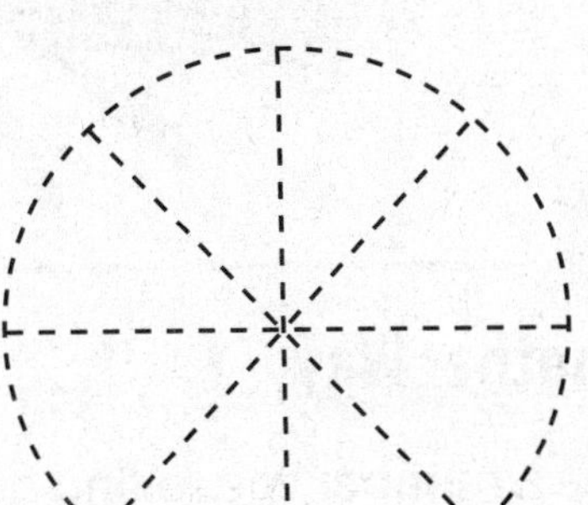

You can use appropriate tools to help find the answer. *Show your work!*

Look Back! **MP.2 Reasoning** Into how many slices of pizza will each ball of dough be divided? What fraction of a whole pizza does 1 slice represent?

How Can You Divide by a Unit Fraction?

A

Joyce is making sushi rolls. She needs $\frac{1}{4}$ cup of rice for each sushi roll. How many sushi rolls can she make if she has 3 cups of rice?

$\frac{1}{4}$ is a unit fraction. A unit fraction is a fraction that describes one part of the whole. So, it has a numerator of 1.

B

One Way

Use an area model to find how many $\frac{1}{4}$s are in 3.

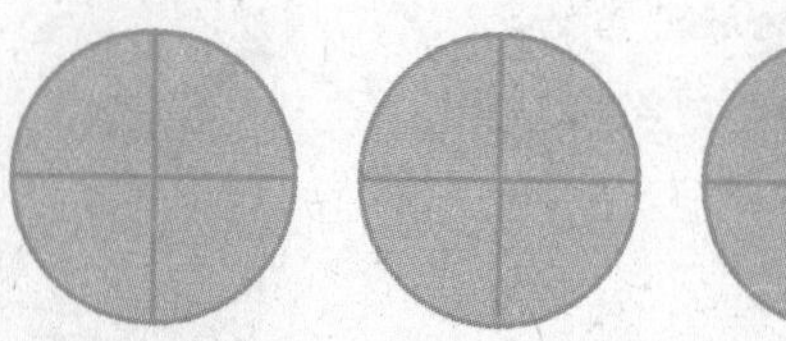

There are four $\frac{1}{4}$s in 1 whole cup. So, there are twelve $\frac{1}{4}$s in three whole cups. So, Joyce can make 12 sushi rolls.

You can also use a number line to represent this problem.

C

Another Way

Use a number line to find how many $\frac{1}{4}$s are in 3.

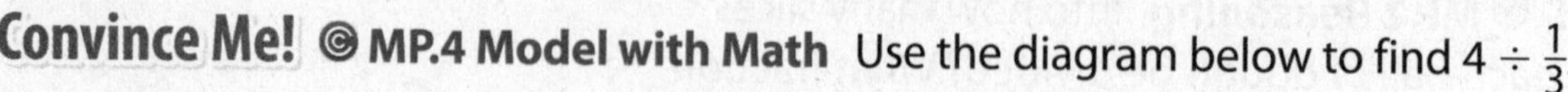

You can see that there are four $\frac{1}{4}$s in between each whole number.

There are four $\frac{1}{4}$s in 1 whole, eight $\frac{1}{4}$s in 2 wholes, and twelve $\frac{1}{4}$s in 3 wholes.

So, $3 \div \frac{1}{4} = 12$.

Joyce can make 12 sushi rolls.

Convince Me! **MP.4 Model with Math** Use the diagram below to find $4 \div \frac{1}{3}$.

 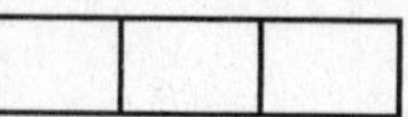 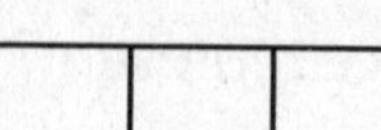

$4 \div \frac{1}{3} =$ ____

Name ______________________

Guided Practice*

Do You Understand?

1. In the example at the top of page 546, if Joyce had 4 cups of rice, how many rolls could she make?

2. In the example at the top of page 546, how does the number line help to show that $3 \div \frac{1}{4}$ is equal to 3×4?

Do You Know How?

In **3** and **4**, use the picture below to find each quotient.

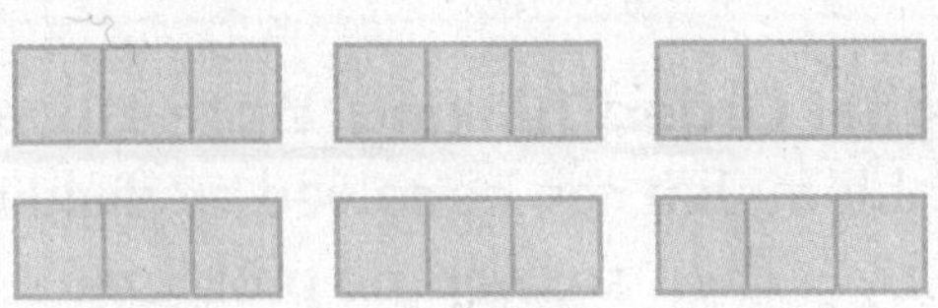

3. How many $\frac{1}{3}$s are in 3?

   $3 \div \frac{1}{3} =$ ____

4. How many $\frac{1}{3}$s are in 6?

   $6 \div \frac{1}{3} =$ ____

Independent Practice

Leveled Practice In **5** and **6**, use the picture to find each quotient.

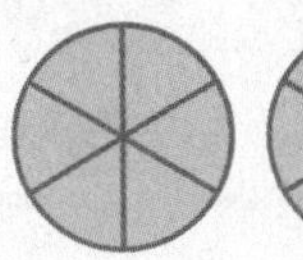 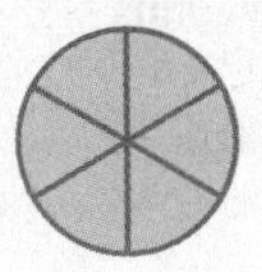 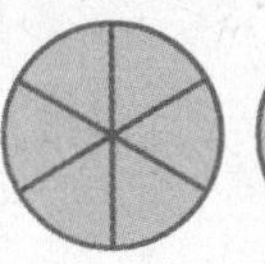 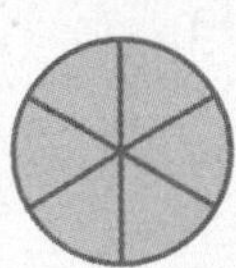 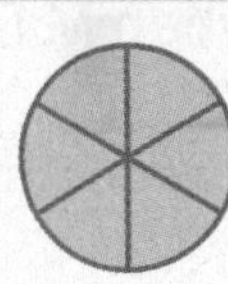

5. How many $\frac{1}{6}$s are in 1?

   $1 \div \frac{1}{6} =$ ____

6. How many $\frac{1}{6}$s are in 5?

   $5 \div \frac{1}{6} =$ ____

In **7–14**, draw a picture or use a number line to find each quotient.

7. $4 \div \frac{1}{2}$
8. $2 \div \frac{1}{8}$
9. $2 \div \frac{1}{3}$
10. $6 \div \frac{1}{4}$
11. $8 \div \frac{1}{3}$
12. $3 \div \frac{1}{10}$
13. $9 \div \frac{1}{8}$
14. $15 \div \frac{1}{5}$

*For another example, see Set B on page 577.

Math Practices and Problem Solving

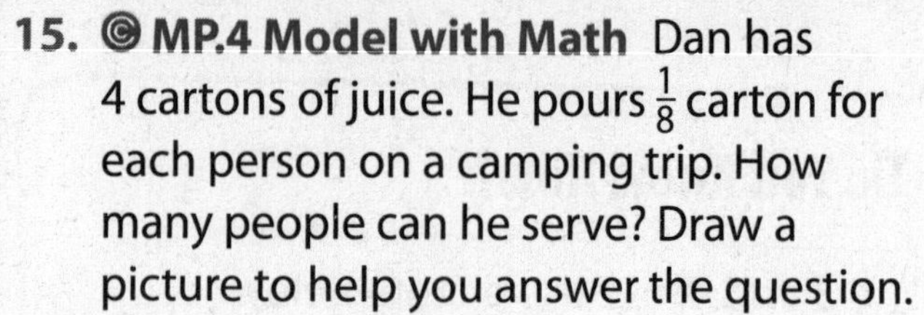

15. **MP.4 Model with Math** Dan has 4 cartons of juice. He pours $\frac{1}{8}$ carton for each person on a camping trip. How many people can he serve? Draw a picture to help you answer the question.

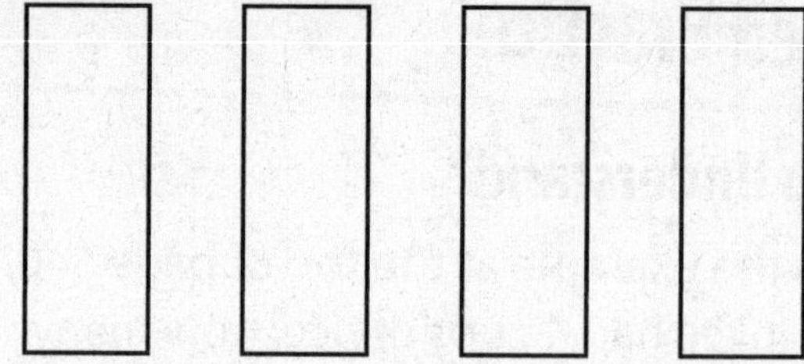

16. **Higher Order Thinking** Write a word problem that can be solved by dividing 10 by $\frac{1}{3}$. Then answer the problem.

17. **Number Sense** The Nile River is the longest river in the world. It is 4,160 miles long. You want to spend three weeks traveling the entire length of the river, traveling about the same number of miles each day. Estimate the number of miles you should travel each day.

18. **MP.1 Make Sense and Persevere** Maria used one bag of flour. She baked two loaves of bread. Then she used the remaining flour to make 48 muffins. How much flour was in the bag when Maria began?

DATA

Recipe	Amount of Flour Needed
Bread	$2\frac{1}{4}$ cups per loaf
Muffins	$3\frac{1}{4}$ cups per 24 muffins
Pizza	$1\frac{1}{2}$ cups per pie

Common Core Assessment

19. Deron is making light switch plates from pieces of wood. He starts with a board that is 18 feet long. How many light switch plates can he make?

   Ⓐ 9 light switch plates
   Ⓑ 24 light switch plates
   Ⓒ 27 light switch plates
   Ⓓ 54 light switch plates

DATA

Wood Projects	
Item	**Length Needed for Each**
Cabinet Shelf	$\frac{3}{4}$ foot
Light Switch Plate	$\frac{1}{3}$ foot
Shingle	$\frac{2}{3}$ foot

Name ______

Homework & Practice 9-4

Divide Whole Numbers by Unit Fractions

Another Look!

Ned has a 2-foot-long piece of rope. He cuts the rope into $\frac{1}{3}$-foot pieces. How many pieces of rope does Ned have now?

Think: How many $\frac{1}{3}$s are in 2? Use a model or a number line to help.

Count how many $\frac{1}{3}$s there are in 2. There are three $\frac{1}{3}$s in 1, so there are six $\frac{1}{3}$s in 2.

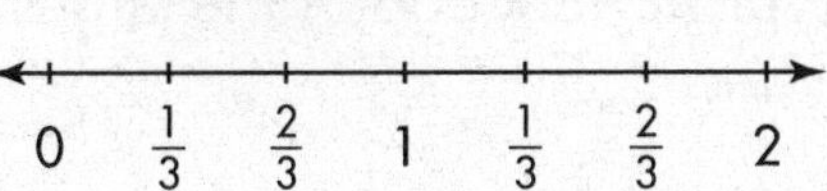

$2 \div \frac{1}{3} = 6$

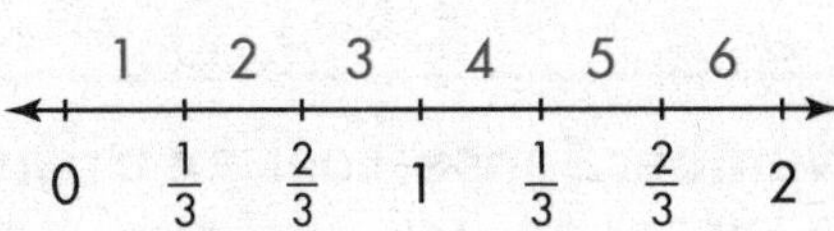

You can use multiplication to check your answer.

$6 \times \frac{1}{3} = 2$

Ned has 6 pieces of rope.

In **1** and **2**, use the picture to find each quotient.

1. How many $\frac{1}{5}$s are in 1? ____

$1 \div \frac{1}{5} =$ ____

2. How many $\frac{1}{5}$s are in 4? ____

$4 \div \frac{1}{5} =$ ____

In **3–10**, find each quotient. You may draw a picture or use a number line to help.

3. $12 \div \frac{1}{2} =$

4. $9 \div \frac{1}{4} =$

5. $3 \div \frac{1}{7} =$

6. $10 \div \frac{1}{10} =$

7. $20 \div \frac{1}{3} =$

8. $7 \div \frac{1}{5} =$

9. $6 \div \frac{1}{6} =$

10. $15 \div \frac{1}{2} =$

11. Use the number line. How many $\frac{1}{4}$-yard long pieces of pipe can be cut from two 1-yard long pieces of pipe?

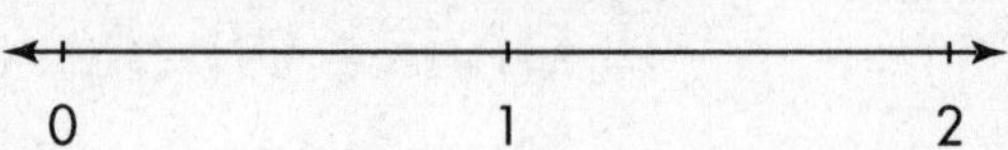

12. **Vocabulary** Define a unit fraction and then give an example.

13. **MP.2 Reasoning** Built in 2005, the world's largest leather work boot is 16 feet tall. A typical men's work boot is $\frac{1}{2}$ foot tall. How many times as tall as a typical work boot is the largest boot?

14. **Higher Order Thinking** When you divide a whole number by a unit fraction, explain how you can find the quotient.

15. **Number Sense** Look for a pattern in the table. Find the missing addends and sums.

Addends	$\frac{1}{8}+\frac{1}{4}$	$\frac{1}{4}+\frac{1}{4}$	$\frac{3}{8}+\frac{1}{4}$	
Sum	$\frac{3}{8}$	$\frac{1}{2}$		

16. **MP.1 Make Sense and Persevere** David made a line plot of how many miles he biked each day for two weeks. How many miles did he bike in all?

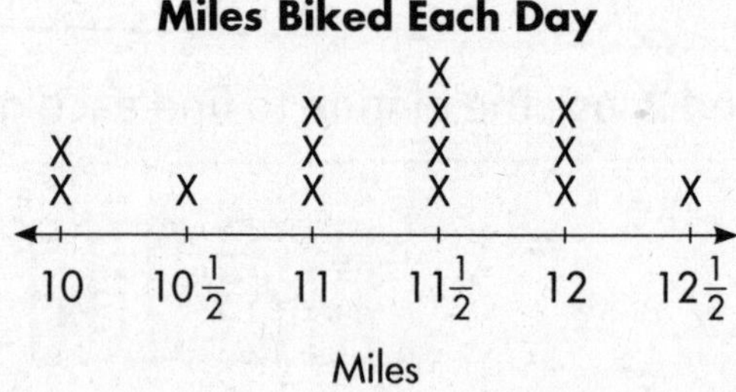

Common Core Assessment

17. Omar has 8 cups of cornmeal. How many batches of corn muffins can he make?

Ⓐ 4 batches

Ⓑ 6 batches

Ⓒ 16 batches

Ⓓ 32 batches

Cornmeal Recipes (DATA)

Item	Amount Needed
Cornbread	$\frac{3}{4}$ cup per loaf
Corn Muffins	$\frac{1}{2}$ cup per batch
Hush Puppies	$\frac{5}{8}$ cup per batch

Name ______________________

Lesson 9-5

Divide Unit Fractions by Non-Zero Whole Numbers

Solve & Share

Yesterday, the cooking club made a pan of lasagna. They left half of the lasagna for 4 members of the photography club to share equally. What fraction of the pan of lasagna did each photography club member get? ***Solve this problem any way you choose.***

I can ...

divide a unit fraction by a non-zero whole number.

Content Standards 5.NF.B.7a, 5.NF.B.7c
Mathematical Practices MP.2, MP.3, MP.4, MP.5, MP.8

You can use appropriate tools to show how to divide what is left. *Show your work!*

Look Back! **MP.4 Model with Math** What equation can you write to model this problem?

How Can You Model Dividing a Unit Fraction by a Whole Number?

A

Half of a pan of cornbread is left over. Ann, Beth, and Chuck are sharing the leftovers equally. What fraction of the original cornbread does each person get?

You can make a drawing to show $\frac{1}{2}$ of the cornbread.

B

One Way

Use a model. Divide $\frac{1}{2}$ into 3 equal parts.

$\frac{1}{2} \div 3$

Each part contains $\frac{1}{6}$ of the whole.

$\frac{1}{2} \div 3 = \frac{1}{6}$

Each person gets $\frac{1}{6}$ of the cornbread.

C

Another Way

Use a number line. Shade $\frac{1}{2}$ on the number line. Partition $\frac{1}{2}$ into 3 equal parts.

$\frac{1}{2} \div 3$

0 $\frac{1}{6}$ $\frac{2}{6}$ $\frac{1}{2}$ $\frac{4}{6}$ $\frac{5}{6}$ 1

Each part is $\frac{1}{6}$.

$\frac{1}{2} \div 3 = \frac{1}{6}$

Each person gets $\frac{1}{6}$ of the cornbread.

Convince Me! **MP.2 Reasoning** In the example above, how is dividing by 3 the same as multiplying by $\frac{1}{3}$?

Name ______

Guided Practice*

Do You Understand?

1. In the example at the top of page 552, suppose that 4 people were sharing half of the cornbread equally. What fraction of the original cornbread would each person get? Draw a picture or use objects to help.

2. MP.8 **Generalize** When you divide a unit fraction by a non-zero whole number greater than 1, will the quotient be greater than or less than the unit fraction?

Do You Know How?

In **3–6**, find each quotient. Use the picture or objects to help.

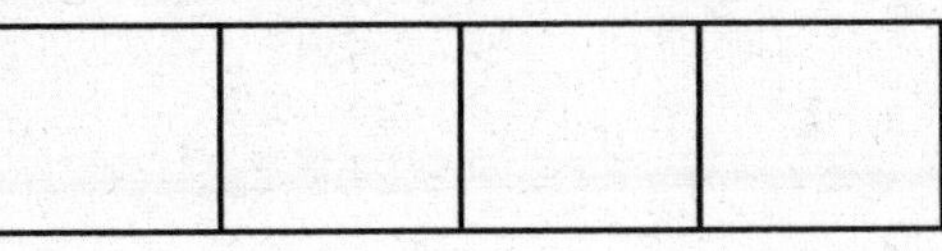

3. $\frac{1}{4} \div 2$

4. $\frac{1}{4} \div 4$

5. $\frac{1}{2} \div 2$

6. $\frac{1}{2} \div 4$

Independent Practice

Leveled Practice In **7** and **8**, find each quotient. Use a picture or objects to help.

7. $\frac{1}{2} \div 5$

8. $\frac{1}{5} \div 2$

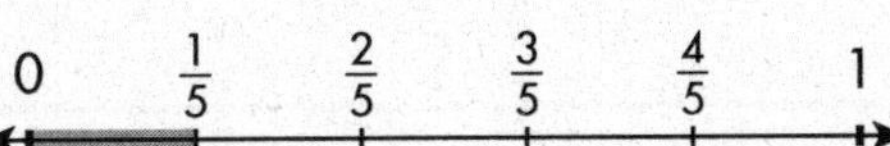

Partitioning pictures or objects can help when dividing fractions by a whole number.

In **9–14**, find each quotient.

9. $\frac{1}{2} \div 7$

10. $\frac{1}{4} \div 3$

11. $\frac{1}{6} \div 2$

12. $\frac{1}{3} \div 4$

13. $\frac{1}{4} \div 5$

14. $\frac{1}{5} \div 3$

*For another example, see Set C on page 577.

Math Practices and Problem Solving

15. Vin, Corrie, Alexa, and Joe equally shared one fourth of a submarine sandwich. What fraction of the original sandwich did each friend get? Use the number line to help you find the answer.

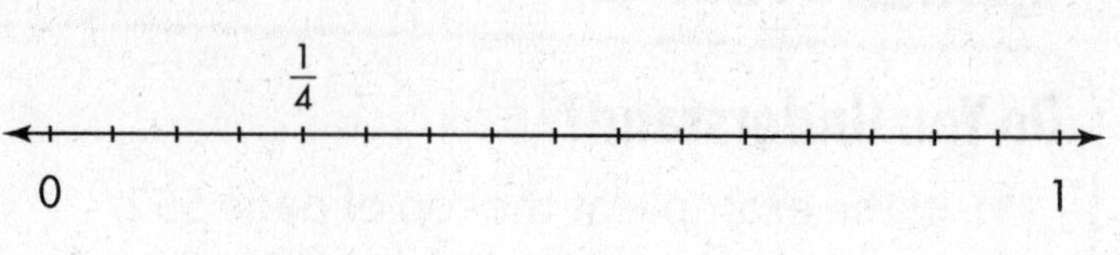

16. Sue has $\frac{1}{2}$ gallon of milk to share evenly among four people. How much milk, in gallons, should she give each person?

17. **MP.3 Construct Arguments** Taryn says that $\frac{1}{4}$ of a cereal bar is larger than $\frac{1}{3}$ of the cereal bar. Is she correct? Explain.

18. **Algebra** On Saturday, Amir ran $1\frac{3}{4}$ miles, and Janie ran $2\frac{1}{2}$ miles. Who ran farther? How much farther? Write an equation to find *d*, the difference of the two distances.

19. **Higher Order Thinking** Five friends equally shared half of one large pizza and $\frac{1}{4}$ of another large pizza. What fraction of each pizza did each friend get? How do the two amounts compare to each other?

Common Core Assessment

20. Jamie cut a rope into thirds. He used two of the pieces to make a swing. He used equal lengths of the leftover rope on four picture frames. What fraction of the original rope did he use for each picture frame?

Ⓐ $\frac{1}{4}$

Ⓑ $\frac{1}{12}$

Ⓒ $\frac{1}{16}$

Ⓓ $\frac{3}{4}$

21. One half of an apple pie is left for 5 family members to share equally. What fraction of the original pie will each member get?

Ⓐ $\frac{1}{10}$

Ⓑ $\frac{1}{7}$

Ⓒ $\frac{1}{3}$

Ⓓ $\frac{2}{5}$

Name ______________________________

Homework & Practice 9-5

Divide Unit Fractions by Non-Zero Whole Numbers

Another Look!

Sal has $\frac{1}{3}$ of a sheet of poster board. Four friends are sharing the $\frac{1}{3}$ sheet equally. What fraction of the original sheet does each friend get?

How can you divide $\frac{1}{3}$ into 4 equal parts?

Step 1

Use a drawing.

Divide 1 whole sheet into 3 equal parts.

Shade to show Sal's $\frac{1}{3}$.

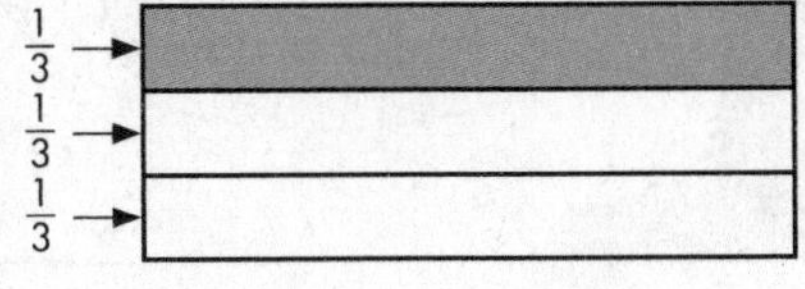

Step 2

Next, divide each third into 4 equal parts.

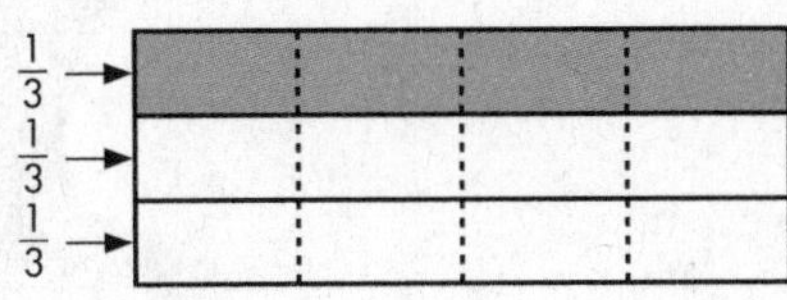

Step 3

Count the total number of parts. The total is the denominator.

$\frac{1}{12}$ ← each friend's part; ← total number of parts

So, each friend gets $\frac{1}{12}$ of the original sheet.

Leveled Practice In **1–11**, find each quotient. Draw a picture or use a number line to help.

1. $\frac{1}{2} \div 4$

2. $\frac{1}{3} \div 2$

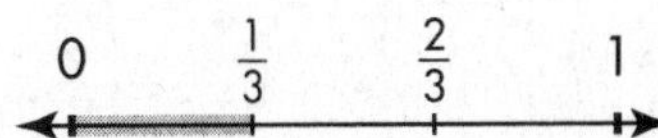

3. $\frac{1}{3} \div 5$

4. $\frac{1}{5} \div 3$

5. $\frac{1}{2} \div 5$

6. $\frac{1}{8} \div 2$

7. $\frac{1}{5} \div 4$

8. $\frac{1}{5} \div 2$

9. $\frac{1}{6} \div 4$

10. $\frac{1}{4} \div 3$

11. $\frac{1}{8} \div 2$

12. Marge and Kimo equally shared one fourth of a pie that was left over. What fraction of the original pie did each friend get? Use the picture to help you find the solution.

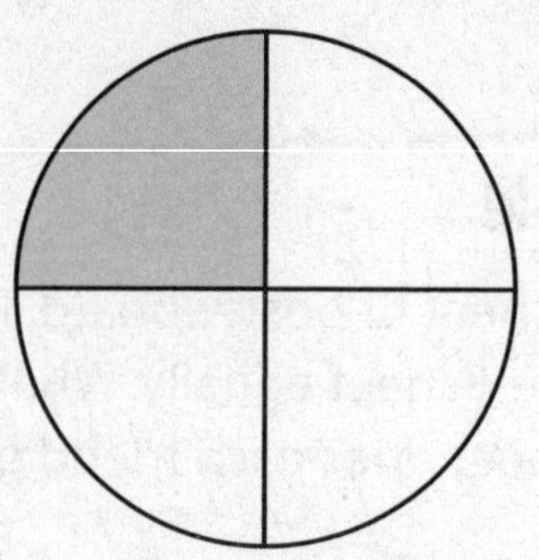

13. **Higher Order Thinking** Eve and Gerard each have $\frac{1}{2}$ of a poster to paint. Eve divided her half into 6 equal sections. She painted one section blue. Gerard divided his half into 5 equal sections. He painted one section blue. Whose blue section is larger? Explain.

14. **Number Sense** What are two decimals whose product is close to 10?

Use compatible numbers to help you find a product.

15. **MP.2 Reasoning** Without multiplying, order the following products from least to greatest.

$2 \times \frac{3}{5}$ $\quad \frac{1}{4} \times \frac{3}{5}$ $\quad 1\frac{2}{5} \times \frac{3}{5}$ $\quad \frac{6}{6} \times \frac{3}{5}$

16. Tom plans to replace a rectangular piece of drywall. Find the area of the piece of drywall that Tom needs to replace.

16 feet

$\frac{3}{4}$ foot

Common Core Assessment

17. Mrs. Sims cut a melon into fifths. She gave 1 piece to each of her four children. She used equal amounts of the leftover melon to make three fruit cups. What fraction of the original melon did she use to make each fruit cup?

Ⓐ $\frac{1}{4}$

Ⓑ $\frac{1}{12}$

Ⓒ $\frac{1}{15}$

Ⓓ $\frac{1}{20}$

18. Steven has $\frac{1}{3}$ of a package of biscuit mix left. He will use equal parts of the leftover mix to make three batches of biscuits. What fraction of the original package will he use for each batch?

Ⓐ $\frac{1}{9}$

Ⓑ $\frac{1}{6}$

Ⓒ $\frac{1}{2}$

Ⓓ $\frac{2}{3}$

Name ______________________________

Lesson 9-6
Divide Whole Numbers and Unit Fractions

I can …
divide with unit fractions.

Content Standards 5.NF.B.7a, 5.NF.B.7b, 5.NF.B.7c
Mathematical Practices MP.1, MP.2, MP.4, MP.8

Solve & Share

The Brown family is planting $\frac{1}{3}$ of their garden with flowers, $\frac{1}{3}$ with berries, and $\frac{1}{3}$ with vegetables. The vegetable section has equal parts of carrots, onions, peppers, and tomatoes. What fraction of the garden is planted with carrots? ***Solve this problem any way you choose.***

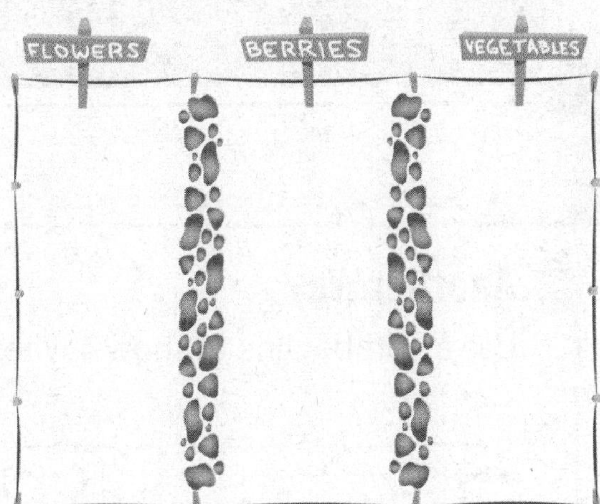

Reasoning
How can you show an equal share of each vegetable?

Look Back! **MP.4 Model with Math** Write an equation that models this problem. Explain your reasoning.

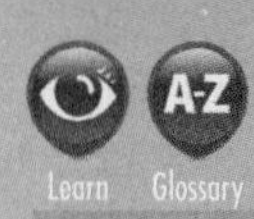

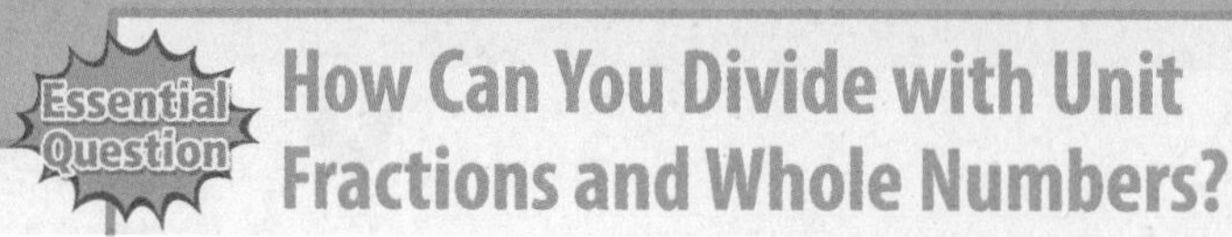

How Can You Divide with Unit Fractions and Whole Numbers?

A

A utility company is planning to install wind turbines on 4 square miles of land. Each turbine requires $\frac{1}{6}$ square mile of land. How many turbines can be installed?

Model the problem with a picture or an equation to help you.

B

One Way

Use an area model to show 4 square miles. Divide each square mile into 6 equal parts to represent $\frac{1}{6}$ square mile.

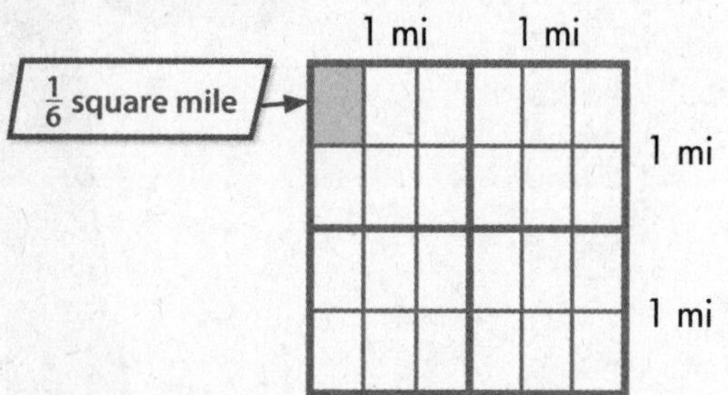

There are 24 parts.
So, 24 wind turbines will fit on the land.

C

Another Way

Use a number line to show 4 wholes.

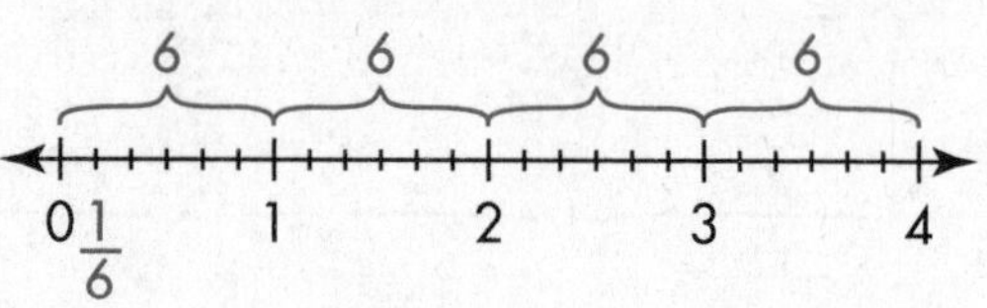

There are 6 $\frac{1}{6}$s in each whole.

So, there are 24 $\frac{1}{6}$s in 4 wholes.

24 wind turbines will fit on the land.

Convince Me! **MP.4 Model with Math** Use an area model to find $2 \div \frac{1}{4}$. Then use multiplication to check your answer.

Name ______________________

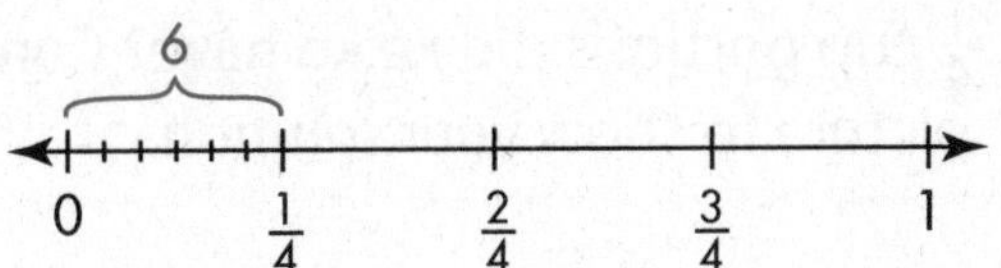

Another Example

Use a number line to find $\frac{1}{4} \div 6$.

If you partition $\frac{1}{4}$ into 6 equal segments, how long is each segment?

$\frac{1}{4} \div 6 = \frac{1}{24}$

Check your answer using multiplication: $\frac{1}{24} \times 6 = \frac{1}{4}$.

Guided Practice*

Do You Understand?

1. MP.8. Generalize When you divide a whole number by a fraction less than 1, will the quotient be greater than or less than the whole number?

2. 4 square miles of land is separated into sections that each have an area of $\frac{1}{2}$ square mile. How many sections are there?

   $4 \div \frac{1}{2}$

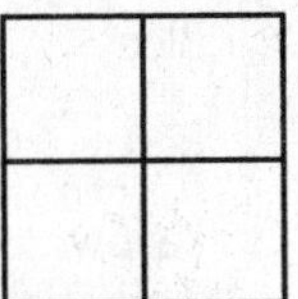

Do You Know How?

In **3–6**, find each quotient.

3. $2 \div \frac{1}{4}$

4. $3 \div \frac{1}{4}$

5. $\frac{1}{6} \div 2$

6. $2 \div \frac{1}{3}$

Draw a number line or use a model to help you find the answers!

Independent Practice

Leveled Practice In **7–10**, find each quotient. Use a model or number line to help.

7. $5 \div \frac{1}{2}$

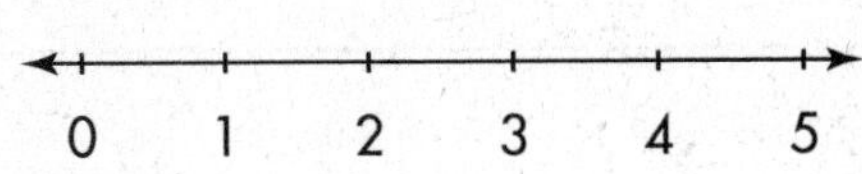

8. $\frac{1}{2} \div 5$

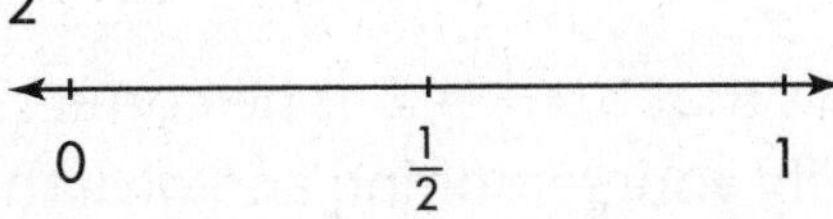

9. $6 \div \frac{1}{3}$

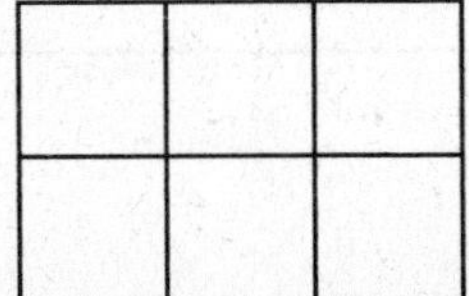

10. $\frac{1}{3} \div 6$

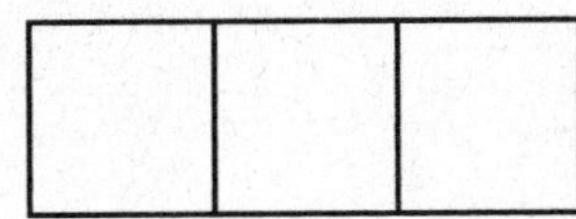

*For another example, see Set C on page 577.

Math Practices and Problem Solving

11. **MP.4 Model with Math** Keiko divided 5 cups of milk into $\frac{1}{4}$-cup portions. How many $\frac{1}{4}$-cup portions did Keiko have? Complete the picture to show your solution.

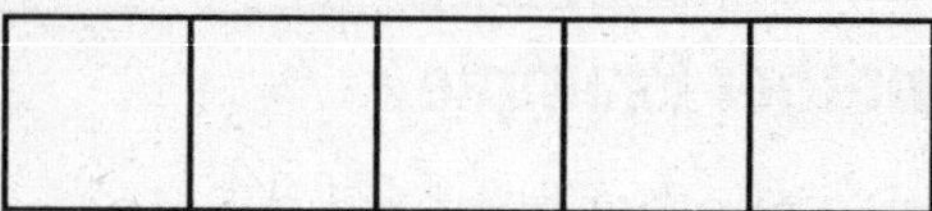

12. **Algebra** Ms. Allen has $\frac{1}{8}$ of a pan of brownies left to divide between 2 children. Draw a picture to find what fraction, *f*, of the original pan of brownies each child gets. Write an equation for *f* that models the solution.

13. A regular polygon has a perimeter of 2 feet. If each side measures $\frac{1}{3}$ foot, what is the name of the polygon?

A regular polygon
has equal side lengths and
equal angle measures.

14. **Higher Order Thinking** Mr. Brent uses $\frac{1}{4}$ cup of blue paint and $\frac{1}{4}$ cup of yellow paint to make each batch of green paint. How many batches of green paint can he make with the amount of paint he has left? Explain how you found your answer.

DATA

Paint Color	Amount Left
Blue	3 cups
Red	2 cups
Yellow	4 cups

Common Core Assessment

15. Jordan says that $6 \div \frac{1}{2} = 3$. Is he correct? If not, justify your reasoning and give the correct quotient.

Name ______________________

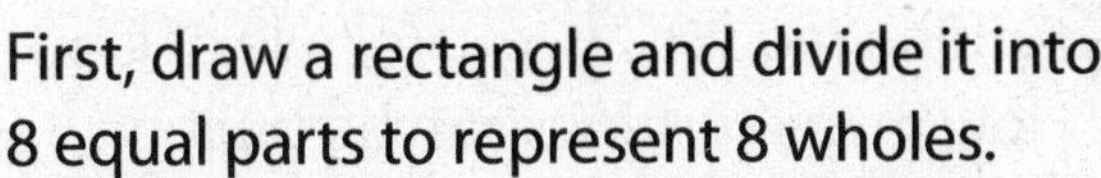

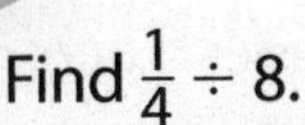

Homework & Practice 9-6

Divide Whole Numbers and Unit Fractions

Another Look!

Find $8 \div \frac{1}{4}$.

You can use an area model to solve the problem.

First, draw a rectangle and divide it into 8 equal parts to represent 8 wholes.

Then use another color to divide each of the 8 parts into fourths and count the total number of fraction parts.

$\frac{1}{4}$

There are 32 small squares, so you know that $8 \div \frac{1}{4} = 32$.

Find $\frac{1}{4} \div 8$.

You can also divide unit fractions by whole numbers.

Think: the quotient times the divisor must equal the dividend.

What times 8 equals $\frac{1}{4}$?

$\frac{1}{32} \times 8 = \frac{1}{4}$

So, $\frac{1}{4} \div 8 = \frac{1}{32}$.

In **1–12**, find each quotient. Use a number line or model to help.

1. $6 \div \frac{1}{2}$

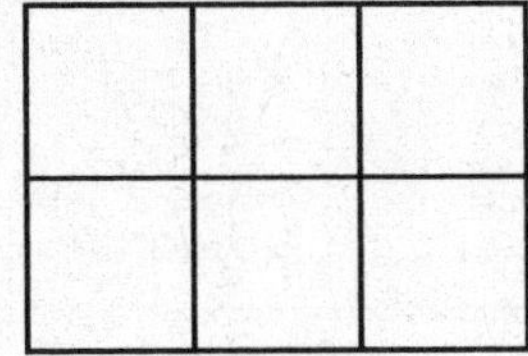

2. $4 \div \frac{1}{4}$

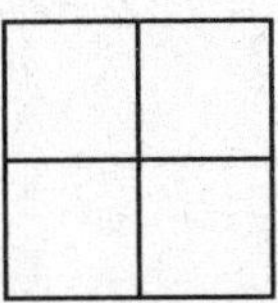

3. $5 \div \frac{1}{3}$

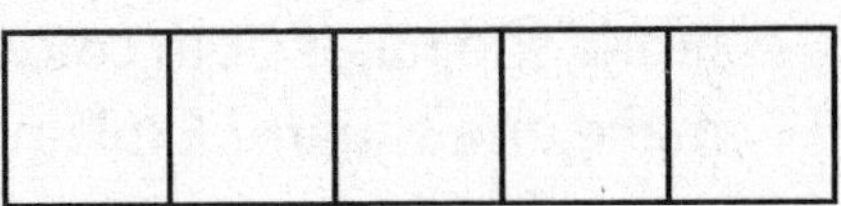

4. $\frac{1}{2} \div 6$

5. $\frac{1}{5} \div 2$

6. $\frac{1}{8} \div 3$

7. $\frac{1}{7} \div 8$

8. $5 \div \frac{1}{5}$

9. $\frac{1}{3} \div 9$

10. $\frac{1}{4} \div 8$

11. $6 \div \frac{1}{7}$

12. $\frac{1}{6} \div 5$

13. Cynthia has a piece of wood that is 6 feet long. She cuts it into $\frac{1}{2}$-foot pieces. How many pieces does she have? Use the number line to help you solve the problem.

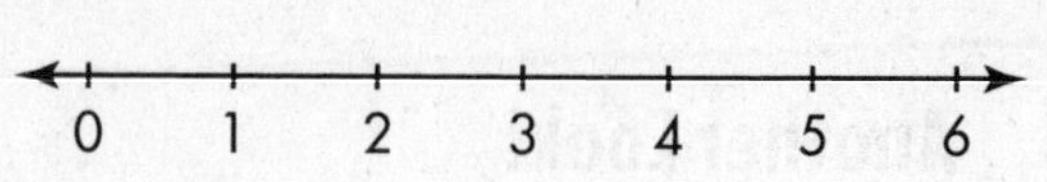

14. **MP.4 Model with Math** Gregg has a coin collection album with 275 pages. Each coin is displayed on $\frac{1}{6}$ of a page. How many coins will fit in the album?

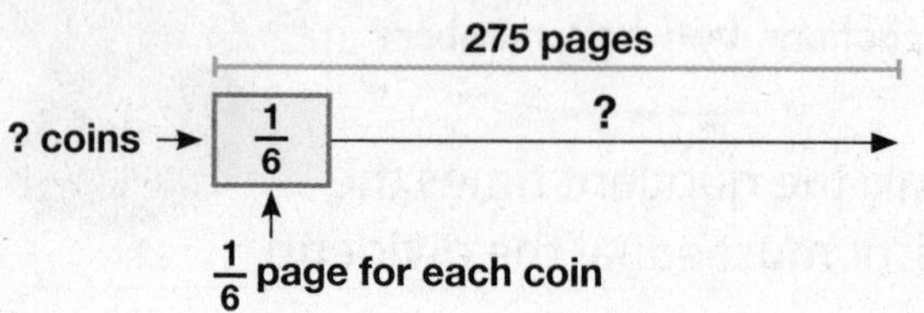

15. **Math and Science** Suppose a wind turbine requires $\frac{1}{6}$ square mile of land. How many turbines can be built on 8 square miles of land?

16. **MP.1 Make Sense and Persevere** Meredith modeled a division problem on the number line. What division problem did she model? Find the quotient.

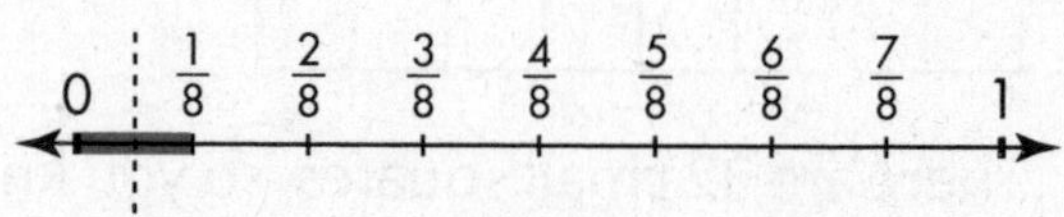

17. **Higher Order Thinking** Millie has 5 yards of blue fabric and 7 yards of pink fabric. How many quilt squares can she make with the fabric she has if both colors are needed to make one square? Explain your reasoning.

DATA

Amount of Fabric Needed for One Quilt Square

Fabric Color	Amount Needed
Blue	$\frac{1}{4}$ yard
Pink	$\frac{1}{3}$ yard

Common Core Assessment

18. Cindy says that $\frac{1}{4} \div 12 = 3$. Is she correct? If not, justify your reasoning and give the correct quotient.

Name ______________________________

Lesson 9-7
Solve Problems Using Division

I can ...
solve division problems involving unit fractions.

Content Standard 5.NF.B.7c
Mathematical Practices MP.1, MP.2, MP.4, MP.6

Solve & Share

Organizers of an architectural tour need to set up information tables every $\frac{1}{8}$ mile along the 6-mile tour, beginning $\frac{1}{8}$ mile from the start of the tour. Each table needs 2 signs. How many signs do the organizers need? ***Solve this problem any way you choose.***

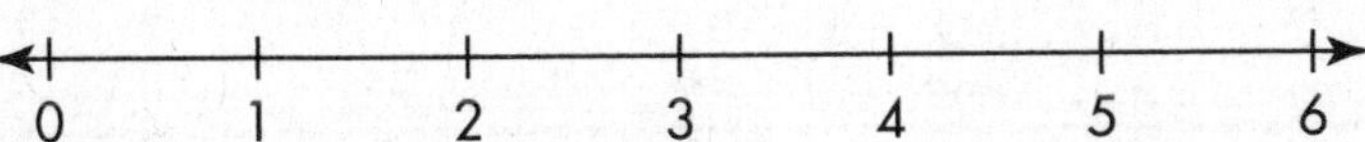

Make Sense and Persevere What steps do you need to do to solve this problem? *Show your work!*

Look Back! **MP.2. Reasoning** How does the number line help you solve this problem?

How Can You Solve Division Problems with Unit Fractions?

A

John plans to buy sheets of plywood like the ones shown to make boxes with lids. Each box is a cube that has $\frac{1}{3}$-foot edges. How many sheets of plywood does John need in order to make 5 boxes with lids?

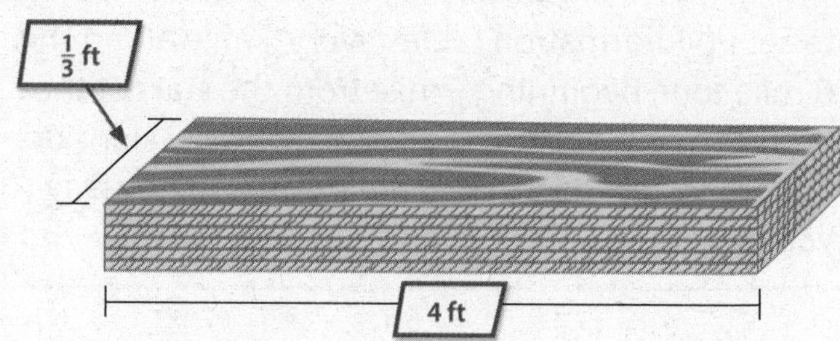

$\frac{1}{3}$ ft

Remember, a cube has 6 identical faces.

B **What do you know?**
Six pieces of plywood are needed for each of the 5 boxes.

Boxes are $\frac{1}{3}$-foot cubes.

Each sheet of plywood is $\frac{1}{3}$ foot wide and 4 feet long.

What are you asked to find?
The number of sheets of plywood John needs to buy

C **Write an equation to help answer each question.**

1. How many pieces of plywood are needed for 5 boxes with lids?

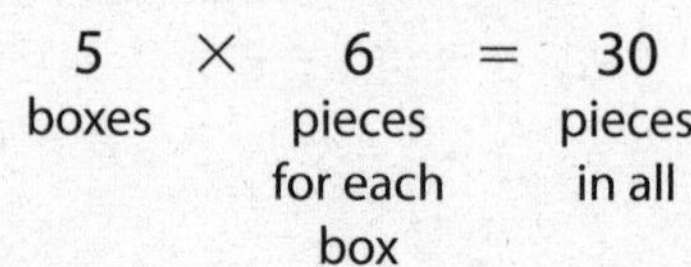

5 boxes × 6 pieces for each box = 30 pieces in all

2. How many pieces can be cut from 1 sheet of plywood?
   $4 \div \frac{1}{3} = 12$

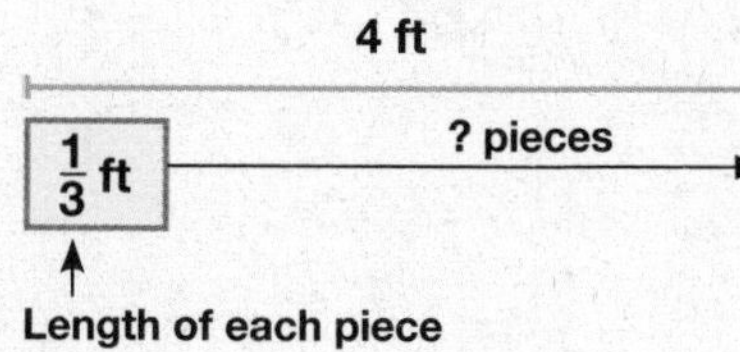

$\frac{1}{3}$ ft

3. How many sheets of plywood does John need for 5 boxes with lids?
   $30 \div 12 = 2$ R6
   John needs 3 sheets of plywood.

Convince Me! © **MP.2 Reasoning** Write a real-world problem that can be solved by first adding 24 and 36 and then dividing by $\frac{1}{4}$. Find the solution to your problem and explain your answer.

Name ______________________________

Practice Buddy Tools Assessment

Guided Practice*

Do You Understand?

1. In the example on page 564, why were additional questions answered to help solve the problem?

2. MP.4 Model with Math What equations were used to solve the example on page 564?

Do You Know How?

3. Tamara needs tiles to make a border for her bathroom wall. The border will be 9 feet long and $\frac{1}{3}$ foot wide. Each tile measures $\frac{1}{3}$ foot by $\frac{1}{3}$ foot. Each box of tiles contains 6 tiles. How many boxes of tiles does Tamara need? Write two equations that can be used to solve the problem.

Independent Practice

Write the equations needed to solve each problem. Then solve.

4. Robert wants to use all the ingredients listed in the table at the right to make trail mix. How many $\frac{1}{2}$-pound packages can he make?

Equations: ______________________________

Answer: ______________________________

DATA

Ingredient	Weight (in pounds)
Dried Apples	$2\frac{1}{2}$
Pecans	4
Raisins	$1\frac{1}{2}$

5. Rachel used $\frac{2}{3}$ of a package of cornbread mix. She will use equal parts of the leftover mix to make 2 batches of cornbread. What fraction of the original package will she use for each batch?

Equations: ______________________________

Answer: ______________________________

*For another example, see Set D on page 578.

Math Practices and Problem Solving

6. MP.1 Make Sense and Persevere
Sandra is making vegetable soup. If she makes 12 cups of soup, how many cups of onions does she need? Use the data table on the right. Write the equations needed to solve the problem. Then solve.

Vegetable	Amount Needed for 3 Cups of Soup
Carrots	$\frac{1}{3}$ cup
Onions	$\frac{1}{8}$ cup
Peas	$\frac{1}{4}$ cup

7. Emily needs to buy fabric to make curtain panels for her windows. Each panel will be 4 feet long and $\frac{1}{2}$ foot wide. Each piece of fabric that she can buy is 4 feet long and 2 feet wide. How many panels can she make from 1 piece of fabric?

8. Algebra Barry buys a package of pasta for \$2.39 and a jar of tomato sauce for \$3.09. He uses a \$0.75 coupon and a \$0.50 coupon. What is the total cost of Barry's purchase? Write an expression to show your work.

9. Higher Order Thinking Mr. Moss had 4 gallons of paint. He painted 8 doors. How many benches can he paint with the paint that is left? Show your work.

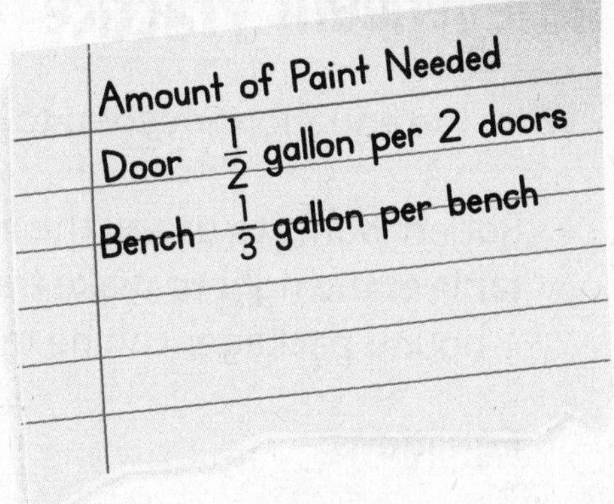

Common Core Assessment

10. Sophia uses $\frac{1}{2}$ pound of white flour to make one loaf of bread and $\frac{1}{4}$ pound of cake flour to make one cake. Which shows how many cakes and loaves of bread Sophia can make with the amount of flour that she has?

Ⓐ 12 cakes, 4 loaves of bread

Ⓑ 6 cakes, 8 loaves of bread

Ⓒ 8 cakes, 6 loaves of bread

Ⓓ 4 cakes, 12 loaves of bread

Flour in Pantry

Kind of Flour	Amount
Cake	3 pounds
White	2 pounds
Whole Wheat	4 pounds

Name ______________________

Homework & Practice 9-7

Solve Problems Using Division

Another Look!

Nell participated in a 3-day charity walk. She raised \$0.50 for each $\frac{1}{3}$ mile that she walked. The first day, Nell walked 12 miles. The second day, she walked 8 miles. The third day, she walked 16 miles. How much money did Nell raise?

What do you know?

Nell walked 12 miles, 8 miles, and 16 miles.

She raised \$0.50 for each $\frac{1}{3}$ mile she walked.

What do you need to find?

How much money Nell raised

How can you use what you know to solve the problem?

Write an equation to answer each question.

a What is the total number of miles Nell walked?

Nell walked $12 + 8 + 16 = 36$, or 36 miles.

b How many $\frac{1}{3}$ miles did Nell walk?

Nell walked $36 \div \frac{1}{3} = 108$, or 108 one-third miles.

c How much money did Nell raise?

Nell raised $108 \times \$0.50 = \$54$.

Write the equations needed to solve each problem. Then solve.

How many steps do you need to solve each problem?

1. Anna plants peas in $\frac{3}{8}$ of her garden and herbs in $\frac{1}{8}$ of it. She divides the rest of the garden into 6 sections. What fraction of the original garden is each section?

   Equations: ______________________

   Answer: ______________________

2. Ryan has 4 cups of grape juice, and Kelsey has 7 cups of lemonade. They want to combine what they have to make punch. How many $\frac{1}{2}$-cup servings of punch can they make?

   Equations: ______________________

   Answer: ______________________

3. **MP.6 Be Precise** Benjamin is making bow ties. How many $\frac{1}{2}$-yard-long bow ties can he make if he has 18 feet of fabric?

4. Cole's rectangular garden has an area of 54 square feet. What could be the dimensions of the garden?

5. **MP.1 Make Sense and Persevere** One batch of fruit punch contains $\frac{1}{4}$ quart grape juice and $\frac{1}{2}$ quart apple juice. Colby makes 9 batches of fruit punch. How much grape juice did he use for 9 batches?

6. **Higher Order Thinking** Ms. James has a 6-square-foot bulletin board and a 12-square-foot bulletin board. She wants to cover both boards with index cards without gaps or overlaps. Each index card has an area of $\frac{1}{4}$ square foot. How many index cards does she need?

7. **Number Sense** Craig has 36 ounces of flour left in one bag and 64 ounces of flour in another bag. Use the Baking Flour Equivalents table to find how many cups of flour Craig has in all.

DATA

Baking Flour Equivalents

Number of Ounces	Number of Cups
16	3.6
10	2.3
8	1.8

8. Doris uses 8 square pieces of fabric to make one scarf. Each side of a square piece of fabric is $\frac{1}{4}$ yard in length. Doris can buy large pieces of fabric that are $\frac{1}{4}$ yard long and 2 yards wide. How many large pieces of fabric should she buy to make 7 scarves? Show your work.

Common Core Assessment

9. Debbie cut a cord into sixths. She used five of the pieces to make necklaces. She used equal lengths of the remaining cord for each of four bracelets. What fraction of the original cord did Debbie use for each bracelet?

Ⓐ $\frac{1}{6}$

Ⓑ $\frac{1}{12}$

Ⓒ $\frac{1}{16}$

Ⓓ $\frac{1}{24}$

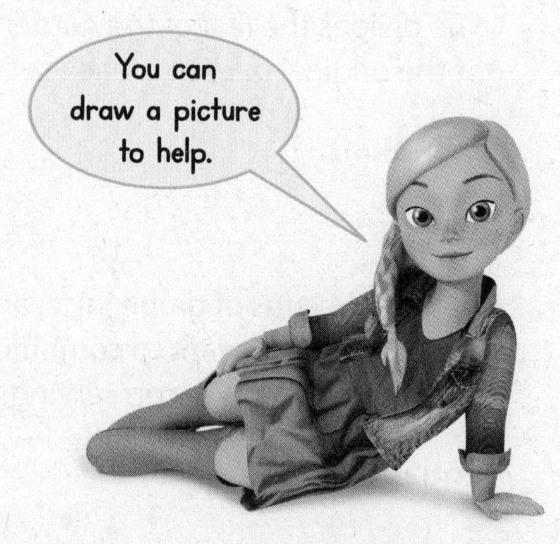
You can draw a picture to help.

Name ______________________________

Solve & Share

What do you notice about the calculations below? Make a generalization about what you notice. Complete the remaining examples.

Sue's Equations		Randy's Equations
$4 \div \frac{1}{3} = 12$	→	$\frac{1}{3} \div 4 = \frac{1}{12}$
$8 \div \frac{1}{10} = 80$	→	$\frac{1}{10} \div 8 = \frac{1}{80}$
$5 \div \frac{1}{4} = 20$	→	$\frac{1}{4} \div 5 = \frac{1}{20}$
$12 \div \frac{1}{2} =$ ___	→	$\frac{1}{2} \div 12 =$ ___
$6 \div \frac{1}{100} =$ ___	→	$\frac{1}{100} \div 6 =$ ___

Math Practices and Problem Solving

Lesson 9-8

Repeated Reasoning

I can ...
notice repetition in calculations and describe a general method for dividing whole numbers and unit fractions.

Mathematical Practices MP.8 Also, MP.2, MP.3, MP.4, MP.6
Content Standards 5.NF.B.7a, 5.NF.B.7b, 5.NF.B.7c

Thinking Habits

Be a good thinker! These questions can help you.

- Are any calculations repeated?
- Can I generalize from examples?
- What shortcuts do I notice?

Look Back! **MP.8 Generalize** Test your general method by writing another pair of equations like Sue's and Randy's equations.

How Do You Use Repeated Reasoning When Dividing Whole Numbers and Unit Fractions?

A

Ali partitioned a 4-foot board into $\frac{1}{2}$-foot pieces. She counted 8 pieces.

Then she partitioned a $\frac{1}{2}$-foot board into 4 equal pieces. Each piece was $\frac{1}{8}$ of a foot.

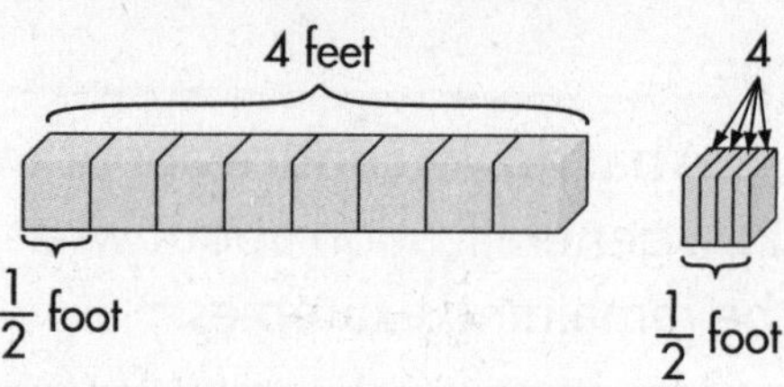

Study the equations below. What generalizations can you make? Explain.

$4 \div \frac{1}{2} = 8$ $\quad \frac{1}{2} \div 4 = \frac{1}{8}$

$4 \times 2 = 8$ $\quad \frac{1}{2} \times \frac{1}{4} = \frac{1}{8}$

What do I need to do?

I need to understand the equations and make generalizations about them.

B

How can I make a generalization from repeated reasoning?

I can

- look for things that repeat in a problem.
- test whether my generalization works for other numbers.

C

I see that

$4 \div \frac{1}{2} = 4 \times 2$ and $\frac{1}{2} \div 4 = \frac{1}{2} \times \frac{1}{4}$.

Check if the same relationship applies to other numbers.

$10 \div \frac{1}{3} = 30$ and $10 \times 3 = 30$

$\frac{1}{3} \div 10 = \frac{1}{30}$ and $\frac{1}{3} \times \frac{1}{10} = \frac{1}{30}$

Dividing a whole number by a unit fraction is the same as multiplying a whole number by the denominator of the unit fraction.

Dividing a unit fraction by a whole number other than zero is the same as multiplying the unit fraction by a unit fraction with the whole number as the denominator.

Convince Me! © **MP.8 Generalize** Marcus made the following generalization: $12 \div \frac{1}{5} = \frac{1}{12} \times \frac{1}{5}$. Is he correct? Explain.

Name ______________________

Guided Practice*

MP.8 Repeated Reasoning

Nathan has two 8-foot boards. He cuts one board into $\frac{1}{4}$-foot pieces. He cuts the other board into $\frac{1}{2}$-foot pieces.

Repeated reasoning can help you find a general method for solving problems that are the same type.

1. Write and solve a division equation to find how many $\frac{1}{4}$-ft pieces can be cut from an 8-foot board. Explain your reasoning.

2. Find how many $\frac{1}{2}$-ft pieces can be cut from the 8-foot board. Can you repeat the method you used in Exercise 1 to solve this problem? Explain.

Independent Practice

MP.8 Repeated Reasoning

A landscaper's truck is filled with $\frac{1}{2}$ ton of gravel. The gravel is shared equally among 3 projects.

Remember, the method for dividing a whole number by a unit fraction is different from the method for dividing a unit fraction by a whole number.

3. Write and solve a division equation to find how much gravel each project will get. Explain your reasoning.

4. Suppose another truck is filled with $\frac{1}{2}$ ton of gravel. Find how much gravel each project will get if the $\frac{1}{2}$ ton of gravel is shared equally among 8 projects. Can you repeat the method you used in Exercise 3 to solve this problem? Explain.

*For another example, see Set E on page 578.

Math Practices and Problem Solving

Common Core Performance Assessment

Pet Food

Karl has a cat and a dog. He buys one bag of cat food and one bag of dog food. How many $\frac{1}{4}$-lb servings of cat food can he get from one bag? How many $\frac{1}{2}$-lb servings of dog food can he get from one bag?

DATA

Pet Food	Bag Size
Fish	5 lb
Cat	12 lb
Dog	20 lb

5. **MP.3 Critique Reasoning** Karl thinks that he will be able to get more servings of dog food than cat food because the bag of dog food weighs more than the bag of cat food. Do you agree with his reasoning? Explain.

6. **MP.4 Model with Math** Write a division and a multiplication equation that Karl could use to find the number of servings of cat food in one bag.

7. **MP.8 Generalize** What generalization can you make that relates the division equation to the multiplication equation you wrote in Exercise 6?

8. **MP.8 Repeated Reasoning** Find how many servings of dog food are in one bag. Can you repeat the method you used in Exercise 6 to solve this problem? Explain.

When you use repeated reasoning, you notice repetition in calculations.

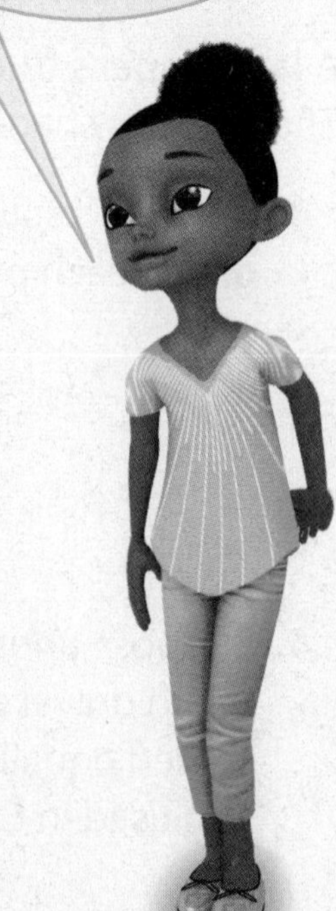

Name ______________________________

Homework & Practice 9-8

Repeated Reasoning

Another Look!

Study each set of problems. Then make a generalization about each set.

Repeated reasoning can help you find general methods for solving division problems involving unit fractions and whole numbers.

Set A

$\frac{1}{4} \div 6 = \frac{1}{24}$ $\frac{1}{4} \times \frac{1}{6} = \frac{1}{24}$

$\frac{1}{3} \div 5 = \frac{1}{15}$ $\frac{1}{3} \times \frac{1}{5} = \frac{1}{15}$

Set B

$6 \div \frac{1}{4} = 24$ $6 \times 4 = 24$

$5 \div \frac{1}{3} = 15$ $5 \times 3 = 15$

Set A

$\frac{1}{4} \div 6 = \frac{1}{4} \times \frac{1}{6}$

$\frac{1}{3} \div 5 = \frac{1}{3} \times \frac{1}{5}$

Generalization:

Dividing a unit fraction by a whole number other than zero is the same as multiplying the unit fraction by a unit fraction with the whole number as the denominator.

Set B

$6 \div \frac{1}{4} = 6 \times 4$

$5 \div \frac{1}{3} = 5 \times 3$

Generalization:

Dividing a whole number by a unit fraction is the same as multiplying a whole number by the denominator of the unit fraction.

Mrs. Miller brought 7 apples to a picnic. She cut each apple in half. How many pieces did she wind up with?

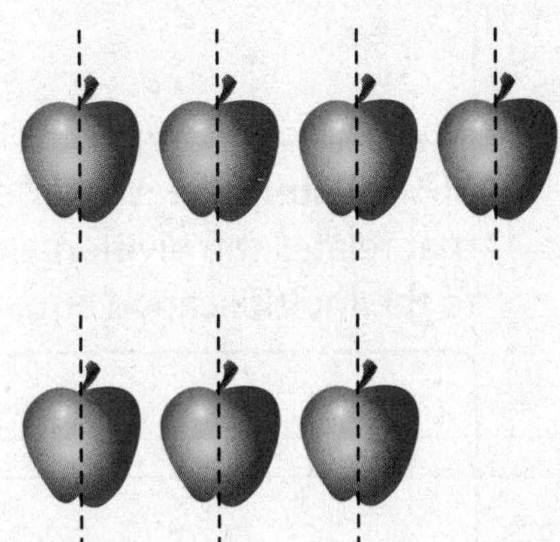

1. Write and solve a division equation to find the total number of apple pieces. Explain your reasoning.

2. Suppose Mrs. Miller decided to cut each apple into fourths rather than into halves. Find how many apple pieces she would have then. Can you repeat the method you used in Exercise 1 to solve this problem? Explain.

3. When you divide a whole number by a unit fraction, how does the quotient compare to the whole number? Explain.

Common Core Performance Assessment

Craft Project

Mariah has the spool of ribbon shown at the right and $\frac{1}{2}$ yard of fabric for a craft project. She wants to cut the ribbon into 6 equal pieces. How long is each piece of ribbon?

$\frac{1}{3}$ yard

?	?	?	?	?	?

$\frac{1}{3}$ yard

4. **MP.4 Model with Math** Find the length of each ribbon piece in yards. Write a division equation to model the problem.

5. **MP.2 Reasoning** Explain how you can use multiplication to check your answer to Exercise 4.

6. **MP.6 Be Precise** Find the length of each ribbon piece in inches. Show your work.

7. **MP.8 Generalize** What generalization can you make that relates the division equation you wrote in Exercise 4 to the multiplication equation you wrote in Exercise 5?

Repeated reasoning can help you find shortcuts.

8. **MP.8 Repeated Reasoning** Mariah has $\frac{1}{3}$ yard of a gold ribbon. She wants to cut this ribbon into 2 equal pieces. How long is each piece of gold ribbon in yards? Can you repeat the method you used in Exercises 4 and 5 to solve this problem? Explain.

Name ______________________________

Fluency Practice Activity

Solve each problem. Follow problems with an answer of 3,456 to shade a path from **START** to **FINISH**. You can only move up, down, right, or left.

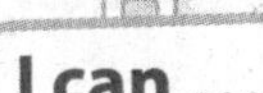

I can ...
multiply multi-digit whole numbers.

Content Standard 5.NBT.B.5

Start

576 × 6	101 × 34	350 × 16	436 × 16	127 × 28
96 × 36	462 × 13	64 × 54	48 × 72	144 × 24
108 × 32	192 × 18	288 × 12	82 × 42	216 × 16
303 × 12	317 × 48	456 × 11	2,586 × 12	128 × 27
66 × 51	286 × 40	360 × 36	230 × 56	384 × 9

Finish

TOPIC 9 Vocabulary Review

Word List

- dividend
- divisor
- factor
- inverse operations
- product
- quotient
- unit fraction

Understand Vocabulary

Write *always, sometimes,* or *never.*

1. A whole number divided by a fraction less than 1 is a mixed number. ____________

2. The answer to a division problem is greater than the dividend. ____________

3. A fraction less than 1 divided by a whole number is a whole number. ____________

4. Dividing by $\frac{1}{2}$ means you are finding how many halves are in the dividend. ____________

5. The dividend is the greatest number in a division problem. ____________

6. A whole number can be written as a fraction with 1 as the denominator. ____________

Draw a line from each number in Column A to the correct answer in Column B.

Column A	Column B
7. $\frac{1}{3} \div 6$	12
8. $3 \div \frac{1}{2}$	2
9. $2 \div \frac{1}{6}$	6
10. $\frac{1}{6} \div 2$	$\frac{1}{18}$
	$\frac{1}{12}$

Use Vocabulary in Writing

11. Explain how to use what you know about whole number division to check your work when you divide with fractions. Use at least three terms from the Word List in your explanation.

Name ____________________

TOPIC 9

Reteaching

Set A pages 527–532, 533–538

You can represent the fraction $\frac{3}{4}$ as division.

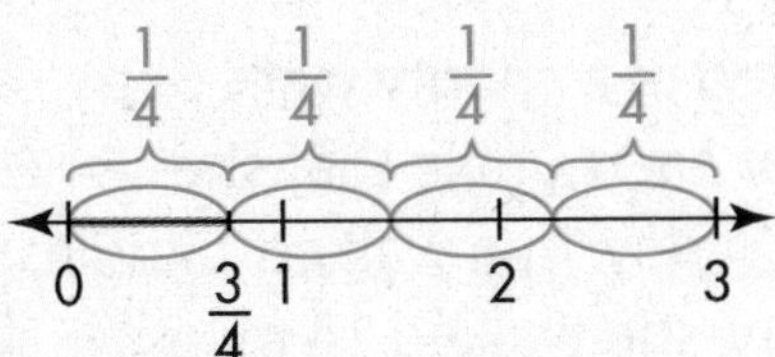

Think: $\frac{1}{4}$ of 3 wholes.

So, $\frac{3}{4} = 3 \div 4$.

Remember that any fraction can be represented as division of the numerator by the denominator.

Write a division expression for each fraction.

1. $\frac{7}{9}$ **2.** $\frac{11}{17}$ **3.** $\frac{10}{3}$

Write each expression as a fraction or mixed number.

4. $7 \div 12$ **5.** $13 \div 20$

6. $9 \div 5$ **7.** $17 \div 7$

Set B pages 539–544, 545–550

A 4-foot board is cut into pieces that are $\frac{1}{2}$ foot in length. How many pieces are there?

length of board → **4 feet**

$\frac{1}{2}$ ft **x pieces**

length of each piece

$4 \div \frac{1}{2} = 4 \times 2 = 8$

There are 8 pieces.

Remember that you can use multiplication to check your answer.

1. A 12-foot-long playground is marked off into $\frac{1}{5}$-foot-long sections for a game. How many sections are there?

2. A 4-pound package of peanuts is divided into $\frac{1}{4}$-pound packages. How many $\frac{1}{4}$-pound packages are there?

Set C pages 551–556, 557–562

Find $\frac{1}{2} \div 4$.

Use a number line. Partition $\frac{1}{2}$ into 4 equal parts.

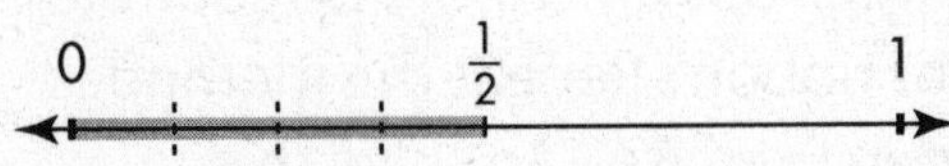

Each part is $\frac{1}{8}$.

So, $\frac{1}{2} \div 4 = \frac{1}{8}$.

Remember that you can use objects or a number line to help you divide.

1. $\frac{1}{3} \div 2$ **2.** $\frac{1}{7} \div 7$

3. $\frac{1}{2} \div 8$ **4.** $\frac{1}{8} \div 2$

5. $7 \div \frac{1}{2}$ **6.** $25 \div \frac{1}{6}$

Set D pages 563–568

Helen has $97 in quarters and half dollars combined. She has $13 in quarters. How many half dollars does she have?

How much does Helen have in half dollars?

$97

$13	?

$\$97 - \$13 = \$84$

How many $\frac{1}{2}$ dollars are in $84?

$84

$\frac{1}{2}$?

$\$84 \div \frac{1}{2} = 84 \times 2 = 168$

Helen has 168 half dollars.

Remember to read the problem carefully and make sure that you answer the right question and that your answer makes sense.

1. Ana participated in a charity walk. She raised $0.25 for each $\frac{1}{2}$ mile that she walked. The first day, Ana walked 11 miles. The second day, she walked 14 miles. How much money did Ana raise?

2. Mr. Holms used $\frac{4}{5}$ of a carton of orange juice. He used equal amounts of the leftover juice for two servings. What fraction of the whole carton of juice did he use for each serving?

Set E pages 569–574

Think about these questions to help you use **repeated reasoning** when solving division problems.

Thinking Habits

- Are any calculations repeated?
- Can I generalize from examples?
- What shortcuts do I notice?

Remember that repeated reasoning can help you find a general method for solving problems that are the same type.

Teresa has two 6-foot pieces of ribbon. One piece she cuts into $\frac{1}{4}$-foot pieces. The other piece she cuts into $\frac{1}{2}$-foot pieces.

1. How many $\frac{1}{4}$-foot pieces can she cut from one piece of ribbon? Explain.

2. How many $\frac{1}{2}$-foot pieces can be cut from the 6-foot ribbon? Repeat the method you used in Exercise 1 to solve this problem.

Name ________________________________

1. If the diameter of a tree trunk is growing $\frac{1}{4}$ inch each year, how many years will it take for the diameter to grow 8 inches?

Ⓐ 2 years
Ⓑ 8 years
Ⓒ 24 years
Ⓓ 32 years

2. For questions 2a–2d, choose Yes or No to tell if the number 4 will make each equation true.

2a. $1 \div 4 = \square$ ○ Yes ○ No

2b. $5 \div \square = \frac{4}{5}$ ○ Yes ○ No

2c. $\square \div 7 = \frac{4}{7}$ ○ Yes ○ No

2d. $2 \div \square = \frac{1}{2}$ ○ Yes ○ No

3. Mrs. Webster wants to divide the milk shown into $\frac{1}{3}$-pint servings. How many servings are possible?

4. How many $\frac{1}{8}$s are in 25?

5. Raven is making pillows. She needs $\frac{1}{5}$ yard of fabric for each pillow. If she has 6 yards of fabric, how many pillows can she make? Use the number line.

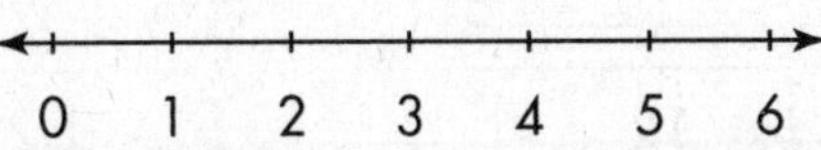

Ⓐ $\frac{1}{30}$ pillow
Ⓑ $\frac{7}{5}$ pillows
Ⓒ 11 pillows
Ⓓ 30 pillows

6. A farmer owns 24 acres of land. He plans to use 6 acres for an entrance into the farm and partition the remaining land into $\frac{1}{3}$-acre lots. How many $\frac{1}{3}$-acre lots will he have?

Ⓐ 6 lots
Ⓑ 18 lots
Ⓒ 54 lots
Ⓓ 72 lots

7. One half of a cantaloupe was shared equally among 3 people. What fraction of the whole cantaloupe did each person get? Explain how you found your answer.

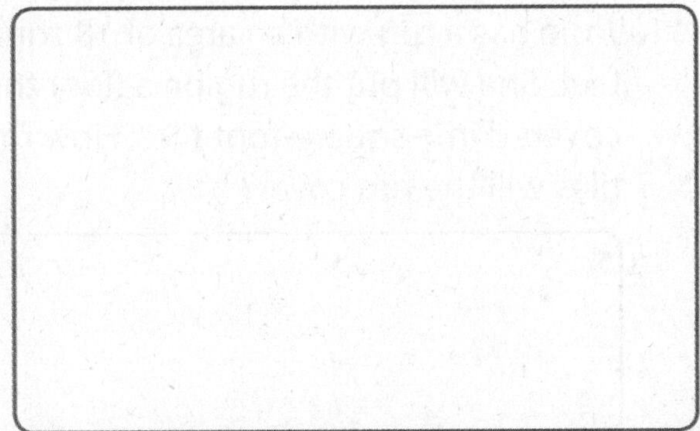

8. Draw lines to match each expression on the left to its quotient on the right.

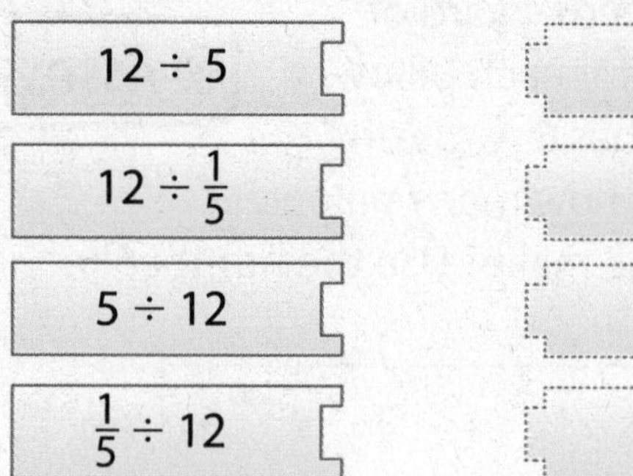

9. Choose all the expressions that are equal to $\frac{1}{6}$.

- ☐ $6 \div 1$
- ☐ $3 \div 18$
- ☐ $2 \div \frac{1}{3}$
- ☐ $1 \div 6$
- ☐ $\frac{1}{3} \div 2$

10. Cecil and three friends ran a 15-mile relay race. Each friend ran an equal distance. What distance did each friend run?

Ⓐ $\frac{4}{15}$ mile

Ⓑ $3\frac{1}{4}$ miles

Ⓒ $3\frac{2}{3}$ miles

Ⓓ $3\frac{3}{4}$ miles

11. Josie has a rug with an area of 18 square feet. She will put the rug on a floor that is covered in $\frac{1}{3}$-square-foot tiles. How many tiles will the rug cover?

12. Ellen says that $1\frac{2}{5}$ equals $5 \div 7$. Is she correct? Explain.

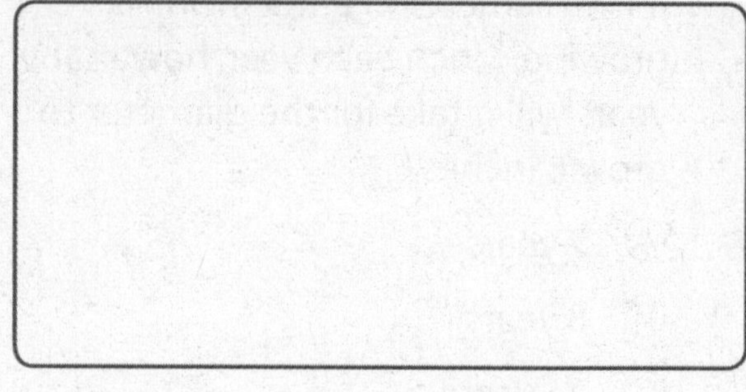

13. Corey has $\frac{1}{4}$ yard of fabric. He cuts the fabric into 2 equal pieces. Write an expression for the number of yards of each piece of fabric.

14. Look at the equations below.

$8 \div \frac{1}{3} = \square$ $\quad 2 \div \frac{1}{9} = \square$

$8 \times 3 = \square$ $\quad 2 \times 9 = \square$

Part A

Write numbers in the boxes above to make each equation true.

Part B

What generalization can you make about the equations? Explain.

Name ____________________

TOPIC 9

Performance Assessment

Making Cloth Dolls

Julie and Erin are making cloth dolls for the craft fair. The figure below shows some of the materials they need for each doll.

1. The **Julie and Erin's Supplies** table shows the amounts they have of some of the materials they need.

Part A

If Julie and Erin use the brown yarn they have to make 4 dolls, how much yarn can they use for each doll? Show your work.

Julie and Erin's Supplies

Supply	Amount
Buttons	9
Brown Yarn	10 yd
Black Velvet	4 yd
White cloth	5 yd

Part B

How many dolls can Julie and Erin make with the amount of black velvet they have? Complete the model to represent the problem.

Part C

How many dolls can Julie and Erin make with the amount of white cloth they have? Write an equation to represent the problem. Use multiplication to check your answer.

Part D

The ribbon used for each doll is divided into 3 equal pieces. What is the length in yards of each piece? Complete the number line to solve.

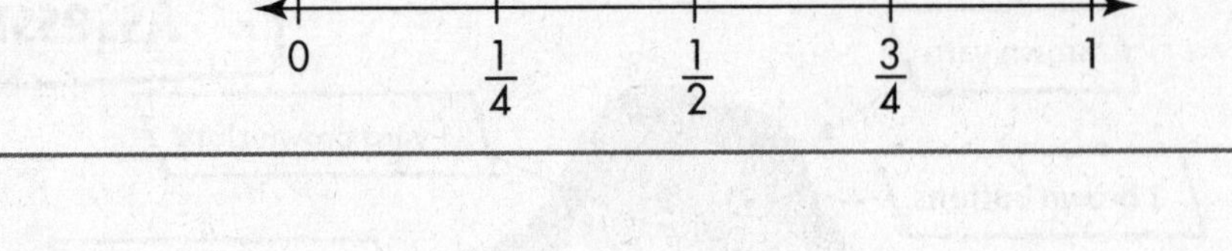

2. Julie and Erin have $6\frac{1}{3}$ yards of red checked cloth. After making dresses for 4 dolls, they use the remaining cloth to make bows for the dolls' hair. They need 8 bows for 4 dolls.

Part A

How much cloth do Julie and Erin have for each bow? Explain.

Part B

Julie wrote the equations shown. What is the pattern in her equations? Explain how to use the pattern to find the quotient you found in Part A.

Julie's Equations

$$\frac{1}{2} \div 3 = \frac{1}{2} \times \frac{1}{3} = \frac{1}{6}$$

$$\frac{1}{3} \div 3 = \frac{1}{3} \times \frac{1}{3} = \frac{1}{9}$$

$$\frac{1}{2} \div 4 = \frac{1}{2} \times \frac{1}{4} = \frac{1}{8}$$

$$\frac{1}{3} \div 4 = \frac{1}{3} \times \frac{1}{4} = \frac{1}{12}$$

TOPIC 10

Understand Volume Concepts

Essential Questions: What is the meaning of volume of a solid? How can the volume of a rectangular prism be found?

You use energy 24/7, from getting out of bed in the morning to texting your friends at night!

Chemical energy from food transforms to mechanical energy to get you out of bed.

That's powerful! And, chemical and mechanical energy move the bus that takes me to school. Here's a project about everyday energy.

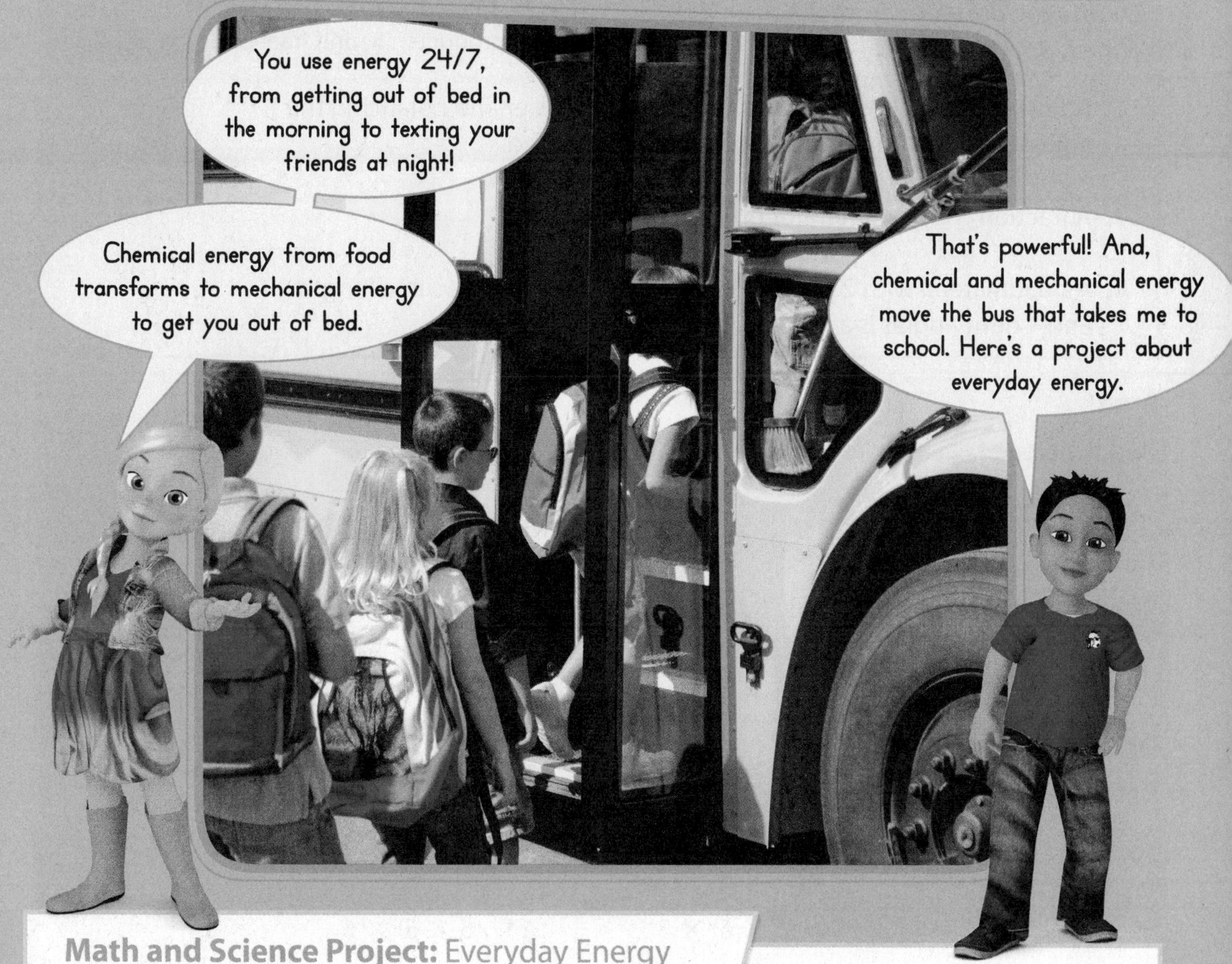

Math and Science Project: Everyday Energy

Do Research Use the Internet and other sources to learn more about these five types of energy: electrical, light, mechanical, sound, and thermal. Make a table of the various types of energy you use every day. Include at least one example of how you use each type of energy.

Journal: Write a Report Include what you found. Also in your report:

- Draw a diagram of your classroom and label where and how 3 types of energy are used.
- Estimate how far your desk is from a light energy source and add this dimension to your sketch.
- Use your diagram to make up and solve problems involving measurements such as the volume of your classroom.

Name ______________________________

Review What You Know

Vocabulary

Choose the best term from the box.
Write it on the blank.

- compensation
- rectangle
- partial products
- unit fraction

1. Adjusting a number to make a computation easier and balancing the adjustment by changing another number is called ____________.

2. A fraction with a numerator of 1 is called a ____________.

3. A quadrilateral with 2 pairs of parallel sides that are the same length and 4 right angles is a ____________.

Area

Find the area of each figure.

4. 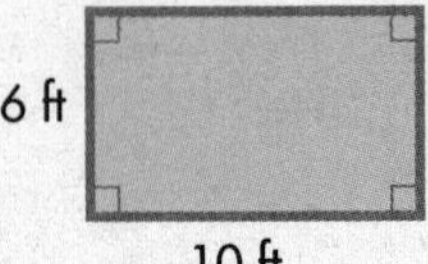

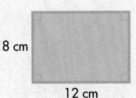

5. 

Operations

Find each product or quotient.

6. 16×6

7. 3×42

8. $216 \div 3$

9. $128 \div 4$

10. $(5 \times 6) \times 3$

11. $(6 \times 6) \times 6$

12. Joanie has two 12-inch-long wood pieces and two 16-inch-long wood pieces. What is the combined length of the wood pieces?

Ⓐ 28 inches Ⓑ 32 inches Ⓒ 56 inches Ⓓ 192 inches

Finding Area

13. Niko used square tiles to make a rectangle with 2 rows and 7 tiles in each row. Explain how you can find the area of the rectangle.

My Word Cards

Use the examples for each word on the front of the card to help complete the definitions on the back.

A-Z Glossary

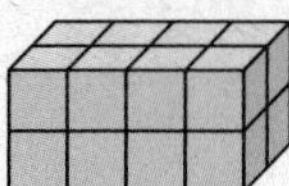

Multiply length by width by height:
Volume $= 4 \times 2 \times 2 = 16$ cubic units

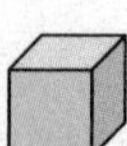

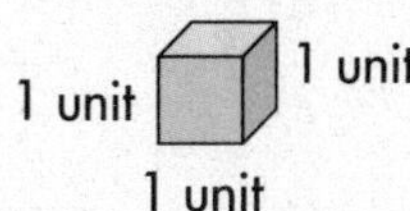

The volume of the cube is 1 cubic unit.

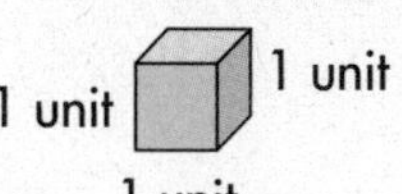

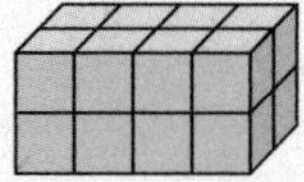

formula for volume of a rectangular prism:

$$V = \ell \times w \times h$$

V = Volume ℓ = length
w = width h = height

My Word Cards

Complete the definition. Extend learning by writing your own definitions.

A __________ is a solid figure with six identical squares as its faces.

______________ is the number of cubic units needed to fill a solid figure.

A _________________ is a cube that measures 1 unit along each edge.

A __________________ is the volume of a cube that measures 1 unit along each edge.

A _________________ is a rule that uses symbols to relate two or more quantities.

A _____________________________ is a solid figure with six rectangular faces.

Name ______________________ Solve

Lesson 10-1
Model Volume

I can ...
find the volume of solid figures.

Content Standards 5.MD.C.3a, 5.MD.C.3b, 5.MD.C.4
Mathematical Practices MP.2, MP.5, MP.7

Solve & Share Gina is building a rectangular prism out of sugar cubes for her art class project. She started by drawing a diagram of the rectangular prism that is 4 cubes high and 4 cubes long. How many cubes does she use to make the prism? ***Solve this problem any way you choose.***

Use Appropriate Tools
You can draw a picture to find the number of cubes in a rectangular prism. *Show your work!*

Side View

Front View

Top View

Look Back! **MP.2 Reasoning** Gina decided to change her art project and build a rectangular prism that is 3 cubes long, 4 cubes wide, and 2 cubes high. Use the picture to determine the number of cubes she used.

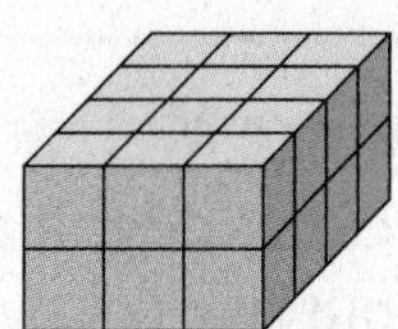

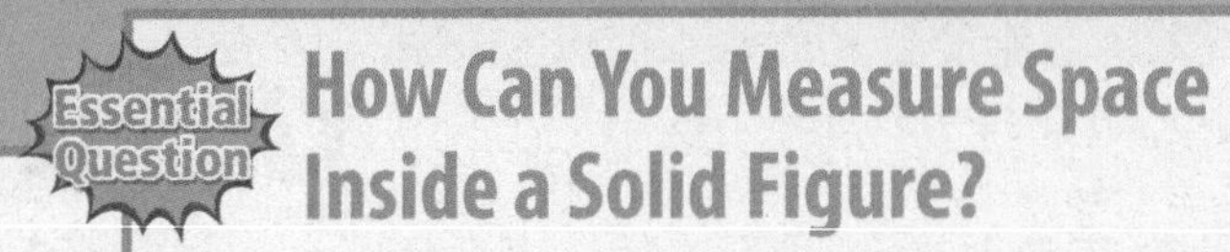

How Can You Measure Space Inside a Solid Figure?

A

Volume is the number of cubic units needed to pack a solid figure without gaps or overlaps. A cubic unit is the volume of a cube measuring 1 unit on each edge. What is the volume of this rectangular prism?

Each cube of a solid figure is 1 cubic unit.

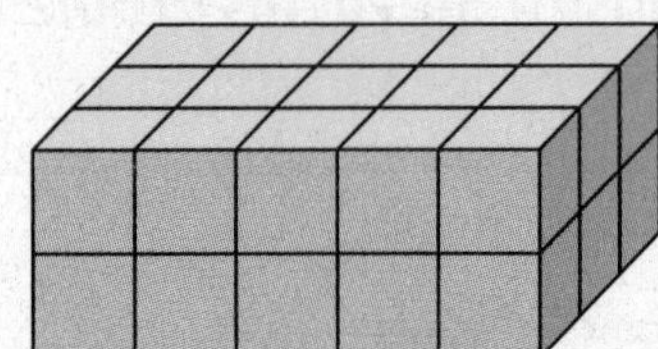

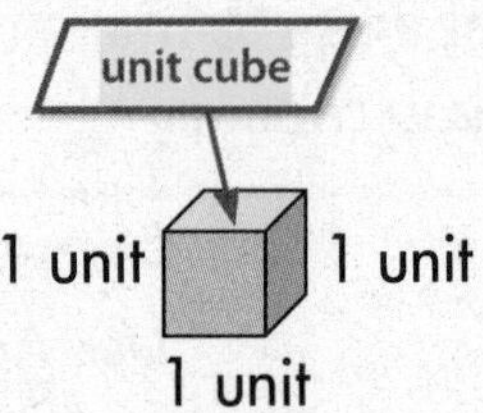

B Use unit cubes to make a model.

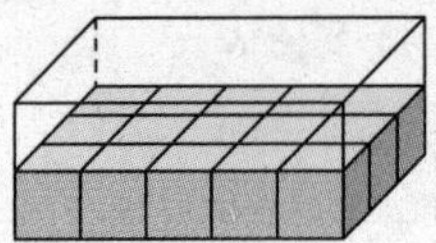

Count the number of cubes.

There are 15 unit cubes in the bottom layer. The volume of the bottom layer is 15 cubic units.

C There are two layers.

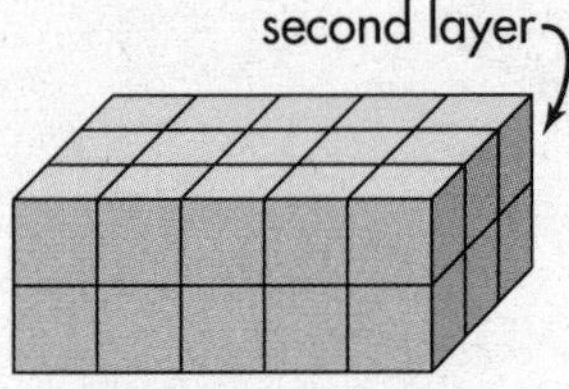

Multiply the volume of the bottom layer by 2.

The volume of the prism is 2×15 or 30 cubic units.

Convince Me! **MP.2 Reasoning** In the picture below, how many unit cubes does it take to make the rectangular prism on the left without gaps or overlaps? How many 2-unit cubes does it take to make the rectangular prism?

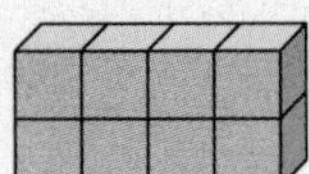
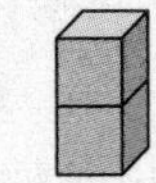

2-unit cube

Name

Practice Buddy Tools Assessment

Guided Practice*

Do You Understand?

1. Make a model of a rectangular prism with a bottom layer that is 3 cubes long by 3 cubes wide. Make a top layer that is the same as the bottom layer. Then draw a picture of your model. What is the volume?

2. **A-Z Vocabulary** What is the difference between a unit cube and a cubic unit?

Do You Know How?

In **3** and **4**, use unit cubes to make a model of each rectangular prism. Find the volume.

3. 

4. 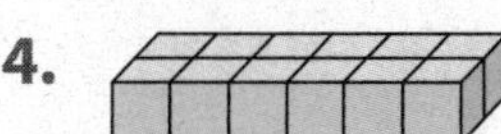

Independent Practice*

In **5–13**, find the volume of each solid. Use unit cubes to help.

5. 

6. 

7. 

8. 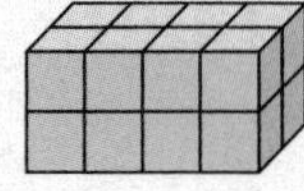

9. 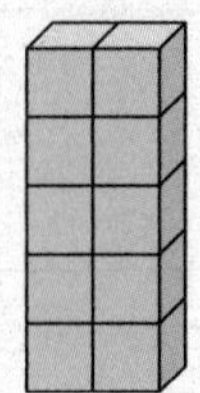

10. 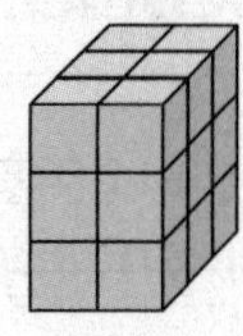

11. 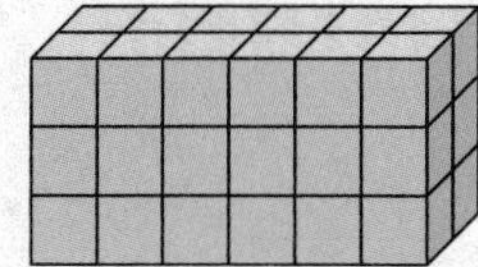

12. 

13. 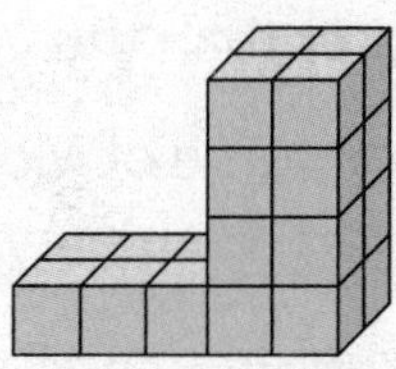

*For another example, see Set A on page 625.

Math Practices and Problem Solving

In **14–18**, use the table.

Compare the volumes of the prisms. Write >, <, or = for each ◯.

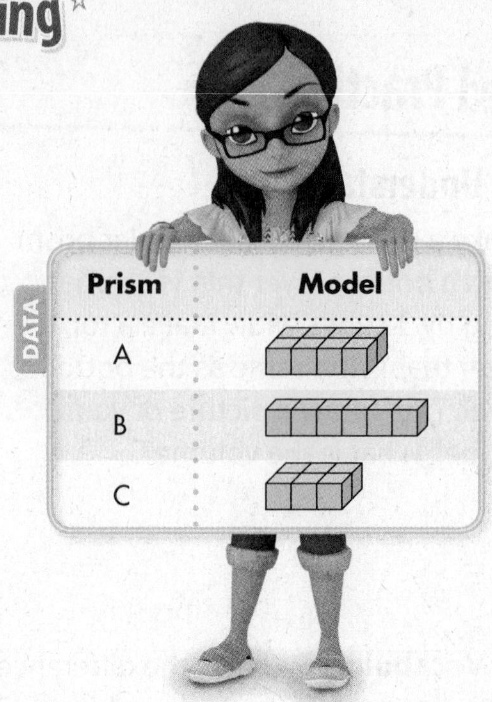

14. Prism A ◯ Prism B

15. Prism B ◯ Prism C

16. Prism C ◯ Prism A

17. If you added another layer of unit cubes on top of Prism A, what would the volume of the new solid be in cubic units?

18. If you put Prism C on top of Prism A, what would the volume of the new solid be in cubic units?

19. **MP.2 Reasoning** In an election, 471 people voted. Candidate B received $\frac{2}{3}$ of the votes. How many votes did Candidate B receive?

20. **Higher Order Thinking** Ms. Kellson's storage closet is 3 feet long, 3 feet wide, and 7 feet high. Can she fit 67 boxes that each have a volume of 1 cubic foot in her closet? Explain your answer.

Common Core Assessment

21. Natalie made the solid figures shown using unit cubes. Which statement about these models is true?

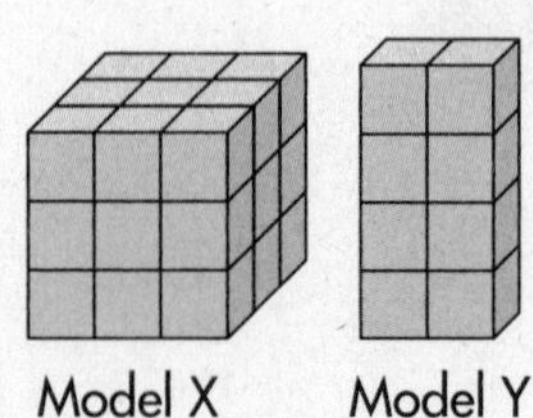

Ⓐ Model X and Model Y have the same volume.

Ⓑ The volume of Model X is 9 cubic units greater than the volume of Model Y.

Ⓒ The volume of Model X is 19 cubic units greater than the volume of Model Y.

Ⓓ The volume of Model X and Model Y combined is 45 cubic units.

Name ______________________

Homework & Practice 10-1
Model Volume

Another Look!

Volume is the measure of space inside a solid figure.

Find the volume of this solid by counting the number of unit cubes.

There are 8 cubes in the bottom layer and there are 4 layers. The total number of unit cubes is 32.

So, the volume is 32 cubic units.

In **1–9**, find the volume of each solid. Use unit cubes to help.

1. 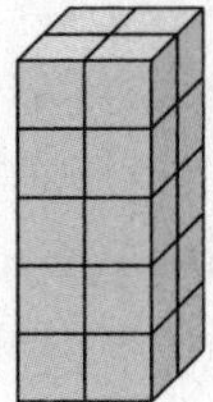

2. 

3. 

4. 

5. 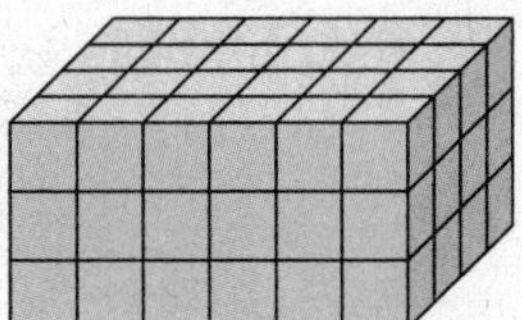

6. 

7. 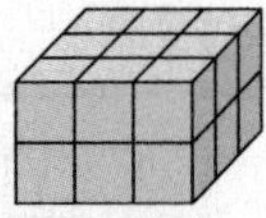

8. 

9. 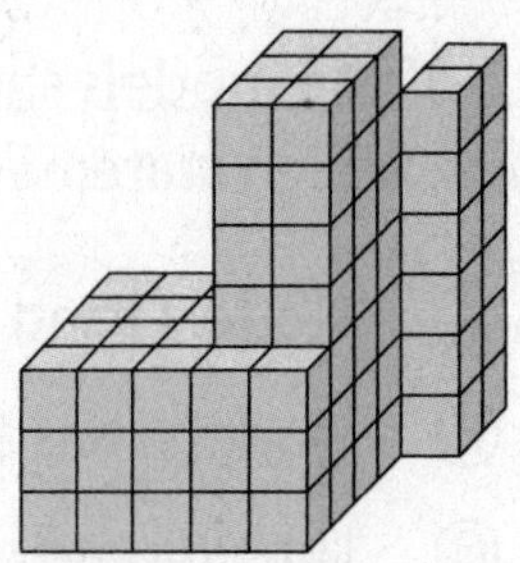

In **10–12**, use the table.

10. Higher Order Thinking Complete the table. Show some different ways that a rectangular prism can have a volume of 12 cubic units.

11. MP.7 Look for Relationships Look across each row of the table. What pattern do you see?

12. Use the table to help. How many unit cubes are needed to make a model of a rectangular prism that is 4 units long, 3 units wide, and 2 units tall?

Number of Cubes Long	Number of Cubes Wide	Number of Cubes Tall
1	1	12
2	2	3
2	3	
2		1
3	1	
3	2	
3		1
4	1	
6		1

13. Number Sense A building is 509 feet tall. Each floor is about 14 feet tall. About how many floors does the building have?

Do you need an estimate or an exact answer?

14. MP.2 Reasoning Velma and Bruce combined their model buildings to make one building. How can they change each building part to make the parts equal in volume? Explain your reasoning.

Common Core Assessment

15. Both of the models shown are made up of 1-inch cubes. Which statement about these models is true?

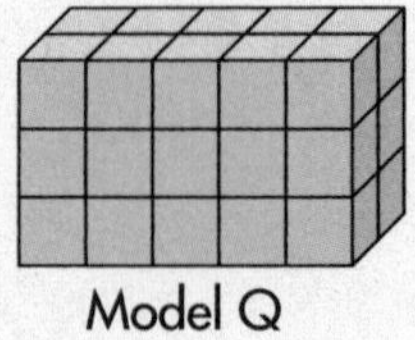

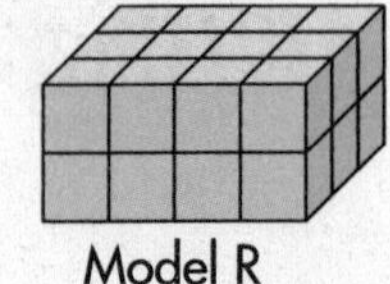

Ⓐ Model Q and Model R have the same volume.

Ⓑ Model R has a greater volume than Model Q.

Ⓒ The volume of Model Q is 7 cubic inches greater than the volume of Model R.

Ⓓ The volume of Model Q and Model R combined is 54 cubic inches.

Name ____________________

Lesson 10-2
Develop a Volume Formula

I can ...
find the volume of rectangular prisms using a formula.

Content Standards 5.MD.C.4, 5.MD.C.5a, 5.MD.C.5b
Mathematical Practices MP.1, MP.2, MP.3, MP.4, MP.6

Solve & Share Kevin needs a new aquarium for his fish. The pet store has a fish tank in the shape of a rectangular prism that measures 5 feet long by 2 feet wide by 4 feet high. Kevin needs a fish tank that has a volume of at least 35 cubic feet. Will this fish tank be big enough? ***Solve this problem any way you choose.***

Make Sense and Persevere
Read the problem carefully to make sure that you understand what you are trying to find. *Show your work!*

Look Back! **MP.3 Critique Reasoning** Malcolm says the volume of the aquarium would change if its dimensions were 2 feet long, 4 feet wide, and 5 feet high. Do you agree? Explain.

How Can You Use a Formula to Find the Volume of a Rectangular Prism?

A

Remember that volume is the number of cubic units (units^3) needed to pack a solid figure without gaps or overlaps.

Find the volume of the rectangular prism if each cubic unit represents 1 cubic foot.

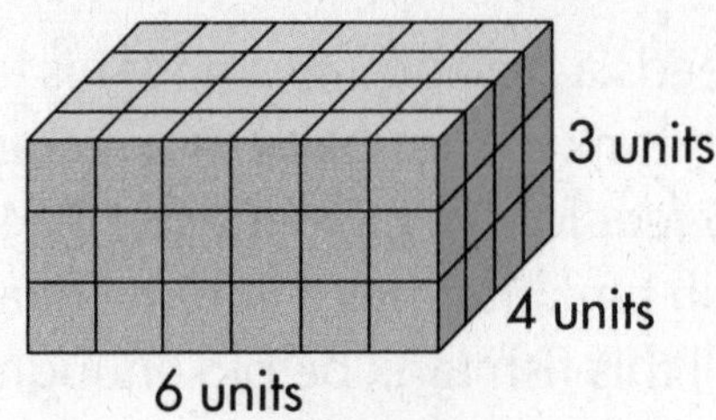

You can find the volume of a rectangular prism by counting cubes or using a formula.

A formula is a rule that uses symbols to relate two or more quantities.

B

If the dimensions of a rectangular prism are given as length ℓ, width w, and height h, then use this formula to find the volume V:

Volume = length × width × height

$V = (\ell \times w) \times h$ or $V = \ell \times (w \times h)$

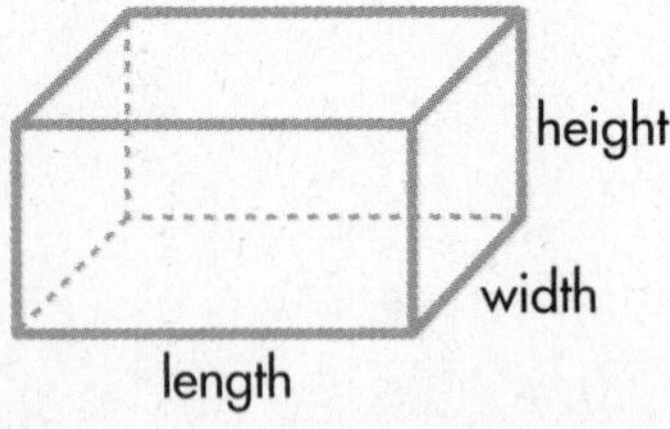

The factors in the formula can be regrouped using the Associative Property.

C

Use the formula to find the volume of the rectangular prism.

$V = \ell \times w \times h$

$V = (6 \times 4) \times 3$

$V = 24 \times 3$

$V = 72$

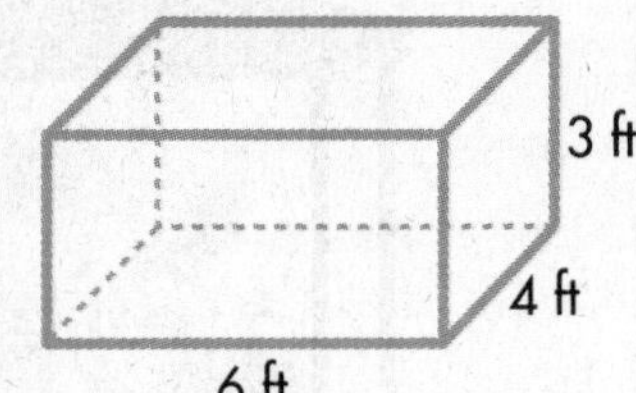

The volume of the rectangular prism is 72 cubic feet or 72 ft^3.

Convince Me! **MP.2 Reasoning** Give the dimensions of a different rectangular prism that also has a volume of 72 ft^3. Explain how you decided.

Name

Guided Practice*

Do You Understand?

1. In the example on page 594, could you first multiply the width by the height? Explain.

2. MP.4 Model with Math A wooden block measures 5 centimeters long, 3 centimeters wide, and 2 centimeters tall. Draw a rectangular prism to show the block and label it. What is the volume of the block?

Do You Know How?

In **3** and **4**, find the volume of each rectangular prism.

3.
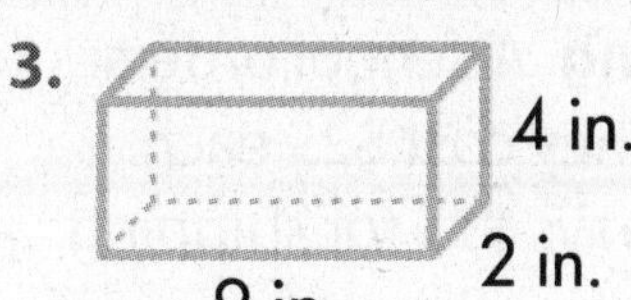

4.
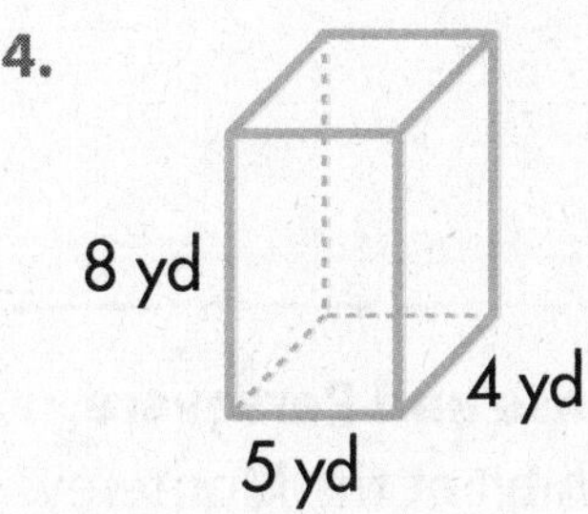

Independent Practice

In **5–10**, find the volume of each rectangular prism.

5.
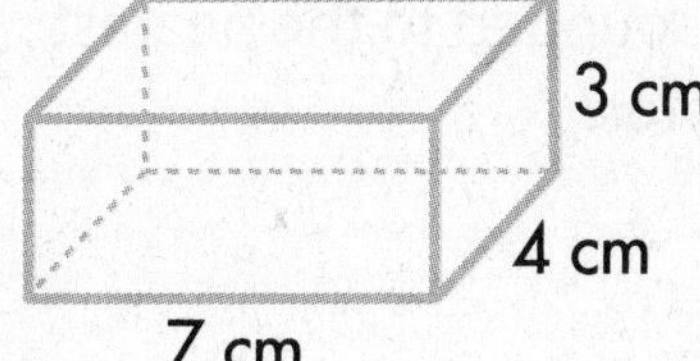

6.
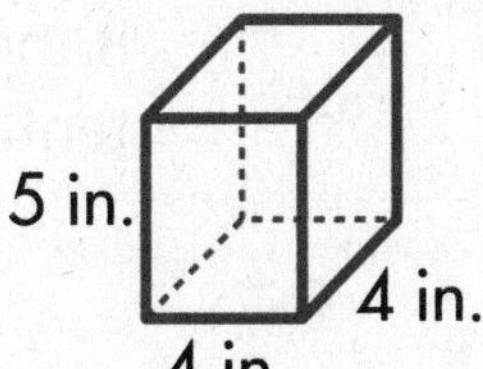

7.
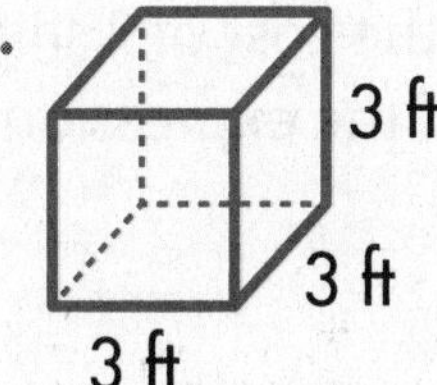

8.
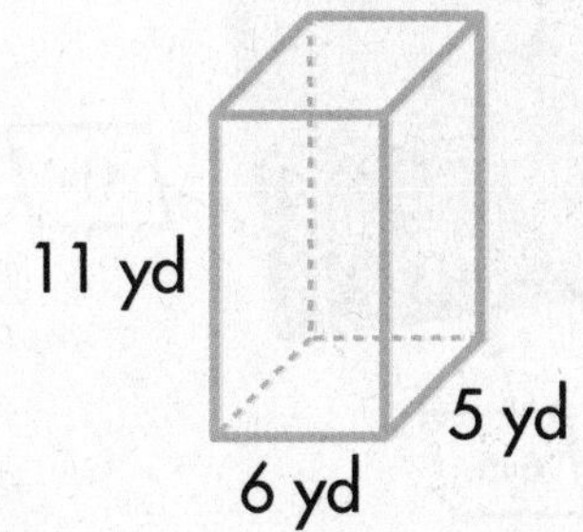

9.
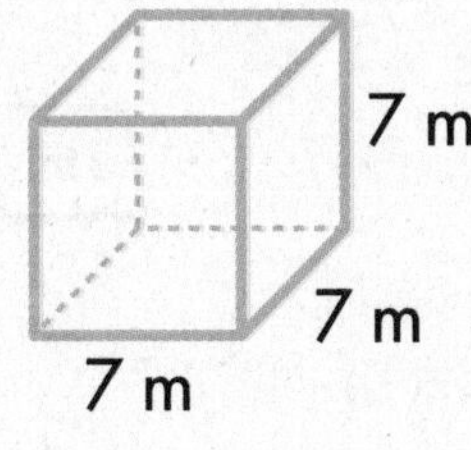

10.
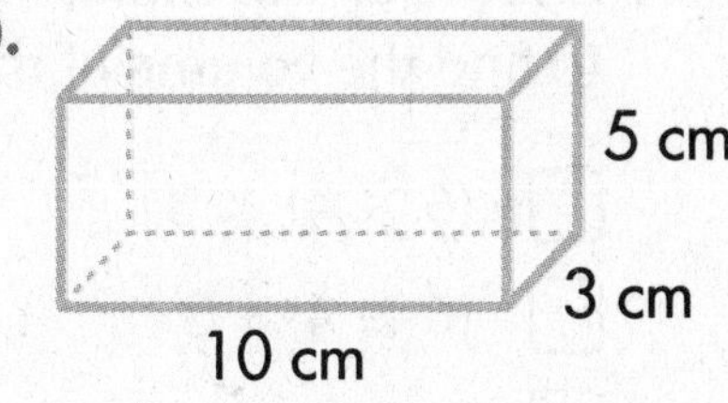

*For another example, see Set B on page 625.

Math Practices and Problem Solving

In **11** and **12**, use the picture of the dictionary.

11. The dictionary is 3 inches thick. What is the volume of the dictionary?

12. **MP.2 Reasoning** A school orders 10 dictionaries. They cost $25 each. The school also pays $15 for shipping. How much does the school pay to get the new dictionaries? Show your work.

13. **MP.1 Make Sense and Persevere** The Outer Bay exhibit at the Monterey Bay Aquarium has a viewing window that is 56.5 feet long, 17 feet tall, and 13 inches thick. Estimate its volume in cubic feet. Remember 12 inches = 1 foot.

14. **Higher Order Thinking** What is the height of a rectangular prism that has a volume of 280 cubic meters, a length of 8 meters, and a width of 7 meters? Show how you found your answer.

15. **Algebra** Nat used the expression $3 \times s$ to find the cost of 3 shirts. What is the value of the expression if $s = \$16$?

16. The height of a tree is 8.194 meters. What is the height rounded to the nearest tenth of a meter?

Common Core Assessment

17. Choose all the expressions that can be used to find the volume of this wooden box.

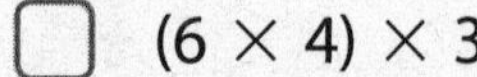

- ☐ $(6 \times 4) \times 3$
- ☐ $(6 \times 4) + 3$
- ☐ 6×4
- ☐ $6 \times (4 \times 3)$
- ☐ $(4 \times 3) \times 6$

Name ______________________

Homework & Practice 10-2

Develop a Volume Formula

Another Look!

What is the volume of a rectangular prism that has a length of 2 centimeters, a width of 4 centimeters, and a height of 3 centimeters?

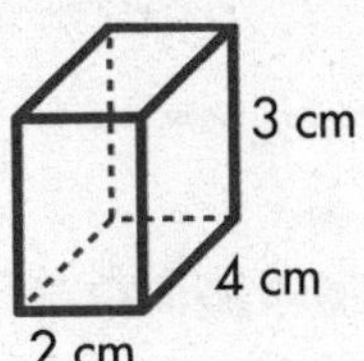

The volume of the prism is the same whether you count unit cubes or multiply its dimensions.

A model with unit cubes can show the meaning of ℓ, w, and h.

ℓ = length
w = width
h = height

$\ell = 2$ cm $w = 4$ cm $h = 3$ cm

Insert the values for ℓ, w, and h in the volume formula.

$V = \ell \times w \times h$
$V = (2 \times 4) \times 3$
$V = 8 \times 3$
$V = 24$

The volume is 24 cm^3.

In **1–6**, find the volume of each rectangular prism.

1.

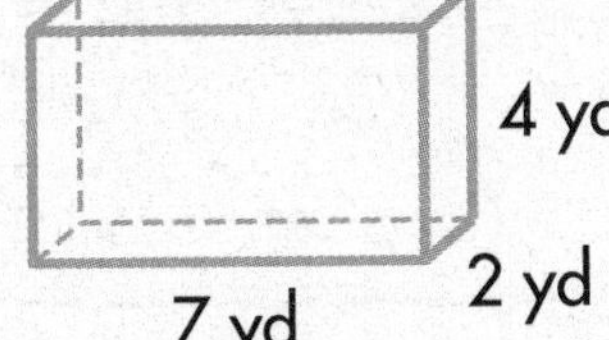

2.

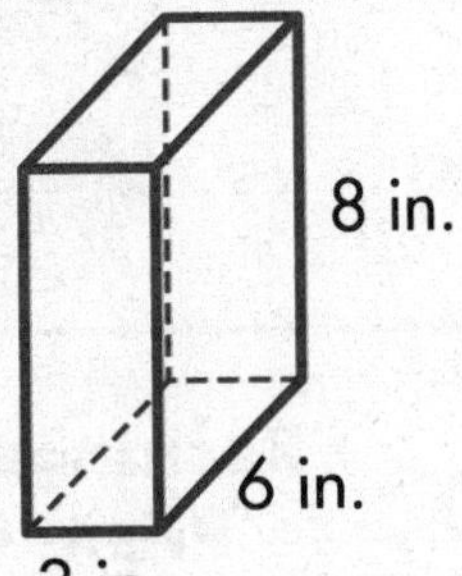

3.

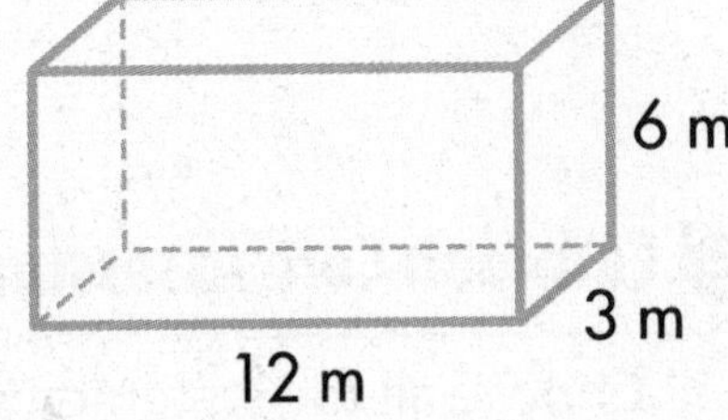

4.

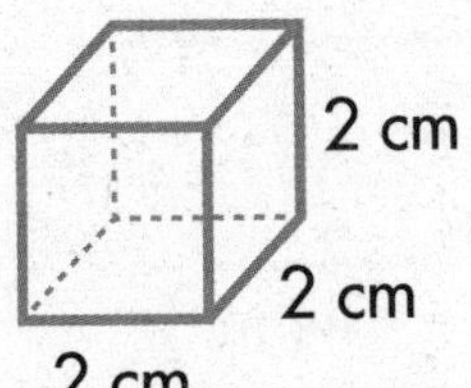

5.

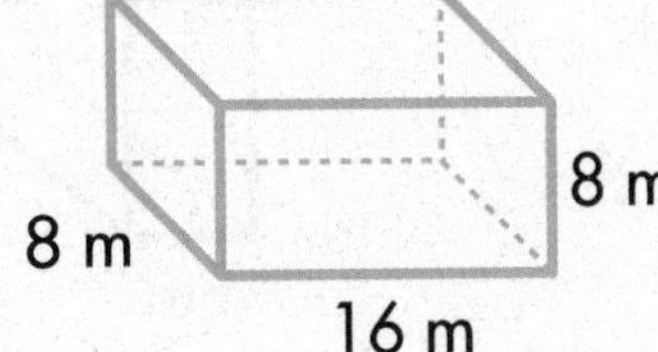

6.

7 yd
5 yd
11 yd

7. **MP.4 Model with Math** Write an expression for the volume of the bar magnet.

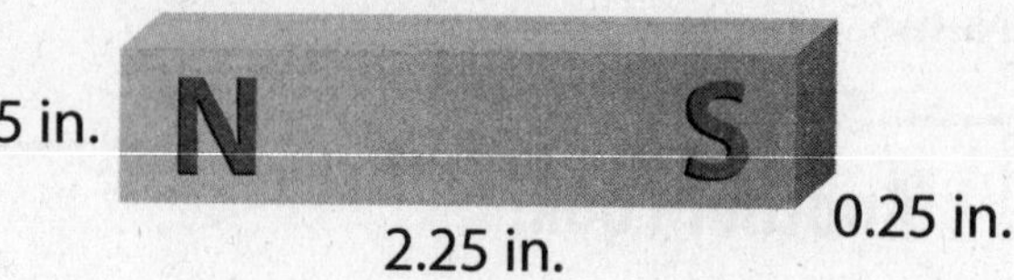

8. **MP.6 Be Precise** The front door of a house is 80 inches tall. What is the volume of the door?

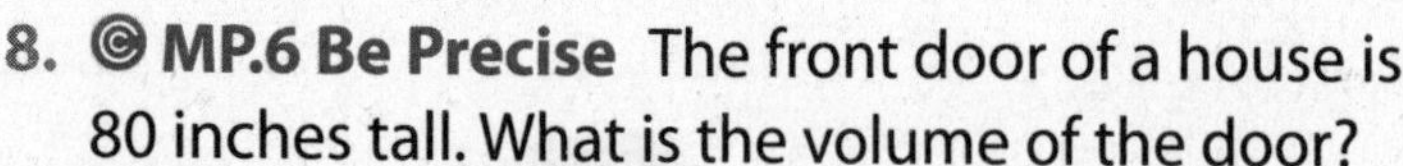

9. A bedroom door in the house has the same dimensions as the front door, but the length is 30 inches rather than 36 inches. How much greater is the volume of the front door than the bedroom door?

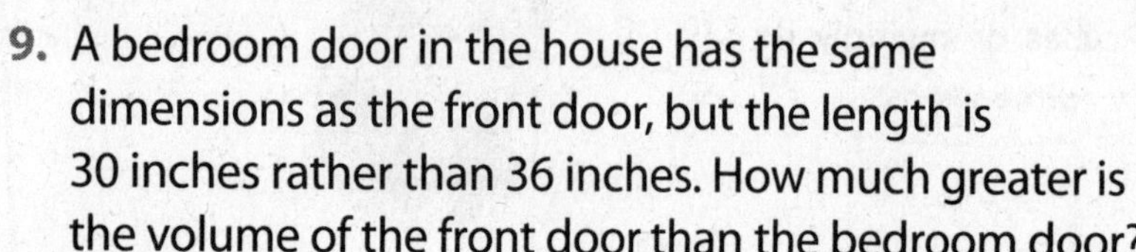

10. The living room in the house has an area of 224 square feet and a width of 14 feet. What is the length of the room?

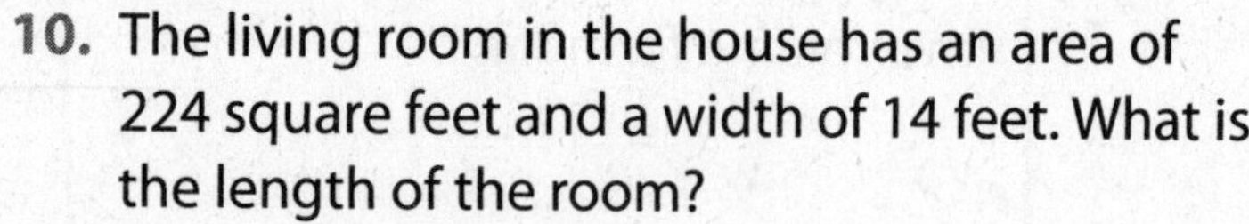

11. **Higher Order Thinking** A cube has a volume of 1,000 cubic feet. What is the length of an edge of the cube? Show how you found your answer.

12. A quadrilateral has all sides the same length and no right angles. What is the name of the quadrilateral?

Common Core Assessment

13. Choose all the statements that are true.

- ☐ Volume of Prism G = (4 + 10) + 12
- ☐ Volume of Prism G = 4 × (10 × 12)
- ☐ Volume of Prism H = 14 × 5 × 7
- ☐ Volume of Prism H = 14 × (5 + 7)
- ☐ Volume of Prism H = (14 × 5) + 7

Rectangular Prism G

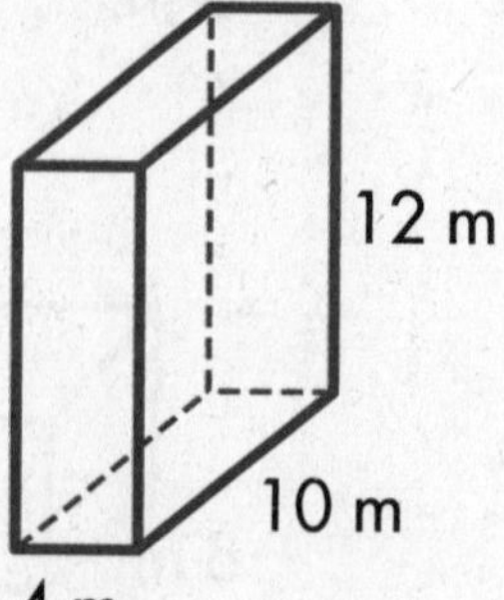

Rectangular Prism H

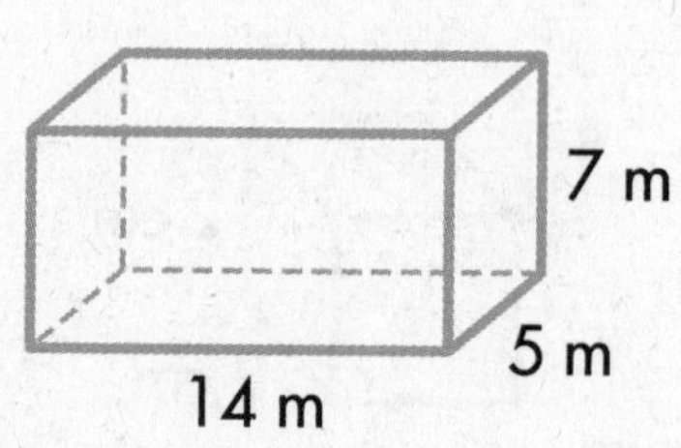

Name ______________________________

Lesson 10-3
Volume of Prisms

I can ...

find the volume of prisms in different ways.

© **Content Standards** 5.MD.C.5a, 5.MD.C.5b
Mathematical Practices MP.1, MP.2, MP.4, MP.7, MP.8

Solve & Share

Rachel built a rectangular prism that has a volume of 24 cubic inches. What are five possible length, width, and height dimensions for her prism? ***Solve this problem any way you choose.***

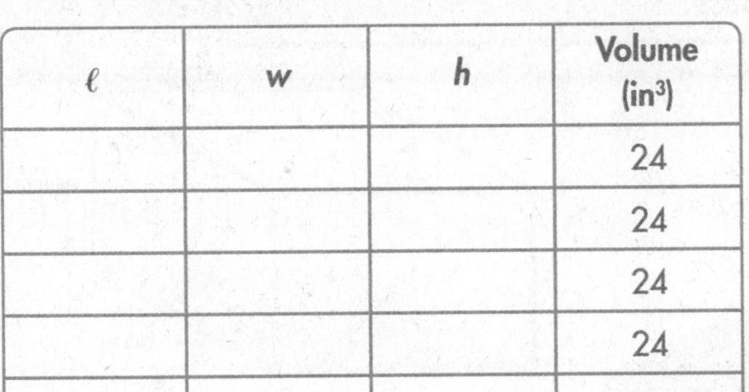

ℓ	w	h	Volume (in^3)
			24
			24
			24
			24
			24

You can use structure to find possible dimensions of the prism. *Show your work!*

Look Back! © **MP.2 Reasoning** What are possible length and width dimensions for the base of the prism if the height is 2 inches?

How Can You Find the Volume of a Rectangular Prism When the Area of the Base Is Given?

A

Carrie needs to know how much sand will fill a rectangular prism for her science project. The area of the base of a rectangular prism is 56 square centimeters. The prism's height is 6 centimeters. You know that $V = \ell \times w \times h$. *Here is another formula for the volume of a rectangular prism:*

Volume $= B \times h$, *where B is the area of the base.*

You can find B, the area of the base of the rectangular prism by using the area formula $A = \ell \times w$.

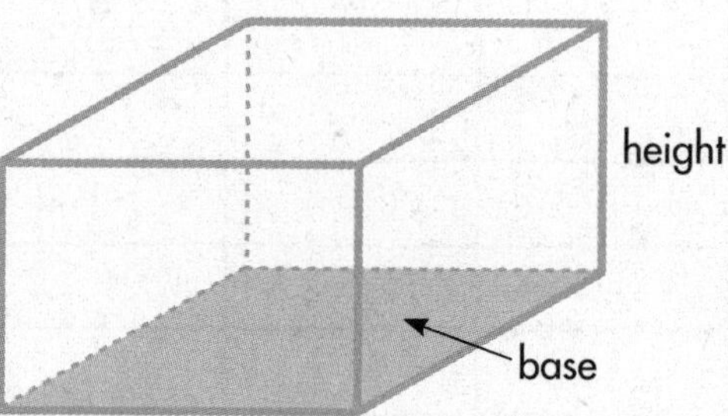

B Find the volume of the rectangular prism if the area of its base is 56 square centimeters and its height is 6 centimeters.

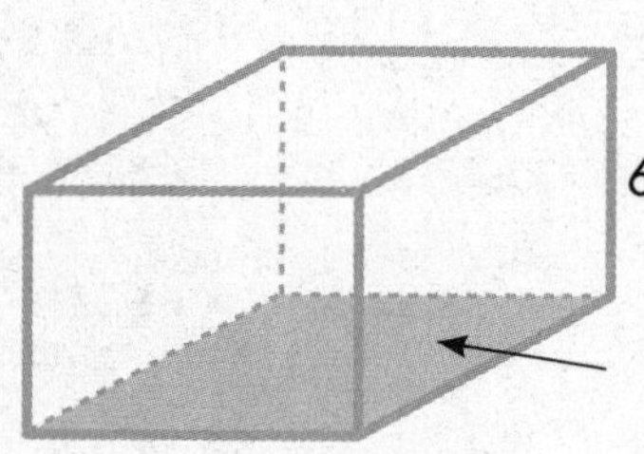

$V = B \times h$
$V = 56 \times 6$
$V = 336 \text{ cm}^3$

So, the volume of the rectangular prism is 336 cm^3.

Convince Me! **MP.2 Reasoning** In the example above, what are possible length and width dimensions of the base of the rectangular prism? Explain.

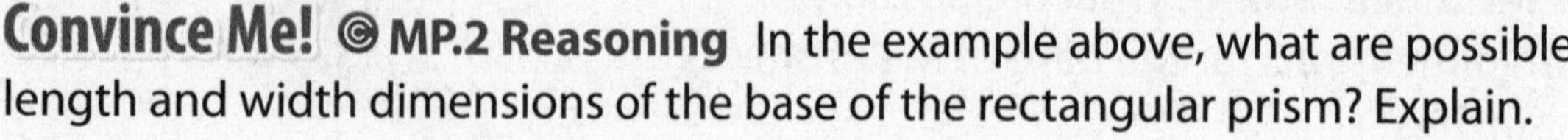

Name ______________________________

Guided Practice*

Do You Understand?

1. **MP.8 Generalize** In the example at the top of page 600, what is the shape of the base of the rectangular prism? How do you find the area of that kind of shape?

2. **MP.4 Model with Math** A cereal box measures 6 inches long, 2 inches wide, and 10 inches tall. The area of the base is 12 square inches. Draw and label a rectangular prism to represent the box. What is the volume of the figure you drew?

Do You Know How?

In **3** and **4**, find the volume of each rectangular prism.

3.
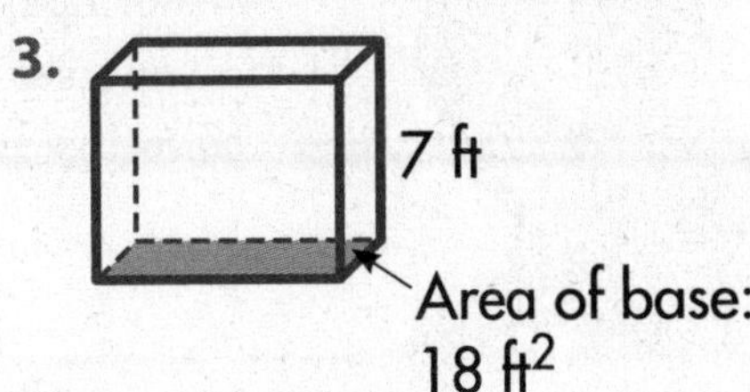

4.
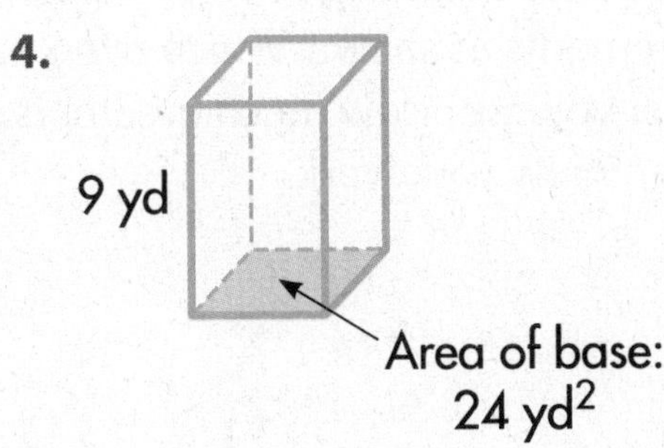

Independent Practice

In **5–10**, find the volume of each rectangular prism.

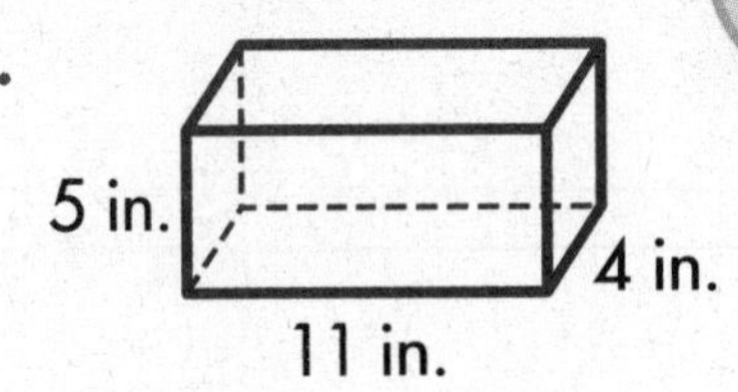

Remember that volume is measured in cubic units!

5. 2 yd, 16 yd^2

6. 3 m, 52 m^2

7. 5 in., 4 in., 11 in.

8.
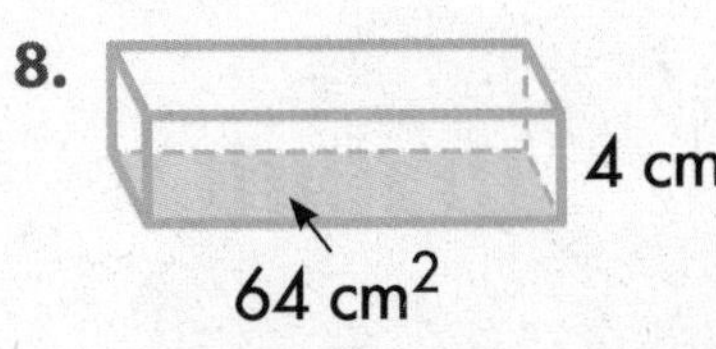

9. 11 yd, 12 yd, 10 yd

10.
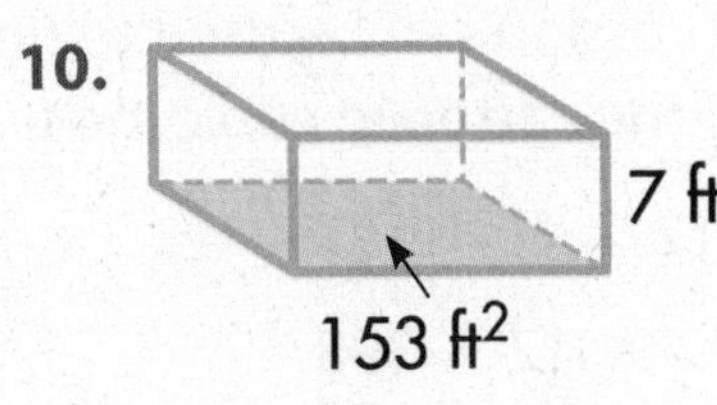

*For another example, see Set B on page 625.

Math Practices and Problem Solving

11. **MP.1 Make Sense and Persevere** Use the drawing of the ice cube tray. Each small ice cube section has a base with an area of 20 square centimeters. What is the volume of all the ice cube sections in the tray?

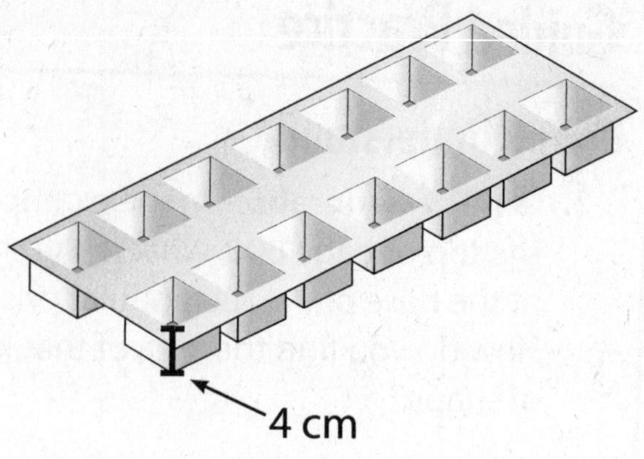

What operation(s) do you need to use to solve this problem?

12. **Higher Order Thinking** Two ovens have measurements as shown. Which oven has a greater volume? How much greater is its volume? Show your work.

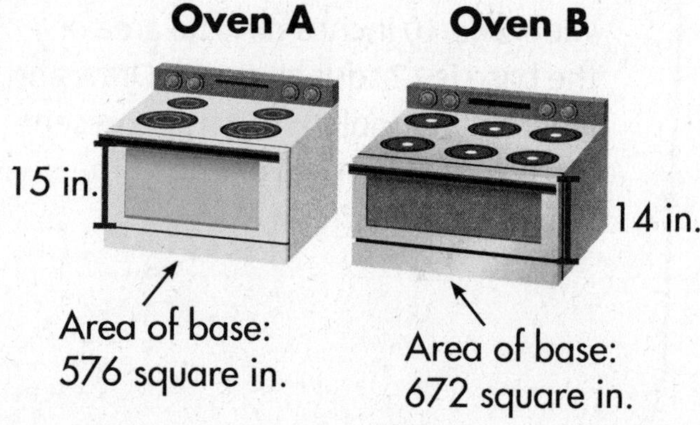

13. **MP.2 Reasoning** The perimeter of an equilateral triangle is 51 feet. What is the length of one of its sides? Explain your work.

14. **Number Sense** Harry is in line at the store. He has 3 items that cost $5.95, $4.25, and $1.05. Explain how Harry can add the cost of the items mentally before he pays for them.

Common Core Assessment

15. Which expression can be used to find the volume of the carton in cubic inches?

Ⓐ $(12 \times 12) + 308$

Ⓑ $12 \times 12 \times 308$

Ⓒ $308 + 12 + 308 + 12$

Ⓓ 308×12

Name ______________________

Homework & Practice 10-3
Volume of Prisms

Another Look!

What is the volume of the rectangular prism?

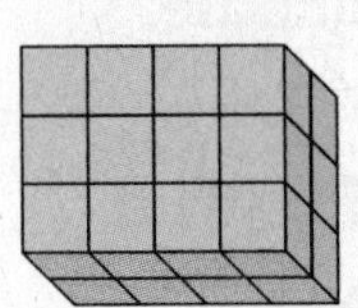

Use the formula $V = B \times h$ and cubes to help.

$V = B \times h$

B = the area of the base

h = height

What is the area of the base?

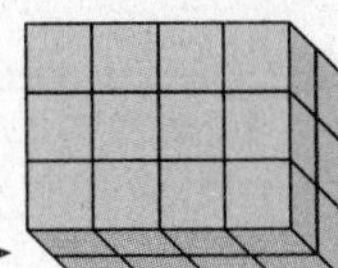

$A = \ell \times w$

$A = 4 \times 2$

$A = 8 \text{ units}^2$

What is the height, h?

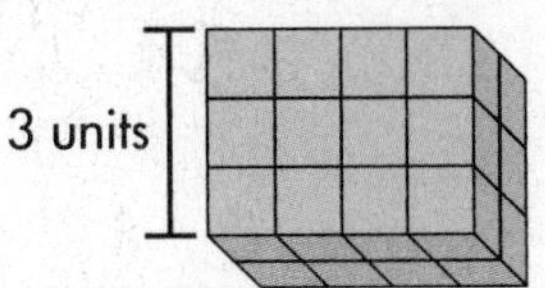

The prism is 3 units tall.

Use the values to complete the formula.

$V = B \times h$

$V = 8 \times 3$

$V = 24 \text{ units}^3$

In **1–6**, find the volume of each rectangular prism.

1.

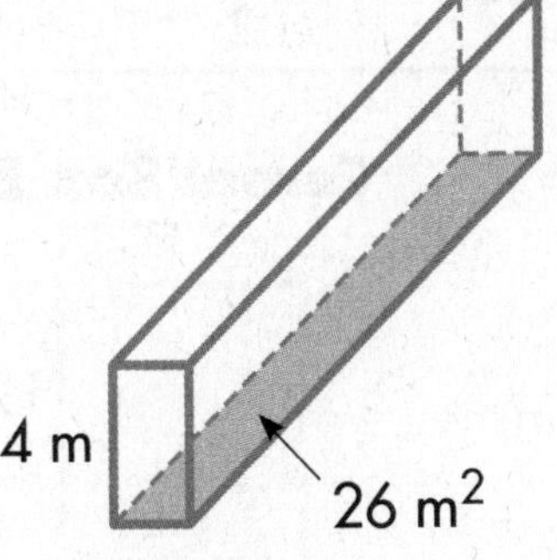

2.

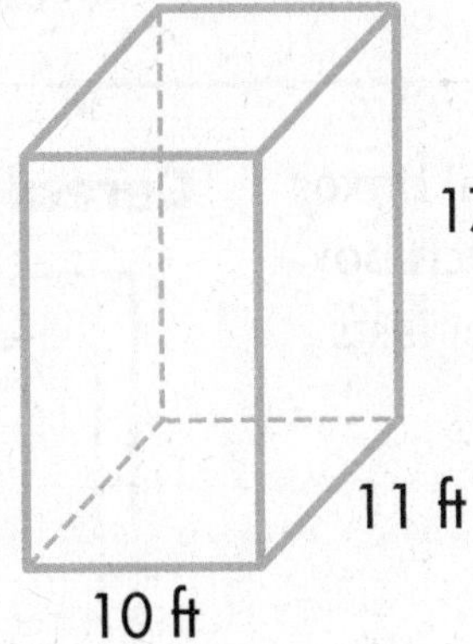

3.

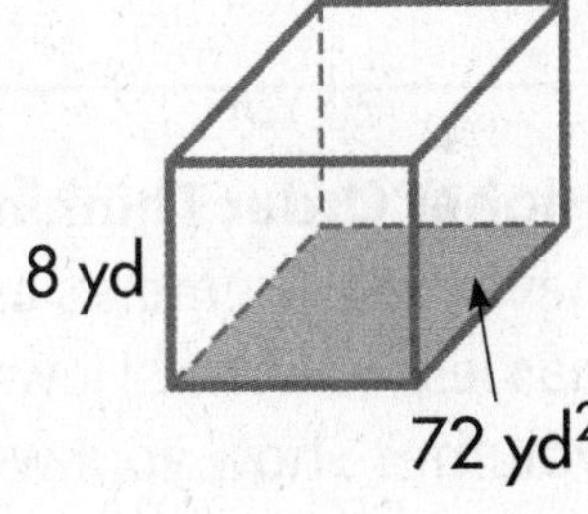

4.

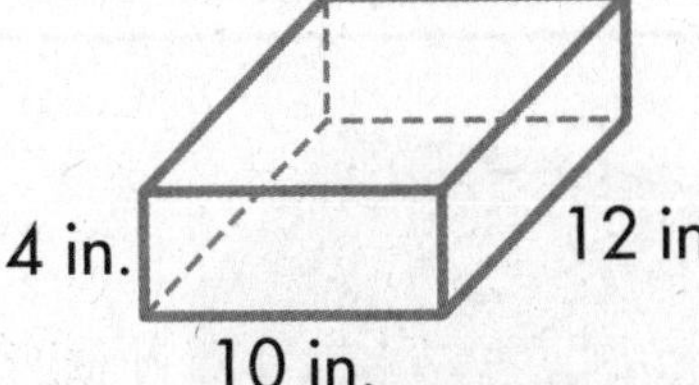

5.

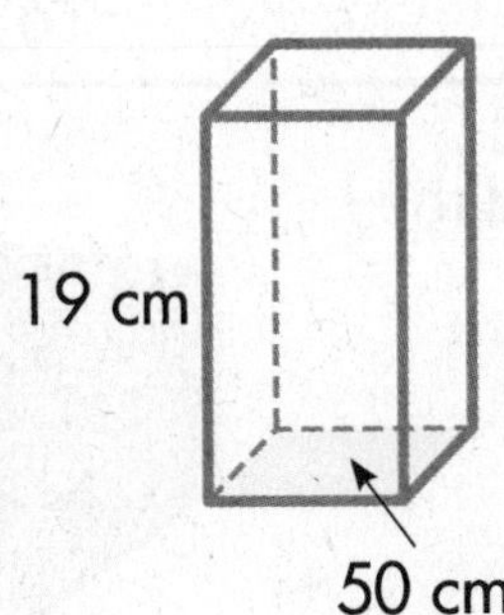

6.

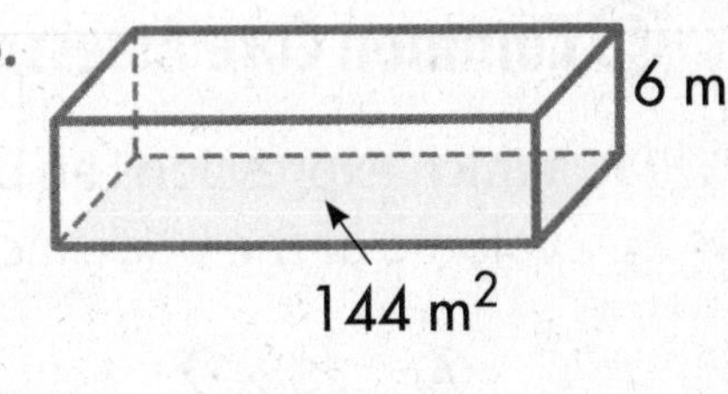

7. **Math and Science** If two objects are pushed by the same amount of force, the one with the greater mass will move more slowly. For a science project, Kendra used centimeter cubes, each with the same mass and volume, to build the two rectangular prisms shown. If each rectangular prism is pushed by the same amount of force, which one will move more slowly? Compare the volumes using > or <.

Rectangular Prism A

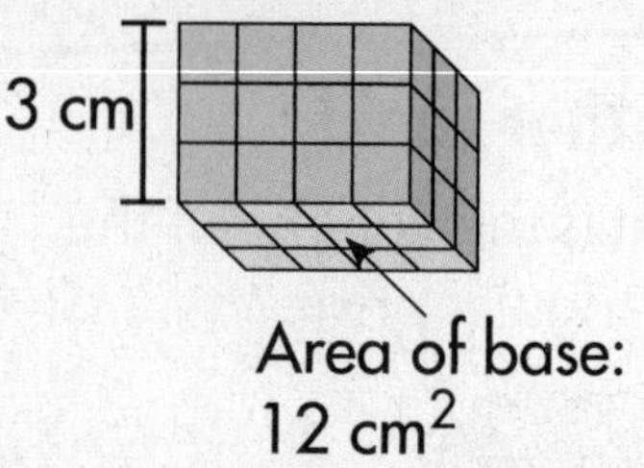

Area of base: 12 cm^2

Rectangular Prism B

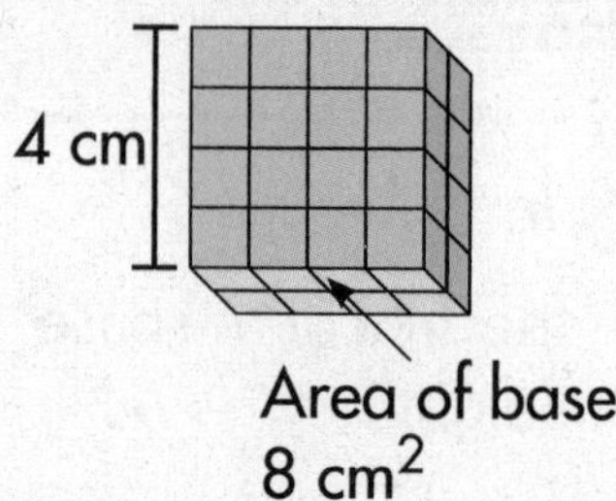

Area of base: 8 cm^2

8. **MP.2 Reasoning** What is the height of a rectangular prism that has a volume of 192 cubic feet and a base with an area of 48 square feet? Explain your work.

9. What is the perimeter of the rectangle shown?

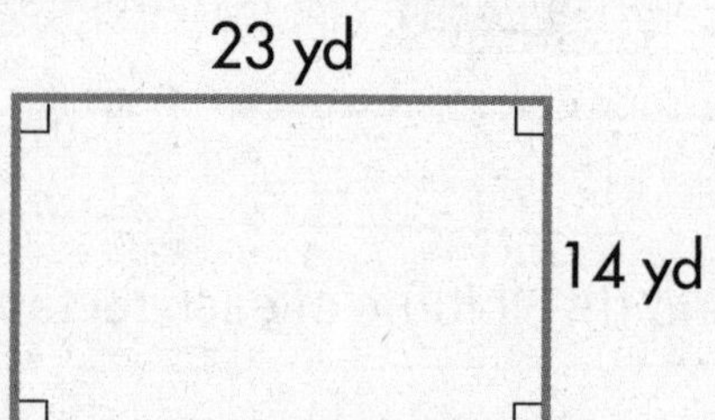

10. **Higher Order Thinking** Two cereal boxes have measurements as shown. Which box has less volume? How much smaller is its volume? Show your work.

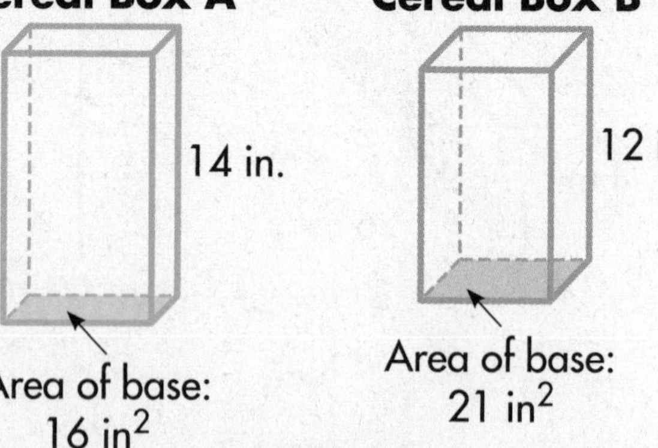

Common Core Assessment

11. Which expression can be used to find the volume of the brick in cubic inches?

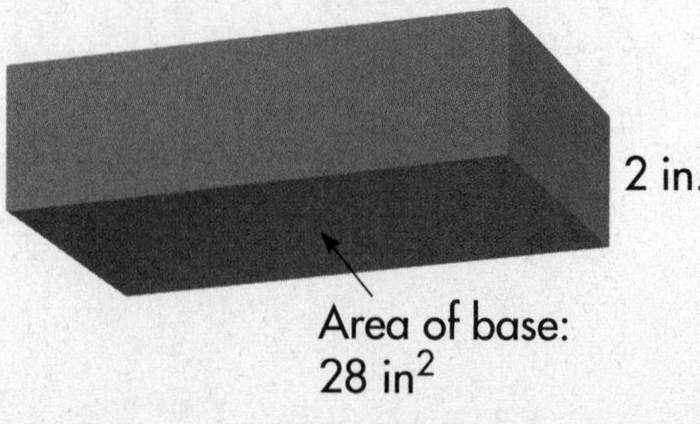

Ⓐ 28×2

Ⓑ $(2 + 2) \times 28$

Ⓒ $(2 \times 2) + 28$

Ⓓ $28 + 2 + 28 + 2$

Name ______________________________

Lesson 10-4
Combine Volumes of Prisms

I can …
find the volume of a solid figure that is the combination of two or more rectangular prisms.

Content Standard 5.MD.C.5c
Mathematical Practices MP.1, MP.2, MP.4, MP.7

Solve & Share Ariel is thinking of a three-dimensional figure that is made by combining two rectangular prisms. What is the volume of this three-dimensional figure? ***Solve this problem any way you choose.***

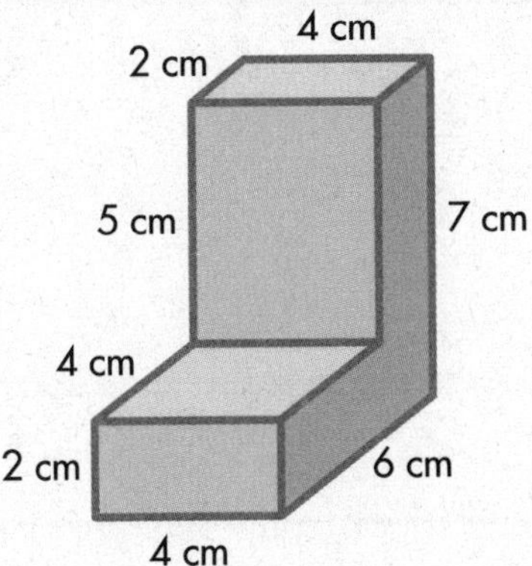

Use Structure
You can find the volumes of the rectangular prisms that make up the solid figure. Show your work!

Look Back! MP.2 Reasoning How did you separate the solid into simpler rectangular prisms? Write the dimensions of each of the prisms.

How Can You Find the Volume of a Solid Figure Composed of Two Rectangular Prisms?

A

The shape and size of a storage building are shown in the figure. The building supervisor wants to find the volume to determine how much storage space is available. What is the volume of the building?

4 m
9 m
5 m
6 m
7 m
12 m
9 m
10 m

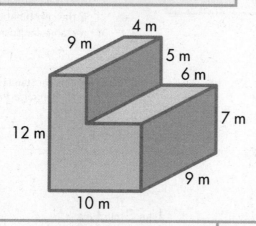

B The building can be separated into two rectangular prisms as shown. Identify the measurements for the length, width, and height of each prism.

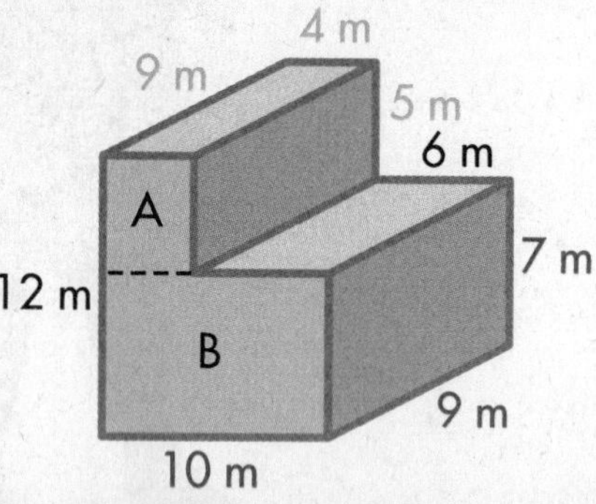

C Use the formula $V = \ell \times w \times h$ to find the volume of each rectangular prism.

Volume of Prism A	Volume of Prism B
$V = \ell \times w \times h$	$V = \ell \times w \times h$
$= 4 \times 9 \times 5$	$= 10 \times 9 \times 7$
$= 180$	$= 630$

Add to find the total volume.

$180 + 630 = 810$

The volume of the storage building is 810 cubic meters.

Convince Me! **MP.2 Reasoning** What is another way to divide the solid above into two rectangular prisms? What are the dimensions of each prism?

Name ______________________________________

Guided Practice*

Do You Understand?

In **1** and **2**, use the solid below. The dashed line separates it into two rectangular prisms, A and B.

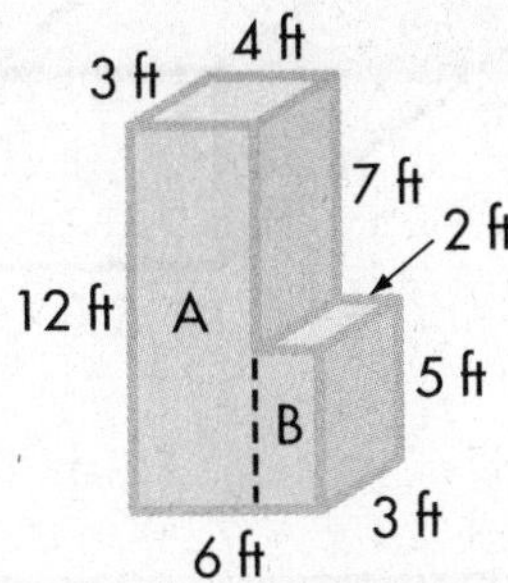

1. What are the length, width, and height of Prism A? What are the length, width, and height of Prism B?

2. What is another way you could separate the shape into two rectangular prisms? What are each prism's dimensions?

Do You Know How?

In **3** and **4**, find the volume of each solid figure.

3.

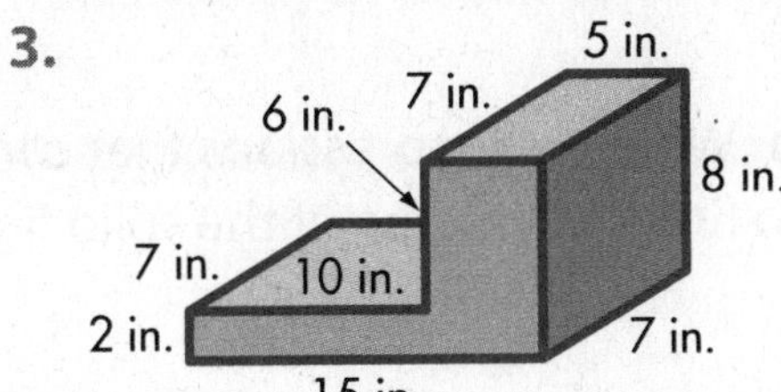

4.

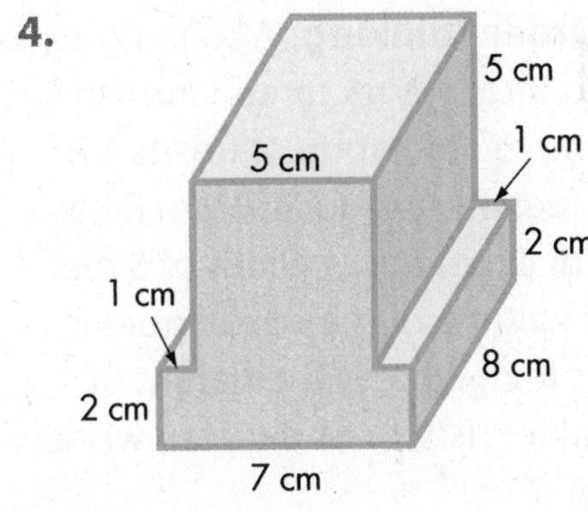

Independent Practice

In **5–7**, find the volume of each solid figure.

5.

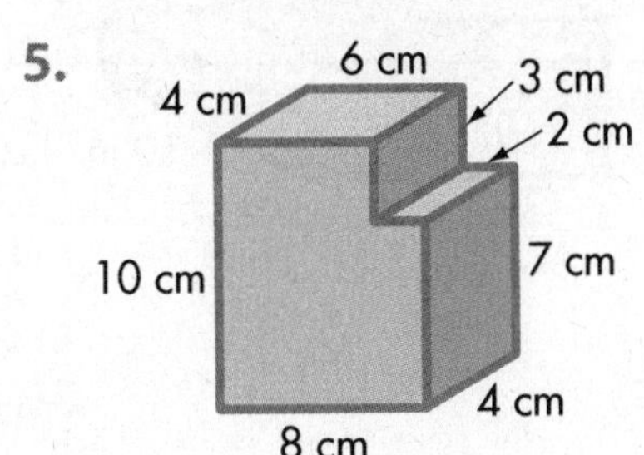

6.

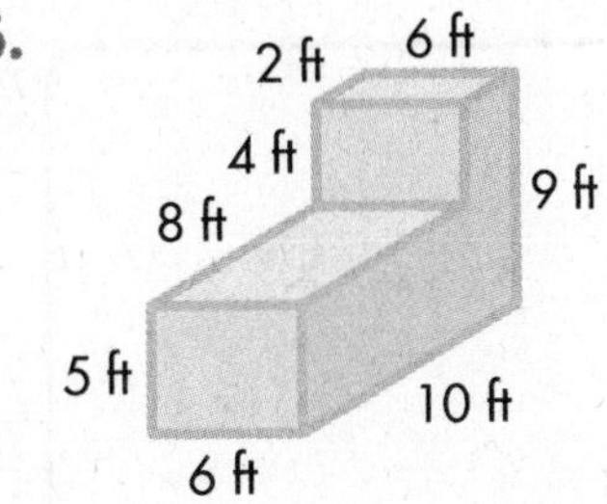

7.

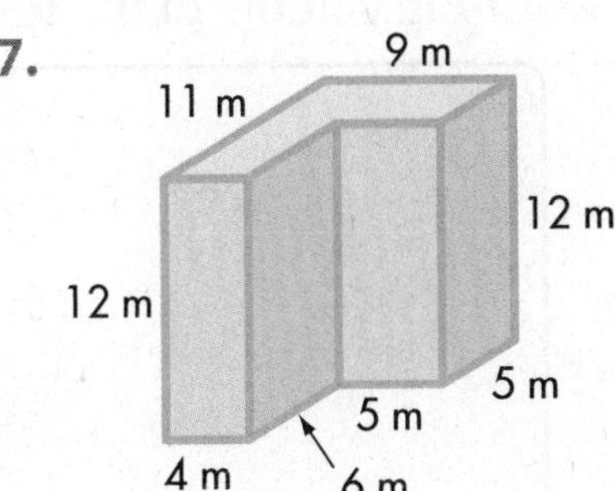

*For another example, see Set C on page 626.

Math Practices and Problem Solving

For **8–10**, use the drawing of the solid figure.

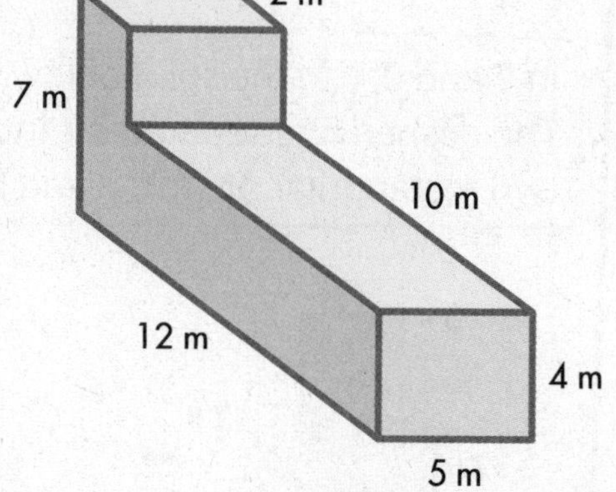

8. MP.1 Make Sense and Persevere How would you find the volume of the figure shown?

9. Algebra Write two expressions that can be added to find the volume of the solid figure.

10. What is the volume of the solid figure?

---

11. Higher Order Thinking A solid figure is separated into two rectangular prisms. The volume of Rectangular Prism A is 80 cubic feet. Rectangular Prism B has a length of 6 feet and a width of 5 feet. The total volume of the solid figure is 200 cubic feet. What is the height of Rectangular Prism B? Show your work.

12. MP.4 Model with Math The Peters family will drive 615 miles to reach their vacation destination. If they drive 389 miles the first day, how many miles will they drive the second day? Complete the bar diagram to help.

____ miles

____ miles	x

Common Core Assessment

13. Draw a line to separate the solid figure at the right into two rectangular prisms. Then write an expression for the volume of the solid figure.

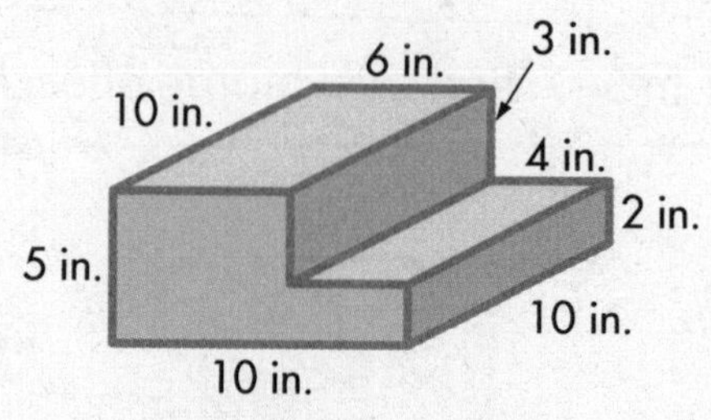

Name ________________________

Homework & Practice 10-4

Combine Volumes of Prisms

Another Look!

What is the volume of the solid figure?

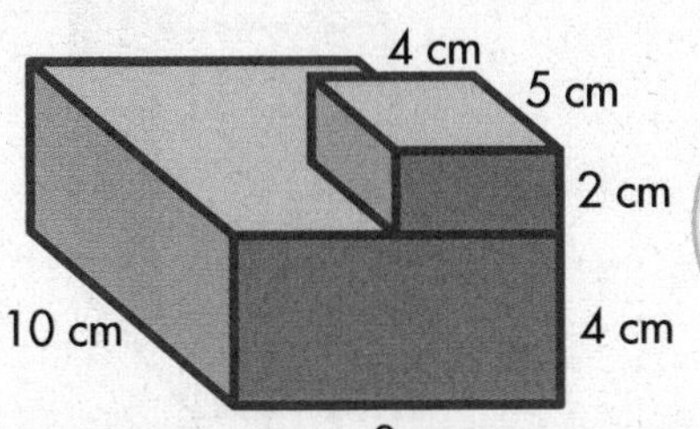

Make sure you find the ℓ, w, and h of each rectangular prism.

Separate the solid figure into rectangular prisms.

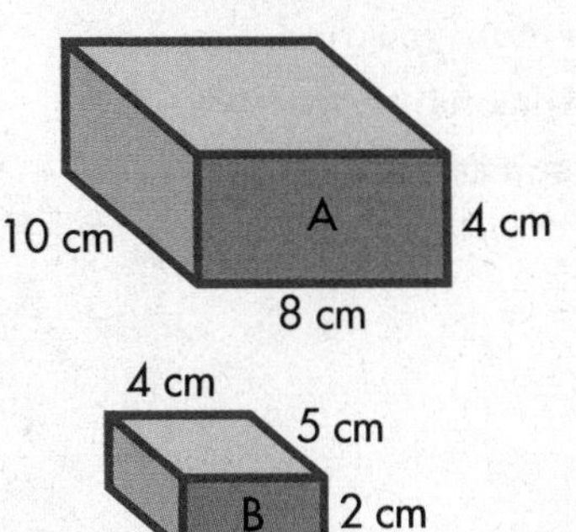

Find the volume of each rectangular prism.

Prism A:
$V = \ell \times w \times h$
$V = 8 \times 10 \times 4$
$V = 80 \times 4$
$V = 320$

Prism B:
$V = \ell \times w \times h$
$V = 4 \times 5 \times 2$
$V = 20 \times 2$
$V = 40$

Add the volumes.

$320 + 40 = 360$

So, the volume of the solid figure is 360 cm^3.

In **1–6**, find the volume of each solid figure.

1.

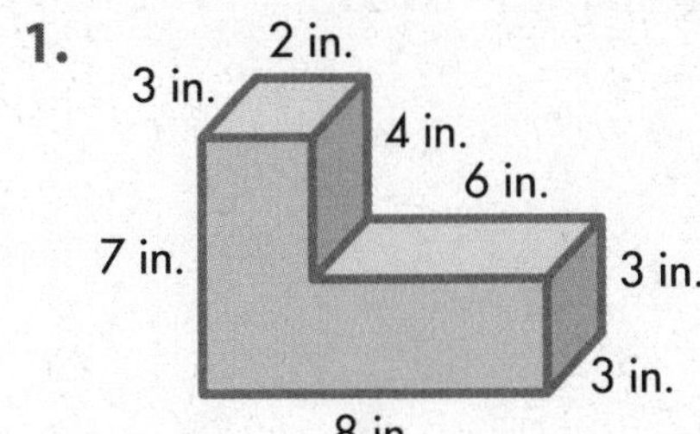

2.

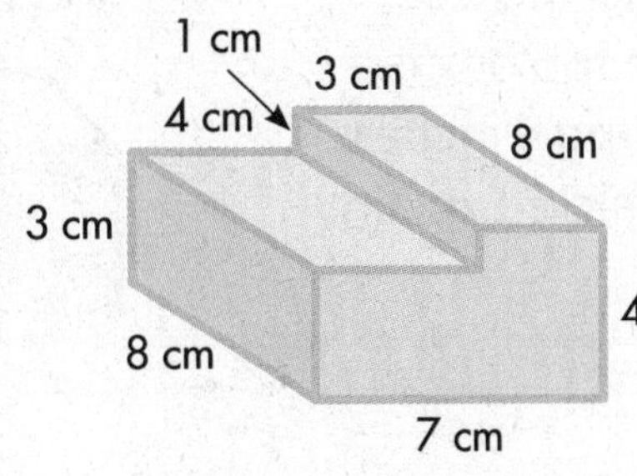

3.

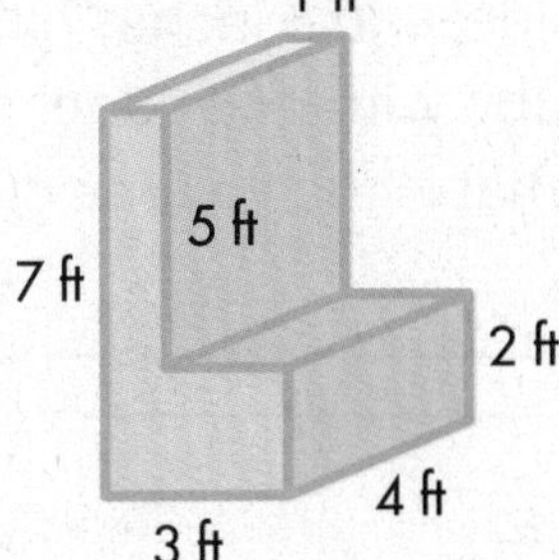

4.

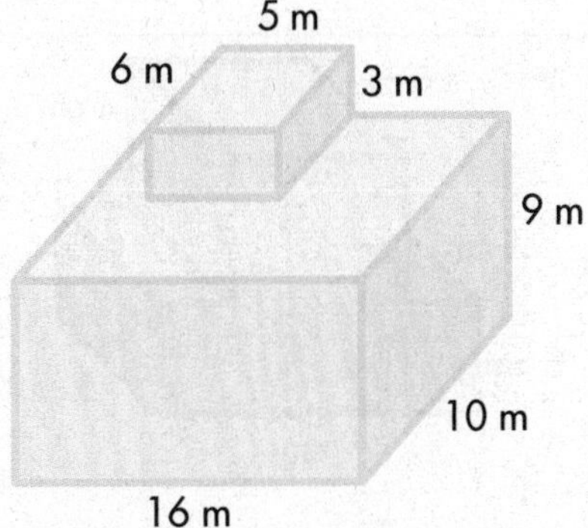

5.

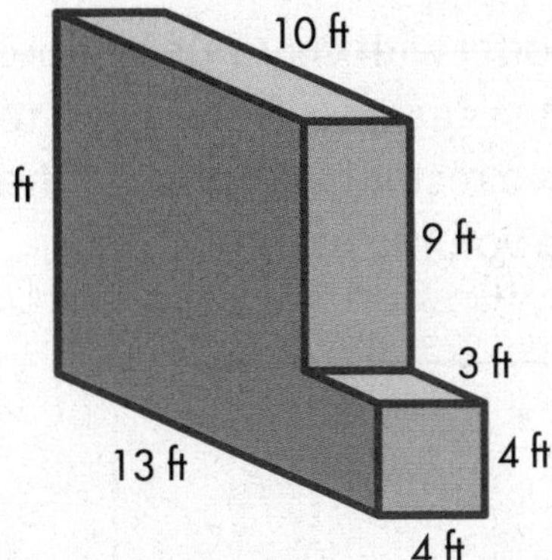

6.

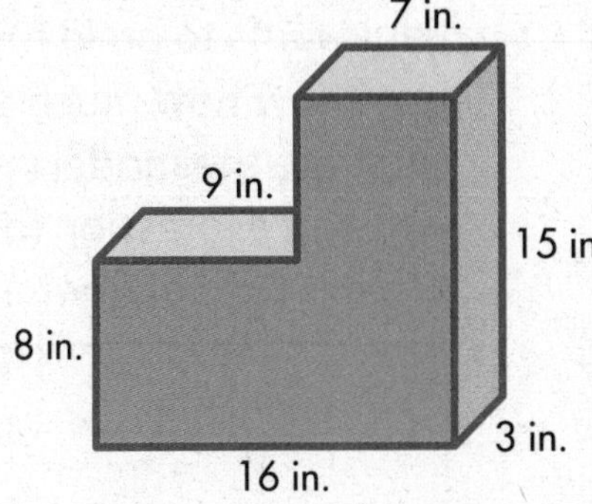

In **7** and **8**, use the drawing of the solid figure.

7. Find two different ways to separate the solid figure into two rectangular prisms. Draw a line on each figure below to show each way.

5 in.
4 in.
7 in.
5 in.
2 in.
2 in.
6 in.
5 in.

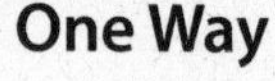

One Way

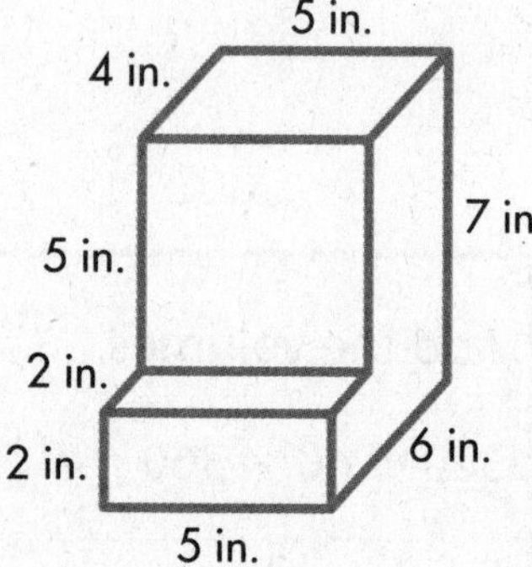

Another Way

5 in.
4 in.
7 in.
5 in.
2 in.
2 in.
6 in.
5 in.

How can you find the dimensions of the two smaller solids?

8. **MP.4 Model with Math** Choose one way that you found. Write and solve an equation for the volume of each rectangular prism. Then find the volume of the solid figure.

9. **Higher Order Thinking** Ashley is stacking two boxes on a shelf. The bottom box measures 6 inches long, 5 inches wide, and 5 inches high. The top box is a cube with one edge measuring 4 inches. What is the volume of this stack? Explain.

10. **Algebra** Write an expression you can use to find the volume of the cube. Then find the volume if $y = 9$ feet.

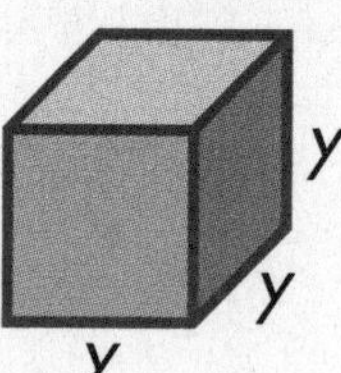

Common Core Assessment

11. Paul wants to build this model with clay, but he does not know how much clay to purchase. Draw a line to separate the model into two rectangular prisms. Then write an expression for the volume of the model. What is the volume?

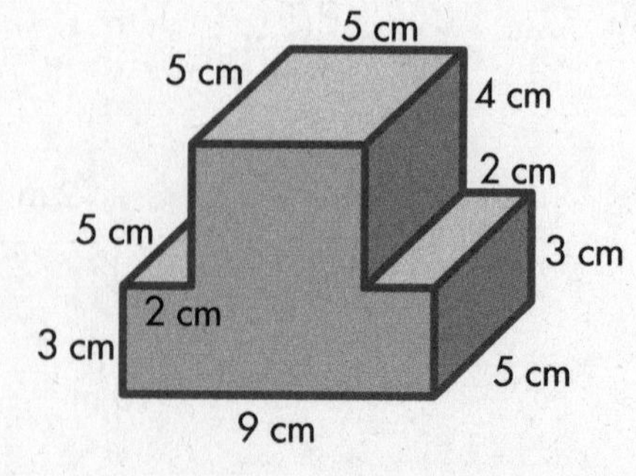

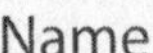

Name

Lesson 10-5

Solve Word Problems Using Volume

I can . . .
solve word problems involving volume.

Content Standard 5.MD.C.5c
Mathematical Practices MP.2, MP.3, MP.4, MP.8

Solve & Share

A school has two wings, each of which is a rectangular prism. The school district is planning to install air conditioning in the school and needs to know its volume. What is the volume of the school? ***Solve this problem any way you choose.***

Model with Math Write a multiplication expression for the volume of each wing of the building.

50 m
10 m
50 m
SCHOOL
14 m
57 m
75 m

Look Back! **MP.4 Model with Math** Write a mathematical expression that can be used to find the total volume of the school.

How Can You Use Volume Formulas to Solve Real-World Problems?

A

The nature center has a large bird cage called an aviary. It consists of two sections, each shaped like a rectangular prism. There needs to be 10 cubic feet of space for each bird. How many birds can the nature center have in the aviary?

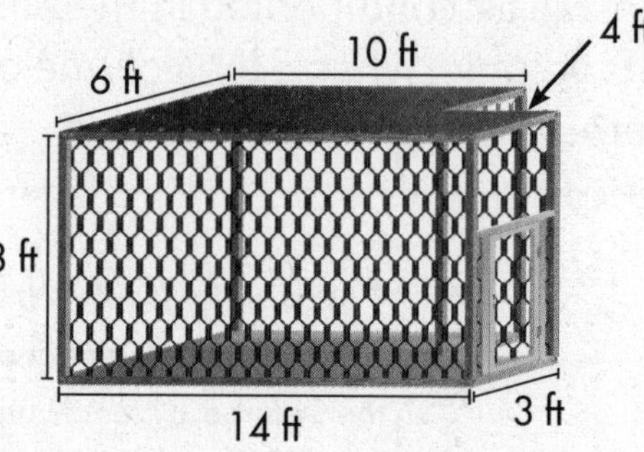

You can make sense of the problem by breaking it apart into simpler problems.

B Find the volume of each section.
Use the formula $V = \ell \times w \times h$.

Small section:
$V = 4 \times 3 \times 8 = 96$

Large section:
$V = 10 \times 6 \times 8 = 480$

Add to find the total volume:
$96 + 480 = 576$

The combined volume is 576 cubic feet.

C Divide to find the number of birds that will fit.

576 cubic feet

10 cu ft | ?

$576 \div 10 = 57.6$

The nature center can put 57 birds in the aviary.

Convince Me! **MP.3 Critique Reasoning** Tom solved the problem a different way. First he found the total area of the floor, and then he multiplied by the height. Does Tom's method work? Explain.

Name

Guided Practice*

Do You Understand?

1. How can you find the volume of the china cabinet?

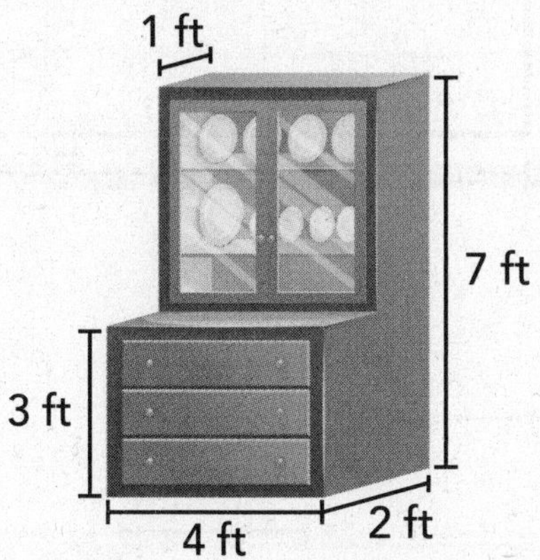

2. MP.2 Reasoning What is the height of the top section of the china cabinet? Explain.

3. Find the volume of the china cabinet.

Do You Know How?

4. Find the volume of the building below.

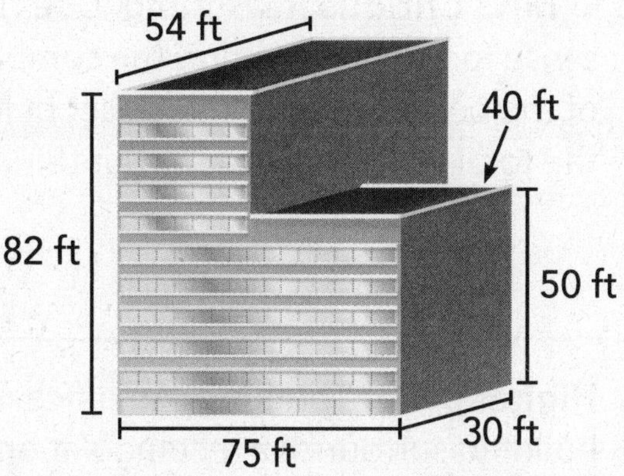

5. The nature center has a fish tank shaped like a rectangular prism that measures 6 feet long by 4 feet wide by 4 feet high. It can be stocked safely with 3 small fish in each cubic foot of water. How many small fish can safely fit in the tank?

Independent Practice

6. Sophie built a house out of building blocks. Find the volume of the house Sophie built.

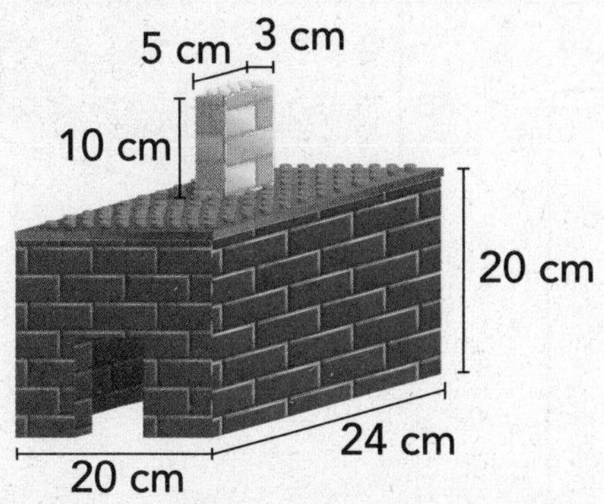

7. How many cubic inches of concrete would it take to make these stairs?

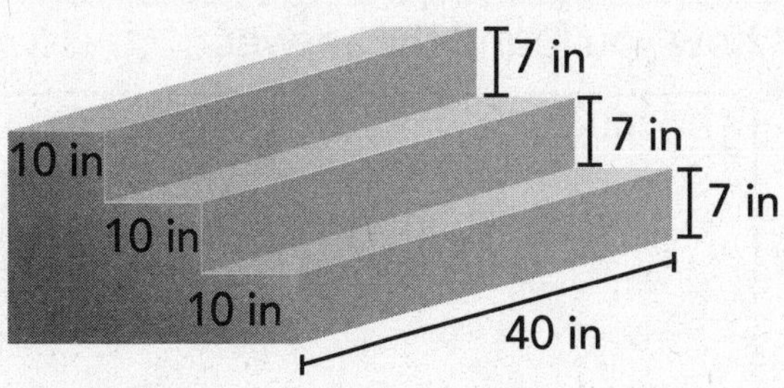

*For another example, see Set C on page 626.

Math Practices and Problem Solving

8. A floor plan of Angelica's bedroom and closet is shown at the right. The height of the bedroom is 9 feet. The height of the closet is 7 feet. What is the total volume of the bedroom and the closet?

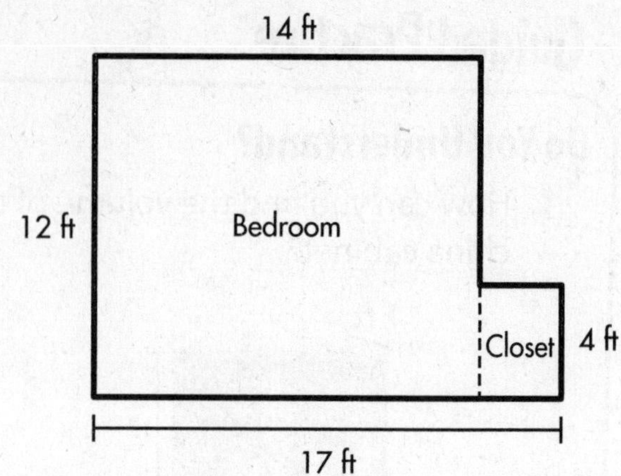

9. **MP.3 Critique Reasoning** Does it make sense for Angelica to find the combined area of the bedroom floor and closet before finding the total volume? Explain your thinking.

10. **Higher Order Thinking** An office building surrounds a rectangular open-air courtyard. What is the volume of the building? How did you find the answer?

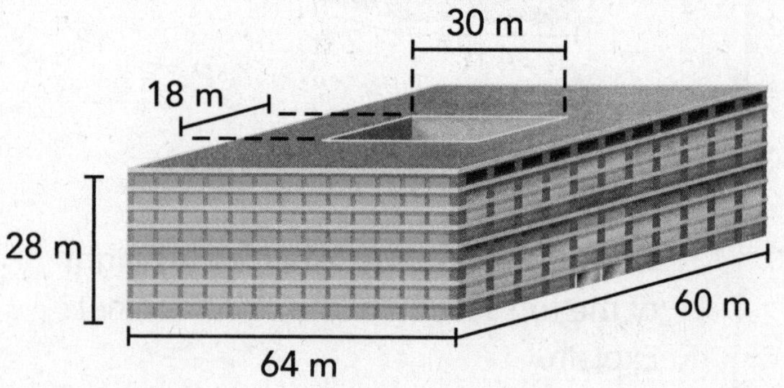

Common Core Assessment

11. Mrs. Bhatia's closet consists of two sections, each shaped like a rectangular prism. She plans to buy mothballs to keep the moths away. She needs one box for every 32 cubic feet of space. How many boxes should she buy? Explain how you found the answer.

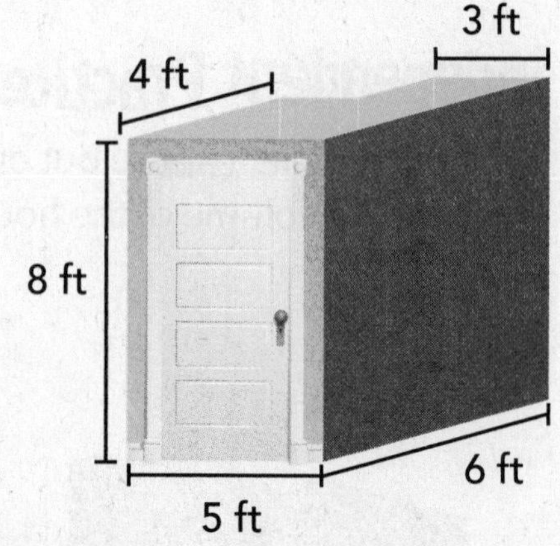

Name

Homework & Practice 10-5

Solve Word Problems Using Volume

Another Look!

The shape of a swimming pool is a rectangular prism. The pool is 9 meters long and 4 meters wide. It holds 108 cubic meters of water. How deep is the pool if the entire pool is the same depth?

Use the volume formula.

$V = \ell \times w \times h$
$108 = 4 \times 9 \times h$
$108 = 36 \times h$

Divide to find the answer.

$108 \div 36 = 3$

The swimming pool is 3 meters deep.

Think about the operation that can help you find a missing factor.

1. A garage is shaped like a rectangular prism. What is the volume of the garage? Show your work.

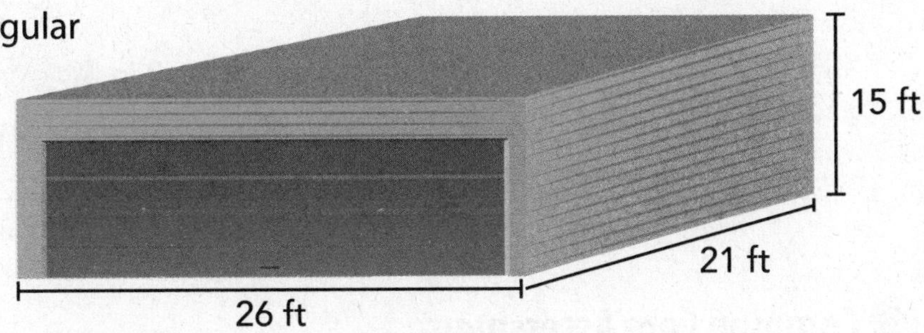

2. Nabeel's sand box is 7 feet wide, 5 feet long and 2 feet deep. What is the volume of the sand box?

3. A box of oat cereal measures 24 centimeters long by 5 centimeters wide by 25 centimeters high. A box of rice cereal measures 26 centimeters long by 4 centimeters wide by 28 centimeters high. Which box has the greater volume? How much greater?

4. Marin has a jewelry box with a volume of 440 cubic inches. The box is 5 inches high and 11 inches long. What is the width of the box?

5. Walter is building a storage shed shaped like a rectangular prism. It will be 7 feet high and 8 feet long. How wide should it be if Walter wants 280 cubic feet of storage space?

6. **MP.8 Generalize** Use multiplication to describe the relationship between the dividend, the divisor, and the quotient. Then use that relationship to show that $\frac{1}{8} \div 6 = \frac{1}{48}$.

7. **Higher Order Thinking** Otis is packing two gift boxes in a shipping carton. The rest of the space in the carton will be filled with packing pellets. What is the volume of the space that needs to be filled with packing pellets? Explain how you found your answer.

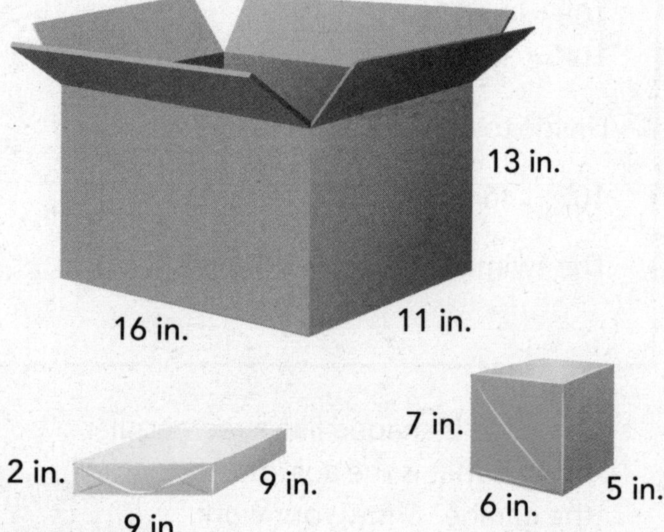

Common Core Assessment

8. Marie built a sand castle that is made of two rectangular prisms. If there are 2,000 cubic inches of sand in a bag of sand, how much sand was left after Marie built her sand castle? Explain how you found your answer.

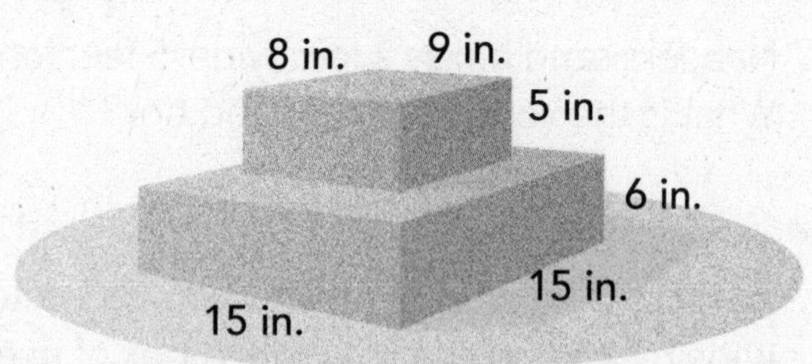

Name ______________________

Solve & Share

A space station is being built from 24 cubic modules. The space station can be any shape but the modules must be placed together so that entire faces match up with each other. Choose a tool to create two different plans for the space station. Explain why you chose the tool you selected.

Math Practices and Problem Solving

Lesson 10-6

Use Appropriate Tools

I can ...

use appropriate tools to solve volume problems.

Mathematical Practices MP.5 Also MP.1, MP.2, MP.3, MP.4, MP.7
Content Standards 5.MD.C.3a, 5.MD.C.3b, 5.MD.C.4

Thinking Habits

Be a good thinker! These questions can help you.

- Which tools can I use?
- Why should I use this tool to help me solve the problem?
- Is there a different tool I could use?
- Am I using the tool appropriately?

Look Back! **MP. 5 Use Appropriate Tools** How did you decide which tool to use?

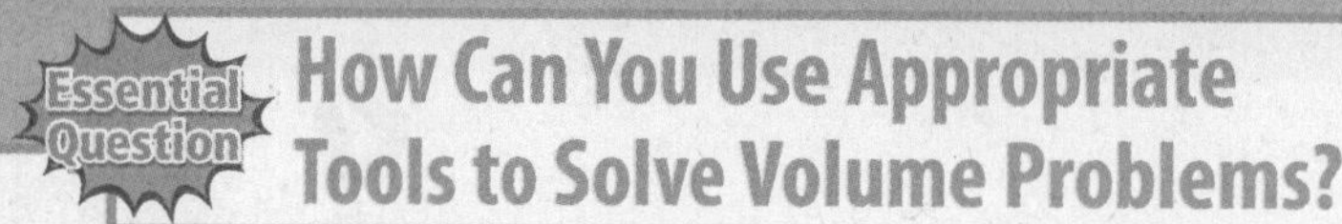

How Can You Use Appropriate Tools to Solve Volume Problems?

A

Jeremiah needs to build a display of boxes that is 4 feet tall.

The boxes he uses are cubes that measure 1 foot on each edge. His display needs to look like a pyramid, with just one box in the top layer.

How many boxes will Jeremiah need to make his display?

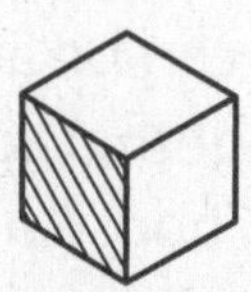

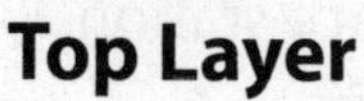

What do I need to do?

I need to choose an appropriate tool to solve this problem.

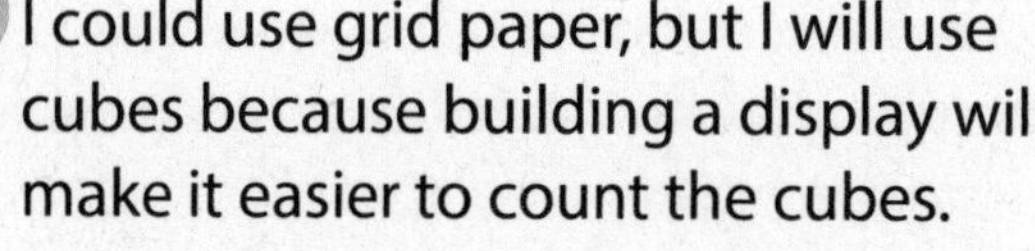

B

How can I use appropriate tools strategically to help me solve this problem?

I can

- decide which tool is appropriate.
- use cubes to solve this problem.
- use the tool correctly.

C

I could use grid paper, but I will use cubes because building a display will make it easier to count the cubes.

Each cube represents 1 box in the display. My display will have 4 layers because it needs to be 4 feet tall, and each box is 1 foot high.

The display has $1 + 4 + 9 + 16 = 30$ cubes.

So, Jeremiah needs 30 boxes in all to make his display.

Convince Me! **MP.5 Use Appropriate Tools** What tools other than cubes could you use to solve this problem? Explain.

Name ______________________________

Guided Practice*

MP.5 Use Appropriate Tools

A paint store manager is going to build a display with same-sized cubes. The display will look like a staircase with 5 steps. Each step in the display will be 6 cubes long. The store manager needs to know the total number of cubes he will need to build the display.

1. What tool might the manager use to be sure that there is enough space for the display? Explain.

2. The store manager will build the staircase display with 1-foot plastic cubes. What is the volume of the display? Explain how you used tools to decide.

Independent Practice

MP.5 Use Appropriate Tools

Cindy plans to make a jewelry box shaped like a rectangular prism. She wants it to have a volume of 96 cubic inches.

Think about a tool you can use to help represent and solve the problem.

3. How can you find possible dimensions of the box?

4. What could the dimensions of that jewelry box be?

5. Can Cindy build the box so that it is twice as wide as it is tall?

6. Cindy has some ribbon to decorate the jewelry box. What tool might help her decide how much of the jewelry box she can decorate?

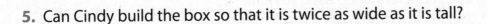

*For another example, see Set D on page 626.

Math Practices and Problem Solving

Common Core Performance Assessment

Flower Planters

An architect is designing flower planters for a park. Each planter consists of a border of 1-foot concrete cubes surrounding a square opening. Each concrete cube weighs 120 pounds. The diagram below shows the top view of some of the planters.

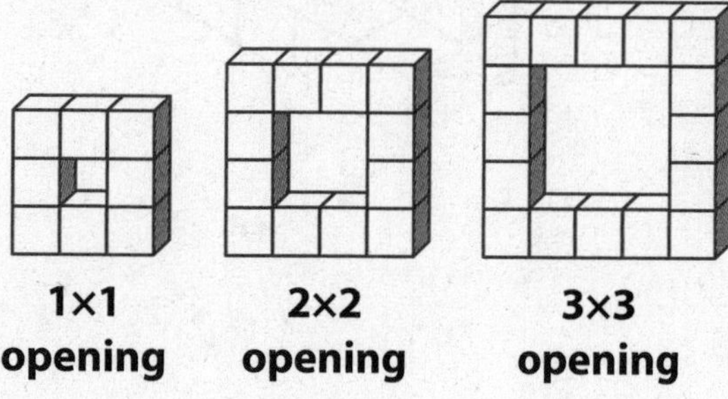

Remember to think about which tools make sense for these problems.

7. **MP.7 Use Structure** What is the total volume of a planter that has a 6 × 6 opening?

8. **MP.7 Use Structure** What is the total volume of a planter that has an 8 × 8 opening?

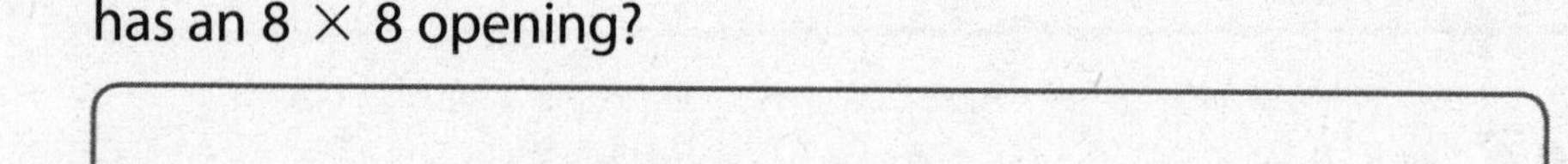

9. **MP.5 Use Appropriate Tools** What will be the total volume of a planter that has a 12 × 12 opening? Can you determine this by just using paper and pencil? Explain.

10. **MP.4 Model with Math** Each concrete cube used to make the planters costs $3.00. What is the total cost of the cubes needed for two planters with 6 × 6 openings, two with 8 × 8 openings, and two with 12 × 12 openings? Write an expression that represents the total cost.

Name ______________________

Homework & Practice 10-6

Use Appropriate Tools

Another Look!

Francine is designing a small birdhouse shaped like a rectangular prism. It needs to have a volume of 120 cubic inches. She wants the height to be 10 inches. What could the length and width of the floor be?

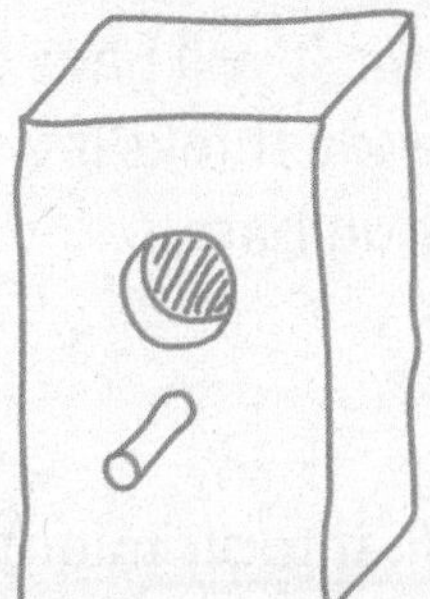

10 in.

One Way

Build a model with cubes. Since the volume is 120 cubic inches, use 120 cubes.

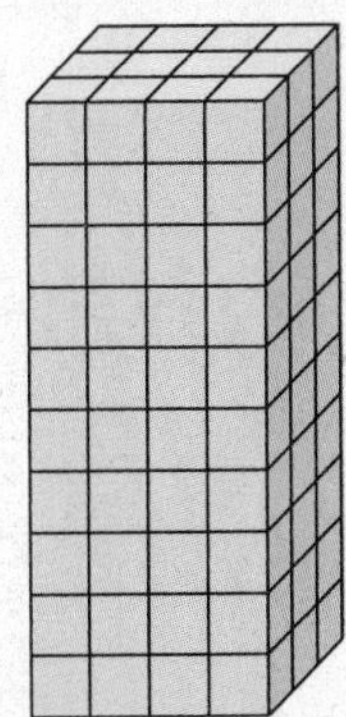

So, one possibility is that the length is 4 inches and the width is 3 inches.

Another Way

Use grid paper to design the floor.

The height is 10 inches, so the area of the floor is $120 \div 10 = 12$. Use grid paper to draw some possible floors with an area of 12 square inches.

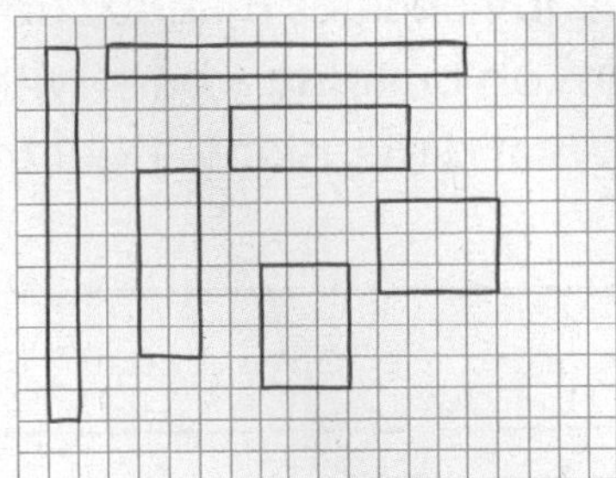

One possibility is that the length is 4 inches and the width is 3 inches.

MP.5 Use Appropriate Tools

An architect is designing different vacation cottages that are shaped like rectangular prisms that are side-by-side.

Sometimes there is more than one tool that can help you solve problems.

1. The height of one cottage will be 3 meters, and the volume will be 108 cubic meters. What tool can help you find different dimensions for the floor? Give two different possible pairs of dimensions for the floor. Explain.

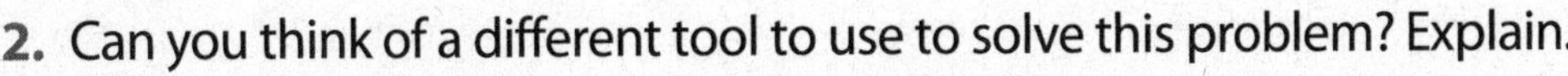

2. Can you think of a different tool to use to solve this problem? Explain.

Ⓒ Common Core Performance Assessment

Making a Bug Barn

Wendy is going to use screening and wood to make a bug barn for her little sister. It will have the shape of a rectangular prism. Wendy thinks it will take about 2 hours to make the bug barn.

3. **MP.5 Use Appropriate Tools** What tools might Wendy use?

4. **MP.2 Reasoning** Wendy wants the volume to be 80 cubic inches. What dimensions could the bug barn have?

5. **MP. 2 Reasoning** Wendy decides that 80 cubic inches is too small. So she plans on building a barn with a volume of 108 cubic inches. What dimensions could this bug barn have?

6. **MP.1 Make Sense and Persevere** Wendy searches the Internet and finds a bug barn that is 7 inches long, 4 inches wide, and 3 inches tall. If she wants to build a bug barn with volume greater than this, would either of the above barns work? Explain.

7. **MP.3 Critique Reasoning** Wendy thinks that if she doubles all of the dimensions of a bug barn, its volume will also double. Do you agree? Use one of the above bug barns to show your work.

Name ____________________

TOPIC 10

Fluency Practice Activity

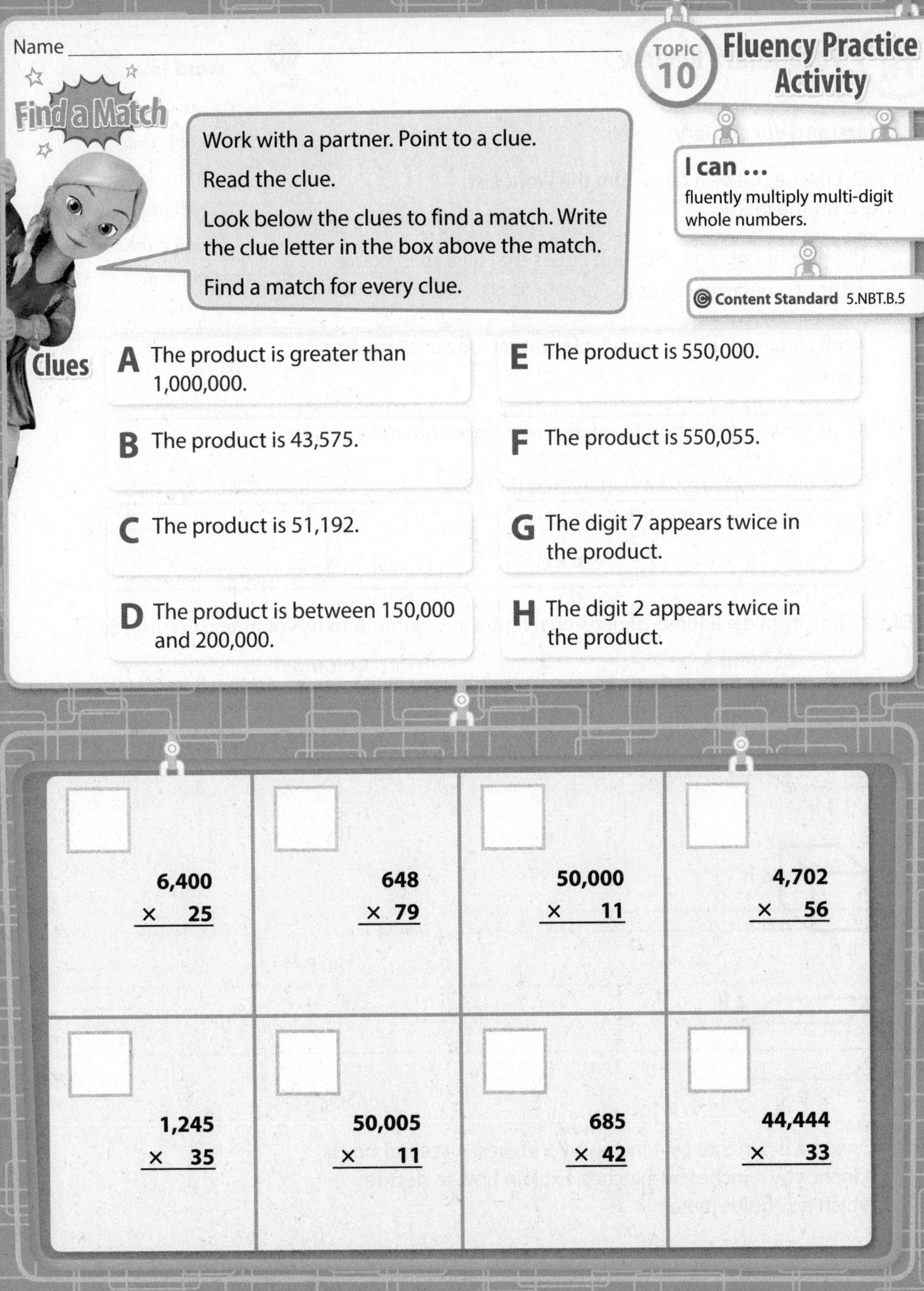

Work with a partner. Point to a clue.

Read the clue.

Look below the clues to find a match. Write the clue letter in the box above the match.

Find a match for every clue.

I can ...
fluently multiply multi-digit whole numbers.

Content Standard 5.NBT.B.5

Clues

A The product is greater than 1,000,000.

B The product is 43,575.

C The product is 51,192.

D The product is between 150,000 and 200,000.

E The product is 550,000.

F The product is 550,055.

G The digit 7 appears twice in the product.

H The digit 2 appears twice in the product.

☐ $6{,}400 \times 25$	☐ 648×79	☐ $50{,}000 \times 11$	☐ $4{,}702 \times 56$
☐ $1{,}245 \times 35$	☐ $50{,}005 \times 11$	☐ 685×42	☐ $44{,}444 \times 33$

TOPIC 10

Vocabulary Review

Word List

- area
- cubic unit
- formula
- rectangular prism
- unit cube
- volume

Understand Vocabulary

In **1–3**, choose the best term from the Word List. Write it on the blank.

1. The number of same-size unit cubes that fill a solid figure without overlaps or gaps is ______.

2. A solid figure with 6 rectangular faces that are not all squares is a(n) ______________.

3. A rule that uses symbols to relate two or more quantities is a(n) ______.

4. Cross out the expressions below that do NOT represent the volume of the prism.

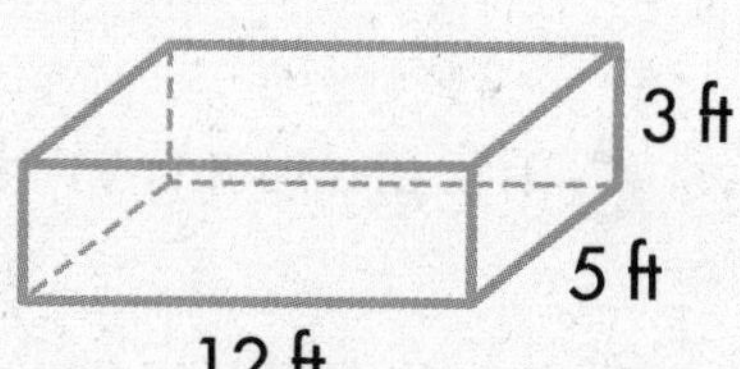

36×5 $\quad 3 \times 5 \times 12$ $\quad 60 \times 3$ $\quad 12 \times (3 + 5)$

Draw a line from each three-dimensional figure in Column A to its volume in Column B.

Column A	Column B
5. 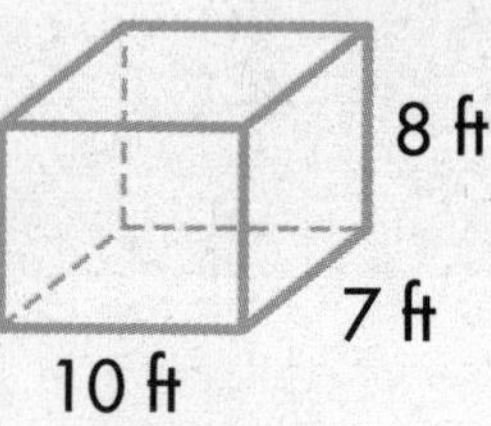	64 ft^3
6. 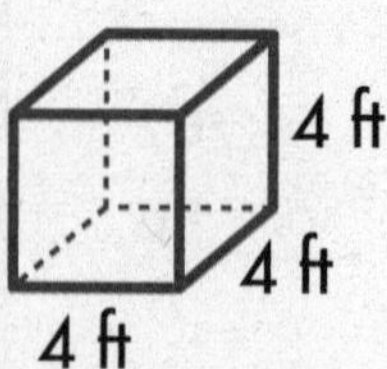	100 ft^3
7. 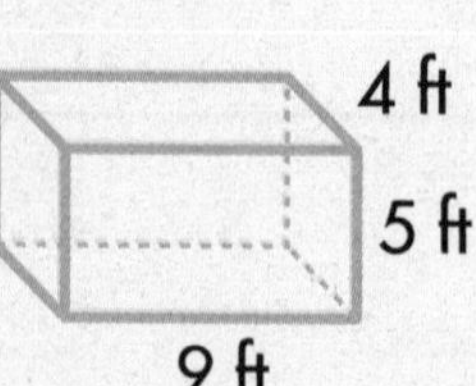	180 ft^3
	560 ft^3

8. One box is 3 inches by 4 inches by 5 inches. A second box is 4 inches by 4 inches by 4 inches. Explain how to decide which box holds more.

Name ______________________________

TOPIC 10

Reteaching

Set A pages 587–592

Find the number of cubes needed to make this rectangular prism.

There are 3 rows of 5 cubes in the bottom layer.
There are 3 layers.

Multiply to find the total number of cubes.

$3 \times 5 \times 3 = 45$

The volume is 45 cubic units.

Remember, you can multiply the numbers in any order!

Remember that you can find the number of cubes in each layer and then multiply by the number of layers.

Find each volume. You may use cubes to help.

1.

2.

3.

Set B pages 593–598, 599–604

Find the volume of this rectangular prism.

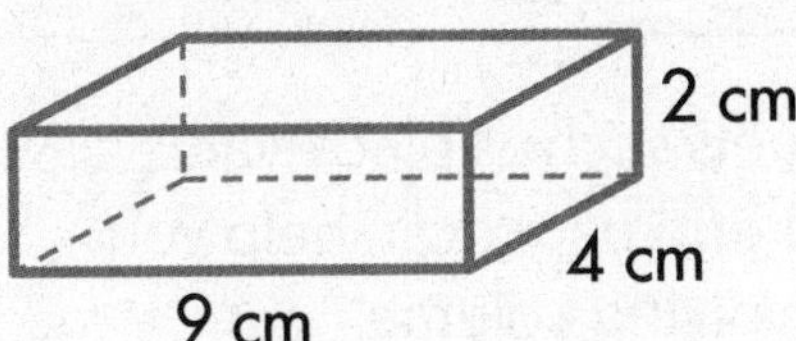

Volume = length × width × height

$V = \ell \times w \times h$
$= 9 \text{ cm} \times 4 \text{ cm} \times 2 \text{ cm}$
$V = 72$ cubic centimeters or 72 cm^3

The volume of the prism is 72 cm^3.

Remember if you know the area of the base of a rectangular prism, use the formula $V = B \times h$, where B is the area of the base.

Find each volume. You may use cubes to help.

1. Area of the base, $B = 42$ square meters and height = 3 meters

2. Area of the base = 75 square inches and height is 15 inches

3.

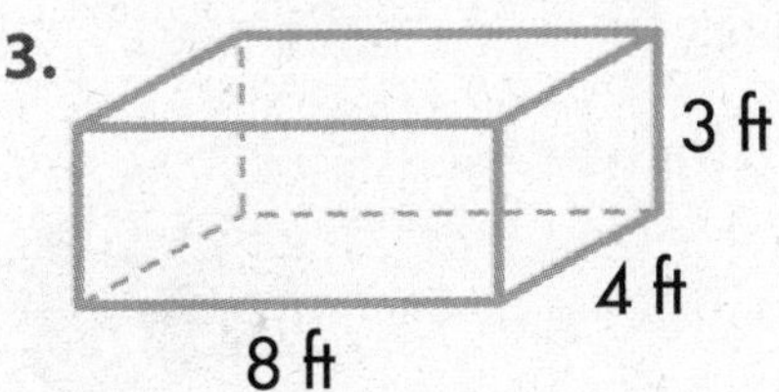

Set C pages 605–610, 611–616

Some solid figures can be separated into two rectangular prisms.

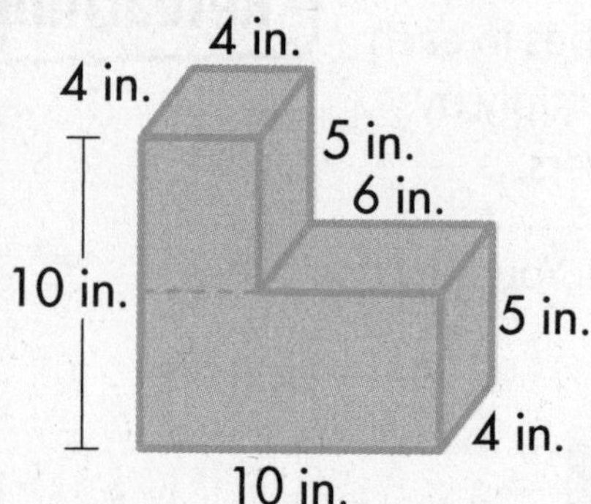

Add the volume of each prism to find the total volume of the solid figure.

$V = (4 \times 4 \times 5) + (10 \times 4 \times 5)$
$= 80 + 200$
$= 280$

The volume of the solid figure is 280 cubic inches.

Remember to identify the length, width, and height of each prism, so that you can calculate the volume of each part.

1. Find the volume.

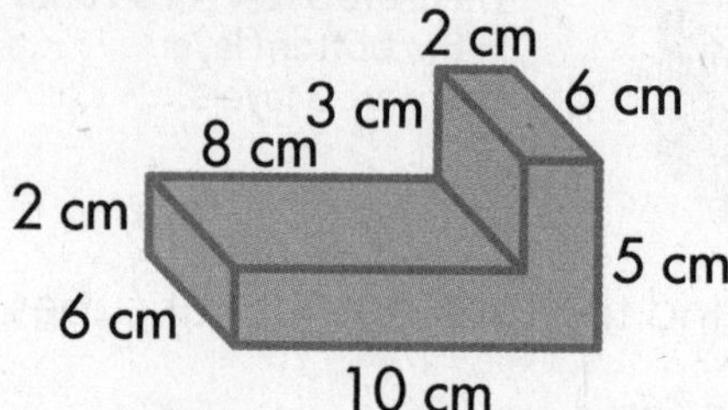

An office building has the dimensions shown. What is the volume of the building?

2. 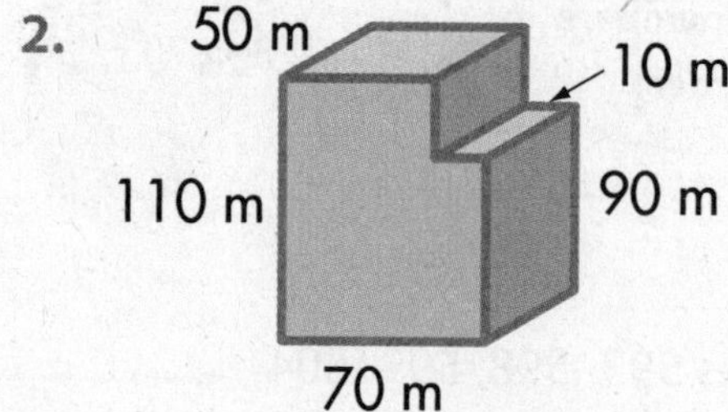

Set D pages 617–622

Think about these questions to help you **use appropriate tools strategically.**

Thinking Habits

- Which tools can I use?
- Why should I use this tool to help me solve the problem?
- Is there a different tool I could use?
- Am I using the tool appropriately?

Remember that tools such as place-value blocks, cubes, and grid paper can help you solve problems involving volume.

Molly used 1-inch cubes to build the structure shown. She left a 3-inch by 1-inch opening in both layers of the structure.

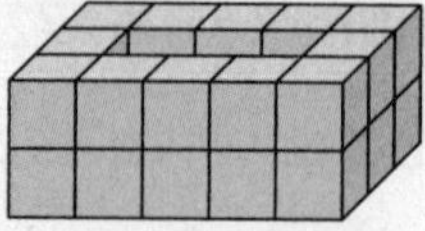

1. What tools could you use to model the problem?

2. What is the total volume of the structure?

Name ______________________________

1. Julio used unit cubes to make a rectangular prism. What is the volume of the prism?

Ⓐ 18 cubic units
Ⓑ 54 cubic units
Ⓒ 72 cubic units
Ⓓ 108 cubic units

---

2. Draw lines to match the volume of a prism on the left with its possible dimensions on the right.

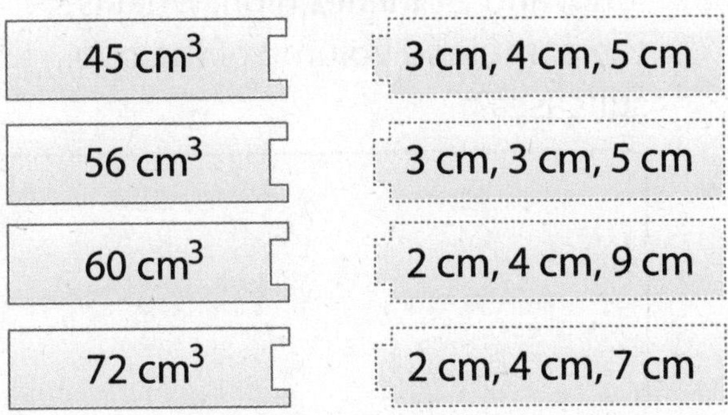

---

3. A swimming pool is 50 meters long, 15 meters wide, and 3 meters deep. What is the volume of the pool?

Ⓐ 4,500 cubic meters
Ⓑ 2,250 cubic meters
Ⓒ 900 cubic meters
Ⓓ 750 cubic meters

4. A small building has the dimensions shown.

Part A

Write an expression for the total volume of the building.

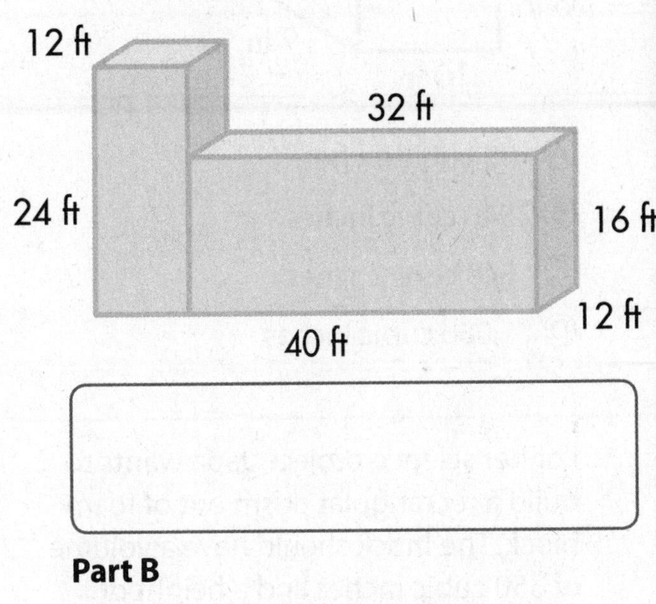

Part B

What is the volume of the building?

---

5. Choose all the expressions that could **NOT** be used to find the volume of the bale of hay.

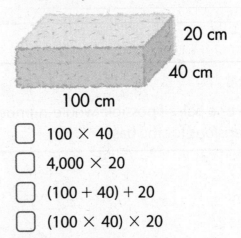

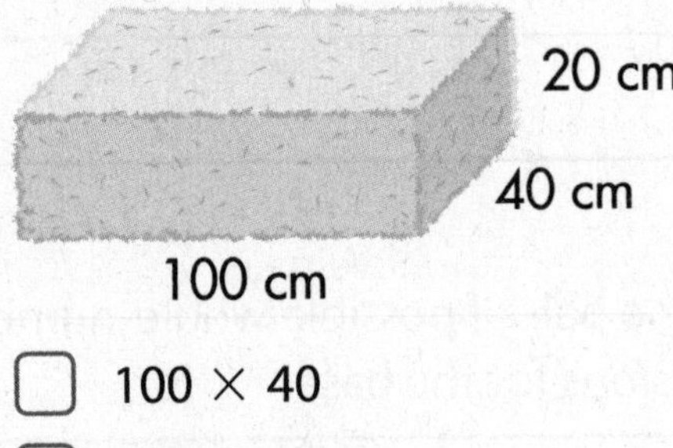

- ☐ 100×40
- ☐ $4{,}000 \times 20$
- ☐ $(100 + 40) + 20$
- ☐ $(100 \times 40) \times 20$
- ☐ $(100 \times 40) + 20$

6. Madeline made the wooden steps shown. What is the volume of the steps?

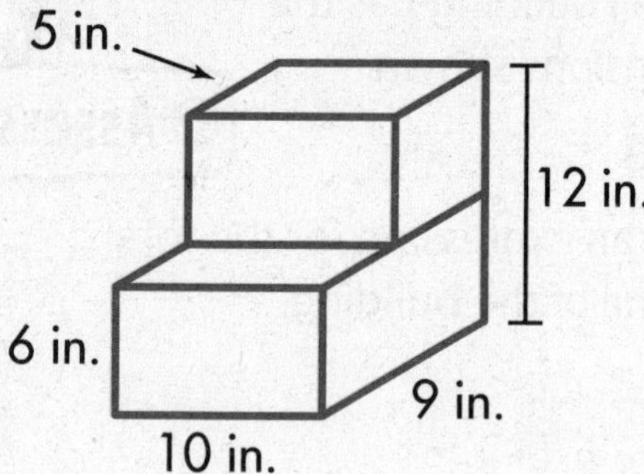

Ⓐ 72 cubic inches

Ⓑ 540 cubic inches

Ⓒ 840 cubic inches

Ⓓ 1,080 cubic inches

---

7. For her science project, Jada wants to build a rectangular prism out of foam block. The block should have a volume of 350 cubic inches and a height of 5 inches.

Part A

What tool can help Jada find possible dimensions for the base of the block? Explain.

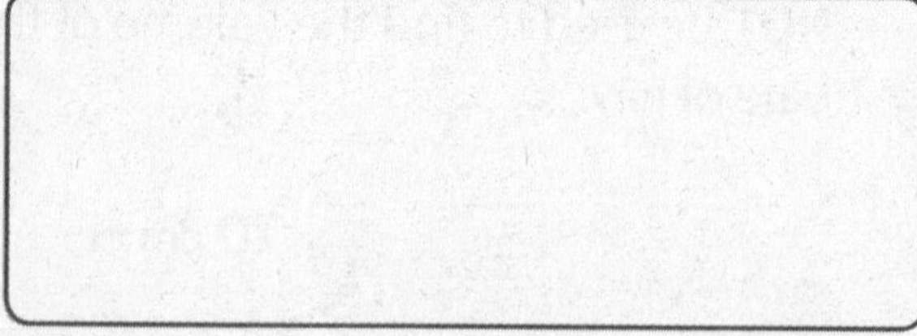

Part B

Give one pair of possible whole-number dimensions for the base.

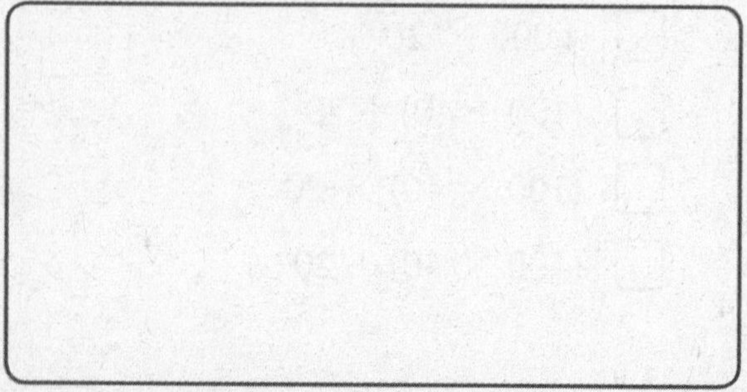

8. What is the volume of the trunk shown?

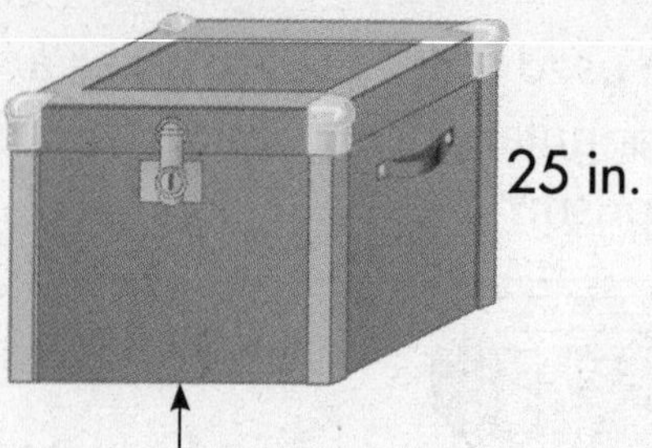

Area of base: 750 in^2

---

9. Martin's suitcase has a volume of 1,080 cubic inches. Lily's suitcase measures 9 inches wide, 13 inches long, and 21 inches high. What is the combined volume of the two suitcases?

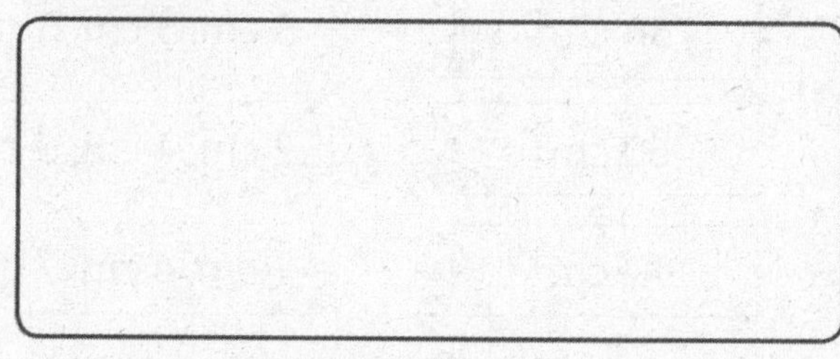

---

10. For questions 10a–10d, choose Yes or No. Can the expression be used to find the volume of the box in cubic centimeters?

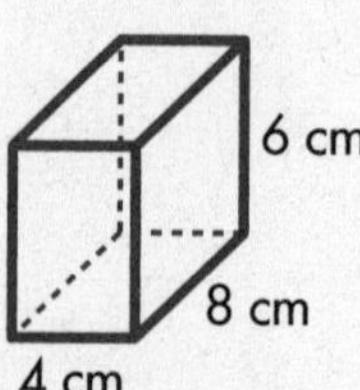

10a. 8×6 ○ Yes ○ No

10b. 32×6 ○ Yes ○ No

10c. $(4 \times 8) + 6$ ○ Yes ○ No

10d. $(4 \times 8) \times 6$ ○ Yes ○ No

Name ______________________________

Sporting Goods

Hiroto works in a sporting goods store.

1. Hiroto stacks identical boxes of golf balls to form a rectangular prism. Each box is a cube.

Golf Ball Display

Part A

How many boxes are in the **Golf Ball Display**?

Part B

Explain how the number of boxes you found in Part A is the same as what you would find by using the formula $V = \ell \times w \times h$.

Part C

Hiroto needs to restack the boxes so the display is 2 layers high, less than 14 inches wide, and less than 30 inches long. The size of each box is shown in at the right. What is one way Hiroto can stack the boxes? Justify your answer.

2 in.

2 in.

2 in.

Part D

What is the volume of the golf ball display in cubic inches? Explain how you solved.

2. Hiroto builds two displays using rectangular foam blocks.

Part A

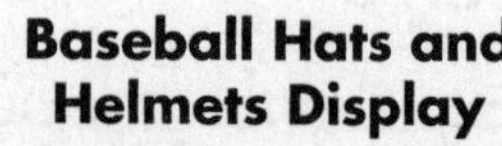

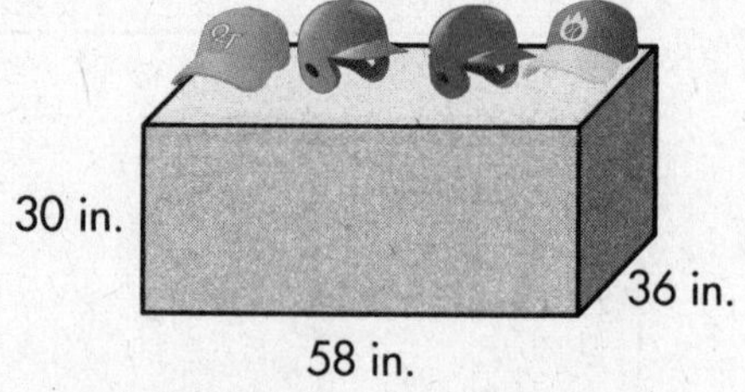

What is the volume of the foam block used for the **Baseball Hats and Helmets Display**? Explain how to solve using the formula $V = B \times h$.

Part B

Hiroto used two blocks to build the **Baseball Uniforms Display**. What is the combined volume of the blocks? Explain how you solved.

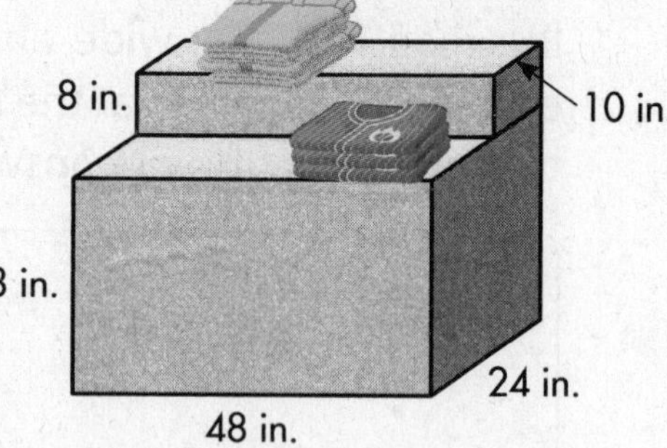

Part C

Explain how you knew which units to use for your answer to Part B.

Convert Measurements

Essential Questions: What are customary measurement units and how are they related? What are metric measurement units and how are they related?

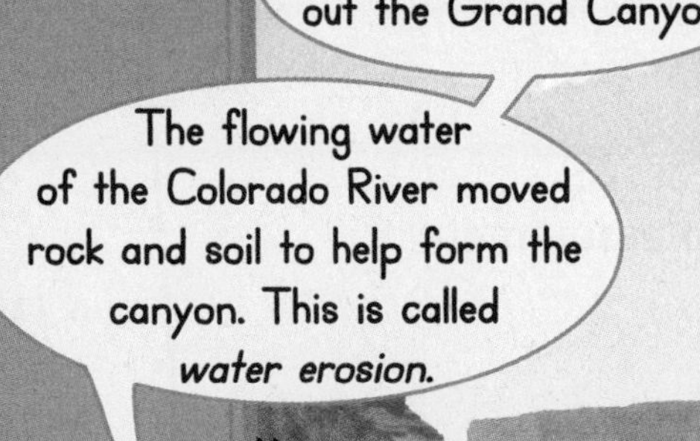

Wind and water carved out the Grand Canyon.
The flowing water of the Colorado River moved rock and soil to help form the canyon. This is called *water erosion.*
That's a lot of movement! Here's a project about the Grand Canyon.

Math and Science Project: Grand Canyon

Do Research Use the Internet and other sources to learn about the Grand Canyon and the Colorado River. Where is the Grand Canyon? How was it formed? What do the different rock layers tell us? Predict how you think the canyon dimensions will change in a million years.

Journal: Write a Report Include what you found. Also in your report:

- Describe the canyon's dimensions.
- Describe the Colorado River's dimensions.
- Define erosion.
- Make up and solve problems involving measurement units and conversions.

Name ______________________________

Review What You Know

Vocabulary

Choose the best term from the box. Write it on the blank.

- customary
- multiplication
- exponent
- subtraction
- metric

1. A meter is a unit of length in the ________ system of measurement.
2. A foot is a unit of length in the ________ system of measurement.
3. Division has an inverse relationship with ________.
4. A(n) ________ shows the number of times a base is used as a factor.

Multiplication

Find each product.

5. 60×6
6. 24×10^3
7. 16×7
8. $10^2 \times 1.6$
9. 100×34
10. $10^4 \times 0.37$
11. 46.102×10^2
12. $10^1 \times 0.005$

Division

Find each quotient.

13. $1{,}000 \div 100$
14. $176 \div 16$
15. $3{,}600 \div 60$
16. $120 \div 24$

Measurement

Circle the more appropriate unit of measure for each item.

17. The capacity of a swimming pool: liters or milliliters
18. The length of an ear of corn: yards or inches
19. The mass of a gorilla: grams or kilograms
20. The weight of a tennis ball: ounces or pounds
21. Would you use more centimeters or meters to measure the length of car? Explain.

My Word Cards

Use the examples for each word on the front of the card to help complete the definitions on the back.

A-Z Glossary

12 inches (in.) = 1 foot

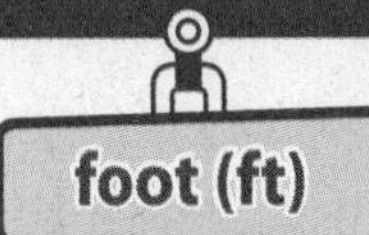

1 foot (ft) = 12 inches

1 yard (yd) = 3 ft = 36 in.

1 mile (mi) = 1,760 yd = 5,280 ft

Cups, fluid ounces, pints, quarts, and gallons are all customary units of capacity.

1 cup (c) = 8 fluid ounces

8 fluid ounces (fl oz) = 1 cup

1 pint (pt) = 2 cups

My Word Cards

Complete the definition. Extend learning by writing your own definitions.

A customary unit of length equal to 12 inches is a ________.

A customary unit of length less than 1 foot is an ________.

A customary unit of length equal to 5,280 feet is a ________.

A customary unit of length equal to 3 feet is a ________.

A customary unit of capacity equal to 8 fluid ounces is a ________.

____________ is the volume of a container measured in liquid units.

A customary unit of capacity equal to 2 cups is a ________.

A customary unit of capacity equal to 8 ________________ is a cup.

Use the examples for each word on the front of the card to help complete the definitions on the back.

1 quart (qt) = 2 pints

1 gallon (gal) = 4 quarts

The weight of the peach is 7 ounces.

1 ton (T) = 2,000 pounds

1 pound (lb) = 16 ounces

16 ounces (oz) = 1 pound

1 kilometer (km) = 1,000 meters

1 meter (m) = 100 centimeters

My Word Cards

Complete the definition. Extend learning by writing your own definitions.

A customary unit of capacity equal to 4 quarts is a ________________.

A customary unit of capacity equal to 2 pints is a __________.

A customary unit of weight equal to 2,000 pounds is a _________.

____________ is a measure of how light or heavy something is.

A customary unit of weight less than 1 pound is an __________.

A customary unit of weight equal to 16 ounces is a ____________.

A metric unit of length equal to 100 centimeters is a _________.

A metric unit of length equal to 1,000 meters is a ________________.

A-Z Glossary

My Word Cards

Use the examples for each word on the front of the card to help complete the definitions on the back.

centimeter (cm)

1 centimeter (cm) = 10 millimeters

millimeter (mm)

1,000 millimeters (mm) = 1 meter

liter (L)

1 liter (L) = 1,000 milliliters

milliliter (mL)

1,000 milliliters (mL) = 1 liter

mass

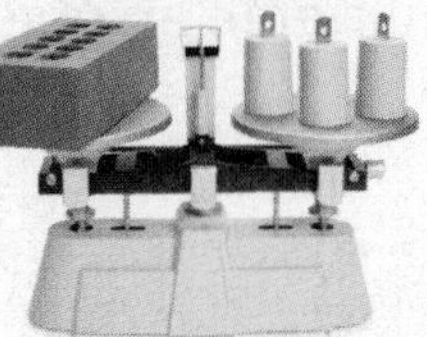

The brick has a mass of 3 kilograms.

milligram (mg)

1,000 milligrams (mg) = 1 gram

gram (g)

1 gram (g) = 1,000 milligrams

kilogram

1 kilogram (kg) = 1,000 grams

My Word Cards

Complete the definition. Extend learning by writing your own definitions.

A metric unit of length less than a centimeter is a ________________.

A metric unit of length equal to 10 millimeters is a ________________.

A metric unit of capacity less than a liter is a ______________.

A metric unit of capacity equal to 1,000 milliliters is a __________.

A metric unit of mass less than a gram is a ________________.

____________ is the measure of the amount of matter in an object.

A metric unit of mass equal to 1,000 grams is a _______________.

A metric unit of mass equal to 1,000 milligrams is a __________.

Name ______________________

Lesson 11-1
Convert Customary Units of Length

I can ...
convert customary units of length.

Content Standards 5.MD.A.1, 5.NBT.B.5, 5.NBT.B.6
Mathematical Practices MP.2, MP.4, MP.6, MP.8

Solve & Share

William has a piece of wire that measures 1 yard long. He will use wire to fix several electrical outlets in his house. How many inches long is the wire? ***Solve this problem by using bar diagrams.***

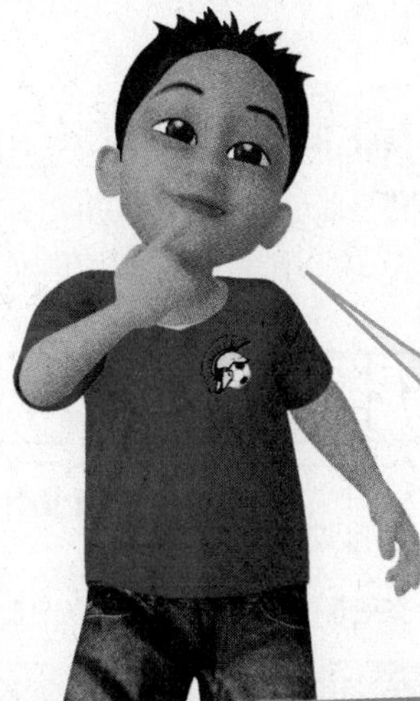

Model with Math
You can show the relationship between yards and inches in a bar diagram. *Show your work!*

Look Back! **MP.8 Generalize** How can you convert inches to yards? Would you multiply or divide when converting from a smaller unit to a larger unit? Explain.

How Do You Change from One Unit of Length to Another?

A

Some frogs can jump $11\frac{1}{4}$ feet. What are some other ways to describe the same distance?

1 foot (ft) = 12 inches (in.)
1 yard (yd) = 3 ft = 36 in.
1 mile (mi) = 1,760 yd = 5,280 ft

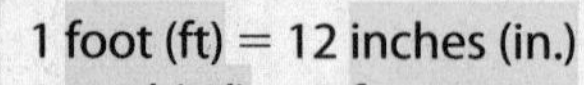

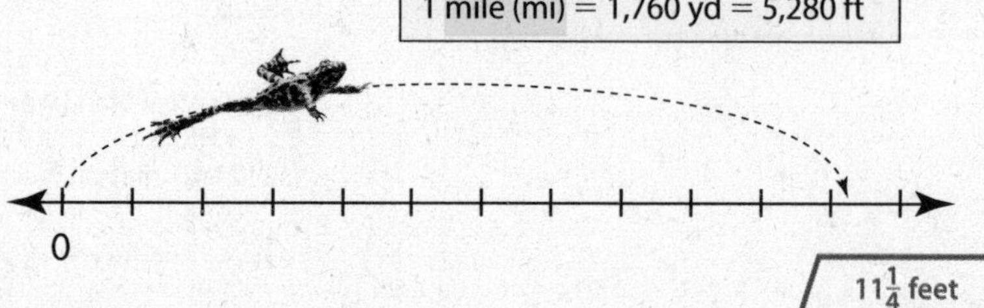

B **To change larger units to smaller units, multiply.**

$11\frac{1}{4}$ ft = ☐ in.

You know 1 foot equals 12 inches.

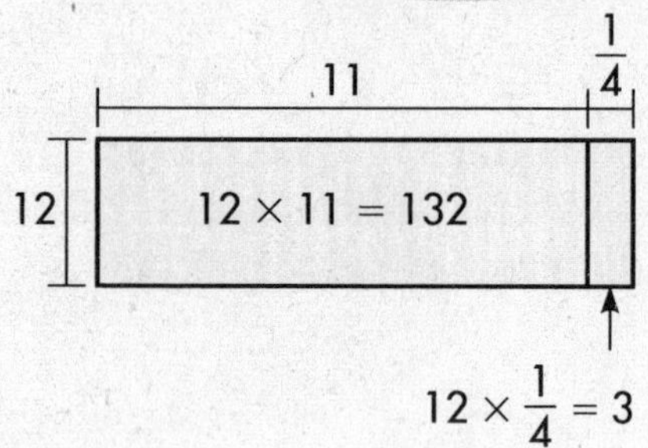

$11\frac{1}{4} \times 12 = 132 + 3 = 135$

So, $11\frac{1}{4}$ feet = 135 inches.

C **To change smaller units to larger units, divide.**

Ed's frog jumped 11 feet. How many yards is this?

11 ft = ☐ yd ☐ ft

You know 3 feet is equal to 1 yard.

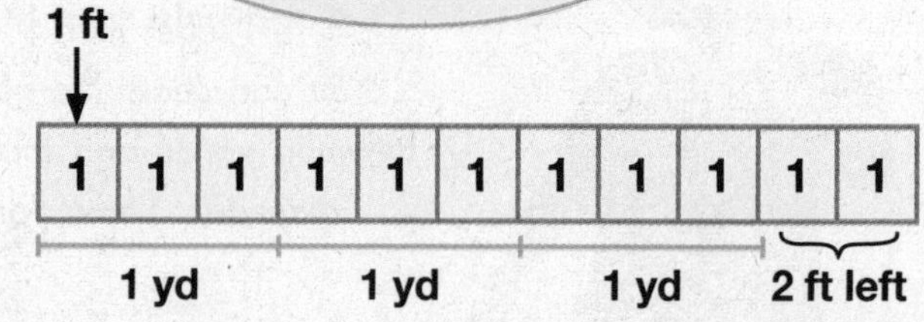

$11 \div 3 = 3$ R2 So, 11 feet = 3 yards, 2 feet.

Convince Me! **MP.8 Generalize** In the example above, explain how you could use a mixed number to write 11 feet as an equivalent measure in yards.

Name ______

Practice Buddy Tools Assessment

Guided Practice*

Do You Understand?

1. If you want to convert yards to feet, what operation would you use?

2. If you want to convert feet to miles, what operation would you use?

3. What are some tools you could select to measure length? Explain when you would use them.

Do You Know How?

In **4–8**, convert each unit of length.

4. 9 ft = ____ yd

5. 8 ft 7 in. = ____ in.

6. $5\frac{1}{2}$ ft = ____ in.

7. 288 in. = ____ yd

8. 219 in. = ____ ft ____ in. or ____ ft

Independent Practice

In **9** and **10**, complete the table to show equivalent measures.

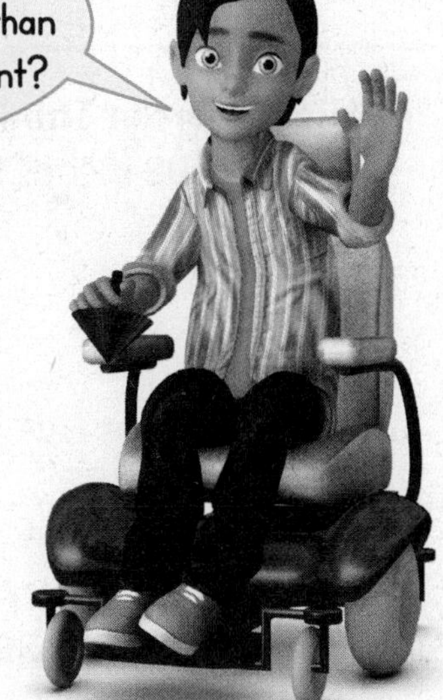

Will your answer be greater than or less than the given measurement?

9.

Feet	Inches
1	
2	
	36
4	

10.

Yards	Feet
1	
	6
3	
4	

In **11–16**, convert each unit of length.

11. 3 yd = ____ in.

12. 324 ft = ____ yd

13. $2\frac{2}{3}$ mi = ________ ft

14. 56 ft = ____ yd ____ ft

15. $12\frac{1}{2}$ ft = ____ in.

16. 6 in. = ____ ft

In **17–19**, compare lengths. Write >, <, or = for each ◯.

17. 100 ft ◯ 3 yd

18. 74 in. ◯ 2 yd 2 in.

19. 5,200 ft 145 in. ◯ 1 mi 40 in.

*For another example, see Set A on page 689.

Math Practices and Problem Solving

20. **Number Sense** Which number would be greater, the height of a tree in feet or the height of the same tree in yards?

21. **MP.2 Reasoning** The dimensions of the nation's smallest post office are 8 feet 4 inches by 7 feet 3 inches. Why would you use the measurement 8 feet 4 inches instead of 7 feet 16 inches?

22. Roger earns $24 a week mowing lawns. He spends $\frac{1}{6}$ of his earnings on lunch and $\frac{2}{3}$ of his earnings on music. He saves the rest. How many dollars does Roger save? Tell how you found the answer.

23. Ariana has 144 peaches. She has to pack 9 boxes with an equal number of peaches. How many peaches should she pack in each box?

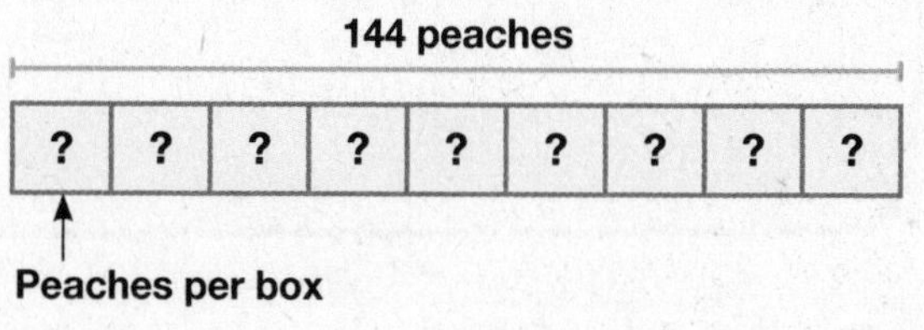

24. **Higher Order Thinking** How do you convert 108 inches to yards?

25. **Vocabulary** What is an appropriate customary unit to use when measuring the length of a driveway? Justify your answer.

Common Core Assessment

26. Is the measurement greater than 7 feet? Choose Yes or No.

2 yards	○ Yes	○ No
2 yards 2 inches	○ Yes	○ No
2 yards 2 feet	○ Yes	○ No
3 yards	○ Yes	○ No

27. Is the measurement less than 435 inches? Choose Yes or No.

37 feet	○ Yes	○ No
36 feet 2 inches	○ Yes	○ No
12 yards 3 inches	○ Yes	○ No
12 feet 3 inches	○ Yes	○ No

Name ______________________

Homework & Practice 11-1

Convert Customary Units of Length

Another Look!

Remember:
1 foot equals 12 inches.
1 yard equals 3 feet, or 36 inches.
1 mile equals 1,760 yards, or 5,280 feet.

How to change from one customary unit of length to another:

Converting from a smaller unit to a larger unit:

6 feet = ______ yards

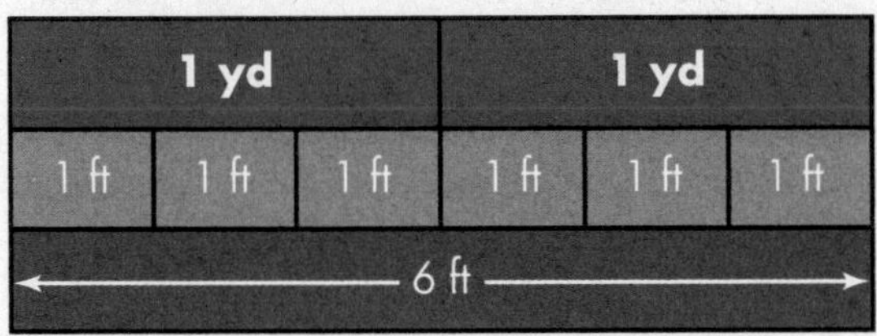

You know 3 ft = 1 yd. **Divide** 6 ÷ 3.

So, 6 ft = 2 yd.

Converting from a larger unit to a smaller unit:

2 feet = ______ inches

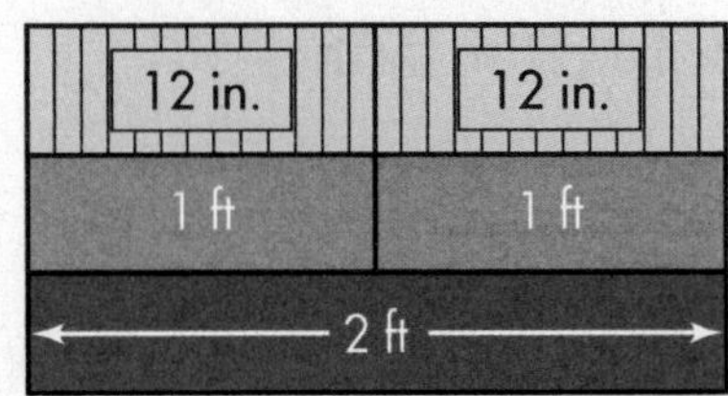

You know 1 ft = 12 in. **Multiply** 2 × 12.

So, 2 ft = 24 in.

In **1–9**, convert each unit of length.

1. 12 ft = ______ yd

2. 2 mi = ______ yd

3. 46 in. = ______ ft ______ in.

4. 7 ft = ______ in.

5. 3 mi = ______ ft

6. 108 in. = ______ ft

7. 72 in. = ______ yd

8. 2 ft 3 in. = ______ in.

9. 45 in. = ______ yd ______ in.

In **10–15**, compare lengths. Write >, <, or = for each ◯.

10. 64 in. ◯ 5 ft

11. 2 mi ◯ 3,333 yd

12. 36 yd 2 ft ◯ 114 ft 2 in.

13. 9 yd ◯ 324 in.

14. 4 ft 7 in. ◯ 56 in.

15. 25 ft ◯ 8 yd 11 in.

16. Find the perimeter of the rectangle in yards.

33 in.

75 in.

17. Lucy wants to make different types of cheesecake. Each cheesecake uses $\frac{2}{3}$ pound of cream cheese. She has 2 pounds of cream cheese. How many cheesecakes can she make?

For **18** and **19**, use the table.

18. Four friends each took a different path walking from the lunchroom to the gymnasium. The table shows the distance that each of them walked. Who walked the farthest?

19. Write the distance Domingo walked in feet and in inches.

Distance Walked

Name	Distance
Rowan	150 yd
Janelle	429 ft 8 in.
Domingo	130 yd 2 ft
Lydia	460 ft

20. **MP.6 Be Precise** Jordan is 4 feet 8 inches tall. Her mother is 5 feet 10 inches tall. How much taller is Jordan's mother than Jordan? Give your answer in feet and inches.

21. **Higher Order Thinking** How can you find the number of inches in 1 mile? Show your work.

Common Core Assessment

22. Is the measurement greater than 100 inches? Choose Yes or No.

8 feet 6 inches	○ Yes	○ No
8 feet	○ Yes	○ No
3 yards	○ Yes	○ No
2 yards 19 inches	○ Yes	○ No

23. Is the measurement less than 4 yards? Choose Yes or No.

143 inches	○ Yes	○ No
47 feet	○ Yes	○ No
12 feet	○ Yes	○ No
11 feet	○ Yes	○ No

Name ____________________

Lesson 11-2
Convert Customary Units of Capacity

I can ...
convert customary units of capacity.

Content Standards 5.MD.A.1, 5.NBT.B.5, 5.NBT.B.6
Mathematical Practices MP.2, MP.8

Solve & Share

A recipe makes 16 cups of soup. How many quarts does the recipe make? Remember, there are 2 cups in a pint and 2 pints in a quart. ***Solve this problem any way you choose!***

____ cups = 1 quart

16 cups = ____ quarts

You can use reasoning to help you convert between different units.

Look Back! **MP.8 Generalize** Is the number of cups greater than or less than the number of quarts? Why do you think that is?

Essential Question

How Do You Convert Customary Units of Capacity?

A

Sue is making punch. She needs $3\frac{3}{4}$ cups of orange juice and 5 pints of lemonade. How many fluid ounces of orange juice and how many quarts of lemonade does she need?

1 gallon (gal) = 4 quarts (qt)
1 quart = 2 pints (pt)
1 pint = 2 cups (c)
1 cup = 8 fluid ounces (fl oz)

You can multiply or divide to convert one unit of capacity to a different one.

B

To change a larger unit to a smaller unit, multiply.

$3\frac{3}{4}$ c = ☐ fl oz

$3\frac{3}{4}$ c

8 fl oz	8 fl oz	8 fl oz	6 fl oz

$3\frac{3}{4} \times 8 = (3 \times 8) + \left(\frac{3}{4} \times 8\right)$

$= 24 + 6 = 30$

So, $3\frac{3}{4}$ cups = 30 fluid ounces.

C

To change a smaller unit to a larger unit, divide.

5 pt = ☐ qt

2 pints equals 1 quart.

1 pt

1	1	1	1	1

1 qt 1 qt $\frac{1}{2}$ qt

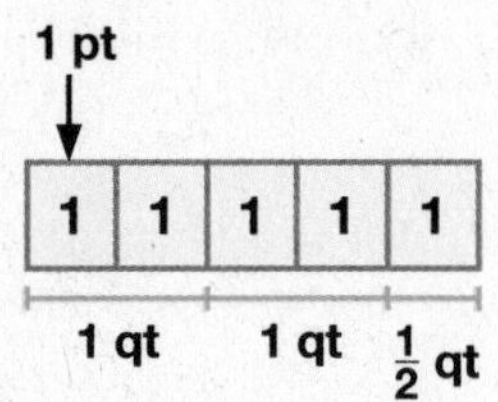

Find 5 ÷ 2.

$5 \div 2 = \frac{5}{2} = 2\frac{1}{2}$

So, 5 pints = $2\frac{1}{2}$ quarts.

Convince Me! **MP.8 Generalize** When you convert from pints to quarts, why do you divide?

Name ___

Practice Buddy | Tools | Assessment

Guided Practice*

Do You Understand?

1. MP.2 Reasoning Why would you change 4 gallons 5 quarts to 5 gallons 1 quart?

2. Why is $\frac{1}{8}$ cup equal to 1 fluid ounce?

Do You Know How?

In **3–8**, convert each unit of capacity.

3. 32 c = ___ gal
4. $\frac{1}{2}$ qt = ___ gal
5. 48 qt = ___ pt
6. $6\frac{1}{8}$ qt = ___ c
7. 3 qt 1 pt = ___ pt
8. 9 pt = ___ qt ___ pt or ___ qt

You may need to convert more than once.

Independent Practice

In **9–20**, convert each unit of capacity.

9. 10 pt = ___ qt
10. 48 fl oz = ___ c
11. $\frac{1}{2}$ c = ___ pt
12. $9\frac{1}{4}$ pt = ___ c
13. 36 pt = ___ qt
14. 30 qt = ___ gal ___ qt
15. 1 qt = ___ gal
16. 5 gal = ___ c
17. 1 gal 1 c = ___ fl oz
18. 7 c = ___ fl oz
19. 72 pt = ___ gal
20. $\frac{1}{3}$ pt = ___ c

21. Complete the table to show equivalent measures.

Gallons	Quarts	Pints	Cups	Fluid Ounces
1		8		
2				256

*For another example, see Set B on page 689.

Math Practices and Problem Solving

For **22–24**, use the aquarium.

22. The class aquarium holds 2 gallons of water. How many cups is this? How many fluid ounces is this?

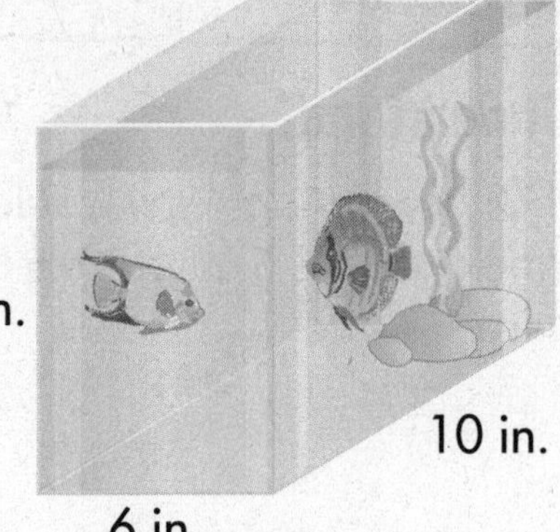

23. Susan finds that 2 pints, 1 cup of water has evaporated from the class aquarium. How many pints of water are left in the aquarium?

24. If all of the dimensions of the aquarium were doubled, what would be the volume of the new aquarium?

25. Carrie has 3 gallons of paint. Bryan has 10 quarts of paint. How many more pints of paint does Carrie have than Bryan?

26. **MP.2 Reasoning** Lorelei filled her 5-gallon jug with water. How many times could she fill her 2-quart canteen with water from the jug? Explain.

27. **Higher Order Thinking** A recipe calls for 3 tablespoons of pineapple juice. A can of pineapple juice is 12 fluid ounces. How many teaspoons of juice are in the can?

DATA
1 tablespoon (tbsp) = 3 teaspoons (tsp)
1 fluid ounce (fl oz) = 2 tablespoons (tbsp)

Common Core Assessment

28. Choose all the measurements that are greater than 4 cups.

- ☐ 30 fluid ounces
- ☐ 2 pints
- ☐ 3 pints
- ☐ 1 quart
- ☐ 1 gallon

29. Choose all the statements that are true.

- ☐ 15 pt $<$ 2 gal
- ☐ 1 gal $<$ 5 qt
- ☐ 12 fl oz $>$ 2 c
- ☐ 2 qt 1 cup $>$ 10 cups
- ☐ 20 pints $=$ 10 quarts

Name ______________________

Help Practice Buddy Tools Games

Homework & Practice 11-2

Convert Customary Units of Capacity

Another Look!

Remember:
1 gallon equals 4 quarts,
1 quart equals 2 pints,
1 pints equals 2 cups, and
1 cup equals 8 fluid ounces.

How to change from one customary unit of capacity to another:

Converting from a smaller unit to a larger unit:

4 pints = ______ quarts

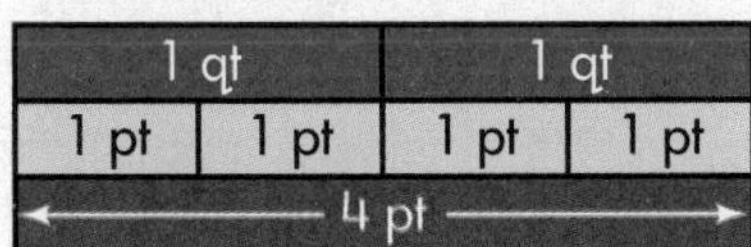

Operation: Divide.

You know 2 pt = 1 qt.

Find 4 ÷ 2; 4 pt = 2 qt

Converting from a larger unit to a smaller unit:

2 gallons = ______ quarts

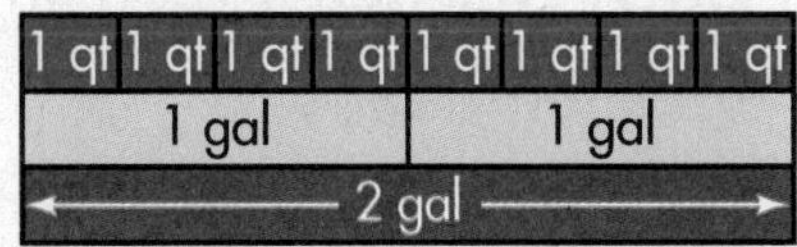

Operation: Multiply.

You know 1 gal = 4 qt.

Find 2 × 4; 2 gal = 8 qt

1. Convert 2 quarts to fluid ounces. Write in the missing amounts.

2 quarts = ____ pints ____ pints = 8 cups ____ cups = ____ fluid ounces

In **2–13**, convert each unit of capacity.

2. 14 fl oz = ______ c

3. 8 gal = ______ qt

4. $3\frac{1}{4}$ pt = ______ fl oz

5. $\frac{1}{4}$ c = ______ pt

6. $6\frac{1}{4}$ qt = ______ pt

7. 28 c = ______ qt

8. 2 qt = ______ pt

9. 5 c = ____ pt ____ c

10. 3 gal = ______ pt

11. 96 fl oz = ______ c

12. 4 qt = ______ c

13. $8\frac{1}{4}$ pt = ______ c

14. **Number Sense** Estimate the number of pints in 445 fluid ounces. Explain your work.

15. If you needed only 1 cup of milk, what is your best choice at the grocery store—a quart container, a pint container, or a $\frac{1}{2}$-gallon container?

In **16** and **17**, use the recipe.

16. Sadie is making punch. How many more quarts of lemon-lime juice will she use than orange juice?

17. **Higher Order Thinking** How many gallons of punch will Sadie make?

Ingredients for Punch

DATA

- 8 quarts lemon-lime juice
- 4 pints vanilla ice cream
- 8 cups orange juice

18. Callie bought 2 gallons of juice for \$2.58 per gallon. She sold the juice in 1-cup servings for \$0.75 each. Each serving is $\frac{1}{16}$ gallon. How much more did she get for selling the juice than she paid to buy it? Tell how you found the answer.

19. **MP.2 Reasoning** How would you convert a measurement given in fluid ounces into pints?

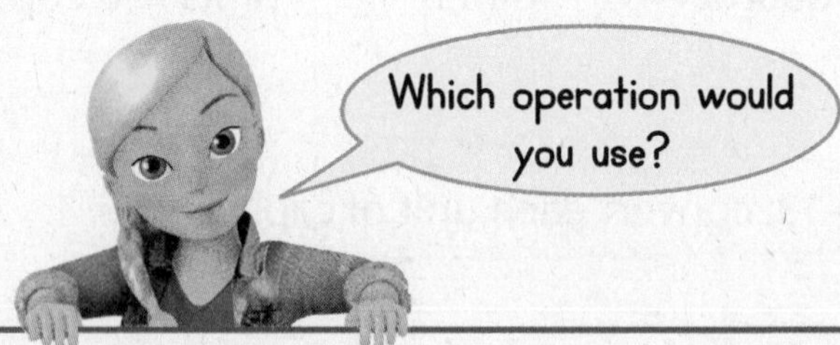
Which operation would you use?

Common Core Assessment

20. Choose all measurements that are equal to 4 quarts.

- ☐ 2 gallons
- ☐ 2 pints
- ☐ 8 pints
- ☐ 16 cups
- ☐ 48 fl oz

21. Choose all statements that are true.

- ☐ 7 pints $>$ 2 quarts
- ☐ 4 pints 1 cup $>$ 10 cups
- ☐ 1 quart $>$ 40 fl oz
- ☐ 1 gallon $<$ 8 pints 1 cup
- ☐ 8 quarts $=$ 32 gallons

Name ______________________

Solve

Lesson 11-3
Convert Customary Units of Weight

I can ...

convert customary units of weight.

Content Standards 5.MD.A.1, 5.NBT.B.5, 5.NBT.B.6

Mathematical Practices MP.4, MP.5, MP.6, MP.8

Solve & Share

Maria adopted 4 dogs. All together they eat $1\frac{3}{4}$ pound of food each day. One pound is equal to 16 ounces. How many ounces of food will the dogs eat in 5 days? ***Solve this problem any way you choose.***

Use Appropriate Tools You can use drawings or equations to solve the problem. *Show your work!*

Look Back! **MP.8 Generalize** Which is the larger unit of weight, an ounce or a pound? How can you use this relationship to find the number of ounces in 5 pounds?

How Can You Convert Units of Weight?

A

An adult African elephant weighs about 5 tons. A baby African elephant weighs about 250 pounds. How many pounds does the adult elephant weigh? How can you convert 250 pounds to tons?

1 ton (T) = 2,000 pounds (lb)
1 pound (lb) = 16 ounces (oz)

To convert from one unit of weight to another, you can use multiplication or division.

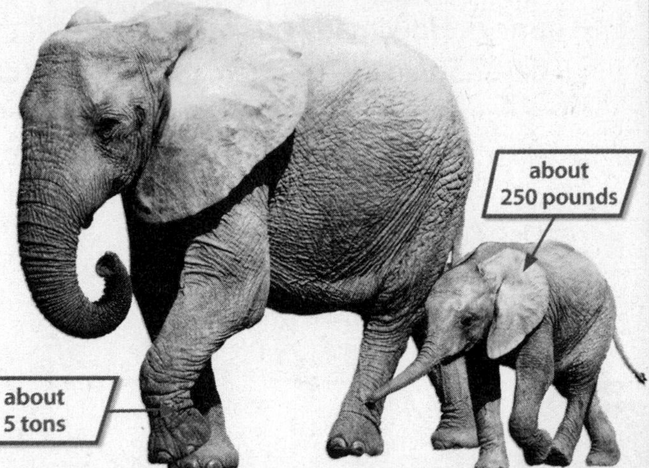

B

To convert from larger units to smaller units, multiply.

5 T = ☐ lb

1 ton equals 2,000 pounds.

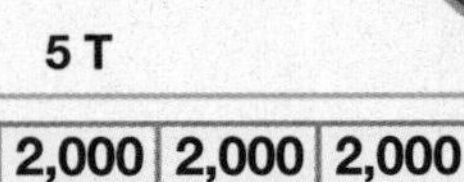

5 T

2,000 lb	2,000 lb	2,000 lb	2,000 lb	2,000 lb

Find 5 × 2,000.

5 × 2,000 = 10,000

So, 5 tons = 10,000 pounds.

C

To convert from smaller units to larger units, divide.

250 lb = ☐ T

2,000 pounds equals 1 ton.

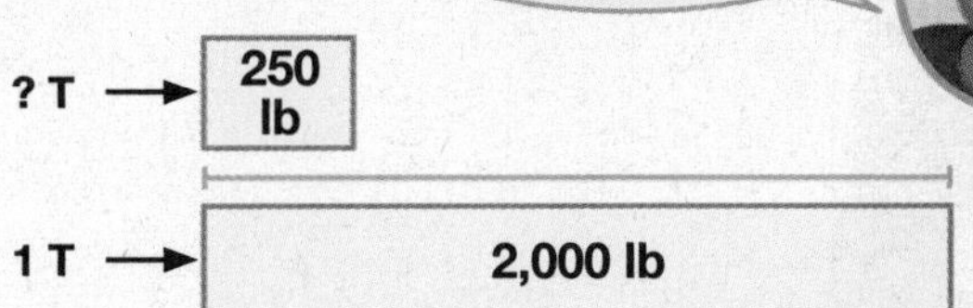

Find $\frac{250}{2,000}$.

$\frac{250 \div 250}{2,000 \div 250} = \frac{1}{8}$ So, 250 pounds = $\frac{1}{8}$ ton.

Convince Me! MP.8 Generalize When you convert 16 pounds to ounces, do you multiply or divide? Explain.

Name ____________________

Guided Practice*

Do You Understand?

1. Would it be best to measure the weight of an egg in tons, pounds, or ounces? Explain.

2. What types of tools do people select to measure weight? Explain your example.

Do You Know How?

In **3–6**, convert each unit of weight.

3. 2,000 lb = ____ T
4. 48 oz = ____ lb
5. 6,500 lb = ____ T
6. $\frac{1}{2}$ lb = ____ oz

In **7** and **8**, compare. Write >, <, or = for each ◯.

7. 2 T ◯ 45,000 lb
8. 4 lb ◯ 64 oz

Independent Practice

Will your answer be greater than or less than the number you started with?

In **9–14**, convert each unit of weight.

9. 240 oz = ______ lb
10. $7\frac{1}{10}$ T = ________ lb
11. 8 lb = ______ oz
12. 4 oz = ______ lb
13. 250 lb = ______ T
14. 1 T = ______ oz

In **15–17**, compare. Write >, <, or = for each ◯.

15. 5,000 lb ◯ 3 T
16. 24 lb ◯ 124 oz
17. 64,000 oz ◯ 2 T

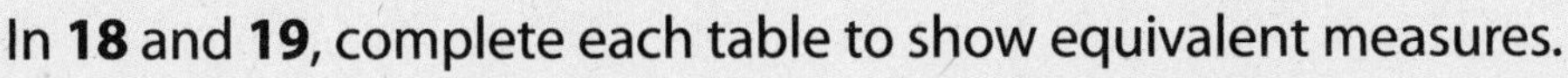

In **18** and **19**, complete each table to show equivalent measures.

18.

pounds	$\frac{1}{2}$		5
ounces		32	

19.

tons	$\frac{1}{2}$	2	
pounds			12,000

*For another example, see Set C on page 689.

Math Practices and Problem Solving

20. **MP.6 Be Precise** The perimeter of the rectangular playground shown below is 160 feet. What is the area of the playground?

21. **Math and Science** Humans exploring space have left behind bags of trash, bolts, gloves, and pieces of satellites. There are currently about 4,000,000 pounds of litter in orbit around Earth. Julia says that this amount using number names is four billion. Do you agree? Explain your thinking.

In **22–25**, use the table.

22. What would be the most appropriate unit to measure the combined weight of 4 horses?

23. About how much would 4 horses weigh? Write the weight two different ways.

24. How many more ounces does the sheep weigh than the ape?

25. **Higher Order Thinking** What is the difference in weight between the horse and the combined weight of the dolphin and the ape? Write your answer in tons.

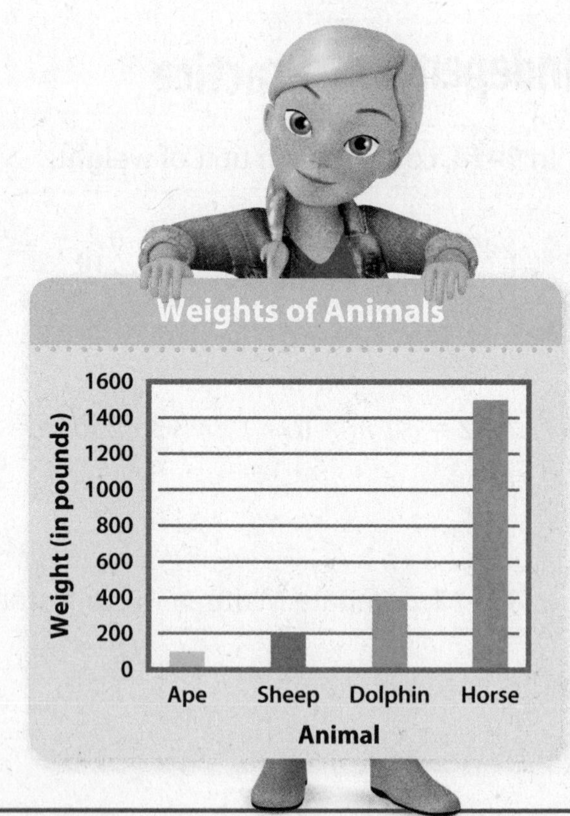

Common Core Assessment

26. **Part A**

The world's heaviest lobster weighed 44 pounds 6 ounces. Write the lobster's weight in ounces in the box below.

44 lb 6 oz = _____ ounces

Part B

Describe the steps you took to find your answer.

Name ______________________

Homework & Practice 11-3

Convert Customary Units of Weight

Another Look!

Remember:
1 ton equals 2,000 pounds and 1 pound equals 16 ounces.

How to change from one unit of weight to another:

Converting from a smaller unit to a larger unit:

32 ounces = ______ pounds

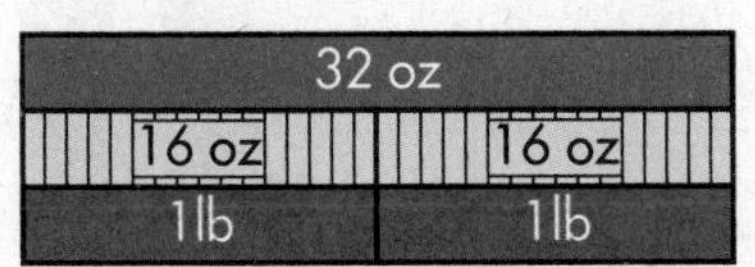

You know 16 oz = 1 lb, so divide.

Find 32 ÷ 16; 32 oz = 2 lb

Converting from a larger unit to a smaller unit:

3 pounds = ______ ounces

3 lb
1 lb | 1 lb | 1 lb
16 oz | 16 oz | 16 oz

You know 1 lb = 16 oz, so multiply.

Find 3 × 16; 3 lb = 48 oz

In **1–6**, convert each unit of weight.

1. 4 T = ______ lb

2. 5 lb = ______ oz

3. 5,500 lb = ______ T

4. $2\frac{1}{2}$ lb = ______ oz

5. 90 lb = ______ oz

6. 224 oz = ______ lb

In **7–12**, compare. Write >, <, or = for each ◯.

7. 16 lb ◯ 16 oz

8. 1,500 lb ◯ 2 T

9. 3 T ◯ 5,999 lb

10. 1,600 oz ◯ 10 lb

11. 19 lb ◯ 300 oz

12. 8 oz ◯ $\frac{1}{2}$ lb

In **13** and **14**, complete each table to show equivalent measures.

13.

pounds	2,000	3,000	
tons			3

14.

ounces	16	48	
pounds			10

In **15** and **16**, use the recipe.

15. Aaron bought these ingredients to make the trail mix recipe. How many pounds of trail mix will he make?

16. **MP.4 Model with Math** Aaron wants to divide the trail mix equally into 6 bags to give to his friends. How much trail mix will be in each bag? Draw a bar diagram and write an equation to help you find the answer.

Trail Mix Recipe

DATA
10 ounces dried bananas
20 ounces raisins
18 ounces nuts

17. **Number Sense** A candy maker buys a bar of chocolate weighing 162 ounces. About how many pounds does the bar weigh?

18. **Higher Order Thinking** Karla bought 2 pounds of broccoli, $1\frac{3}{4}$ pounds of green beans, and 10 ounces of kale. How much do Karla's vegetables weigh in all? Write your answer two different ways.

19. Students visited a zoo where they learned that a large white rhinoceros could weigh as much as 6,000 pounds. How many tons is this?

20. **Algebra** Complete the table. Write the expression that can be used to find the missing value in the second row.

n	12	15	21	28
n + ___	18	21	27	

Common Core Assessment

21. **Part A**

Paula's kitten weighs $3\frac{1}{2}$ pounds. Write this weight in the boxes using pounds and ounces.

____ pounds ____ ounces

Part B

Explain how you found your answer.

Name ______________________________ Solve

Lesson 11-4
Convert Metric Units of Length

I can ...
convert metric units of length.

Content Standards 5.MD.A.1, 5.NBT.A.2
Mathematical Practices MP.2, MP.3, MP.5, MP.7

Solve & Share Measure the length of your book in centimeters. Then measure it in millimeters. What do you notice about the two measurements?

1 cm = ____ mm

length of book: ____ cm

length of book: ____ mm

Use Appropriate Tools
You can select appropriate units and tools to measure the length of objects!

Look Back! **MP.7 Use Structure** How many meters long is your textbook? How do you know?

How Do You Convert Metric Units of Length?

A

The most commonly used metric units of length are the kilometer (km), meter (m), centimeter (cm), and millimeter (mm).

$1 \text{ km} = 10^3 \text{ m} = 1{,}000 \text{ m}$
$1 \text{ m} = 10^2 \text{ cm} = 100 \text{ cm}$
$1 \text{ m} = 10^3 \text{ mm} = 1{,}000 \text{ mm}$
$1 \text{ cm} = 10 \text{ mm}$

DATA

1 kilometer	1 hectometer	1 decameter	1 meter	1 decimeter	1 centimeter	1 millimeter
10^3 m	10^2 m	10 m	1 m	0.1 m	0.01 m	0.001 m

Every metric unit is 10 times as great as the next smaller unit.

B The distance between two towns is 3 kilometers. How many meters apart are they?

3 km = ☐ m

To change from larger units to smaller units, multiply.

One kilometer equals 1,000 meters.

Find 3×10^3.
3 km = 3,000 m

So, the towns are 3,000 meters apart.

C 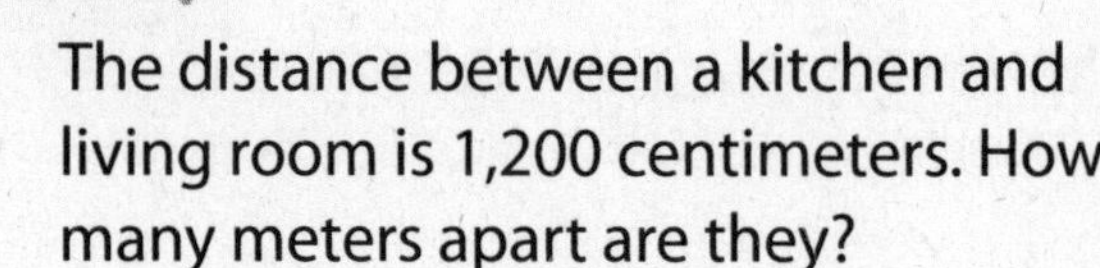

The distance between a kitchen and living room is 1,200 centimeters. How many meters apart are they?

1,200 cm = ☐ m

To change from smaller units to larger units, divide.

Find $1{,}200 \div 10^2$.
1,200 cm = 12 m

So, the kitchen and the living room are 12 meters apart.

Convince Me! **MP.3 Critique Reasoning** Elena says that 25 cm is equal to 250 mm. Do you agree? Why or why not?

Name ________________________

Practice Buddy   Tools   Assessment

Guided Practice*

Do You Understand?

1. To find the number of meters in six kilometers, why do you multiply 6×10^3?

2. Convert 12.5 centimeters to millimeters. Explain.

Do You Know How?

In **3–6**, convert each unit of length.

3. 10^3 cm = ____ m
4. 58 m = ________ mm
5. 1,000 mm = ____ cm
6. 3 km = ________ m

In **7** and **8**, compare lengths. Write >, <, or = for each ◯.

7. 9,000 m ◯ 20 km
8. 400 cm ◯ 4 m

Independent Practice

In **9–14**, convert each unit of length.

9. 7.5 cm = ____ mm
10. 6 m = ____ cm
11. 0.8 km = ________ cm
12. 17,000 m = ____ km
13. 48,000 mm = ____ m
14. 4 km = ________ m

In **15–20**, compare lengths. Write >, <, or = for each ◯.

15. 25,365 cm ◯ 30 m
16. 3.6 km ◯ 3,600 m
17. 1,200 mm ◯ 12 m
18. 52,800 cm ◯ 1 km
19. 7,500,000 m ◯ 750 km
20. 800 m ◯ 799,999 mm

In **21** and **22**, complete each table.

21.

km	1		0.1
m		500	

22.

m		5	0.5
cm	5,000		

*For another example, see Set D on page 689.

Math Practices and Problem Solving

23. Number Sense Let x = the length of an object in meters and y = the length of the same object in millimeters. Which is a smaller number, x or y?

24. Higher Order Thinking How many millimeters are equal to one kilometer? Show your work.

25. MP.2 Reasoning Which fraction is greater: $\frac{7}{8}$ or $\frac{9}{12}$? Explain how you know.

How do you compare fractions?

26. A week ago, Trudy bought the pencil shown. Now the pencil measures 12.7 centimeters.

How many centimeters of the pencil have been used?

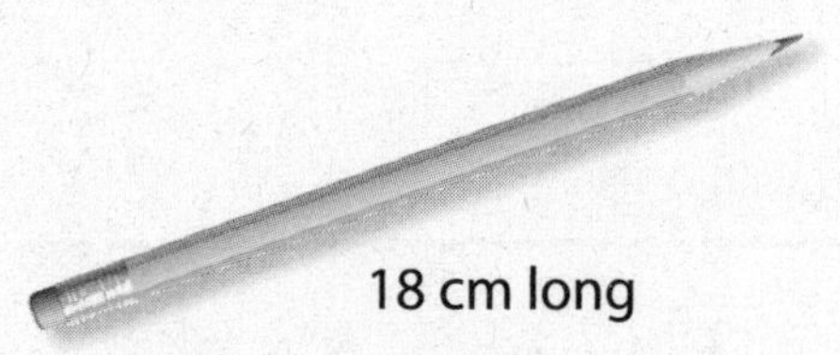
18 cm long

27. Math and Science Mount St. Helens, located in Washington, erupted on May 18, 1980. Before the eruption, the volcano was 2.95 kilometers high. After the eruption, the volcano was 2.55 kilometers high. Use the bar diagram to find the difference in height of Mount St. Helens before and after the eruption, in meters.

2.95 km

2.55 km	?

Common Core Assessment

28. Eileen plants a tree that is 2 meters tall in her yard. Which of the following is equivalent to 2 meters?

Ⓐ 200 mm

Ⓑ 20 cm

Ⓒ 200 km

Ⓓ 2,000 mm

29. Which of these number sentences is **NOT** true?

Ⓐ 600 cm = 6 m

Ⓑ 1 m < 9,000 mm

Ⓒ 900 mm = 9 cm

Ⓓ 10 km > 5,000 m

Name ______________________

Homework & Practice 11-4

Convert Metric Units of Length

Another Look!

Remember:
1 km = 10^3 m = 1,000 m
1 m = 10^2 cm = 100 cm
1 m = 10^3 mm = 1,000 mm
1 cm = 10 mm

How to change from one metric unit of length to another:

Converting a length from a smaller to a larger metric unit:

200 centimeters = ______ meters

1 m	1 m
100 cm	100 cm
← 200 cm →	

You know 10^2 cm = 1 m, so divide.

Find 200 ÷ 100; 200 cm = 2 m

Converting a length from a larger to a smaller metric unit:

2 kilometers = ______ meters

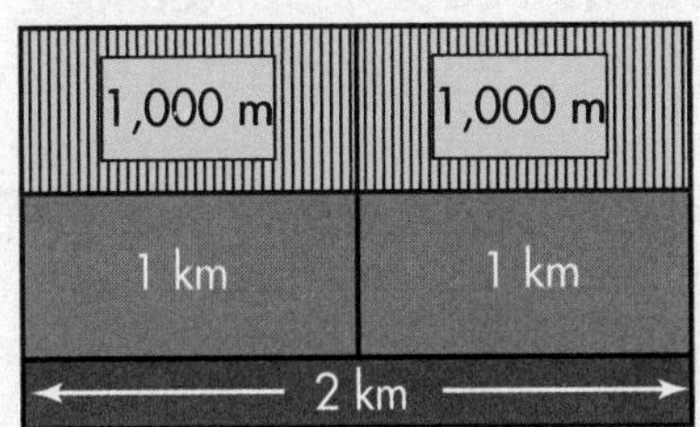

You know 1 km = 10^3 m, so multiply.

Find 2 × 1,000; 2 km = 2,000 m

In **1–6**, convert each unit of length.

How can you double check that your answers are correct?

1. 25 m = ______ cm

2. 345 cm = ______ m

3. 4.5 m = ______ cm

4. 10 m = ______ mm

5. 987 mm = ______ cm

6. 5 km = ______ m

In **7–9**, compare lengths. Write >, <, or = for each ◯.

7. 3 km ◯ 5,000 m

8. 800 cm ◯ 8 m

9. 38.5 mm ◯ 10 cm

In **10** and **11**, complete each table to show equivalent measures.

10.

mm	5	85	
cm			90

11.

km	0.4		25
m		7,000	

12. **Higher Order Thinking** Park rangers at the North Rim of the Grand Canyon recorded the amounts of rainfall over 12 months. What was the total amount of rainfall in centimeters?

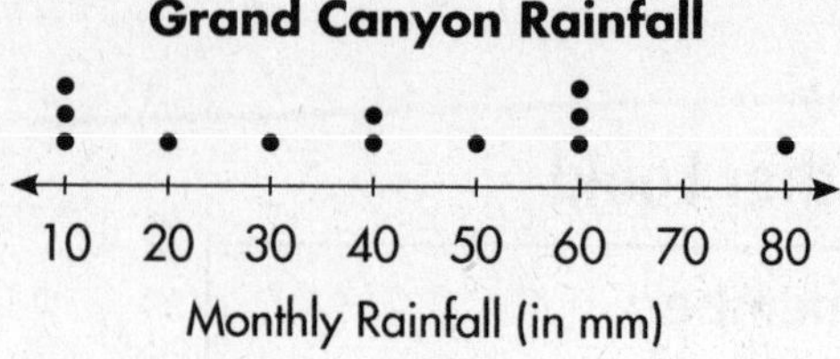

13. What is the difference between the greatest and least amounts of monthly rainfall? Write an equation to model your work.

14. Arturo builds a cube that measures 5 inches on each side. What is the volume of Arturo's cube? Write an equation to show your work.

15. **MP.7 Use Structure** List three measurements with different units that are equal to 5 meters.

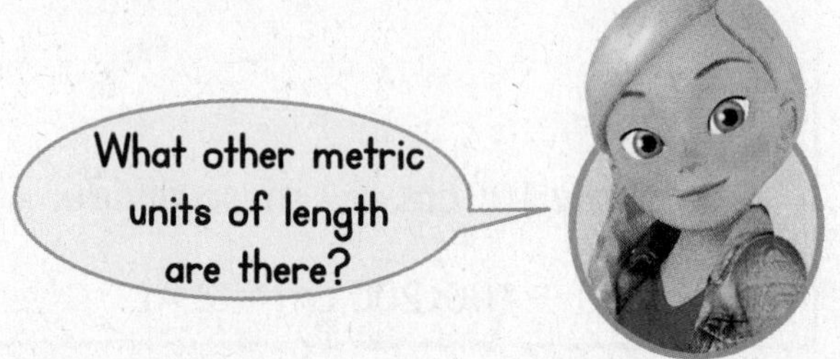

What other metric units of length are there?

16. If you walked all three trails in one day, how far would you walk? Write the answer in meters and in kilometers.

DATA

Trail	Length
Spring Hollow	2 km
Brookside	2,400 m
Oak Ridge	1 km 600 m

17. **MP.2 Reasoning** Explain how you can move the decimal point to convert 3,200 meters to kilometers.

Common Core Assessment

18. Cory finds a leaf that is 5 cm long. Which measurement is equivalent to 5 cm?

Ⓐ 0.05 mm
Ⓑ 0.5 mm
Ⓒ 50 mm
Ⓓ 500 mm

19. Which of these number sentences is **NOT** true?

Ⓐ 4,000,000 mm = 4 km
Ⓑ 300 mm > 3 cm
Ⓒ 5 m > 5,000 mm
Ⓓ 2,000 m < 20 km

Name ______________________

Lesson 11-5

Convert Metric Units of Capacity

I can . . .
convert metric units of capacity.

Content Standards 5.MD.A.1, 5.NBT.A.2
Mathematical Practices MP.2, MP.3, MP.7, MP.8

Solve & Share

A pitcher holds 4 liters of water. How many milliliters does the pitcher hold? ***Solve this problem any way you choose.***

Generalize You can convert metric units of capacity using multiplication or division. *Show your work!*

1 liter = ________ milliliters

4 liters = ________ milliliters

Look Back! **MP.7 Look for Relationships** Juanita shares a one-liter bottle of water with 3 friends. How much water does each person get? Give your answer in liters and milliliters.

How Do You Convert Metric Units of Capacity?

Essential Question

A

The most commonly used units of capacity in the metric system are the liter (L) and the milliliter (mL).

Can you find
a liter or milliliter in
the real world?
1 liter equals
1,000 milliliters

B Susan has 1.875 liters of water. How many milliliters is this?

1.875 L = ☐ mL

To change a larger unit to a smaller unit, multiply.

Find 1.875×10^3.
$1.875 \times 10^3 = 1,875$
1.875 L = 1,875 mL

So, Susan has 1,875 milliliters of water.

C Jorge has 3,500 milliliters of water. How many liters is this?

3,500 mL = ☐ L

To change a smaller unit to a larger unit, divide.

Find $3,500 \div 10^3$.
$3,500 \div 10^3 = 3.5$
3,500 mL = 3.5 L

So, Jorge has 3.5 liters of water.

Convince Me! **MP.2 Reasoning** Order these measurements from greatest to least. Explain how you decided.

2,300 L   500 mL   3,000 mL   2 L   22 L

Name ______________________

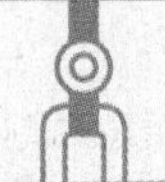

Practice Buddy Tools Assessment

Guided Practice*

Do You Understand?

1. MP.8 Generalize Explain how you can convert milliliters to liters.

2. What types of tools would you select to measure capacity? Give an example and explain how that tool could be used.

Do You Know How?

In **3–8**, convert each unit of capacity.

3. 2.75 L = ______ mL

4. 3,000 mL = ______ L

5. 5 L = ______ mL

6. 250 mL = ______ L

7. 0.027 L = ______ mL

8. 400 mL = ______ L

Independent Practice

In **9–20**, convert each unit of capacity.

9. 5,000 mL = ______ L

10. 45,000 mL = ______ L

11. 4.27 L = ______ mL

12. 13 L = ______ mL

13. 3,700 mL = ______ L

14. 0.35 L = ______ mL

15. 2,640 mL = ______ L

16. 314 mL = ______ L

17. 0.06 L = ______ mL

18. 2,109 mL = ______ L

19. 85 mL = ______ L

20. 9.05 L = ______ mL

In **21** and **22**, complete each table to show equivalent measures.

21.

liters	0.1	1	10
milliliters			

22.

milliliters	500	5,000	50,000
liters			

*For another example, see Set E on page 690.

Math Practices and Problem Solving

23. MP.2 Reasoning Carla's famous punch calls for 3 liters of mango juice. The only mango juice she can find is sold in 500-milliliter cartons. How many cartons of mango juice does Carla need to buy?

24. Carla makes 6 liters of punch. She pours the punch into 800 mL bottles. How many bottles can she fill?

25. Bobby filled the jug with water for soccer practice. If each player gets 250 milliliters of water, how many players will the water jug serve?

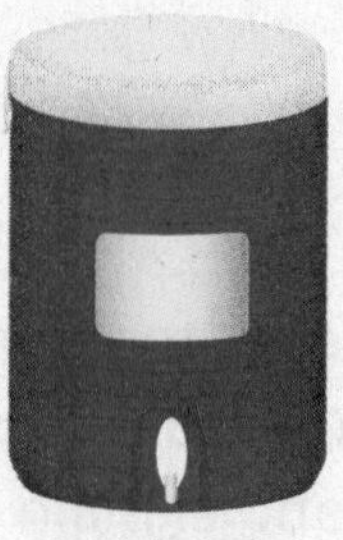

holds 5 L

26. **Higher Order Thinking** One cubic centimeter will hold 1 milliliter of water. How many milliliters will the aquarium below hold? How many liters will it hold?

27. Terry is buying juice. He needs 3 liters. A half-liter of juice costs \$2.39. A 250-milliliter container of juice costs \$1.69. What should Terry buy so he gets 3 liters at the lowest price? Explain.

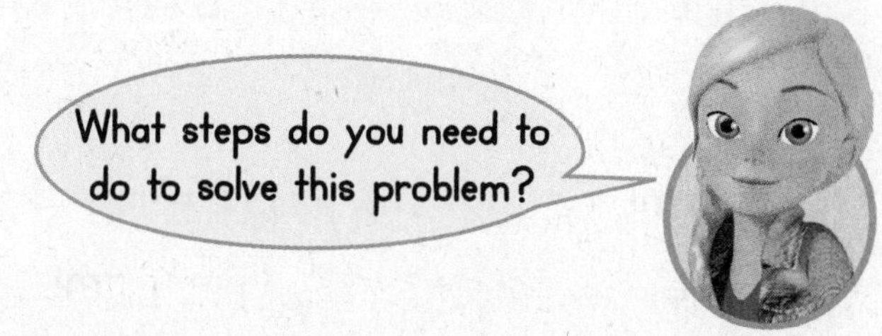

What steps do you need to do to solve this problem?

Common Core Assessment

28. A bird bath holds 4 liters of water. How many milliliters of water does it hold?

Ⓐ 400 mL
Ⓑ 800 mL
Ⓒ 4,000 mL
Ⓓ 8,000 mL

29. You are filling a 2-liter bottle with liquid from full 80-milliliter containers. How many containers will it take to fill the 2-liter bottle?

Ⓐ 400
Ⓑ 250
Ⓒ 40
Ⓓ 25

Name ______

Homework & Practice 11-5

Convert Metric Units of Capacity

Another Look!

Remember:
To change from liters to milliliters, multiply by 10^3. To change from milliliters to liters, divide by 10^3.

How to change from one metric unit of capacity to another:

Converting a capacity from a smaller to a larger metric unit:

2,000 milliliters = ______ liters

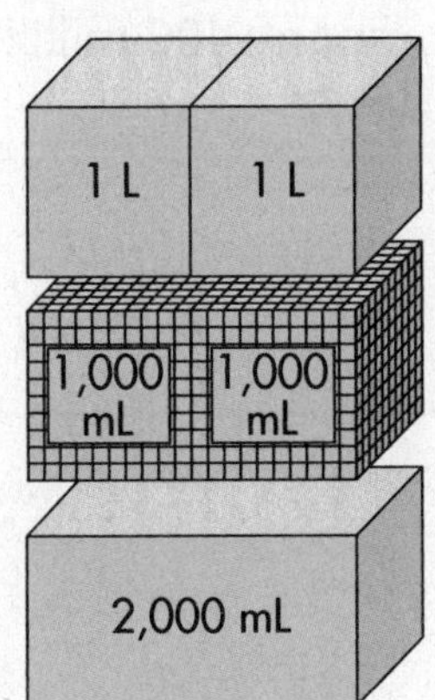

You know 10^3 mL = 1L, so divide.

Find 2,000 ÷ 1,000; 2,000 mL = 2 L

Converting a capacity from a larger to a smaller metric unit:

3 liters = ______ milliliters

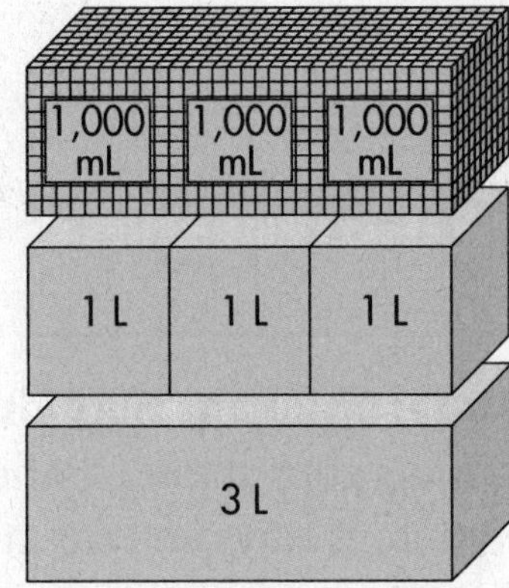

You know 1 L = 10^3 mL, so multiply.

Find 3 × 1,000; 3 L = 3,000 mL

In **1–9**, convert each unit of capacity.

1. 5 L = ______ mL

2. 13,000 mL = ______ L

3. 1.6 L = ______ mL

4. 4,750 mL = ______ L

5. 950 mL = ______ L

6. 0.4 L = ______ mL

7. 2.7 L = ______ mL

8. 8,400 mL = ______ L

9. 0.071 L = ______ mL

In **10** and **11**, complete each table to show equivalent measures.

10.

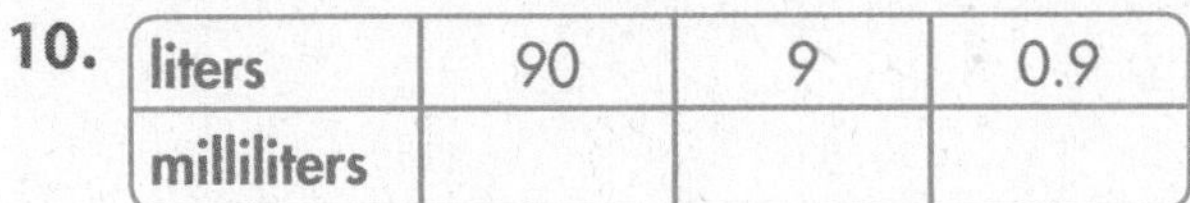

liters	90	9	0.9
milliliters			

11.

milliliters	250	2,500	25,000
liters			

12. **MP.3 Construct Arguments** Tell whether you would use multiplication or division to convert milliliters to liters. Explain your answer.

13. **Algebra** Complete the following table. Then write an equation that can be used to convert *p* pounds to *o* ounces.

Pounds	3	4	5	6	7
Ounces	48				

14. The length of a rectangular garden is 10 yards and its width is 10 feet. What is the perimeter of the garden in feet?

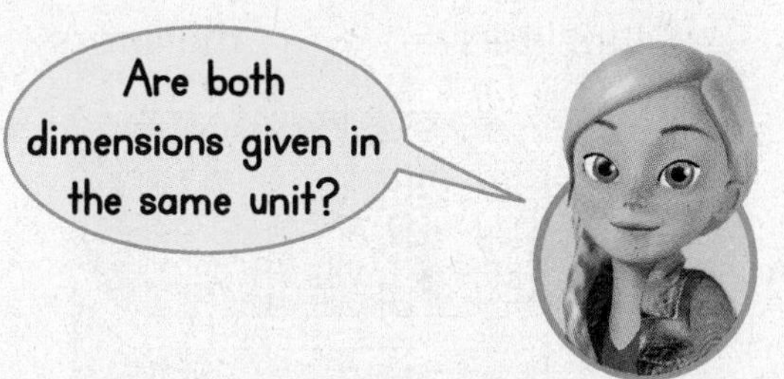

Are both dimensions given in the same unit?

15. You are preparing for a breakfast party and need enough milk for 20 people. Each person will drink about 200 milliliters of milk. Which is the better estimate of the amount of milk you should prepare: 400 milliliters or 4 liters? Why?

16. **Higher Order Thinking** Suppose you have the 3 cups shown at the right. List two different ways you can measure exactly 1 liter.

Common Core Assessment

17. A community center has a swimming pool that holds 29,000,000 milliliters of water. How many liters of water can the pool hold?

Ⓐ 290,000,000 L
Ⓑ 2,900,000 L
Ⓒ 290,000 L
Ⓓ 29,000 L

18. There are 1.5 liters of punch in a pitcher. How many milliliters of punch are in the pitcher?

Ⓐ 100 mL
Ⓑ 1,500 mL
Ⓒ 1,000 mL
Ⓓ 15,000 mL

Name ______________________________

Lesson 11-6
Convert Metric Units of Mass

I can ...
convert metric units of mass.

Content Standards 5.MD.A.1, 5.NBT.A.2
Mathematical Practices MP.1, MP.2, MP.7

Solve & Share In Chemistry class, Rhonda measured 9.5 grams of a substance. How many milligrams is this? ***Solve this problem any way you choose.***

Look for Relationships
You can use patterns to help you see a relationship between the units.

Look Back! **MP.7 Use Structure** How many kilograms did Rhonda measure? Write an equation to model your work.

Learn Glossary

How Do You Convert Metric Units of Mass?

A

The three most commonly used units of mass are the milligram (mg), the gram (g), and the kilogram (kg).

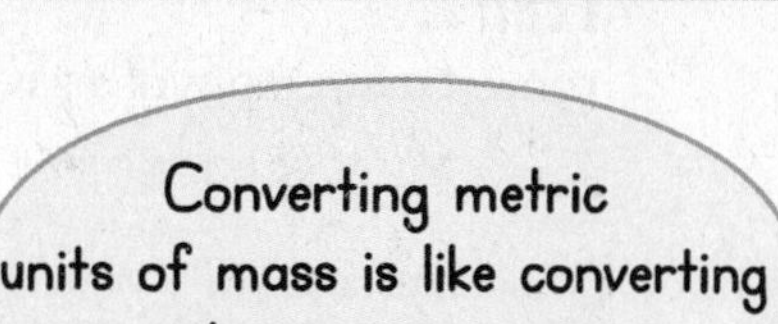

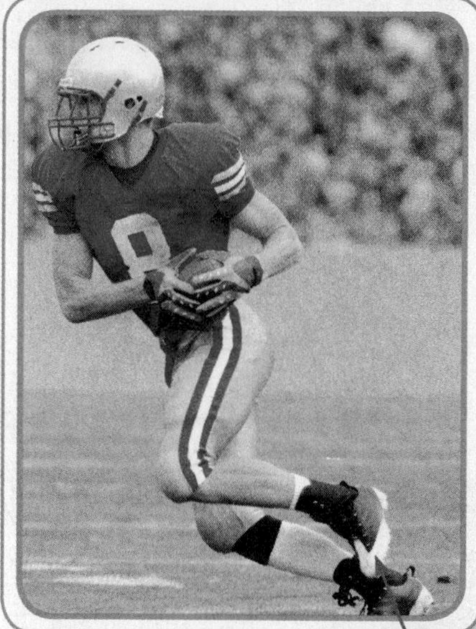

Converting metric units of mass is like converting other metric units.

10^3 mg = 1 g
10^3 g = 1 kg

B A whistle has a mass of about 5 grams. How many milligrams is this?

To change from a larger unit to a smaller unit, multiply.

Find 5×10^3.
$5 \times 10^3 = 5 \times 1{,}000 = 5{,}000$
So, 5 g = 5,000 mg.

So, a whistle has a mass of about 5,000 milligrams.

C How many kilograms is the whistle?

To change from a smaller unit to a larger unit, divide.

Find $5 \div 10^3$.
$5 \div 10^3 = 5 \div 1{,}000 = 0.005$
So, 5 g = 0.005 kg.

So, a whistle has a mass of about 0.005 kilogram.

Convince Me! MP.7 Use Structure In the picture above, what is the football player's mass in grams and in milligrams? How can you tell?

Name ________________________________

Guided Practice*

Practice Buddy Tools Assessment

Do You Understand?

1. **Vocabulary** How does the relationship between meters and millimeters help you understand the relationship between grams and milligrams?

2. Which has the greater mass: 1 kilogram or 137,000 milligrams? Explain how you made your comparison.

Do You Know How?

In **3** and **4**, convert each unit of mass.

3. 9.25 g = ______ mg

4. 190 g = ______ kg

In **5** and **6**, compare. Write >, <, or = for each ◯.

5. 7,000 mg ◯ 7,000 g

6. 10^2 kg ◯ 10^4 g

Independent Practice

In **7–12**, convert each unit of mass.

7. 17,000 g = ______ kg

8. 18 kg = ______ g

9. 4,200 mg = ______ g

10. 0.276 g = ______ mg

11. 4.08 kg = ______ g

12. 43 mg = ______ g

In **13–18**, compare. Write >, <, or = for each ◯.

13. 2,000 g ◯ 3 kg

14. 4 kg ◯ 4,000 g

15. 10^4 mg ◯ 13 g

16. 7 kg ◯ 7,000 g

17. 9,000 g ◯ 8 kg

18. 8,000 g ◯ 5 kg

In **19** and **20**, complete each table.

19.

grams		10	
milligrams	1,000		100,000

20.

grams	500		50,000
kilograms		5	

*For another example, see Set F on page 690.

Math Practices and Problem Solving

21. **MP.1 Make Sense and Persevere** Sheryl has a recipe for pasta with vegetables. The recipe calls for 130 grams of vegetables and twice as much pasta as vegetables. What is the total mass in grams of the recipe?

22. Terri is beginning a science experiment in the lab. The instructions call for 227 milligrams of potassium. Calculate the difference between this amount and 1 gram.

23. **Number Sense** One of the world's heaviest hailstones weighed 2.2 pounds. Which is more appropriate to express its mass, 1 kilogram or 1 gram?

24. **Higher Order Thinking** A cook has 6 onions that have a total mass of 900 grams and 8 apples that have a total mass of 1 kilogram. All onions are the same size, and all apples are the same size. Which has the greater mass, an onion or an apple? Explain.

In **25** and **26**, use the given information and the picture.

Math and Science If a man weighs 198 pounds on Earth, his mass on Earth is 90 kilograms.

25. What is this man's weight on the Moon?

26. What is his mass on the Moon? Explain.

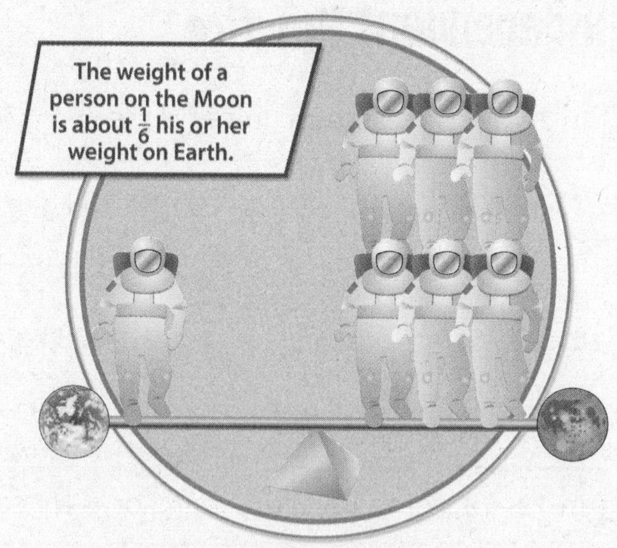

The weight of a person on the Moon is about $\frac{1}{6}$ his or her weight on Earth.

Common Core Assessment

27. Write the following masses on the lines from least to greatest.
500 g 50 kg 5,000 mg

______ < ______ < ______

28. If you convert grams to milligrams, what operation would you use?

Name ____________________

Homework & Practice 11-6

Convert Metric Units of Mass

Another Look!

Remember:
10^3 milligrams equals 1 gram and
10^3 grams equals 1 kilogram.

How to convert from one metric unit of mass to another:

Smaller metric unit to a larger unit:
6,000 grams = ____ kilograms

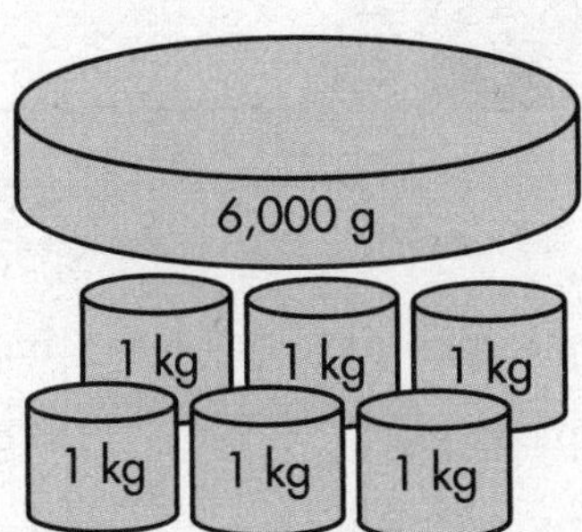

You know 10^3 g = 1 kg, so divide.

Find 6,000 ÷ 1,000; 6,000 g = 6 kg

Larger metric unit to a smaller unit:
2 grams = ____ milligrams

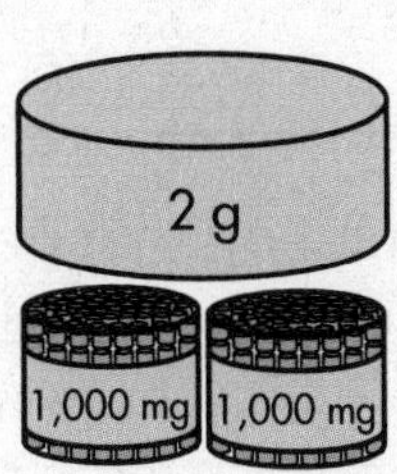

You know 1 g = 10^3 mg, so multiply.

Find 2 × 1,000; 2 g = 2,000 mg

In **1–6**, convert each unit of mass.

1. 72 g = ______ mg

2. 8,000 g = ______ kg

3. 2,000 mg = ______ kg

4. 490 g = ______ kg

5. 0.648 g = ____ mg

6. 0.061 kg = ______ g

In **7–12**, compare. Write >, <, or = for each ◯.

7. 4,000 mg ◯ 5 g

8. 64 kg ◯ 64,000 g

9. 3 kg ◯ 40,000 mg

10. 6,000 g ◯ 6 kg

11. 93 g ◯ 92,000 mg

12. 90 kg ◯ 90,000 mg

In **13** and **14**, complete each table to show equivalent measures.

13.

grams	2		200
milligrams		20,000	

14.

grams		1,000	
kilograms	0.1		10

15. **MP.1 Make Sense and Persevere** A recipe that serves two people calls for 1,600 milligrams of baking soda. You want to make enough for 10 people. How many grams of baking soda will you need? Write an equation to show your work.

16. **MP.2 Reasoning** What steps would you take to compare 2 kilograms and 3,200 grams?

Is there more than one way to compare them?

17. Nutritionists recommend that people eat 25,000 milligrams of fiber each day. The table shows the amount of fiber Jodi has eaten today. How many more grams of fiber does she need to get the recommended daily amount of fiber?

DATA

Food	Amount of Fiber
1 cup raspberries	8 grams
1 cup oatmeal	4 grams
2 cups orange juice	1 gram

18. Classify the triangle by its sides and its angles.

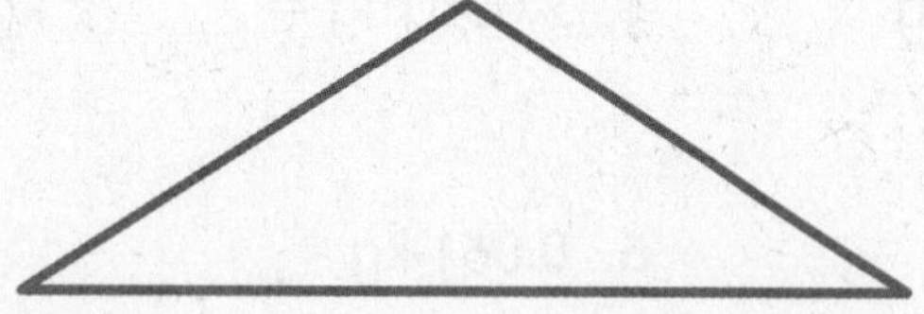

19. **Higher Order Thinking** How is converting grams to milligrams similar to converting pounds to ounces? How is it different?

Common Core Assessment

20. Write the following masses on the lines from greatest to least.
30 g   2 kg   60,000 mg

_______ > _______ > _______

21. If you convert grams to kilograms, what operation would you use?

Name ______________________

Lesson 11-7
Solve Word Problems Using Measurement Conversions

I can ...
solve real-world problems with measurement conversions.

Content Standards 5.MD.A.1, 5.NBT.B.5
Mathematical Practices MP.1, MP.2, MP.3, MP.6, MP.8

Solve & Share

Amy wants to frame a poster that has a width of 8 inches and a length of 1 foot. What is the perimeter of the poster? ***Solve this problem any way you choose.***

Make Sense and Persevere
You can use measurement conversions in real-world situations.
Show your work!

1 foot = ____ inches

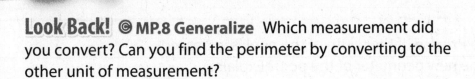

Look Back! **MP.8 Generalize** Which measurement did you convert? Can you find the perimeter by converting to the other unit of measurement?

How Can You Convert Units of Measurement to Solve a Problem?

A

A city pool is in the shape of a rectangle with the dimensions shown. What is the perimeter of the pool?

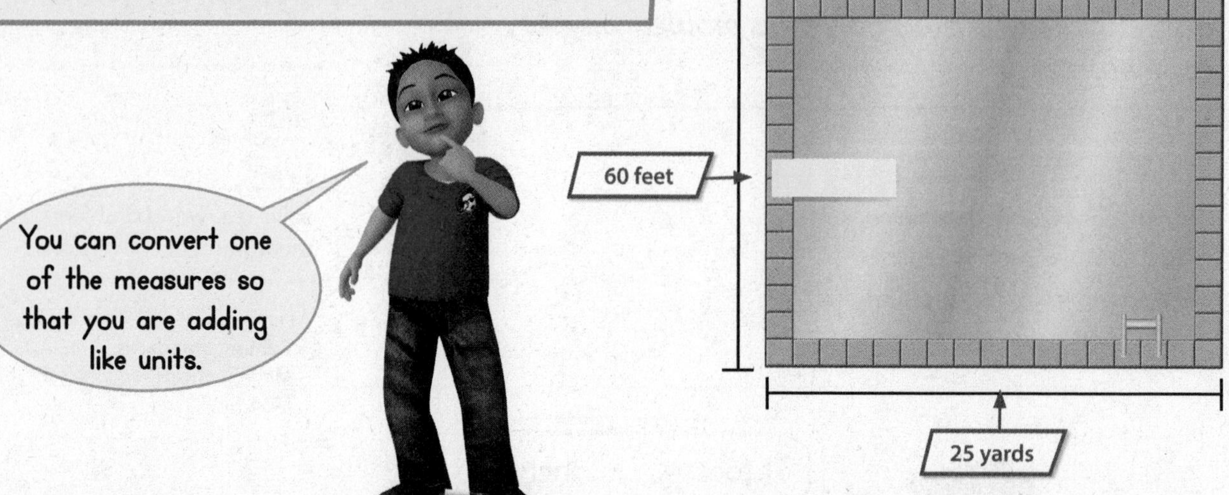

You can convert one of the measures so that you are adding like units.
60 feet
25 yards

B *What do you know?*

The dimensions of the pool:
$\ell = 25$ yards
$w = 60$ feet

What are you asked to find?

The perimeter of the pool

You can use feet for perimeter.

C Convert 25 yards to feet so you can add like units.

1 yard = 3 feet

To change from larger units to smaller units, multiply.

25×3 feet = 75 feet

So, 25 yards = 75 feet.

D Substitute like measurements into the perimeter formula.

Perimeter = $(2 \times \text{length}) + (2 \times \text{width})$

$P = (2 \times \ell) + (2 \times w)$

$P = (2 \times 75) + (2 \times 60)$

$P = 150 + 120$

$P = 270$ feet

The perimeter of the pool is 270 feet.

Convince Me! **MP.6 Be Precise** If the width of the pool is increased by 3 feet, what would be the new perimeter of the pool? Explain.

Name

Guided Practice*

Do You Understand?

1. In the example on the previous page, how could you find the perimeter by converting all measurements to yards?

2. Write a real-world multiple-step problem that involves measurement.

Do You Know How?

3. Stacia needs enough ribbon to wrap around the length (ℓ) and height (h) of a box. If the length is 2 feet and the height is 4 inches, how much ribbon will she need?

4. If ribbon is sold in whole number yards and costs $1.50 per yard, how much will it cost Stacia to buy the ribbon?

Independent Practice

In **5–7**, use conversions to solve each problem.

5. Becca wants to edge her hexagonal garden with brick. All sides are equal. The brick costs $6 per yard. What is the perimeter of the garden? How much will it cost to buy the edging she needs?

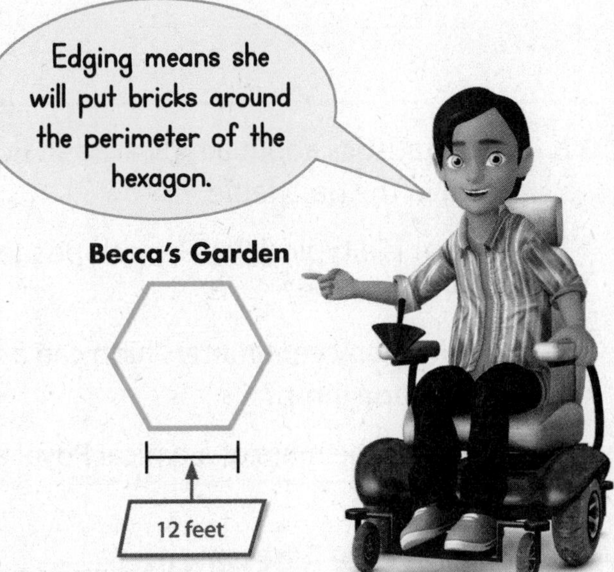

Edging means she will put bricks around the perimeter of the hexagon.
Becca's Garden
12 feet

6. Isaac buys milk to make milkshakes for his friends. He buys 1 quart of milk and $\frac{1}{2}$ gallon of milk. How many cups of milk does he buy?

7. Maggie buys $1\frac{1}{2}$ pounds of walnuts, 8 ounces of pecans, and $\frac{3}{4}$ pound of almonds. How much do the nuts weigh in all?

*For another example, see Set G on page 690.

Math Practices and Problem Solving

8. **MP.2 Reasoning** Matt's family is thinking about buying a family pass to the city pool. The pass is $80 for a family of 4. Individual passes are $25 each. How much money can Matt's family save by purchasing a family pass instead of 4 individual passes?

9. Marcia walked 900 meters on Friday. On Saturday, she walked 4 kilometers. On Sunday, she walked 3 kilometers, 600 meters. How many kilometers did Marcia walk over the weekend?

10. **Higher Order Thinking** Raul wants to put wood shavings in his rabbit's cage. The floor of the cage measures 1 yard wide by 5 feet long. One bag of shavings covers 10 square feet.

    How many bags will Raul have to buy to cover the floor of the cage? Explain.

11. Cheryl's fish tank is 2 yards long by 24 inches wide by 3 feet high. What is the volume of Cheryl's tank in cubic inches?

12. Some statistics about a typical adult Royal antelope are shown in the data table.

    a What is a typical Royal antelope's tail length in millimeters?

    b How many centimeters high can a typical Royal antelope jump?

    c What is the mass of a typical Royal antelope in grams?

An Adult Royal Antelope (DATA)

Head and body length	43 cm
Tail length	6 cm
Mass	2.4 kg
Vertical leap	2 m

Common Core Assessment

13. Joann wants to put a wallpaper border around her room. The border costs $3 per foot. The diagram shows Joann's room. How much money will the border cost?

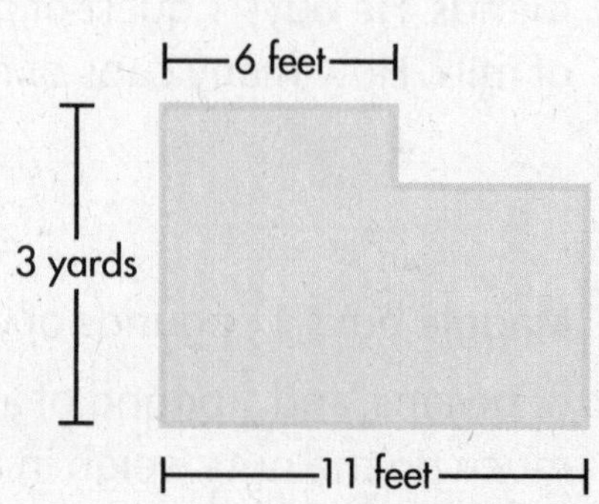

Ⓐ $120

Ⓑ $102

Ⓒ $84

Ⓓ $60

Name ______________________

Homework & Practice 11-7
Solve Word Problems Using Measurement Conversions

Another Look!

Kyle hiked 10 miles on Saturday. He hiked half as many miles on Sunday. How many total yards did Kyle hike?

What question needs to be answered first?
How many miles did Kyle hike on Sunday?

Answer this question.
$10 \div 2 = 5$ miles

What is the total number of miles hiked?
$10 + 5 = 15$ miles

Convert the answer to yards.
1 mi = 1,760 yd, so 15 miles is $15 \times 1,760 = 26,400$ yd

Kyle hiked a total of 26,400 yards.

Read the problem. Underline what you know. Circle what you are asked to find.

1. Kendra biked 10 kilometers on Monday. She biked twice as many kilometers on Tuesday. How many total meters did she bike?

   Underline what you know. Circle what you need to find.

   What question do you need to answer first?

   ____

   How many meters did Kendra bike in all? __________

Remember to check your calculations and make sure you answered the correct question.

2. Wilson made fruit punch. He used 2 quarts of orange juice and 1 pint of cranberry juice. He used one quart more ginger ale than orange juice. How many cups of fruit punch did Wilson make?

3. Claire's backyard is in the shape of a rectangle and has a length of 19.5 feet. It cost her $945 to fence in the yard. If fencing costs $15 per foot, what is the width of Claire's backyard?

4. Zayna is putting ribbon around a picture of her dog. The picture is 300 millimeters wide and 150 millimeters tall. How many meters of ribbon will she need?

5. Ann is putting carpet in a room that is 12 feet long and 10 feet wide. The carpet costs $3.00 per square foot. How much will the carpet for the room cost?

6. For every 3 cans of vegetables purchased, you get 1 free can. Tessie went home with 32 cans of vegetables. How many cans did she have to pay for?

7. **MP.1 Make Sense and Persevere** Isabel ran around the track 6 times at the same rate of speed. It took her 24 minutes to run. John took 3 minutes to run around the track once. Which student ran faster? Explain.

8. **MP.3 Construct Arguments** Badal has 120 cubic centimeters of water. He wants to pour it into a rectangular vase that is 4 centimeters high, 40 millimeters wide, and 5 centimeters long. Will all the water fit into the vase? Explain.

9. **Higher Order Thinking** Nancy is saving $2 from her allowance every week. Marco is saving $1 the first week, $2 the second week, $3 the third week, and so on. At the end of 10 weeks, who will have saved more money? How much more?

10. José is painting a backdrop for the school play. The rectangular backdrop is 60 inches by 45 inches. If his container of paint can cover 25 square feet, does he have enough to paint the backdrop?

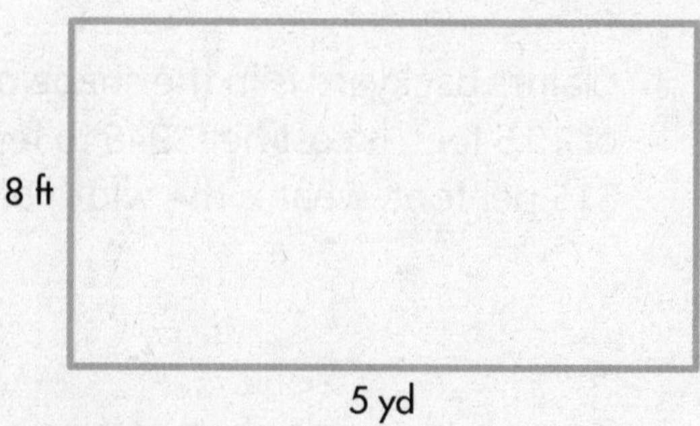

HINT: Convert the dimensions from inches to feet.

Common Core Assessment

11. Darin wants to put a fence around his garden. How much fencing should he buy?

Ⓐ 26 yards
Ⓑ 40 yards
Ⓒ 46 feet
Ⓓ 120 feet

8 ft

5 yd

Name ____________________

Solve

Math Practices and Problem Solving

Lesson 11-8
Precision

I can ...
be precise when solving measurement problems.

Mathematical Practices MP.6. Also MP.1, MP.2, MP.4
Content Standards 5.MD.A.1, 5.NBT.B.5

Solve & Share

Beth wants to make a picture frame like the one pictured below. She recorded the outside dimensions as 5 cm by 7 cm. Measure the outside dimensions of the frame in millimeters. Compare your measurements to Beth's. Do you think her measurements are precise enough? Explain.

Thinking Habits

*Think about these questions to help you **attend to precision.***

- Am I using numbers, units, and symbols appropriately?
- Am I using the correct definitions?
- Am I calculating accurately?
- Is my answer clear?

Look Back! **MP.6 Be Precise** What is the difference between the perimeter based on the measurements Beth made and the perimeter based on the measurements you made? Explain how you found the answer.

Learn Glossary

Essential Question

How Can You Be Precise When Solving Math Problems?

A

Chad and Rhoda are hanging a swing. Chad cut a piece of chain 6 feet 2 inches long. Rhoda cut a piece of chain 72 inches long. When they hung the swing, it was crooked.

Use precise language to explain why.

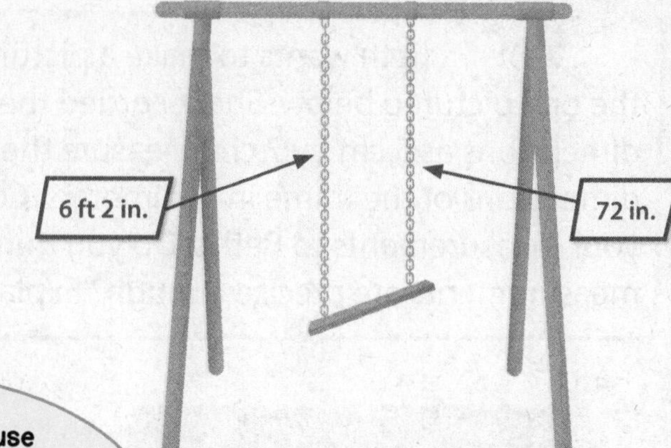

Be Precise means that you use appropriate math words, symbols, and units as well as accurate calculations when you solve problems.

B

How can I be precise in solving this problem?

I can

- calculate accurately.
- give a clear answer.
- use the correct units.

C

Here's my thinking...

Convert 6 ft 2 inches to inches to see if Chad and Rhoda cut equal lengths of chain.

6 ft 2 in. = ☐ in.

$6 \times 12 = 72$, so 6 ft = 72 in.

6 ft 2 in. $= 72 + 2 = 74$ in.

Chad's chain is 74 inches long, but Rhoda's chain is only 72 inches long. Since Chad and Rhoda used unequal lengths of chain, the swing is crooked.

Convince Me! © **MP.6 Be Precise** What recommendations would you make to Chad and Rhoda so that the swing hangs level?

Name ______

Practice Buddy Tools Assessment

Guided Practice*

MP.6 Precision

Mary needs a board 4 feet 8 inches long. She cut a board 56 inches long.

Remember to be precise by converting measurements accurately.

1. What measurements are given? Are the same units used for each measurement? Explain.

2. Explain how you can convert one of the measurements so that both use the same unit.

3. Is the board Mary cut the right length? Give a clear and appropriate answer.

Independent Practice

MP.6 Be Precise

Sean is making meat loaf. He used the amount of catsup shown in the measuring cup.

Meat Loaf

2 lb ground beef
1 egg
6 fl oz catsup
$\frac{1}{2}$ c bread crumbs
salt and pepper to taste

4. Are the units that Sean used to measure the catsup the same as those given in the recipe? Explain.

5. How can you convert one of the measurements so that both use the same unit?

6. Did Sean use the right amount of catsup? Give a clear and appropriate answer.

*For another example, see Set H on page 690.

Math Practices and Problem Solving

Common Core Performance Assessment

Shipping a Package

A customer is using regular delivery to ship a package. Northside Shipping Company discovered that its old scale is not very accurate. It registers a weight that is 2 ounces too heavy. A new, accurate scale shows that the actual weight of the customer's package is 2 pounds 11 ounces.

Northside Shipping Company

Regular Delivery
$0.75 first ounce
$0.60 each additional ounce

Rush Delivery
$1.45 first ounce
$0.75 each additional ounce

7. **MP.1 Make Sense and Persevere** Which information do you need to determine the total shipping cost using either scale?

8. **MP.6 Be Precise** Why do you need to convert measurements to determine total shipping costs?

To be precise, you need to check that the words, numbers, symbols, and units you use are correct and that your calculations are accurate.

9. **MP.4 Model with Math** Show how to convert the measurements you described in Exercise 8.

10. **MP.6 Be Precise** What would the total cost be if the package is weighed on the new scale? What would the total cost be if the package is weighed on the old scale? Show your work.

Name ______________________

Homework & Practice 11-8

Precision

Another Look!

Meg and Tina measured the length of their classroom. They wondered how the measurements compare.

Meg	Tina
Our classroom is $9\frac{1}{3}$ yards long	Length of classroom = 28 ft

Tell how you can use precision to compare the measurements.

- I can use numbers, units, and symbols correctly.
- I can calculate accurately.
- I can give a clear answer.

Use precision to compare the measurements.

Convert $9\frac{1}{3}$ yards to feet.

$9\frac{1}{3}$ yd = _____ ft

$9\frac{1}{3} \times 3 = \frac{28}{3} \times \frac{3}{1} = \frac{84}{3} = 28$

So, $9\frac{1}{3}$ yd = 28 ft.

Since $9\frac{1}{3}$ yd = 28 ft, the measurements are equal.

MP.6 Be Precise

William bought a 0.5-liter bottle of liquid plant food. He uses 40 milliliters a week.

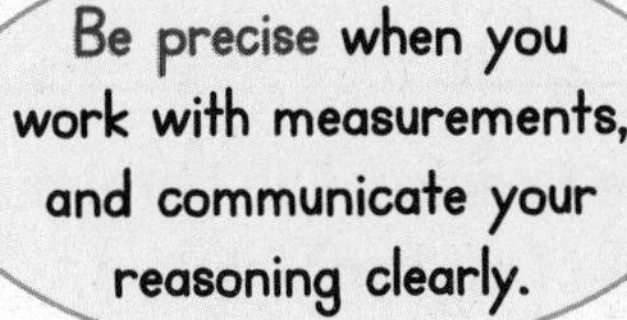

Be precise when you work with measurements, and communicate your reasoning clearly.

1. What measurements are given? Are the same units used for each measurement? Explain.

2. Explain how you can convert one of the measurements so that both use the same unit.

3. How much plant food does William need for 12 weeks? Explain.

4. Is one bottle enough for 12 weeks? Give a clear answer.

Common Core Performance Assessment

Buying Ribbon
Mimi needs eleven 18-inch pieces of rhinestone ribbon. She purchased 5 yards of the ribbon shown at the right.

10 yd

$6 per yard
or
$55 for the whole spool

5. **MP.6 Be Precise** What is the total amount of ribbon Mimi needs? Explain.

6. **MP.2 Reasoning** Do you need to convert measurements to determine if Mimi purchased the right amount of ribbon? Explain.

7. **MP.4 Model with Math** Show how to convert the measurements you described in Exercise 6.

8. **MP.6 Be Precise** Did Mimi purchase the correct amount of ribbon? Explain.

9. **MP.1 Make Sense and Persevere** If Mimi purchases the additional ribbon she needs, what will be the total cost of all the ribbon? Show two different ways to find the answer.

To be precise, you need to check that you are using units of measure correctly and that your conversions are accurate.

Name ____________________

Fluency Practice Activity

Find a partner. Get paper and a pencil. Each partner chooses light blue or dark blue.

At the same time, Partner 1 and Partner 2 each point to one of their black numbers. Both partners find the product of the two numbers.

The partner who chose the color where the product appears gets a tally mark. Work until one partner has seven tally marks.

I can ...
multiply multi-digit whole numbers.

Content Standard 5.NBT.B.5

Partner 1

1,000
25
57
75
100

14,250	275,937	363,075	4,841,000
67,650	18,750	652,700	121,025
6,527,000	750,000	57,000	22,550
42,750	56,250	163,175	75,000
484,100	90,200	372,039	489,525
32,490	51,414	570,000	902,000

Partner 2

570
750
902
4,841
6,527

Tally Marks for Partner 1

Tally Marks for Partner 2

TOPIC 11 Vocabulary Review

Understand Vocabulary

Choose the best term from the Word List. Write it on the blank.

Word List

- Capacity
- Centimeter
- Cup
- Fluid ounce
- Foot
- Gallon
- Gram
- Inch
- Kilogram
- Kilometer
- Liter
- Mass
- Meter
- Mile
- Milligram
- Milliliter
- Millimeter
- Ounce
- Pint
- Pound
- Quart
- Ton
- Weight
- Yard

1. One ________ is equivalent to twelve ________.
2. The measure of the amount of matter in an object is known as ________.
3. The volume of a container measured in liquid units is its ________.
4. There are 1,000 meters in one ________.
5. Finding how light or how heavy an object is means measuring its ________.
6. There are 2 cups in one ________.

For each of these objects, give an example and a non-example of a unit of measure that could be used to describe it.

	Example	Non-example
7. Milk	________	________
8. Person's height	________	________
9. Shoe size	________	________

Use Vocabulary in Writing

10. Explain the relationship among the metric units of mass in the Word List.

Name ____

TOPIC 11

Reteaching

Set A pages 639–644

Convert 3 yards to inches.

1 foot (ft) = 12 inches (in.)
1 yard (yd) = 3 ft = 36 in.
1 mile (mi) = 1,760 yd = 5,280 ft

1 yard = 36 inches. To change larger units to smaller units, multiply: $3 \times 36 = 108$.

So, 3 yards = 108 inches.

Remember to divide when changing smaller units to larger units.

Convert.

1. 7 ft = ____ in.
2. $1\frac{1}{2}$ mi = ____ ft
3. $5\frac{2}{3}$ yd = ____ ft
4. 54 in. = ____ ft

Set B pages 645–650

Convert 16 cups to pints.

2 cups = 1 pint. To change smaller units to larger units, divide: $16 \div 2 = 8$.

So, 16 cups = 8 pints.

Remember that 1 gal = 4 qt, 1 qt = 2 pt, 1 pt = 2 c, and 1 cup = 8 fl oz.

Convert.

1. 36 c = ____ gal
2. 7 pt = ____ qt
3. $1\frac{1}{2}$ gal = ____ fl oz
4. 6 pt = ____ c

Set C pages 651–656

Convert 6 pounds to ounces.

1 pound = 16 ounces. To change larger units to smaller units, multiply: $6 \times 16 = 96$.

So, 6 pounds = 96 ounces.

Remember that 2,000 pounds = 1 ton.

Convert.

1. $2\frac{3}{4}$ lb = ____ oz
2. 56 oz = ____ lb
3. 4,000 lb = ____ T
4. $6\frac{1}{2}$ T = ____ lb
5. $\frac{1}{4}$ T = ____ oz
6. 200 lb = ____ T

Set D pages 657–662

Convert 2 meters to centimeters.

1 km = 1,000 m   1 m = 100 cm
1 m = 1,000 mm   1 cm = 10 mm

1 meter = 100 centimeters. To change larger units to smaller units, multiply: $2 \times 100 = 200$.

So, 2 meters = 200 centimeters.

Remember to multiply or divide by a power of 10 to convert metric measurements.

Convert.

1. 5.4 m = ____ cm
2. 2.7 km = ____ m
3. 0.02 km = ____ cm
4. 0.025 m = ____ mm
5. 675 mm = ____ m
6. 7,435 cm = ____ m

Set E pages 663–668

Convert 6,000 milliliters to liters.

1,000 milliliters = 1 liter. To change milliliters to larger units, divide: 6,000 ÷ 1,000 = 6.

So, 6,000 milliliters = 6 liters.

Remember that the most commonly used metric units of capacity are the liter and milliliter.

Convert.

1. 6 L = ______ mL
2. 0.15 L = ______ mL
3. 2,000 mL = __ L
4. 900 mL = ____ L

Set F pages 669–674

Convert 6 kilograms (kg) to grams (g).

1 kilogram = 1,000 grams. To change larger units to smaller units, multiply: 6 × 1,000 = 6,000.

So, 6 kg = 6,000 g.

Remember that to convert metric units, you can annex zeros and move the decimal point.

Convert.

1. 30 kg = ______ g
2. 3,000 mg = __ g
3. 560 g = ____ kg
4. 0.17 g = ____ mg

Set G pages 675–680

In a contest, Lina jumped 3 yards and Ed jumped 8 feet. Who jumped farther?

Convert each measurement to the same unit. Then compare.

Find how many feet are in 3 yards:
1 yd = 3 ft, so 3 yd = 9 ft.

Lina jumped 9 feet, Ed jumped 8 feet. So, Lina jumped farther.

Remember to check if the units in the problem are the same.

1. Max wants to put a fence around his triangular garden. If each side is 6 yards, how many feet of fencing does Max need?

Set H pages 681–686

Think about these questions to help you **be precise** in your work.

Thinking Habits

- Am I using numbers, units, and symbols appropriately?
- Am I using the correct definitions?
- Am I calculating accurately?
- Is my answer clear?

Remember that the problem might have more than one step.

Solve. Show your work.

1. Monica bought a 40-pound bag of dog food for her pet. Twice a day, she gives the dog 6 ounces of food. How much dog food will she use in 1 week? Explain.

Name ______________________________

1. The nutrition label on a carton of soy milk says that one glass contains 7 grams of protein. How many milligrams of protein does one glass contain?

Ⓐ 7 milligrams

Ⓑ 70 milligrams

Ⓒ 700 milligrams

Ⓓ 7,000 milligrams

2. Justin's garden is shown below.

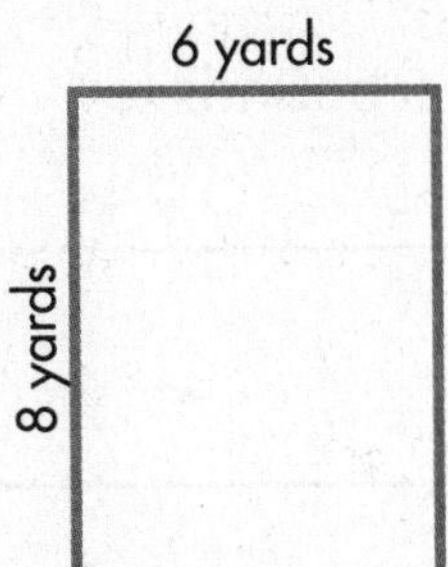

Part A

How can you convert the dimensions of Justin's garden from yards to inches?

Part B

What is the perimeter of Justin's garden in inches?

3. Which of the following expressions can be used to find how many kilograms of sweet potatoes are needed for the recipe?

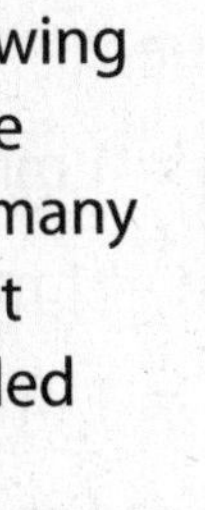

DATA

Soup Recipe
1 onion
2,000 grams sweet potatoes
3 liters water
15 milliliters chicken stock

Ⓐ $1{,}000 \div 2{,}000$

Ⓑ $2{,}000 \div 1{,}000$

Ⓒ $2{,}000 \times 1{,}000$

Ⓓ $2{,}000 \times 100$

4. Ten bales of cotton weigh about 5,000 pounds. Which comparison is true?

Ⓐ 5,000 pounds < 10,000 ounces

Ⓑ 5,000 pounds = 3 tons

Ⓒ 5,000 pounds < 3 tons

Ⓓ 5,000 pounds > 3 tons

5. Tyrell bought 4 liters of fruit punch for a party. He will serve the punch in glasses that can hold 200 milliliters. How many full glasses of fruit punch can he serve?

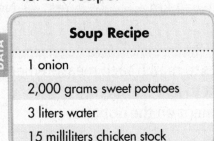

6. For questions 6a–6d, choose Yes or No to tell if the number 10^3 will make each equation true.

6a. ☐ km = 1 mm ○ Yes ○ No

6b. ☐ mm = 1 m ○ Yes ○ No

6c. ☐ cm = 1 m ○ Yes ○ No

6d. ☐ m = 1 km ○ Yes ○ No

7. Draw lines to match each measurement on the left to its equivalent measurement on the right.

1 gallon	2 cups
1 cup	2 pints
1 quart	8 fl oz
1 pint	4 quarts

8. Choose all lengths that are equal to 6 feet 12 inches.

☐ 3 yd 1 ft

☐ 7 ft

☐ 7 ft 2 in.

☐ 2 yd 1 ft

☐ 1 yd 4 ft

9. Juanita has a pail with a capacity of 3.4 liters. How many milliliters will the pail hold?

10. Mason made 5 quarts of salsa. Which of the following can be used to find the number of cups of salsa Mason made?

Ⓐ $5 \times 2 \times 2$

Ⓑ $5 \times 4 \times 4$

Ⓒ $5 \div 2 \div 2$

Ⓓ $5 \times 4 \div 2$

11. Alicia bought 5 pounds of potting soil. She wants to put 10 ounces of soil in each flower pot.

Part A

How can she convert 5 pounds to ounces?

Part B

How many flower pots can she fill?

12. The tail of a Boeing 747 is $63\frac{2}{3}$ feet. How many inches tall is the tail?

13. A model ship is 0.38 meter long. How long is the ship in centimeters?

Name ______________________________

TOPIC 11

Performance Assessment

Orange Juice

Heidi sells freshly-squeezed orange juice in **Heidi's Orange Juice** cups.

1. Use the **Information about Oranges**. Answer the questions below to find how many pounds of oranges Heidi needs for her orange juice.

Part A

How many oranges does Heidi need to make one large orange juice? Explain. Show your work.

Part B

How many pounds of oranges does Heidi need to make one large orange juice? Show your work.

Heidi's Orange Juice

Large = $2\frac{1}{4}$ cups

Information about Oranges

One medium orange has about 2 fl oz of juice and weighs about 5 ounces.

2. Answer the following to find the area of **Heidi's Display Shelf**.

Part A

What units can you use for the area? Explain.

Heidi's Display Shelf

4 ft

15 in.

Part B

What is the area of **Heidi's Display Shelf**? Show your work.

3. The **Orange Nutrition** table shows nutrients in one medium-sized orange that weighs 5 ounces or 140 grams. All the nutrients in the orange are also in Heidi's orange juice.

Orange Nutrition

Nutrient	Amount
Carbohydrates	16 g
Fiber	3.5 g
Potassium	250 mg

Part A

How many grams of potassium are in one large cup of Heidi's orange juice? Explain how you solved.

Part B

How many milligrams of fiber are in one large cup of Heidi's orange juice? Use an exponent when you explain the computation you used to solve.

4. Heidi also sells cartons of orange juice. Use the picture of **Heidi's Orange Juice Carton.** Find the volume of the carton in cubic centimeters. Explain.

Heidi's Orange Juice Carton

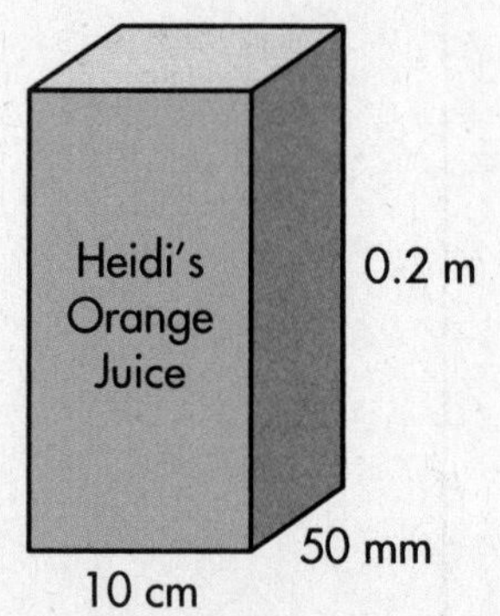

Represent and Interpret Data

Essential Question: How can line plots be used to represent data and answer questions?

Wildfires help nature by burning away dead plant material.

Lightning can cause wildfires. But did you know human activities cause 9 out of 10 wildfires?

I'm shocked! It's time for some trailblazing research! Here's a project about wildfires.

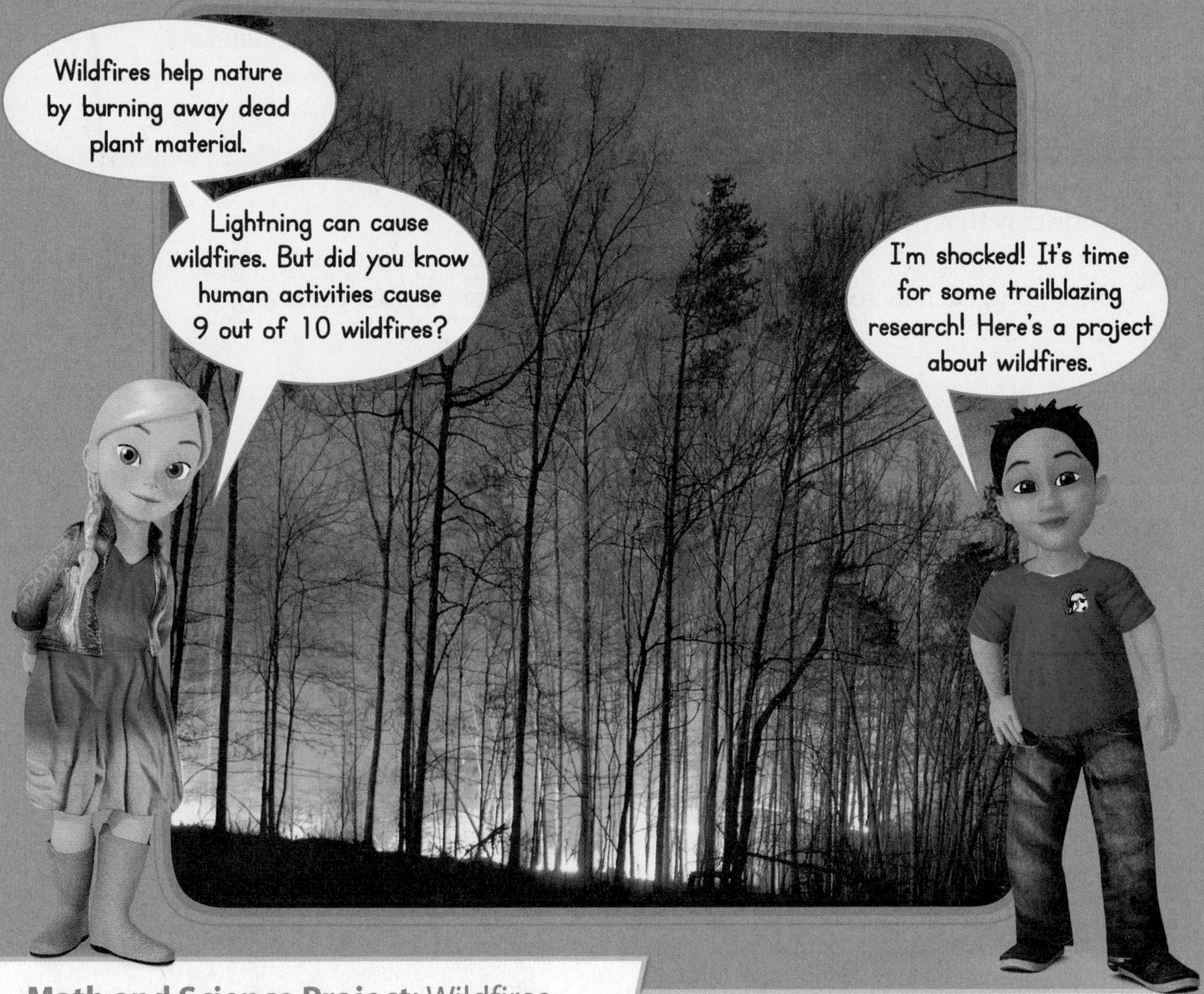

Math and Science Project: Wildfires

Do Research Use the Internet and other sources to learn more about wildfires. Investigate how wildfires affect ecosystems. Explore the costs and benefits of wildfires. List five living things in an ecosystem. Research how long each one takes to recover from a wildfire.

Journal: Write a Report Include what you found. Also in your report:

- Make a pamphlet to show how wildfires affect ecosystems.
- Suggest ways to prevent wildfires.
- Make a line plot to show your data.
- Make up and solve problems using line plots.

Name ____________________

Review What You Know

Vocabulary

Choose the best term from the Word List. Write it on the blank.

- bar graph
- compare
- frequency table
- overestimate
- underestimate

1. A display that shows how many times an event occurs is a(n) ____________.

2. A display that uses bars to show data is a(n) ____________.

3. Rounding each factor in a multiplication to a greater number gives a(n) ____________ of the actual product.

4. You can use the length of the bars in a bar graph to ____________ two similar data sets.

Fraction Computation

Find each answer.

5. $2\frac{1}{2} + 5\frac{1}{3}$

6. $13\frac{3}{10} - 8\frac{1}{5}$

7. $8\frac{1}{3} + 7\frac{11}{12}$

8. $15 - 5\frac{2}{9}$

9. $7\frac{5}{8} + 13\frac{11}{20}$

10. $15\frac{4}{5} + 1\frac{2}{3}$

11. $\frac{7}{8} \times 4$

12. $5 \times 1\frac{2}{3}$

13. $2\frac{1}{8} \times \frac{2}{3}$

Bar Graphs

Use the bar graph to answer the questions.

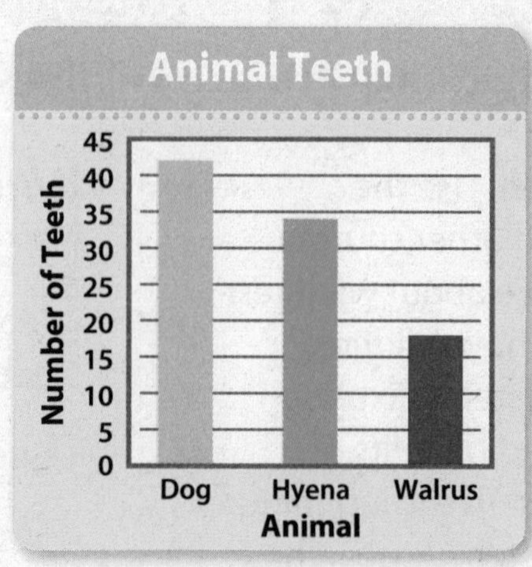

14. Which animal has about 34 teeth?

15. About how many more teeth does a dog have than a hyena?

16. About how many more teeth does a hyena have than a walrus?

My Word Cards

Use the examples for each word on the front of the card to help complete the definitions on the back.

A-Z Glossary

line plot

Pet Ownership

Number of Pets	0	1	2	3
Dots	•••	••••	••••	••

Number of Pets

Amount of Rainfall (in.):

$\frac{1}{4}, \frac{1}{2}, 1, 1\frac{1}{2}, \frac{3}{4}, 0, \frac{5}{8}, 0$

$0, 1\frac{1}{4}, \frac{7}{8}, \frac{1}{2}, 1$

outlier

2, 3, 3, 1, 4, 15, 4, 1, 2, 2

15 is an outlier.

My Word Cards

Complete the definition. Extend learning by writing your own definitions.

Collected information is called

________________.

A display of responses along a number line, with dots or Xs recorded above the responses to indicate the number of times a response occurred, is called a

________________________.

An ________________ is a value that is much greater or much less than the other values in a data set.

Name ______________________________

Lesson 12-1
Analyze Line Plots

I can ...
read a line plot.

Content Standard 5.MD.B.2
Mathematical Practices MP.1, MP.2, MP.5, MP.6, MP.7

Solve & Share

Several students were asked how many blocks they walk from home to school each day. The results are shown in the line plot below. How many students were asked the question? ***Use the line plot to solve this problem.***

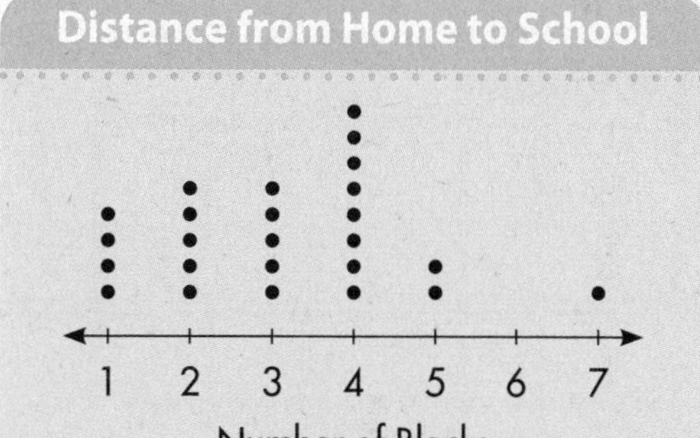

Make Sense and Persevere How can you analyze data in a line plot? *Show your work!*

Look Back! MP.2 **Reasoning** What can you tell about the distance most of the students in the group walk to school each day?

Essential Question How Can You Analyze Data Displayed in a Line Plot?

A

A line plot, or dot plot, shows data along a number line. Each dot or X represents one value in the data set.

In science class, Abby and her classmates performed an experiment in which they used different amounts of vinegar.

The table below shows how much vinegar each person used.

A line plot shows how often each value occurs.

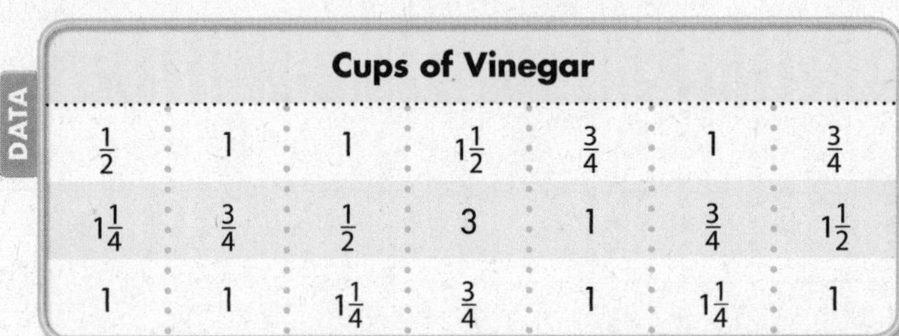

DATA

Cups of Vinegar						
$\frac{1}{2}$	1	1	$1\frac{1}{2}$	$\frac{3}{4}$	1	$\frac{3}{4}$
$1\frac{1}{4}$	$\frac{3}{4}$	$\frac{1}{2}$	3	1	$\frac{3}{4}$	$1\frac{1}{2}$
1	1	$1\frac{1}{4}$	$\frac{3}{4}$	1	$1\frac{1}{4}$	1

B Read the line plot.

A line plot can be used to organize the amount of vinegar each person used.

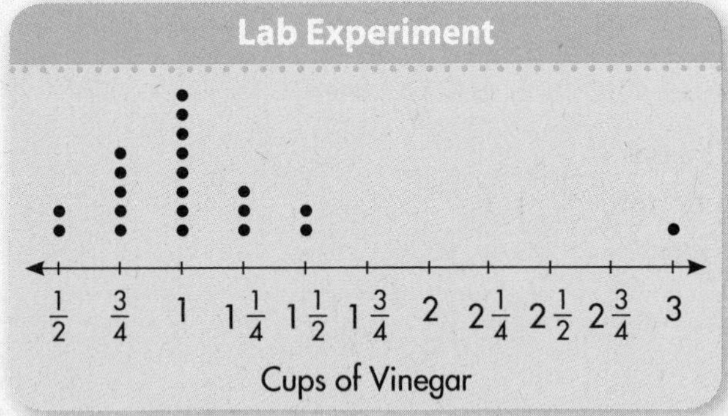

C Analyze the data.

Identify any outliers.

An outlier is any value that is very different from the rest of the values.

The dot above 3 is far from the rest of the dots. This value is an outlier.

Convince Me! **MP.2 Reasoning** How does the line plot show which amount of vinegar was used most often in this experiment?

Name ______________________________

Guided Practice*

Do You Understand?

1. **Vocabulary** What is an outlier in a set of data?

2. In the line plot on the previous page, do any values occur the same number of times? Explain.

3. **MP.7 Look for Relationships** Describe any patterns in the line plot on the previous page.

Do You Know How?

In **4** and **5**, use the data set to answer the questions.

4. Mr. Rice's students ran a 40-yard dash in the following times, in seconds.

   6.8 7.3 7.1 7.0 7.2 7.3 7.0 6.9

   6.9 7.1 7.1 7.2 7.1 7.0 7.1 7.2

   How many race times are recorded?

5. Use the line plot that shows the data.

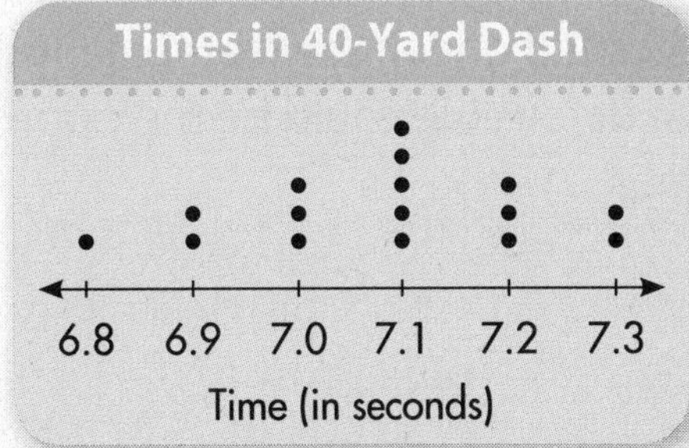

Which time occurred most often?

Independent Practice

In **6–8**, use the line plot to answer the questions.

6. How many orders for cheese does the line plot show?

7. Which amount of cheese was ordered most often?

8. How many more orders for cheese were for $\frac{3}{4}$ pound or less than for 1 pound or more?

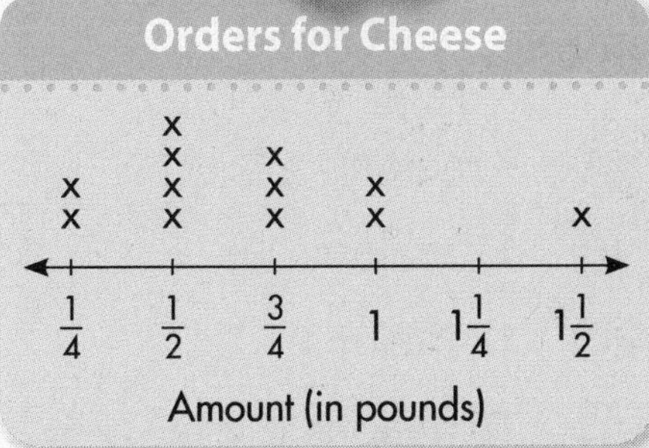

*For another example, see Set A on page 725.

Math Practices and Problem Solving

In **9–11**, use the data set and line plot.

DATA

Fox Sparrow Feather Lengths (in inches)				
$2\frac{1}{2}$	$2\frac{1}{4}$	2	$2\frac{1}{2}$	$2\frac{3}{4}$
2	$2\frac{1}{2}$	$\frac{3}{4}$	$2\frac{1}{4}$	$2\frac{1}{4}$
$2\frac{3}{4}$	2	$2\frac{1}{2}$	$2\frac{1}{2}$	$2\frac{3}{4}$
$2\frac{1}{4}$	$2\frac{1}{4}$	$2\frac{1}{4}$	2	$2\frac{1}{4}$

9. **MP.6 Be Precise** Jerome studied the feather lengths of some adult fox sparrows. How long are the longest feathers in the data set?

10. How many feathers are $2\frac{1}{4}$ inches or longer? Explain.

11. **Higher Order Thinking** Jerome discovered he had made an error when he recorded one of the feather lengths. Which data value could be the error? Explain.

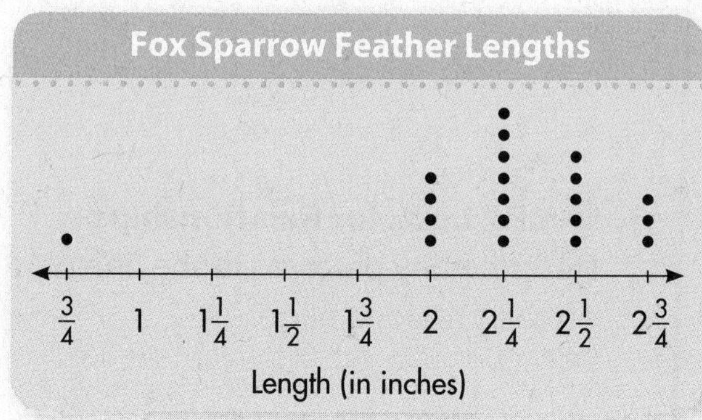

12. **MP.2 Reasoning** How can you find the value that occurs most often by looking at a line plot?

13. **MP.5 Use Appropriate Tools** Draw and label a rectangle with a perimeter of 24 inches.

Common Core Assessment

14. Use the information shown in the line plot. How many melons weigh more than 4 pounds and less than $5\frac{1}{2}$ pounds?

Ⓐ 7 melons

Ⓑ 11 melons

Ⓒ 13 melons

Ⓓ 16 melons

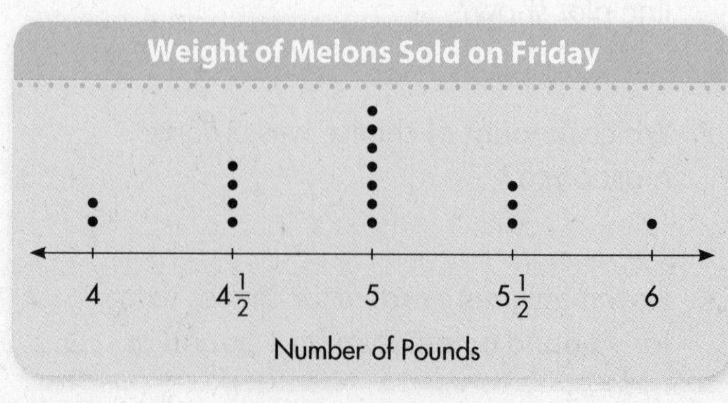

Name ______________________________

Homework & Practice 12-1

Analyze Line Plots

Another Look!

For an experiment, Bea recorded how much each of 14 seedlings grew in one month. She made a line plot to show the data. Which value occurred most often?

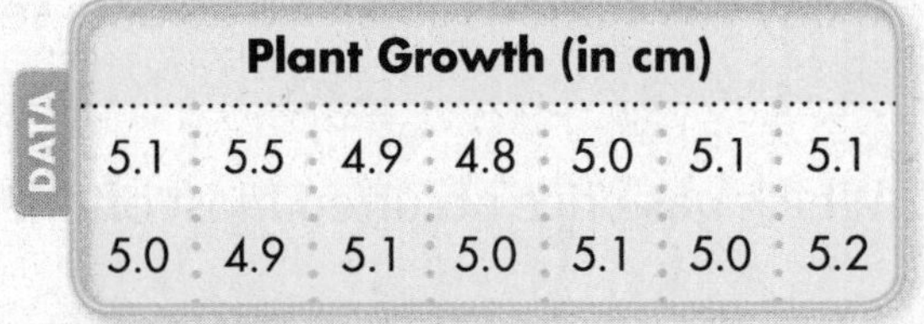

DATA

Plant Growth (in cm)						
5.1	5.5	4.9	4.8	5.0	5.1	5.1
5.0	4.9	5.1	5.0	5.1	5.0	5.2

Step 1

Read the labels on the line plot. Values are listed in order on a number line.

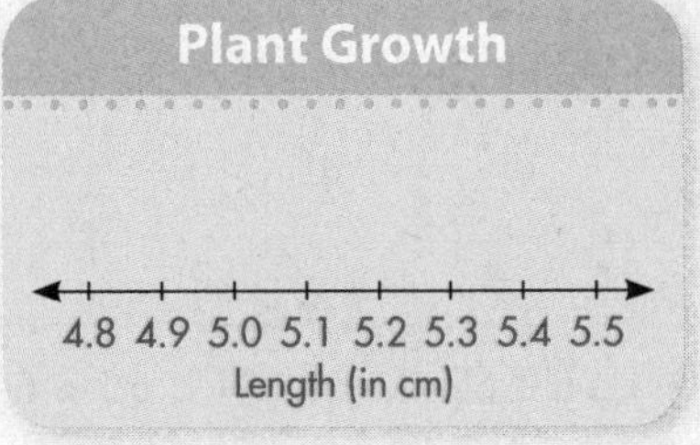

Step 2

Each dot stands for 1 time the value occurred. Dots are stacked when a value occurs more than once.

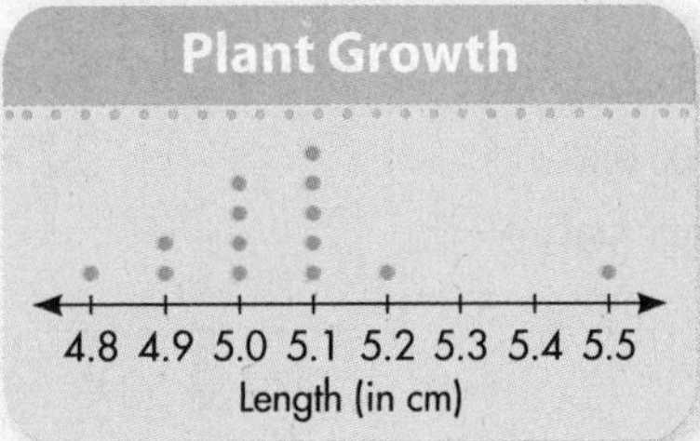

Step 3

Use the dot plot to solve.

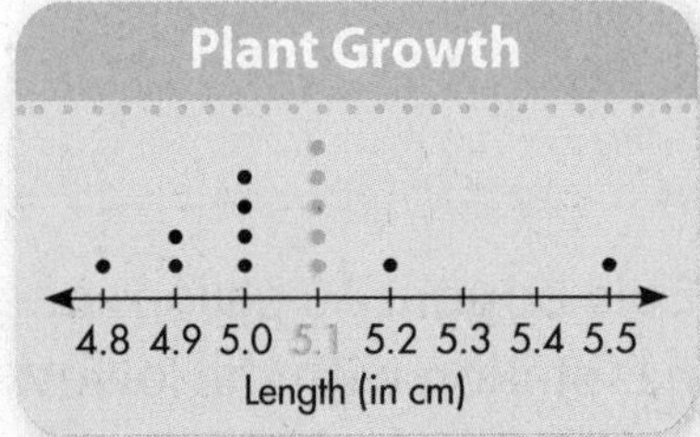

The value of 5.1 has the most dots, so 5.1 cm growth occurred most often.

In **1–4**, use the line plots to solve.

1. Ani and her friends recorded their bowling shoe sizes. Which two bowling shoe sizes occurred most often?

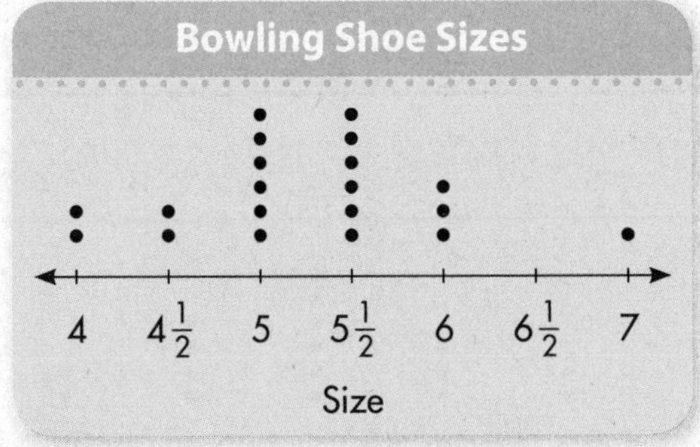

2. A pearl diver recorded the sizes of the pearls in a batch. Which three pearl sizes occurred least often?

Pearl Sizes

5.5 6.0 6.5 7.0 7.5 8.0

Size (in millimeters)

3. In Exercise 1, how many of Ani's bowling friends have size $6\frac{1}{2}$ shoes? Explain how you know.

4. In Exercise 2, how many pearls were in the batch? Explain how you know.

In **5–8**, use the data set and line plot.

5. On Thursday, Cole collected data on the gas prices at different gas stations. How many gas stations are in Cole's data set?

6. Which gas price occurred most often?

7. **Higher Order Thinking** What is the outlier in the data? Give a reason why you think this outlier occurred.

DATA

Prices of 1 Gallon of Gas on Thursday (in dollars)

3.61	3.60	3.59	3.58	3.59
3.59	3.60	3.61	3.62	3.66
3.58	3.57	3.59	3.60	3.59

8. Cole bought 10 gallons of gas at the gas station with the lowest price. He paid with two $20 bills. Write and solve an equation to find his change.

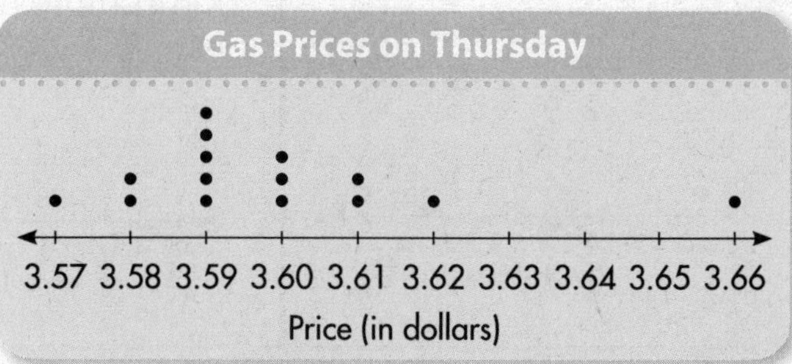

9. **MP.6 Be Precise** Mrs. Dugan plans to serve 100 barbecue sandwiches at the company picnic. How many packages of barbecue buns will she need if buns come in packages of 8? packages of 12?

10. **Algebra** Janet had $9.25 this morning. She spent $4.50 for lunch and then spent $3.50 on school supplies. Write and solve an equation to find m, the amount of money Janet had left at the end of the day.

Common Core Assessment

11. Use the line plot at the right. How many players on the soccer club are older than 11 years and younger than $11\frac{3}{4}$ years?

Ⓐ 6 players

Ⓑ 9 players

Ⓒ 10 players

Ⓓ 13 players

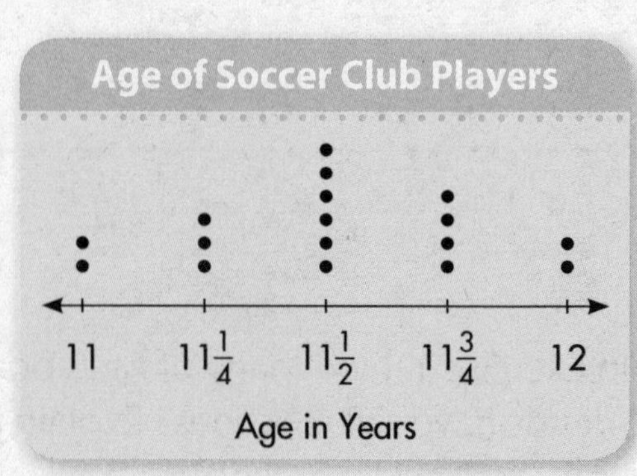

Name ____________________

Lesson 12-2
Make Line Plots

I can ...
display data in a line plot.

Content Standard 5.MD.B.2
Mathematical Practices MP.1, MP.2, MP.4, MP.6, MP.7, MP.8

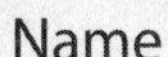

Solve & Share

A fifth-grade class recorded the height of each student. How could you organize the data? ***Make a line plot to solve this problem.***

Heights of Students in Grade 5 (to the nearest $\frac{1}{2}$ inch):

55, 52, $50\frac{1}{2}$, $50\frac{1}{2}$, 55, $50\frac{1}{2}$, 50, 55, $50\frac{1}{2}$, 55, $58\frac{1}{2}$, 60, 52, $50\frac{1}{2}$, $50\frac{1}{2}$, 50, 55, 55, $58\frac{1}{2}$, 60

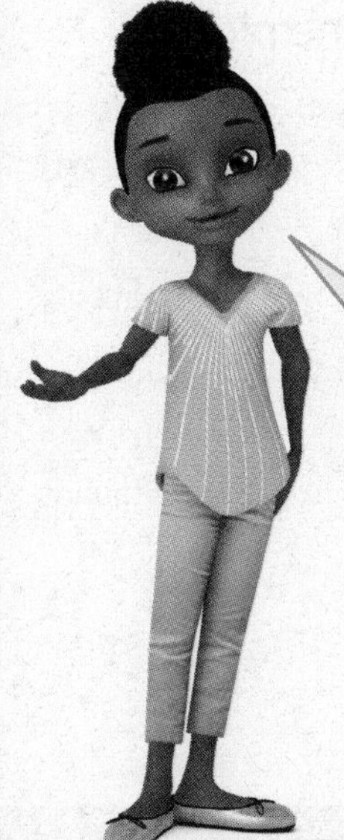

Make Sense and Persevere
You can make a line plot to organize data. *Show your work!*

Look Back! **MP.8 Generalize** How does organizing the data help you see the height that occurs most often? Explain.

How Can You Use a Line Plot to Organize and Represent Measurement Data?

A

The dogs in Paulina's Pet Shop have the following weights. The weights are in pounds.

How can you organize this information in a line plot?

Measurement data that is organized is easier to use.

DATA

Weights of Dogs (in pounds)					
$8\frac{1}{2}$	$12\frac{1}{4}$	6	$11\frac{1}{2}$	$7\frac{1}{4}$	$12\frac{1}{4}$
$8\frac{1}{2}$	$12\frac{1}{4}$	$8\frac{1}{2}$	$12\frac{1}{4}$	$12\frac{1}{4}$	6

B

Organize the data.

Write the weights from least to greatest.

$6, 6, 7\frac{1}{4}, 8\frac{1}{2}, 8\frac{1}{2}, 8\frac{1}{2}, 11\frac{1}{2}, 12\frac{1}{4}, 12\frac{1}{4}, 12\frac{1}{4}, 12\frac{1}{4}, 12\frac{1}{4}$

You can also organize the data in a frequency table. The frequency is how many times a given response occurs.

DATA

Dog Weight (pounds)	Tally	Frequency
6	||	2
$7\frac{1}{4}$	|	1
$8\frac{1}{2}$	|||	3
$11\frac{1}{2}$	|	1
$12\frac{1}{4}$	~~||||~~	5

C

Make a line plot.

First draw the number line using an interval of $\frac{1}{4}$. Then mark a dot for each value in the data set. Write a title for the line plot.

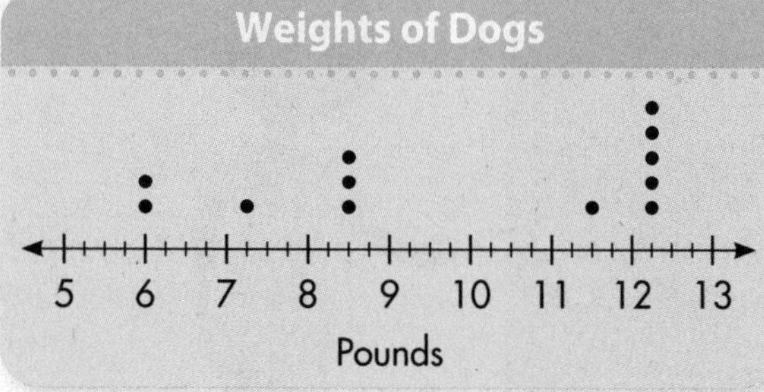

Convince Me! **MP.2 Reasoning** Which weight occurs most often? Which weight occurs least often? How can you tell from the line plot?

Name ____________________

Practice Buddy | Tools | Assessment

Guided Practice*

Do You Understand?

1. In the line plot of dog weights on the previous page, what does each dot represent?

2. In a line plot, how do you determine the values to show on the number line?

Do You Know How?

3. Draw a line plot to represent the data.

DATA

Weights of Pumpkins	Tally	Frequency
$3\frac{1}{2}$ lb	||	2
$5\frac{1}{4}$ lb	|||	3
7 lb	||||	4
$8\frac{1}{2}$ lb	|	1

Independent Practice

In **4** and **5**, complete the line plot for each data set.

Double check that you have a dot for each value.

4. 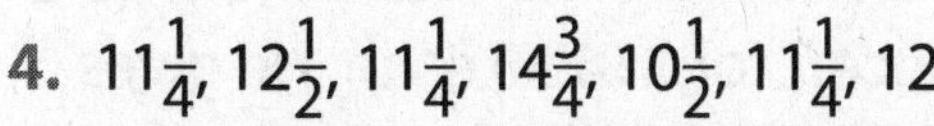
$11\frac{1}{4}, 12\frac{1}{2}, 11\frac{1}{4}, 14\frac{3}{4}, 10\frac{1}{2}, 11\frac{1}{4}, 12$

5. 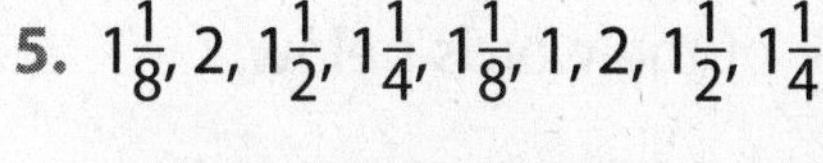
$1\frac{1}{8}, 2, 1\frac{1}{2}, 1\frac{1}{4}, 1\frac{1}{8}, 1, 2, 1\frac{1}{2}, 1\frac{1}{4}$

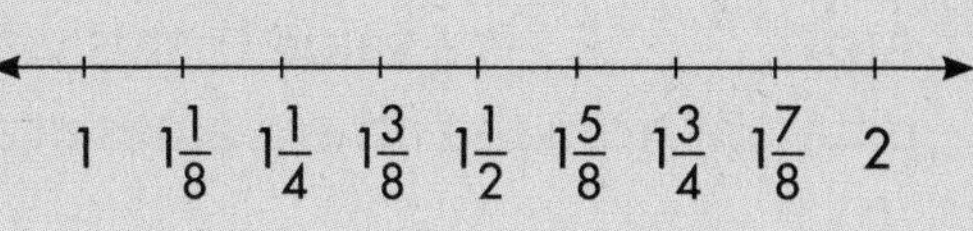

In **6** and **7**, construct a line plot for each data set.

6. $\frac{1}{2}, \frac{3}{4}, \frac{3}{4}, 1, 1, 0, \frac{1}{2}, \frac{1}{2}, \frac{3}{4}$

7. $5\frac{1}{2}, 5, 5, 5\frac{1}{8}, 5\frac{3}{4}, 5\frac{1}{4}, 5\frac{1}{2}, 5\frac{1}{8}, 5\frac{1}{2}, 5\frac{3}{8}$

*For another example, see Set B on page 725.

Math Practices and Problem Solving

In **8–10**, use the data set.

8. MP.1 Make Sense and Persevere Martin's Tree Service purchased several spruce tree saplings. Draw a line plot of the data showing the heights of the saplings.

Heights of Saplings (in.)

$26\frac{1}{2}$	27	$26\frac{3}{4}$	$27\frac{1}{2}$	$26\frac{3}{4}$
$27\frac{1}{2}$	$27\frac{3}{4}$	$27\frac{1}{4}$	$27\frac{1}{2}$	$27\frac{1}{4}$
$27\frac{3}{4}$	$27\frac{1}{2}$	$26\frac{1}{2}$	$26\frac{1}{2}$	$27\frac{1}{2}$
$27\frac{1}{4}$	$27\frac{1}{4}$	$27\frac{1}{2}$	27	$26\frac{3}{4}$

9. MP.7 Look for Relationships How many more saplings with a height of $27\frac{1}{4}$ inches or less were there than saplings with a height greater than $27\frac{1}{4}$ inches?

10. Higher Order Thinking Suppose Martin's Tree Service bought two more saplings that were each $27\frac{1}{4}$ inches tall. Would the value that occurred most often change?

11. Vocabulary Complete the sentence using one of the words below.

line plot   data   outlier

A(n) ________ is a value that is very different from the other values in a data set.

12. MP.6 Be Precise Randall buys 3 tickets for a concert for $14.50 each. He gives the cashier a $50 bill. How much change does he get? Write equations to show your work.

Common Core Assessment

13. Amy measured how many centimeters the leaves on her houseplants grew in July. Use the leaf growth data below to complete the line plot on the right.

$2\frac{1}{2}, 4\frac{1}{2}, 4, 4, 3, 1, 3, 3\frac{1}{2}, 3\frac{1}{2}, 3\frac{1}{2}, 2\frac{1}{2}, 3, 3\frac{1}{2}, 3\frac{1}{2}, 5\frac{1}{2}$

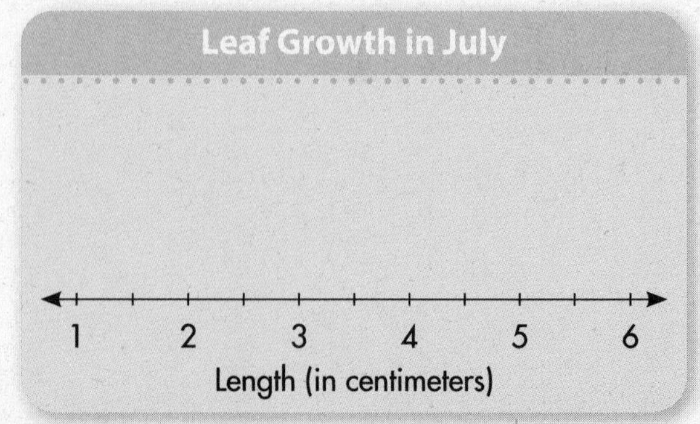

Name ____________________

Homework & Practice 12-2
Make Line Plots

Another Look!

Mick recorded the lengths of 10 Steller sea lions. Which length occurs most often?

DATA

Steller Sea Lion Lengths (in feet)				
$9\frac{1}{4}$	$9\frac{1}{8}$	$8\frac{3}{4}$	$9\frac{1}{4}$	$9\frac{1}{4}$
$9\frac{3}{8}$	$9\frac{1}{4}$	$9\frac{1}{8}$	$9\frac{1}{4}$	$9\frac{1}{8}$

Step 1

Make a frequency table to organize the data.

Value	Tally	Frequency
$8\frac{3}{4}$	|	1
$9\frac{1}{8}$	|||	3
$9\frac{1}{4}$	~~||||~~	5
$9\frac{3}{8}$	|	1

Step 2

Make a line plot. Draw a dot for each value. Stack dots for values that occur more than once.

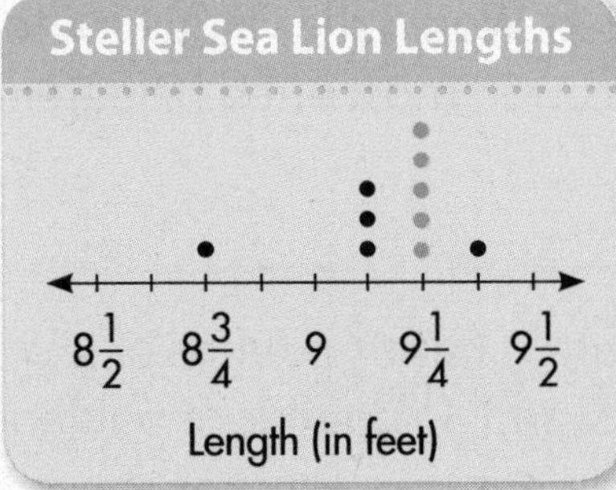

The length $9\frac{1}{4}$ feet occurs most often.

1. Jacob and his father measured the lengths of scrap wood in their yard. Make a line plot of their data.

DATA

Scrap Wood Lengths (in inches)					
$4\frac{1}{2}$	$4\frac{7}{8}$	5	$4\frac{1}{4}$	$4\frac{1}{2}$	$4\frac{3}{8}$
$4\frac{1}{8}$	$4\frac{1}{2}$	$4\frac{1}{4}$	$4\frac{3}{4}$	$4\frac{1}{2}$	$4\frac{1}{2}$
$4\frac{5}{8}$	$4\frac{3}{4}$	$4\frac{1}{4}$	$4\frac{1}{8}$	$4\frac{1}{2}$	$4\frac{7}{8}$

2. What is the difference between the longest and shortest piece of scrap wood?

In **3** and **4**, use the table showing data from recipes used in a chili cooking contest.

3. MP.1 Make Sense and Persevere Draw a line plot of the data.

Cups of Beans in 1 Batch				
5	$5\frac{1}{2}$	$4\frac{1}{2}$	$4\frac{1}{2}$	$4\frac{1}{2}$
$4\frac{1}{2}$	$4\frac{1}{2}$	$4\frac{1}{2}$	$4\frac{3}{4}$	$4\frac{1}{2}$

4. Higher Order Thinking Suppose the contestants were asked to make two batches of their recipe instead of one batch. Would the value for the amount of beans that occurred most often be different? Explain.

5. A restaurant has $6\frac{1}{2}$ pounds of jalapeño peppers, $4\frac{3}{4}$ pounds of red bell peppers, and $5\frac{1}{4}$ pounds of poblano peppers. How many pounds of peppers does the restaurant have in all?

6. MP.4 Model with Math Jessica and her friend measured the lengths of the fish they caught one day. Make a line plot of their data.

Fish Lengths (in cm)			
10.25	10.50	11.75	12.00
10.75	11.00	11.25	11.50
11.25	11.25	11.50	11.00

Common Core Assessment

7. The list below shows the weight in ounces of various rock samples. Use the data to complete the line plot on the right.

$8\frac{1}{4}, 7\frac{1}{2}, 5\frac{1}{4}, 6\frac{3}{4}, 7, 7, 8\frac{1}{4}, 5\frac{1}{4},$
$5\frac{1}{4}, 7\frac{1}{2}, 7, 7, 6\frac{3}{4}, 7$

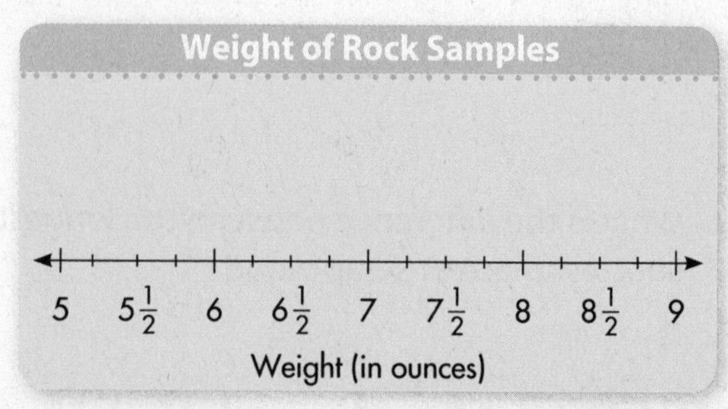

Name ____________________

Lesson 12-3
Solve Word Problems Using Measurement Data

I can ...
solve problems using data in a line plot.

Content Standards 5.MD.B.2, 5.NF.A.2, 5.NF.B.6
Mathematical Practices MP.1, MP.2, MP.3, MP.4, MP.8

Solve & Share

Rainfall for the Amazon was measured and recorded for 30 days. The results were displayed in a line plot. What can you tell about the differences in the amounts of rainfall? ***Use the line plot to solve this problem.***

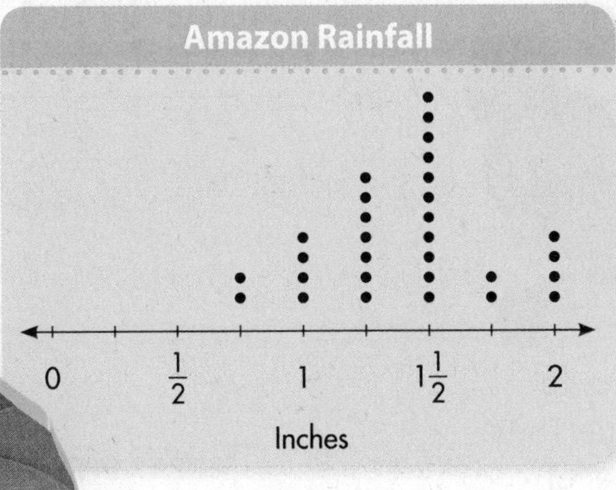

Make Sense and Persevere You can use a representation to analyze data. *Show your work!*

Look Back! **MP.2 Reasoning** What is the difference between the greatest amount of rain in a day and the least amount of rain in a day? How can you tell?

How Can You Use Measurement Data Represented in a Line Plot to Solve Problems?

A

Bruce measured the daily rainfall while working in Costa Rica. His line plot shows the rainfall for each day in September. What was the total rainfall for the month?

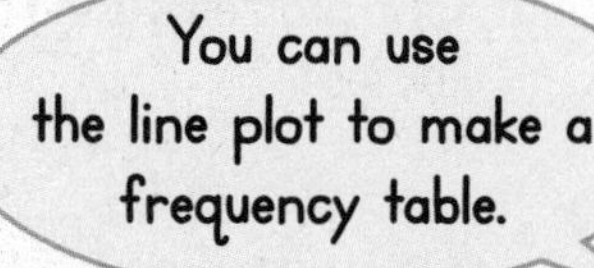

You can use the line plot to make a frequency table.

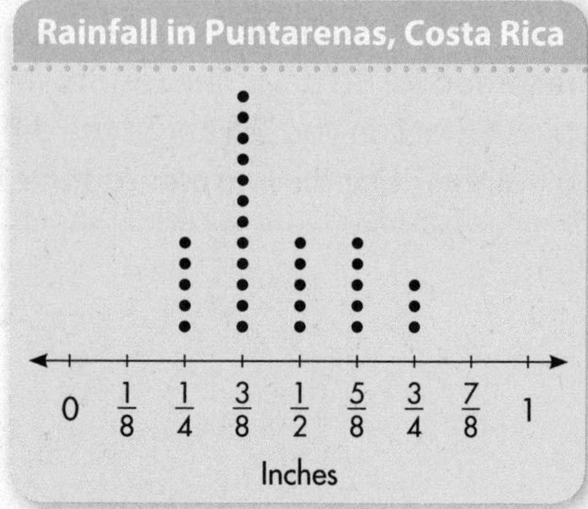

B Multiply each value by the frequency to find the amount of rain for that value. Then add the products to find the number of inches of rainfall for the month.

DATA

Rainfall (inches)	Frequency	Multiplication
$\frac{1}{4}$	5	$5 \times \frac{1}{4} = 1\frac{1}{4}$
$\frac{3}{8}$	12	$12 \times \frac{3}{8} = 4\frac{1}{2}$
$\frac{1}{2}$	5	$5 \times \frac{1}{2} = 2\frac{1}{2}$
$\frac{5}{8}$	5	$5 \times \frac{5}{8} = 3\frac{1}{8}$
$\frac{3}{4}$	3	$3 \times \frac{3}{4} = 2\frac{1}{4}$

The table helps you organize the numerical data for your calculations.

$1\frac{1}{4} + 4\frac{1}{2} + 2\frac{1}{2} + 3\frac{1}{8} + 2\frac{1}{4} =$

$1\frac{2}{8} + 4\frac{4}{8} + 2\frac{4}{8} + 3\frac{1}{8} + 2\frac{2}{8} = 13\frac{5}{8}$

The total rainfall was $13\frac{5}{8}$ inches.

Convince Me! **MP.3 Critique Reasoning** Rosie says she can find the total rainfall in the example above without multiplying. Do you agree? Explain.

Name

Practice Buddy | Tools | Assessment

Guided Practice*

Do You Understand?

In **1–4**, use the line plot showing how many grams of salt were left after liquids in various containers evaporated.

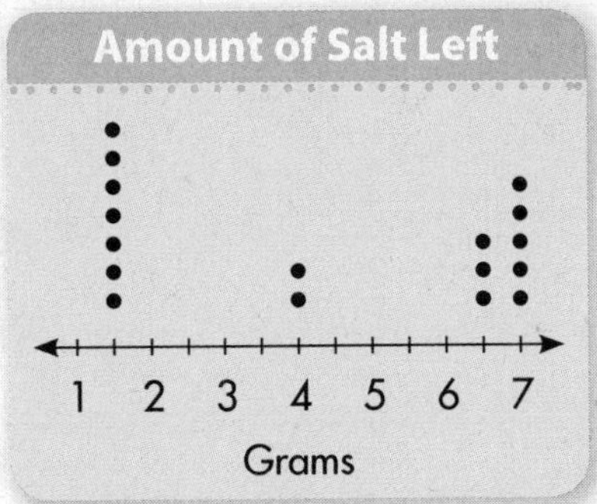

1. **MP.8 Generalize** How could you find the difference between the greatest amount and the least amount of salt left?

Do You Know How?

2. Write a problem that can be answered using the line plot.

3. **MP.4 Model with Math** Write and solve an equation that represents the total number of grams of salt left.

4. How many grams of salt would be left if two of each container were used?

Independent Practice

In **5** and **6**, use the line plot Allie made to show the lengths of strings she cut for her art project.

5. Write an equation for the total amount of string.

6. What is the difference in length between the longest and the shortest lengths of string?

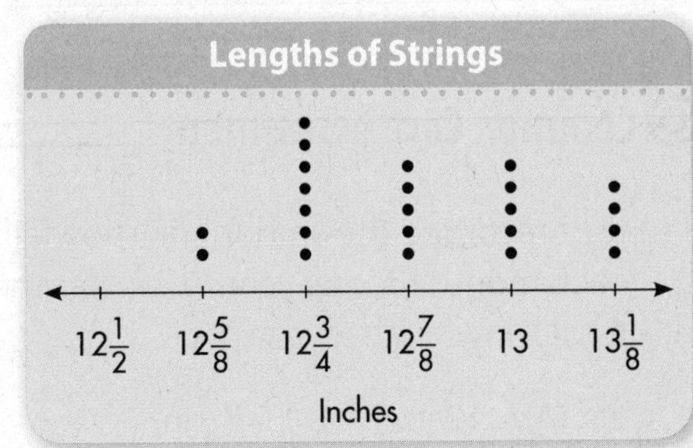

*For another example, see Set C on page 726.

Math Practices and Problem Solving

In **7** and **8**, use the line plot Susannah made to show the amount of rainfall in one week.

7. Algebra Write and solve an equation for the total amount of rainfall, r, Susannah recorded.

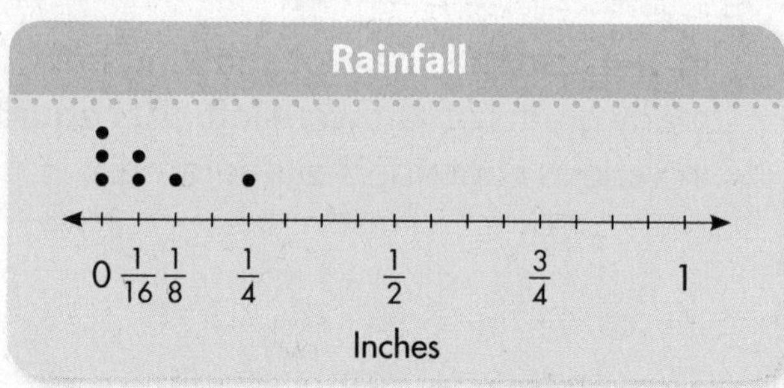

8. Higher Order Thinking Suppose the same amount of rain fell the following week, but the same amount of rain fell each day. How much rain fell each day?

9. MP.1 Make Sense and Persevere The area of a square deck is 81 square feet. How long is each side of the deck?

How does knowing the shape of the deck help you?

10. Althea recorded the amount she earned from T-shirt sales each day for 14 days. She made a frequency table to organize the data. Write a problem that can be answered by using the frequency table.

DATA

Amount Earned (in $)	Frequency	Multiplication
7.50	3	$3 \times 7.50 = 22.50$
15.00	4	$4 \times 15.00 = 60.00$
22.50	5	$5 \times 22.50 = 112.50$
30.00	1	$1 \times 30.00 = 30.00$
37.50	1	$1 \times 37.50 = 37.50$

Common Core Assessment

11. Kurt recorded the amount of snowfall in each month for one year. What was the total snowfall that year?

Ⓐ 12 in. Ⓒ $7\frac{3}{4}$ in.

Ⓑ $10\frac{1}{4}$ in. Ⓓ $7\frac{1}{2}$ in.

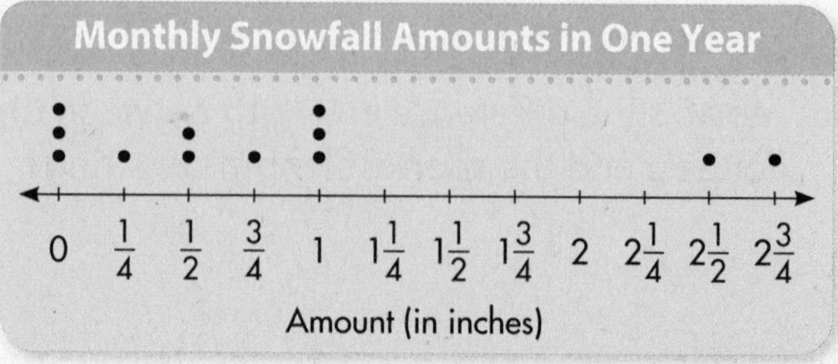

Name ______________________________

Homework & Practice 12-3

Solve Word Problems Using Measurement Data

Another Look!

Mr. Culver made a line plot to show the number of hours students worked on a class project. What was the total number of hours that the students worked?

Number of Hours Spent on Class Project

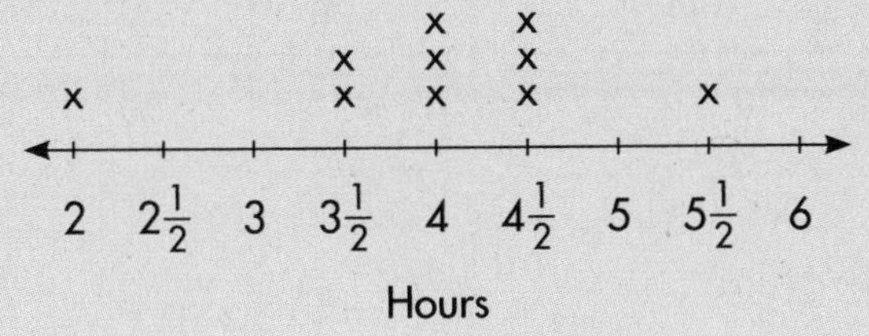

Use the line plot to make a frequency table.

Multiply each number of hours by its frequency. The product is the total amount for that value.

Add the products.

$$2 + 7 + 12 + 13\frac{1}{2} + 5\frac{1}{2} = 40$$

The students spent a total of 40 hours on the project.

Hours	Frequency	Multiplication
2	1	$1 \times 2 = 2$
$3\frac{1}{2}$	2	$2 \times 3\frac{1}{2} = 7$
4	3	$3 \times 4 = 12$
$4\frac{1}{2}$	3	$3 \times 4\frac{1}{2} = 13\frac{1}{2}$
$5\frac{1}{2}$	1	$1 \times 5\frac{1}{2} = 5\frac{1}{2}$

In **1** and **2**, use each line plot to answer the question.

1. Wai recorded the length of each wire needed for a science project. What is the total length of wire needed?

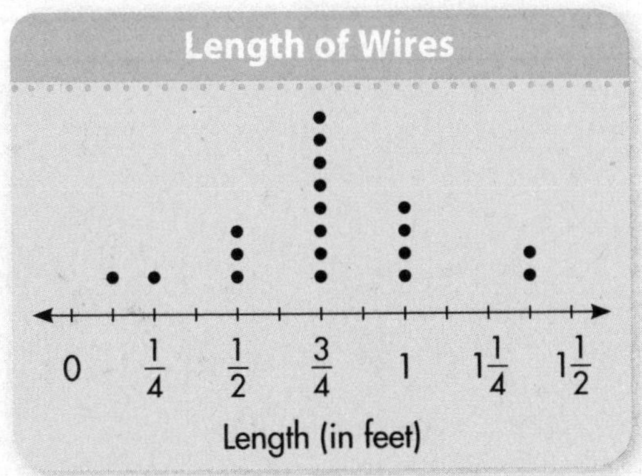

2. Trey measured the mass of some pebbles. What is the combined mass of the pebbles that are $4\frac{1}{2}$ grams or more?

Pebble Masses

3 4 5 6 7

Mass (in grams)

In **3** and **4**, Dominick's class flew toy gliders. He recorded the flight distances in a line plot.

3. What is the difference between the longest and shortest distances the gliders flew?

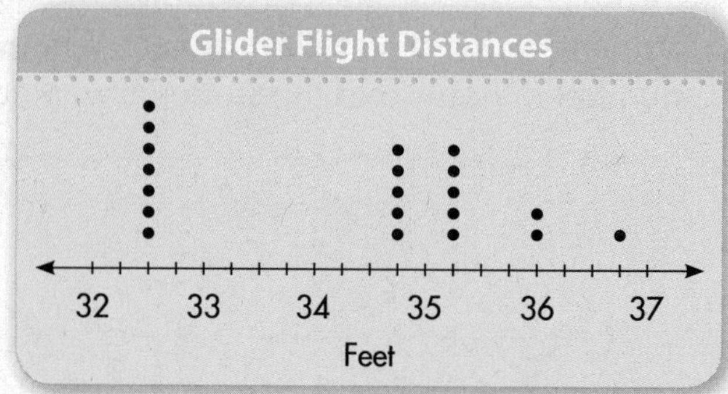

4. Higher Order Thinking Dominick said that $32\frac{1}{2}$ is an outlier. Do you agree with him? Explain.

---

5. Math and Science On June 1, 2013, the number of hours of daylight in Anchorage, Alaska was $18\frac{1}{4}$ hours. What was the number of hours without daylight?

6. Number Sense How could you estimate the quotient $162 \div 19$?

---

7. MP.2 Reasoning Nolan listed the weights of oranges in a box in the frequency table. Which is greater, the total weight of the 6.25-ounce oranges or the total weight of the 7.25-ounce oranges? How much more? Explain.

DATA

Weight (in ounces)	Frequency	Multiplication
6.25	13	?
6.5	16	$16 \times 6.5 = 104$
6.75	20	$20 \times 6.75 = 135$
7.0	14	$14 \times 7.0 = 98$
7.25	9	?

Common Core Assessment

8. Anita recorded the amount of rainfall each day for 14 days. What was the total amount of rainfall in the 14 days?

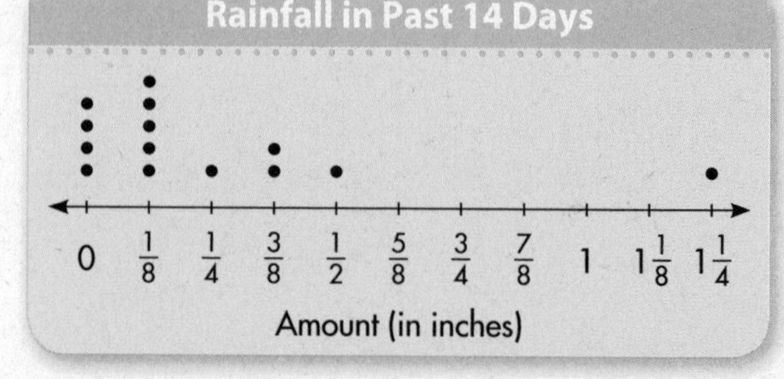

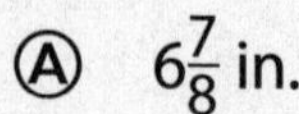

Ⓐ $6\frac{7}{8}$ in.

Ⓑ $4\frac{1}{2}$ in.

Ⓒ $3\frac{3}{8}$ in.

Ⓓ $\frac{1}{8}$ in.

Name ___________________________________

Math Practices and Problem Solving

Lesson 12-4
Critique Reasoning

I can ...
critique the reasoning of others by using what I know about line plots and fractions.

Mathematical Practices MP.3. Also MP.1, MP.2, MP.4, MP.6
Content Standards 5.MD.B.2, 5.NF.A.2, 5.NF.B.6

Solve & Share

A cross country coach recorded the team's practice runs and made the line plot below. The coach had each runner analyze the line plot and write an observation. Read the statements and explain whether you think each runner's reasoning makes sense.

September Practice Runs

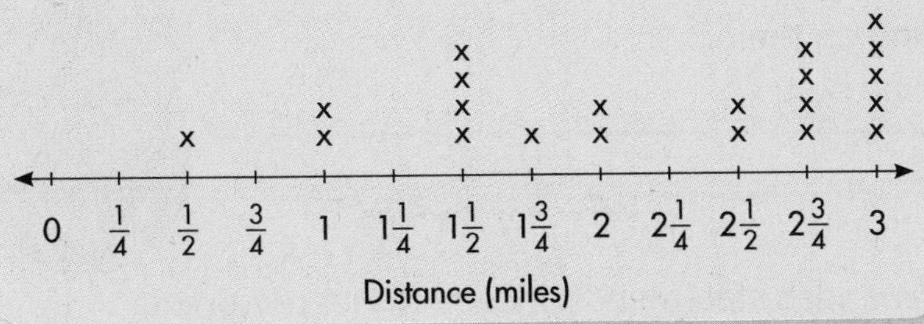

Olivia
The distance we ran the most often was 3 miles.

Natalie
The team ran 8 different times, each time for a different distance.

Michelle
The team ran different distances on different days. We usually ran for 2 miles or more.

Peter
Each day the team ran the same distance or a little farther than the day before.

Thinking Habits

Be a good thinker!
These questions can help you.

- What questions can I ask to understand other people's thinking?
- Are there mistakes in other people's thinking?
- Can I improve other people's thinking?

Look Back! MP.3 Critique Reasoning Quinn said that to find the total distance the team ran in September, you add each number that has an X above it: $\frac{1}{2} + 1 + 1\frac{1}{2} + 1\frac{3}{4} + 2 + 2\frac{1}{2} + 2\frac{3}{4} + 3$. Do you agree? Explain why or why not.

Essential Question

How Can You Critique the Reasoning of Others?

A

Ms. Kelly's class made a line plot showing how many hours each student spent watching television the previous evening. Amanda said, "No one watched TV for 3 hours." Drake said, "No, 3 of us watched no TV." Who is correct? Explain your reasoning.

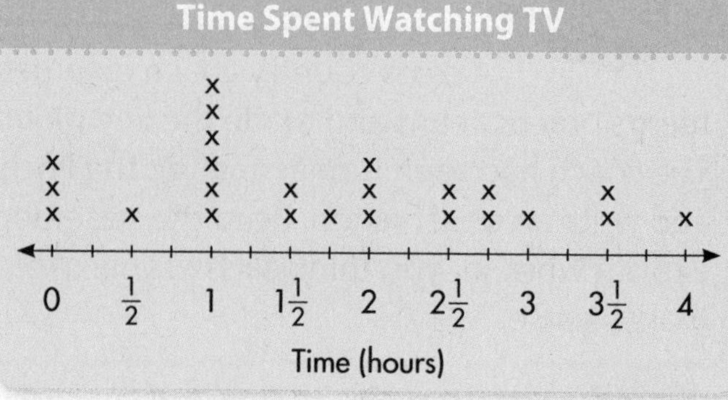

What information do Amanda and Drake use for reasoning?

Amanda and Drake base their reasoning on their analysis of the data displayed on the line plot.

B

How can I critique the reasoning of others?

I can

- decide if the statements make sense.
- look for mistakes in calculations.
- clarify or correct flaws in reasoning.

C

Here's my thinking...

Amanda's statement is incorrect. Her reasoning has flaws. She sees the 3 Xs above the zero and thinks that means that zero people watched 3 hours of TV. The labels on the number line tell how many hours, and the Xs tell how many students. So, Amanda should have said, "There are 3 people who watched 0 hours of TV."

Drake's statement is correct. Since there are 3 Xs above the 0, he is correct when he says that 3 people watched no TV.

Convince Me! **MP.3 Critique Reasoning** Andre said, "More than half of us watched TV for less than 2 hours." Explain how you can critique Andre's reasoning to see if his thinking makes sense.

Name ____________________

Guided Practice*

MP.3 Critique Reasoning

Renee works for a sand and gravel company. She made a line plot to show the weight of the gravel in last week's orders. She concluded that one third of the orders were for more than 6 tons.

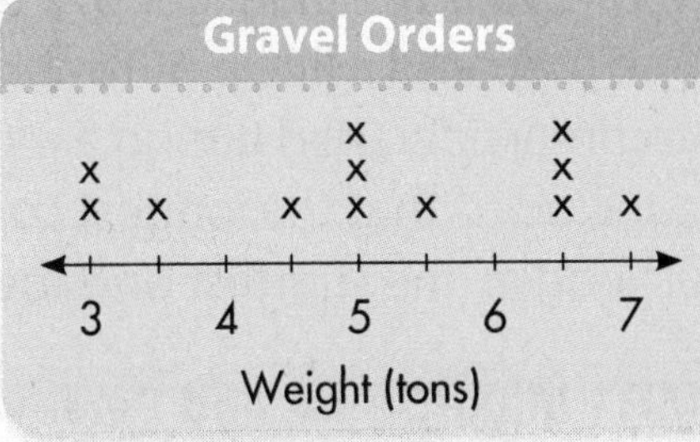

1. What is Renee's conclusion? How did she support it?

2. Describe at least one thing you would do to critique Renee's reasoning.

3. Does Renee's conclusion make sense? Explain.

Independent Practice

MP.3 Critique Reasoning

Aaron made a line plot showing the weights of the heads of cabbage he picked from his garden. He said that since $1\frac{1}{2} + 2 + 2\frac{1}{4} + 2\frac{3}{4} = 8\frac{1}{2}$, the total weight of the cabbages is $8\frac{1}{2}$ pounds.

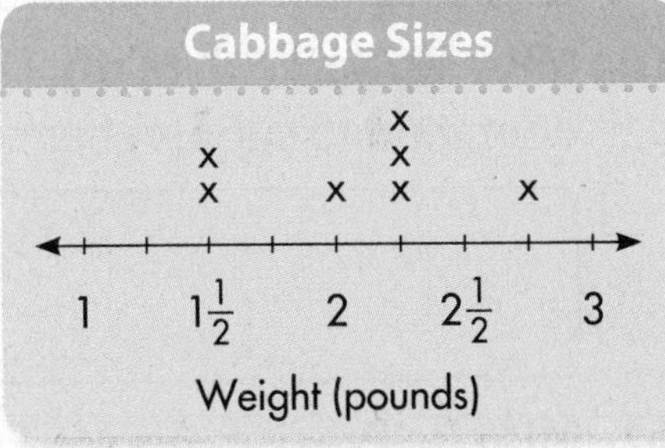

4. Describe at least one thing you would do to critique Aaron's reasoning.

5. Is Aaron's addition accurate? Show how you know.

6. Can you identify any flaws in Aaron's thinking? Explain.

7. Does Aaron's conclusion make sense? Explain.

When you critique reasoning, you need to explain if someone's method makes sense.

*For another example, see Set D on page 726.

Math Practices and Problem Solving

Common Core Performance Assessment

Television Commercials

Ms. Fazio is the manager of a television station. She prepared a line plot to show the lengths of the commercials aired during a recent broadcast. She concluded that the longest commercials were 3 times as long as the shortest ones because $3 \times \frac{1}{2} = 1\frac{1}{2}$.

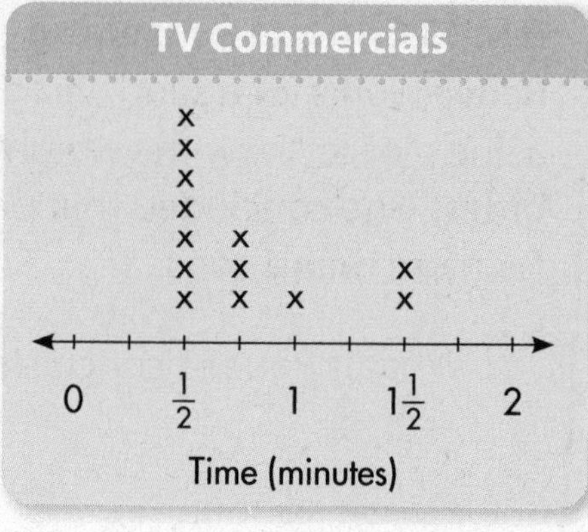

8. **MP.1 Make Sense and Persevere** Which information in the line plot did Ms. Fazio need to use in order to draw her conclusion?

9. **MP.2 Reasoning** Did the number of Xs above the number line affect Ms. Fazio's conclusion? Explain.

10. **MP.4 Model With Math** Did Ms. Fazio use the correct operation to support her conclusion? Explain.

11. **MP.6 Be Precise** Are Ms. Fazio's calculations accurate? Show how you know.

12. **MP.3 Critique Reasoning** Is Ms. Fazio's conclusion logical? How did you decide? If not, what can you do to improve her reasoning?

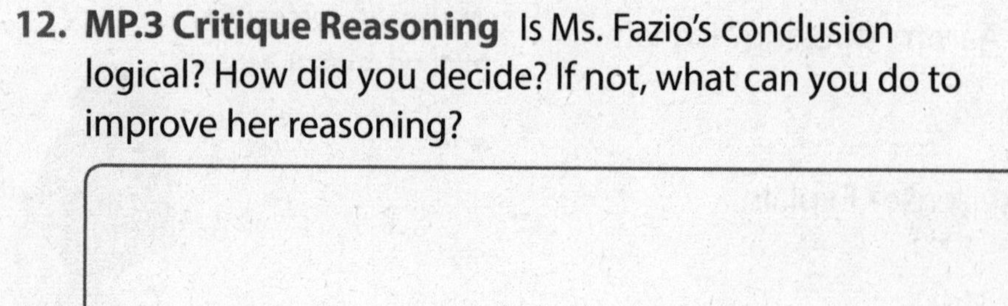

To use math precisely, you need to check that the words, numbers, symbols, and units you use are correct and that your calculations are accurate.

Name ______________________________

Homework & Practice 12-4
Critique Reasoning

Another Look!

A cooking class needs 20 quarts of raspberries. The instructor, Mr. Romano, made a line plot to show how many quarts of raspberries each student picked at a raspberry farm. Then he said, "We need another $\frac{3}{4}$ quart." He showed the class:

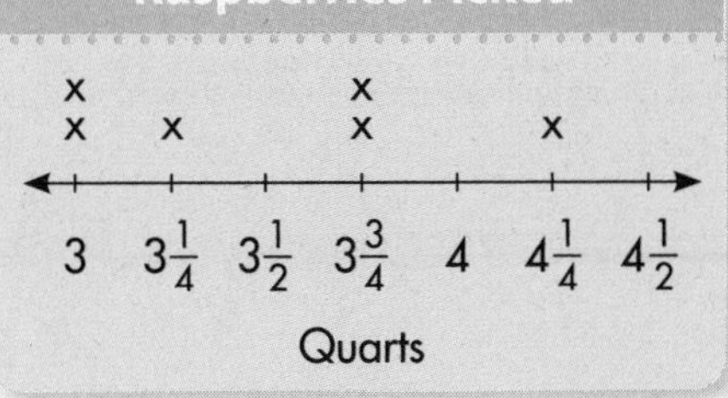

$$(2 \times 3) + 3\frac{1}{4} + \left(2 \times 3\frac{3}{4}\right) + 4\frac{1}{4} =$$

$$6 + 3\frac{1}{4} + 5\frac{3}{4} + 4\frac{1}{4} = 19\frac{1}{4}.$$

Tell how you can critique Mr. Romano's reasoning.

- I can decide if his strategy makes sense.
- I can look for flaws in his calculations.
- I can clarify or correct his reasoning.

Critique Mr. Romano's reasoning.

Mr. Romano's strategy makes sense, but he made a careless mistake in his calculations. $\left(2 \times 3\frac{3}{4}\right) = 7\frac{1}{2}$, not $5\frac{3}{4}$. So, the class picked $6 + 3\frac{1}{4} + 7\frac{1}{2} + 4\frac{1}{4} = 21$ quarts. They have enough raspberries.

When you critique reasoning, you explain why someone's thinking is correct or incorrect.

MP.3 Critique Reasoning

Gillian said that if all the students and Mr. Romano had each picked just $2\frac{1}{2}$ quarts of raspberries, they would have had enough. She estimated $7 \times 3 = 21$.

1. Tell how you can critique Gillian's reasoning.

2. Critique Gillian's reasoning.

3. Identify the flaw in Gillian's thinking.

Common Core Performance Assessment

Video Game

Lydia is playing *Galaxy 8RX*. After three misses, the game is over. Last week, Lydia kept track of how long her games lasted. She made a line plot of her data. Lydia said, "My best time is $2\frac{3}{4}$ minutes longer than my worst time because $4\frac{1}{4} - 1\frac{1}{2} = 2\frac{3}{4}$."

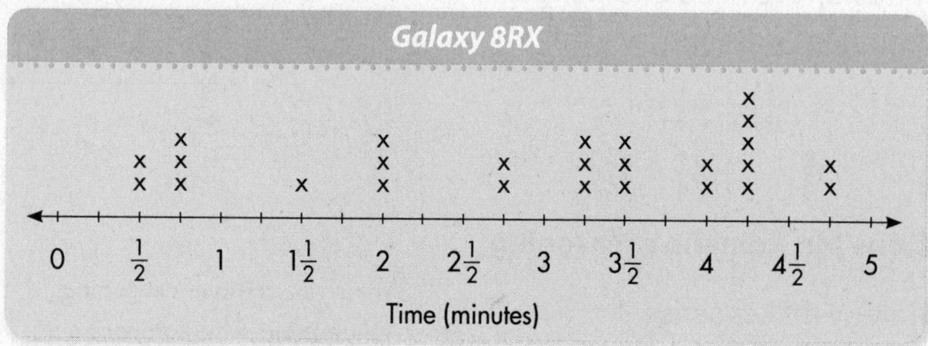

4. **MP.4 Model With Math** Is subtraction the correct operation to compare Lydia's best and worst times? Explain.

5. **MP.6 Be Precise** Are Lydia's calculations accurate? Show how you know.

6. **MP.1 Make Sense and Persevere** In the line plot, what do the numbers Lydia subtracted represent?

7. **MP.3 Critique Reasoning** Does Lydia's conclusion make sense? How did you decide? If not, what can you do to improve her reasoning?

When you critique reasoning, you need to carefully consider all parts of a person's reasoning.

Name ____________________

Topic 12 Fluency Practice Activity

Solve each problem. Follow problems with an answer of 29,160 to shade a path from **START** to **FINISH**. You can only move up, down, right, or left.

I can …
multiply multi-digit whole numbers.

Content Standard 5.NBT.B.5

Start

729 × 40	2,430 × 12	360 × 81	1,620 × 18	540 × 54
1,234 × 25	712 × 55	704 × 40	596 × 50	1,215 × 24
663 × 45	454 × 65	810 × 36	3,645 × 8	486 × 60
740 × 27	1,816 × 15	405 × 72	430 × 71	412 × 70
731 × 40	1,164 × 25	1,080 × 27	972 × 30	648 × 45

Finish

TOPIC 12

Vocabulary Review

Glossary

Word List

- Bar graph
- Data
- Frequency table
- Line plot
- Outlier

Understand Vocabulary

Choose the best term from the Word List. Write it on the blank.

1. Another name for collected information is ______________.

2. A value that is very different from the other values in a particular data set is a(n) ______________.

3. A(n) ______________ is a display of responses on a number line with a dot or X used to show each time a response occurs.

Circle the outlier in each data set.

4. 4 16 17 20

5. 37.2 42.1 43.9 50 76.5

6. $1\frac{1}{2}$ $1\frac{3}{4}$ 0 $1\frac{2}{3}$ $13\frac{1}{2}$

7. 101.2 37.2 40 42.5 33.05

Write **always**, **sometimes**, or **never**.

8. The value closest to 0 on a line plot is ______________ an outlier.

9. A data display ______________ has an outlier.

10. Cross out the words that are **NOT** examples of items that contain *data*.

Encyclopedia Alphabet Email address MP3 Player Phone number Grocery list

Use Vocabulary in Writing

11. Twenty students measured their heights for an experiment in their science class. How can a line plot help the students analyze their results?

Name ______________________________

TOPIC 12

Reteaching

Set A pages 699–704

The data set below shows the number of goals scored by 20 teams in a soccer tournament.

4, 8, 7, 0, 3, 3, 7, 4, 6, 1,

2, 7, 6, 4, 2, 7, 2, 6, 7, 4

The line plot shows how often each data value occurs.

Remember that an outlier is a value that is very different from most of the values in a line plot.

Use the Goals Scored line plot.

1. How many soccer teams scored 3 goals?
2. How many teams scored more than 5 goals?
3. What was the greatest number of goals scored by a team?
4. How many teams scored only 2 goals?
5. What is the difference between the greatest and least number of goals scored?

Set B pages 705–710

Twelve people were surveyed about the number of hours they spend reading books on a Saturday. The results are:

$\frac{3}{4}$ $1\frac{1}{2}$ 1 $\frac{1}{2}$ $1\frac{1}{2}$ $2\frac{3}{4}$

$1\frac{3}{4}$ $\frac{1}{2}$ $2\frac{1}{2}$ 2 $1\frac{1}{2}$ 2

Draw a number line from 0 to 3. Mark the number line in fourths because the survey results are given in $\frac{1}{4}$ hours. Then for each response, place a dot above the value on the number line.

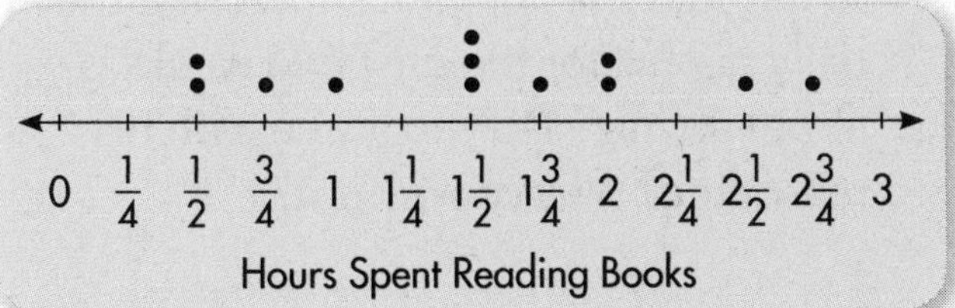

Remember that you can make a line plot to show and compare data.

Use the information below to make a line plot about Patrick's plants.

Patrick listed how many inches his plants grew in one week: 1 $\frac{1}{2}$ $\frac{3}{4}$ $1\frac{1}{2}$ $\frac{1}{2}$ $1\frac{1}{4}$ $1\frac{1}{4}$ $\frac{1}{2}$ 1

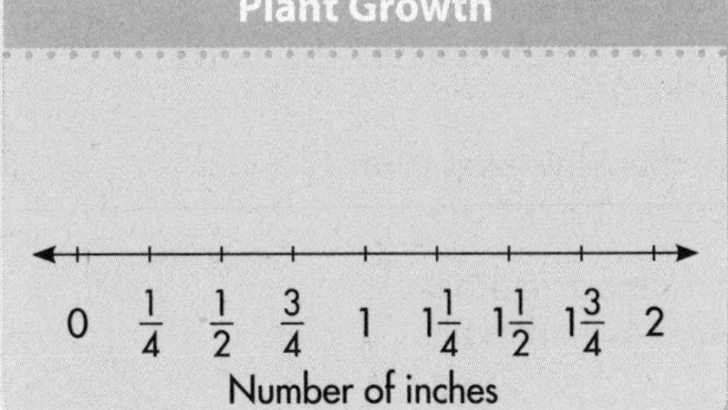

1. Complete the line plot.
2. How many dots are on the line plot?
3. How many inches of plant growth was the most common?

Set C pages 711–716

This line plot shows the amount of flour Cheyenne needs for several different recipes. She organizes the data in a frequency table to calculate the total amount of flour she needs.

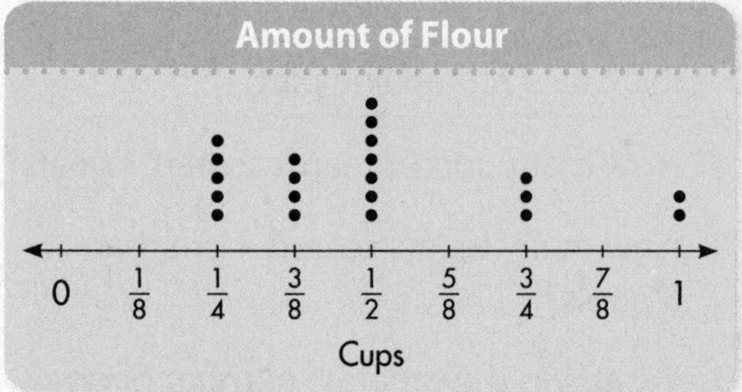

DATA

Amount of Flour (cups)	Frequency	Multiplication
$\frac{1}{4}$	5	$5 \times \frac{1}{4} = 1\frac{1}{4}$
$\frac{3}{8}$	4	$4 \times \frac{3}{8} = 1\frac{1}{2}$
$\frac{1}{2}$	7	$7 \times \frac{1}{2} = 3\frac{1}{2}$
$\frac{3}{4}$	3	$3 \times \frac{3}{4} = 2\frac{1}{4}$
1	2	$2 \times 1 = 2$

Remember that you can multiply each data value by its frequency to find the total amount.

Use the line plot and frequency table at the left.

1. What values are multiplied in the third column of the table?

2. Write and solve an equation to find the total amount of flour Cheyenne needs.

Set D pages 717–722

Think about these questions to help you **critique the reasoning of others.**

Thinking Habits

- What questions can I ask to understand other people's thinking?
- Are there mistakes in other people's thinking?
- Can I improve other people's thinking?

Remember you need to carefully consider all parts of an argument.

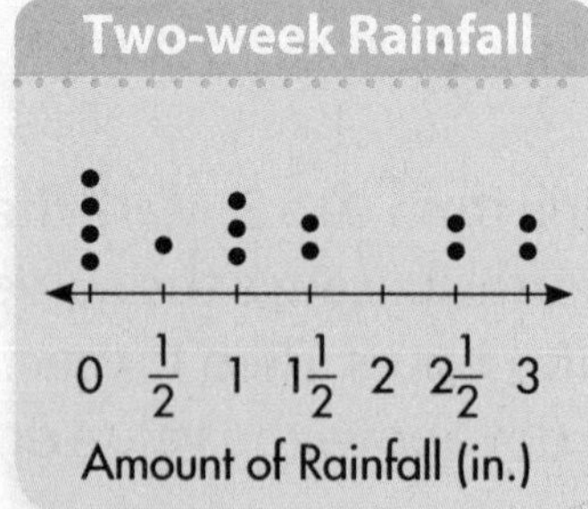

1. Justin says the line plot shows that the daily rainfall for the past two weeks is about an inch. Do you agree with his reasoning? Why or why not?

Name ____________________

1. Which line plot shows the data?

8	$7\frac{1}{2}$	$8\frac{3}{4}$	$7\frac{1}{4}$	$7\frac{1}{4}$	$8\frac{3}{4}$	$8\frac{3}{4}$
$8\frac{3}{4}$	$8\frac{3}{4}$	8	$8\frac{3}{4}$	$9\frac{1}{4}$	$9\frac{1}{4}$	$7\frac{1}{4}$

Ⓐ
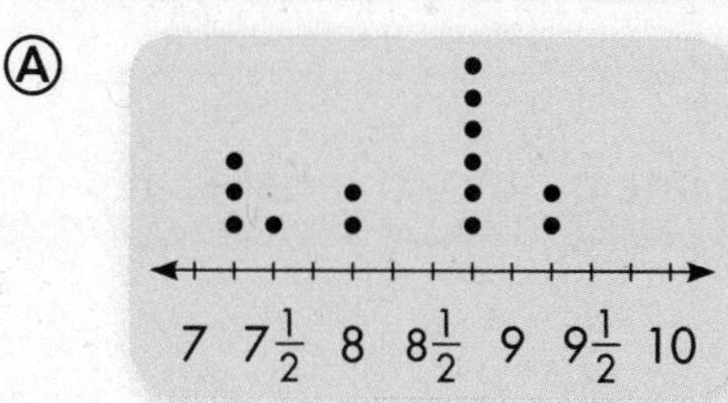

Ⓑ
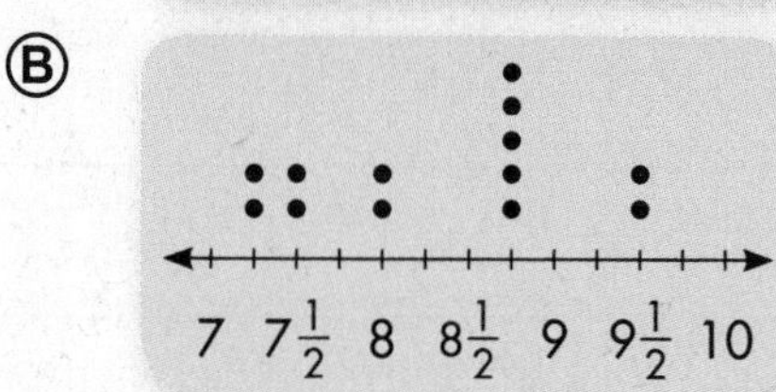

Ⓒ
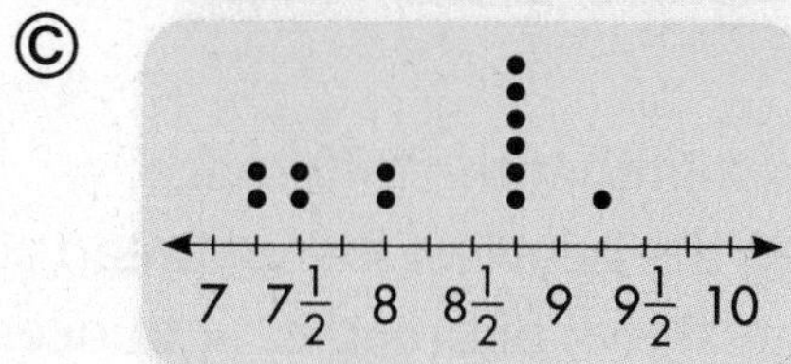

Ⓓ
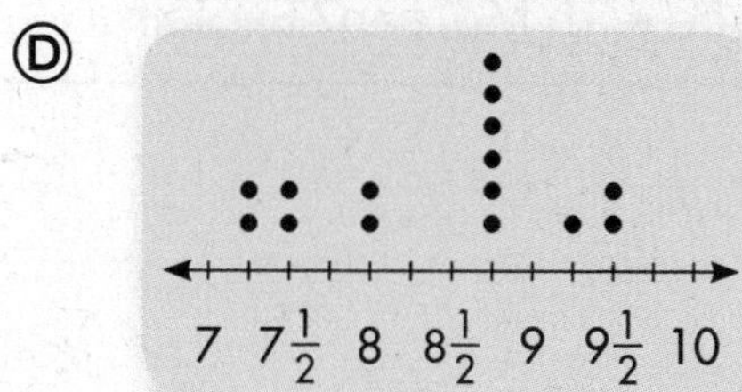

2. The line plot shows the results from a survey asking parents how many children they have in school. How many parents have two children in school?

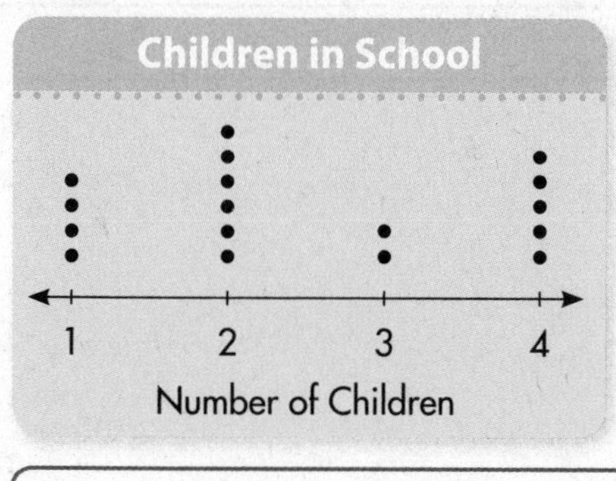

3. Georgiana made a line plot of the amount of time she spent practicing her violin each day in the past two weeks.

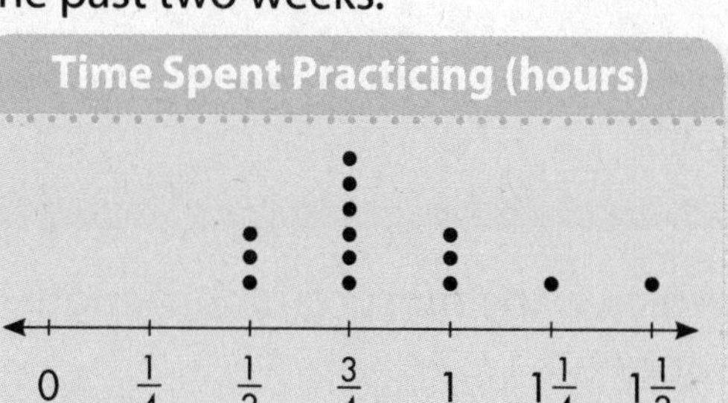

Part A

What is the difference between the greatest and least times spent practicing?

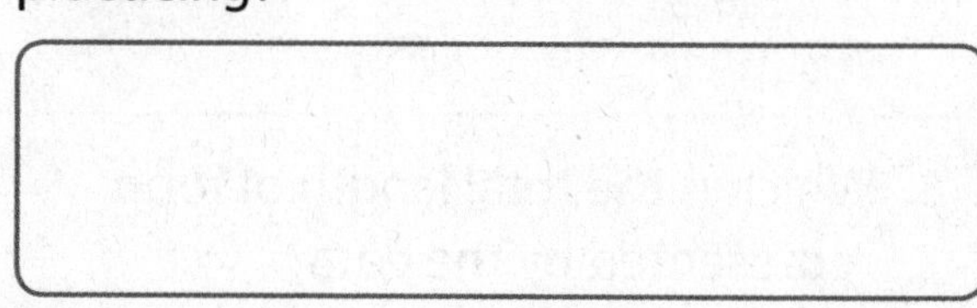

Part B

What is the most common amount of time she spent practicing?

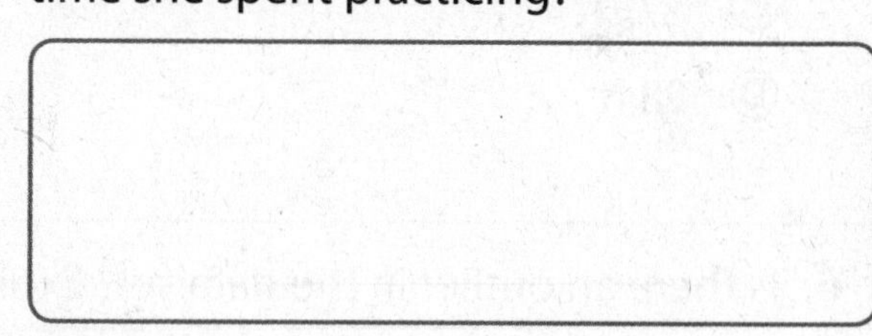

Part C

What is the total amount of time Georgiana practiced? Write and solve an equation to show your work.

Ashraf and Melanie cut rope into different lengths for an art project. They made a line plot to display their data. Use the line plot to answer **4–6**.

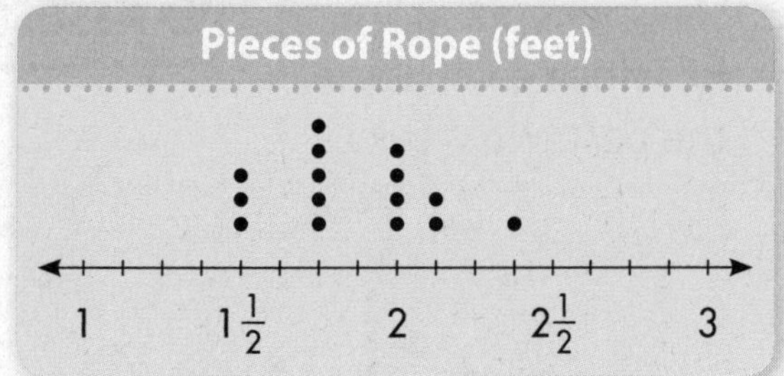

4. Which is the most common length of rope?

Ⓐ $1\frac{5}{8}$ ft

Ⓑ $1\frac{3}{4}$ ft

Ⓒ $1\frac{7}{8}$ ft

Ⓓ $2\frac{3}{8}$ ft

---

5. Which is the total length of rope represented by the data?

Ⓐ $25\frac{1}{8}$ ft

Ⓑ $27\frac{5}{8}$ ft

Ⓒ $27\frac{7}{8}$ ft

Ⓓ 28 ft

---

6. Is there an outlier in the data set? Explain your reasoning.

7. Terry works at a bakery. This morning he recorded how many ounces each loaf of bread weighed.

$23\frac{1}{2}$	24	$23\frac{3}{4}$	$23\frac{1}{2}$	$24\frac{1}{4}$	$23\frac{1}{2}$
24	$23\frac{1}{4}$	$24\frac{1}{2}$	$22\frac{3}{4}$	$24\frac{1}{4}$	$23\frac{1}{2}$

Part A

Make a line plot for the data set.

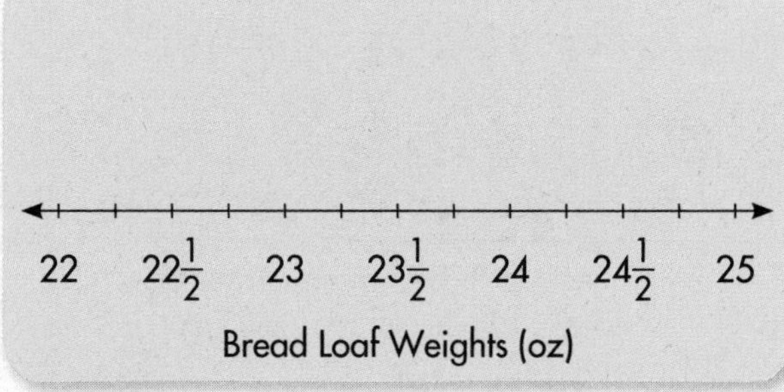

Part B

Morgan said that the difference between the heaviest loaf of bread and the lightest loaf of bread is $1\frac{1}{2}$ ounces. Do you agree with Morgan? Explain.

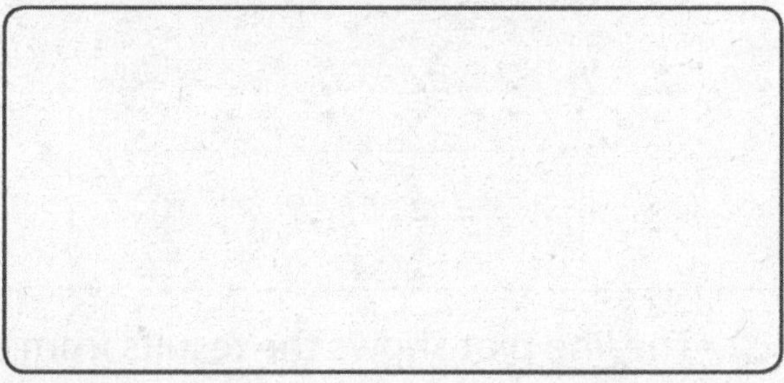

Part C

What is the combined weight of all the loaves of bread? Show your work.

Name ____

TOPIC 12

Performance Assessment

Measuring Bugs

Ms. Wolk's class measured the length and weight of Madagascar Hissing Cockroaches.

1. The **Cockroach Lengths** line plot shows the lengths the class found.

Part A

Which length did the most students get? How can you tell from the line plot?

Cockroach Lengths

Inches	$\frac{1}{2}$	$\frac{3}{4}$	1	$1\frac{1}{4}$	$1\frac{1}{2}$	$1\frac{3}{4}$	2	$2\frac{1}{4}$	$2\frac{1}{2}$	$2\frac{3}{4}$	3
	x					xxx	xxxxx	xxxxxxx	xxxxxx	xxxx	xx

Part B

Jordan said that all of the Madagascar Hissing Cockroaches were between 2 and 3 inches long.
Is he correct? Explain your reasoning.

Part C

Ginny said that twice as many students found a length of $2\frac{1}{2}$ inches as found a length of $1\frac{3}{4}$ inches. Is she correct? Explain your reasoning.

Part D

Is there an outlier? If so, what length is it?

2. The **Cockroach Weights** table shows the weights the class found.

Part A

Complete the line plot to represent the cockroach weights.

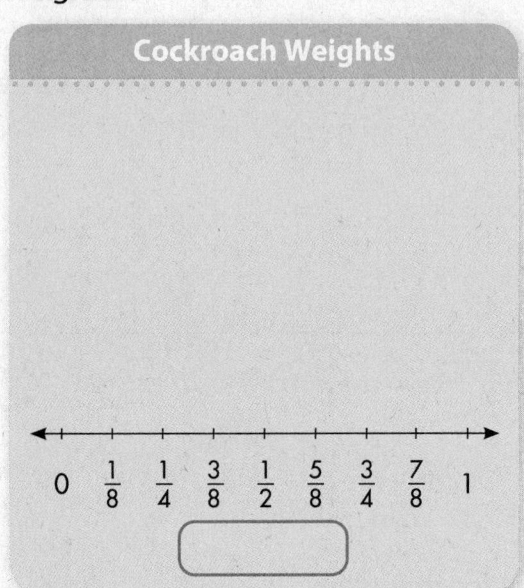

DATA

Cockroach Weights
(In ounces)

$\frac{3}{8}$	$\frac{5}{8}$	$\frac{1}{2}$	$\frac{3}{4}$	$\frac{5}{8}$	$\frac{1}{2}$	$\frac{5}{8}$
$\frac{1}{2}$	$\frac{3}{4}$	$\frac{3}{8}$	$\frac{3}{4}$	$\frac{1}{2}$	$\frac{3}{8}$	$\frac{3}{4}$
$\frac{3}{4}$	$\frac{3}{8}$	$\frac{3}{4}$	$\frac{5}{8}$	$\frac{1}{4}$	$\frac{3}{4}$	$\frac{1}{2}$
$\frac{5}{8}$	$\frac{1}{4}$	$\frac{1}{2}$	$\frac{1}{2}$	$\frac{3}{4}$	$\frac{3}{8}$	$\frac{5}{8}$

Part B

What is the total weight of all the cockroaches the students measured? Complete the table to help you. Show your work.

Cockroach Weights
(In ounces)

Weight (ounces)	Frequency	Multiplication

Algebra: Write and Interpret Numerical Expressions

Essential Question: How is the value of a numerical expression found?

So when I drink milk, I am part of that food chain. Yum! Here's a project on food chains and food webs.

A *food chain* shows a path of energy moving through an ecosystem.

For example, plants capture the Sun's energy and convert it into food energy. Cows eat plants.

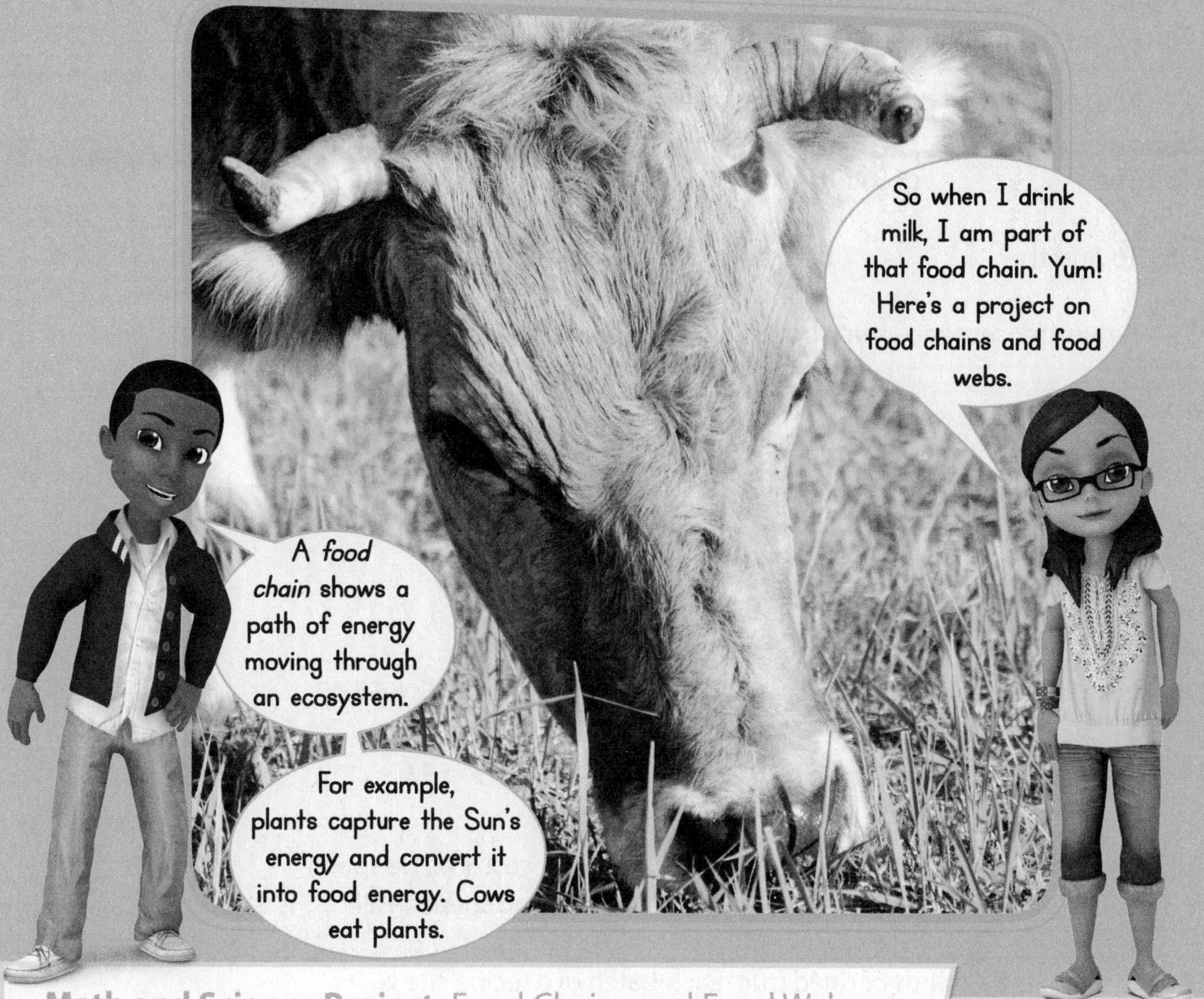

Math and Science Project: Food Chains and Food Webs

Do Research Use the Internet or other sources to find out more about food chains and food webs. Investigate the roles of producers, consumers, and decomposers. Explain how energy from sunlight is transferred to consumers.

Journal: Write a Report Include what you found. Also in your report:

- Draw a food web from an ecosystem near your home.
- Draw arrows on your food web to show how energy moves. Explain why the order is important.
- On one food chain of your food web, label each organism as a producer, consumer, or decomposer.

Name ______________________________

Review What You Know

Vocabulary

Choose the best term from the box. Write it on the blank.

- difference
- product
- sum
- equation
- quotient

1. The answer to a division problem is the __________.

2. The __________ of 5 and 7 is 12.

3. To find the __________ between 16 and 4, you subtract.

4. A number sentence that shows two equivalent values is a(n) __________.

Mixed Review

Find each answer.

5. $648 \div 18$

6. 35×100

7. $47.15 + 92.9$

8. $\frac{1}{4} + \frac{1}{4} + \frac{1}{4}$

9. $3.4 - 2.7$

10. $1.9 + 7$

11. $3\frac{2}{5} + \frac{1}{2}$

12. $75 \div \frac{1}{5}$

13. $\$3.75 + \$2.49$

14. $8\frac{5}{8} - 1\frac{2}{8}$

15. 31.8×2.3

16. $9 - 4.6$

17. Jackson bought 2 tickets to the state fair. Each ticket cost $12. He spent $15 on rides and $8.50 on food. How much did Jackson spend in all?

18. A baker has 3 pounds of dried fruit. Each batch of a recipe she is making uses $\frac{1}{2}$ pound of the fruit. How many batches can she make?

Ⓐ 9 batches Ⓑ 6 batches Ⓒ 2 batches Ⓓ $1\frac{1}{2}$ batches

Multiplication

19. What equation comes next in the pattern below? Explain.

$7 \times 10 = 70$
$7 \times 100 = 700$
$7 \times 1{,}000 = 7{,}000$

My Word Cards

Use the examples for each word on the front of the card to help complete the definitions on the back.

A-Z Glossary

numerical expression

$15 - 7$

evaluate

$5 \times (6 + 2) = 5 \times 8 = 40$

order of operations

$6 \times 5 + 12 \div 3$

$30 + 4$

34

parentheses

$3 \times (15 - 7)$

brackets

$3 \times [(15 - 7) \div 2]$

$\{6 + [3 \times (15 - 7) \div 2]\} \div 9$

My Word Cards

Complete the definition. Extend learning by writing your own definitions.

To ______________ means doing the calculations to find the value of an expression.

A ______________ is a mathematical phrase that contains numbers and at least one operation.

Curved symbols used in mathematical expressions and equations to group numbers or variables together are called ______________.

The ______________ tells which calculations to do before others. First, simplify inside parentheses, brackets, and braces. Then multiply and divide in order from left to right. Finally, add and subtract in order from left to right.

Symbols used with parentheses and brackets in mathematical expressions and equations to group numbers or variables together are called ______________.

Square symbols used in mathematical expressions and equations to group numbers or variables together are called ______________.

Name

Lesson 13-1
Order of Operations

I can ...
use the order of operations to evaluate expressions.

Content Standard 5.OA.A.1
Mathematical Practices MP.2, MP.3, MP.4, MP.5

Solve & Share

Two students evaluated the expression 15 + 12 ÷ 3 + 5 and got two different answers. Neither student made a mistake in the calculations, so how did they get different results? ***Solve this problem any way you choose.***

$15 + 12 \div 3 + 5$

Reasoning
You can use the order of operations to evaluate expressions that have more than one operation. *Show your work!*

Look Back! **MP.3 Construct Arguments** Why is it important to use the order of operations when evaluating an expression?

How Can You Evaluate a Numerical Expression with More Than One Operation?

A

Two students evaluated the same numerical expression but got different answers. To avoid getting more than one answer, use the order of operations. Rebecca used the correct order.

Rebecca's Way	Juan's Way
$36 + 9 \div 3 \times 5$	$36 + 9 \div 3 \times 5$
$36 + 3 \times 5$	$45 \div 3 \times 5$
$36 + 15$	15×5
51	75

You can evaluate or find the value of $12 \div 4 + (9 - 2) \times (3 + 5)$ by using the order of operations.

B

Step 1

In using order of operations, do the operations inside parentheses first.

$12 \div 4 + (9 - 2) \times (3 + 5)$

$12 \div 4 + 7 \times 8$

Remember to rewrite the calculations that still need to be done.

C

Step 2

Then, multiply and divide in order from left to right.

$12 \div 4 + 7 \times 8$

$3 + 56$

D

Step 3

Finally, add and subtract in order from left to right.

$3 + 56$

59

$12 \div 4 + (9 - 2) \times (3 + 5) = 59$

Convince Me! **MP.3 Critique Reasoning** In the first example, why was Juan's answer incorrect?

Name ____________________

Practice Buddy Tools Assessment

Guided Practice*

Do You Understand?

1. Insert parentheses to make the following statement true.
3 + 5 × 2 − 10 = 6

2. **Vocabulary** Write a numerical expression with **parentheses**. Then find the value of the expression.

Remember to always use the order of operations.

Do You Know How?

In **3–7**, name the operation you should do first.

3. 6 + 27 ÷ 3

4. 5 × 2 + 12 ÷ 6

5. 17.25 − (4.5 + 3.75)

6. (14 − 7) + (3 + 5)

7. 4 ÷ 2 × 8

Independent Practice

In **8–19**, use the order of operations to find the value of each expression.

8. 3 + 7 × 6 ÷ 3

9. 2 × 9 + (2 × 14)

10. 64 ÷ 8 × $\frac{1}{2}$

11. (19 − 5) × 3 + 4

12. 15.3 − 12 + 2.5

13. 36 − 5 + (16 − 11)

14. 8 × (3 + 2) − 6

15. 3 ÷ (9 − 6) + 4 × 2

16. (3 + 4) × (3 + 5)

17. 0.7 + 1.8 ÷ 6

18. 4 × (3 − 2) + 18

19. 8 × 6 − 4 × 3

In **20–25**, insert parentheses to make each statement true.

20. 30 − 4 × 2 + 5 = 2

21. 17 − 8 − 5 = 14

22. 10 ÷ 2 − 3 + 1 = 3

23. 30 − 4 × 2 + 5 = 57

24. 17 − 8 − 5 = 4

25. 10 ÷ 2 − 3 + 1 = 1

*For another example, see Set A on page 767.

Math Practices and Problem Solving

26. **MP.4 Model with Math** Find the difference. Use the model.

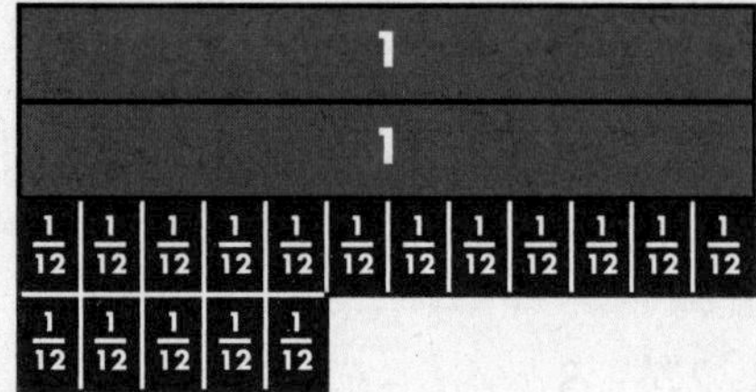

$3\frac{5}{12} - 1\frac{7}{12}$

27. A small cruise ship has 220 passengers. At the Port of San Juan, 2 groups of 12 passengers go ashore to shop and 5 groups of 6 passengers go sightseeing. Evaluate $220 - (2 \times 12) - (5 \times 6)$ to find the number of passengers that are left on the ship.

28. **Higher Order Thinking** Joe says that the following statement is true. Do you agree? Explain.
$4 \times (3 + 5) - 10 = 4 \times 3 + 5 - 10$

29. **Number Sense** How many hundredths are in five tenths? How many thousandths are in five hundredths? Explain.

30. **MP.2 Reasoning** Ralph bought 3 boxes with 20 pencils each and 4 boxes with 10 pens each. To find the total number of pencils and pens, Ralph evaluated $3 \times 20 + 4 \times 10 = 100$. Is his answer reasonable? Explain.

31. **MP.5 Use Appropriate Tools** Tina wants to use rope to decorate a rectangular picture frame. The frame measures 18 inches wide and 12 inches tall. Tina has 4 feet of rope. Does she have enough rope to go around the perimeter of the frame? Explain.

Remember,
1 foot = 12 inches.

Common Core Assessment

32. What is the value of the expression $3 \times 5 + (3 \times 9)$?

Ⓐ 35
Ⓑ 42
Ⓒ 96
Ⓓ 162

33. Which expression has a value of 8?

Ⓐ $11 - 6 - 3$
Ⓑ $4 + 30 \div 6$
Ⓒ $(9 + 7) \div 2$
Ⓓ $1 + 1 \times (2 + 2)$

Name ______________________

Help Practice Buddy Tools Games

Homework & Practice 13-1
Order of Operations

Another Look!

Evaluate $8 \div 2 + 3 \times (6 - 1) - 7$.

You need to use the order of operations, so you will get the correct answer.

Step 1	Step 2	Step 3
Do the operations inside the parentheses. $(6 - 1) = 5$ $8 \div 2 + 3 \times 5 - 7$	Multiply and divide in order from left to right. $8 \div 2 = 4$ and $3 \times 5 = 15$ $4 + 15 - 7$	Add and subtract in order from left to right. $4 + 15 = 19$ and $19 - 7 = 12$ So, $8 \div 2 + 3 \times (6 - 1) - 7 = 12$.

In **1–12**, use the order of operations to find the value of each expression.

1. $6 \times (3 + 2) \div 10$

2. $12 - (3 \times 3) + 11$

3. $(10 \times 0.4) + (10 \times 0.8)$

4. $(8 \div 4) \times (4 - 2)$

5. $8.5 - 10 \div 2$

6. $18 - (8 \div 2) + 25$

7. $12 \div 3 + 4 \times 5$

8. $50 - (5 \times 5) + 13$

9. $(14 - 8) \times (15 - 4)$

10. $\frac{3}{4} + \frac{1}{2} \times 2$

11. $20 - 12 + 8 \times 5$

12. $31 - (75 \div 3) \div 5$

In **13–18**, insert parentheses to make each statement true.

13. $15 - 3 \times 4 + 9 = 12$

14. $21 - 8 - 6 = 7$

15. $18 \div 3 - 5 + 1 = 2$

16. $15 - 3 \times 4 + 9 = 57$

17. $21 - 8 - 6 = 19$

18. $18 \div 3 - 5 + 1 = 0$

19. Dion bought 3 pounds of oranges and 2 pounds of grapefruit. Write an expression to represent the amount of money Dion spent on the fruit. Then evaluate the expression. How much did Dion spend?

DATA

Fruit Prices

Fruit	Cost (per pound)
Lemons	\$0.79
Oranges	\$0.99
Limes	\$1.09
Grapefruit	\$1.59

20. Dion paid with a \$20 bill. How much change did she get?

21. Insert parentheses in the expression $6 + 10 \times 2$ so that

a the expression equals 32.

b the expression equals $(12 + 1) \times 2$.

22. **Higher Order Thinking** Carlos evaluated $20 - (2 \times 6) + 8 \div 4$ and got 29. Is his answer correct? If not, explain what Carlos did wrong and find the correct answer.

23. **Number Sense** The highest point in Colorado is Mount Elbert, at 14,433 feet. About how many miles is that?

Remember, there are 5,280 feet in 1 mile.

24. **MP.2 Reasoning** Susan is 50 inches tall. Myra is 3 inches taller than Elaine, who is 2 inches shorter than Susan. How tall is Myra?

Common Core Assessment

25. What is the value of the expression $(25 - 7) \times 2 \div 4 + 2$?

Ⓐ 18
Ⓑ 11
Ⓒ 6
Ⓓ 5

26. Which expression has a value of 11?

Ⓐ $13 - 5 - 3$
Ⓑ $1 + (8 \times 2)$
Ⓒ $5 + 2 \times (4 - 1)$
Ⓓ $15 - 1 + (6 \div 2)$

Name ______________________

Lesson 13-2
Evaluate Expressions

I can ...
evaluate expressions with parentheses, brackets, and braces.

Content Standard 5.OA.A.1
Mathematical Practices MP.1, MP.3, MP.6, MP.7

Solve & Share

Evaluate the expression $3 + (6 - 2) \times 4$.
Solve this problem using the order of operations.

$$3 + (6 - 2) \times 4$$

You can use structure to evaluate expressions with more than one term.
Show your work!

Look Back! **MP.3 Construct Arguments** Are parentheses needed in the expression $(8 \times 5) - 9 + 6$? Explain your answer.

What Order Should You Use When You Evaluate an Expression?

A

Jack evaluated
$[(7 \times 2) - 3] + 8 \div 2 \times 3$.

To avoid getting more than one answer, he used the order of operations given at the right.

Parentheses, brackets, and braces are all used to group numbers in numerical expressions.

Order of Operations

1. Evaluate inside parentheses ( ), brackets [ ], and braces { }.
2. Multiply and divide from left to right.
3. Add and subtract from left to right.

B

Step 1

First, do the operations inside the parentheses.

$[(7 \times 2) - 3] + 8 \div 2 \times 3$

$[14 - 3] + 8 \div 2 \times 3$

Then, evaluate the terms inside the brackets.

$[14 - 3] + 8 \div 2 \times 3$

$11 + 8 \div 2 \times 3$

C

Step 2

Next, multiply and divide in order from left to right.

$11 + 8 \div 2 \times 3$

$11 + 4 \times 3$

$11 + 12$

D

Step 3

Finally, add and subtract in order from left to right.

$11 + 12 = 23$

So, the value of the expression is 23.

Convince Me! **MP.3 Construct Arguments** Would the value of $\{2 + [(15 - 3) - 6]\} \div 2$ change if the braces were removed? Explain.

Name ______

Practice Buddy   Tools   Assessment

Guided Practice*

Do You Understand?

1. Explain the steps involved in evaluating the expression [(4 + 2) − 1] × 3.

2. Would the value of (12 − 4) ÷ 4 + 1 change if the parentheses were removed? Explain.

Do You Know How?

In **3–6**, use the order of operations to evaluate the expression.

3. [7 × (6 − 1)] + 100

4. 17 + 4 × 3

5. (8 + 1) + 9 × 7

6. {[(4 × 3) ÷ 2] + 3} × 6

Independent Practice

Remember to evaluate inside parentheses, brackets, and braces first.

Leveled Practice In **7–21**, use the order of operations to evaluate the expression.

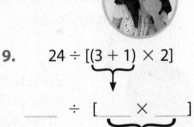

7. 8 × (3 + 4) ÷ 2

   8 × ____ ÷ 2

   ____ ÷ 2 = 28

8. 39 + 6 ÷ 2

   39 + ____ = 42

9. 24 ÷ [(3 + 1) × 2]

   ____ ÷ [____ × ____]

   ____ ÷ ____ = 3

10. 5 ÷ 5 + 4 × 12

11. [6 − (3 × 2)] + 4

12. (4 × 8) ÷ 2 + 8

13. (18 + 7) × (11 − 7)

14. 2 + [4 + (5 × 6)]

15. (9 + 11) ÷ (5 + 4 + 1)

16. 90 − 5 × 5 × 2

17. 120 − 40 ÷ 4 × 6

18. 22 + (96 − 40) ÷ 8

19. (7.7 + 0.3) ÷ 0.1 × 4

20. 32 ÷ (12 − 4) + 7

21. {8 × [1 + (20 − 6)]} ÷ $\frac{1}{2}$

*For another example, see Set A on page 767.

Math Practices and Problem Solving

22. Dan and his 4 friends want to share the cost of a meal equally. They order 2 large pizzas and 5 small drinks. If they leave a tip of $6.30, how much does each person pay?

DATA

Menu	
Small pizza	$8.00
Large pizza	$12.00
Small drink	$1.50
Large drink	$2.25

23. Higher Order Thinking Use the operation signs +, −, ×, and ÷ once each in the expression below to make the number sentence true.

6 ▢ (3 ▢ 1) ▢ 5 ▢ 1 = 17

24. MP.6 Be Precise Carlotta needs $12\frac{1}{2}$ yards of ribbon for a project. She has $5\frac{1}{4}$ yards of ribbon on one spool and $2\frac{1}{2}$ yards on another spool. How much more ribbon does she need?

25. Theresa bought three containers of tennis balls at $2.98 each. She had a coupon for $1 off. Her mom paid for half of the remaining cost. How much did Theresa pay? Evaluate the expression [(3 × 2.98) − 1] ÷ 2.

26. Math and Science Giraffes are *herbivores*, or plant eaters. A giraffe can eat up to 75 pounds of leaves each day. Write and evaluate an expression to find how many pounds of leaves 5 giraffes can eat in a week.

Common Core Assessment

27. Using the order of operations, which operation should you perform last to evaluate this expression?

(1 × 2.5) + (52 ÷ 13) + (6.7 − 5) − (98 + 8)

Ⓐ Addition

Ⓑ Subtraction

Ⓒ Multiplication

Ⓓ Division

28. Draw lines to match each expression to its value.

29 − (5 − 3)	4
25 − 5 ÷ 5	21
(2 × 6) − (2 × 4)	24
[5 × (6 − 2)] + 1	27

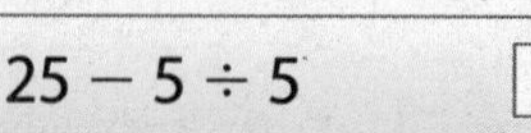
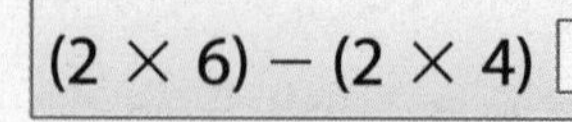

Name ______________________

Homework & Practice 13-2

Evaluate Expressions

Another Look!

When an expression contains more than one operation, **parentheses** ( ) can be used to show which operation should be done first. Parentheses are one type of **grouping symbol**.

Do the operation inside the parentheses first.

Operations in grouping symbols are always done first.

Evaluate $(2 + 8) \times 3$.

$10 \times 3 = 30$

Evaluate $2 + (8 \times 3)$.

$2 + 24 = 26$

Brackets and **braces** are other types of **grouping symbols**.
Evaluate terms inside brackets after doing operations within parentheses.

Evaluate $[(4 + 9) - (30 \div 5)] \times 10$.

$[13 - 6] \times 10$

$7 \times 10 = 70$

In **1–12**, evaluate the expression.

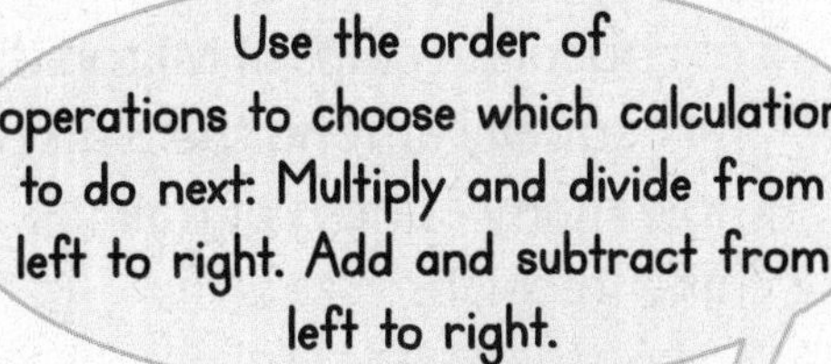

Use the order of operations to choose which calculation to do next: Multiply and divide from left to right. Add and subtract from left to right.

1. $(16 + 4) \div 10$

_____ $\div 10 =$ _____

2. $60 \div (3 \times 4)$

$60 \div$ _____ $=$ _____

3. $(16 \div 4) + (10 - 3)$

4. $64 \div (10 \times 0.8)$

5. $27 - (7.5 \times 2)$

6. $[(4 \times 6) + 6] \div 6$

7. $(5 + 2) \times (14 - 9) - 1$

8. $5 + \{[2 \times (14 - 9)] - 1\}$

9. $(52 + 48) \div (8 + 17)$

10. $[52 + (48 \div 8)] + 17$

11. $(80 + 16) \div (4 + 12)$

12. $80 + 16 \div 4 + 12$

13. Keisha bought a new pair of skis for \$450. She made a payment of \$120 and got a student discount of \$40. Her mother paid $\frac{1}{2}$ of the balance. How much does Keisha have left to pay?

14. **MP.6 Be Precise** Ellen is $5\frac{1}{2}$ feet tall. Her sister is $\frac{3}{4}$ foot shorter than Ellen. How tall is Ellen's sister?

15. **Higher Order Thinking** Rewrite using parentheses to make each statement true.

a $42 + 12 \div 6 = 9$

b $33 - 14\frac{1}{2} + 3\frac{1}{2} = 15$

c $32 \div 8 \times 2 = 2$

16. **Algebra** What steps would you use to solve the equation $n = 7 + (32 \div 16) \times 4 - 6$? Solve the equation.

17. **MP.1 Make Sense and Persevere** Milton makes trail mix for his hiking group. He mixes $1\frac{1}{4}$ pound of peanuts, 14 ounces of raisins, 12 ounces of walnuts, and 10 ounces of chocolate chips. If Milton divides the trail mix equally among the 8 hikers in the group, how many ounces of trail mix does each hiker receive?

Remember:
There are 16 ounces in 1 pound.

Common Core Assessment

18. Using the order of operations, which operation should you perform last to evaluate this expression?

$8 + \{[14 \div 2 \times (3 - 1)] - 1\}$

Ⓐ Addition

Ⓑ Division

Ⓒ Multiplication

Ⓓ Subtraction

19. Draw lines to match each expression to its value.

Expression	Value
$16 + 6 \div 3$	18
$20 - (4 \times 2)$	15
$(3 \times 3) + (3 \times 2)$	12
$[(8 - 3) \times 4] - 12$	8

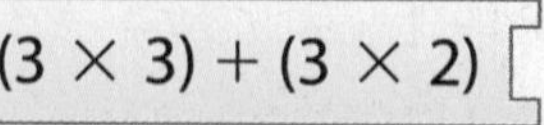

Name ___________________________________

Lesson 13-3
Write Numerical Expressions

I can ...
write simple expressions that show calculations with numbers.

Content Standards 5.OA.A.2, 5.OA.A.1
Mathematical Practices MP.2, MP.3, MP.4, MP.8

Solve & Share

A baker packages 12 cupcakes to a box. Sean orders 5 boxes for his sister's graduation party and 3.5 boxes for the Variety Show party. Write an expression that shows the calculations you could use to find the number of cupcakes Sean orders.

Model with Math
You can write a numerical expression to model this situation.

Look Back! **MP.4 Model with Math** Write a different expression to model Sean's order. Evaluate both expressions to check that they are equivalent. How many cupcakes does Sean order?

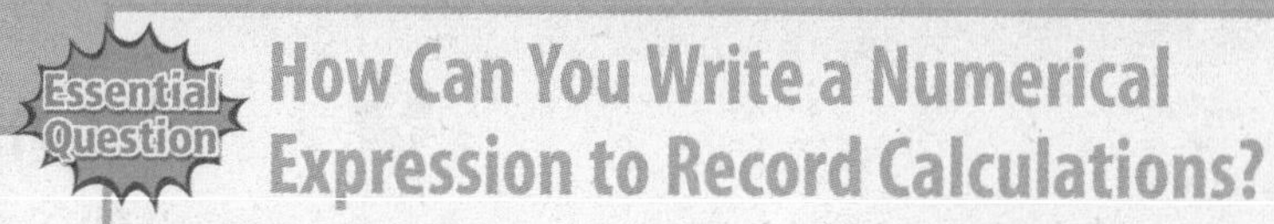

How Can You Write a Numerical Expression to Record Calculations?

A

The school auditorium has 546 seats on the main floor and 102 in the balcony. Every seat is filled for all of the Variety Show performances. Write an expression that shows the calculations you could use to determine how many tickets were sold.

Variety Show
Tickets $4.50
Performances:
·Friday, March 18, 7:00 P.M.
·Saturday, March 19, 2:00 P.M.
·Saturday, March 19, 7:00 P.M.
·Sunday, March 20, 2:00 P.M.

B

Think about how you would calculate the total number of tickets.

Add 546 + 102 to find the total number of seats.
Then **multiply** by the number of performances, 4.

So, you need to write a numerical expression that represents:

"Find 4 times the sum of 546 and 102."

C

Use numbers and symbols to write the numerical expression.

The sum of 546 and 102: 546 + 102

4 times the sum: 4 × (546 + 102)

Remember, parentheses show which calculation to do first.

The expression 4 × (546 + 102) shows the calculations for the number of tickets sold.

Convince Me! **MP.2 Reasoning** Two students wrote different expressions to find the total number of tickets sold. Is their work correct? Explain.

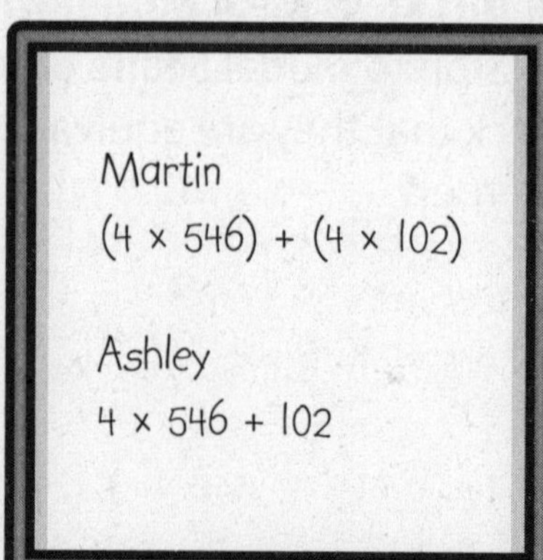

Name

Guided Practice*

Do You Understand?

1. **MP.8 Generalize** Why do some numerical expressions contain parentheses?

2. **MP.2 Reasoning** Show how to use a property to write an equivalent expression for $9 \times (7 + 44)$. Can you use a different property to write another equivalent expression? Explain.

Do You Know How?

In **3–6**, write a numerical expression for each calculation.

3. Add 8 and 7, and then multiply by 2.

4. Find triple the difference between 44.75 and 22.8.

5. Multiply 4 times $\frac{7}{8}$ and then add 12.

6. Add 49 to the quotient of 125 and 5.

Independent Practice

In **7–11**, write a numerical expression for each calculation.

7. Add 91, 129, and 16, and then divide by 44.

8. Find 8.5 times the difference between 77 and 13.

9. Subtract 55 from the sum of 234 and 8.

10. Multiply $\frac{2}{3}$ by 42, and then multiply that product by 10.

11. Write an expression to show the calculations you could use to determine the total area of the rectangles at the right.

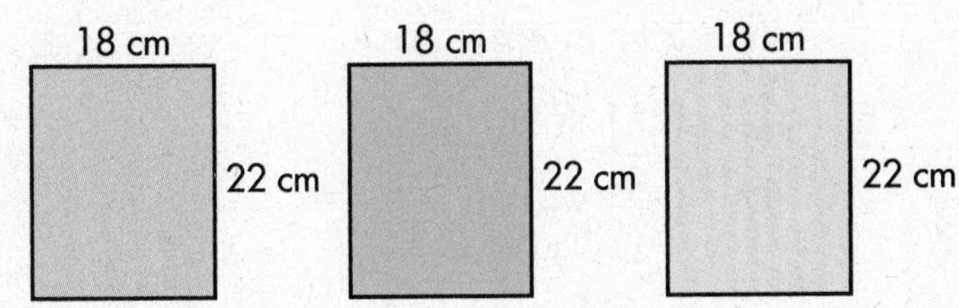

*For another example, see Set B on page 767.

Math Practices and Problem Solving

12. **MP.4 Model with Math** Ronnie's Rentals charges \$25 plus \$15 per hour to rent a chain saw. David rented a chain saw for 5 hours. Write an expression to show how you could calculate the total amount David paid.

13. **MP.4 Model with Math** Fourteen students bought their art teacher a new easel for \$129 and a set of blank canvases for \$46. Sales tax was \$10.50. They shared the cost equally. Write an expression to show how you could calculate the amount each student paid.

14. **Vocabulary** When evaluating an expression, why is it important to use the **order of operations**?

15. A storage shed is shaped like a rectangular prism. The width is 8 yards, the height is 4 yards, and the volume is 288 cubic yards. Explain how to find the length of the storage shed.

16. **Higher Order Thinking** Danielle has a third of the amount needed to pay for her choir trip expenses. Does the expression $(77 + 106 + 34) \div 3$ show how you could calculate the amount of money Danielle has? Explain.

Choir Trip Expenses

Train ticket \$77
Hotel \$106
Meals \$34

Common Core Assessment

17. Which expression represents the following calculation?

    Subtract 214 from 721 and then divide by 5.

    Ⓐ $(721 \div 214) - 5$
    Ⓑ $721 - 214 \div 5$
    Ⓒ $(721 \div 5) - 214$
    Ⓓ $(721 - 214) \div 5$

18. Last winter, Kofi earned \$47.50 shoveling snow and \$122 giving ice-skating lessons. During the summer, he earned twice as much by doing yard work.

    Which expression shows how you could calculate the amount of money Kofi earned during the summer?

    Ⓐ $2 + (47.50 + 122)$
    Ⓑ $2 \times 47.50 + 122$
    Ⓒ $2 \times (47.50 + 122)$
    Ⓓ $2 \times (47.50 \times 122)$

Name ___________________________

Homework & Practice 13-3

Write Numerical Expressions

Another Look!

Cole is $11\frac{1}{2}$ years old. Uncle Frank is 4 times as old as Cole. Write an expression to show how you could calculate Uncle Frank's age in 6 years.

Uncle Frank's current age:
$4 \times 11\frac{1}{2}$

Uncle Frank's age in 6 years:
$\left(4 \times 11\frac{1}{2}\right) + 6$

The expression $\left(4 \times 11\frac{1}{2}\right) + 6$ shows the calculations that will determine Uncle Frank's age in 6 years.

You could use properties to write other expressions for Frank's age.

In **1–7**, write a numerical expression for each calculation.

1. Multiply 16, 3, and 29, and then subtract 17.

2. Add 13.2 and 0.9, and then divide by 0.6.

3. Subtract $12\frac{1}{2}$ from the product of $\frac{9}{10}$ and 180.

4. Add the quotient of 120 and 60 to the quotient of 72 and 9.

5. Multiply 71 by 8, and then add 379.

6. Find 3 times the difference of 7.25 and 4.5.

7. Write an expression to show the calculations you could use to determine how much greater the area of the yellow rectangle is than the area of the green rectangle.

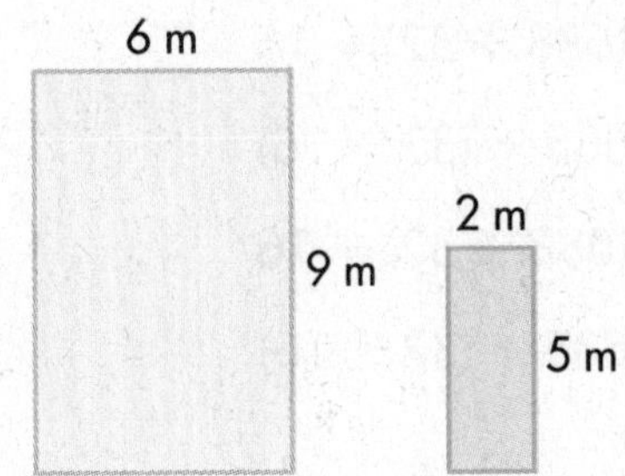

8. **MP.4 Model with Math** Lola uses 44 beads to make a bracelet and 96 beads to make a necklace. Write an expression to show how you could calculate the total number of beads Lola used to make 13 bracelets and 8 necklaces.

9. **MP.3 Construct Arguments** Bart works 36 hours a week and makes \$612. Charles works 34 hours a week and makes \$663. Who makes more per hour? How do you know?

10. **MP.2 Reasoning** Use a property to write an equivalent expression for $12 \times (100 - 5)$. Which property did you use?

11. Doreen solved the following problem: $\frac{1}{6} \div 5 = \frac{1}{30}$
Show how to use multiplication to check Doreen's answer.

12. **Higher Order Thinking** Stephen is combining all of the juice shown to make fruit punch. Does the expression $(64 + 28 + 76) \div 6$ show how you could calculate the number of $\frac{3}{4}$-cup servings? Explain.

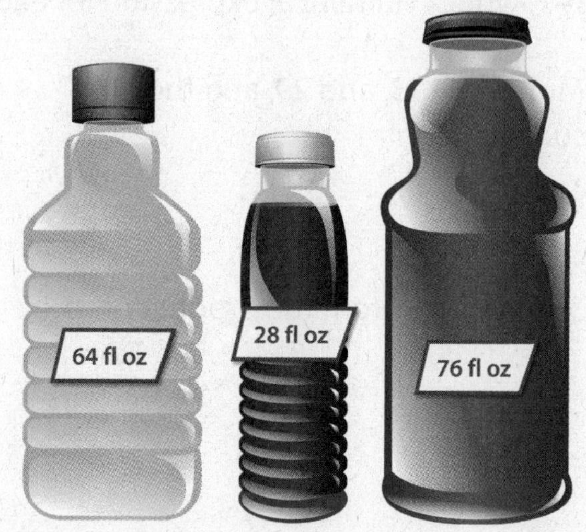

Common Core Assessment

13. Which expression represents the following calculation?

Divide 688 by 32, and then add 16.

Ⓐ $(688 \div 32) + 16$
Ⓑ $688 + (32 \div 16)$
Ⓒ $(688 + 32) \div 16$
Ⓓ $688 \div (32 + 16)$

14. Missy bought 7 pairs of socks for \$2.85 a pair. She had a coupon for \$2.25 off her total purchase.

Which calculation shows the total amount Missy paid for the socks, not including sales tax?

Ⓐ $7 \times (2.85 - 2.25)$
Ⓑ $2.85 \times (7 - 2.25)$
Ⓒ $(2.85 \times 7) - 2.25$
Ⓓ $(2.85 \times 7) \div 2.25$

Name ______________________

Lesson 13-4
Interpret Numerical Expressions

I can ...
interpret numerical expressions without evaluating them.

Content Standard 5.OA.A.2
Mathematical Practices MP.2, MP.3, MP. 7

Solve & Share

Mrs. Katz is planning her family's trip to the museum. She made a list of the expenses. Then she wrote the following expression to show how she can calculate the total cost.

$6 \times (4.20 + 8 + 12 + 3.50)$

How many people do you think are in the family? How can you tell?

Museum Trip Expenses (per person)

Roundtrip bus fare: \$4.20
Buffet lunch: \$8
Entrance fee: \$12
Dinosaur lecture: \$3.50

Use Structure
You can interpret the relationships in numerical expressions without doing any calculations.

Look Back! **MP.7 Use Structure** While they are at the museum, the family decides to watch a movie about earthquakes for \$2.75 per person. Jana and Kay disagree as to how they should adjust Mrs. Katz's expression to find the total expenses for the trip.

Jana says the expression should be $6 \times (4.20 + 8 + 12 + 3.50) + 2.75$.
Kay says the expression should be $6 \times (4.20 + 8 + 12 + 3.50 + 2.75)$.

Who is correct? Explain.

How Can You Interpret Numerical Expressions Without Evaluating Them?

A

Jimmy's clown costume requires $\frac{7}{8} + \frac{1}{2} + 1\frac{3}{4}$ yards of fabric.

His dad's matching clown costume requires $3 \times \left(\frac{7}{8} + \frac{1}{2} + 1\frac{3}{4}\right)$ yards.

How does the amount of fabric needed for the dad's costume compare to the amount needed for Jimmy's costume?

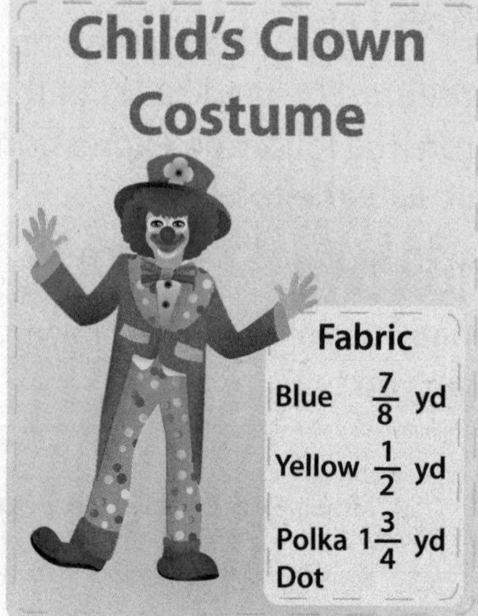

You can compare the expressions and solve the problem without doing any calculations.

B Interpret the part of each expression that is the same.

$$\frac{7}{8} + \frac{1}{2} + 1\frac{3}{4}$$

$$3 \times \left(\frac{7}{8} + \frac{1}{2} + 1\frac{3}{4}\right)$$

Both expressions contain the sum $\frac{7}{8} + \frac{1}{2} + 1\frac{3}{4}$. This is the amount of fabric needed for Jimmy's costume.

C Interpret the part of each expression that is different.

$$\frac{7}{8} + \frac{1}{2} + 1\frac{3}{4}$$

$$3 \times \left(\frac{7}{8} + \frac{1}{2} + 1\frac{3}{4}\right)$$

The second expression shows that the sum is multiplied by 3.

So, the dad's costume requires 3 times as much fabric as Jimmy's costume.

Remember, multiplying by 3 means "3 times as much."

Convince Me! **MP.2 Reasoning** The 7 students in a sewing class equally share the cost of fabric and other supplies. Last month, each student paid (\$167.94 + \$21.41) ÷ 7. This month, each student paid (\$77.23 + \$6.49) ÷ 7. Without doing any calculations, in which month did each student pay more? Explain.

Name ______________________________

Practice Buddy Tools Assessment

Guided Practice*

Do You Understand?

1. The number of yards of fabric needed for Rob's costume is $\left(\frac{7}{8} + \frac{1}{2} + 1\frac{3}{4}\right) \div 2$. How does the amount of fabric needed for Rob's costume compare to the amount needed for Jimmy's costume? Explain.

2. **MP.2 Reasoning** Without doing any calculations, explain why the following number sentence is true.

   $14 + (413 \times 7) > 6 + (413 \times 7)$

Do You Know How?

Without doing any calculations, describe how Expression A compares to Expression B.

3. **A** $8 \times (41{,}516 - 987)$
   B $41{,}516 - 987$

In **4** and **5**, without doing any calculations, write >, <, or =.

4. $7 \times \left(4\frac{3}{8} + 3\frac{1}{2}\right)$ ◯ $22 \times \left(4\frac{3}{8} + 3\frac{1}{2}\right)$

5. $8.2 + (7.1 \div 5)$ ◯ $(7.1 \div 5) + 8.2$

Independent Practice

In **6** and **7**, without doing any calculations, describe how Expression A compares to Expression B.

6. **A** $(613 + 15{,}090) \div 4$
   B $613 + 15{,}090$

7. **A** $\left(418 \times \frac{1}{4}\right) + \left(418 \times \frac{1}{2}\right)$
   B $418 \times \frac{3}{4}$

In **8–11**, without doing any calculations, write >, <, or =.

8. $(284 + 910) \div 30$ ◯ $(284 + 7{,}816) \div 30$

9. $\frac{1}{3} \times (5{,}366 - 117)$ ◯ $5{,}366 - 117$

10. $71 + (13{,}888 - 4{,}296)$ ◯ $70 + (13{,}888 - 4{,}296)$

11. $15 \times (3.6 + 9.44)$ ◯ $(15 \times 3.6) + (15 \times 9.44)$

*For another example, see Set C on page 768.

Math Practices and Problem Solving

12. **MP.7 Use Structure** A 4-story parking garage has spaces for 240 + 285 + 250 + 267 cars. While one floor is closed for repairs, the garage has spaces for 240 + 250 + 267 cars. How many spaces are there on the floor that is closed? Explain.

13. **MP.3 Construct Arguments** Peter bought $4 \times \left(2\frac{1}{4} + \frac{1}{2} + 2\frac{7}{8}\right)$ yards of ribbon. Marilyn bought $4 \times \left(2\frac{1}{4} + \frac{1}{2} + 3\right)$ yards of ribbon. Without doing any calculations, determine who bought more ribbon. Explain.

14. Brook's score in a card game is 713 + 102 + 516. On her next turn, she draws one of the cards shown. Now her score is (713 + 102 + 516) ÷ 2. Which card did Brook draw? Explain.

15. Marta bought a 0.25-kilogram box of fish food. She uses 80 grams a week. Is one box of fish food enough for 4 weeks? Explain.

16. **Higher Order Thinking** How can you tell that (496 + 77 + 189) × 10 is twice as large as (496 + 77 + 189) × 5 without doing complicated calculations?

Common Core Assessment

17. The area of Sally's classroom is 21.5 × 41 square feet. The area of Georgia's classroom is (21.5 × 41) − 56 square feet. Without doing any calculations, determine how the area of Georgia's classroom compares to the area of Sally's classroom. Explain.

Name ______________________

Help
Practice Buddy
Tools
Games

Homework & Practice 13-4

Interpret Numerical Expressions

Another Look!

Audrey and Donald played a video game. The expressions below show the number of points each player scored.

Audrey: 32,700 + 6,140 + 5,050

Donald: (32,700 + 6,140 + 5,050) − 8,815

How does Donald's score compare to Audrey's?

You can compare some expressions without doing any calculations.

Both expressions contain the same sum. Audrey: 32,700 + 6,140 + 5,050 Donald: (32,700 + 6,140 + 5,050) − 8,815	The expression for Donald's score shows 8,815 subtracted from the sum. So, Donald's score is 8,815 points less than Audrey's score.

In **1** and **2**, without doing any calculations, describe how Expression A compares to Expression B.

1. **A** (23,000 − 789) × 19
B 23,000 − 789

2. **A** $6\frac{4}{5} + \left(88 \times \frac{3}{10}\right)$
B $88 \times \frac{3}{10}$

In **3–6**, without doing any calculations, write >, <, or =.

3. (714 ÷ 32) − 20 ◯ (714 ÷ 32) − 310

4. 0.1 × (716 + 789) ◯ 716 + 789

5. $\frac{1}{2}$ × (228 + 4,316) ◯ (228 + 4,316) ÷ 2

6. (3.9 × 8) + (3.9 × 4) ◯ 3.9 × 15

7. Which expression is 16 times as large as 18,233 − 4,006?

Ⓐ (18,233 − 4,006) + 16
Ⓑ (18,233 − 4,006) × 16
Ⓒ (18,233 − 4,006) ÷ 16
Ⓓ (18,233 × 16) − 4,006

8. **MP.7 Use Structure** Sid paid $6.80 for wrapping paper and $7.35 for ribbon. He wrapped identical gifts for all of his cousins. Sid wrote the expression $(6.80 + 7.35) \div 8$ to help him calculate how much it cost him to wrap each gift. How many gifts did Sid wrap? Explain.

9. **MP.3 Construct Arguments** Yolanda bought $3 \times \left(\frac{1}{4} + \frac{7}{8} + 1\frac{1}{2}\right)$ pounds of cheese. Sam bought $2 \times \left(\frac{1}{4} + \frac{7}{8} + 1\frac{1}{2}\right)$ pounds of cheese. Without doing any calculations, determine who bought more cheese. Explain.

10. Jack bought the fishing gear pictured. The sales tax was calculated by multiplying the total cost of the fishing gear by 0.07 and rounding to the nearest cent. How much did Jack pay for the fishing gear including sales tax?

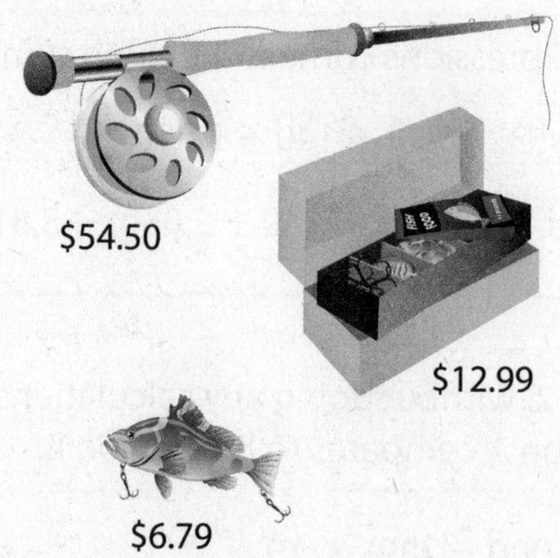

$6.79

11. Cy bought a laptop computer, a printer, and a router. Cy used a $35 coupon to make the purchase. He wrote $(1{,}415.00 + 277.50 + 44.95) - 35$ to show how he can calculate the final cost, not including sales tax. Write an expression that can be used to find the total price of the items he bought before sales tax and the coupon.

12. **Higher Order Thinking** Arrange expressions A, B, C, D, and E in order from least to greatest.

A $(9{,}311 + 522) \times 4.8$

B $9{,}311 + 522$

C $(9{,}311 + 522) \times \frac{1}{2}$

D $25 \times (9{,}311 + 522)$

E $(9{,}311 \times 5) + (522 \times 5)$

Common Core Assessment

13. Last month, Ms. Jeffers flew $1{,}716 + 984 + 2{,}058$ miles for work. This month, she flew $4 \times (1{,}716 + 984 + 2{,}058)$ miles. Without doing any calculations, determine how the number of miles Ms. Jeffers flew this month compares to the number of miles she flew last month. Explain.

Name ______________________________

Math Practices and Problem Solving

Lesson 13-5
Reasoning

I can ...
make sense of quantities and relationships in problem situations.

Mathematical Practices MP.2 Also MP.1, MP.3, MP.4, MP.6
Content Standards 5.OA.A.1, 5.OA.A.2

Solve & Share The camp cook has 6 dozen eggs. He uses 18 eggs to bake some brownies. Then he uses twice as many eggs to make pancakes. How many eggs does the cook have left? Use reasoning to write and evaluate an expression that represents the problem.

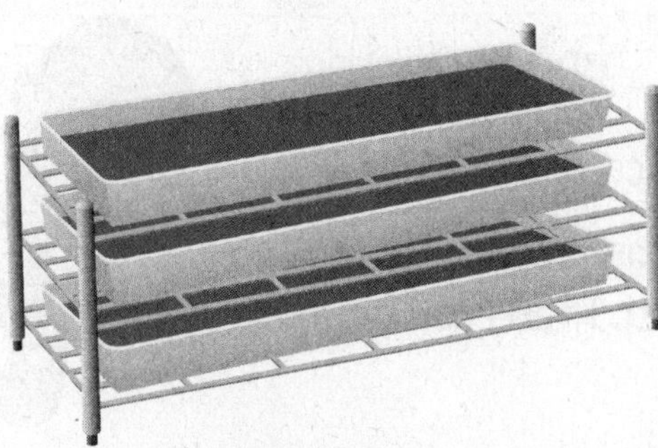

Thinking Habits

Be a good thinker! These questions can help you.

- What do the numbers and symbols in the problem mean?
- How are the numbers or quantities related?
- How can I represent a word problem using pictures, numbers, or equations?

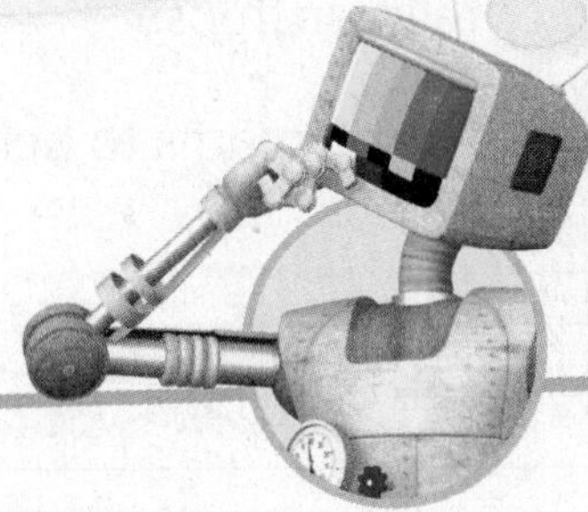

Look Back! **MP.2 Reasoning** Explain how the numbers, symbols, and operations in your expression represent this problem.

Essential Question

How Can You Use Reasoning to Solve Problems?

A

Rose has 3 albums for her soccer cards. She gets 7 more cards for each of her albums for her birthday. How many cards does Rose have in all?

What do I need to do to solve the problem?

I need to find how many cards, including Rose's new cards, will be in each album. Then I need to multiply to find the number of cards in 3 albums.

You can use tools or draw a diagram to help solve the problem.

B

How can I use reasoning to solve this problem?

I can

- identify the quantities I know.
- use mathematical properties, symbols, and operations to show relationships.
- use diagrams to help.

C

Here's my thinking...

I need to find how many cards Rose has in all.

I can use a diagram to show how the quantities in the problem are related. Then I can write an expression.

There are 22 cards in each of her 3 albums.
She gets 7 more cards for each of her 3 albums.

22	7	22	7	22	7

$$3 \times (22 + 7) = 3 \times 29$$
$$= 87$$

Rose has 87 cards.

Convince Me! **MP.2 Reasoning** How can you use the Distributive Property to write an expression equivalent to the one given above? Use reasoning to explain how you know the expressions are equivalent.

Name ______

Practice Buddy | Tools | Assessment

Guided Practice*

MP.2 Reasoning

Todd has 4 baseball card albums like the one pictured. He lets his best friend Franco choose 5 cards from each album. How many cards does Todd have now?

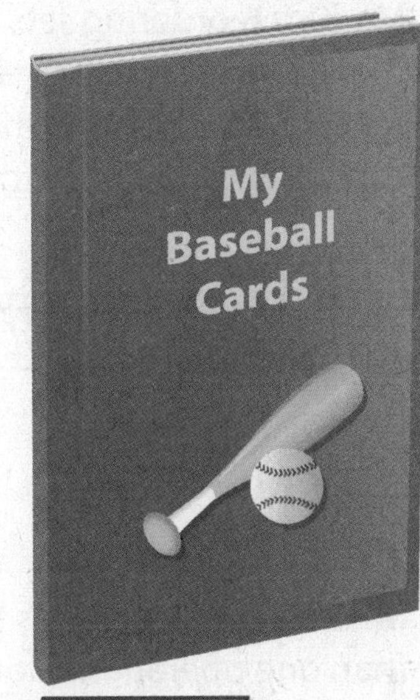

42 cards in each album

1. Write an expression to represent the total number of cards in Todd's albums before he gives some cards to Franco. Explain how your expression represents the quantities and the relationship between the quantities.

2. Write an expression to represent the total number of cards in Todd's albums after he gives some cards to Franco.

3. How many cards does Todd have after he gives some cards to Franco? Explain how you solved the problem.

Independent Practice

MP.2 Reasoning

Brandon is filling a flower order for a banquet. He needs 3 large arrangements and 12 small arrangements. The large arrangements each contain 28 roses. The small arrangements each contain 16 roses. How many roses does Brandon need in all?

Remember to think about the meaning of each number before solving the problem.

4. Write an expression to represent the total number of roses Brandon needs. You can use a diagram to help.

5. Explain how the numbers, symbols, and operations in your expression represent the problem.

6. How many roses does Brandon need? Explain how you solved the problem.

*For another example, see Set D on page 768.

Math Practices and Problem Solving

Common Core Performance Assessment

Math Supplies

Ms. Kim is ordering sets of place-value blocks for the 3rd, 4th, and 5th graders. She wants one set for each student, and there are 6 sets of blocks in a carton. How many cartons should Ms. Kim order?

DATA

Grade	Number of Students
3rd	48
4th	43
5th	46
6th	50

7. **MP.1 Make Sense and Persevere** What information in the problem do you need?

8. **MP.2 Reasoning** Does this problem require more than one operation? Does the order of the operations matter? Explain.

9. **MP.4 Model with Math** Write an expression to represent the number of cartons Ms. Kim needs to order. You can use a diagram to help.

10. **MP.3 Construct Arguments** Did you use grouping symbols in your expression? If so, explain why they are needed.

11. **MP.6 Be Precise** Find the total number of cartons Ms. Kim should order. Explain how you found the answer.

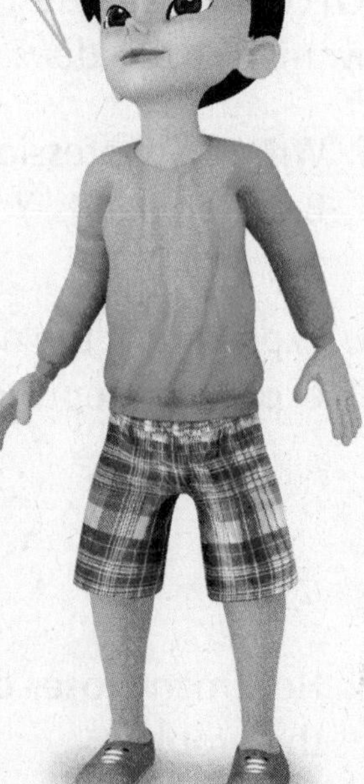

Use reasoning to make sense of the relationship between the numbers.

Name ____________________

Homework & Practice 13-5
Reasoning

Another Look!

There are 37 cars parked in the school parking lot at 5:00. There are 9 more cars at 5:30. At 6:00, there are twice as many cars as at 5:30. How many cars are in the lot at 6:00?

Use expressions to represent the quantities and relationships in the problem. You can use diagrams to help.

37 cars at 5:00	**9 more at 5:30**	**Twice as many at 6:00**
[37]	[37 | 9]	[37 | 9] [37 | 9]
37	37 + 9	(37 + 9) × 2

$(37 + 9) \times 2 = 46 \times 2 = 92$

So, there are 92 cars at 6:00.

Reasoning can help you understand how the quantities in a problem are related.

MP.2 Reasoning

Ms. Lang lives In St. Paul, Minnesota. Last year, she made 4 round trips to Madison, Wisconsin, and 3 round trips to Bismarck, North Dakota. How many more miles did she travel in her trips to Bismarck than in her trips to Madison?

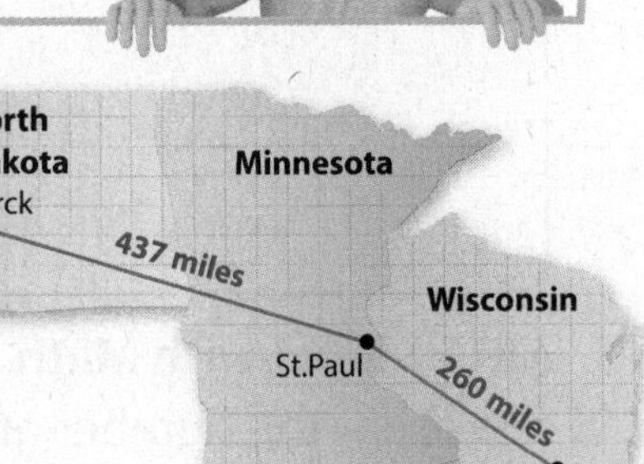

1. Write an expression to represent the difference between the total number of miles in the Bismarck trips and the total number of miles in the Madison trips. You can use a diagram to help.

2. Explain how the numbers, symbols, and operations in your expression represent the problem.

3. How many more miles did Mrs. Lang travel in her trips to Bismarck than in her trips to Madison? Explain how you solved the problem.

Common Core Performance Assessment

Camping Trip
Ross is planning a camping trip for 136 scouts. He has reserved 4 buses. The scouts will sleep in tents or cabins. If they fill every bed in the cabins, how many campers will sleep in tents?

State Park
14 cabins
Each cabin has 4 single beds.

4. **MP.1 Make Sense and Persevere** What information in the problem do you need?

5. **MP.2 Reasoning** Describe the calculations needed to solve the problem and explain the order in which you need to do them. You can use a diagram to help.

6. **MP.4 Model with Math** Write an expression to represent the number of campers that will sleep in tents.

7. **MP.3 Critique Reasoning** Ross says he does not need grouping symbols in the expression that represents this problem. Is he correct? Explain.

8. **MP.6 Be Precise** Find the number of campers that will sleep in tents. Explain how you found the answer.

When you use reasoning, you can use properties and diagrams to help make sense of the quantities.

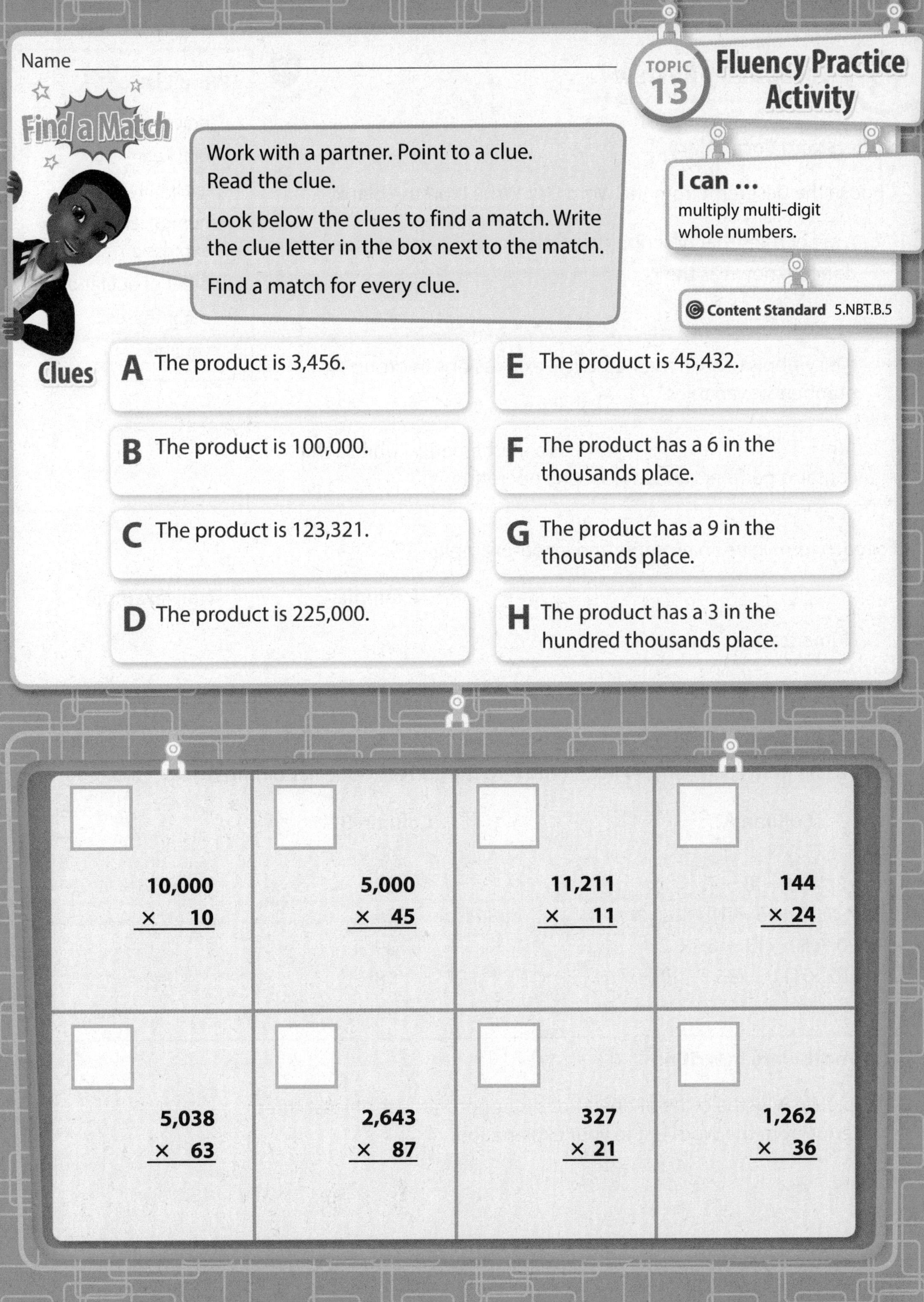

Name ______________________

Find a Match

TOPIC 13
Fluency Practice Activity

Work with a partner. Point to a clue. Read the clue.

Look below the clues to find a match. Write the clue letter in the box next to the match.

Find a match for every clue.

I can ... multiply multi-digit whole numbers.

Content Standard 5.NBT.B.5

Clues

A The product is 3,456.

B The product is 100,000.

C The product is 123,321.

D The product is 225,000.

E The product is 45,432.

F The product has a 6 in the thousands place.

G The product has a 9 in the thousands place.

H The product has a 3 in the hundred thousands place.

☐ $10{,}000 \times 10$	☐ $5{,}000 \times 45$	☐ $11{,}211 \times 11$	☐ 144×24
☐ $5{,}038 \times 63$	☐ $2{,}643 \times 87$	☐ 327×21	☐ $1{,}262 \times 36$

TOPIC 13

Vocabulary Review

Word List

- braces
- brackets
- evaluate
- numerical expression
- order of operations
- parentheses
- variable

Understand Vocabulary

Choose the best term from the Word List. Write it on the blank.

1. A set of rules that describes the order in which calculations are done is known as the ____________.

2. ____________, ____________, and ____________ are symbols used in mathematical expressions to group numbers or variables.

3. A(n) ____________ is a mathematical phrase that contains numbers and at least one operation.

For each term, give an example and a non-example.

	Example	Non-example
4. Numerical expression	____________	____________
5. Expression with parentheses	____________	____________

Draw a line from each number in Column A to the correct value in Column B.

Column A	Column B
6. $3 + 6 \times 2$	49
7. $12 \times (8 - 5) - 7$	20
8. $7 \times [5 + (3 - 1)]$	15
9. $20 \div 5 + (13 - 6) \times 2$	29
10. $\{10 \times [11 - (36 \div 4)]\}$	18

Use Vocabulary in Writing

11. Explain why the order of operations is important. Use at least three terms from the Word List in your explanation.

Name ______________________________

Reteaching

Set A pages 735–740, 741–746

Use the order of operations to evaluate $50 + (8 + 2) \times (14 - 4)$.

Order of Operations

1. Calculate inside parentheses, brackets, and braces.
2. Multiply and divide from left to right.
3. Add and subtract from left to right.

Perform the operations inside the parentheses, brackets, and braces.

$50 + (8 + 2) \times (14 - 4) = 50 + 10 \times 10$

Multiply and divide in order from left to right.

$50 + 10 \times 10 = 50 + 100$

Add and subtract in order from left to right.

$50 + 100 = 150$

Remember that if the parentheses are inside brackets or braces, perform the operations inside the parentheses first.

Evaluate each expression.

1. $(78 + 47) \div 25$
2. $4 + 8 \times 6 \div 2 + 3$
3. $[(8 \times 25) \div 5] + 120$
4. $312 \times (40 + 60) \div 60$
5. $80 - (0.4 + 0.2) \times 10$
6. $(18 - 3) \div 5 + 4$
7. $8 \times 5 + 7 \times 3 - (10 - 5)$
8. $22 - \{[(87 - 32) \div 5] \times 2\}$

Set B pages 747–752

Write a numerical expression for the phrase: "Subtract 15 from the product of 12 and 7".

Think:

Sum → Addition (+)

Difference → Subtraction (−)

Product → Multiplication (×)

Quotient → Division (÷)

Product of 12 and 7: 12×7

Subtract 15 from the product: $(12 \times 7) - 15$

So, a numerical expression for the phrase is: $(12 \times 7) - 15$.

Remember that you can use parentheses to show which calculation to do first.

Write a numerical expression for each phrase.

1. Add 15 to the product of $\frac{3}{4}$ and 12.
2. Find the difference of 29 and 13, and then divide by 2.
3. Add $1\frac{1}{2}$ and $\frac{3}{4}$, and then subtract $\frac{1}{3}$.
4. Multiply 1.2 by 5 and then subtract 0.7.
5. Add the quotient of 120 and 3 to the product of 15 and 10.

Set C pages 753–758

The expressions below show how many miles each student ran this week. How does Alex's distance compare to Kim's distance?

Kim: $\left(4 \times 3\frac{1}{2}\right)$

Alex: $\left(4 \times 3\frac{1}{2}\right) + 2\frac{1}{2}$

What is the **same** about the expressions? Both contain the product $4 \times 3\frac{1}{2}$.

What is **different** about the expressions? $2\frac{1}{2}$ is added in Alex's expression.

So, Alex ran $2\frac{1}{2}$ miles farther than Kim this week.

Remember that sometimes you can compare numerical expressions without doing any calculations.

Without doing any calculations, write >, <, or =.

1. $72 \times (37 - 9)$ ◯ $69 \times (37 - 9)$
2. $(144 \div 12) - 6$ ◯ $144 \div 12$
3. $\left(4 + \frac{1}{2} + 3\right) \times 2$ ◯ $2 \times \left(4 + \frac{1}{2} + 3\right)$
4. Describe how Expression A compares to Expression B.

   A \$3.99 + (\$9.50 × 2) **B** \$9.50 × 2

Set D pages 759–764

Think about these questions to help you **reason abstractly and quantitatively.**

Thinking Habits

- What do the numbers and symbols in the problem mean?
- How are the numbers or quantities related?
- How can I represent a word problem using pictures, numbers, or equations?

Remember that you can use diagrams to help solve the problem.

1. Kerry has 5 metal and 3 wood paperweights in her collection. She has twice as many glass paperweights as metal paperweights. Write an expression to represent the total number of paperweights in her collection. Then find the total number of paperweights.
2. Reese had 327 baseball cards. Then he lost 8 of them and gave 15 of them to his brother. Write an expression to represent the number of baseball cards he has left. Then find how many baseball cards he has left.

Name ______________________________

TOPIC 13

Assessment

1. In questions 1a–1d, is the expression equal to 10? Choose Yes or No.

1a. $2 \times (45 \div 9)$ ○ Yes ○ No

1b. $24 - 7 \times 2$ ○ Yes ○ No

1c. $1 + 4 \times 2$ ○ Yes ○ No

1d. $(2 \times 25) \div (9 - 4)$ ○ Yes ○ No

2. Choose all of the expressions that are equal to 8×65.

- ☐ $3 + 5 \times 60$
- ☐ $8 \times (60 + 5)$
- ☐ $8 \times (50 + 15)$
- ☐ $(8 + 60) \times (8 + 5)$
- ☐ $(8 \times 60) + (8 \times 5)$

3. Which is the value of the expression $[7 + (3 \times 4)] - 2$?

Ⓐ 38

Ⓑ 20

Ⓒ 17

Ⓓ 12

4. Which expression represents the following calculation?

Add 16 to the quotient of 72 and 8.

Ⓐ $(72 - 8) + 16$

Ⓑ $(72 \div 8) + 16$

Ⓒ $(16 + 72) \div 8$

Ⓓ $(16 + 72) + 8$

5. A factory shipped 100 boxes with 15 skateboards in each box and 10 boxes with 15 helmets in each box.

Part A

Write an expression for the total number of items they shipped.

Part B

Evaluate the expression that represents the number of items that were shipped.

6. Describe how the value of Expression A compares to the value of Expression B.

A $1\frac{1}{2} + \left(54 \div \frac{2}{5}\right)$

B $54 \div \frac{2}{5}$

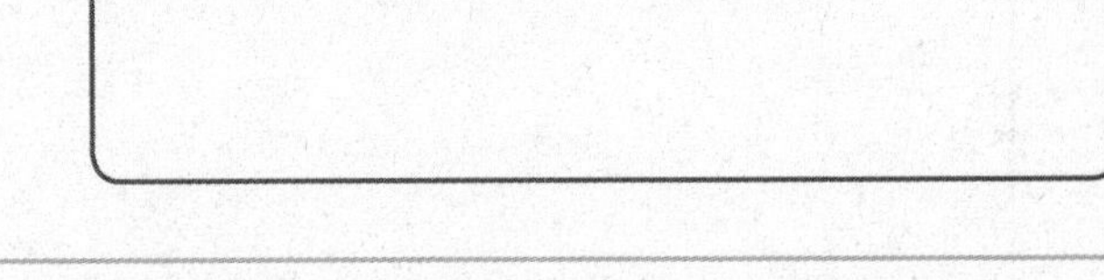

7. Write >, <, or = in the circle to make the statement true.

$(368 \times 19) - 24$ ◯ $(368 \times 19) - 47$

8. Insert parentheses to make the statement true.

$7 + 6 \times 14 - 9 = 37$

9. Which expression represents the following calculation?

Subtract 1.9 from the product of 7.4 and 3.

Ⓐ $(7.4 + 3) - 1.9$

Ⓑ $7.4 \times (3 - 1.9)$

Ⓒ $(7.4 \times 3) - 1.9$

Ⓓ $(7.4 \times 1.9) - 3$

10. Maya read 9 books last month and 3 books this month. Her teacher read twice as many books as Maya. Write an expression for the number of books Maya's teacher read. Then find the number of books that the teacher read.

11. Janice says that the value of the expression $6 + 12 \div 2 + 4$ is 13.

Part A

Why is her answer incorrect?

Part B

What is the correct value for the expression? Show your work.

12. Write $>$, $<$, or $=$ in the circle to make the statement true.

$(249 + 1{,}078) \times \frac{1}{3}$ ◯ $(249 + 1{,}078) \div 3$

13. The table shows the cost for day care for Lucy's dog. This week her dog went to 3 full days of day care and 2 half days of day care. Write an expression for the total cost of this week's day care. Then evaluate the expression to find the total cost.

DATA

Day Care	Cost
Full day	\$28
Half day	\$15

14. Mr. Haugh wrote the following expression on the board.

$6 + (24 - 4) + 8 \div 2$

Part A

What step do you perform first in evaluating this expression?

Part B

What step do you perform second in evaluating this expression?

Part C

What is the value of the expression?

Name ______________________________

TOPIC 13

Performance Assessment

Decorating

Jackie is decorating her room. She wants to put a border around the ceiling. She will put wallpaper on one wall and paint the other three walls.

1. The drawing of **Jackie's Room** shows the width of the room. The expression $[13.2 - (2 \times 2.8)] \div 2$ represents the length of her room.

Part A

How much border does Jackie need to go around the entire ceiling of her room? Explain how you can tell from the expression.

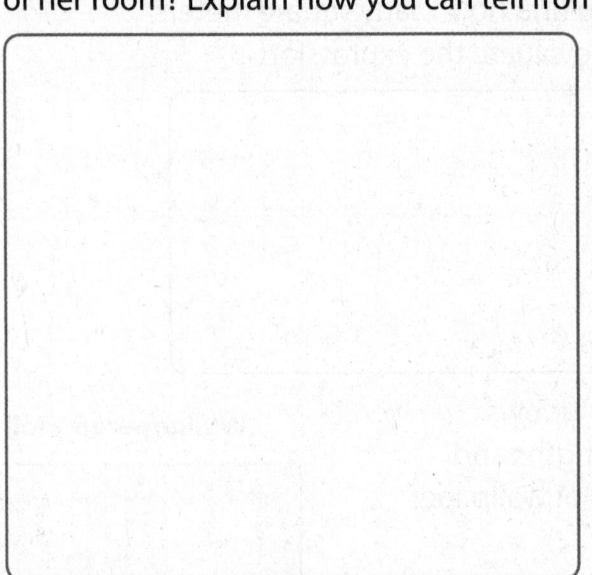

Jackie's Room

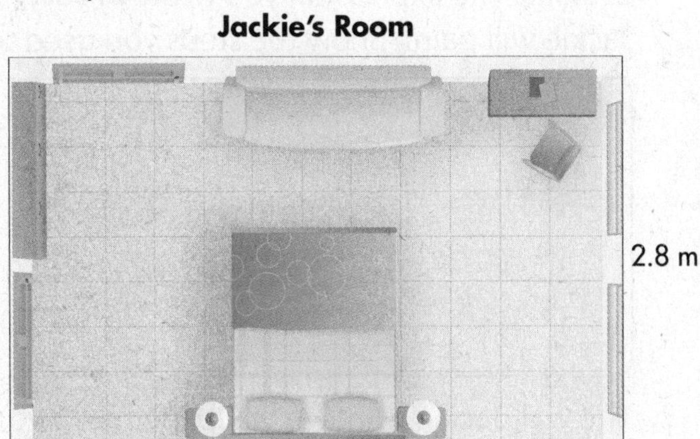

Part B

What is the length of Jackie's room? Show the steps you use to evaluate the expression.

2. The **Painted Walls** drawing shows the three walls Jackie wants to paint. One wall is 2.8 meters long. The length of each of the other walls is the answer you found in Question 1, Part B.

Painted Walls

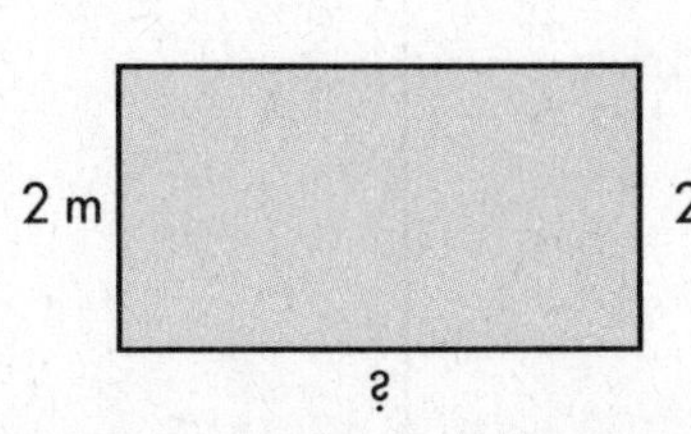

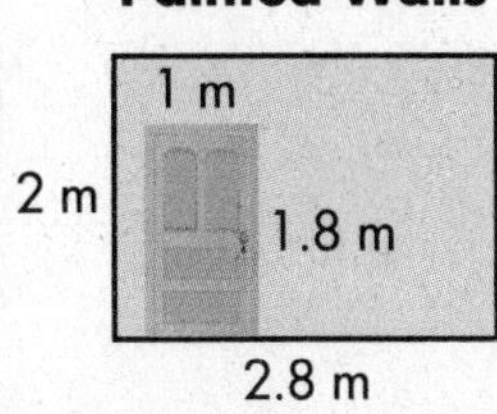

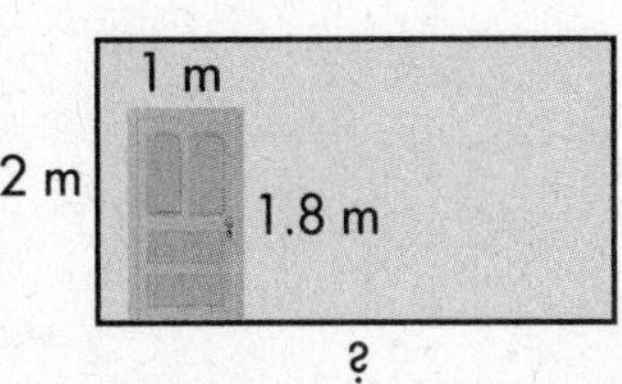

Part A

Write an expression to represent how many square meters Jackie will paint.

Part B

Evaluate the expression you wrote in Part A to find how many square meters Jackie will paint. Show the steps you used to evaluate the expression.

3. The wall Jackie wants to wallpaper has two windows. The **Wallpapered Wall** drawing shows the lengths and widths of the wall and the windows. Each roll of wallpaper covers 0.8 square meter.

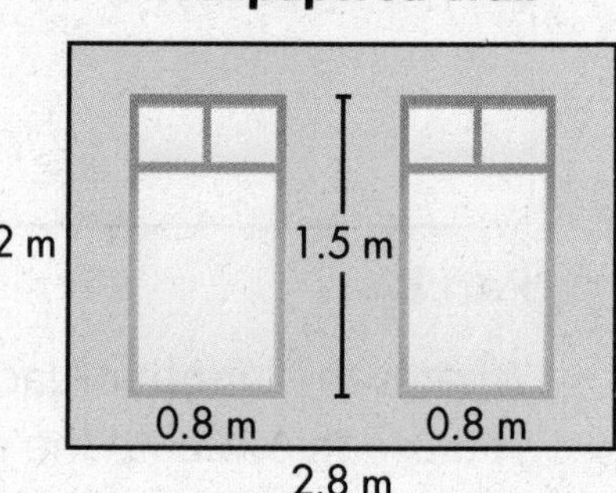

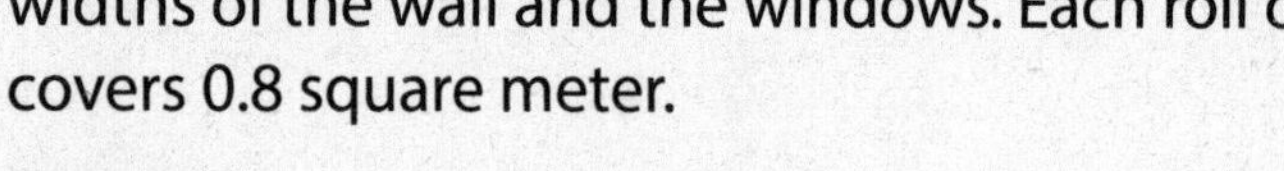

Part A

What does the expression $2 \times (1.5 \times 0.8)$ represent? What does the expression $(2.8 \times 2) - [2 \times (1.5 \times 0.8)]$ represent?

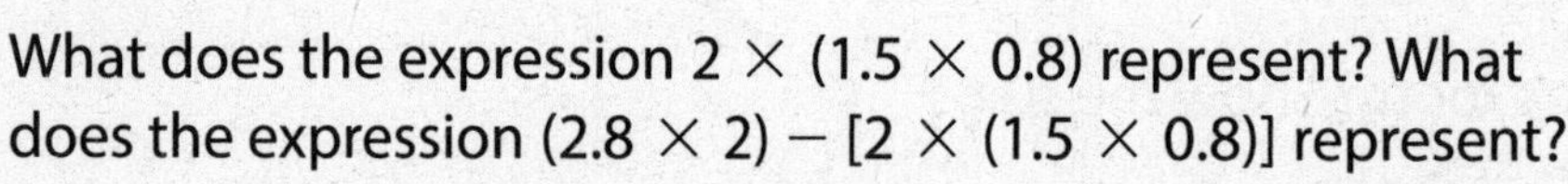

Part B

Write an expression to find how many rolls of wallpaper Jackie needs to buy. Show the steps you used to evaluate the expression.

Graph Points on the Coordinate Plane

Essential Questions: How are points plotted? How are relationships shown on a graph?

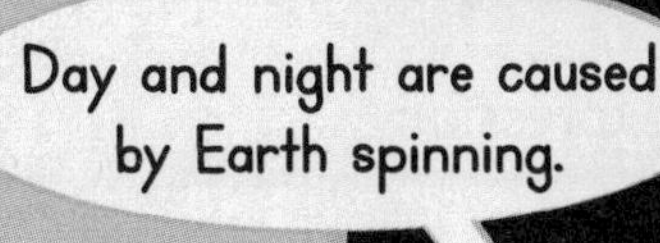

Day and night are caused by Earth spinning.
The imaginary line through Earth's center is Earth's *axis*. The spinning of Earth on its axis is called *rotation*.

I'm getting dizzy thinking about it! Here's a project about Earth's rotation.

Math and Science Project: Earth's Rotation

Do Research Use the Internet or other sources to find out more about Earth's rotation. Investigate why it appears that the Sun is moving across the sky. Design a model to explain Earth's day/night cycle. Compare Earth's rotation to another planet's rotation.

Write a Report: Journal Include what you found. Also in your report:

- Write a step-by-step procedure of how to use a ball and a flashlight to represent the day/night cycle.
- Explain what happens if the ball rotates slowly. What happens if the ball rotates quickly?
- Make up and solve problems for plotting points and using graphs to show relationships.

Name ______________________________

Review What You Know

Vocabulary

- equation
- factor
- line plot
- numerical expression
- variable

Choose the best term from the Word List. Write it on the blank.

1. A(n) ______________________ contains numbers and at least one operation.
2. A letter or symbol that represents an unknown amount is a(n) ________.
3. A number sentence that uses the = symbol is a(n) ________.
4. A display that shows *X*s or dots above a number line is a(n) ________.

Evaluate Expressions

Evaluate each numerical expression.

5. $3 \times 4 \times (10 - 7) \div 2$
6. $(8 + 2) \times 6 - 4$
7. $8 + 2 \times 6 - 4$
8. $40 \div 5 + 5 \times (3 - 1)$
9. $15 \div 3 + 2 \times 10$
10. $21 \times (8 - 6) \div 14$

Write Expressions

Write a numerical expression for each word phrase.

11. Three less than the product of eight and six
12. Thirteen more than the quotient of twenty and four
13. Four times the difference between seven and two

Compare Expressions

14. Use < or > to compare $13 \times (54 + 28)$ and $13 \times 54 + 28$ without calculating. Explain your reasoning.

My Word Cards

Use the examples for each word on the front of the card to help complete the definitions on the back.

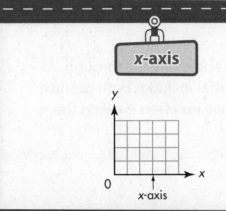

A-Z Glossary

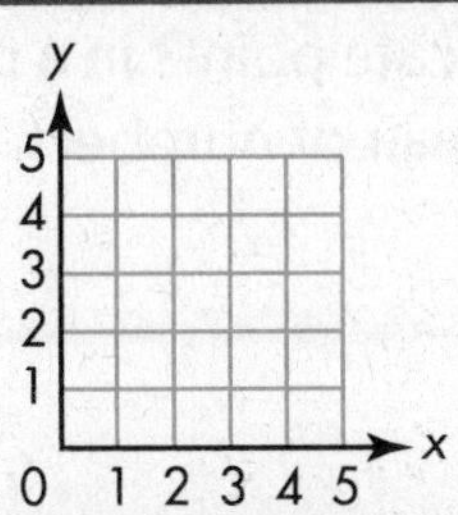

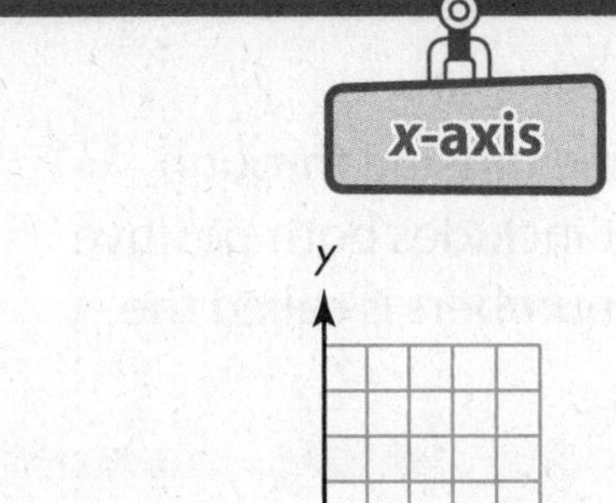

y-axis

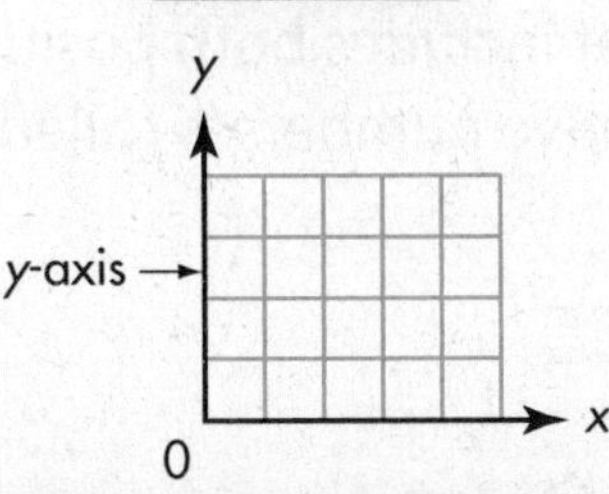

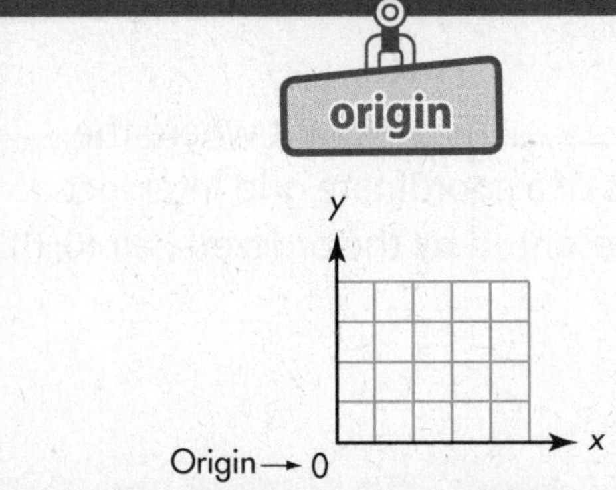

ordered pair

(4, 2)

(4, 2)

x-coordinate

y-coordinate

(4, 2)

y-coordinate

My Word Cards

Complete the definition. Extend learning by writing your own definitions.

A horizontal line passing through the origin that includes both positive and negative numbers is called the

__________.

A ____________________ is used to locate points in a plane using an ordered pair of numbers.

The __________ is the point where the two axes of a coordinate grid intersect. It is represented by the ordered pair (0, 0).

A vertical line passing through the origin that includes both positive and negative numbers is called the

__________.

The first number in an ordered pair, which names the distance to the right or left from the origin along the x-axis,

is called the ____________________.

An ____________________ is pair of numbers used to locate a point on a coordinate grid.

The second number in an ordered pair, which names the distance up or down from the origin along the y-axis, is

called the ____________________.

Name

Lesson 14-1

The Coordinate System

I can ...
locate points on a coordinate grid.

Content Standard 5.G.A.1
Mathematical Practices MP.2, MP.3, MP.4, MP.5, MP.6

Solve & Share

On the first grid, plot a point where two lines intersect. Name the location of the point. Plot and name another point. Work with a partner. Take turns describing the locations of the points on your first grid. Then plot the points your partner describes on your second grid. Compare your first grid with your partner's second grid to see if they match. ***Use the grids below to solve this problem.***

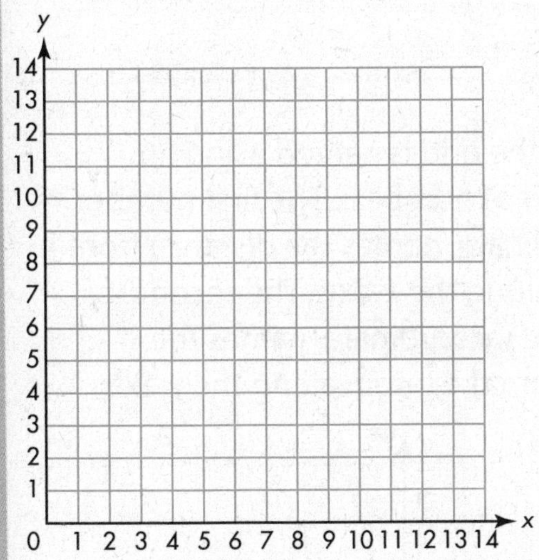

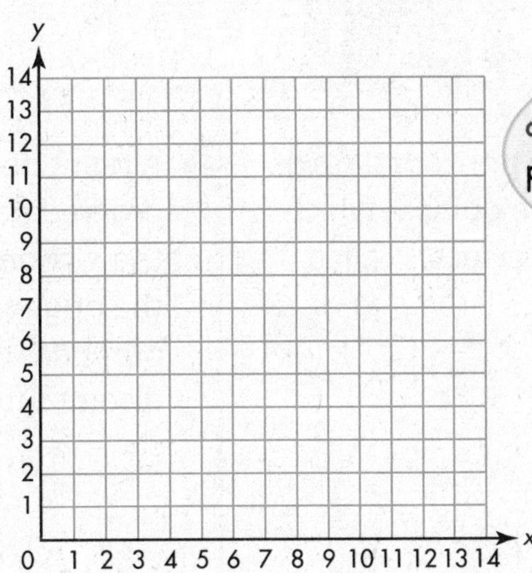

You can use appropriate tools such as grid paper to graph ordered pairs. *Show your work!*

Look Back! **MP.3 Construct Arguments** Why does the order of the two numbers that name a point matter? Explain your thinking.

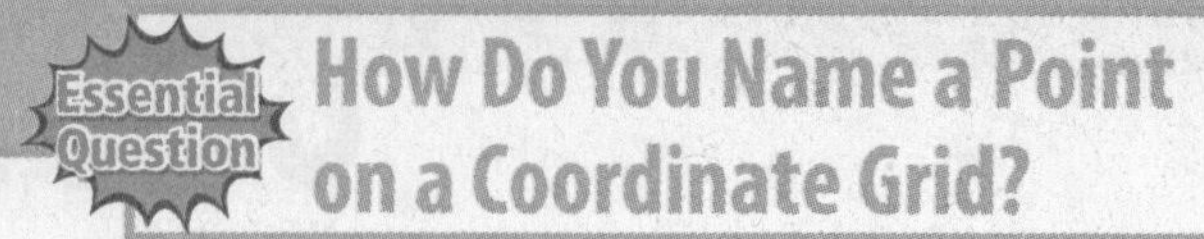

How Do You Name a Point on a Coordinate Grid?

A

A map shows the locations of landmarks and has guides for finding them. In a similar way, a coordinate grid is used to graph and name the locations of points in a plane.

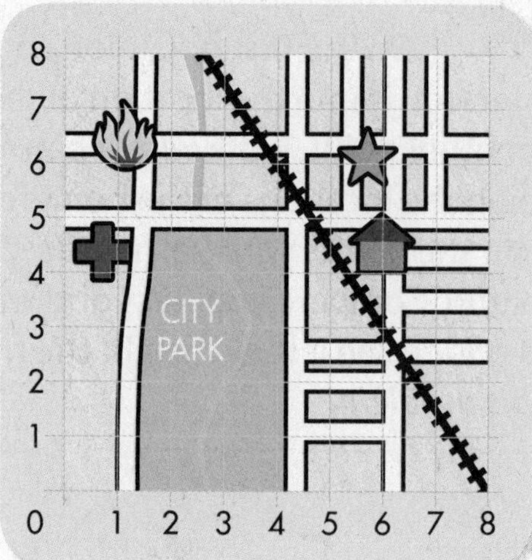

You can use ordered pairs to locate points on a coordinate grid.

B A coordinate grid has a horizontal *x*-axis and a vertical *y*-axis. The point at which the *x*-axis and *y*-axis intersect is called the origin.

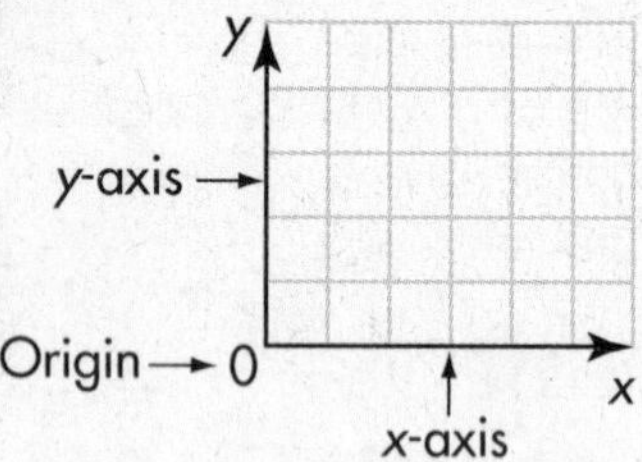

C A point on the grid is named using an ordered pair of numbers. The first number, the *x*-coordinate, names the distance from the origin along the *x*-axis. The second number, the *y*-coordinate, names the distance from the origin along the *y*-axis.

A (1, 3)

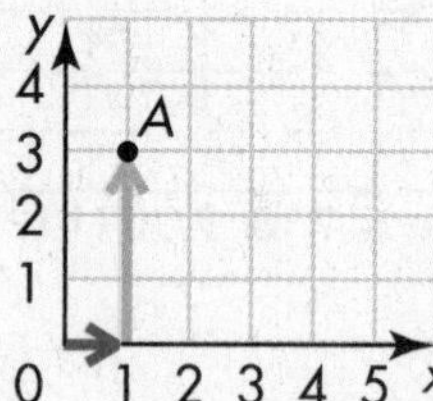

Convince Me! **MP.2 Reasoning** In the example above, name the ordered pair for Point *B* if it is 3 units to the right of Point *A*. Tell how you decided.

Name

Guided Practice*

Do You Understand?

1. You are graphing Point *E* at (0, 5). Do you move to the right zero units, or up zero units? Explain.

2. **Vocabulary** What ordered pair names the origin of any coordinate grid?

3. **MP.6 Be Precise** Describe how to graph Point *K* at (5, 4).

Do You Know How?

In **4** and **5**, write the ordered pair for each point. Use the grid.

4. *B*

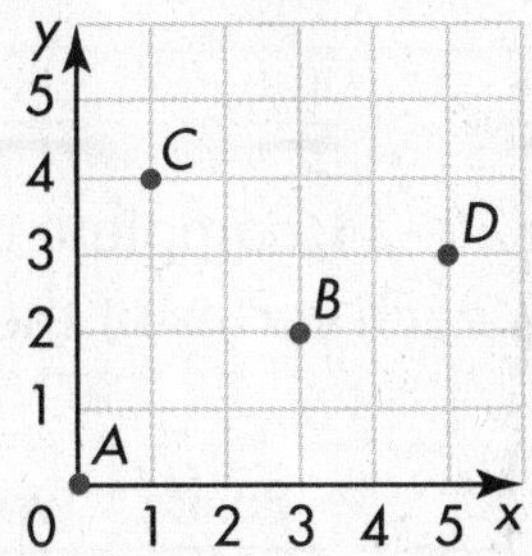

5. *A*

In **6** and **7**, name the point for each ordered pair on the grid above.

6. (5, 3)

7. (1, 4)

Independent Practice

In **8–13**, write the ordered pair for each point. Use the grid.

8. *T*

9. *X*

10. *Y*

11. *W*

12. *Z*

13. *S*

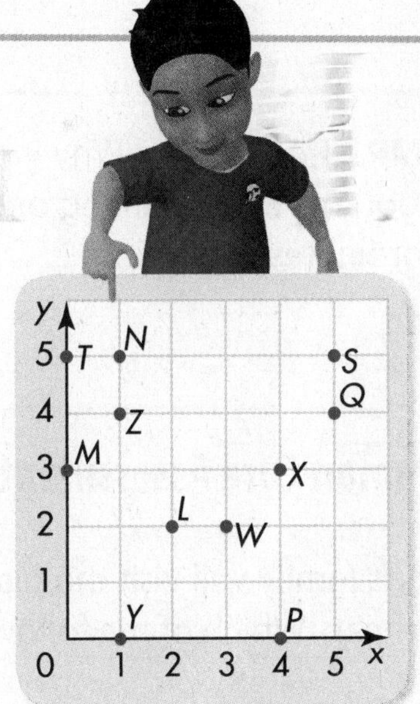

In **14–18**, name the point for each ordered pair on the grid above.

14. (2, 2)

15. (5, 4)

16. (1, 5)

17. (0, 3)

18. (4, 0)

*For another example, see Set A on page 803.

Math Practices and Problem Solving

19. Higher Order Thinking Describe to a friend how to find and name the ordered pair for Point *R* on the grid.

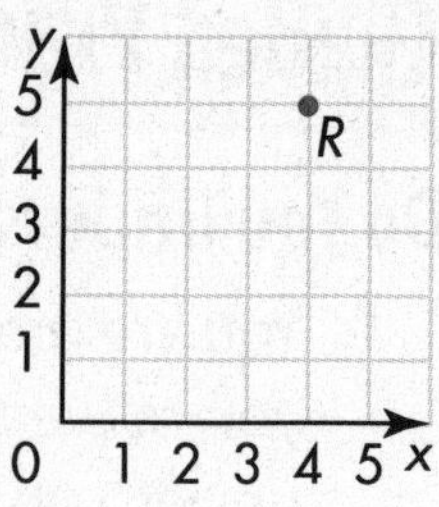

In **20–24**, complete the table. List the point and ordered pair for each vertex of the pentagon at the right.

	Point	Ordered Pair
20.		
21.		
22.		
23.		
24.		

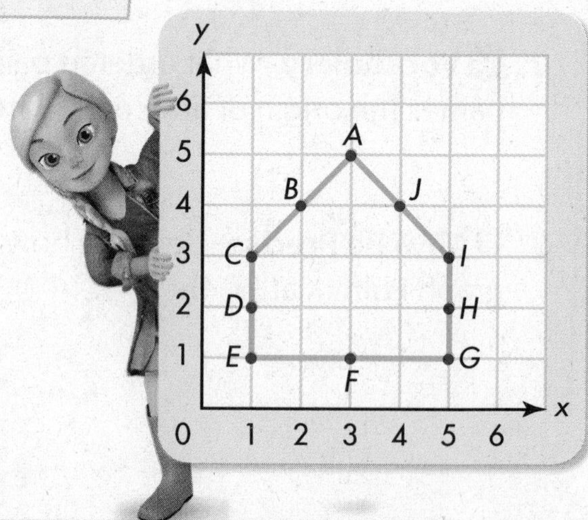

25. 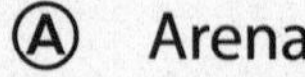 **MP.2 Reasoning** Why is the order important when naming or graphing the coordinates of a point?

26. How are the *x*-axis and the *y*-axis related on a coordinate grid?

Common Core Assessment

27. Dina's family will visit the place located at (4, 2) on the city map. Which of the following places is located at (4, 2)?

Ⓐ Arena

Ⓑ Museum

Ⓒ Bridge

Ⓓ Park

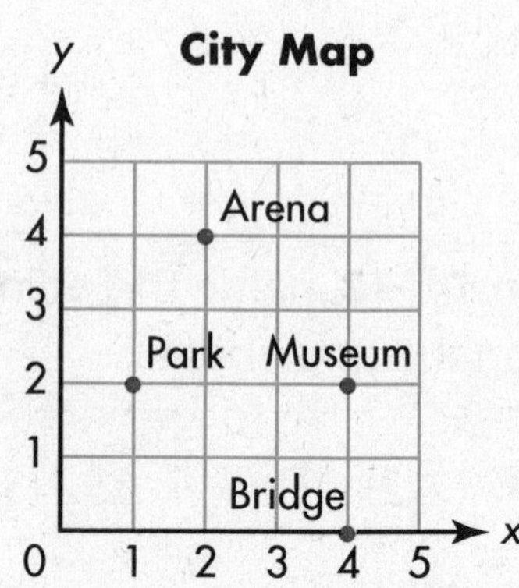

Name ______________________

Homework & Practice 14-1

The Coordinate System

Another Look!

Point *P* gives the location of the playground. Find the coordinates of Point *P*.

Start at (0, 0). Move a distance of 4 units to the right along the *x*-axis.

Move a distance of 3 units up.

The coordinates of Point *P* are (4, 3).

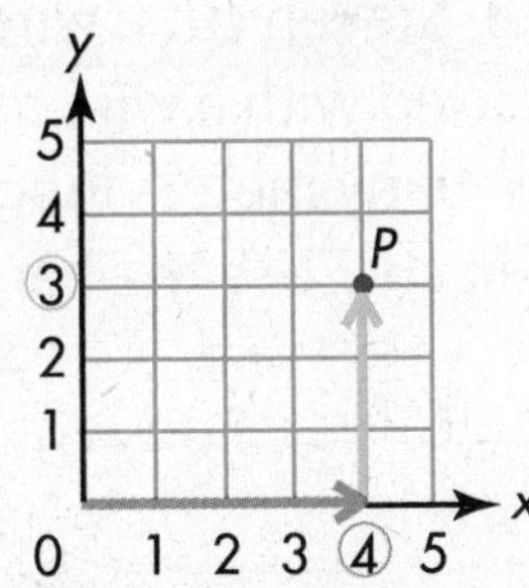

In **1–6**, write the ordered pair for each point on the grid.

1. *A*

2. *B*

3. *C*

4. *D*

5. *E*

6. *F*

In **7–18**, name the point that is located at each ordered pair.

7. (4, 3) Point ______

8. (3, 7) Point ______

9. (0, 3) Point ______

10. (5, 2) Point ______

11. (6, 8) Point ______

12. (6, 4) Point ______

13. (4, 5) Point ______

14. (2, 8) Point ______

15. (5, 5) Point ______

16. (2, 6) Point ______

17. (2, 3) Point ______

18. (3, 2) Point ______

19. Describe to a friend how to graph a point at (2, 5).

20. **MP.2 Reasoning** How are the locations on a coordinate grid different for the ordered pairs (7, 0) and (0, 7)?

21. **MP.4 Model with Math** Steven cut a wire into 5 equal pieces. He started with a wire that was 6.8 meters long. How many meters long was each piece that Steven cut? Use the bar diagram to help you.

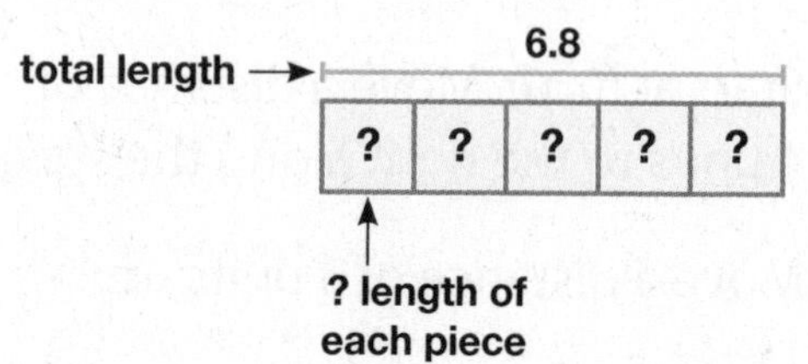

In **22** and **23**, use the chessboard.

22. **Higher Order Thinking** A chessboard is similar to a coordinate grid. The pieces that look like horses are knights. What letter-number combinations name the locations of the white knights?

23. Andre moves the pawn located at (e, 7) down 2 units. What letter-number combination names the pawn's new location? Explain.

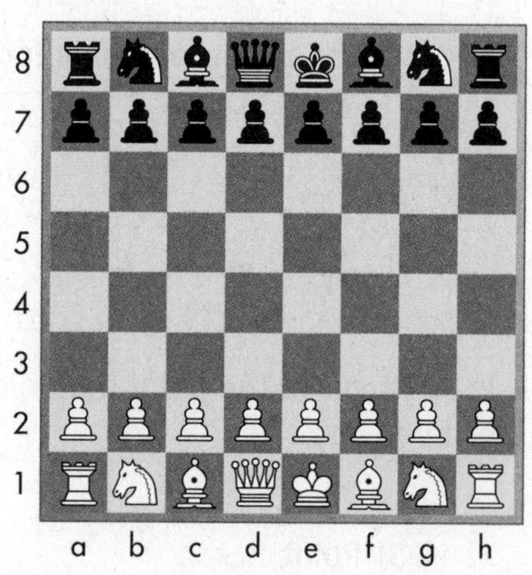

Common Core Assessment

24. Jeremy wants to visit the Duck Pond. Which is a correct description of how to find the ordered pair for the Duck Pond?

Ⓐ From (0, 0), go 4 units along the x-axis. Go 2 units up. Write (4, 2).

Ⓑ From (0, 2), go 2 units along the y-axis. Go 2 units right. Write (2, 2).

Ⓒ From (0, 0), go 2 units along the x-axis. Go 4 units up. Write (2, 4).

Ⓓ From (0, 0), go 2 units along the y-axis. Go 4 units right. Write (4, 2).

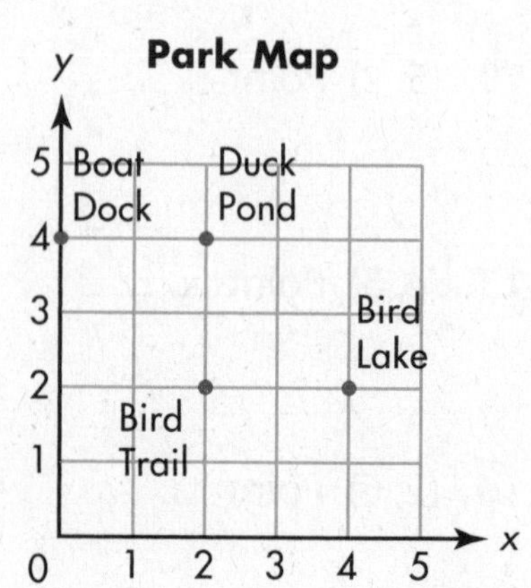

Name

Lesson 14-2

Graph Data Using Ordered Pairs

I can ...
graph points on a coordinate grid.

Content Standard 5.G.A.1
Mathematical Practices MP.1, MP.2, MP.3, MP.5, MP.6, MP.8

Solve & Share Graph and label the point for each ordered pair below on the grid. Then connect the points with line segments to form a shape. What shape did you draw?

Use Appropriate Tools
You can graph points on a coordinate grid. Show your work!

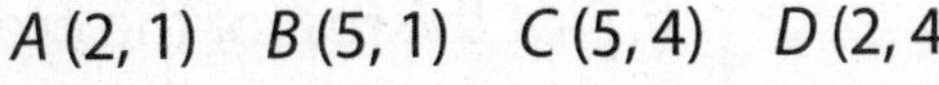

A (2, 1) *B* (5, 1) *C* (5, 4) *D* (2, 4)

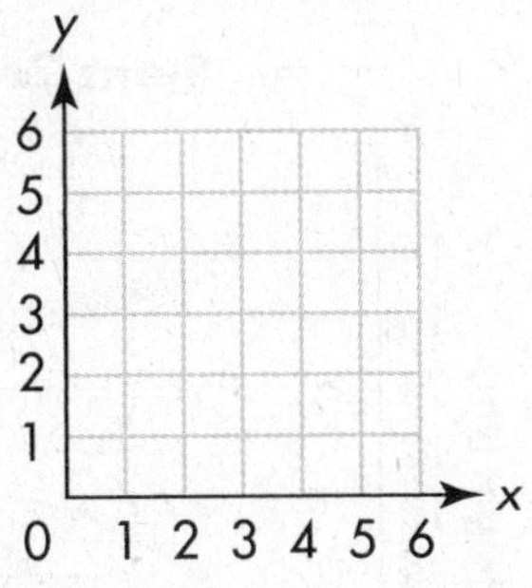

Look Back! **MP.5 Use Appropriate Tools** What tool could you use to help connect points *A*, *B*, *C*, and *D*? Explain.

How Do You Graph a Point on a Coordinate Grid?

A

The table below shows the growth of a plant over a period of several days. Graph ordered pairs to show the plant's growth.

Let x be the number of days and let y be the height of the plant in centimeters.

DATA

Time (days)	1	3	5	7	9
Height (cm)	4	8	10	11	14

The ordered pairs are (1, 4), (3, 8), (5, 10), (7, 11), and (9, 14).

B

Step 1

Graph the first point (1, 4).

Start at (0, 0). Move 1 unit to the right along the x-axis. Then move 4 units up.

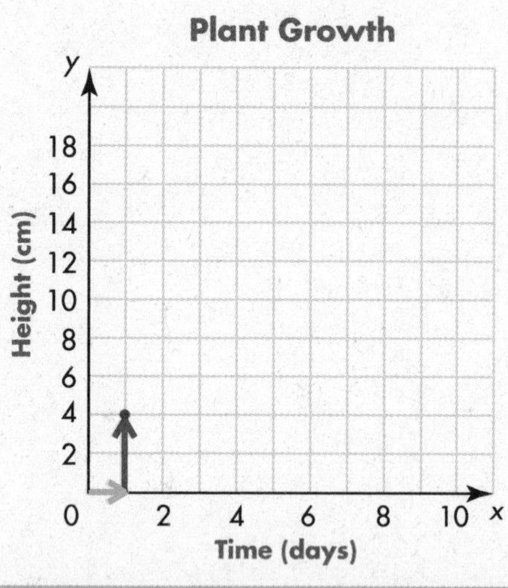

C

Step 2

Plot the rest of the ordered pairs from the table. Use a ruler to connect the points.

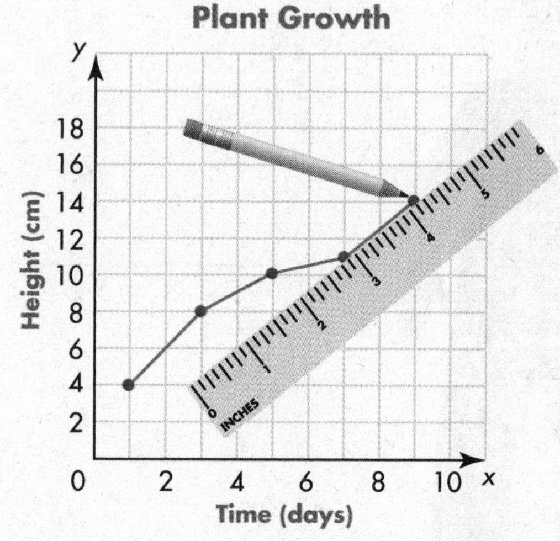

Convince Me! **MP.2 Reasoning** Based on the data, about how tall was the plant on day 4? Day 8?

Name ____

Guided Practice*

Do You Understand?

1. **MP.3 Construct Arguments** Natalie is graphing Point *T* at (1, 8). Should she move to the right 8 units or up 8 units? Explain.

2. **MP.8 Generalize** Describe how to graph the point (*c*, *d*).

Do You Know How?

In **3–6**, graph each point on the grid and label it with the appropriate letter.

3. *E* (1, 3)

4. *F* (4, 4)

5. *G* (5, 2)

6. *H* (0, 2)

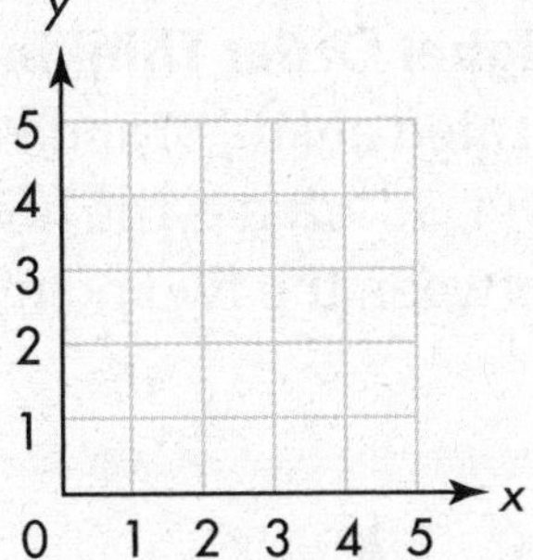

Independent Practice

In **7–18**, graph and label each point on the grid at the right.

7. *J* (2, 6)

8. *K* (6, 2)

9. *L* (4, 5)

10. *M* (0, 8)

11. *N* (3, 9)

12. *V* (6, 6)

13. *P* (1, 4)

14. *Q* (5, 0)

15. *R* (7, 3)

16. *S* (7, 8)

17. *T* (8, 1)

18. *U* (3, 3)

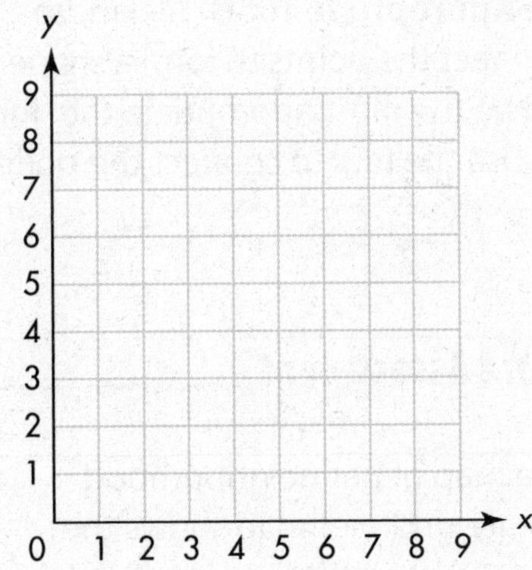

*For another example, see Set B on page 803.

Math Practices and Problem Solving

19. **MP.2 Reasoning** How is graphing (0, 2) different from graphing (2, 0)?

20. **Number Sense** Shane took a test that had a total of 21 items. He got about $\frac{3}{4}$ of the items correct. About how many items did he get correct?

21. **Higher Order Thinking** Point *C* is located at (10, 3) and Point *D* is located at (4, 3). What is the horizontal distance between the two points? Explain.

22. Laurel buys 3 balls of yarn. Each ball of yarn costs $4.75. She also buys 2 pairs of knitting needles. Each pair costs $5.75. She pays for her purchase with two 20-dollar bills. What is her change?

23. Graph the points below on the grid at the right.

A (2, 4) *B* (1, 2) *C* (2, 0)
D (3, 0) *E* (4, 2) *F* (3, 4)

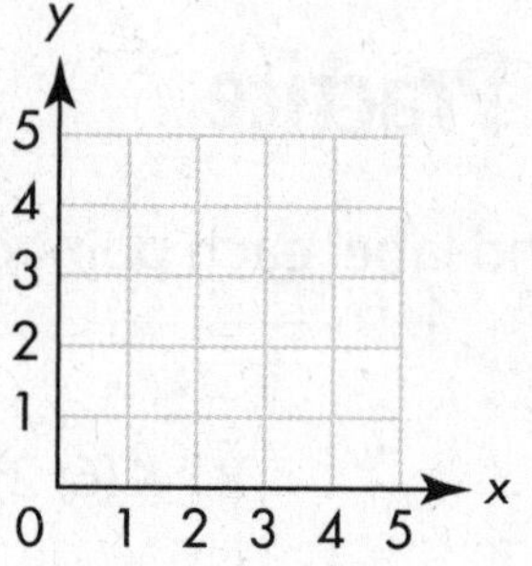

24. **MP.5 Use Appropriate Tools** Alejandro wants to connect the points to form a shape. What would be the most appropriate tool for him to use? Use the tool to connect the points.

Common Core Assessment

25. Talia draws a map of her neighborhood on a coordinate grid. Her map shows the school at *S* (1, 6), her house at *H* (4, 3), and the library at *L* (7, 2). Graph and label each location on the grid at the right.

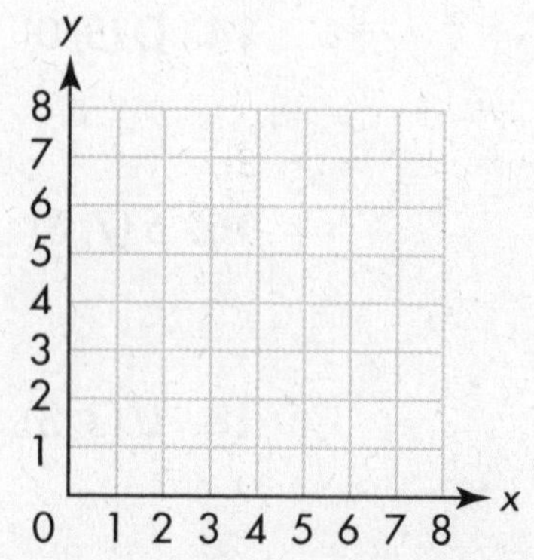

Name ______________________________________

Homework & Practice 14-2

Graph Data Using Ordered Pairs

Another Look!

Graph the following four points and connect them to form a parallelogram.

M (2, 1)   *N* (4, 1)   *O* (5, 4)   *P* (3, 4)

Graph (2, 1) first. Start at (0, 0). Move 2 units to the right from the *y*-axis. Then move one unit up. Draw a dot to represent (2, 1) and label the point *M*.

Graph the remaining 3 points in the same way. Then draw line segments between the points to form a parallelogram.

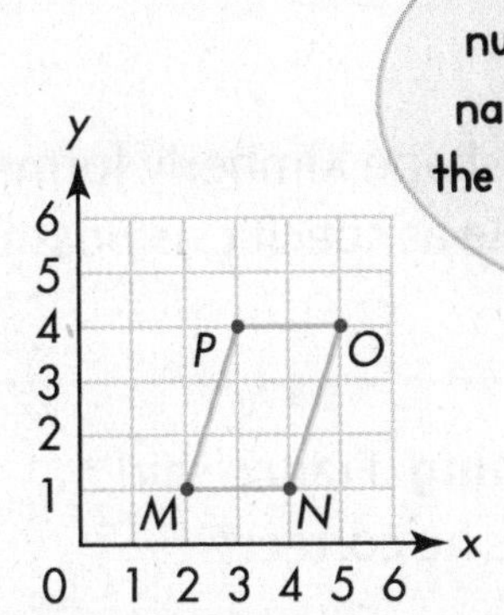

Remember that the first number in an ordered pair names the *x*-coordinate and the second number names the *y*-coordinate.

1. Explain to a friend how to graph the point (1, 5).

In **2–13**, graph and label each point on the grid at the right.

2. *A* (1, 2)

3. *B* (0, 7)

4. *C* (3, 3)

5. *D* (8, 9)

6. *E* (6, 0)

7. *F* (5, 4)

8. *G* (2, 8)

9. *H* (1, 6)

10. *I* (7, 4)

11. *J* (0, 0)

12. *K* (1, 4)

13. *L* (4, 1)

14. Explain the difference in how you graphed points *K* and *L* on the coordinate grid.

15. Graph the points below on the grid at the right.

D (1, 1) *E* (4, 1) *F* (3, 3) *G* (2, 3)

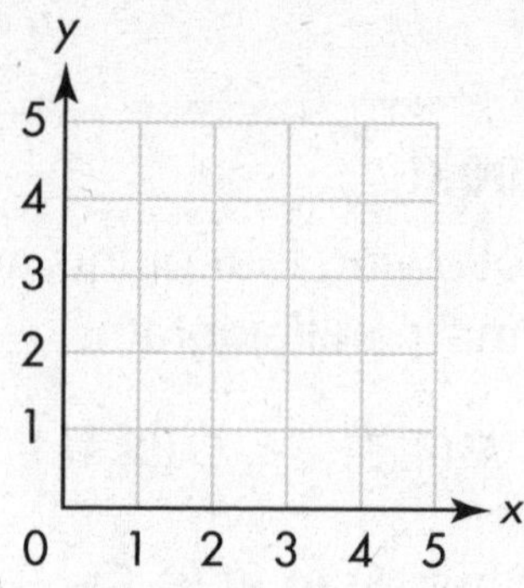

16. **MP.5 Use Appropriate Tools** Kimberly wants to draw line segments to connect the points to form a shape. What would be the most appropriate tool for her to use?

17. What is the name of the shape Kimberly forms by connecting the points? Be as specific as possible.

18. **MP.3 Critique Reasoning** Franco said that $5 + 2 \times 30 = 210$. Is he correct? Explain.

19. **MP.1 Make Sense and Persevere** At a ski lift, 47 people are waiting to board cars. Each car can hold 6 people. How many cars will be completely filled? How many people are left to board the last car?

20. **Higher Order Thinking** One side of a rectangle is parallel to the *x*-axis. One vertex of the rectangle is located at (5, 2) and another vertex at (1, 4). What are the coordinates of the other two vertices?

21. **MP.6 Be Precise** Andi needs $5\frac{1}{2}$ yards of fabric for a project. She has a piece that is $3\frac{1}{4}$ yards at school and a piece that is $1\frac{1}{2}$ yards at home. How much more fabric does she need?

Common Core Assessment

22. Connor visits the following locations: museum at *M* (4, 0), sports center at *S* (5, 2), and bookstore at *B* (7, 8). Graph and label each location on the grid at the right.

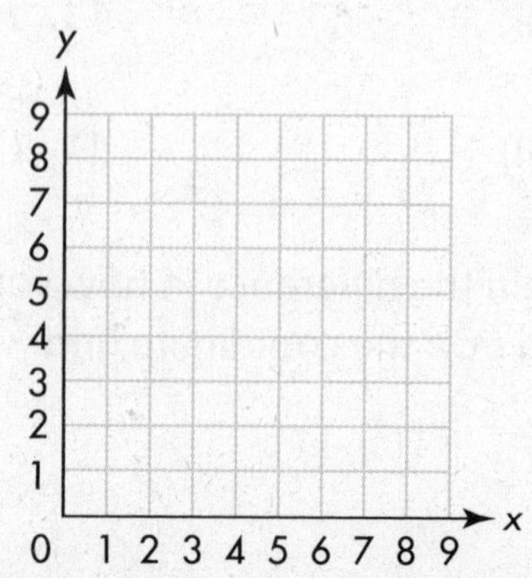

Name ______________________________

Lesson 14-3
Solve Problems Using Ordered Pairs

I can ...
solve real-world problems by graphing points.

Content Standards 5.G.A.1, 5.G.A.2
Mathematical Practices MP.4, MP.6, MP.7

Solve & Share

The table below uses number patterns to describe changes in the width and length of a rectangle. Let *x* be the width and *y* be the length. Then plot each of the four ordered pairs in the table on the coordinate grid. What do you think the length is if the width is 5?

	Rule	Start			
Width	*Add 1*	1	2	3	4
Length	*Subtract 1*	11	10	9	8

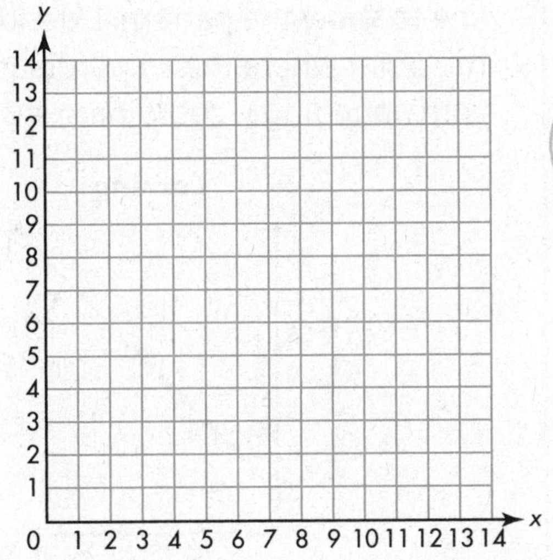

Model with Math
You can make a graph to help solve the problem. *Show your work!*

Look Back! **MP.7 Look for Relationships** What pattern do the points form on your graph?

Essential Question How Can You Use Ordered Pairs to Solve Problems?

A

Both Ann and Bill earn the amount shown each week. Ann starts with no money, but Bill starts with $5. How much will Bill have when Ann has $30? Represent this situation using a table and a graph.

You know that when Ann has $0, Bill has $5.

B Make a table showing how much money Ann and Bill have after each week.

DATA

Week	Start	1	2	3	4	5
Ann's earnings in $	0	3	6	9	12	15
Bill's earnings in $	5	8	11	14	17	20

Let x = Ann's earnings and y = Bill's earnings.

C Plot the ordered pairs from the table. Draw a line to show the pattern. Extend your line to the point where the x-coordinate is 30. The corresponding y-coordinate is 35.

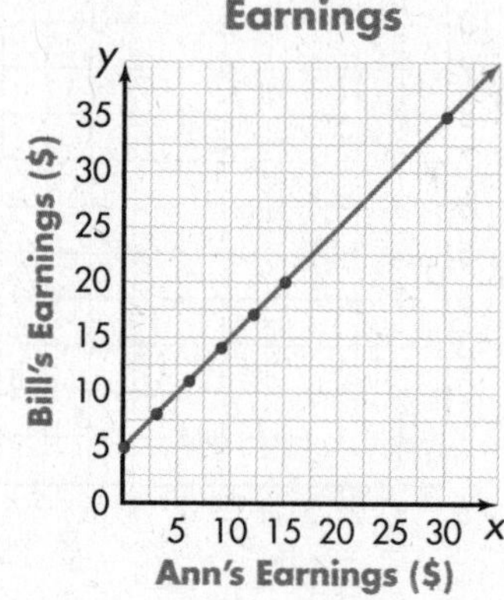

So, Bill has $35 when Ann has $30.

Convince Me! © **MP.7 Look for Relationships** What is the relationship between Bill's earnings and Ann's earnings?

Name ___

Practice Buddy Tools Assessment

☆ Guided Practice*

Do You Understand?

1. In the example on page 790, find another point on the line. What does this point represent?

2. **Algebra** In the example on page 790, write an equation to show the relationship between Ann's earnings and Bill's earnings. Remember to let x = Ann's earnings and y = Bill's earnings.

Do You Know How?

Write the missing coordinates and tell what the point represents.

3.

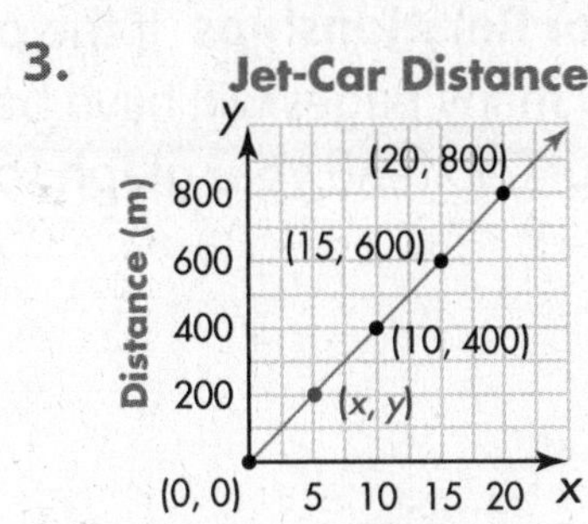

Independent Practice ☆

In **4** and **5**, find the missing coordinates and tell what the point represents.

4.

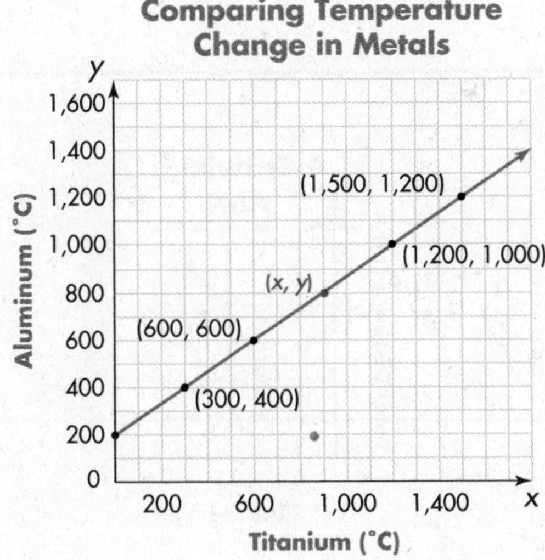

5.

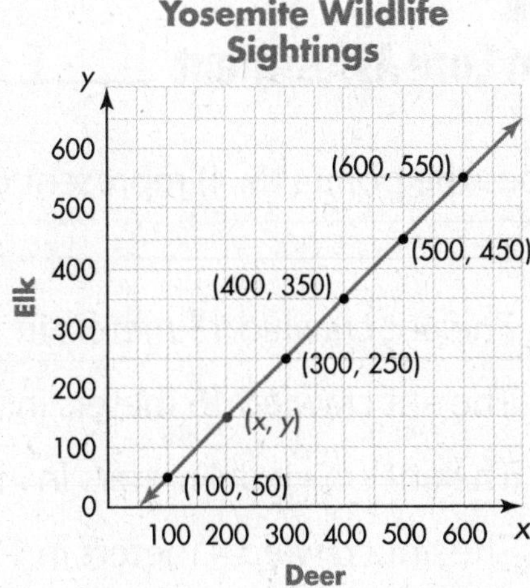

6. For Exercise 5, find two other points on the line. Then graph and label them. Describe the relationship between deer sightings and elk sightings.

*For another example, see Set B on page 803.

Math Practices and Problem Solving

In **7** and **8**, use the table at the right.

Reading Log					
Time (h)	1	2	3	4	5
Pages Read	20	40	60	80	100

7. Graph the points in the table on the grid at the right. Then draw a line through the points.

8. **MP.7 Look for Relationships** If the pattern continues, how many pages will have been read after 6 hours? Extend your graph to solve.

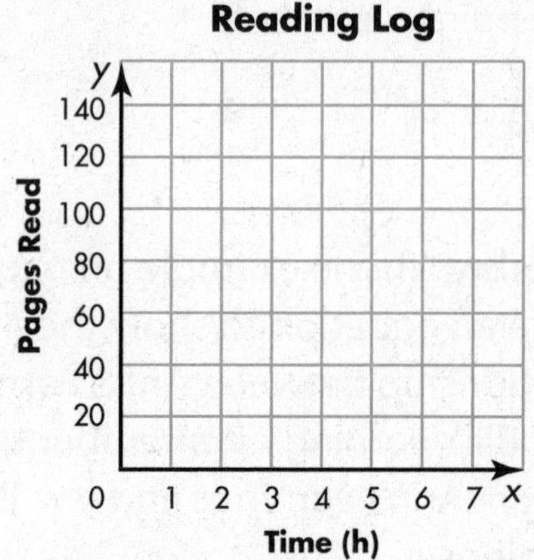

9. **Higher Order Thinking** Suppose you have a graph of speed that shows a lion can run four times as fast as a squirrel. Name an ordered pair that shows this relationship. What does this ordered pair represent?

10. **Number Sense** Candace drives a total of 48 miles each day to get to work and back home. She works 5 days a week. Her car gets 21 miles per gallon of gas. About how many gallons of gas does she need to drive to work and back home each week?

Common Core Assessment

11. What does the point (15, 4) represent on the graph at the right?

Ⓐ The ant crawled 15 meters in 19 seconds.

Ⓑ The ant crawled 15 meters in 4 seconds.

Ⓒ The ant crawled 4 meters in 19 seconds.

Ⓓ The ant crawled 4 meters in 15 seconds.

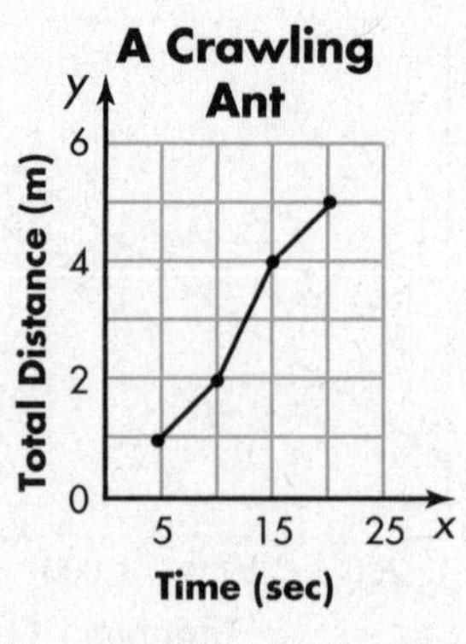

12. What does the point (20, 5) represent on the graph?

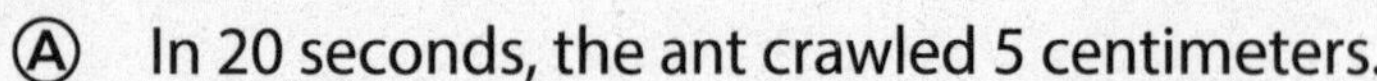

Ⓐ In 20 seconds, the ant crawled 5 centimeters.

Ⓑ In 20 seconds, the ant crawled 5 meters.

Ⓒ In 5 seconds, the ant crawled 20 meters.

Ⓓ In 5 seconds, the ant crawled 15 meters.

Name ___________________________

Homework & Practice 14-3

Solve Problems Using Ordered Pairs

Another Look!

Allison can hike 2 miles in an hour. At that speed, how far would she walk in 7 hours?

DATA

Time (h)	1	2	3
Distance (mi)	2	4	6

Plot the ordered pairs from the table. Draw a line to show the pattern. Then extend the line to where the x-coordinate is 7. Read the y-coordinate when the x-coordinate is 7. The y-coordinate is 14.

So, Allison can hike 14 miles in 7 hours.

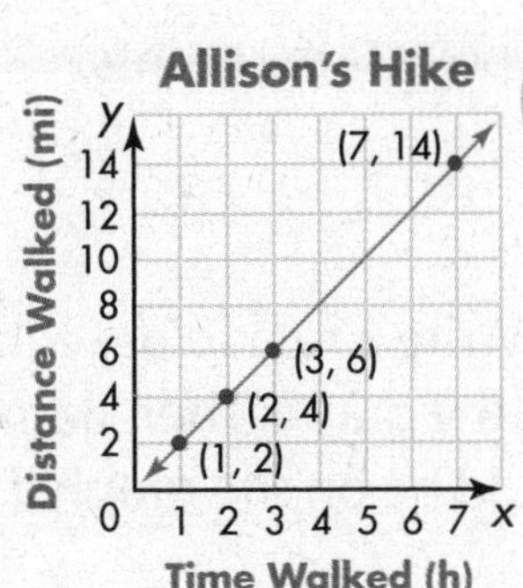

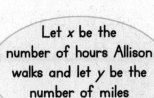

Let x be the number of hours Allison walks and let y be the number of miles she walks.

In **1** and **2**, find the missing coordinates and tell what the point represents.

1.

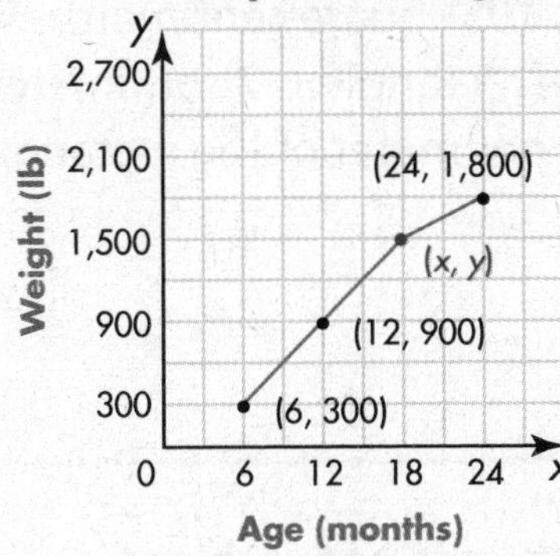

2.

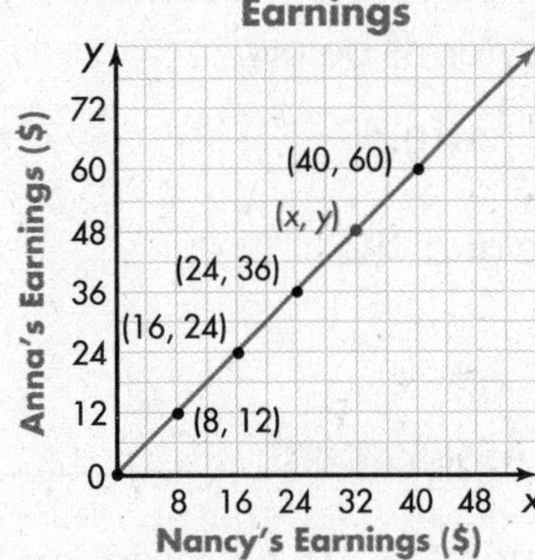

3. For Exercise 2, find another point on the line. Then graph and label the point.

4. What does the ordered pair for the point you found in Exercise 3 represent?

In **5–7**, use the graph at the right.

5. Jamie is making a graph to show her total earnings, *y*, after babysitting for *x* hours. Graph Jamie's first four points below on the grid at the right. Use a ruler to draw a line connecting the points.

(1, 6) (2, 12) (3, 18) (4, 24)

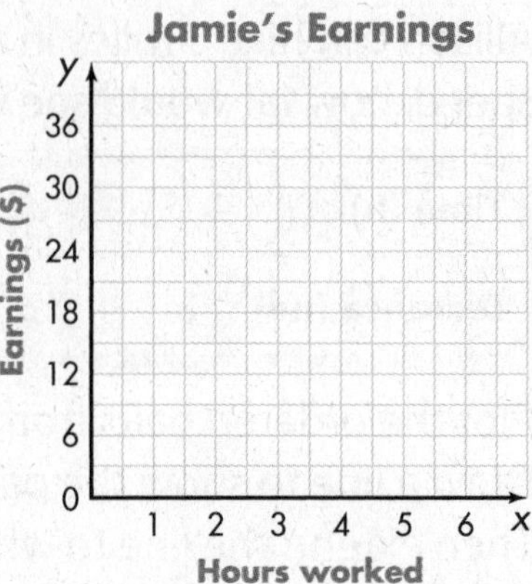

6. Describe what one of the points represents.

7. Higher Order Thinking Write a rule to describe the relationship shown in the graph. Then name two other points that would be on the graph if the line were extended.

---

8. Vocabulary Complete the sentence using one of the terms below.

***x*-axis** ***y*-axis** **origin**

On a coordinate grid, the ____________ is horizontal.

9. MP. 6 Be Precise The area of a rectangle is 105 square centimeters. The width of the rectangle is 7 centimeters. What is the perimeter of the rectangle?

Common Core Assessment

10. What does the point (3, 10) represent on the graph at the right?

Ⓐ After 3 months, the total rainfall was 7 inches.

Ⓑ After 3 months, the total rainfall was 10 inches.

Ⓒ After 10 months, the total rainfall was 3 inches.

Ⓓ After 10 months, the total rainfall was 7 inches.

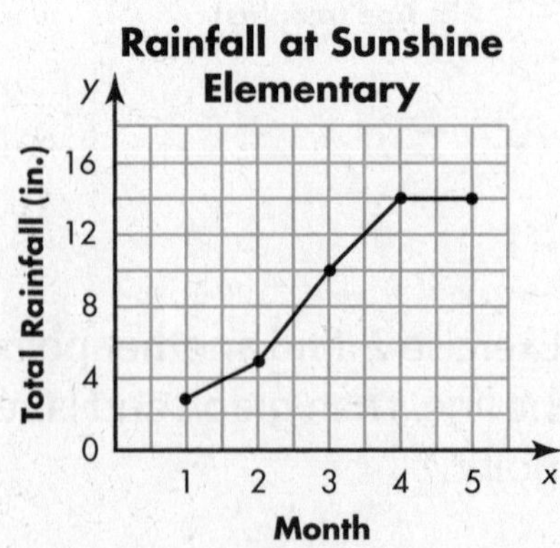

Name ___________________

Solve

Math Practices and Problem Solving

Lesson 14-4
Reasoning

I can ...
use reasoning to solve problems.

Mathematical Practices MP.2, Also MP.1, MP.4, MP.5, MP.7
Content Standards 5.G.A.1, 5.G.A.2

Solve & Share

Six clowns apply for a circus job. The specific job requires the clown to have a clown shoe size less than 15 inches and to be shorter than 5 ft 8 in. tall.

How many clowns meet the size requirements for the job? Complete the graph below to help you decide.

DATA

Clown	Tippy	Yippy	Dippy	Zippy	Fippy	Gippy
Shoe	15	13	13	16	12	16
Height	5′9″	5″10″	5′3″	5′2″	5′4″	5′11″

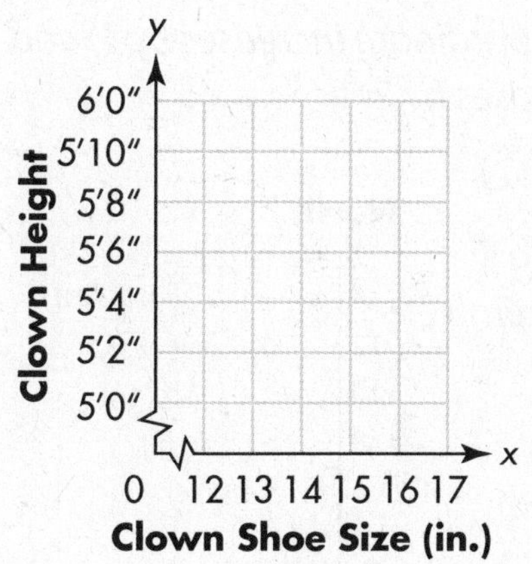

Thinking Habits

Be a good thinker!
These questions can help you.

- What do the numbers and symbols in the problem mean?
- How are the numbers or quantities related?
- How can I represent a word problem using pictures, numbers, or equations?

Look Back! **MP.2 Reasoning** How can you use reasoning about the completed graph to find the number of clowns that meet the requirements? Explain.

How Can You Use Reasoning to Solve Mathematical Problems?

A

In 1705, a ship sank in the ocean at the point shown. Every year the ocean currents moved the ship 1 mile east and 2 miles north. Where was the ship located after 4 years? Where was the ship located after 10 years? Tell how you decided.

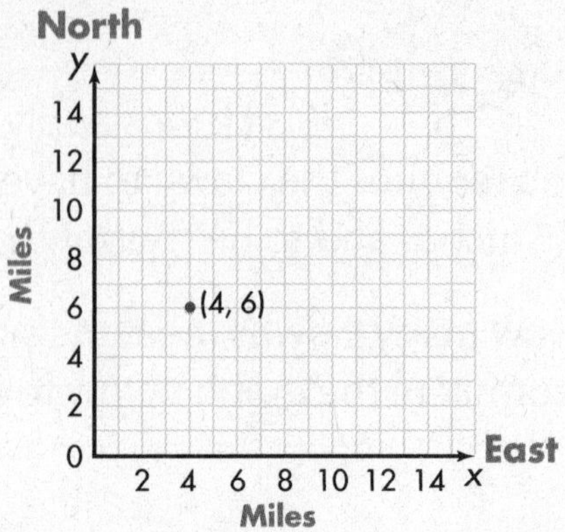

What do I need to do to solve the problem?

I need to find the ship's location after 4 years and after 10 years.

B

How can I use reasoning to solve this problem?

I can

- use what I know about graphing points.
- graph ordered pairs.
- look for relationships in the coordinates.
- decide if my answer makes sense.

C

Here's my thinking...

I will use the graph to show the location each year for 4 years. Each point is 1 mile east and 2 miles north from the previous point.

After 4 years the ship was at (8, 14).

I see a pattern. The x-coordinate increases by 1, and the y-coordinate increases by 2:

(4, 6), (5, 8), (6, 10), (7, 12), (8, 14)

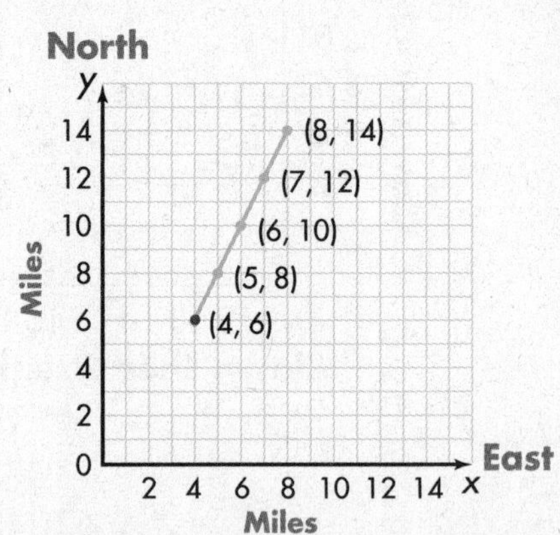

I can continue the pattern for another 6 years:

(9, 16), (10, 18), (11, 20), (12, 22), (13, 24), (14, 26)

After 10 years, the ship was at (14, 26).

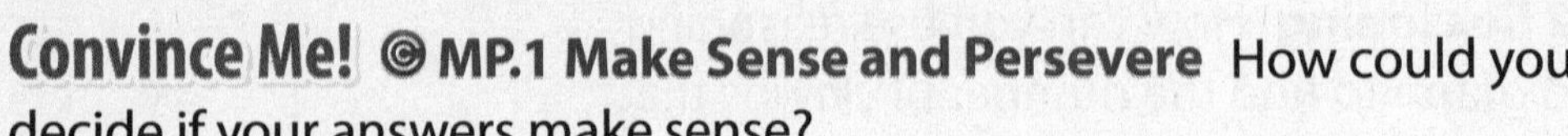

Convince Me! **MP.1 Make Sense and Persevere** How could you decide if your answers make sense?

Name ____________________

Guided Practice*

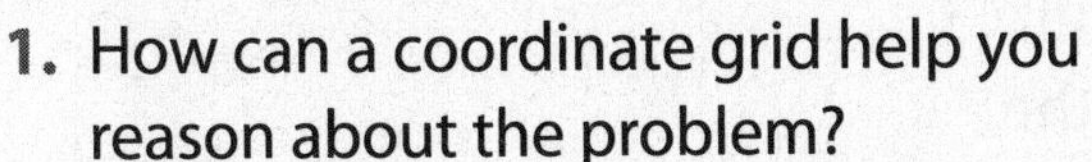

MP.2 Reasoning

Tanya marked a grid in her garden. She planted a rose bush at (3, 1). She moved 2 feet east and 1 foot north and planted the second rose bush. She continued planting rose bushes so that each bush is 2 feet east and 1 foot north of the previous bush.

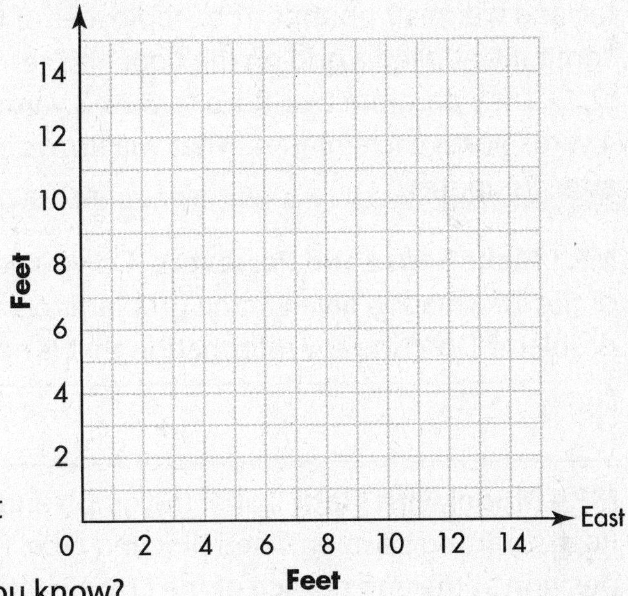

1. How can a coordinate grid help you reason about the problem?

2. Draw and label the locations of the first four bushes on the grid. Do Tanya's bushes lie on a straight line? How do you know?

3. What are the locations of the fifth and ninth rose bushes?

Independent Practice

MP.2 Reasoning

A marching band uses a grid to determine the members' positions. Juan starts at (2, 2). Every 15 seconds, he moves 4 yards east and 3 yards north.

4. How can you model this problem?

5. Draw and label the locations of Juan's first four positions. Do the points form a pattern? How can you tell?

6. What will Juan's location be after 60 seconds? 90 seconds? How does the coordinate grid help you reason about the locations?

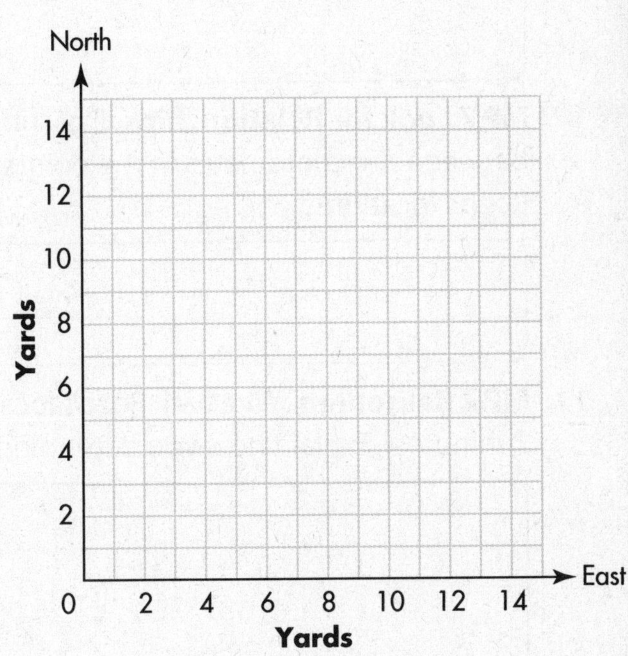

*For another example, see Set C on page 804.

Math Practices and Problem Solving

Common Core Performance Assessment

Rozo Robot

A toy company is testing Rozo Robot. Rozo is 18 inches tall and weighs 2 pounds. The employees of the company marked a grid on the floor and set Rozo at (2, 5). They programmed Rozo to walk 3 yards east and 4 yards north each minute. What will Rozo's location be after 7 minutes?

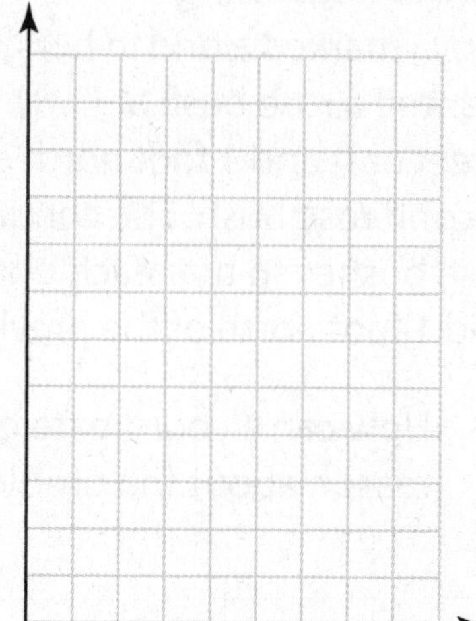

7. **MP.1 Make Sense and Persevere** Do you need all of the information given in the problem to solve the problem? Describe any information that is not needed.

8. **MP.4 Model with Math** Label the graph and plot Rozo's starting position. Then plot and label Rozo's position at the end of each of the first 4 minutes.

9. **MP.5 Use Appropriate Tools** What tool would you choose for drawing a line segment between points on a coordinate grid? Explain your thinking.

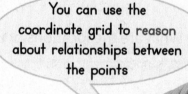

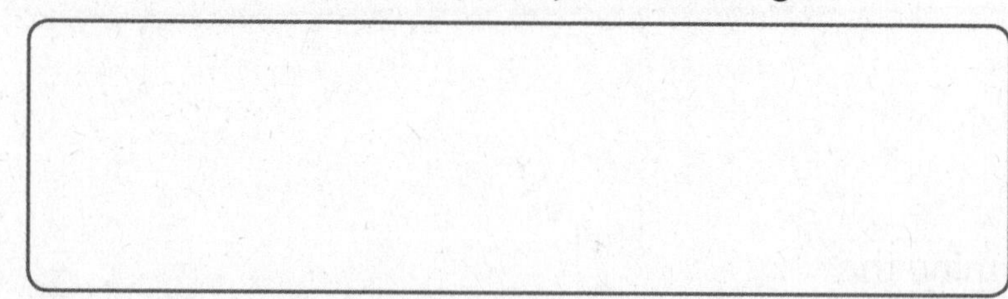

10. **MP.7 Look for Relationships** Describe the relationships between the coordinates in the points that represent Rozo's locations.

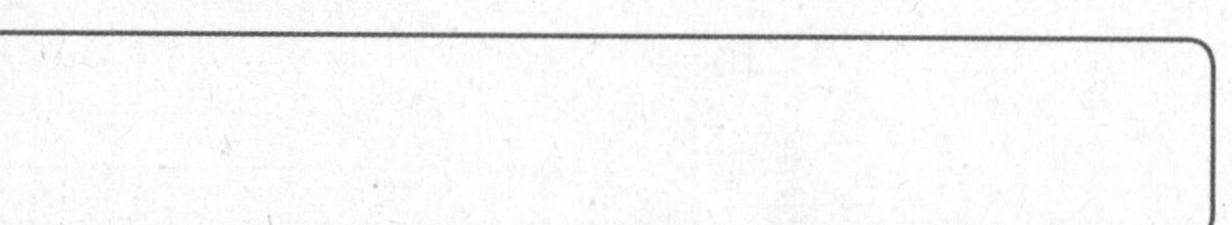

11. **MP.2 Reasoning** What will Rozo's location be after 7 minutes? Explain how you determined your answer.

You can use the coordinate grid to reason about relationships between the points

Name ______________________________

Homework & Practice 14-4

Reasoning

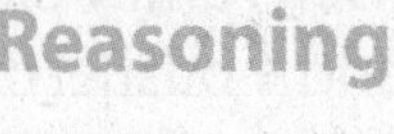

Another Look!

A blue swimming pool contains 5 inches of water. It is filled with 2 more inches of water each hour. A red swimming pool contains 25 inches of water. The water is drained 3 inches each hour. How much water will be in the red pool when the blue pool has 19 inches of water?

You can use a table and graph to model the math.

Depth of Water (in.)

Hour	Start	1	2	3	4
Blue Pool	5	7	9	11	13
Red Pool	25	22	19	16	13

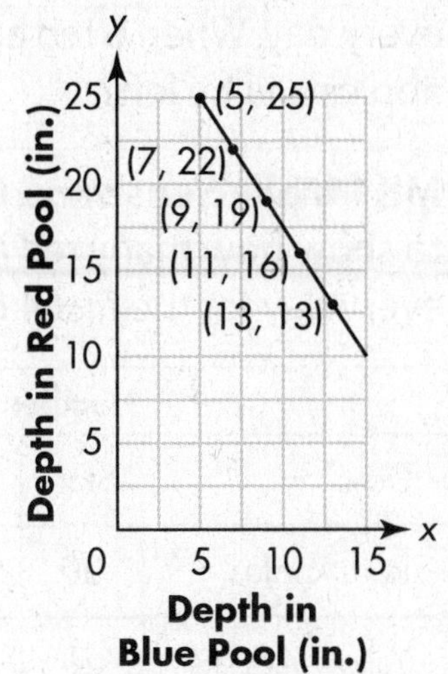

The ordered pairs show a pattern. Each hour, the *x*-coordinate increases by 2, and the *y*-coordinate decreases by 3.

Extend the pattern until the *x*-coordinate is 19:
(15, 10), (17, 7), (19, 4)

When the blue pool has 19 inches of water, the red pool will have 4 inches of water.

MP.2 Reasoning

A tree farm owner uses a grid to mark where to plant trees in the spring. The first tree is planted at (2, 3). Each of the other trees is planted 3 feet east and 2 feet north of the previous tree.

1. Draw and label the locations of the first four trees on the grid.

2. Describe the pattern of the points that represent the tree's locations.

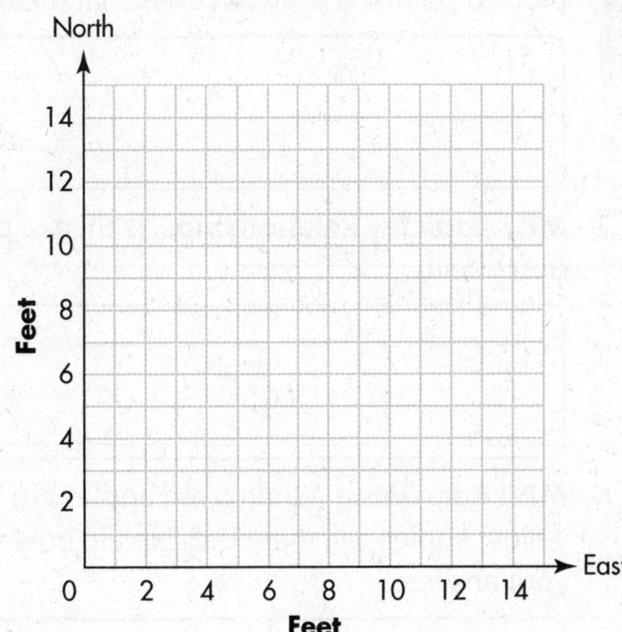

3. What is the location of the seventh tree? Explain how you determined your answer.

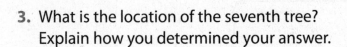

Common Core Performance Assessment

Apple Picking

The Bransen Family picked 20 red apples, 28 yellow apples, and $\frac{1}{2}$ bushel of green apples. Starting the following day, they ate 2 red apples and 3 yellow apples every day. When 6 red apples are left, how many yellow apples will be left?

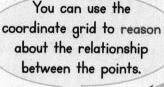

You can use the coordinate grid to reason about the relationship between the points.

4. **MP.1 Make Sense and Persevere** Complete the table to show how many red and yellow apples there are every day for the first 4 days.

Number of Apples					
Day	Start	1	2	3	4
Red Apples	20				
Yellow Apples	28				

5. **MP.4 Model with Math** Label the graph and then plot the data points from your table.

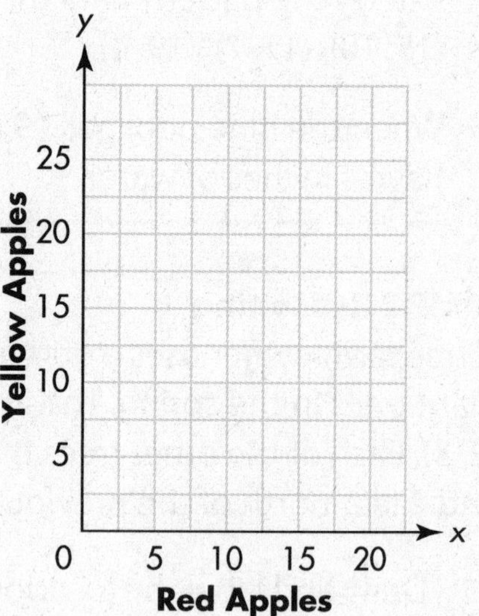

6. **MP.2 Reasoning** Can you draw a line through the plotted points? If so, what does that mean?

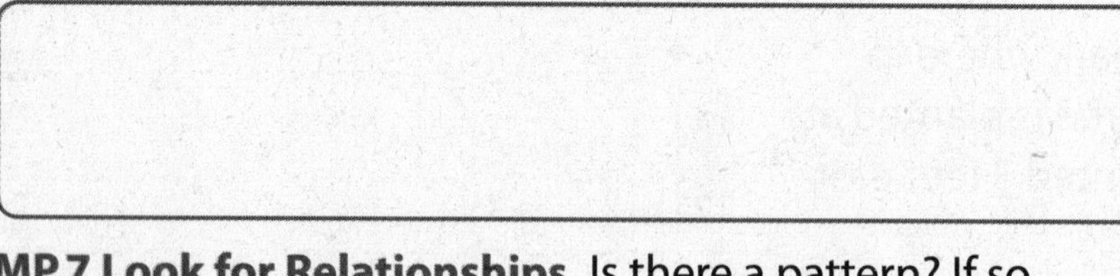

7. **MP.7 Look for Relationships** Is there a pattern? If so, describe it.

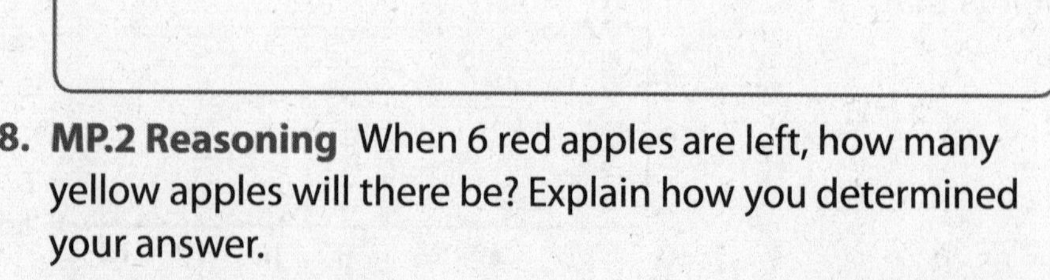

8. **MP.2 Reasoning** When 6 red apples are left, how many yellow apples will there be? Explain how you determined your answer.

Name ______________________________

Fluency Practice Activity

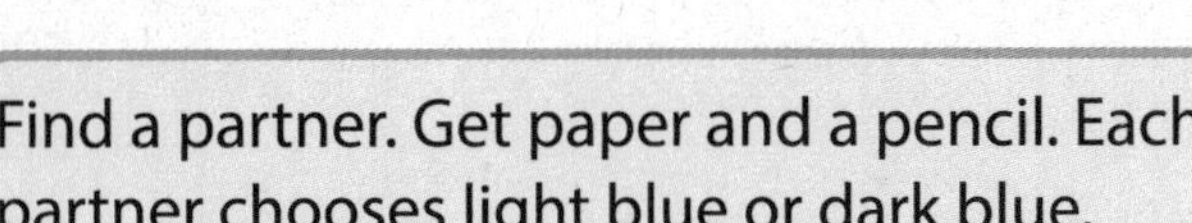

Find a partner. Get paper and a pencil. Each partner chooses light blue or dark blue.

At the same time, Partner 1 and Partner 2 each point to one of their black numbers. Both partners find the product of the two numbers.

The partner who chose the color where the product appears gets a tally mark. Work until one partner has seven tally marks.

I can ...

multiply multi-digit whole numbers.

Content Standard 5.NBT.B.5

Partner 1

85
79
91
44
59

24,024	94,435	11,616	90,100
101,101	8,712	20,856	11,682
30,345	18,018	22,440	83,740
15,576	87,769	21,063	28,203
15,642	62,540	32,487	96,460
48,884	16,830	65,549	46,640

Partner 2

264
198
357
1,060
1,111

Tally Marks for Partner 1

Tally Marks for Partner 2

TOPIC 14

Vocabulary Review

Word List

- coordinate grid
- ordered pair
- origin
- *x*-axis
- *x*-coordinate
- *y*-axis
- *y*-coordinate

Understand Vocabulary

Choose the best term from the Word List. Write it on the blank.

1. The point where the axes of a coordinate grid intersect is the ________________.

2. A(n) ________________ names an exact location on a coordinate grid.

3. The first number of an ordered pair describes the distance from the origin along the ________________.

4. The second number of an ordered pair is the ________________.

5. A ________________ is formed by two number lines that intersect at a right angle.

Draw a line from each lettered point in Column A to the ordered pair it represents.

	Column A	Column B
6.	*A*	(5, 2)
7.	*B*	(1, 7)
8.	*C*	(2, 3)
9.	*D*	(0, 7)
10.	*E*	(7, 1)
11.	*F*	(0, 6)

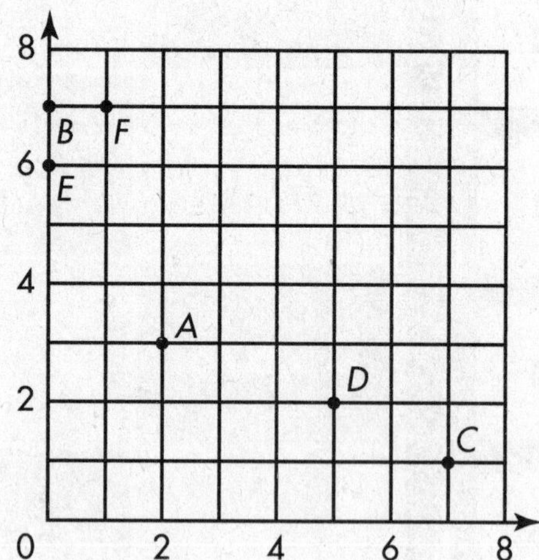

Use Vocabulary in Writing

12. Why is the order of the coordinates important in an ordered pair? Use terms from the Word List in your explanation.

Name ______________________________

TOPIC 14

Reteaching

Set A pages 777–782

What ordered pair names Point *A*?

Start at the origin. The *x*-coordinate is the horizontal distance along the *x*-axis. The *y*-coordinate is the vertical distance along the *y*-axis.

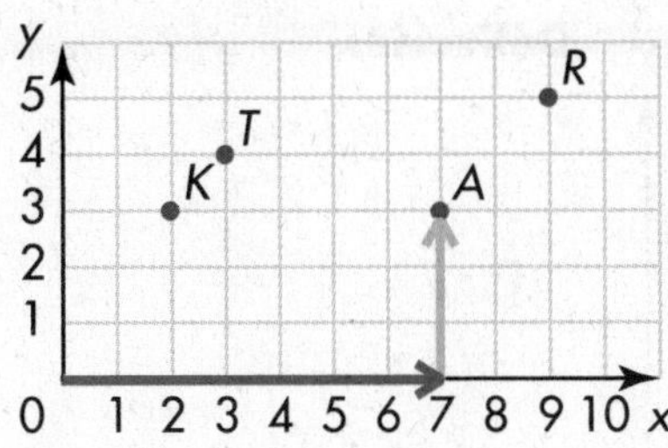

Point *A* is at (7, 3).

Remember to first find the *x*-coordinate. Then find the *y*-coordinate. Write the coordinates in (*x*, *y*) order.

Use the grid to answer the questions.

1. Which point is located at (9, 5)?

2. Which point is located at (2, 3)?

3. What ordered pair names Point *T*?

4. What is the ordered pair for the origin?

Set B pages 783–788, 789–794

In the table, the *x*-coordinate is in the left column and the *y*-coordinate is in the right column. Use the table to plot the ordered pairs. Then draw a line to connect the points.

x	*y*
1	1
2	4
3	7

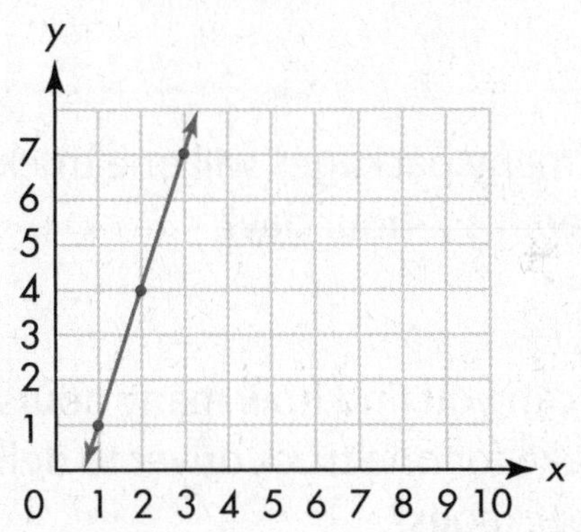

Remember that you can use a tool, such as a ruler, to draw a line to connect the points on the graph.

1. Use the table below to plot the ordered pairs. Then complete the graph by connecting the points.

x	*y*
2	1
4	2
6	3
8	4

y
7
6
5
4
3
2
1
0 1 2 3 4 5 6 7 8 9 10 x

2. Write two ordered pairs with *x*-coordinates greater than 10 that are on the line.

Set C pages 795–800

Think about these questions to help you **use reasoning to solve problems.**

Thinking Habits

- What do the numbers and symbols in the problem mean?
- How are the numbers or quantities related?
- How can I represent a word problem using pictures, numbers, or equations?

Remember that you can use a graph or a table to reason about and solve word problems.

A company uses the graph to show how many packages each truck driver delivers. How many packages will one truck driver deliver in a 7-hour day?

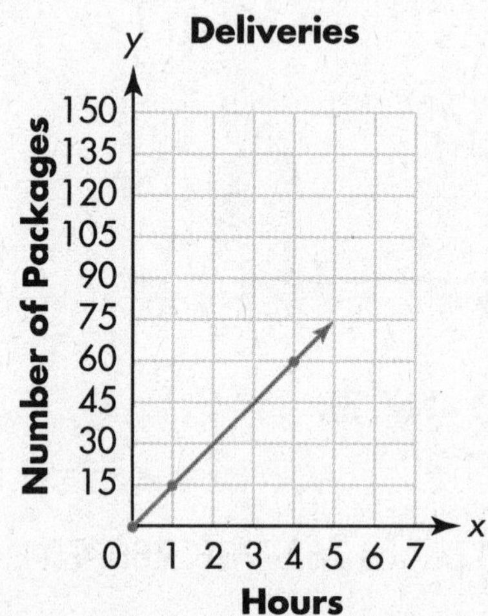

1. What information can help you solve the problem?

2. How can you find the number of packages a driver delivers in 3 hours?

3. How many packages will one truck driver deliver in a 7-hour day?

4. How can you find how many hours it will take for one truck driver to deliver 120 packages?

Name ______________________________

Use the coordinate grid below to answer **1–4**.

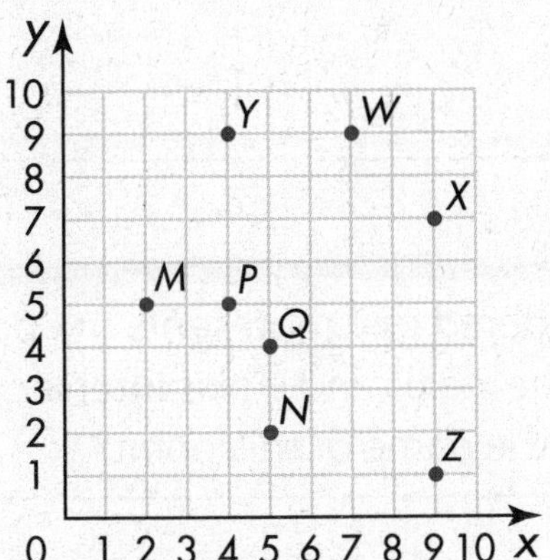

1. Which is the ordered pair for Point *Y*?

Ⓐ (4, 5)

Ⓑ (4, 9)

Ⓒ (7, 9)

Ⓓ (9, 4)

2. Martin graphed a point at (5, 2). Which point did he graph?

Ⓐ *M*

Ⓑ *N*

Ⓒ *Q*

Ⓓ *P*

3. What is the ordered pair for Point *Z*?

4. What is the ordered pair for Point *P*?

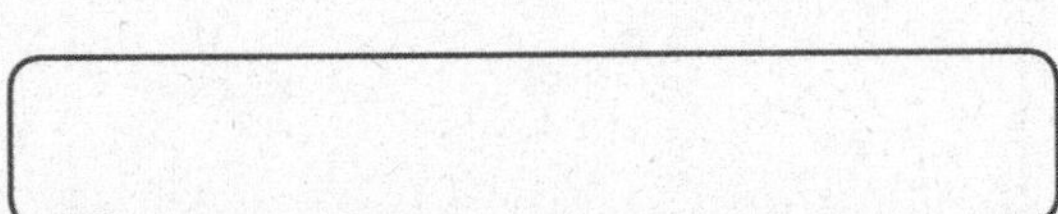

5. Each year, Ginny recorded the height of a tree growing in her front yard. The graph below shows her data.

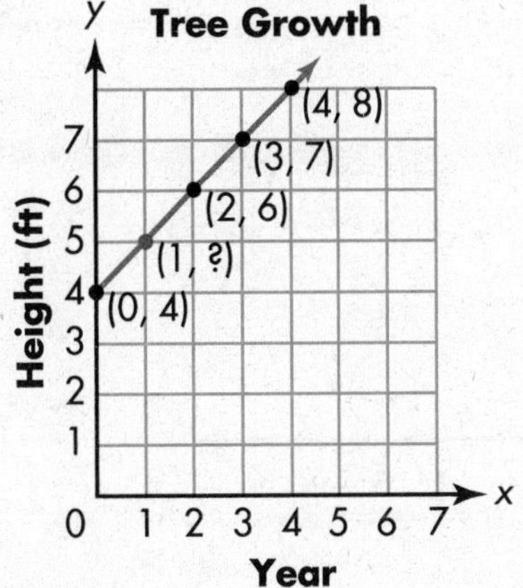

Part A

What was the height of the tree after the first year?

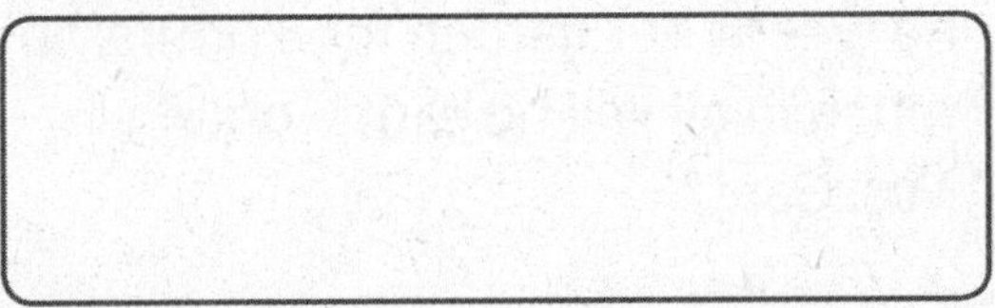

Part B

What does the point (3, 7) represent on the graph?

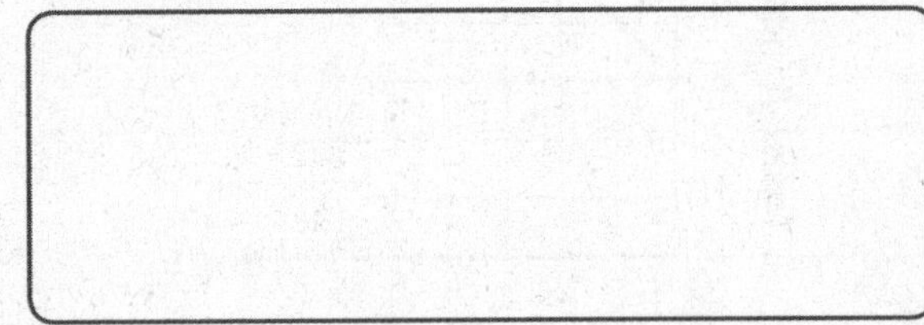

6. Explain how to graph the point (6, 4) on a coordinate plane.

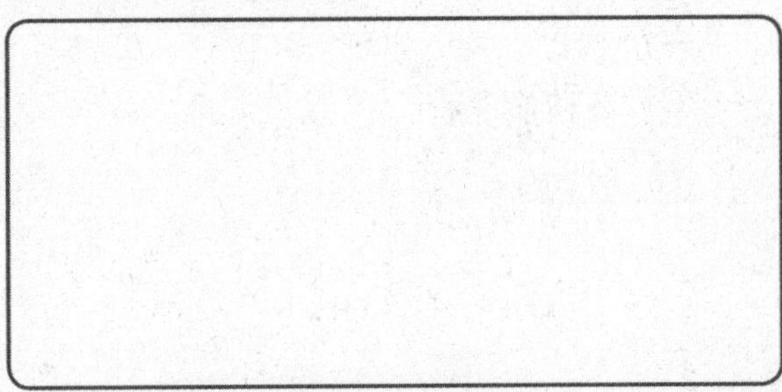

7. Varsha draws a map of her neighborhood on a coordinate plane. Her map shows the park at *P* (3, 1), her house at *H* (5, 6), and the soccer field at *S* (2, 4). Graph and label each location below.

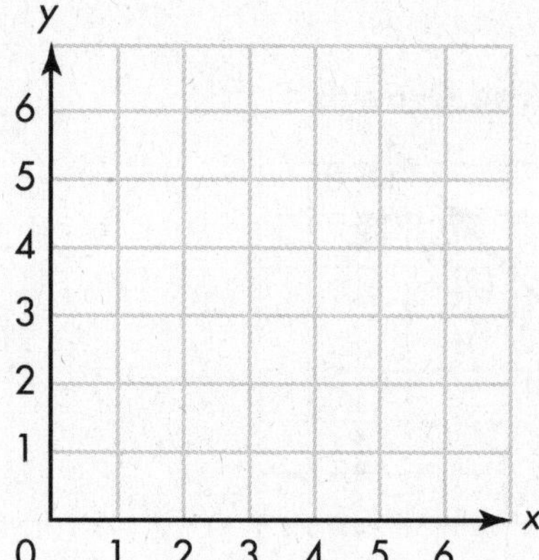

8. Yesterday Billy earned $30 trimming hedges for Mrs. Gant. Today he will earn $10 an hour for weeding her garden. If he weeds her garden for 8 hours, how much in all will he earn working for Mrs. Gant?

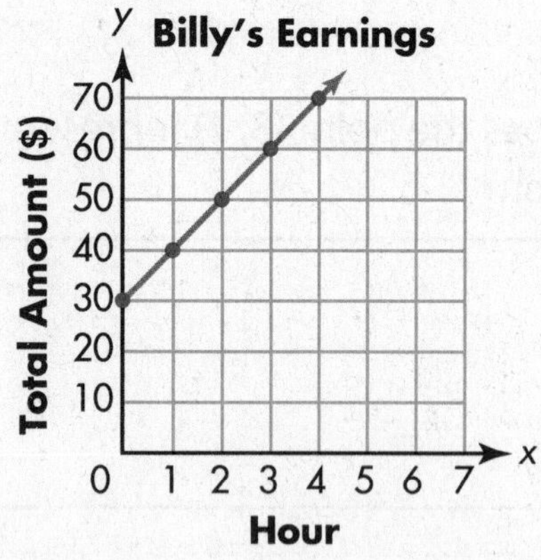

Ⓐ $40

Ⓑ $80

Ⓒ $110

Ⓓ $120

9. How is graphing (0, 12) different from graphing (12, 0)?

10. What ordered pair represents the point where the *x*-axis and *y*-axis intersect? What is the name of this point?

11. Three vertices of a rectangle are located at (1, 4), (1, 2), and (5, 2).

Part A

Graph and label each of the three vertices below.

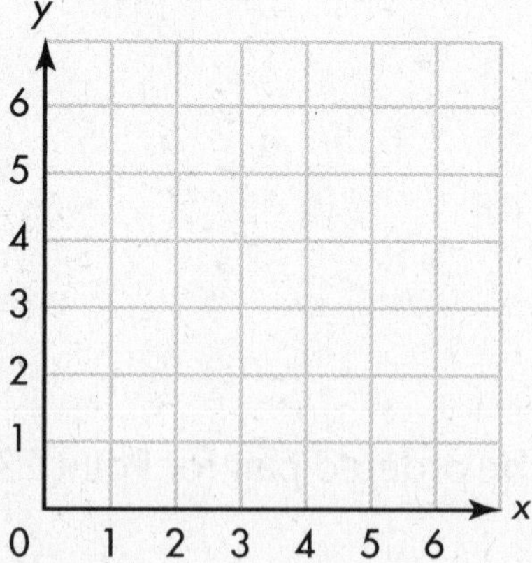

Part B

What are the coordinates of the fourth vertex of the rectangle?

Name ______________________________

Digging for Dinosaur Bones

Omar's mother is a paleontologist. She digs up and studies dinosaur bones. Omar is helping at the dig site.

1. The **Dinosaur Bone Dig 1** grid shows the location of the tent and the triceratops skull Omar's mother found.

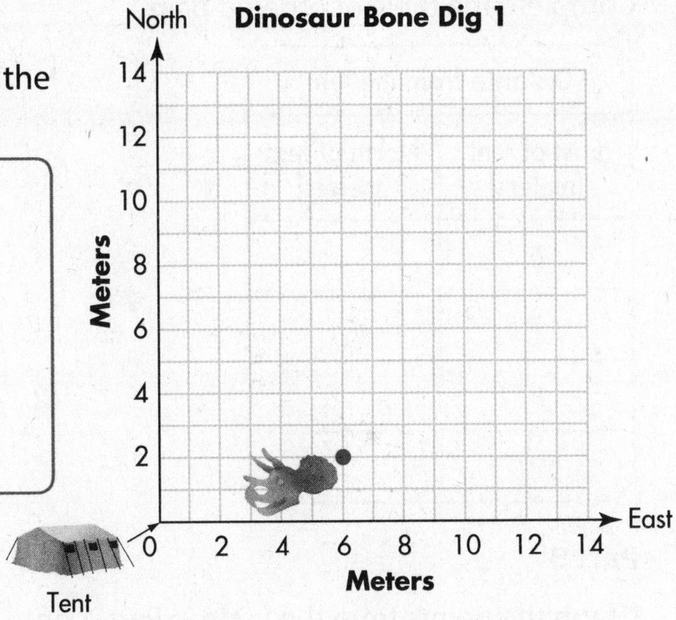

Part A

What ordered pair names the location of the triceratops skull? Explain how you know.

Part B

Omar found a leg bone at (4, 12). Graph this point on the coordinate grid and label it *L*. Explain how you located the point using the terms origin, *x*-coordinate, *x*-axis, *y*-coordinate, and *y*-axis.

Part C

Next, Omar dug 3 meters east and 1 meter south from the leg bone. Graph a point where Omar dug and label it *A*. What ordered pair names the point?

2. Omar's mother started at the triceratops skull. She kept moving east 1 meter and north 2 meters to dig for more dinosaur bones. Complete the table and the graph to find how far north she was when she was 11 meters east of the tent.

Part A

Complete the table of ordered pairs.

Distance from the Tent	
East of tent (meters)	North of tent (meters)
6	
7	
8	
9	

Part B

Graph the points from the table in Part A on the coordinate grid in the **Dinosaur Bone Dig 2** grid. Draw a line through the points. Extend the line past 11 meters east.

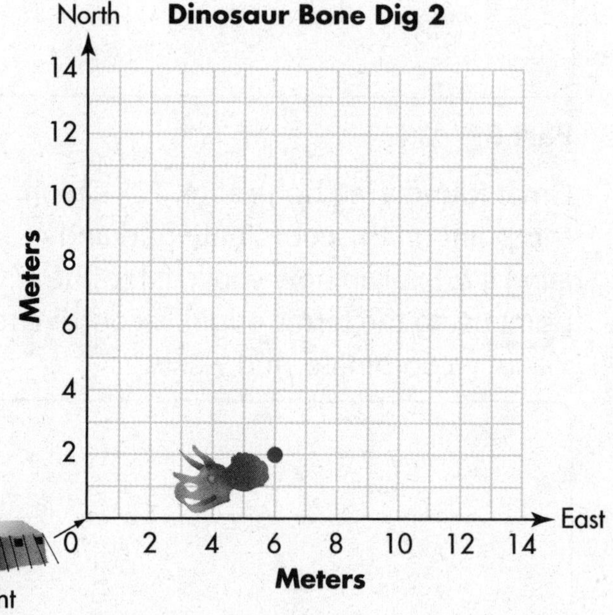

Part C

How far north was Omar's mother when she was 11 meters east of the tent? Explain how to use the graph to solve and why your answer makes sense.

Algebra: Analyze Patterns and Relationships

Essential Questions: How can number patterns be analyzed and graphed? How can number patterns and graphs be used to solve problems?

Buildings can be many different shapes and can have more than 100 floors.

Many buildings have a pattern of glass and concrete for every floor.

Patterns occur in different places and things. Here is a project about finding pattens.

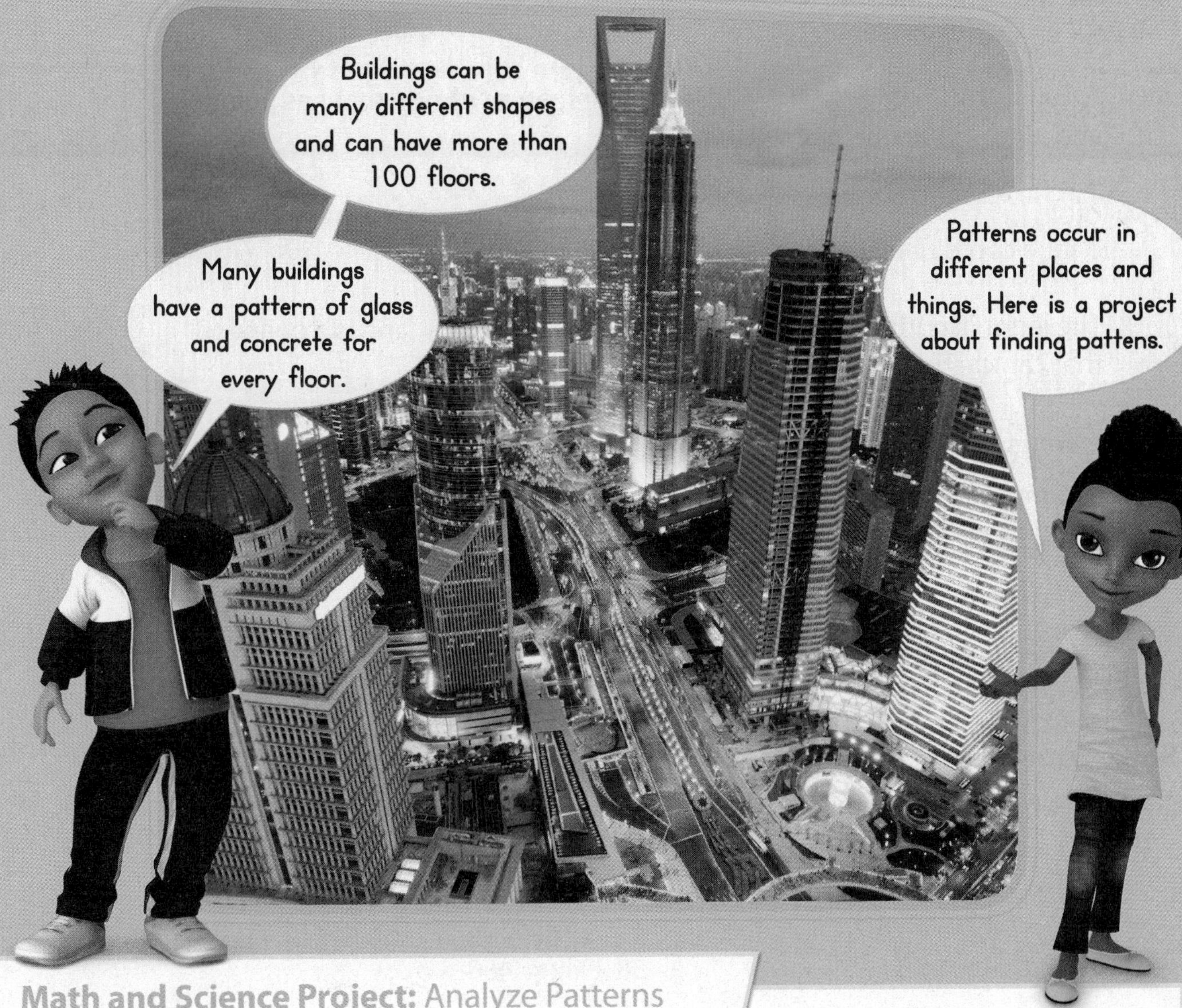

Math and Science Project: Analyze Patterns

Do Research Use the Internet or other sources to find patterns in cities and buildings in other parts of the world.

Journal: Write a Report Include what you found. Also in your report:

- Describe types of patterns found in nature.
- Describe types of patterns found in cities.
- Make a graph to show relationships between some of the patterns you found.

Name ____________________

Review What You Know

Vocabulary

Choose the best term from the Word List. Write it on the blank.

- equation
- expression
- variable
- evaluate
- ordered pair

1. A numerical ____________ is a mathematical phrase that has numbers and at least one operation.

2. A(n) ____________ can be used to show the location of a point on the coordinate plane.

3. The letter n in $\$10 \times n$ is called a(n) ____________ and is a quantity that can change.

Expressions

Write a numerical expression for each calculation.

4. Add 230 and 54, and then divide by 7.

5. Subtract 37 from the product of 126 and 4.

Solve Equations

Solve each equation.

6. $7{,}200 + x = 13{,}000$

7. $6{,}000 = 20 \times g$

8. $105 + 45 = w \times 3$

9. $38 + 42 = 480 \div b$

10. Janine has 85 hockey cards in one book and 105 hockey cards in another book. The hockey cards come in packages of 5 cards. If Janine bought all of her hockey cards in packages, how many packages did she buy?

Ⓐ 21 packages Ⓑ 38 packages Ⓒ 190 packages Ⓓ 195 packages

Evaluate Expressions

11. Explain how to evaluate the expression $9 + (45 \times 2) \div 10$.

A-Z Glossary

My Word Cards

Use the examples for each word on the front of the card to help complete the definitions on the back.

number sequence

0, 3, 6, 9, 12, 15

corresponding terms

0, 3, 6, 9, 12, 15

0, 4, 8, 12, 16, 20

12 and 16 are an example of corresponding terms.

My Word Cards

Complete the definition. Extend learning by writing your own definitions.

Terms that are in the same relative position as one another in a pair of number sequences are

______________________________.

A set of numbers that follows a rule is a

______________________________.

Name ______________________

Lesson 15-1
Numerical Patterns

I can ...
analyze numerical patterns.

Content Standard 5.OA.B.3
Mathematical Practices MP.2, MP.3, MP.4, MP.5, MP.7

Solve & Share

Emma has $100 in her savings account. Jorge has $50 in his savings account. They each put $10 in their accounts at the end of each week. Complete the tables to see how much each of them has saved after 5 weeks. What patterns do you notice?

Week	Emma
Start	$100
1	
2	
3	
4	
5	

Week	Jorge
Start	$50
1	
2	
3	
4	
5	

Look for Relationships to see what is alike and what is different in the two tables.

Look Back! MP.3 Construct Arguments If the savings patterns continue, will Jorge ever have as much saved as Emma? Explain.

How Can You Solve Problems Involving Numerical Patterns?

A

Lindsey has a sage plant that is 3.5 inches tall. She also has a rosemary plant that is 5.2 inches tall. Both plants grow 1.5 inches taller each week. How tall will the plants be after 5 weeks? What is the relationship between the heights of the plants?

You can model with math by creating tables to help identify relationships between corresponding terms in the number sequences.

B You can use the rule "add 1.5" to complete the tables.

Sage Plant

Week	Height (in inches)
Start	3.5
1	5
2	6.5
3	8
4	9.5
5	11

Rosemary Plant

Week	Height (in inches)
Start	5.2
1	6.7
2	8.2
3	9.7
4	11.2
5	12.7

The rosemary plant is always 1.7 inches taller than the sage plant!

Convince Me! **MP.2 Reasoning** If the patterns continue, how can you tell that the rosemary plant will always be taller than the sage plant?

Name ___

Guided Practice*

Do You Understand?

1. Anthony says, "The pattern is that the sage plant is always 1.7 inches shorter than the rosemary plant." Do you agree? Explain.

2. **MP.7 Look for Relationships** How does making tables help you identify relationships between terms in patterns?

Do You Know How?

3. If the plants continue to grow 1.5 inches each week, how tall will each plant be after 10 weeks?

4. If the plants continue to grow 1.5 inches each week, how tall will each plant be after 15 weeks?

Independent Practice

In **5–7**, use the rule "add $0.50" to help you.

5. **MP.4 Model with Math** Tim and Jill each have a piggy bank. Tim starts with $1.25 in his bank and puts in $0.50 each week. Jill starts with $2.75 in her bank and also puts in $0.50 each week. Complete the table to show how much money each has saved after five weeks.

Piggy Bank Savings		
Week	**Tim**	**Jill**
Start	$1.25	$2.75
1		
2		
3		
4		
5		

6. What relationship do you notice between the amount Tim has saved and the amount Jill has saved each week?

7. **MP.3 Construct Arguments** If Tim and Jill continue saving in this way, how much will each have saved after 10 weeks? Explain how you decided.

*For another example, see Set A on page 839.

Math Practices and Problem Solving

For **8–10**, use the table.

Tree Heights (in feet)		
Year	Bur Oak	Hickory
Start	$25\frac{1}{2}$	30
1		
2		
3		
4		
5		

8. Math and Science Bur oak and hickory trees are *deciduous* which means that they lose their leaves seasonally. A bur oak is $25\frac{1}{2}$ feet tall and grows $1\frac{1}{2}$ feet each year. A hickory is 30 feet tall and grows $1\frac{1}{2}$ feet each year. Complete the chart to show the heights of the two trees each year for five years.

9. If each tree continues to grow $1\frac{1}{2}$ feet each year, how tall will each tree be after 15 years?

10. Higher Order Thinking What relationship do you notice between the height of the bur oak and the height of the hickory each year? Explain.

11. Ⓒ MP.2 Reasoning Each small square on the chessboard is the same size. The length of a side of a small square is 2 inches. What is the area of the chessboard? Explain.

Ⓒ Common Core Assessment

12. Jessica has saved \$50. She will add \$25 to her savings each week. Ron has saved \$40 and will add \$25 to his savings each week. How much will each person have saved after 5 weeks?

Ⓐ Jessica: \$275; Ron: \$225

Ⓑ Jessica: \$250; Ron: \$240

Ⓒ Jessica: \$175; Ron: \$165

Ⓓ Jessica: \$165; Ron: \$175

13. Which of the following statements are true?

☐ Jessica has always saved \$25 more than Ron.

☐ Jessica has always saved \$10 more than Ron.

☐ Ron has always saved \$25 less than Jessica.

☐ Ron has always saved \$10 less than Jessica.

Name ______________________________

Homework & Practice 15-1

Numerical Patterns

Another Look!

Cara started with $2. Her sister Chloe started with $7. Both will earn $2 each day for doing chores. How much will each have after five days? What relationship do you notice between how much each sister has after each day?

Step 1

Complete the table. Use the rule "add $2" to help you.

Total Earnings		
Day	**Cara**	**Chloe**
Start	$2	$7
1	$4	$9
2	$6	$11
3	$8	$13
4	$10	$15
5	$12	$17

So, after five days, Cara has $12 and Chloe has $17.

Step 2

Look at each row to compare corresponding terms.

After each day, Chloe has $5 more than Cara.

In **1** and **2**, use the table.

1. Becky and Anton work at an apple orchard. At noon, Becky had picked 75 apples and Anton had picked 63 apples. Each of them picks 20 more apples each hour after noon. How many apples will each of them have picked at 5 P.M.? Use the rule "add 20" to help you complete the table.

Total Apples Picked		
	Becky	**Anton**
Noon	75	63
1 P.M.		
2 P.M.		
3 P.M.		
4 P.M.		
5 P.M.		

2. **MP.3 Construct Arguments** What relationship do you notice between how many apples Becky has picked and how many apples Anton has picked at the end of each hour? Explain.

3. Susie had received 9 text messages when she turned her phone on. She received 15 text messages each hour after that. Victor had received 27 text messages when he turned his phone on. He received 15 text messages each hour after that. How many messages did each person receive after 4 hours? Use the rule "add 15" to help you complete the table.

Total Text Messages Received

Hour	Susie	Victor
Start	9	27
1		
2		
3		
4		

4. **Higher Order Thinking** What relationship do you notice between the total number of text messages each person had received after each hour? Explain.

5. **Number Sense** Mr. Kim has a pitcher that contains 16 cups of juice. How many one-third cup servings are in 16 cups?

6. **MP.5 Use Appropriate Tools** Pierre is using centimeter cubes to build a model. He makes a rectangular prism that is 20 cubes long, 8 cubes tall, and 12 cubes wide. What is the volume of Pierre's model?

Common Core Assessment

7. Brian and Christina started keeping track of their workouts. Brian did 85 sit-ups the first week and 90 sit-ups each week after that. Christina did 65 sit-ups the first week and 90 sit-ups each week after that.

How many sit-ups will each person have done after 5 weeks?

Ⓐ Brian: 425 sit-ups
Christina: 325 sit-ups

Ⓑ Brian: 450 sit-ups
Christina: 450 sit-ups

Ⓒ Brian: 425 sit-ups
Christina: 445 sit-ups

Ⓓ Brian: 445 sit-ups
Christina: 425 sit-ups

8. Which of the following are true statements about the relationship between the numbers of sit-ups Brian and Christina have done after each week?

☐ Christina has always done 20 more sit-ups than Brian.

☐ Brian has always done 25 more sit-ups than Christina.

☐ Christina has always done 20 fewer sit-ups than Brian.

☐ Brian has always done 20 more sit-ups than Christina.

Name ______________________________

Lesson 15-2
More Numerical Patterns

I can ...
use tables to identify relationships between patterns.

Content Standard 5.OA.B.3
Mathematical Practices MP.2, MP.3, MP.4, MP.7, MP.8

Solve & Share During summer vacation, Julie read 45 pages each day. Her brother Bret read 15 pages each day. Complete the tables to show how many pages each of them read after 5 days. What relationship do you notice between the terms in each pattern?

Total Pages Read	
Day	Julie
1	45
2	
3	
4	
5	

Total Pages Read	
Day	Bret
1	15
2	
3	
4	
5	

Look for Relationships Find a rule to help you complete each table.

Look Back! MP.2 Reasoning Explain why this relationship exists between the terms.

How Can You Identify Relationships Between Patterns?

A

Jack is training for a race. Each week, he runs 30 miles and bikes 120 miles. He created a table to record his progress. How many total miles will he run and bike after 5 weeks? Can you identify any relationship between the miles run and the miles biked?

You can use the rules "add 30" and "add 120" to help you complete the table.

B

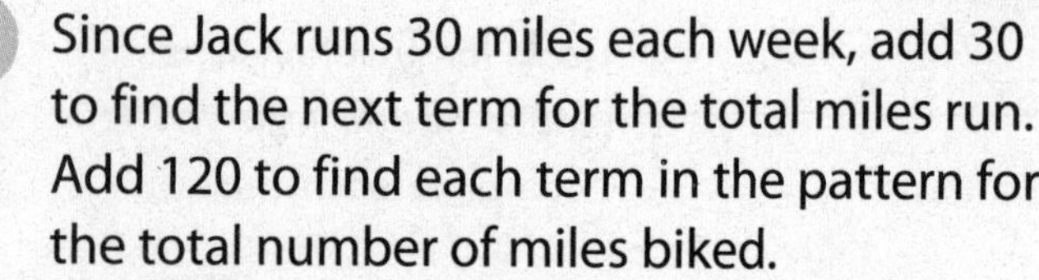

Since Jack runs 30 miles each week, add 30 to find the next term for the total miles run. Add 120 to find each term in the pattern for the total number of miles biked.

DATA

Week	Total Miles Run	Total Miles Biked
1	30	120
2	60	240
3	90	360
4	120	480
5	150	600

C

Compare the corresponding terms in the patterns:

$$30 \times 4 = 120$$
$$60 \times 4 = 240$$
$$90 \times 4 = 360$$
$$120 \times 4 = 480$$
$$150 \times 4 = 600$$

So, the total number of miles biked is always 4 times the total number of miles run.

Convince Me! **MP.8 Generalize** Do you think the relationship between the corresponding terms in the table Jack created will always be true? Explain.

Name ________________

Practice Buddy | Tools | Assessment

Guided Practice*

Do You Understand?

In **1–3**, use the table on page 820.

1. **MP.3 Critique Reasoning** Neko says that the relationship between the terms is that the number of miles run is $\frac{1}{4}$ the number of miles biked. Do you agree? Explain.

Do You Know How?

2. How many total miles will Jack have run and biked after 10 weeks? 15 weeks?

3. **MP.2 Reasoning** Miguel says that he can use multiplication to find the terms in the patterns. Do you agree? Explain.

Independent Practice

In **4–6**, use the rules "add 250" and "add 125" to help you.

4. Maria and Henry are each starting a savings account. Maria puts $250 into her account each month. Henry puts $125 into his account each month. How much money will each of them have saved after 6 months? Complete the table to solve.

Total Amount Saved ($)

Month	Maria	Henry
1		
2		
3		
4		
5		
6		

5. What relationship do you notice between the total amount Maria has saved after each month and the total amount Henry has saved after each month?

6. If Maria and Henry continue saving this way for a full year, how much more will Maria have saved than Henry?

*For another example, see Set B on page 839.

Math Practices and Problem Solving

7. Sheila and Patrick are making a table to compare gallons, quarts, and pints. Use the rule "add 4" to complete the column for the number of quarts. Then use the rule "add 8" to complete the column for the number of pints.

Gallons	Quarts	Pints
1		
2		
3		
4		
5		
6		

8. Patrick has a 12-gallon fish tank at home. How many quarts of water will fill his fish tank? How many pints?

9. **MP.7 Look for Relationships** What relationship do you notice between the number of quarts and the number of pints?

---

10. **Higher Order Thinking** At their family's pizzeria, Dan makes 8 pizzas in the first hour they are open and 6 pizzas each hour after that. Susan makes 12 pizzas in the first hour and 6 pizzas each hour after that. If the pizzeria is open for 6 hours, how many pizzas will they make in all? Complete the table using the rule "add 6" to help you.

Number of Pizzas Made		
Hour	Dan	Susan
1		
2		
3		
4		
5		
6		

11. **MP.7 Look for Relationships** Compare the total number of pizzas made by each person after each hour. What relationship do you notice?

Common Core Assessment

12. Mike and Sarah are packing boxes at a factory. Mike packs 30 boxes each hour. Sarah packs 15 boxes each hour.

How many boxes will each person have packed after an 8-hour shift?

Ⓐ Mike: 38 boxes; Sarah: 23 boxes

Ⓑ Mike: 86 boxes; Sarah: 71 boxes

Ⓒ Mike: 120 boxes; Sarah: 240 boxes

Ⓓ Mike: 240 boxes; Sarah: 120 boxes

13. Which of the following are true statements about the number of boxes Mike and Sarah have packed after each hour?

- ☐ Mike has always packed a total of 15 more boxes than Sarah.
- ☐ Mike has always packed twice as many boxes as Sarah.
- ☐ Sarah has always packed twice as many boxes as Mike.
- ☐ Sarah has always packed one half as many boxes as Mike.

Name ______________________

Homework & Practice 15-2

More Numerical Patterns

Another Look!

Ira makes a table showing the relationship between the number of yards, feet, and inches. How many feet and inches are in 6 yards? What do you notice about the number of feet and inches?

Step 1

Complete the table.

Yards	Feet	Inches
1	3	36
2	6	72
3	9	108
4	12	144
5	15	180
6	18	216

There are 18 feet or 216 inches in 6 yards.

Step 2

Compare the number of feet to the number of inches to find a relationship.

$3 \times 12 = 36$
$6 \times 12 = 72$
$9 \times 12 = 108$
$12 \times 12 = 144$
$15 \times 12 = 180$
$18 \times 12 = 216$

So, there are 12 inches for every foot.

In **1** and **2**, use the rules "add 12" and "add 6" to help you.

1. Each team in a youth hockey league has 12 forwards and 6 defensemen. Complete the table to show how many forwards and defensemen are on 6 teams.

Team	Forwards	Defensemen
1		
2		
3		
4		
5		
6		

2. What relationship do you notice between the number of forwards and the number of defensemen?

3. Jamie makes a table to show the relationship between meters, centimeters, and millimeters. Use the rule "add 100" to complete the column for the number of centimeters. Then use the rule "add 1,000" to complete the column for the number of millimeters. How many centimeters are in 15 meters? How many millimeters?

Meters	Centimeters	Millimeters
1	100	1,000
2		
3		
4		
5		

4. **Higher Order Thinking** The distance between Jamie's house and her friend's house is 75 meters. If Jamie walks to her friend's house and back, how many centimeters does she walk? Explain.

5. **MP.7 Look for Relationships** What relationship do you notice between the number of centimeters and the number of millimeters?

6. **MP.4 Model with Math** A recipe for bread uses $5\frac{3}{4}$ cups of white flour and $3\frac{1}{3}$ cups of wheat flour. How many more cups of white flour than wheat flour are used in the recipe? Write an equation and complete the bar diagram to solve.

Common Core Assessment

At Ashley's Nursery, there are 12 rows of trees. In each row, there are 21 pine trees and 7 spruce trees. Make a table to help you solve the following.

7. How many of each type of tree are there in all?

   Ⓐ 252 pine trees; 84 spruce trees
   Ⓑ 231 pine trees; 74 spruce trees
   Ⓒ 84 pine trees; 252 spruce trees
   Ⓓ 33 pine trees; 19 spruce trees

8. Which of the following are true statements about the relationship between the number of pine trees and spruce trees?

   ☐ There are always 14 more pine trees than spruce trees.
   ☐ There are always 3 times as many spruce trees as pine trees.
   ☐ There are always 3 times as many pine trees as spruce trees.
   ☐ There are always $\frac{1}{3}$ as many spruce trees as pine trees.

Name ______________________________

Lesson 15-3
Analyze and Graph Relationships

I can ...
analyze patterns and graph ordered pairs generated from number sequences.

Content Standards 5.OA.B.3, 5.G.A.2
Mathematical Practices MP.1, MP.3, MP.4, MP.7

Solve & Share

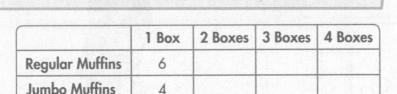

A bakery can fit either 6 regular muffins or 4 jumbo muffins in each box. Each box will contain either regular or jumbo muffins. Complete the table to show how many of each muffin will fit in 2, 3, or 4 boxes. Then generate ordered pairs and graph them.

	1 Box	2 Boxes	3 Boxes	4 Boxes
Regular Muffins	6			
Jumbo Muffins	4			

Look for Relationships
Find a rule that describes the relationship between the number of boxes and the number of muffins.

Look Back! **MP.7 Look for Relationships** The bakery can fit 12 mini-muffins in a box. How many mini-muffins will fit in 4 boxes? Without extending the table, what relationship do you notice between the number of mini-muffins and the number of boxes?

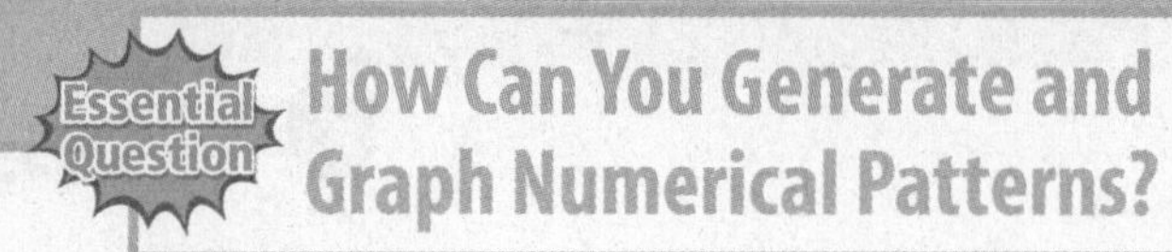

How Can You Generate and Graph Numerical Patterns?

A

Jill earns $5 per hour babysitting. Robin earns $15 per hour teaching ice skating lessons. The girls made a table using the rule "Add 5" to show Jill's earnings and the rule "Add 15" to show Robin's earnings. Complete the table, compare their earnings, and graph the ordered pairs of the corresponding terms.

Hours	0	1	2	3	4
Jill's Earnings	$0	$5	$10	$15	
Robin's Earnings	$0	$15	$30	$45	

B Compare the numbers in Jill's and Robin's sequences.

Each sequence begins with zero. Then each term in Robin's pattern is 3 times as great as the corresponding term in Jill's pattern.

Generate ordered pairs from the total amount Jill and Robin have earned after each hour.

(0, 0), (5, 15), (10, 30), (15, 45), (20, 60)

C Graph the ordered pairs.

Jill's Earnings (x)	Robin's Earnings (y)
0	0
5	15
10	30
15	45
20	60

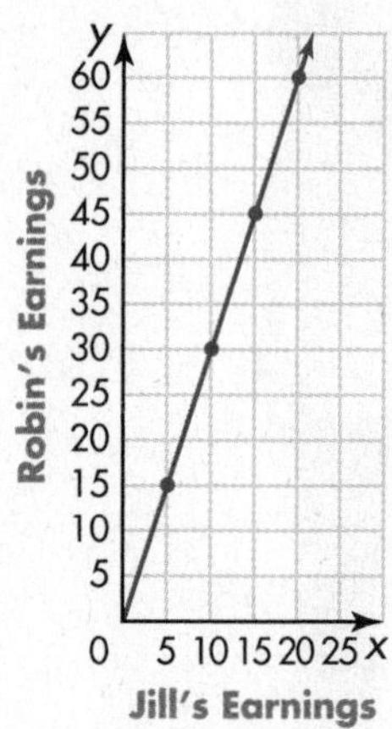

Convince Me! © **MP.1 Make Sense and Persevere** What does the point (0, 0) represent?

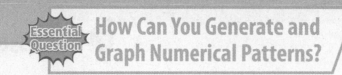

Name ______________________________

Practice Buddy   Tools   Assessment

☆Guided Practice*

Do You Understand?

1. In the example on page 826, what ordered pair would you write for how much Jill and Robin have each earned after 5 hours?

2. MP.3 **Critique Reasoning** Ben says that the relationship is that Jill earns $\frac{1}{3}$ as much as Robin. Do you agree? Explain.

Do You Know How?

Sam and Eric record the total number of miles they walk in one week. Sam walks 2 miles each day. Eric walks 4 miles each day.

3. What ordered pair represents the number of miles each has walked in all after 7 days?

4. **MP.7 Look for Relationships** What relationship do you notice between the total number of miles Sam and Eric have each walked?

Independent Practice

In **5–8**, use the rule "add 4" to help you.

5. Megan and Scott go fishing while at camp. Megan catches 3 fish in the first hour and 4 fish each hour after that. Scott catches 5 fish in the first hour and 4 fish each hour after that. Complete the table to show the total number of fish each has caught after each hour.

Total Fish Caught		
Hours	**Megan**	**Scott**
1	3	5
2		
3		
4		

6. What ordered pair represents the total number of fish they each caught after 4 hours?

7. What relationship do you notice between the total number of fish each has caught after each hour?

8. Graph the ordered pairs of the total number of fish each has caught after each hour.

9. The pattern continues until Scott's total is 29 fish. What ordered pair represents the total number of fish they each caught when Scott's total is 29 fish?

*For another example, see Set C on page 840.

Math Practices and Problem Solving

In **10–12**, use the rules "add 15" and "add 10" to help you.

10. The Snack Shack made a table to track the amount of money from sales of frozen yogurt and fruit cups for four hours. What are the missing values in the table?

	9 A.M.	10 A.M.	11 A.M.	12 P.M.
Money from Yogurt Sales	$0	$15		$45
Money from Fruit Cup Sales	$0		$20	$30

11. **MP.7 Use Structure** If sales continue in the same manner, what ordered pair would represent the money from sales of yogurt and fruit cups at 1 P.M.? Explain how you know.

12. Graph the ordered pairs for the money from sales of yogurt and fruit cups from 9 A.M. to 1 P.M.

13. **Vocabulary** Write two **number sequences**. Then, circle **corresponding terms** in the two sequences.

14. **Higher Order Thinking** Pedro runs $2\frac{1}{2}$ miles each day for 5 days. Melissa runs 4 miles each day for 5 days. How many more miles will Melissa run in 5 days than Pedro? Make a table to help you.

Common Core Assessment

15. Every month, Leonard pays $240 for a car payment. He spends $60 each month for a gym membership.

Write an ordered pair to represent how much Leonard spends in 12 months for car payments and the gym membership.

16. What relationship do you notice between how much Leonard spends in 12 months on car payments and the gym membership?

Name ____________________

Homework & Practice 15-3

Analyze and Graph Relationships

Another Look!

Mary and Sasha kept track of the money they earned at their jobs each week. They used the rules "add 100" and "add 50" to complete the table. Then they graphed ordered pairs of the total amounts they have earned after each week.

Total Amount Earned ($)		
Week	Mary	Sasha
1	100	50
2	200	100
3	300	150
4	400	200

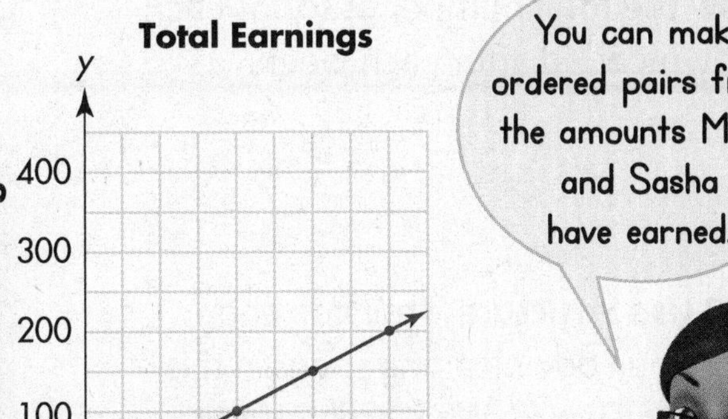

You can make ordered pairs from the amounts Mary and Sasha have earned.

Mary earned $400 after 4 weeks.
Sasha earned $200 after 4 weeks.
Mary earned twice as much as Sasha.

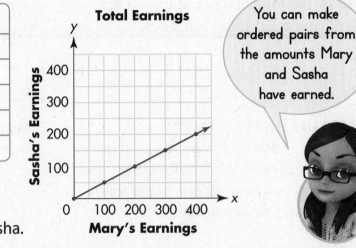

In **1–4**, use the rules "add 6" and "add 12" to help you.

1. Every hour at his bakery, Dennis makes 6 everything bagels and 12 blueberry bagels. Complete the table to show how many of each bagel he makes in all after each hour.

Total Bagels Made		
Hour	Everything	Blueberry
1		
2		
3		
4		

2. What ordered pair would represent the total number of each type of bagel Dennis makes in 8 hours?

3. What relationship do you notice between the total number of everything bagels and the total number of blueberry bagels made after each hour?

4. Graph the ordered pairs of the total number of each type of bagel made after each hour.

In **5–7**, use the rules "add 5" and "add 15" to help you.

5. Thurston and Kim kept track of how many songs they downloaded each week for a month. Thurston downloaded 5 songs each week. Kim downloaded 15 songs each week. Complete the table to show the total number of songs each has downloaded after each week.

Total Number of Songs Downloaded		
Week	**Thurston**	**Kim**
1		
2		
3		
4		

6. **MP.7 Use Structure** Thurston and Kim continue downloading songs in this manner for 8 weeks. What ordered pair would represent the total number of songs they have each downloaded?

7. Graph the ordered pairs of the total number of songs each has downloaded after each week.

8. **MP.4 Model with Math** Diego makes a rectangular prism that is 2 cubes long, 2 cubes wide, and 2 cubes tall. Each dimension of June's rectangular prism is twice as many cubes as Diego's prism. What is the volume of June's prism? Use an equation to show your work.

9. **Higher Order Thinking** There are 347 students going on a field trip. Each bus holds 44 students. If the school pays $95 per bus, will they need to spend more than $1,000 for the buses? How can you decide without using division?

Common Core Assessment

10. Claire makes bracelets using blue and red beads. Each bracelet has 20 red beads and 5 blue beads. Write an ordered pair to represent the number of red beads and blue beads Claire will use to make 8 bracelets.

11. What relationship do you notice between the number of red beads and blue beads Claire uses to make all the bracelets?

Name ______________________________

Solve & Share

Val is planning a bowling-and-pizza party. Including herself, there will be no more than 10 guests. Val wonders which bowling alley offers the less expensive party plan.

Complete the tables for Leonard's Lanes and Southside Bowl. On the same grid, graph the ordered pairs in each table. Use a different color for the values in each table. Which bowling alley would be less expensive? Explain how you know.

Math Practices and Problem Solving

Lesson 15-4

Make Sense and Persevere

I can ...
make sense of problems and keep working if I get stuck.

Mathematical Practices MP.1. Also MP.2, MP.5, MP.6
Content Standard 5.OA.B.3

Leonard's Lanes
Bowling and Pizza: $25 plus $10 per person

Guests	1	2	3	4	5	6	7	8	9	10
Cost ($)	35	45								

Southside Bowl
Bowling and Pizza: $15 per person

Guests	1	2	3	4	5	6	7	8	9	10
Cost ($)	15	30								

Thinking Habits

*Think about these questions to help you **make sense and persevere**.*

- What do I need to find?
- What do I know?
- What else can I try if I get stuck?
- How can I check that my solution makes sense?

Look Back! **MP.1 Make Sense and Persevere** How did the graph help you answer the question?

How Can You Make Sense of a Problem and Persevere in Solving It?

A

Make Sense of the Problem

On Aiden's farm, there are 12 acres of soybeans and 8 acres of corn. Aiden plans to replace his other crops with more acres of soybeans and corn. Will his farm ever have the same number of acres of soybeans and corn? Explain.

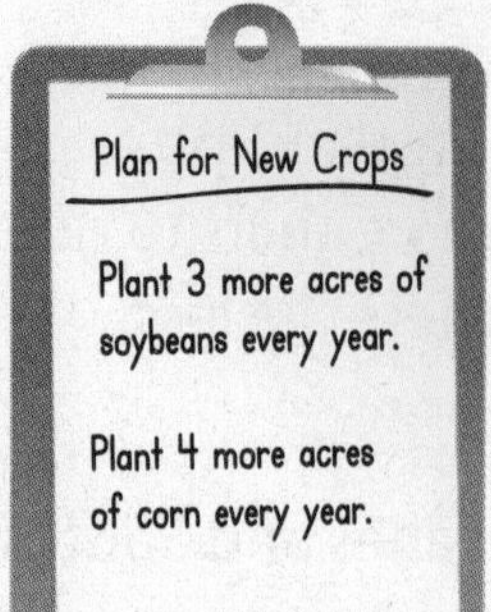

Plan for New Crops
Plant 3 more acres of soybeans every year.
Plant 4 more acres of corn every year.

You can make sense of the problem by answering these questions. What do you know? What are you asked to find?

B

How can I make sense of and solve this problem?

I can

- choose and implement an appropriate strategy.
- use ordered pairs to make graphs.
- identify and analyze patterns.
- check that my work and answer make sense.

C

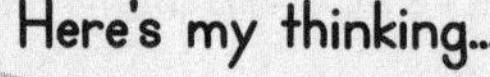

For each crop, I can write a rule, make a table, and plot the ordered pairs. Then I can see if the number of acres is ever the same.

Soybeans
Rule: Start at 12 and add 3.

Years	Start	1	2	3	4	5
Acres	12	15	18	21	24	27

Corn
Rule: Start at 8 and add 4.

Years	Start	1	2	3	4	5
Acres	8	12	16	20	24	28

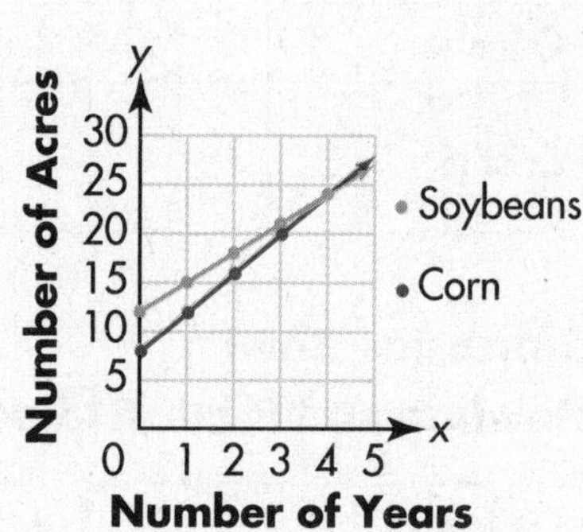

Where the lines intersect, at 4 years, Aiden's farm has 24 acres of each crop.

Convince Me! **MP.1 Make Sense and Persevere** How can you check your work? Does your answer make sense? Explain.

Name ______________________________

Practice Buddy | Tools | Assessment

Guided Practice*

MP.1 Make Sense and Persevere

Mindy has already saved $20 and plans to save $8 each month. Georgette has no money saved yet but plans to save $5 each month. Will the girls ever have saved the same amount? Explain.

Month	Start	1	2	3		
$ Saved	20	28	36	44		

Month	Start	1	2	3	4	
$ Saved						

1. Write a rule and complete each table.

   Rule: ______________________________

   Rule: ______________________________

2. On the same grid, graph the ordered pairs in each table.

3. Explain whether the girls will ever have the same amount of money saved.

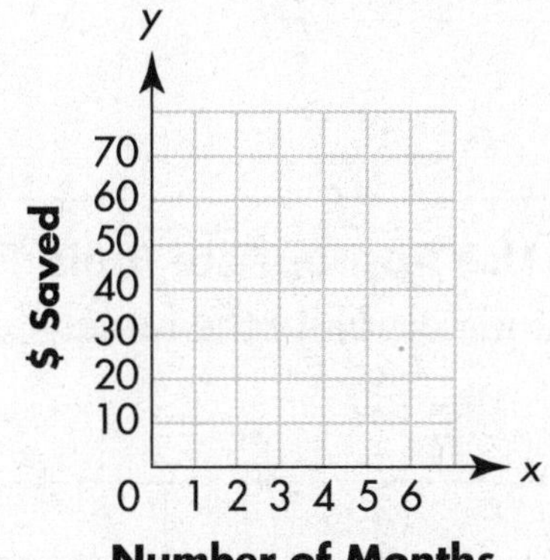

Independent Practice

MP.1 Make Sense and Persevere

O'Brien's Landscaping pays employees $15 plus $12 per lawn. Carter's Landscaping pays $25 plus $10 per lawn. Which company pays more? Explain.

Lawns	Start					
Pay ($)	15					

Lawns	Start					
Pay ($)	25					

4. Write a rule and complete each table.

   Rule: ______________________________

   Rule: ______________________________

5. On the grid, graph the ordered pairs in each table. Explain which company pays more.

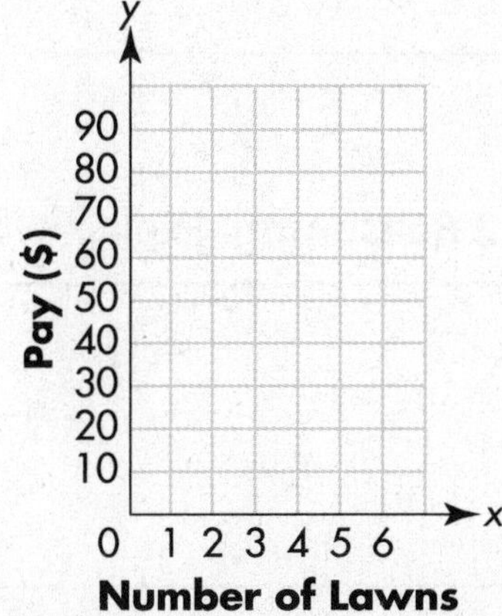

*For another example, see Set D on page 840.

Math Practices and Problem Solving

Common Core Performance Assessment

Track-a-Thon

Jordan is running in a track-a-thon to raise money for charity. Who will make a larger donation, Aunt Meg or Grandma Diane? Explain.

Track-a-Thon Pledges	
Aunt Meg	$8 plus $2 per lap
Grandma Diane	$15 + $1 per lap

6. **MP.1 Make Sense and Persevere** How can you use tables and a graph to solve the problem?

7. **MP.5 Use Appropriate Tools** For each pledge, write a rule and complete the table.

Rule: ______________________

Laps	Start							
Donation ($)	8							

Rule: ______________________

Laps	Start							
Donation ($)	15							

8. **MP.5 Use Appropriate Tools** On the grid, graph the ordered pairs in each table.

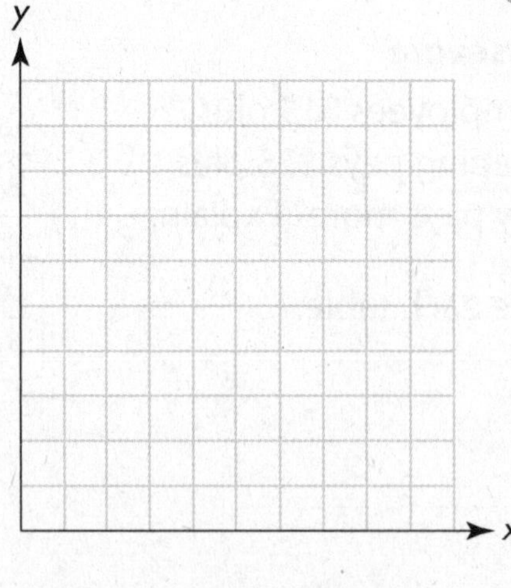

9. **MP.2 Reasoning** Explain whose donation will be greater.

When you make sense and persevere, you choose and implement an appropriate strategy.

Name ______________________

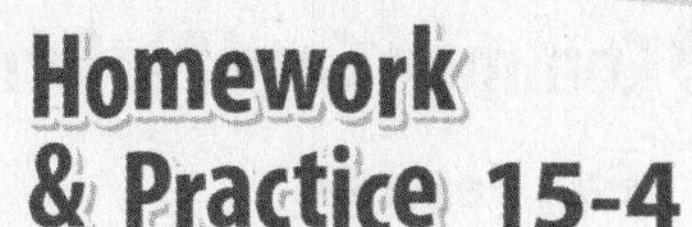

Homework & Practice 15-4
Make Sense and Persevere

Another Look!

Simon has 28 baseball cards and 16 soccer cards. Each month he plans to get 6 more baseball cards and 4 more soccer cards. Will he ever have the same number of baseball cards and soccer cards? Explain.

To make sense and persevere, graph ordered pairs then analyze the graph.

For each type of card, write a rule and make a table. On the same grid, graph the ordered pairs in each table.

Baseball Cards: Start at 28 and add 6.

Months	Start	1	2	3	4	5	6
Baseball Cards	28	34	40	46	52	58	64

Soccer Cards: Start at 16 and add 4.

Months	Start	1	2	3	4	5	6
Soccer Cards	16	20	24	28	32	36	40

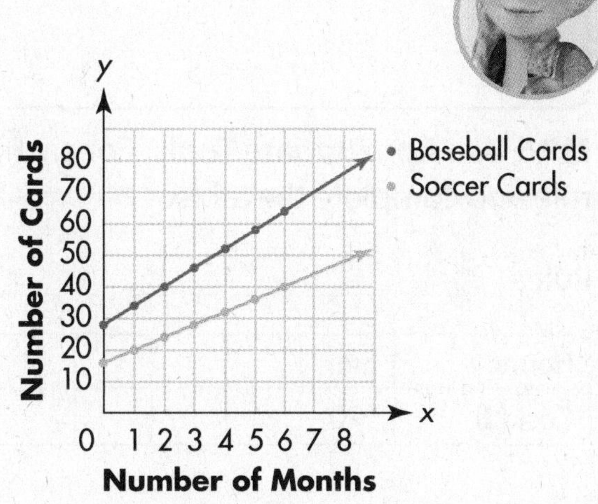

He will never have the same number of baseball cards and soccer cards. The lines are getting farther apart, so the number of soccer cards will never catch up.

MP.1 Make Sense and Persevere

The stingray tank contains 6 inches of water. The shark tank is empty. Each hour, 4 inches of water are added to the stingray tank and 6 inches are added to the shark tank. Will the water in the shark tank ever be as deep as the water in the stingray tank? Explain.

Hours	Start						
Depth (in.)	6						

Hours	Start						
Depth (in.)	0						

1. Write a rule and complete each table.

   Rule: ______________________

   Rule: ______________________

2. Graph the ordered pairs in each table.

3. Explain whether the depth of water in the two tanks will ever be equal.

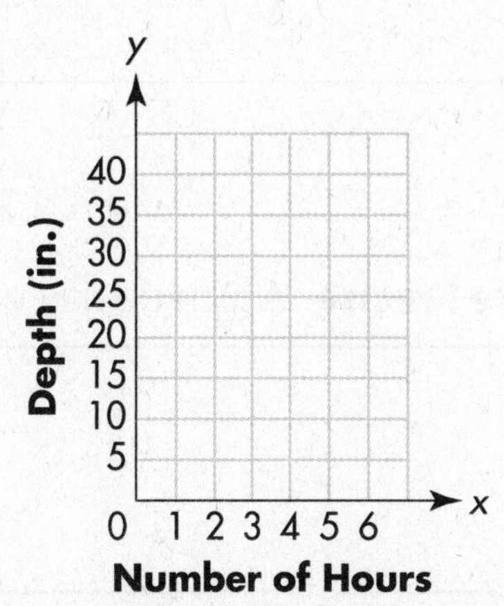

Common Core Performance Assessment

Fall Festival

The park district wants to hire a deejay for the Fall Festival. They expect the Festival to last no more than 6 hours. Which deejay would be less expensive?

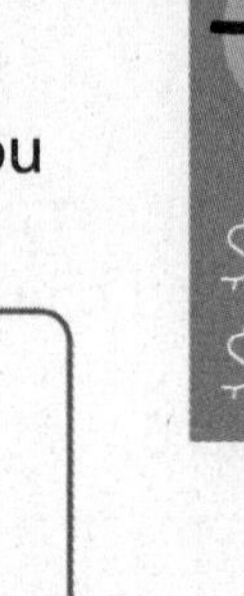

4. **MP.1 Make Sense and Persevere** How can you use tables and a graph to solve the problem?

5. **MP.5 Use Appropriate Tools** For each deejay, write a rule and complete the table.

Rule: ______________________________

Hours	Start					
Cost ($)	90					

Rule: ______________________________

Hours	Start					
Cost ($)	20					

6. **MP.5 Use Appropriate Tools** On the grid, graph the ordered pairs in each table.

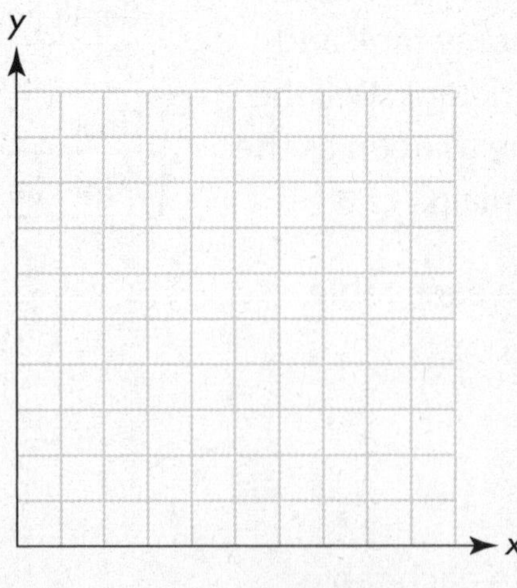

When you make sense and persevere, you use a strategy that makes sense for the problem.

7. **MP.6 Be Precise** Which deejay would be less expensive?

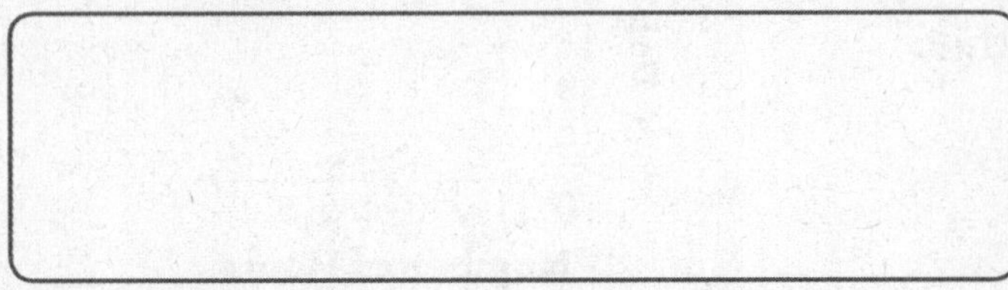

Name ___________________________________

Fluency Practice Activity

Solve each problem. Follow problems with an answer of 72,072 to shade a path from **START** to **FINISH**. You can only move up, down, right, or left.

I can ...
multiply multi-digit whole numbers.

Content Standard 5.NBT.B.5

Start				
5,544 × 13	819 × 88	1,144 × 63	1,716 × 42	792 × 91
2,012 × 36	4,059 × 18	2,007 × 36	6,562 × 11	1,287 × 56
728 × 99	1,092 × 66	3,432 × 21	2,772 × 26	936 × 77
2,574 × 28	4,504 × 16	1,002 × 71	6,311 × 12	4,039 × 18
1,386 × 52	924 × 78	1,638 × 44	1,848 × 39	1,001 × 72
				Finish

Word List

- coordinate grid
- corresponding terms
- number sequence
- ordered pair
- origin
- *x*-axis
- *x*-coordinate
- *y*-axis
- *y*-coordinate

Understand Vocabulary

Write *always, sometimes,* or *never* on each blank.

1. Corresponding terms are ______________ in the same position in a pair of number sequences.

2. An ordered pair can ______________ be plotted on the origin of a coordinate grid.

3. The origin is ______________ any other location on a coordinate grid besides (0, 0).

4. Two number lines that form a coordinate grid ______________ intersect at a right angle.

5. The second number of an ordered pair ______________ describes the distance to the right or left of the origin.

In **6–8**, use the lists of numbers below.

0 4 9 12 15	0 5 10 15 20	0 10 20 30 40
1 4 7 10 10	7 11 15 19 23	

	Example	Non-example
6. Number sequence	______________	______________
7. Another number sequence	______________	______________
8. Identify one pair of corresponding terms in your examples in Exercises 6 and 7.	______________	______________

Use Vocabulary in Writing

9. Explain how to identify corresponding terms in two number sequences. Use terms from the Word List in your explanation.

Name ____

Set A pages 813–818

Maria has $4. She will save $10 each week. Stephen has $9 and will also save $10 each week.

Maria uses the rule "add 10" to create tables to see how much each will have saved after each week. What relationship do you notice between the **corresponding terms**?

Week	Maria
Start	$4
1	$14
2	$24
3	$34
4	$44

Week	Stephen
Start	$9
1	$19
2	$29
3	$39
4	$49

After each week, Stephen has $5 more saved than Maria. Or, Maria's savings are always $5 less than Stephen's savings.

Remember to compare corresponding terms to see if there is a relationship.

1. Two groups of students went hiking. After 1 hour, Group A hiked $1\frac{1}{2}$ miles and Group B hiked $2\frac{1}{2}$ miles. After that, each group hiked 2 miles each hour. Complete the tables to show how far each group had hiked after 3 hours.

Hour	Group A (mi)
1	$1\frac{1}{2}$
2	
3	

Hour	Group B (mi)
1	$2\frac{1}{2}$
2	
3	

2. What relationship do you notice between the corresponding terms?

Set B pages 819–824

Each week, Andre lifts weights twice and runs 4 times. Andre uses the rules "add 2" and "add 4" to complete the table. What relationship do you notice between the corresponding terms?

Week	Lift Weights	Run
1	2	4
2	4	8
3	6	12
4	8	16

The number of times Andre went running is always 2 times the number of times he lifted weights.

Remember to use the rules to help you complete the tables.

1. A garden center sells 15 trees and 45 shrubs each day for one week. Complete the table to show how many trees and shrubs in all were sold in 4 days. Use the rules "add 15" and "add "45" to help you.

Days	Trees	Shrubs
1	15	45
2		
3		
4		

2. What is the relationship between the corresponding terms of the sequences?

Set C pages 825–830

Kelly uses 3 pounds of nuts and 2 pounds of cereal to make each batch of trail mix. The chart shows how many total pounds of each she will need for 4 batches. Graph ordered pairs of the corresponding terms. What does the point (12, 8) represent?

Batch	Nuts (lb)	Cereal (lb)
1	3	2
2	6	4
3	9	6
4	12	8

The chart and graph both represent the problem. The point (12, 8) shows that when Kelly uses 12 pounds of nuts, she will use 8 pounds of cereal.

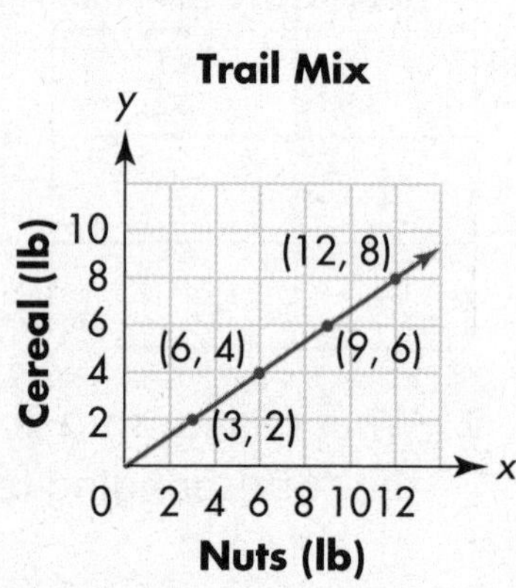

Remember to make ordered pairs from corresponding terms.

1. Lauren has \$6 and saves \$5 each week. Derrick has \$3 and saves \$5 each week. How much will each have saved after 4 weeks? Use the rule "add 5" to complete the table.

Week	Lauren	Derrick
Start	\$6	\$3
1		
2		
3		
4		

2. What does the point (26, 23) represent?

3. What is the relationship between the corresponding terms?

Set D pages 831–836

Think about these questions to help you **make sense and persevere** in solving problems.

Thinking Habits

- What do I need to find?
- What do I know?
- What else can I try if I get stuck?
- How can I check that my solution makes sense?

Remember that you can use patterns, tables, and graphs to represent and solve problems.

1. Sam starts with 5 stamps and buys 10 more each month. Pat starts with 9 stamps and buys 9 more each month. Complete the table using the rules "add 10" and "add 9".

Month	Sam
Start	5
1	
2	
3	
4	

Month	Pat
Start	9
1	
2	
3	
4	

2. Make a graph from the data in the tables. Will Sam ever have more stamps than Pat?

Name ______________________________

TOPIC 15

Assessment

1. Liz and Fareed each start a new savings account. Liz starts her account with $75. Fareed starts his account with $100. Each month, both save another $50.

Part A

Complete the table to show the total amount each has saved after each month. Use the rule "add 50".

Month	Liz	Fareed
Start	$75	$100
1		
2		
3		
4		

Part B

Choose all the ordered pairs that represent amounts Liz and Fareed have each saved.

- ☐ (50, 75)
- ☐ (75, 100)
- ☐ (125, 150)
- ☐ (150, 200)
- ☐ (275, 300)

Part C

Describe the relationship between the amount each person has saved after each month.

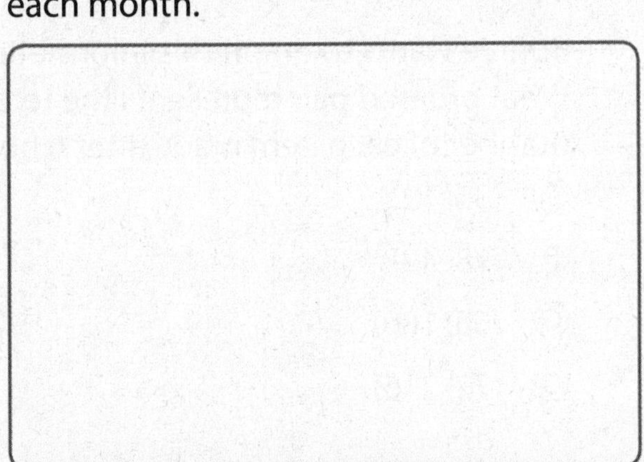

2. There are 16 pawns and 2 kings in each chess set.

Part A

Complete the table to show how many pawns and kings in all are in different numbers of chess sets. Use the rules "add 16" and "add 2".

Sets	Pawns	Kings
1		
2		
3		
4		
5		

Part B

Use the total number of pawns and kings to form ordered pairs. Graph the ordered pairs below.

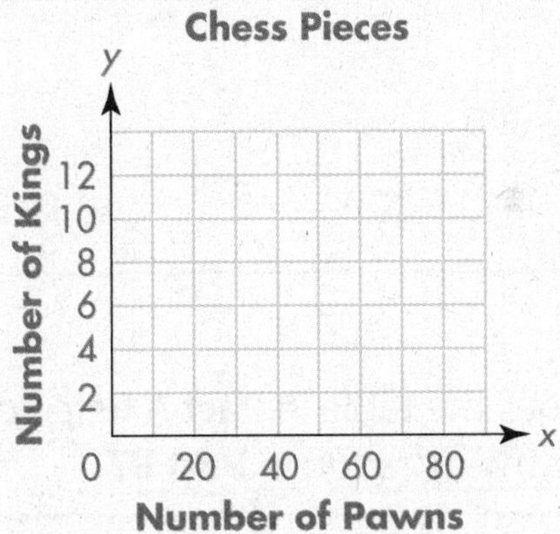

Part C

What would the ordered pair (96, 12) represent?

3. Luis kept track of the heights of his basil and chive plants. His basil plant was 15.5 cm tall and grew 1.5 cm each week. His chive plant was 18.5 cm tall and grew 0.5 cm each week.

Part A

Complete the table to show the heights of each plant after each week. Use the rules "add 1.5" and "add 0.5".

Plant Heights (cm)		
Week	**Basil**	**Chive**
Start	15.5	18.5
1		
2		
3		
4		

Part B

Will the basil plant ever be taller than the chive plant? If so, when?

Part C

How does the table in **Part A** help you answer the question in **Part B?**

4. Bonnie's Bakery makes 12 cakes and 36 muffins each hour.

Part A

Complete the table to show how many cakes and muffins in all the bakery has made after each hour. Use the rules "add 12" and "add 36".

Hour	Cakes	Muffins
1		
2		
3		
4		
5		

Part B

Miles says "the total number of muffins made is always 24 more than the total number of cakes made." Do you agree? Explain your reasoning.

Part C

Bonnie wants to graph this information. What ordered pair represents the total number of each item made after 6 hours?

Ⓐ (36, 12)

Ⓑ (18, 42)

Ⓒ (60, 180)

Ⓓ (72, 216)

Name ___________________________________

TOPIC 15

Performance Assessment

Butterfly Patterns

Use the **Butterflies** picture to explore patterns.

Butterflies

Butterflies have 4 wings and 6 legs.

1. Jessie and Jason use their cell phones to take pictures of butterflies. Jessie had 3 pictures of butterflies stored in her cell phone and Jason had 1 picture in his. On Saturday, they each took a picture of 1 butterfly every hour.

Part A

How many butterfly wings are in each photo collection after 3 hours? Complete the table.

Butterfly Wings		
Hour	Jessie's Pictures	Jason's Pictures
0		
1		
2		
3		

Part B

What is the relationship between the corresponding terms of the two patterns in Part A?

Part C

Write rules for the number of butterfly wings in Jessie's pictures and in Jason's pictures.

2. Compare the number of wings to the number of legs in different numbers of butterflies.

Part A

Complete the table.

Number of Butterflies	Wings	Legs
0	0	0
1		
2		
3		

Part B

What is the relationship between the number of wings and the number of legs you found in Part A?

3. Tomika has no pictures of butterflies in her cell phone, but Kyle has 3 pictures in his. On Saturday, Tomika takes 2 pictures of butterflies every hour and Kyle takes 1 picture every hour. Answer the following to find whether or not their collections of butterfly pictures will ever have the same number of wings.

Tomika's Pictures	
Hours	Wings
0	
1	
2	
3	

Part A

Write a rule and complete the **Tomika's Pictures** table.

Part B

Write a rule and complete the **Kyle's Pictures** table.

Kyle's Pictures	
Hours	Wings
0	
1	
2	
3	

Part C

Graph the ordered pairs from Part A and Part B on the same coordinate grid and draw lines through each set.

Part D

Will Tomika and Kyle ever have the same number of wings in their pictures? Explain.

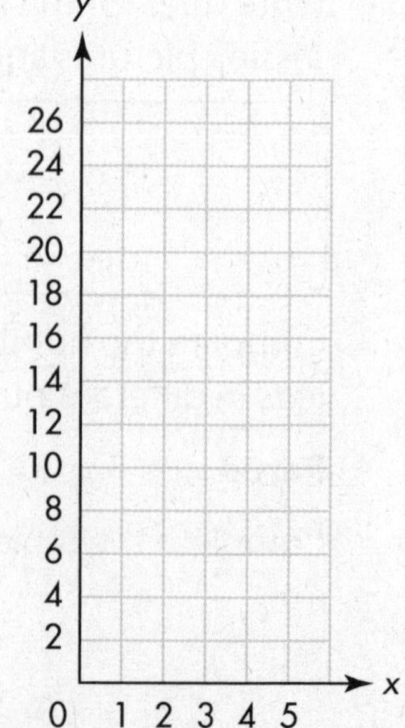

Geometric Measurement: Classify Two-Dimensional Figures

Essential Question: How can triangles and quadrilaterals be described, classified, and named?

Prickly pears, coyotes, scorpions, sand, and rocks are all part of the desert ecosystem of the Guadalupe Mountains.

An *ecosystem* is an interaction of all living organisms in a particular environment.

Hey, did you ever think of school as a kind of ecosystem? Here's a project about ecosystems.

Math and Science Project: Ecosystems

Do Research Use the Internet or other sources to learn more about ecosystems. Look for examples of changes that living organisms might cause. List three different ecosystems and describe any changes that humans might have made to each one.

Journal: Write a Report Include what you found. Also in your report:

- Compare two ecosystems. List 10 living things and 5 non-living things you might find in each one.
- Think about changes that can occur in an ecosystem. Are the changes positive or negative? Why?
- Use two-dimensional shapes to make a map or diagram of an ecosystem.

Name ______________________________

Review What You Know

Vocabulary

Choose the best term from the box. Write it on the blank.

- degree
- line segment
- parallel
- perimeter
- polygon
- quadrilateral
- vertex

1. A ____________ is a polygon with four sides.

2. The point where two sides of a polygon intersect is a ____________.

3. The distance between ____________ sides of a polygon is always the same.

4. The ____________ is a unit of measure for angles.

Decimals

Find each answer.

5. $2.75 + 9.08$

6. $17.6 - 3.08$

7. 83.2×0.1

8. 24.27×10^3

Fractions

Find each answer.

9. $3\frac{2}{3} + 6\frac{9}{10}$

10. $8\frac{1}{2} - 4\frac{4}{5}$

11. $8 \div \frac{1}{2}$

12. $\frac{1}{3} \div 6$

Write an Equation

13. Louisa drew a polygon with six sides of equal length. If the perimeter of Louisa's polygon is 95.4 centimeters, how long is each side? Use an equation to solve.

14. The area of a rectangle is 112 square inches. If the length of the rectangle is 16 inches, what is the width of the rectangle? Use an equation to solve.

Glossary

My Word Cards

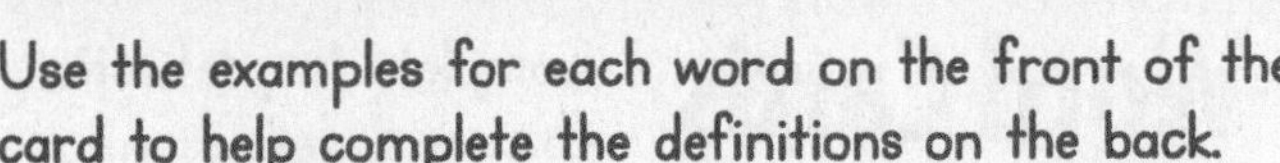
Use the examples for each word on the front of the card to help complete the definitions on the back.

equilateral triangle

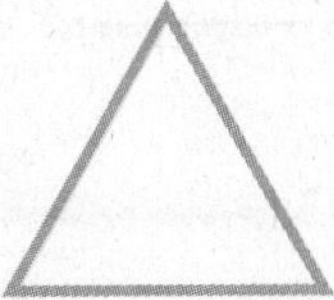

isosceles triangle

scalene triangle

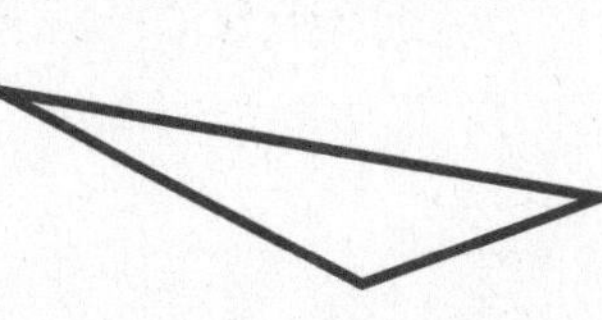

right triangle

acute triangle

obtuse triangle

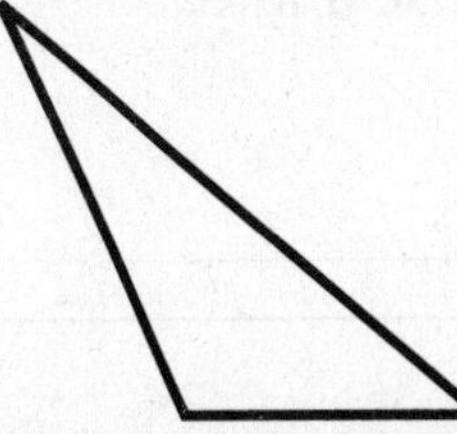

parallelogram

trapezoid

My Word Cards

Complete the definition. Extend learning by writing your own definitions.

An ______________________
has at least two sides of the same length.

In an ______________________
______________________, all sides are the same length.

A ______________________
has one right angle.

In a ______________________,
no sides are the same length.

An ______________________
has one obtuse angle.

An ______________________
has three acute angles.

A ______________________
is a quadrilateral that has one pair of parallel sides.

A ______________________
is a quadrilateral with both pairs of opposite sides parallel and equal in length.

A-Z
Glossary

My Word Cards

Use the examples for each word on the front of the card to help complete the definitions on the back.

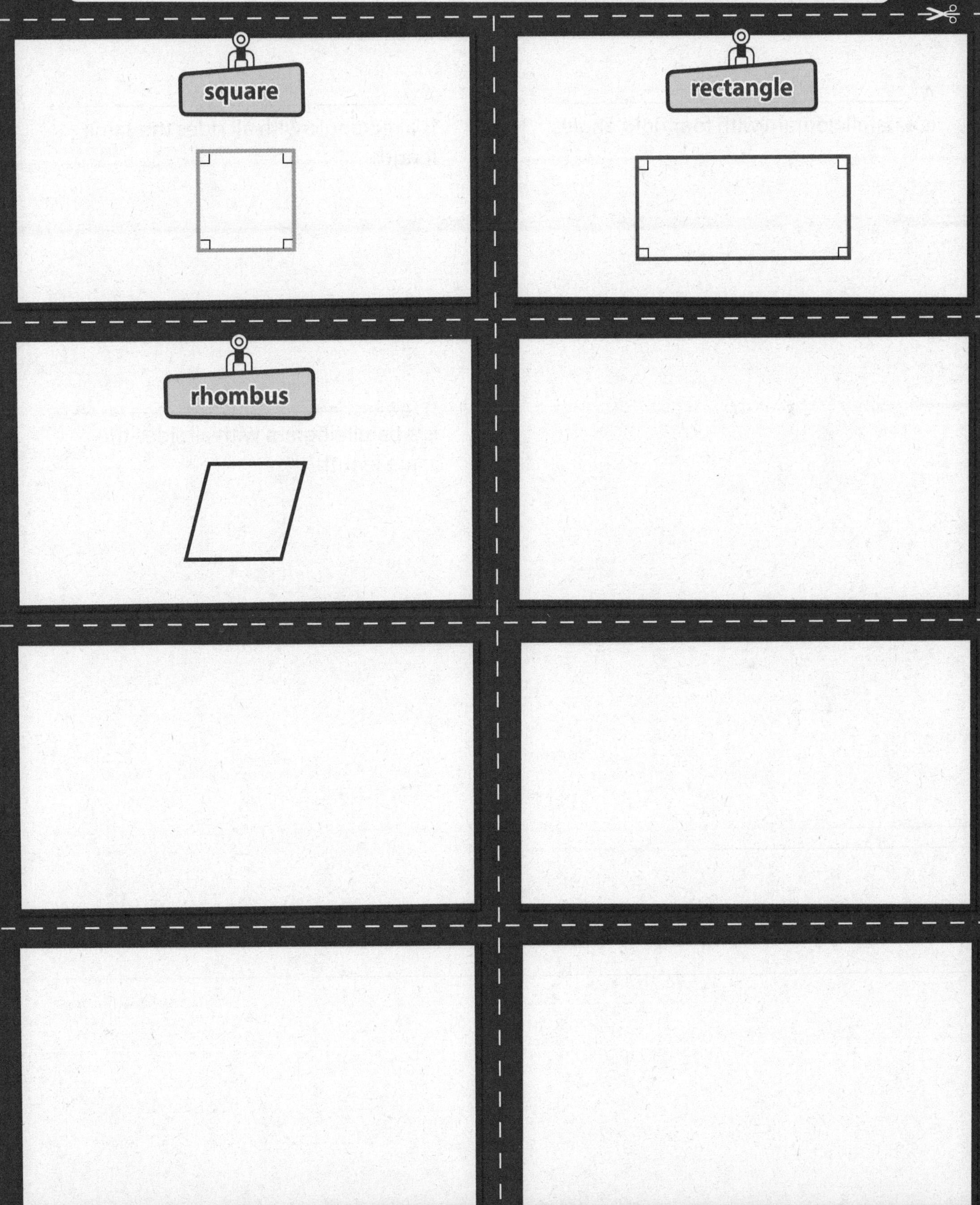

My Word Cards

Complete the definition. Extend learning by writing your own definitions.

A ______________________
is a parallelogram with four right angles.

A ______________________
is a rectangle with all sides the same length.

A ______________________
is a parallelogram with all sides the same length.

Name ______________________

Lesson 16-1
Classify Triangles

I can ...
classify triangles by their angles and sides.

Content Standards 5.G.B.3, 5.G.B.4
Mathematical Practices MP.1, MP.2, MP.3, MP.4

Solve & Share

One triangle is shown below. Draw five more triangles with different properties. Next to each triangle, list the properties, such as 2 equal sides, 1 right angle, 3 acute angles, and so on. ***Work with a partner to solve this problem.***

Construct Arguments How can you tell which properties describe a triangle? *Show your work!*

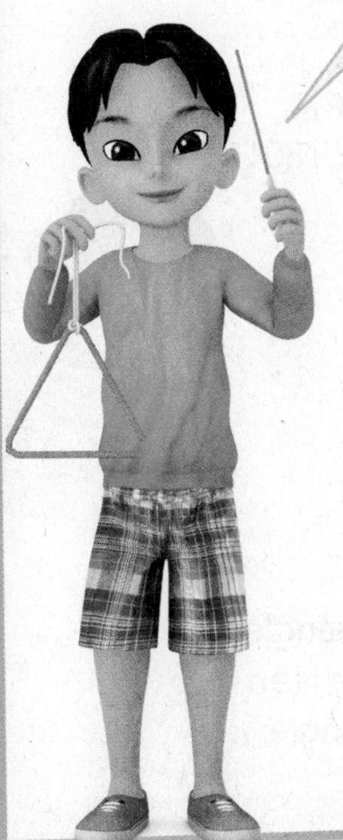

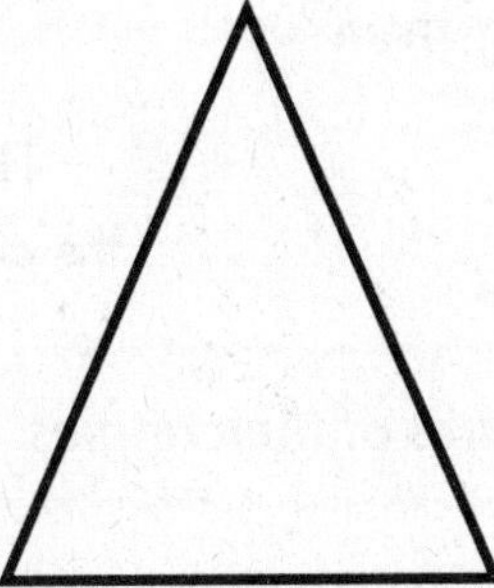

Look Back! **MP.2 Reasoning** Can you classify the triangles you created based on their properties? Do some triangles have more than one classification? Tell how you know.

A

Triangles can be classified by the lengths of their sides.

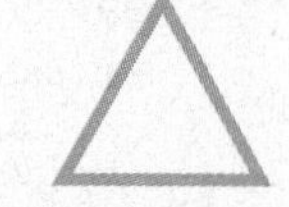

Equilateral triangle
All sides are the same length.

Isosceles triangle
At least two sides are the same length.

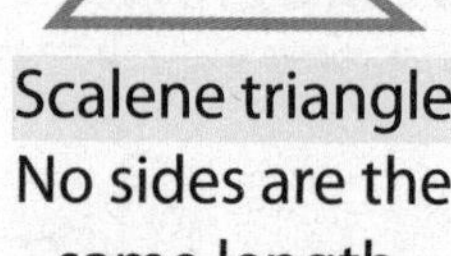

Scalene triangle
No sides are the same length.

Can you tell if the sides of a triangle are the same length without measuring them?

B

The total measure of all the angles in a triangle is 180°.

Triangles can also be classified by the measures of their angles.

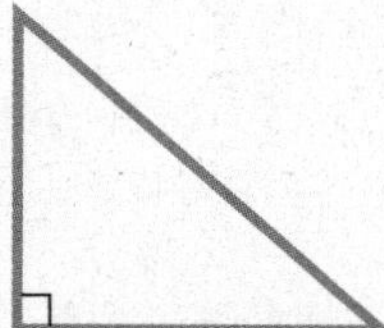

Right triangle
One angle is a right angle.

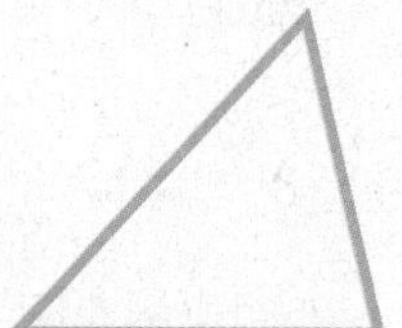

Acute triangle
All three angles are acute angles.

Obtuse triangle
One angle is an obtuse angle.

Convince Me! © **MP.3 Construct Arguments**
Can you draw an equilateral right triangle? Explain using precise mathematical language.

To justify a mathematical argument, you must use precise mathematical language and ideas to explain your thinking.

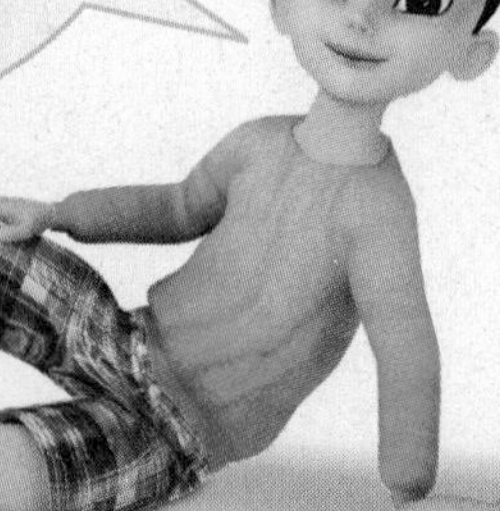

Name ______________________________

Guided Practice*

Do You Understand?

1. MP.3 Construct Arguments Can a right triangle have an obtuse angle? Why or why not?

2. Can an equilateral triangle have only two sides of equal length? Why or why not?

Do You Know How?

In **3** and **4**, classify each triangle by its sides and then by its angles.

3.
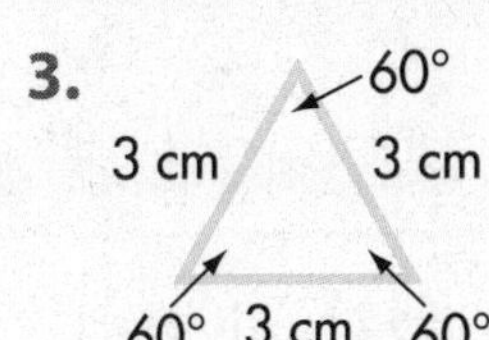

4.
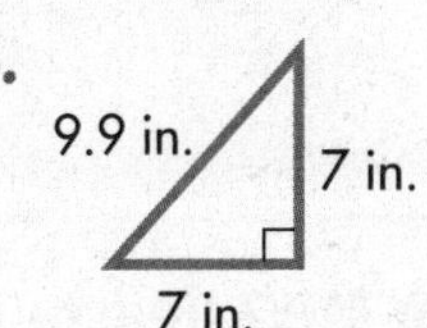

Independent Practice

In **5–10**, classify each triangle by its sides and then by its angles.

5.
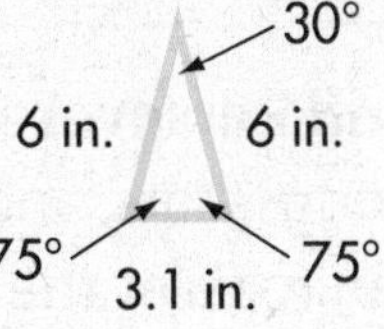

6.
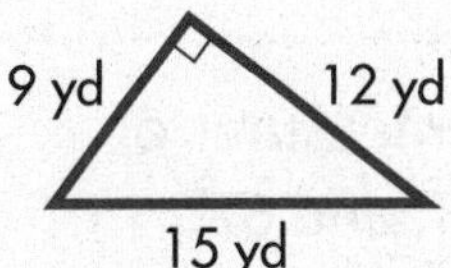

7.
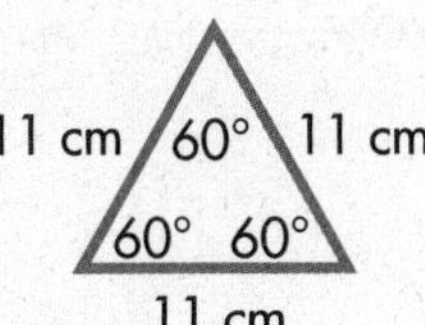

8.

9.
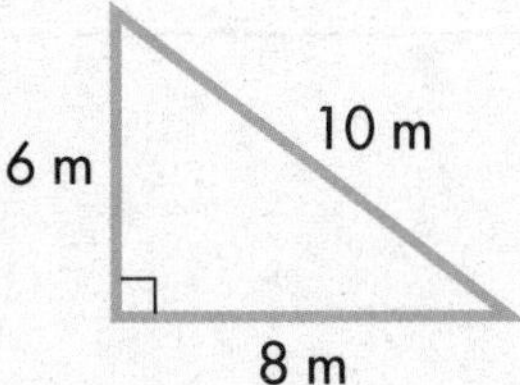

10.
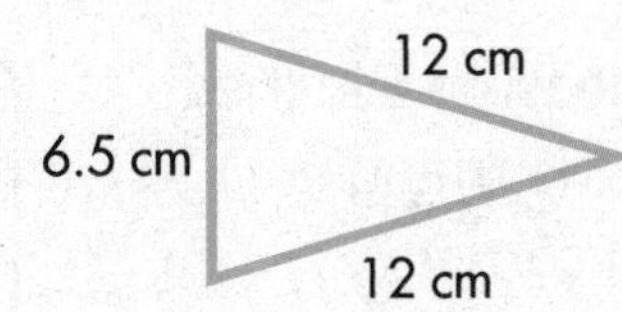

Think about what you need to compare to classify the triangle correctly.

*For another example, see Set A on page 877.

Math Practices and Problem Solving

11. The Louvre Pyramid serves as an entrance to the Louvre Museum in Paris. The base of the pyramid is 35 meters long and the sides are 32 meters long. Classify the triangle on the front of the Louvre Pyramid by the lengths of its sides and the measures of its angles.

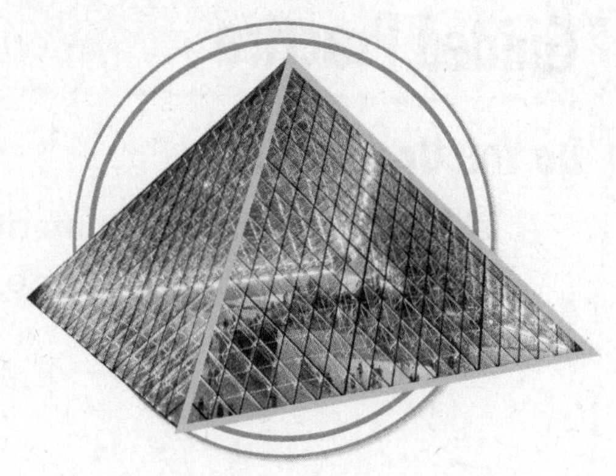

12. **MP.2 Reasoning** A pizza is divided into twelve equal slices. Glenn and Ben each ate $\frac{1}{6}$ of the pizza on Monday. The next day Ben ate $\frac{1}{2}$ of the pizza that was leftover. How many slices of the original pizza remain? Explain your reasoning.

13. During a sale at the bookstore, books sold for \$3 and magazines sold for \$2.50. Jan spent \$16 and bought a total of 6 books and magazines. How many of each did she buy?

14. **Higher Order Thinking** The measures of two angles of a triangle are 23° and 67°. Is the triangle acute, right, or obtuse? Use geometric terms in your explanation.

15. **MP.1 Make Sense and Persevere** An animal shelter houses dogs, cats, and rabbits. There are 126 animals at the shelter. Of the animals, $\frac{1}{3}$ are cats. Three fourths of the remaining animals are dogs. How many of the animals are rabbits? Show your work.

Common Core Assessment

16. Two sides of a triangle measure 5 inches and 6 inches. Jason says the triangle must be scalene. Is Jason correct? Explain.

Name ____________________

Homework & Practice 16-1

Classify Triangles

Another Look!

You can classify triangles by the lengths of their sides and the measures of their angles.

Measures of Angles	Lengths of Sides
Acute All angles are less than 90°.	**Equilateral** All sides are the same length.

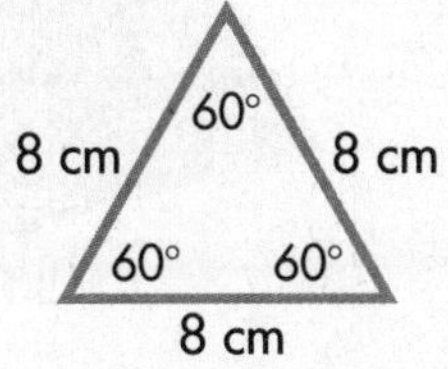

This triangle is both equilateral and acute.

Remember that the sum of the angle measures in a triangle is 180°.

Right One right angle	**Isosceles** At least two sides are the same length.

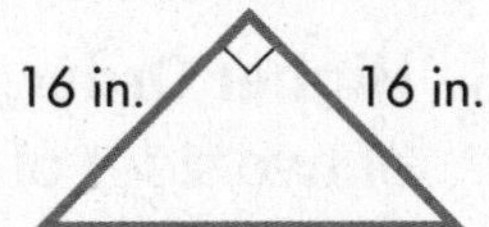

This triangle is both isosceles and right.

Obtuse One obtuse angle	**Scalene** No sides are the same length.

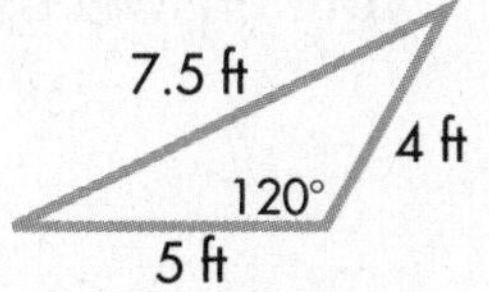

This triangle is both scalene and obtuse.

In **1–9**, classify each triangle by its sides and then by its angles.

1.

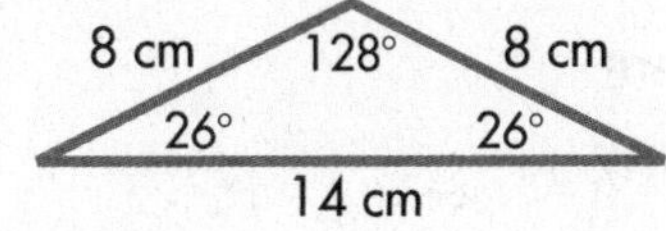

2.

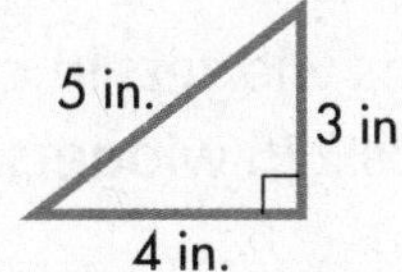

3.

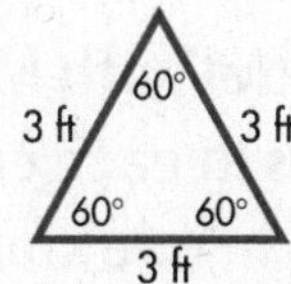

4.

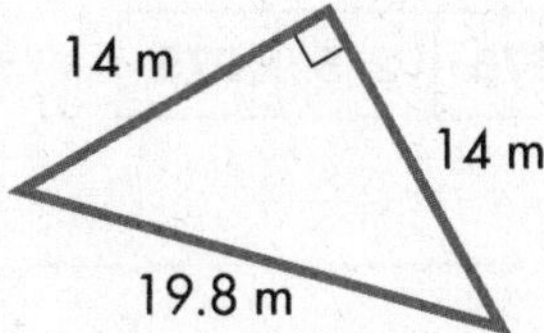

5.

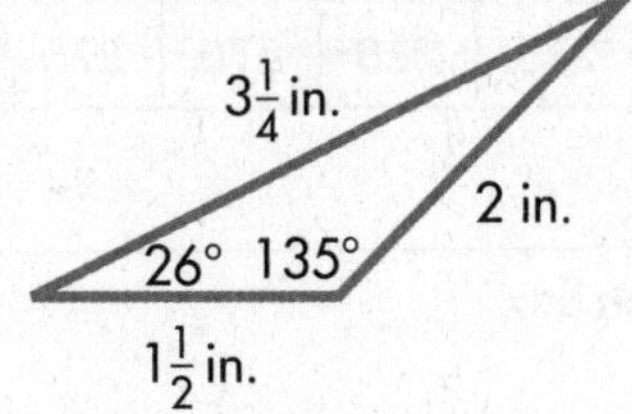

6.

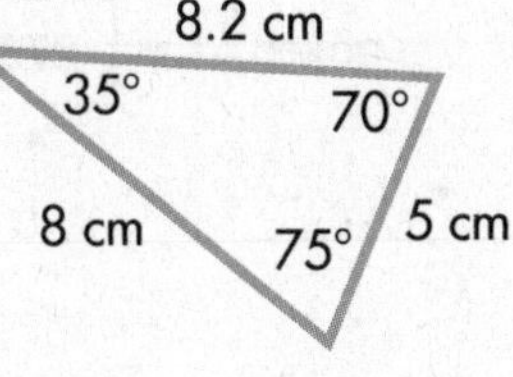

7.

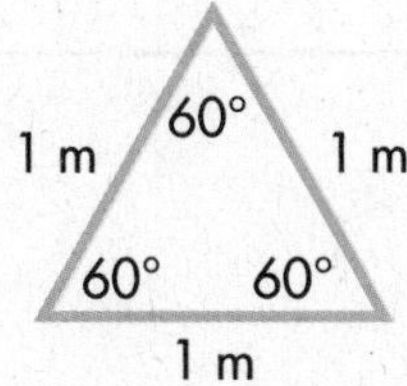

8.

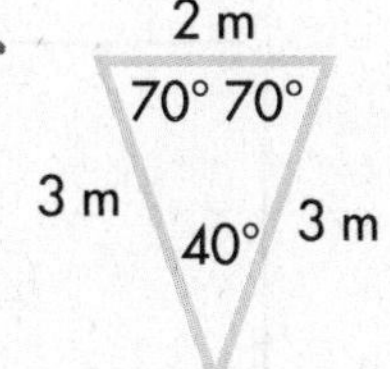

9.

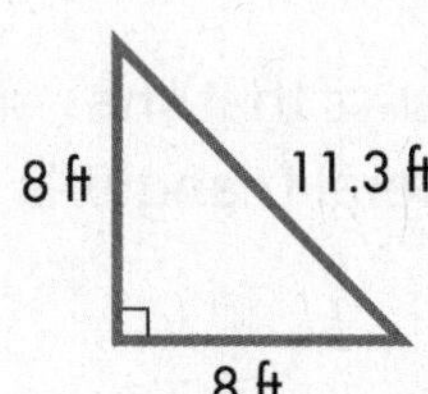

10. Judy bought a new tent for a camping trip. Look at the side of the tent with the opening. Classify the triangle by its sides and its angles.

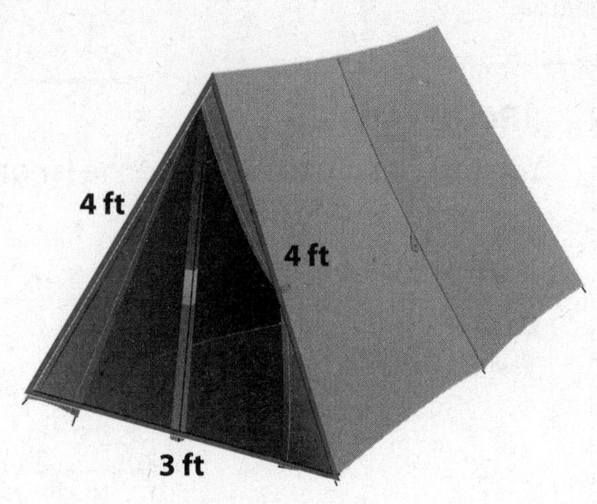

11. **MP.4 Model with Math** Judy bought her tent on sale. The sale price was $70 off the original price. Judy also used a coupon for an extra $15 off. If Judy paid $125 for the tent, what was its original price? Write an equation to show your work.

12. **MP.3 Critique Reasoning** Ted says that the triangle below cannot be classified because all sides are different lengths. Is Ted correct? Explain why or why not.

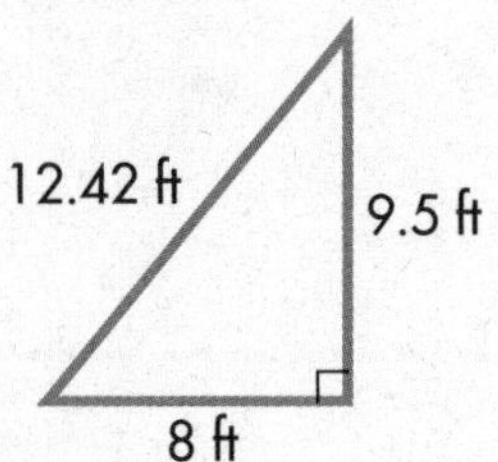

13. **Higher Order Thinking** The lengths of two sides of a triangle are 15 inches each. The third side measures 10 inches. What type of triangle is this? Explain your answer using geometric terms.

14. **MP.4 Model with Math** A factory ships widgets in crates. There are 12 boxes in each crate. Each box holds 275 widgets. How many widgets are in one crate?

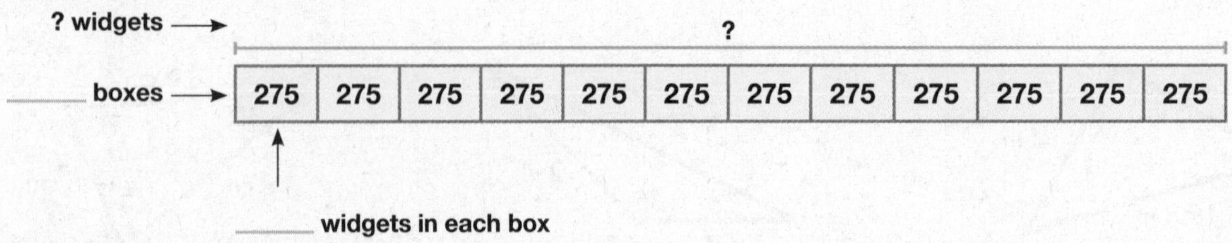

Common Core Assessment

15. Claire says that she can draw an obtuse equilateral triangle. Is she correct? Explain.

Name ______________________________

Lesson 16-2
Classify Quadrilaterals

I can ...
classify quadrilaterals by their properties.

Content Standards 5.G.B.3, 5.G.B.4
Mathematical Practices MP.1, MP.2, MP.3, MP.6, MP.8

Solve & Share

Draw any length line segment that will fit in the space below. The line segment can go in any direction, but it must be straight. Draw another line segment of any length that is parallel to the first one. Connect the ends of each line segment with line segments to make a closed four-sided figure. What does your shape look like? Can you classify it? ***Discuss your ideas with a partner.***

You can use reasoning to find the differences and similarities between shapes when classifying quadrilaterals. *Show your work!*

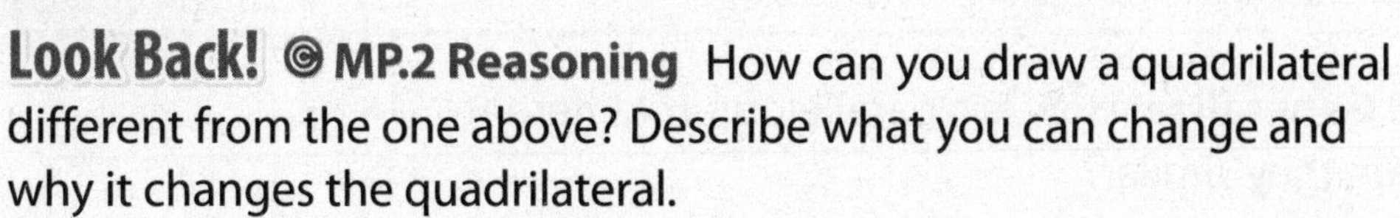

Look Back! **MP.2 Reasoning** How can you draw a quadrilateral different from the one above? Describe what you can change and why it changes the quadrilateral.

What Are Some Properties of Quadrilaterals?

A

Categories of quadrilaterals are classified by their properties.

Think about the questions below when you are classifying quadrilaterals.

- How many pairs of opposite sides are parallel?
- Which sides have equal lengths?
- How many right angles are there?

B

A trapezoid has one pair of parallel sides.

A parallelogram has two pairs of opposite sides parallel and equal in length.

C

A rectangle has four right angles.

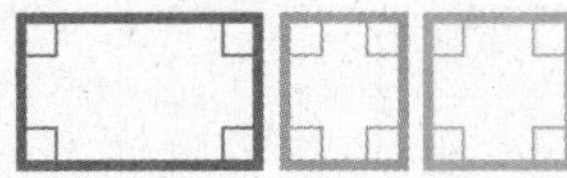

A rhombus has all sides the same length.

D

A square has all sides the same length.

A square has four right angles.

Convince Me! **MP.8 Generalize** How is a parallelogram different from a rhombus? How are they similar?

Name ____________________

Guided Practice*

Do You Understand?

1. **Vocabulary** How are a square and a rhombus alike?

2. **Vocabulary** How is a trapezoid different from a parallelogram?

Use the questions at the top of page 858 to help you classify the quadrilaterals.

Do You Know How?

In **3–6**, use as many names as possible to identify each polygon. Tell which name is most specific.

3. 

4. 

5.

6.

Independent Practice

7. Identify the polygon using as many names as possible.

8. Identify the polygon using as many names as possible.

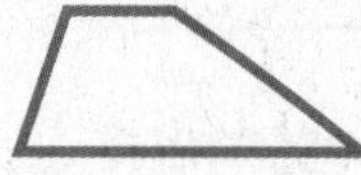

9. Why is a square also a rectangle?

10. Which special quadrilateral is both a rectangle and a rhombus? Explain how you know.

*For another example, see Set B on page 877.

Math Practices and Problem Solving

11. Each time Sophie makes a cut to a polygon, she can make a new type of polygon. What kind of polygon is left if Sophie cuts off the top of the isosceles triangle shown?

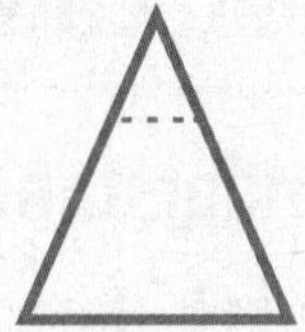

12. **Number Sense** Donald's car gets about 30 miles per gallon. About how many miles can Donald drive on 9.2 gallons of gas? At $3.15 a gallon, about how much would that amount of gas cost?

13. **MP.2 Reasoning** Is it possible to draw a quadrilateral that is not a rectangle but has at least one right angle? Explain.

14. The area of a quadrilateral is 8.4 square feet. Find two decimals that give a product close to 8.4.

15. **MP.6 Be Precise** Suppose you cut a square into two identical triangles. What type of triangles will you make?

16. **Higher Order Thinking** A parallelogram has four sides that are the same length. Is it a square? Explain how you know.

What do you know about the sides of a parallelogram?

Common Core Assessment

17. Which could be the side lengths of a parallelogram?

Ⓐ 5 m, 5 m, 5 m, 1 m

Ⓑ 1 m, 5 m, 1 m, 5 m

Ⓒ 4 m, 1 m, 1 m, 1 m

Ⓓ 1 m, 1 m, 1 m, 5 m

18. Which of the following statements is **NOT** true?

Ⓐ A rhombus has all sides the same length.

Ⓑ A square has 4 right angles.

Ⓒ A trapezoid has no parallel sides.

Ⓓ A rectangle has 4 right angles.

Name ____________________

Homework & Practice 16-2

Classify Quadrilaterals

Another Look!

Some quadrilaterals have special properties.

A **trapezoid** has one pair of parallel sides.

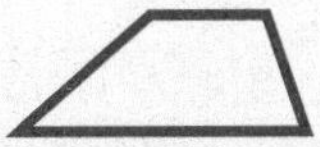

A **parallelogram** has two pairs of opposite sides parallel and equal.

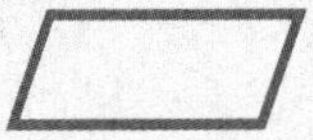

A **rectangle** is a parallelogram with 4 right angles.

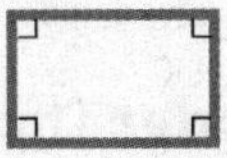

A **rhombus** is a parallelogram with 4 equal sides.

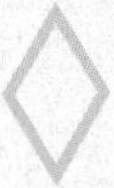

A **square** is a parallelogram with 4 right angles and 4 equal sides.

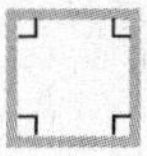

In **1–6**, identify each polygon. Describe each polygon by as many names as possible.

1.

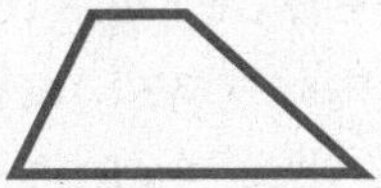

2.

3.

4.

5.

6.

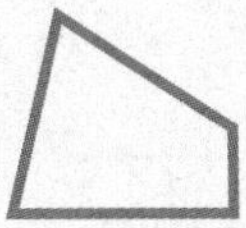

7. **MP.6 Be Precise** A parallelogram has one side that is 4 centimeters long and one side that is 6 centimeters long. What is the perimeter of the parallelogram? Explain.

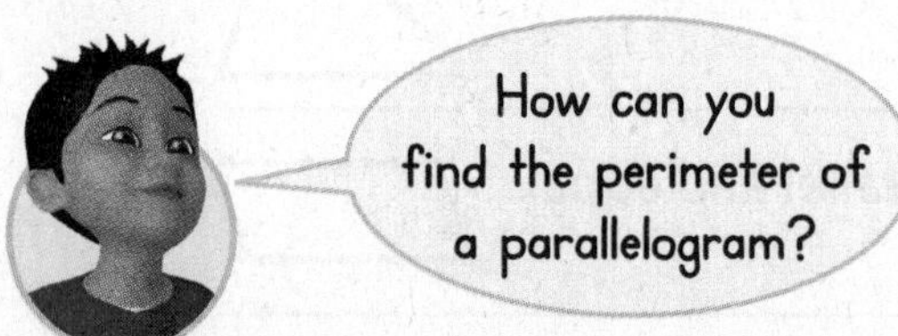

How can you find the perimeter of a parallelogram?

8. **Math and Science** In 2013, a wildfire near Yosemite National Park burned about 400 square miles of forest. If one square mile equals 640 acres, about how many acres of forest were burned? Show your work.

9. **Higher Order Thinking** Marvin says that all rhombuses are squares. Aretha says that all squares are rhombuses. Who is correct? Explain.

10. **MP.3 Construct Arguments** What characteristics help you tell the difference between a rhombus and a rectangle? Explain.

11. Bella is putting 576 cicadas into 8 different terrariums. The same number of cicadas will be put into each one. How many cicadas will be in each terrarium?

576 cicadas							
?	?	?	?	?	?	?	?

12. **MP.1 Make Sense and Persevere** A store has caps on display. Five of the caps are red. There are 4 more blue caps than green caps. There are 3 fewer yellow caps than green caps. If there are 24 caps in all, how many caps are there of each color?

Common Core Assessment

13. What is the length of side a?

Ⓐ 9 mm
Ⓑ 13 mm
Ⓒ 22 mm
Ⓓ 44 mm

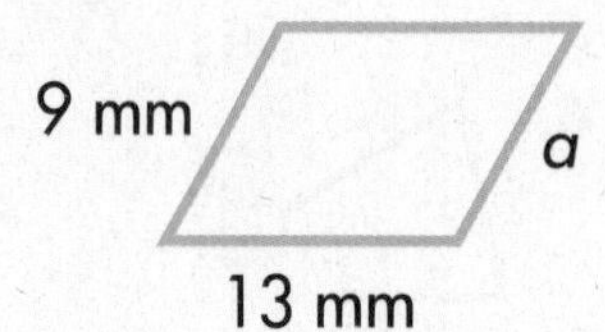

14. Which of the following statements is **NOT** true?

Ⓐ A trapezoid is a rectangle.
Ⓑ A square is also a rectangle.
Ⓒ A rectangle is a quadrilateral.
Ⓓ A square is also a rhombus.

Name ______________________

Lesson 16-3
Continue to Classify Quadrilaterals

Solve & Share

Look at the quadrilaterals below. In the table, write the letters for all the figures that are trapezoids. Then do the same with each of the other quadrilaterals.
Work with a partner to solve this problem.

I can ...
classify quadrilaterals using a hierarchy.

Content Standards 5.G.B.3, 5.G.B.4
Mathematical Practices MP.2, MP.3, MP.4, MP.5, MP.7

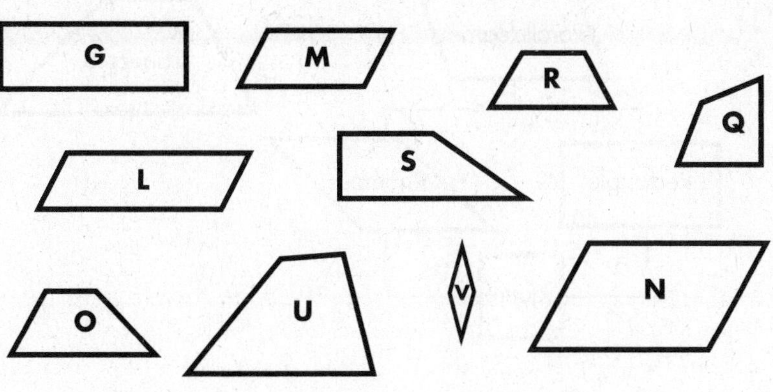

You can use reasoning to classify quadrilaterals that have more than one property. *Show your work!*

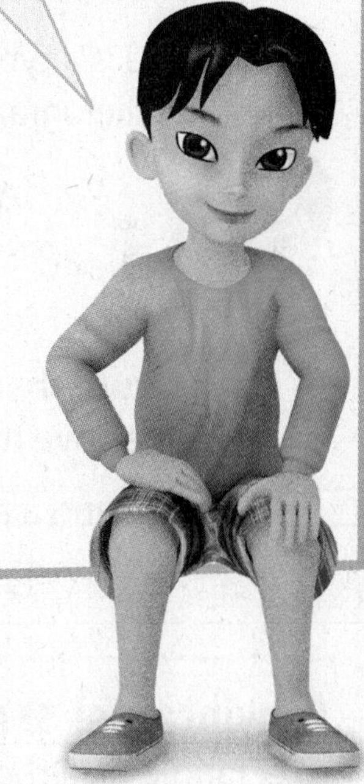

List the letter of each figure in each group.

Trapezoids	
Parallelograms	
Rectangles	
Squares	
Rhombuses	

Look Back! **MP.3 Construct Arguments** Which quadrilateral had the most figures listed? Explain why this group had the most.

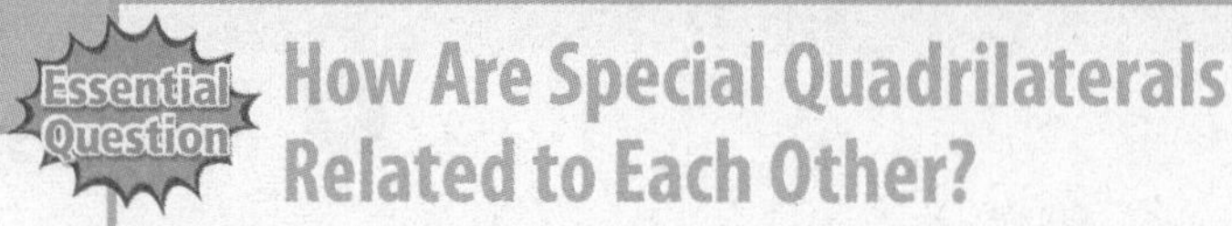

A

This "family tree" shows how special quadrilaterals are related to each other.

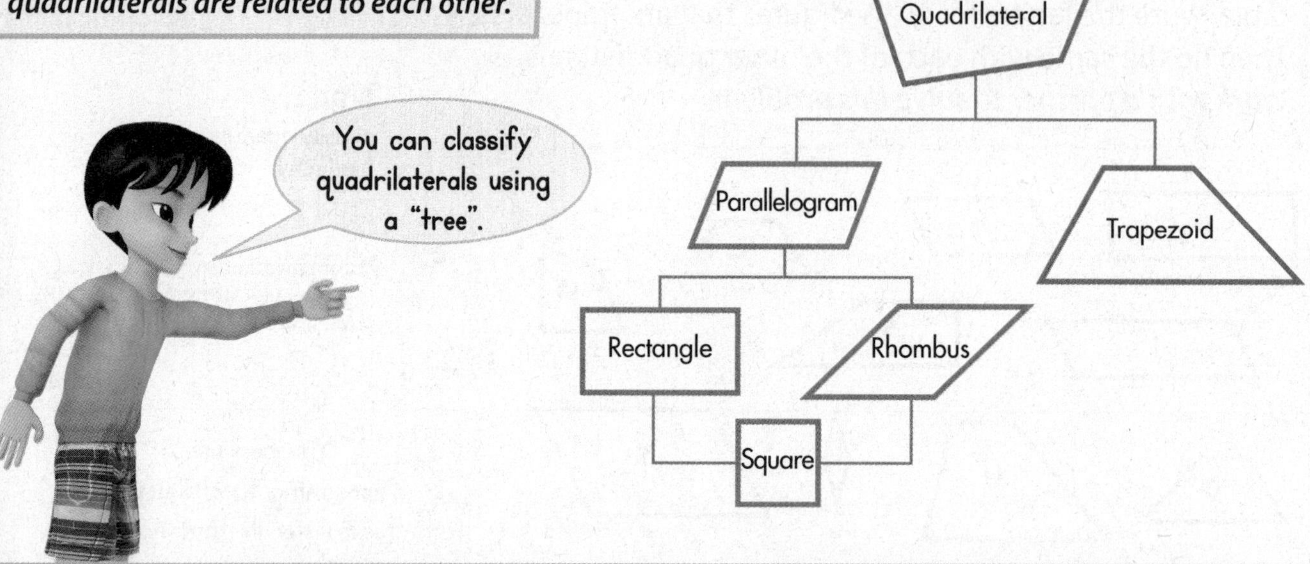

B

Each branch of the tree shows a subcategory of the figure above.

A square is a type of rectangle. All rectangles are parallelograms.

A category can have more than one subcategory.

Each figure shares all of the properties of the figures above it.

A square and a rectangle have four right angles.

C

All of the figures below the parallelogram have two pairs of parallel opposite sides.

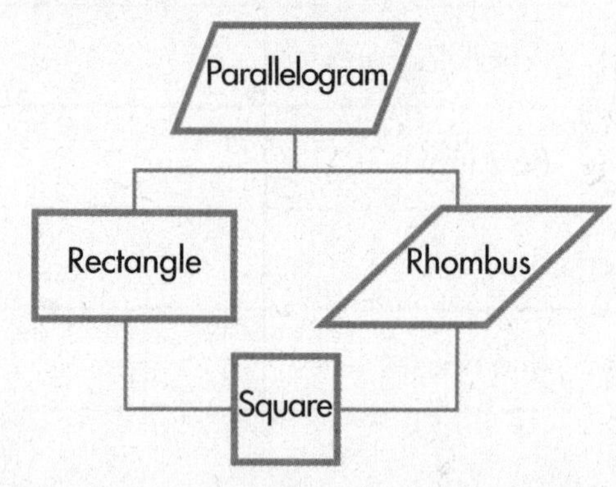

Convince Me! **MP.3 Construct Arguments** When can a rectangle be a rhombus? Can a rhombus be a rectangle? Explain using examples.

Name

Practice Buddy Tools Assessment

Guided Practice*

Do You Understand?

1. Explain how the family tree diagram on page 864 shows that every square is a rectangle.

2. How are a rectangle and a rhombus alike?

Do You Know How?

In **3–6**, tell whether each statement is true or false.

3. All rectangles are squares.

4. Every rhombus is a parallelogram.

5. Parallelograms are special rectangles.

6. A trapezoid can be a square.

Independent Practice

In **7–10**, write whether each statement is true or false.

7. All rhombuses are rectangles.

8. Every trapezoid is a quadrilateral.

9. Rhombuses are special parallelograms.

10. All rectangles are quadrilaterals.

11. What properties does the shape have? Why is it not a parallelogram?

12. Why is a square also a rhombus?

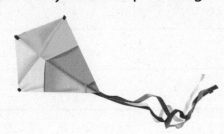

*For another example, see Set C on page 878.

Math Practices and Problem Solving

13. **MP.3 Construct Arguments** Draw a quadrilateral with one pair of parallel sides and two right angles. Explain why this figure is a trapezoid.

14. **MP.5 Use Appropriate Tools** A reflecting pool is shaped like a rhombus with a side length of 6 meters. What is the perimeter of the pool? Explain how you found your answer.

Think about the properties of a rhombus to help you solve.

15. **MP.4 Model with Math** A bakery sold 31 bagels in the first hour of business and 42 bagels in the second hour. If the bakery had 246 bagels to start with, how many bagels were left after the second hour?

246 bagels

31	42	?

16. **Higher Order Thinking** Ann says the figure below is a square. Pablo says that it is a parallelogram. Felix says that it is a rectangle. Can they all be right? Explain.

Common Core Assessment

17. Jeff says that the figure below is a rhombus.

Part A

Is Jeff correct? Explain.

Part B

What names could he use to describe the figure?

Name ______________________

Homework & Practice 16-3

Continue to Classify Quadrilaterals

Another Look!

You can use the family tree to classify quadrilaterals and understand their relationships.

All squares are rectangles.
All squares are rhombuses.
All rectangles are parallelograms.
All rhombuses are parallelograms.
All parallelograms are quadrilaterals.
All trapezoids are quadrilaterals.

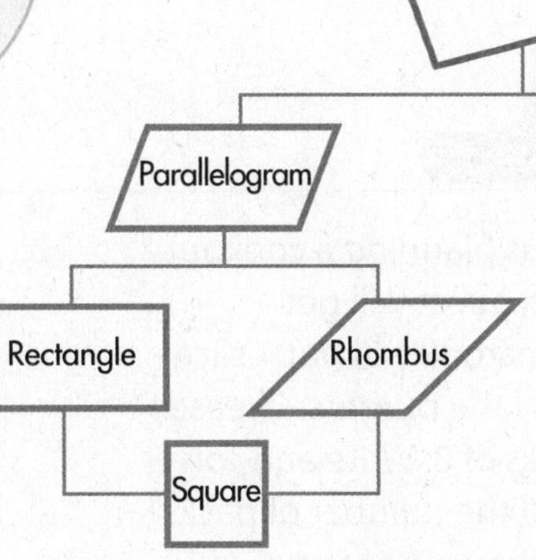

In **1–4**, write whether each statement is true or false.

1. All trapezoids are parallelograms.

2. Every trapezoid is a rectangle.

3. Squares are special parallelograms.

4. All quadrilaterals are squares.

5. The figure shown below is an isosceles trapezoid. The two sides that are not parallel have the same length. How could you add this shape to the family tree diagram?

6. Why is a parallelogram not the same type of quadrilateral as a trapezoid? Explain how you know.

Look at the relationships in the family tree to help you answer.

7. **MP.3 Construct Arguments** Harriet says that it is not possible to draw a quadrilateral that is not a trapezoid and not a parallelogram. Is Harriet correct? Explain why or why not.

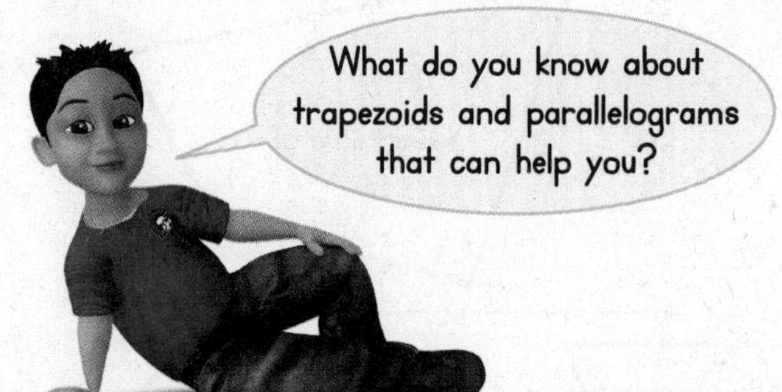

What do you know about trapezoids and parallelograms that can help you?

8. **MP.7 Use Structure** The table shows Henry's savings over several weeks. If the pattern continues, what will Henry's savings be in Week 10? Tell how you know.

DATA

Week	Savings
0	$6.50
1	$7.50
2	$8.50
3	$9.50

9. **Algebra** Sharona is planning a cookout for 42 people. Each guest will get 1 veggie burger. Sharona will put 1 slice of cheese on half of the burgers. Cheese slices come in packs of 8. Write and solve an equation to find the number of packs of cheese, p, that Sharon needs to buy.

10. **Higher Order Thinking** Suppose a trapezoid is defined as a quadrilateral with at least one pair of parallel sides. How would the quadrilateral "family tree" change?

Common Core Assessment

11. Marissa says that the figure below is a rectangle.

Part A

Is Marissa correct? Explain.

Part B

What names could she use to describe the figure?

Name ________________________________

Math Practices and Problem Solving

Lesson 16-4

Construct Arguments

I can ...
construct arguments about geometric figures.

Mathematical Practices MP.3 Also MP.1, MP.2, MP.6, MP.7
Content Standards 5.G.B.3, 5.G.B.4

Solve & Share

Alfie thinks that if he cuts a parallelogram along a diagonal, he will get two triangles that have the same shape and size. Is he correct? ***Solve this problem any way you choose.*** Construct a math argument to justify your answer.

Thinking Habits

Be a good thinker! These questions can help you.

- How can I use numbers, objects, drawings, or actions to justify my argument?
- Am I using numbers and symbols correctly?
- Is my explanation clear and complete?
- Can I use a counterexample in my argument?

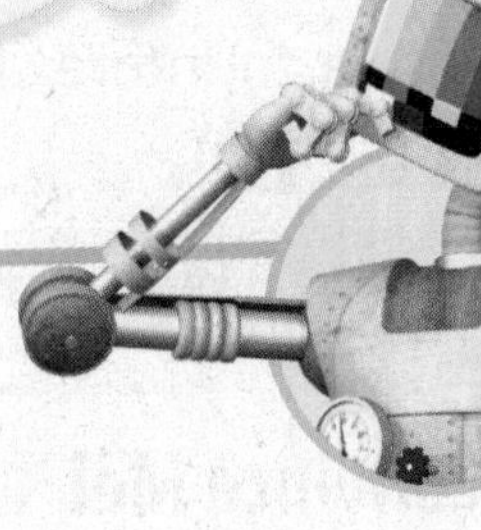

Look Back! **MP.3 Construct Arguments** Suppose you cut along a diagonal of a rhombus, a rectangle, or a square. Would you get two triangles that have the same shape and size? Construct an argument to justify your answer.

A-Z
Learn Glossary

Essential Question

How Can You Construct Arguments?

A

Anika says, "If I draw a diagonal in a parallelogram, I will always form two right triangles." Is she correct? Construct a math argument to justify your answer.

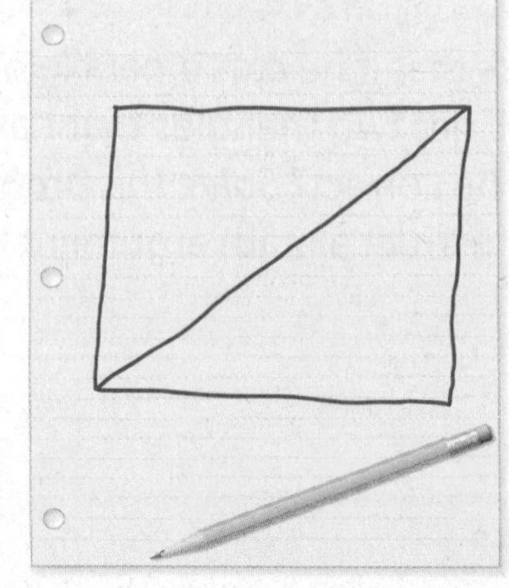

You can construct an argument using what you know about triangles and quadrilaterals.

What do I need to do to solve the problem?

I need to examine several cases, including special parallelograms. Then I need to state my conclusion and write a good argument to justify it.

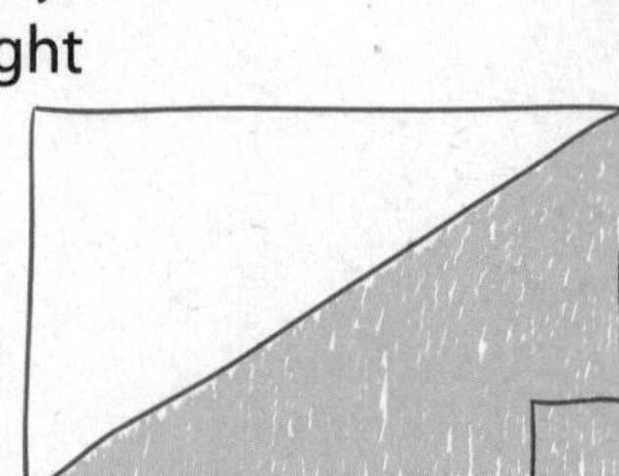
Here's my thinking...

B

How can I construct an argument?

I can

- use math to explain my reasoning.
- use the correct words and symbols.
- give a complete explanation.
- use a counterexample in my argument.

C

Anika is incorrect. The triangles are right triangles only when the parallelogram is a rectangle or square.

Rectangles and squares have four right angles. So, each triangle formed by drawing a diagonal will have a right angle and be a right triangle. But if the parallelogram does not have right angles, each triangle will not have a right angle.

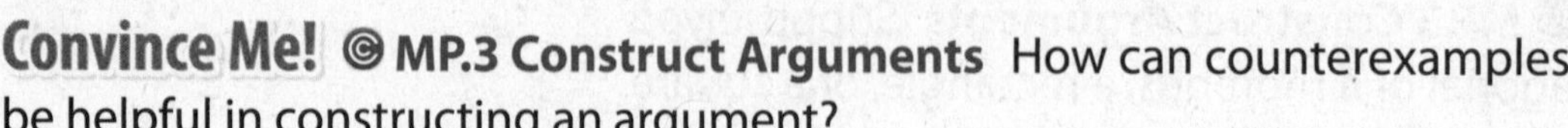

Convince Me! © **MP.3 Construct Arguments** How can counterexamples be helpful in constructing an argument?

Name ____________________

Guided Practice*

MP.3 Construct Arguments

Jamal says, "Two equilateral triangles that are the same size can be joined to make a rhombus."

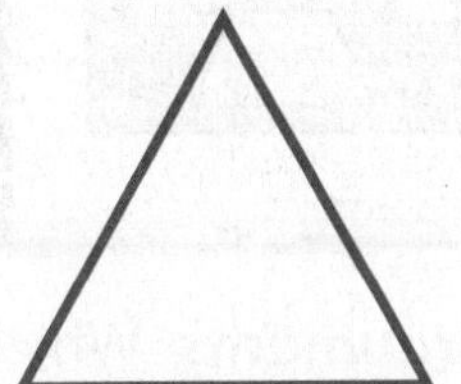

1. What is the definition of an equilateral triangle? What is the definition of a rhombus?

2. How could knowing these definitions help in constructing your argument?

3. Is Jamal correct? Construct an argument to justify your answer.

Independent Practice

MP.3 Construct Arguments

Lauren says, "If I draw a diagonal in a trapezoid, neither of the triangles formed will have a right angle."

4. What is the definition of a trapezoid?

5. Draw examples of a diagonal in a trapezoid.

6. How can you use a drawing to construct an argument?

7. Is Lauren correct? Construct a math argument to justify your answer.

Stuck? Answering this question might help. *Have I interpreted all word meanings correctly?*

A diagram can help you construct arguments.

*For another example, see Set D on page 878.

Math Practices and Problem Solving

Common Core Performance Assessment

Flag Making

Mr. Herrera's class is studying quadrilaterals. The class worked in groups, and each group made a "quadrilateral flag."

8. **MP.3 Construct Arguments** Which flags show parallelograms? Construct a math argument to justify your answer.

9. **MP.2 Reasoning** Explain how you would classify the quadrilaterals on the green flag. on the blue flag.

The definitions of the different quadrilaterals will help you construct arguments.

10. **MP.3 Critique Reasoning** Marcia's group made the red flag. Bev's group made the orange flag. Both girls say their flag shows all rectangles. Critique the reasoning of both girls and explain who is correct.

11. **MP.1 Make Sense and Persevere** Does it make sense for this quadrilateral to be on any of the flags?

Name ____________________

Homework & Practice 16-4

Construct Arguments

Another Look!

If two angles in a triangle each measure 40°, the triangle is an obtuse triangle.

Tell how you can construct a math argument to justify the statement above.

- I can make a drawing to support my argument.
- I can make my explanation clear and complete.

To help you find the measure of the third angle, remember that the sum of the measures of the angles in a triangle is 180°.

Construct a math argument to justify the statement.

The sum of the measures of two angles is $2 \times 40° = 80°$. The measure of the third angle is $180° - 80° = 100°$. An angle that measures more than 90° is an obtuse angle, so the third angle is obtuse. Since the triangle contains an obtuse angle, it is an obtuse triangle.

100°

40° 40°

MP.3 Construct Arguments

Samantha says, "A triangle can have three right angles."

1. List some properties of a triangle. How does knowing the properties of a triangle help in constructing your argument?

Think about whether properties, definitions, and diagrams would help you construct arguments.

2. How can you use a drawing to construct an argument?

3. Is Samantha correct? Construct a math argument to justify your answer.

Ⓒ Common Core Performance Assessment

Stained-Glass Window

Quentin took a picture of a stained-glass window he saw at the library. He is using what he has learned about triangles to classify the triangles in the window.

4. **MP.3 Construct Arguments** Which triangles are right triangles? Construct a math argument to justify your answer.

5. **MP.3 Construct Arguments** Which triangles are right isosceles triangles? Construct a math argument to justify your answer.

6. **MP.3 Construct Arguments** Which triangles are obtuse isosceles triangles? Construct a math argument to justify your answer.

Using definitions of geometric figures can help you to construct arguments.

7. **MP.6 Be Precise** How should Quentin classify Triangles 6, 7, and 8? Use the most precise name you can.

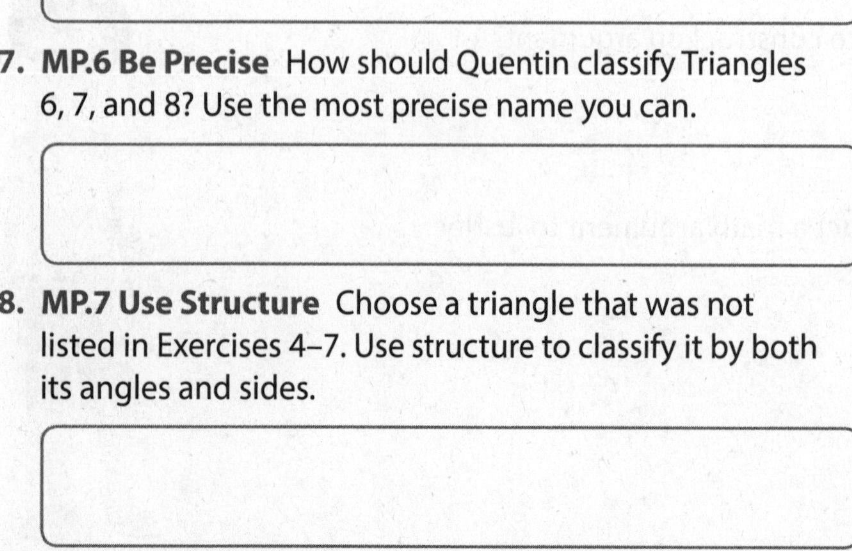

8. **MP.7 Use Structure** Choose a triangle that was not listed in Exercises 4–7. Use structure to classify it by both its angles and sides.

Name ________________________________

Fluency Practice Activity

Find a partner. Get paper and a pencil. Each partner chooses light blue or dark blue.

At the same time, Partner 1 and Partner 2 each point to one of their black numbers. Both partners find the product of the two numbers.

The partner who chose the color where the product appears gets a tally mark. Work until one partner has seven tally marks.

I can ...

multiply multi-digit whole numbers.

Partner 1

29

76

84

91

100

12,264	77,532	204,204	70,499
612,339	64,752	195,141	14,600
4,234	672,900	13,286	11,096
85,200	1,292	71,568	243,100
184,756	565,236	493	221,221
1,547	24,708	511,404	1,428

Partner 2

17

146

852

2,431

6,729

Tally Marks for Partner 1	Tally Marks for Partner 2

TOPIC 16

Vocabulary Review

Word List

- acute triangle
- equilateral triangle
- isosceles triangle
- obtuse triangle
- parallelogram
- rectangle
- rhombus
- right triangle
- scalene triangle
- square
- trapezoid

Understand Vocabulary

Choose the best term from the Word List. Write it on the blank.

1. A 3-sided polygon with at least two sides the same length is a(n) ______________.

2. A polygon with one pair of parallel sides is a(n) ______________.

3. A(n) ______________ has four right angles and all four sides the same length.

4. All three sides of a(n) ______________ are different lengths.

5. The measure of each of the three angles in a(n) ______________ is less than 90°.

6. A rectangle is a special type of ______________.

For each of these terms, draw an example and a non-example.

	Example	Non-example
7. Obtuse triangle	______________	______________
8. Rhombus with no right angle	______________	______________
9. Isosceles right triangle	______________	______________

Use Vocabulary in Writing

10. Alana claims that not all 4-sided polygons with 2 pairs of equal sides are parallelograms. Is Alana correct? Use terms from the Word List in your answer.

Name ___________________________________

Reteaching

Set A pages 851–856

Classify the triangle by the measures of its angles and the lengths of its sides.

Since one of the angles is right, this is a right triangle. Since two of the sides are the same length, this is an isosceles triangle.

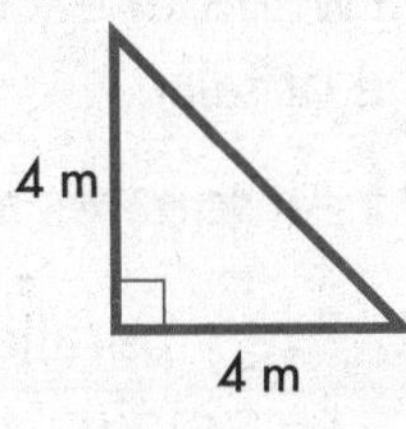

It is a right, isosceles triangle.

Remember that right, obtuse, and acute describe the angles of a triangle. Equilateral, scalene, and isosceles describe the sides of a triangle.

Classify each triangle by the measures of its angles and the lengths of its sides.

1. 60° 60° 60°

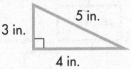

2. 3 in. 5 in. 4 in.

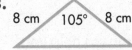

3. 8 cm 105° 8 cm

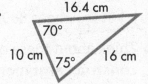

4. 16.4 cm 70° 10 cm 75° 16 cm

Set B pages 857–862

Quadrilaterals are classified by their properties.

A **trapezoid** has one pair of parallel sides.

A **parallelogram** has two pairs of equal parallel sides.

A **rectangle** is a parallelogram with 4 right angles.

A **rhombus** is a parallelogram with 4 equal sides.

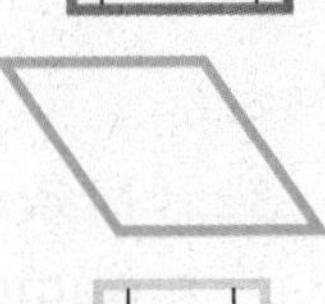

A **square** is a parallelogram with 4 right angles and 4 equal sides.

Remember that some quadrilaterals can be identified by more than one name.

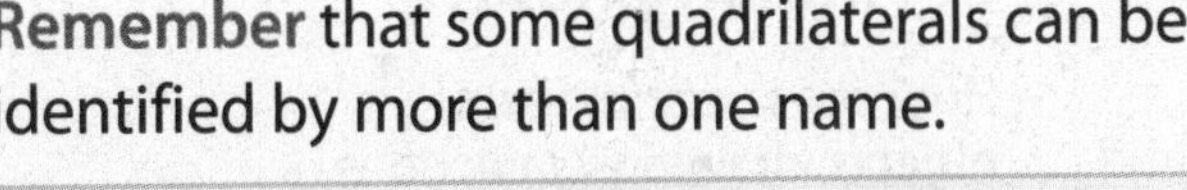

Identify each quadrilateral. Describe each quadrilateral by as many names as possible.

1.

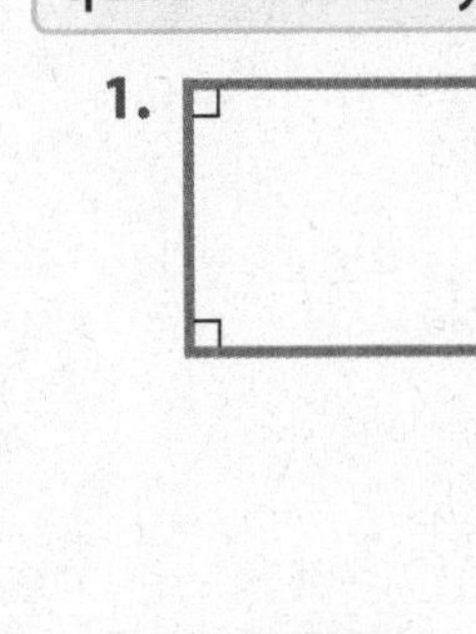

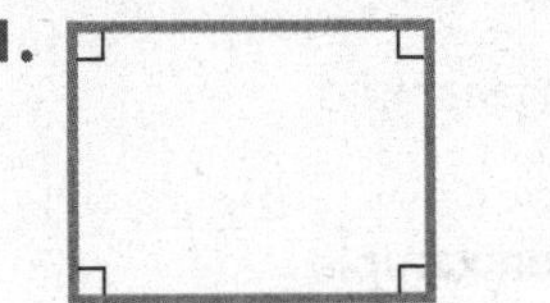

2.

3. **4.**

Set C pages 863–868

This family tree diagram shows how special quadrilaterals are related to each other.

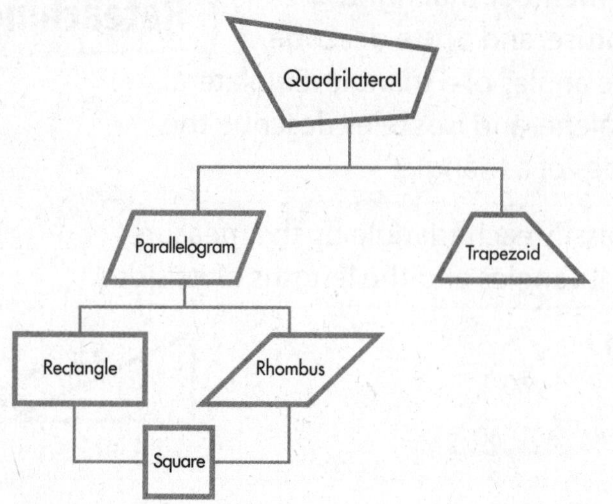

Remember that each branch of the family tree shows a subgroup of the figure above.

Tell whether each statement is true or false.

1. All squares are rectangles.
2. Every parallelogram is a rectangle.
3. Rhombuses are special parallelograms.
4. All trapezoids are quadrilaterals.

Set D pages 869–874

Think about these questions to help you **construct arguments.**

Thinking Habits

- How can I use numbers, objects, drawings, or actions to justify my argument?
- Am I using numbers and symbols correctly?
- Is my explanation clear and complete?
- Can I use a counterexample in my argument?

Remember that using definitions of geometric figures can help you construct arguments.

Malcolm says, "The sum of the angle measures in any rectangle is 180°."

1. What is the definition of a rectangle?
2. Draw a picture of a rectangle and label its angles.
3. Is Malcolm correct? Construct a math argument to justify your answer.

Name ______________________________

TOPIC 16

Assessment

1. Harry drew the triangles shown. Which of the following correctly describes the triangles?

Ⓐ Both triangles have a right angle.

Ⓑ Only one triangle has an acute angle.

Ⓒ Both triangles have at least two obtuse angles.

Ⓓ Both triangles have at least two acute angles.

2. A right triangle has an angle whose measure is 35°. What is the measure of the third angle in the triangle?

Ⓐ 35°

Ⓑ 55°

Ⓒ 72.5°

Ⓓ 145°

3. Choose all the shapes that are parallelograms.

☐

☐

☐

☐

☐

4. The necklace charm shown has one pair of parallel sides. What type of quadrilateral is the charm?

5. Which of the following can be used to describe the square below?

Ⓐ Opposite sides are perpendicular.

Ⓑ All angles are obtuse.

Ⓒ It has 2 acute angles.

Ⓓ All sides are the same length.

6. Nat says that a square is a rectangle because it has 4 right angles. Amy says that a square is a rhombus because it has 4 equal sides. Who is correct? Explain.

7. Look at the rhombus and square below.

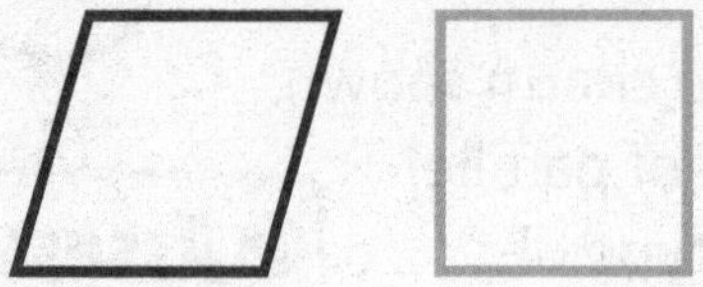

Part A

How are the two figures the same?

Part B

How are the two figures different?

8. Identify the figure below using as many names as possible.

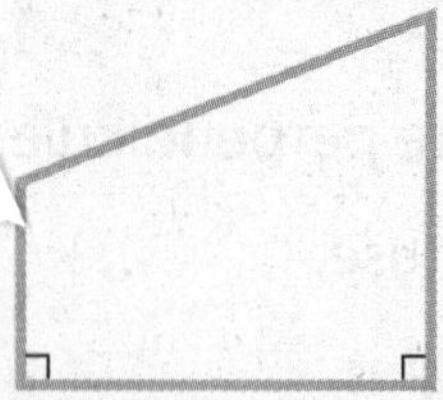

9. Identify the figure below using as many names as possible.

10. A sail on a sailboat is a triangle with two sides perpendicular, and each side is a different length. Which two terms describe the triangular sail?

Ⓐ Isosceles, right

Ⓑ Isosceles, acute

Ⓒ Scalene, right

Ⓓ Scalene, obtuse

11. Anwar says that the shape below is a parallelogram. Is he correct? Explain.

12. Triangle *HJK* is an isosceles triangle. The measures of angles *J* and *K* are equal. The measure of angle *H* is 100°. What is the degree measure of angle *J*?

H

J K

Name ______________________________

Geometry in Art

Artists often use triangles and quadrilaterals in their pictures.

1. Use the **Poster** to answer the following questions.

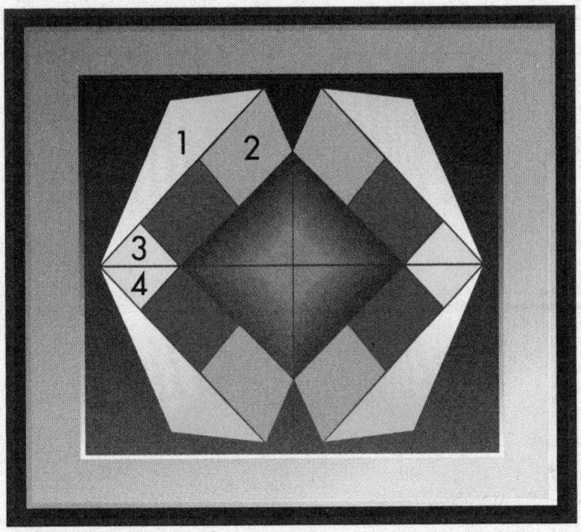

Part A

Classify Triangle 1 in the **Poster** by its angles and by its sides.

Part B

What are all of the names you can use to describe Shape 2 in the **Poster**?

Part C

Triangles 3 and 4 are identical. They are joined in the **Poster** to form a square. Construct a math argument to show why Triangles 3 and 4 are isosceles right triangles.

Part D

If Triangle 3 is joined with another triangle that is the same size and shape, do the two triangles always form a square? Construct a math argument to explain your reasoning.

Part E

What are the measures of the angles of Triangle 3? Note that two angles in an isosceles triangle always have the same measure. Explain.

2. Classify the triangles and quadrilaterals in the **Houses** drawing to answer the following questions.

Part A

Are all the triangles shown in the design isosceles? Are they all equilateral? Construct a math argument, using properties, to explain why or why not.

Part B

All of the quadrilaterals in the **Houses** drawing are rectangles. Does that mean all of the quadrilaterals are parallelograms? Does that mean all are squares? Construct a math argument, using properties, to explain your reasoning.

Step Up to Grade 6

Here's a preview of next year. These lessons help you step up to Grade 6.

Lessons

Name ______________________________

Step Up to Grade 6

Lesson 1
Understand Integers

I can ...
recognize positive numbers and their opposites.

Content Standards 6.NS.C.5, 6.NS.C.6a
Mathematical Practices MP.2, MP.3, MP.5

Solve & Share Leila and Erik recorded these temperatures during an experiment: 10°C, 4°C, 0°C, −4°C, and −10°C. Make a mark on the thermometer at each of these temperatures. Tell how you decided where to place each mark. ***Solve this problem any way you choose.***

5
0
–5
°C

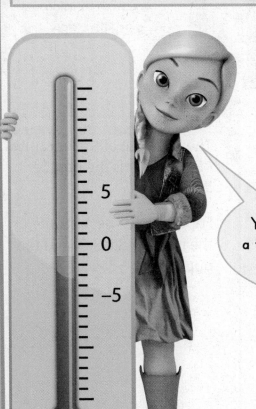

Use Appropriate Tools
You can use a tool, such as a thermometer, to understand how the quantities are related.

Look Back! **MP.2 Reasoning** In what other situations have you seen negative numbers used?

What Are Different Ways to Represent Integers?

A

You can compare integers to degrees of temperature measured on a thermometer. When the temperature goes below zero, it is written with a negative sign.

6°C is 6°C warmer than 0°C.

– 6°C is 6°C colder than 0°C.

The distance from 0°C is the same.

B

A number line can also show numbers greater than and less than 0.

Integers are the set of numbers that includes the counting numbers, their opposites, and zero.

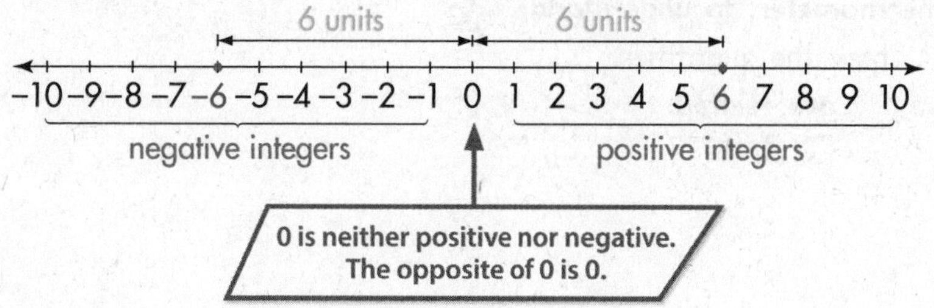

0 is neither positive nor negative. The opposite of 0 is 0.

C

The opposite of the opposite of a number is the number itself.

For example, the opposite of the number 3 is -3, and the opposite of -3 is 3.

Convince Me! © **MP.2 Reasoning** What is the value of $-(-9)$? Explain your reasoning.

Name ____________

Tools Assessment

Guided Practice

Do You Understand?

1. MP.2 Reasoning Which is warmer, 2°C or −5°C? Tell how you know.

2. Which integers do you use for counting?

3. How would you read the number −30?

Do You Know How?

In **4–9**, use the number line below. Give the integer that each point represents. Then write its opposite and tell how many units the number is from 0.

4. *A*
5. *B*
6. *C*
7. *D*
8. *E*
9. *F*

A F D C E B

−10 −5 0 5 10

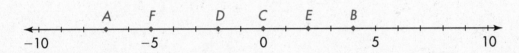

Independent Practice

In **10–25**, write the opposite of each integer and tell how many units the number is from 0.

10. 10
11. −17
12. 22
13. −(−24)
14. −160
15. 48
16. 45
17. −70
18. 80
19. −21
20. 125
21. −5,846
22. −(−100)
23. 472
24. −225
25. −35,425

Math Practices and Problem Solving

26. Ella picked the polygon with the greatest perimeter. Which of the following polygons did she pick?

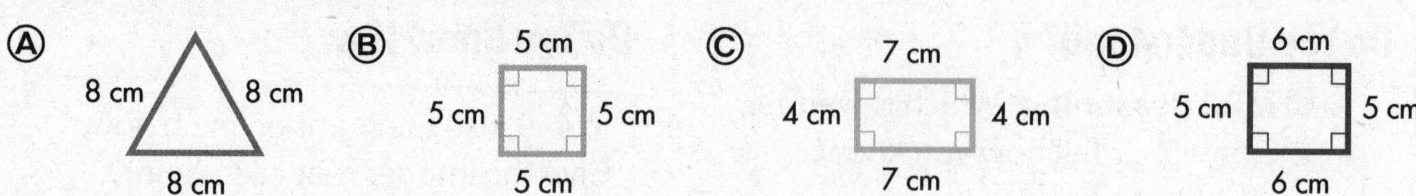

27. **MP.3 Critique Reasoning** Sam said that any integer is the same distance from zero as the opposite of its opposite. Is Sam correct? Critique Sam's reasoning.

28. **Higher Order Thinking** What could the number -18 represent? Using the same situation, what would its opposite represent? What would 0 represent?

29. A dolphin jumps 3 feet above sea level to go through a ring. The dolphin starts at the opposite distance below sea level. How far does the dolphin travel from its starting position to the top of its jump? Tell how you know.

A dolphin can swim to 150 feet below sea level.

Common Core Assessment

30. Choose all the equations that are true.

- ☐ $-5 = 5$
- ☐ $-(9) = -9$
- ☐ $-(-2) = 2$
- ☐ $-3 = -(-3)$
- ☐ $-[-(-6)] = 6$

31. Choose all the statements that are true.

- ☐ 3 steps backward is written -3.
- ☐ 12 feet above sea level is written -12.
- ☐ Leah owes Katy \$5, so Katy has $-\$5$.
- ☐ Thomas owes Joey \$6, so Thomas has $-\$6$.
- ☐ 356 feet below sea level is written -356

Name ______________________________

Solve & Share Write the integers −7, 4, −2, and 5 in order from least to greatest. Explain how you decided. ***Solve this problem any way you choose.***

Step Up to Grade 6

Lesson 2
Compare and Order Integers

I can ...
compare and order integers.

Content Standards 6.NS.C.7a, 6.NS.C.7b
Mathematical Practices MP.2, MP.4, MP.5

Use Appropriate Tools
How can you use a number line or thermometer to solve this problem?
Show your work!

Look Back! **MP.2 Reasoning** How can you use a number line to compare two integers?

Learn
Glossary

Essential Question

How Can You Compare and Order Integers?

A

The table shows the low temperatures during a cold week. Find which day had the lowest temperature. Then order the temperatures from least to greatest.

You can use a number line to help compare and order integers.

DATA

Day	Temperature
Monday	3°C
Tuesday	−6°C
Wednesday	5°C
Thursday	1°C
Friday	−5°C

B

First, locate the integers on a number line.

Number line from −8 to 8 with points marked at −6, −5, 1, 3, 5:
−8 −7 −6 −5 −4 −3 −2 −1 0 1 2 3 4 5 6 7 8

When comparing integers on a number line, the integer that is farthest to the left is the least.

−6 is farther to the left than −5, so −6 is less.

It was colder on Tuesday than on Friday.

You can use symbols to compare integers. Write:

$$-6 < -5 \text{ or } -5 > -6$$

C

Integer values on a number line increase as you move from left to right.

The temperature farthest to the left is −6.

Moving left to right, you can write the temperatures from least to greatest.

−6, −5, 1, 3, 5

Tuesday was the coldest day.

Convince Me! **MP.2 Reasoning** The temperature on Saturday was −8°C. Was the temperature colder on Saturday or on Tuesday? How do you know?

Name ____________________

Guided Practice

Do You Understand?

1. MP.5 Use Appropriate Tools Is -7 to the right or to the left of -2 on a number line? What does that tell you about their values?

2. MP.2 Reasoning If a positive integer a is greater than positive integer b, is the opposite of a greater than or less than the opposite of b. Explain your answer.

3. In the table on the previous page, which day had the warmest temperature?

Do You Know How?

In **4–7**, use <, >, or = to compare.

4. $7 \bigcirc -12$ **5.** $-3 \bigcirc -9$

6. $-8 \bigcirc 0$ **7.** $-(-2) \bigcirc -2$

In **8–11**, order the numbers from least to greatest.

8. $-6, 5, -7$ **9.** $8, -6, -2$

10. $-21, -(-15), -12$ **11.** $3, -3, -19, 11$

Independent Practice

You can use a number line to help.

In **12–19**, use <, >, or = to compare.

12. $5 \bigcirc -18$ **13.** $-(-7) \bigcirc 7$ **14.** $0 \bigcirc 9$ **15.** $18 \bigcirc 9$

16. $-19 \bigcirc -23$ **17.** $4 \bigcirc -6$ **18.** $-25 \bigcirc -32$ **19.** $-1 \bigcirc 3$

In **20–25**, order the numbers from least to greatest.

20. $-1, 9, -8, 11$ **21.** $19, 12, -21, -3$ **22.** $17, 14, -10, 4, -2, -4$

23. $3, -4, 6, -5, 7$ **24.** $-37, 15, 11, -3, 8, 12$ **25.** $57, -21, 43, -6, 7, 23$

Math Practices and Problem Solving

In **26–28**, use the table.

Player	Par Score
Martha	0 (par)
Madison	−2
Tom	−3
Emma	4
Ben	1
Quincy	−4
Jackson	6

26. In miniature golf, the lowest score wins. Scores can be compared to par, which is the number of strokes set for the course. List the top five finishers in order from first place to fifth place.

27. Which players' scores are opposites?

28. Which player's score is farther from 0 on a number line than Quincy's score?

For **29** and **30**, use the number line.

29. MP.4 Model with Math The variables on the number line represent integers. Order the variables from least to greatest value.

x z y

−8 −7 −6 −5 −4 −3 −2 −1 0 1 2 3 4 5 6 7 8

30. Higher Order Thinking Write a statement using > or < to compare x and the opposite of y when $x = -7$ and $y = 4$. Explain.

Common Core Assessment

31. Avery wrote her friends' game scores in order from least to greatest. What did she write?

Ⓐ −4, −7, −9, 6, 10

Ⓑ −4, 6, −7, −9, 10

Ⓒ −4, −7, −9, 6, 10

Ⓓ −9, −7, −4, 6, 10

32. Which number sentence is true?

Ⓐ $-18 > -14$

Ⓑ $-29 < -27$

Ⓒ $4 < -4$

Ⓓ $-(-5) > 7$

Name ________________________________

Solve & Share A grid map of Washington, D.C., is shown below. Kayla wants to visit the White House and the FBI Building. What ordered pairs represent these two locations? ***Solve this problem any way you choose.***

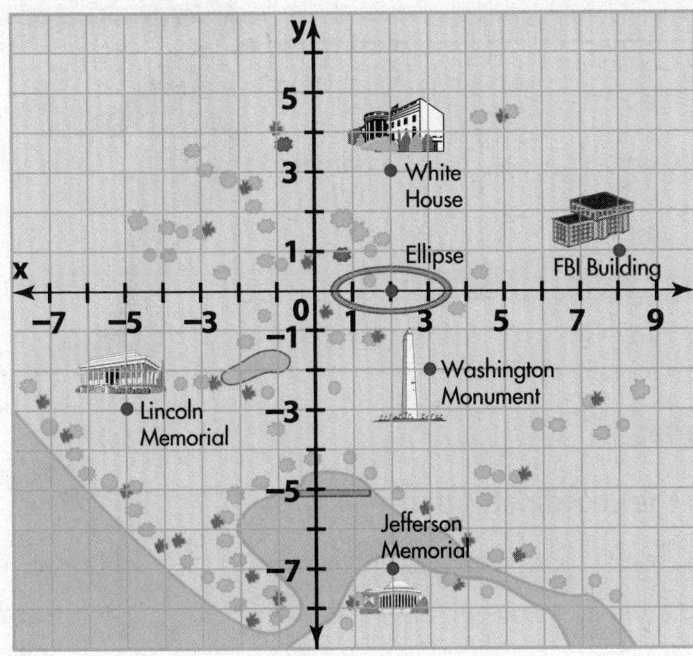

Step Up to Grade 6

Lesson 3
Rational Numbers on the Coordinate Plane

I can ...
graph rational numbers on a coordinate plane.

Content Standards 6.NS.C.6b, 6.NS.C.6c
Mathematical Practices MP.1, MP.2, MP.3

You can make sense and persevere to solve this problem. *Show your work!*

Look Back! **MP.2 Reasoning** Using the grid, give directions on how to move from the Jefferson Memorial to the Washington Monument.

How Can You Graph a Point on a Coordinate Plane?

A

Graph the points Q(2, −3), R(−1, 1), and S(0, 2) on a coordinate plane.

A coordinate plane is a grid containing two number lines that intersect at a right angle at zero. The number lines, called the *x*- and *y*-axes, divide the plane into four quadrants.

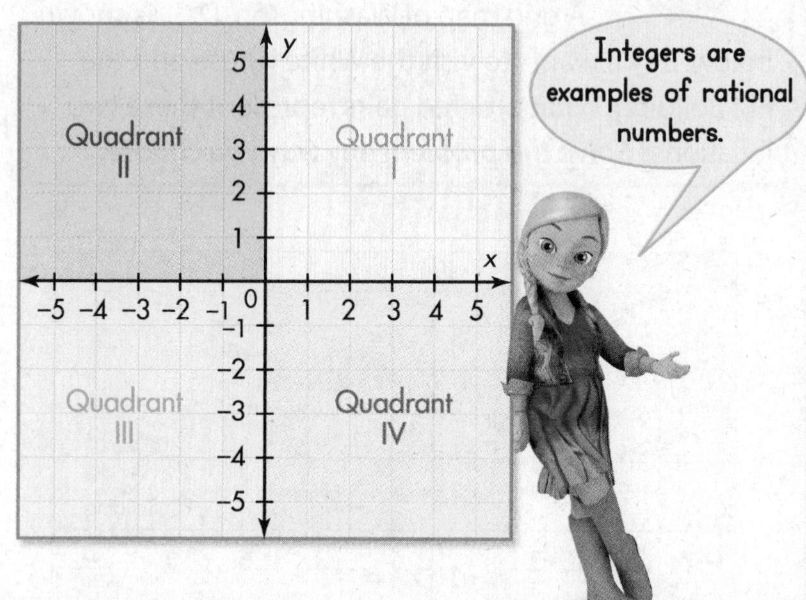

B

Graphing points on a coordinate plane:

An ordered pair (x, y) of numbers gives the coordinates that locate a point relative to each axis.

To graph any point *P* with coordinates (x, y):

- Start at the origin, (0, 0).
- Use the *x*-coordinate to move right (if positive) or left (if negative) along the *x*-axis.
- Then use the *y*-coordinate to move up (if positive) or down (if negative) along the *y*-axis.
- Plot a point on the coordinate grid and label the point.

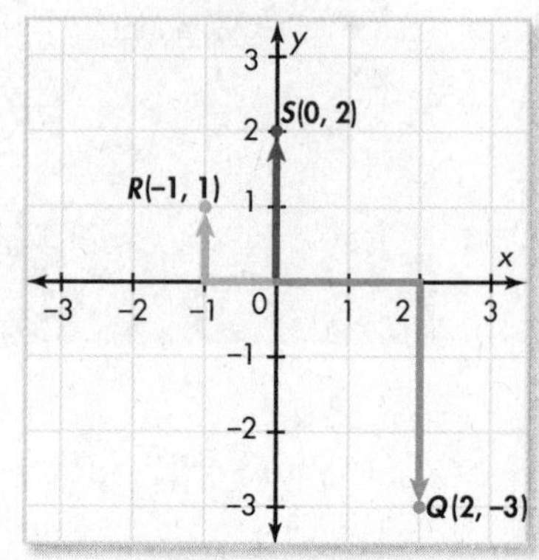

Convince Me! **MP.3 Critique Reasoning** Kayla says that the Lincoln Memorial is located at (−3, −5) on the grid map of Washington, D.C. Do you agree? Critique Kayla's reasoning.

Name ______________________________________

Guided Practice

Do You Understand?

1. In which quadrant does a point lie if its *x*- and *y*- coordinates are negative?

2. MP.3 Construct Arguments Do (4, 5) and (5, 4) locate the same point? Explain.

Do You Know How?

In **3–5**, graph and label the points given.

3. $W(-5, 1)$

4. $X(4, 3)$

5. $Z(-2, 0)$

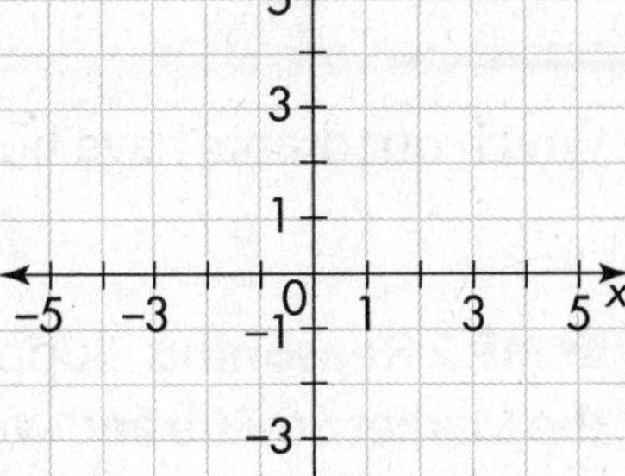

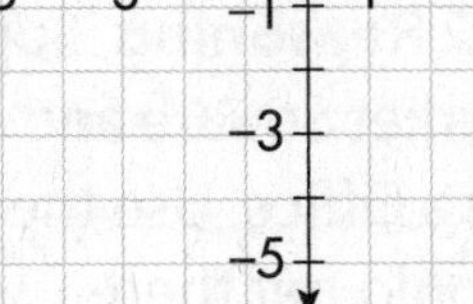

Independent Practice

In **6–13**, graph and label the points given.

6. $A(1, -1)$
7. $B(5, 3)$
8. $C(-3, 2)$
9. $D(5, -2)$
10. $E\left(-4\frac{1}{2}, -4\right)$
11. $F\left(1, 3\frac{1}{4}\right)$
12. $G\left(-5\frac{1}{3}, 0\right)$
13. $H(5, -5)$

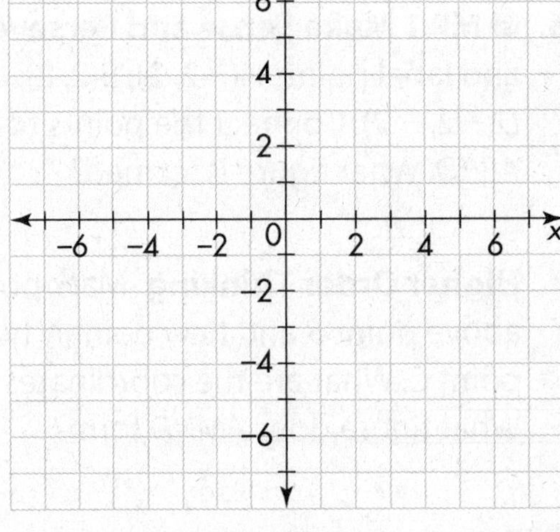

In **14–21**, give the ordered pair of each point.

14. *P*
15. *Q*
16. *R*
17. *S*
18. *H*
19. *J*
20. *K*
21. *L*

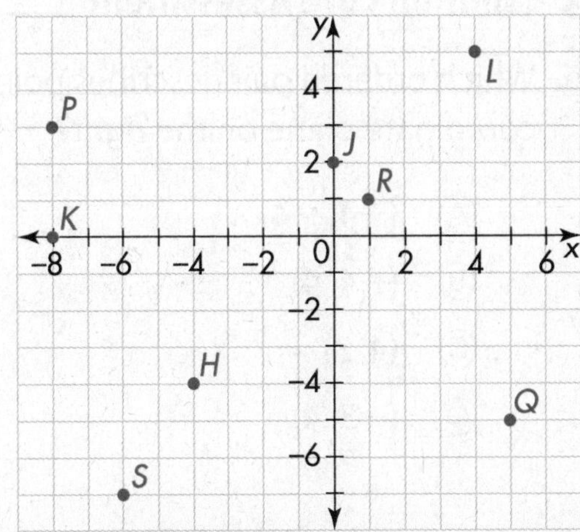

Math Practices and Problem Solving

In **22–25**, use the map at the right. The Market Square is at the origin.

Use the red dots to locate the coordinates of the buildings.

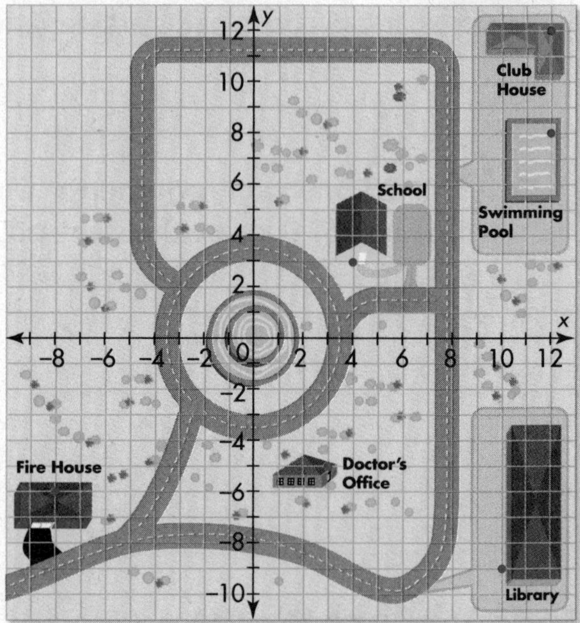

22. Give the coordinates of the Library.

23. What building is located in Quadrant III?

24. Which quadrants have buildings in them?

25. **MP.2 Reasoning** Suppose you were at the Market Square and wanted to get to the Doctor's Office. Use the map to explain how you would get there.

In **26–27**, use the grid to the right.

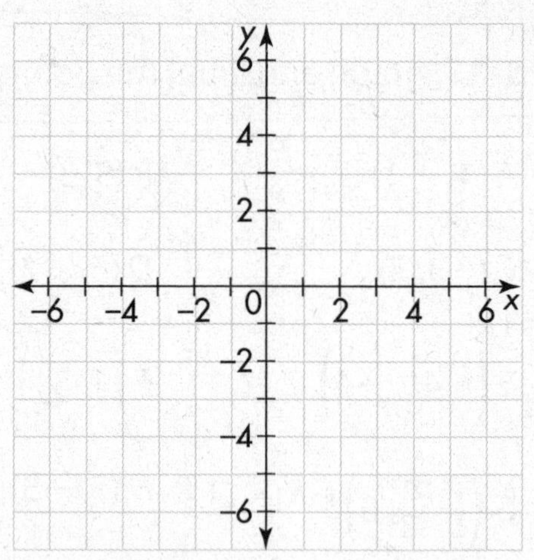

26. **MP.1 Make Sense and Persevere** Graph and label points $A(-2, 2)$, $B(2, 2)$, $C(2, -2)$, and $D(-2, -2)$. Connect the points to form figure *ABCD*. What figure is formed?

27. **Higher Order Thinking** Mark point *M* two units above point *B* and new point *N* two units above point *C*. What are the coordinates of points *M* and *N*? What figure does *AMND* form?

Common Core Assessment

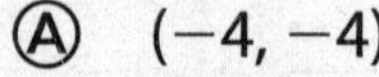

28. Which ordered pair describes point *P* on the coordinate plane on the right?

Ⓐ $(-4, -4)$

Ⓑ $(-4, 4)$

Ⓒ $(4, 3)$

Ⓓ $(-3, 4)$

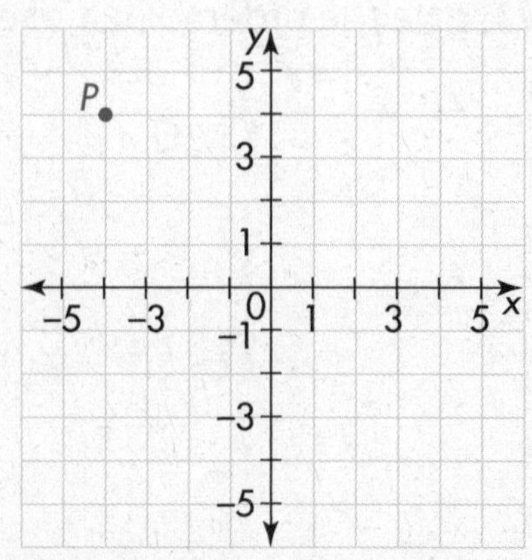

Name ____________________  Solve

Solve & Share There are 15 laptop computers in the computer lab. There are 45 students in the lab. Write an expression that represents the relationship between the number of students and the number of computers. ***Solve this problem any way you choose.***

Step Up to Grade 6

Lesson 4

Understand Ratios

I can ...
use a ratio to describe the relationship between two quantities.

Content Standard 6.RP.A.1
Mathematical Practices MP.2, MP.6

You can use reasoning to compare the number of students and the number of computers.

Look Back! **MP.6 Be Precise** How would your expression be different if you are comparing the number of computers to the number of students?

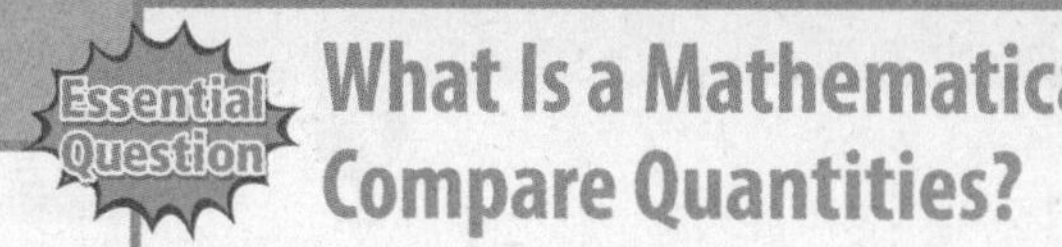

What Is a Mathematical Way to Compare Quantities?

A

Tom's Pet Service takes care of cats and dogs. Currently, there are more dogs than cats. Compare the number of cats to the number of dogs. Then compare the number of cats to the total number of pets at Tom's Pet Service.

B

A ratio is a relationship where for every *x* units of one quantity, there are y units of another quantity.

A ratio can be written three ways: *x* to *y*, *x*:*y*, or $\frac{x}{y}$.

The quantities *x* and *y* in a ratio are called terms.

C

Use a ratio to compare the number of cats to the number of dogs:

14 to 17,

14:17, or

$\frac{14}{17}$

This ratio compares one part to another part.

D

Use a ratio to compare the number of cats to the total number of pets:

14 to 31,

14:31, or

$\frac{14}{31}$

This ratio compares one part to the whole.

Convince Me! ◎ **MP.2 Reasoning** Is the ratio of dogs to cats the same as the ratio of cats to dogs? Explain.

Name ______________________________

Guided Practice

Do You Understand?

1. MP.2 Reasoning Some ratios compare a part to a part. How is this different from a fraction?

2. In the example on the previous page, what is the ratio of total animals to dogs? Write the ratio three ways.

Do You Know How?

In **3** through **5**, use the information below to write a ratio for each comparison in three different ways.

A fifth-grade basketball team has 2 centers, 3 forwards, and 5 guards.

3. Forwards to centers

4. Guards to total team members

5. Centers to guards

Independent Practice

In **6–14**, use the data table to write a ratio for each comparison in three different ways.

A person's blood type is denoted with the letters A, B, and O, and the symbols + and −. The blood type A+ is read as *A positive*. The blood type B− is read as *B negative*.

6. O+ donors to B+ donors

7. A− donors to B+ donors

8. AB+ donors to total donors

9. O− donors to total donors

10. A+ and AB+ donors to O+ donors

11. A− and AB− donors to total donors

12. A+ and B+ donors to A− and B− donors

13. O+ and O− donors to all other donors

14. What comparison does the ratio 6 to 21 represent?

DATA

Blood Donors

Type	Donors
A+	45
B+	20
AB+	6
O+	90
A−	21
B−	0
AB−	4
O−	9
Total	195

Name ______________________

Step Up to Grade 6

Lesson 5
Understand Rates

I can ...
explain what a rate is and solve problems involving rates.

Content Standard 6.RP.A.2
Mathematical Practices MP.1, MP.2, MP.3, MP.4, MP.6

Solve & Share Suppose that you walk 3,540 feet in 20 minutes. How many feet do you walk in 1 minute? ***Solve this problem any way you choose.***

You can model with math by using a bar diagram to help you solve the problem. *Show your work!*

Look Back! **MP.1 Make Sense and Persevere** How do you know your answer is reasonable?

Are There Special Types of Ratios?

A

A rate is a special type of ratio that compares quantities with unlike units of measure.

How far does the car travel in 1 minute?

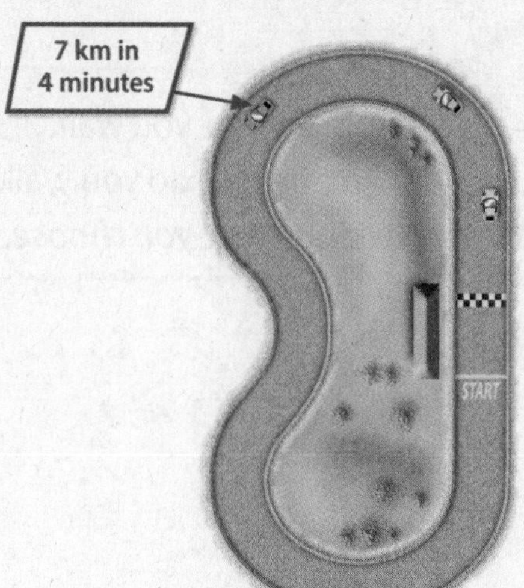

If the comparison is to 1 unit, the rate is called a unit rate.

B

First, write how fast the car travels as a rate.

Write 7 km in 4 minutes as $\frac{7 \text{ km}}{4 \text{ min}}$.

Remember, fractions represent division.

Divide 7 kilometers by 4 minutes.

$$\begin{array}{r} 1.75 \\ 4\overline{)7.00} \\ -\,4 \\ \hline 30 \\ -\,28 \\ \hline 20 \\ -\,20 \\ \hline 0 \end{array}$$

C

To understand why it works, remember that you can divide the terms of any ratio by the same number to find an equal ratio.

$$\frac{7 \div 4}{4 \div 4} = \frac{1.75}{1}$$

The unit rate is $\frac{1.75 \text{ km}}{1 \text{ min}}$.

The car travels 1.75 kilometers in 1 minute.

Convince Me! **MP.2 Reasoning** What is the car's rate for 1 hour? Explain.

Math Practices and Problem Solving

15. **MP.6 Be Precise** A math class surveyed the musical preferences of 42 students. Use the data table to write a ratio for each comparison in three different ways for **a**, **b**, and **c**.

a Students who prefer jazz to students who prefer country

b Students who prefer classic rock to the total number of students surveyed

c Students who prefer rock or classic rock to students who prefer all other types of music

DATA

Favorite Music Type	Number of Students
Rock	12
Classic rock	4
Country	18
Jazz	2
Heavy metal	6

16. **Higher Order Thinking** Use the data table for Problem 15. Write two equivalent ratios using four different types of music. How do you know the ratios are equivalent?

17. On average, about 45,000,000 gallons of water flow over the Niagara Falls in 60 seconds. About how much water flows over the Niagara Falls in one second?

Common Core Assessment

18. There are 12 girls and 18 boys in Martine's class. There are 24 computers in the computer lab. What ratio represents the total number of students compared to the number of computers?

Ⓐ 12:18

Ⓑ 12:24

Ⓒ 18:24

Ⓓ 30:24

19. If the ratio of goldfish to other fish is 8 to 16, which is the ratio of other fish to all fish?

Ⓐ 2 to 3

Ⓑ 3 to 2

Ⓒ 16 to 8

Ⓓ 8 to 24

Name ____________________

Guided Practice

Do You Understand?

1. **MP.6 Be Precise** What is special about a unit rate?

2. Explain the difference in meaning between these two rates: $\frac{\text{5 trees}}{\text{1 chimpanzee}}$ and $\frac{\text{1 tree}}{\text{5 chimpanzees}}$.

Do You Know How?

In **3–6**, write each as a rate and as a unit rate.

3. 20 km in 4 hours

4. 26 cm in 13 s

5. 230 miles on 10 gallons

6. $12.50 for 5 lb

Independent Practice

In **7–18**, write each as a rate and a unit rate.

How are each rate and unit rate related?

7. 35 minutes to run 5 laps

8. 24 butterflies on 12 flowers

9. 112 days for 4 full moons

10. 18 eggs laid in 3 days

11. 56 points scored in 8 games

12. 216 apples growing on 9 trees

13. 125 giraffes on 50 square miles

14. 84 mm in 4 seconds

15. 123 miles driven in 3 hours

16. 210 miles in 7 hours

17. 250 calories in 10 crackers

18. 15 countries visited in 12 days

Math Practices and Problem Solving

In **19–21**, use the bar graph at the right.

19. **MP.2 Reasoning** Give three equivalent rates that describe the top speed of a tuna.

20. At top speeds, how much faster can a swordfish swim than a killer whale?

21. **MP.3 Construct Arguments** Which animal swims at a top speed of about 0.5 mile per minute? Explain how you found your answer.

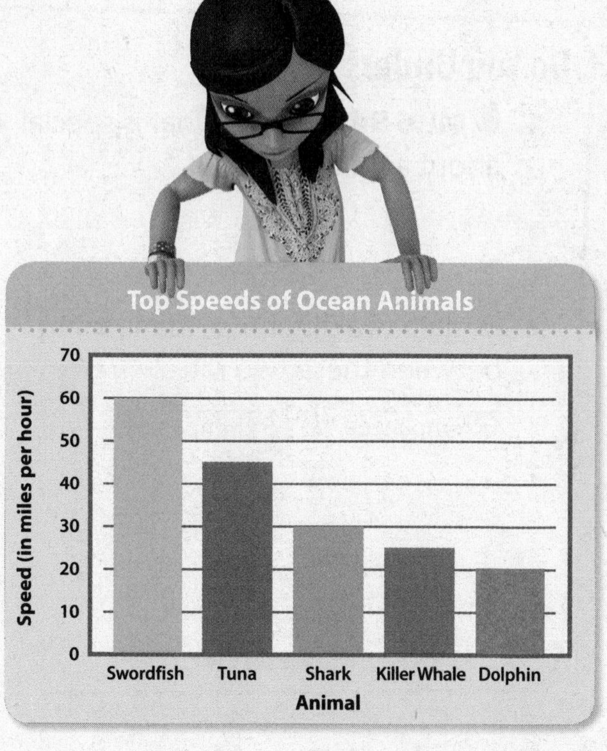

22. **Higher Order Thinking** The *X-43 Hyper-X* is one of the fastest aircraft in the world. It can reach a maximum speed of 6,750 mph. What is its maximum rate of speed in miles per second?

23. Make a list of three rates that describe things that you do. For example, you could describe how many classes you attend in a day. For each example, explain why it is a rate.

Common Core Assessment

24. Doug caught 10 fish over a period of 4 hours. Which of the following is a unit rate per hour for this situation?

- Ⓐ 2.5 fish per hour
- Ⓑ 5 fish per 2 hours
- Ⓒ 2 hours per 5 fish
- Ⓓ 4 hours per 10 fish

25. Ava found that 5 cars passed her house in 10 minutes. Which of the following is a unit rate per hour for this situation?

- Ⓐ 10 cars per hour
- Ⓑ 20 cars per hour
- Ⓒ 30 cars per hour
- Ⓓ 40 cars per hour

Name ______________________________

Step Up to Grade 6

Lesson 6
Understand Percents

I can ...
represent and find the percent of a whole.

Content Standard 6.RP.A.3c
Mathematical Practices MP.2, MP.3, MP.4, MP.7, MP.8

Solve & Share For every group of 20 students, 5 bring their lunch from home and 15 buy their lunch. How many students out of 100 bring their lunch? ***Solve this problem any way you choose.***

You can use structure and what you have learned about equivalent fractions to find the solution. *Show your work!*

Look Back! **MP.4 Model with Math** Model your solution another way. Explain your strategy.

Learn Glossary

Essential Question What Is a Percent?

A

A percent is a special kind of ratio in which the first term is compared to 100.

What percent of people prefer Bright White Toothpaste?

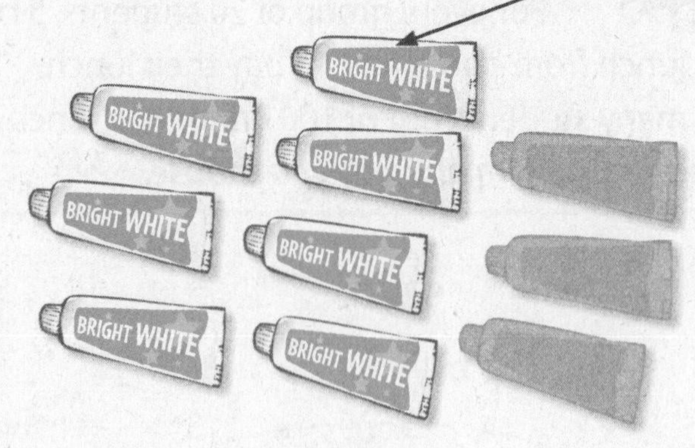

The percent is the number of hundredths that represents the part of the whole.

There are different ways to show a percent.

B Use a grid to model the percent.

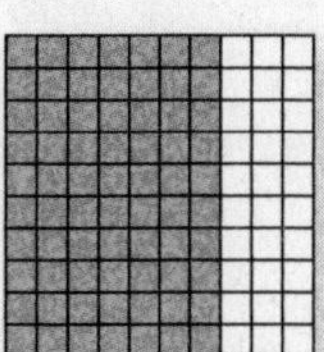

$\frac{7}{10} = \frac{70}{100} = 70\%$

C Use number lines to model the percent.

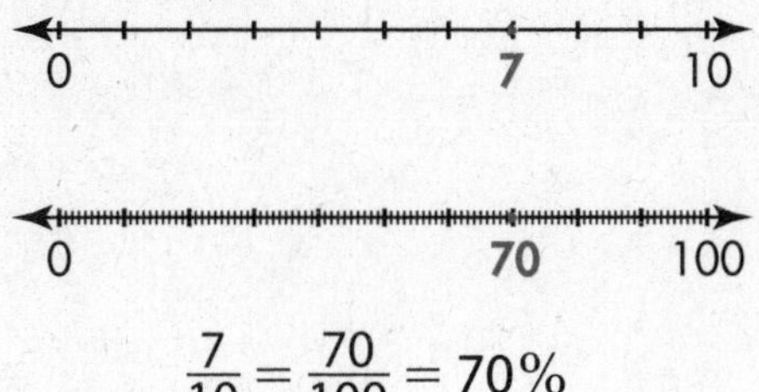

$\frac{7}{10} = \frac{70}{100} = 70\%$

D Use equivalent fractions to find the percent.

$\frac{7}{10} = \frac{x}{100}$

$\frac{7}{10} = \frac{70}{100}$

$\frac{7}{10} = \frac{70}{100} = 70\%$

70% of people prefer Bright White Toothpaste.

Convince Me! **MP.2 Reasoning** What percent of people do not prefer Bright White Toothpaste? How do you know?

hundredth One part of 100 equal parts of a whole

kilometer (km) A metric unit of length; one kilometer is equal to 1,000 meters.

Identity Property of Addition The sum of any number and zero is that number.

Identity Property of Multiplication The product of any number and one is that number.

inch (in.) A customary unit of length; 12 inches are equal to one foot.

intersecting lines Lines that pass through the same point

interval (on a graph) The difference between consecutive numbers on an axis of a graph

inverse operations Operations that undo each other
Example: Adding 6 and subtracting 6 are inverse operations.

isosceles triangle A triangle with at least two sides of the same length

kilogram (kg) A metric unit of mass; one kilogram is equal to 1,000 grams.

less than symbol (<) A symbol that points towards a lesser number or expression
Example: $305 < 320$

line A straight path of points that goes on forever in two directions

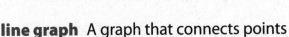

line graph A graph that connects points to show how data change over time

line of symmetry The line on which a figure can be folded so that both halves are the same

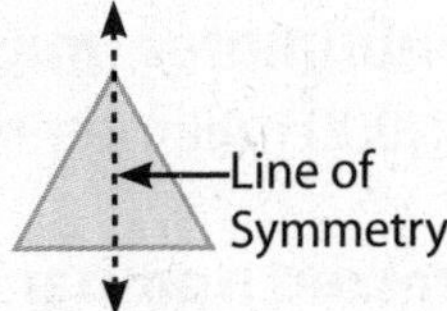

line plot A display of responses along a number line, with dots or Xs recorded above the responses to indicate the number of times a response occurred

line segment Part of a line having two endpoints

liter (L) A metric unit of capacity; one liter is equal to 1,000 milliliters

mass The measure of the quantity of matter in an object

meter (m) A metric unit of length; One meter is equal to 100 centimeters.

metric units of measure Units of measure commonly used by scientists

mile (mi) A customary unit of length equal to 5,280 feet

milligram (mg) A metric unit of mass; 1,000 milligrams is equal to one gram.

milliliter (mL) A metric unit of capacity; 1,000 milliliters is equal to one liter.

millimeter (mm) A metric unit of length; 1,000 millimeters is equal to one meter.

mixed number A number that has a whole-number part and a fraction part

multiple The product of a given whole number and any whole number

multiple of 10 A number that has 10 as a factor

Multiplication Property of Equality Both sides of an equation can be multiplied by the same nonzero number and the sides remain equal.

multiplicative inverse (reciprocal) Two numbers whose product is one

number name A way to write a number using words

number sequence A set of numbers that follows a rule

numerator The number above the fraction bar in a fraction

numerical data Data involving numbers including measurement data

numerical expression A mathematical phrase that contains numbers and at least one operation
Example: 325 + 50

obtuse angle An angle whose measure is between 90° and 180°

135°

obtuse triangle A triangle in which one angle is an obtuse angle

octagon A polygon with 8 sides

order of operations The order in which operations are done in calculations. Work inside parentheses, brackets, and braces is done first. Next, terms with exponents are evaluated. Then, multiplication and division are done in order from left to right, and finally addition and subtraction are done in order from left to right.

ordered pair A pair of numbers used to locate a point on a coordinate grid

origin The point where the two axes of a coordinate grid intersect; the origin is represented by the ordered pair (0, 0).

ounce (oz) A customary unit of weight; 16 ounces is equal to one pound.

outlier A value that is much greater or much less than the other values in a data set

overestimate An estimate that is greater than the actual answer

parallel lines In a plane, lines that never cross and stay the same distance apart

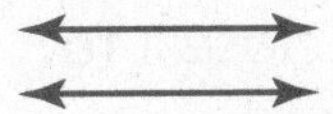

parallelogram A quadrilateral with both pairs of opposite sides parallel and equal in length

parentheses The symbols (and) used to group numbers or variables in mathematical expressions
Example: 3(15 − 7)

partial products Products found by breaking one of two factors into ones, tens, hundreds, and so on, and then multiplying each of these by the other factor

pentagon A polygon with 5 sides

perfect square A number that is the product of a counting number multiplied by itself

perimeter The distance around a figure

period In a number, a group of three digits, separated by commas, starting from the right

perpendicular lines Two lines that intersect to form square corners or right angles

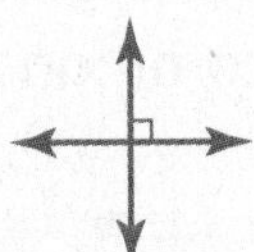

pint (pt) A customary unit of capacity equal to 2 cups

place value The position of a digit in a number that is used to determine the value of the digit
Example: In 5,318, the 3 is in the hundreds place. So, the 3 has a value of 300.

plane An endless flat surface

point An exact location in space

polygon A closed plane figure made up of line segments

pound (lb) A customary unit of weight equal to 16 ounces

power The product that results from multiplying the same number over and over

prime number A whole number greater than 1 that has exactly two factors, itself and 1

prism A solid figure with two identical parallel bases and faces that are parallelograms

product The number that is the result of multiplying two or more factors

protractor A tool used to measure and draw angles

pyramid A solid figure with a base that is a polygon whose faces are triangles with a common vertex

quadrilateral A polygon with 4 sides

quart (qt) A customary unit of capacity equal to 2 pints

quotient The answer to a division problem

ray Part of a line that has one endpoint and extends forever in one direction.

reciprocal A given number is a reciprocal of another number if the product of the numbers is one. *Example:* The numbers $\frac{1}{8}$ and $\frac{8}{1}$ are reciprocals because $\frac{1}{8} \times \frac{8}{1} = 1$.

rectangle A parallelogram with four right angles

rectangular prism A solid figure with 6 rectangular faces

regular polygon A polygon that has sides of equal length and angles of equal measure

remainder The amount that is left after dividing a number into equal parts

rhombus A parallelogram with all sides the same length

right angle An angle whose measure is 90°

right triangle A triangle in which one angle is a right angle

rounding A process that determines which multiple of 10, 100, 1,000, and so on, a number is closest to

sample A representative part of a larger group

scale (in a graph) A series of numbers at equal intervals along an axis on a graph

scalene triangle A triangle in which no sides have the same length

sides (of an angle) The two rays that form an angle

sides of a polygon The line segments that form a polygon

solid figure (also: solid) A figure that has three dimensions (length, width, and height)

solution The value of the variable that makes the equation true

square A rectangle with all sides the same length

square unit A square with sides one unit long used to measure area

standard form A common way of writing a number with commas separating groups of three digits starting from the right
Example: 3,458,901

stem-and-leaf plot A way to organize numerical data using place value

straight angle An angle measuring 180°

Subtraction Property of Equality The same number can be subtracted from both sides of an equation and the sides remain equal.

sum The result of adding two or more addends

survey A question or questions used to gather information

symmetric A figure is symmetric if it can be folded on a line to form two halves that fit exactly on top of each other.

tablespoon (tbsp) A customary unit of capacity; two tablespoons is equal to one fluid ounce.

tenth One of ten equal parts of a whole

terms Numbers in a sequence or variables, such as x and y, in an algebraic expression

thousandth One of 1,000 equal parts of a whole

three-dimensional shape A solid with three dimensions that has volume, such as a rectangular prism

ton (T) A customary unit of weight equal to 2,000 pounds

trapezoid A quadrilateral that has exactly one pair of parallel sides

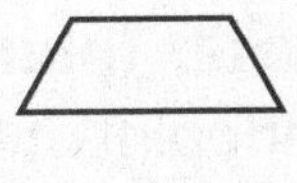

trend A relationship between two sets of data that shows up as a pattern in a graph

triangle A polygon with 3 sides

underestimate An estimate that is less than the actual answer

unknown A symbol or letter, such as x, that represents a number in an expression or equation

unit cube A cube that measures one unit on each side

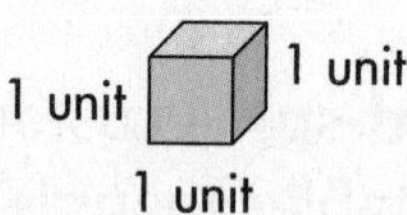

unit fraction A fraction with a numerator of 1

value (of a digit) The number a digit represents, which is determined by the position of the digit; see also *place value*

variable A letter, such as *n*, that represents a number in an expression or an equation

vertex (plural: vertices) **a.** The common endpoint of the two rays in an angle; **b.** A point at which two sides of a polygon meet; **c.** The point at which three or more edges meet in a solid figure

volume The number of cubic units needed to fill a solid figure

weight A measure of how light or how heavy something is

whole numbers The numbers 0, 1, 2, 3, 4, and so on

word form A way to write a number using words; see also *number name*

***x*-axis** A horizontal number line on a coordinate grid

***x*-coordinate** The first number in an ordered pair, which names the distance to the right or left from the origin along the *x*-axis

***y*-axis** A vertical number line on a coordinate grid

***y*-coordinate** The second number in an ordered pair, which names the distance up or down from the origin along the *y*-axis

yard (yd) A customary unit of length equal to 3 feet

Zero Property of Multiplication The product of any number and 0 is 0.

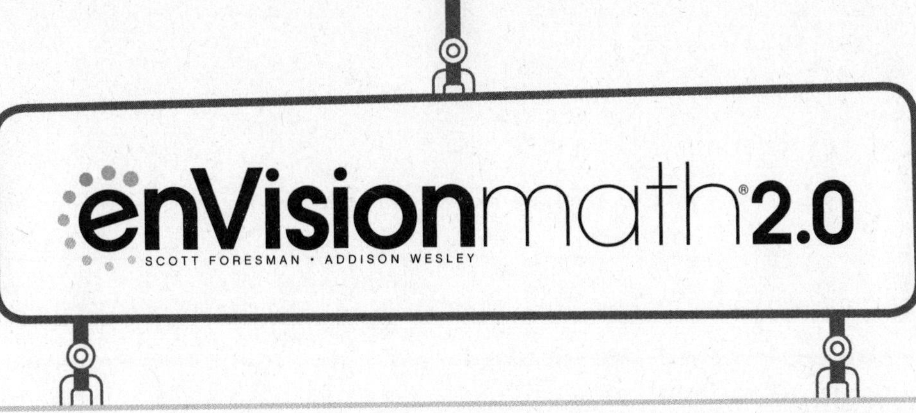

Photographs

Photo locators denoted as follows: Top (T), Center (C), Bottom (B), Left (L), Right (R), Background (Bkgd)

001 Daniel Prudek/Shutterstock; **006** Risteski Goce/Shutterstock; **014** John Foxx/Thinkstock; **024** Vladislav Gajic/Fotolia; **030C** Hemera Technologies/Getty Images; **030L** James Steidl/Fotolia; **030R** Ivelin Radkov/Fotolia; **055** Ilyas Kalimullin/Shutterstock; **060** Pearson Education; **084L** Corbis; **084R** Robert Marien/Corbis; **109** Leungchopan/Shutterstock; **126** Pearson Education; **132** Cphoto/Fotolia; **143** Tatiana Popova/Shutterstock; **163** Smileus/Shutterstock; **166** Pearson Education; **172** Pearson Education; **183** Viacheslav Krylov/Fotolia; **195** Alisonhancock/Fotolia; **237** Tom Wang/Shutterstock; **246** Pearson Education; **258** Pearson Education; **264** Visions of America/Alamy; **299** Lisastrachan/Fotolia; **332BL** Pearson Education; **332BR** Pearson Education; **332TL** Pearson Education; **332TR** Pearson Education; **336L** Getty Images; **336R** Getty Images; **367** Marcio Jose Bastos Silva/Shutterstock; **372** Pearson Education; **390** Pearson Education; **414L** Pearson Education; **414R** Esanbanhao/Fotolia; **426** Image Source/Jupiter images; **437B** by-studio/Fotolia; **437T** Paul Orr/Shutterstock; **455** Simone van den Berg/Fotolia; **462** Bikeriderlondon/Shutterstock; **476** Pearson Education; **523** Zest_Marina/Fotolia; **546** Pearson Education; **558** Bev/Fotolia; **583** Morgan Lane Photography/Shutterstock; **596** Pearson Education; **631** Iktomi/Fotolia; **633L** Pearson Education; **633R** Pavlo Sachek/Fotolia; **635** Pearson Education; **637** Pearson Education; **646C** Pearson Education; **646L** Pearson Education; **646R** Pearson Education; **652** Getty Images; **664** Pearson Education; **666** Pearson Education; **670L** Marianne de Jong/Shutterstock; **670R** Brocreative/Fotolia; **693B** Volff/Fotolia; **693T** Evgeny Karandaev/Shutterstock; **695** Jon Beard/Shutterstock; **731** Natalia Pavlova/Fotolia; **773** Solarseven/Shutterstock; **790** Pearson Education; **809** kalafoto/Fotolia; **843** leekris/Fotolia; **845** Michael J Thompson/ShutterStock; **854** 2010/Photos to Go/Photolibrary; **888** Corbis; **920B** hotshotsworldwide/Fotolia; **920TL** Jupiter Images; **920TR** Jupiter Images.